Introducing Art

Teacher Wraparound Edition

Gene Mittler, Ph.D.
Professor Emeritus
Texas Tech University

Rosalind Ragans, Ph.D.
Associate Professor Emerita
Georgia Southern University

Jean Morman Unsworth, M.F.A.
Professor of Fine Arts Emerita
Loyola University of Chicago

Faye Scannell
Specialist, Art and Technology
Bellevue, Washington Public Schools

McGraw Hill Glencoe

New York, New York   Columbus, Ohio   Chicago, Illinois   Peoria, Illinois   Woodland Hills, California

Teacher Manual

Glencoe

The McGraw-Hill Companies

Send all inquiries to:
Glencoe/McGraw-Hill
21600 Oxnard Street, Suite 500
Woodland Hills, CA 91367

ISBN 0-07-846499-4 (Student Text)
ISBN 0-07-846504-4 (Teacher Wraparound Edition)

Printed in the United States of America.

1 2 3 4 5 6 7 8 9 043/027 08 07 06 05 04

About the Authors

Gene Mittler

Gene Mittler is one of the authors of Glencoe's middle school art series, *Introducing Art, Exploring Art*, and *Understanding Art*. He is also author of *Art in Focus*, a chronological approach to art for Glencoe's senior high program, and *Creating and Understanding Drawings*. He has taught at both the elementary and secondary levels and at Indiana University. He received an M.F.A. in sculpture from Bowling Green State University and a Ph.D. in art education from the Ohio State University. Dr. Mittler is currently Professor Emeritus at Texas Tech University.

Jean Morman Unsworth

Jean Morman Unsworth author, teacher, and consultant, is one of the authors of Glencoe's middle school book *Introducing Art*. Educated at the Art Institute of Chicago, University of Notre-Dame, and the University of Georgia, she has taught elementary through graduate levels and was Professor of Fine Arts at Loyola University of Chicago until 1987. She initiated and designed Chicago Children's Museum and the Interdisciplinary Arts Masters program at Columbia College in Chicago. She now gives full time to writing and consulting.

Rosalind Ragans

Rosalind Ragans is one of the authors of Glencoe's middle school art series, *Introducing Art, Exploring Art*, and *Understanding Art*. She serves as senior author on the elementary program of *Art Connections* for the SRA division of McGraw-Hill, and wrote the multi-level, comprehensive *ArtTalk* text for Glencoe's senior high program. She received a B.F.A at Hunter College, CUNY, New York, and earned a M.Ed. in Elementary Education at Georgia Southern College and a Ph.D. in Art Education at the University of Georgia. Dr. Ragans was named National Art Educator of the Year for 1992.

Faye Scannell

Faye Scannell is an art specialist, lead art technology teacher, and teacher educator in the Bellevue, Washington Public Schools, the Bellevue Art Museum, and through Seattle Pacific University. She is a frequent presenter at art education conferences and has written technology activities for Glencoe's art programs. She was educated at Kutztown State University of Pennsylvania, Lesley College, and several Washington universities. In 1993 she received the Art Educator of the Year Award from the Washington Art Education Association.

About Artsource®

The materials provided in the Performing Arts Handbook are excerpted from Artsource®: The Center's Study Guide to the Performing Arts, a project of the Music Center Education Division. Based in Los Angeles, the Music Center is one of the three largest performing arts centers in the United States. It established the Education Division in 1979 as part of its commitment to engaging new and diverse audiences in the arts—in the Center's theatres, in schools, and throughout the community. The Music Center Education Division is dedicated to providing opportunities for lifelong learning in the arts and advancing quality arts education as integral to the core curriculum in Southern California schools. For additional information, visit www.musiccenter.org/artsource.

Editorial Consultants

Claire B. Clements, Ph.D.
Specialist, Special Needs
Associate Professor and Community Education
Director at the Program on Human Development and Disability
The University of Georgia
Athens, Georgia

Robert D. Clements, Ph.D.
Specialist, Special Needs
Professor Emeritus of Art
The University of Georgia
Athens, Georgia

Cris Guenter, Ed.D.
Specialist, Portfolio and Assessment
Professor, Fine Arts/Curriculum and Instruction
California State University, Chico
Chico, California

Dede Tisone-Bartels, M.A.
Specialist, Curriculum Connections
Crittenden Middle School
Mountain View, California

Contributors/Reviewers

Max A. Butler
Fine Arts Instructor
Cedar Valley Middle School
Austin, TX

Gail F. Enkey
Art Teacher
Chiaravelle Montessori School
Evanston, IL

Stacey Hendrickson
Art Instructor
Gates Intermediate School
Scituate, MA

Joy Jones
Art Teacher
Chisholm Trail Middle School
Round Rock, TX

Barbara A. Perez
Art Teacher
St. Athanasius Grammar School
Evanston, IL

Irene Wettermark Porter
Visual Arts Teacher
Hayes Middle School
Birmingham, AL

Teri Power
Art Specialist & G&T Coordinator
East Elementary School
New Richmond, WI

Margaret Powers
Art Teacher
McAdory Elementary School
McCalla, AL

Wandra Merritt Sanders
Art Teacher
Hyde Park Elementary
Jacksonville, FL

Sylvia L. Thompson
Art Instructor
Cammack Middle School
Huntington, WV

Performing Arts Handbook Contributors

Mark Slavkin
Vice President for Education, The Music Center of Los Angeles County

Michael Solomon
Managing Director, Music Center Education Division

Melinda Williams
Concept Originator and Project Director

Susan Cambigue-Tracey
Project Coordinator

Arts Discipline Writers:
Dance—Susan Cambigue-Tracey, Diana Cummins, Madeline Dahm, Carole Valleskey
Music—Rosemarie Cook-Glover, Mando Fonseca, Marilyn Wulliger, Barbara Leonard
Theatre—Barbara Leonard, Susan Cambigue-Tracey

Studio Lesson Consultants

The authors wish to express their gratitude to the following art teachers whose students provided exemplary work for the Studio Lessons.

Jeff Bender
Park Plaza Middle School
Evansville, IN

Vickie Berk
Memorial Middle School
Houston, TX

Susan A. Clark
Washington Middle School
Vista, CA

Jill Cornell
Akron Central School
Akron, NY

Norman Dexter
Dougherty Middle School
Albany, GA

John Edwards
Southside Middle School
Albany, GA

Susan Green
Spring Branch Middle School
Houston, TX

Donald Gruber
Clinton Junior High
Clinton, IL

Peggy Harris
Albany Middle School
Albany, GA

Cathy Kayrouz
Stuart Middle School
Louisville, KY

Audrey Komroy
Akron Central School
Akron, NY

Janine Nathan
Spring Oaks Middle School
Houston, TX

Gerald Obregon
Norland Middle School
Miami, FL

Charles L. Osten
Whittle Springs Middle School
Knoxville, TN

Cynthia Pate
McGary Middle School
Evansville, IN

Barbara A. Perez
St. Athanasius Grammar School
Evanston, IL

Irene Wettermark Porter
Hayes Middle School
Birmingham, AL

Faye Scannell
Medina Elementary
Medina, WA

Leslee Smith
Cammack Middle School
Huntington, WV

Sherry M. Taylor
Savannah Grove Elementary
Effingham, SC

Curtis R. Uebelhor
Perry Heights Middle School
Evansville, IN

Janice Rentz
Radium Springs Middle School
Albany, GA

Robin M. Whitelock
Henry H. Filer Middle School
Hialeah, FL

Student Contributors

The following students contributed exemplary work for the Studio Lesson pages:

Fig. 1–13, Kim Truong, Washington Middle School, Vista, CA; Fig. 1–13, Carmen Lopez, Washington Middle School, Vista, CA; Fig. 1–19, Kaylie Hodge, Medina Elementary, Medina, WA; Fig. 2–5, Benjamin Trinka, Medina Elementary, Medina, WA; Fig. 2–13, Leigh Nordstrom, Medina Elementary, Medina, WA; Fig. 3–7, Marium Kureishy, Clinton Junior High, Clinton, IL; Fig. 3–11, Mead Scofield, Memorial Middle School, Houston, TX; Fig. 3–17, Kristina Smith, Cammack Middle School, Huntington, WV; Fig. 4–9, Jason Johnson, Albany Middle School, Albany, GA; Fig. 4–11, Chelsea Bingiel, Clinton Junior High, Clinton, IL; Fig. 4–13, Florian Kimpel, Plaza Park Middle School, Evansville, IN; Fig. 4–13, Jing Liu, Plaza Park Middle School, Evansville, IN; Fig. 5–6, Kate Morrisson, St. Athanasius Grammar School, Evanston, IL; Fig. 5–10, Katie Harr, St. Athanasius Grammar School, Evanston, IL; Fig. 5–16, Manuel Dominguez, Henry H. Filer Middle School, Hialeah, FL; Fig. 5–20, William Bissell, Medina Elementary, Medina, WA; Fig. 6–5, Adam McGuire, Plaza Park Middle School, Evansville, IN; Fig. 6–9, Jancy Buffington, Medina Elementary, Medina, WA; Fig. 6–17, Nathan Faulks, Clinton Junior High, Clinton, IL; Fig. 7–5, Vincent Carioscia, St. Athanasius Grammar School, Evanston, IL; Fig. 7–13, Molly Cook, Cammack Middle School, Huntington, WV; Fig. 7–17, Brandie Rawlinson, Perry Heights Middle School, Evansville, IN; Fig. 7–17, Darrell Ray Morris, Perry Heights Middle School, Evansville, IN; Fig. 8–5; Charlie Kemp, Medina Elementary, Medina, WA; Fig. 8–9, Vanessa Thomas, Dougherty Middle School, Albany, GA; Fig. 8–17, Samantha Wells, Stuart Middle School, Louisville, KY; Fig. 9–10, Kara Lucas, Springs Oaks Middle School, Houston, TX; Fig. 9–14, Lucy Arndt, St. Athanasius Grammar School, Evanston, IL; Fig. 9–18, Charley Will, McGary Middle School, Evansville, IN; Fig. 10–9, Ashley Whitesell, Akron Central School, Akron, NY; Fig. 10–13, Lindsey Helton, Spring Oaks Middle School, Houston, TX; Fig. 10–17, Graem Gulick, Medina Elementary. Medina, WA; Figure 11–5, Julian Robinson, Savannah Grove Elementary, Effingham, SC; Fig. 11–7, Spring Branch Middle School art students, Houston, TX; Fig. 11–9, Joshua R. Reynolds, Whittle Springs Middle School, Knoxville, TN; Fig. 11–17, Louise and Katherine Galuski, Akron Central School, Akron, NY; Fig. 12–5, Latoya Jackson, Southern Middle School, Louisville, KY; Fig. 12–9, Emily Kirk, McGary Middle School, Evansville, IN; Fig. 12–17, Chele Kent, Radium Springs Middle School, Albany, GA; Fig. 13–5, 6th, 7th, and 8th grade class at Henry H. Filer School, Hialeah, FL; Fig. 13–9, Tina Sheppard, Hayes Middle School, Birmingham Middle School, Birmingham, AL; Fig. 13–17, Nicole Vasquez, Norland Middle School, Miami, FL; Fig. 14–5, Shanterika Toombs, Southside Middle School, Albany, GA; Fig, 14–9, Paul Goderis, St. Athanasius Grammar School, Evanston, IL.

A Comprehensive Art Program to Meet All Your Needs

Welcome to Glencoe's *Introducing Art*—a lively, inviting, quality art program.

Table of Contents

Glencoe's Middle School Art Programs: ART is for All Students

Promotes Student Success

A quality, comprehensive art program enriches students' lives and allows for discovery and creative problem solving. Whether pursued as a career or as an avocational interest, involvement with the arts contributes to the development of lifelong skills such as creative expression, making informed judgments, and developing problem-solving skills. It provides students with a broader perception of their environment and a greater understanding of historical and cultural perspectives. Students are encouraged to express their thoughts and ideas creatively, while challenging their imagination, fostering reflective thinking, and developing disciplined effort and critical-thinking skills.

Provides a Comprehensive Art Program

Glencoe provides three programs designed specifically for the middle school student. These programs are structured around the belief that students learn best in a classroom that is engaging, meaningful, and focused on art as a core curriculum subject, one that is built on their everyday experiences and enriches their learning in all areas.

- Each book in the series allows teachers to customize their lesson plans around a specific emphasis—the study of themes in art, art media and techniques, or the chronology and history of art.
- All programs in the series present various artistic styles, historical periods, and traditions as contributions of diverse cultures.
- Each text is sequentially developed with age-appropriate individual and group activities in order that art can be taught as a core subject.
- Cross-curricular features throughout each text provide students the opportunity to see how art is integrated with other disciplines.
- All programs cover a wide range of media, techniques, processes, and artistic styles.

Provides Inclusion Strategies for All Learning Styles and Ability Levels

Glencoe's middle school art programs present engaging, relevant, and appropriate content and creative expressive activities for the widest range of learners. The content and features of Glencoe's middle school art programs are presented in a dynamic design that will motivate and engage your students. The Teacher Wraparound Edition offers a variety of teaching strategies to address different learning abilities. Inclusion strategies to meet students' individual needs are also provided.

Links to the Performing Arts and Other Curriculum Areas

- **Music, Dance, Theatre** The visual and performing arts are mutually reinforcing. Glencoe's art programs are designed to underscore that unity by emphasizing how the foundation of all areas of art are built upon corresponding concepts and principles.
- **Cross-Curriculum Connections** Students learn how concepts in one subject area, in this case art, can enhance and increase their interest in and knowledge of other subject areas such as math, social studies, and language arts.

Introducing Art offers learning opportunities that incorporate a variety of media, artistic styles, historical periods, and cultural backgrounds. There are four basic components that provide the overall structure for student learning objectives in *Introducing Art*:

PERCEPTION The process of learning the basic skills and knowledge to express their ideas and feelings creatively are important to student success in the visual arts. By learning the elements and principles of art, students learn to develop and organize ideas from the environment.

CREATIVE EXPRESSION Studio lesson and activities give students the opportunity to create works of art by elaborating on direct observation, personal experience, and traditional events. Students are challenged to demonstrate technical skills effectively using various media, tools, and techniques including digital media.

HISTORICAL AND CULTURAL HERITAGE Throughout the program, works of art from various historical periods and diverse cultures are presented to encourage student understanding of art history and cultural history.

EVALUATION By interpreting and evaluating their own artworks and those of their peers, students apply the art criticism process. *Introducing Art* offers multiple opportunities to analyze artworks to form conclusions about formal properties, and historical and cultural contexts.

Expands the Arts Through Technology

Advances in digital media and other new technologies offer exciting opportunities for art teachers and students. Through CD-ROMs and the Internet, students can sharpen their visual perception and have access to an infinite variety of artworks. With digital art software programs, students expand the limits of their creative expression and build skills for the modern workplace. New activities and resource components provide a range of technology options that encourage exploration of new possibilities both in art education and production.

Meets National Standards for Arts Education

The National Standards for Arts Education provides guidelines that set benchmark standards for grade-appropriate competency in the performing and visual arts. The Glencoe art programs are correlated to the National Standards (see the Scope and Sequence on pages TM 16–TM 22), and helps teachers design their lessons around the National Standards.

Includes Assessment Strategies

Throughout the Glencoe art programs students are encouraged to keep sketchbooks, or visual art journals, and develop portfolios featuring their selected works of art. In addition, the frequent self-evaluation of completed artworks provides ongoing assessment of each student's progress, fostering a sense of accomplishment and a commitment to high standards of art production. Building self-assessment skills prepares students for the eventual transition to the workplace.

Glencoe's Middle School Art Series at a Glance

Glencoe provides comprehensive art programs with a 3-text middle school art series. This Series at a Glance displays a complete listing of chapters in the series.

Introducing Art

Chapter 1	The Elements of Art
Chapter 2	The Principles of Art
Chapter 3	Art Media and Techniques
Chapter 4	Looking at Art
Chapter 5	Art Through the Ages
Chapter 6	Perceiving Nature
Chapter 7	Observing Animals
Chapter 8	Portraying People
Chapter 9	Visiting Places
Chapter 10	Examining Objects
Chapter 11	Recording Events
Chapter 12	Telling a Story
Chapter 13	Celebrations
Chapter 14	Creating Fantasy

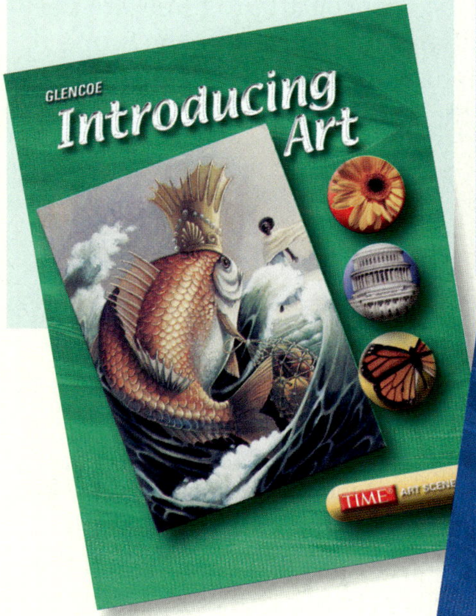

Exploring Art

Chapter 1	Art in Your World
Chapter 2	The Elements of Art
Chapter 3	The Principles of Art
Chapter 4	Exploring Art Media
Chapter 5	Art Criticism and Aesthetics
Chapter 6	Art History and You
Chapter 7	Drawing
Chapter 8	Printmaking
Chapter 9	Painting
Chapter 10	Photography
Chapter 11	Graphic Design
Chapter 12	Sculpture
Chapter 13	Crafts
Chapter 14	Architecture
Chapter 15	Film, Video, and Digital Art

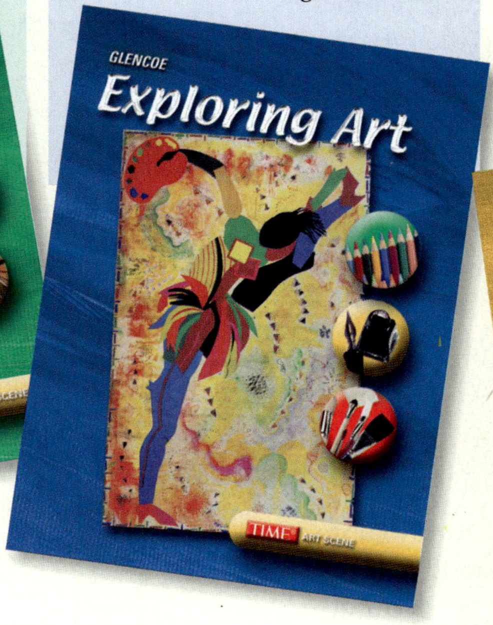

Understanding Art

Chapter 1	Art Across the World
Chapter 2	The Language of Art
Chapter 3	The Media of Art
Chapter 4	Art Criticism, Aesthetics, and Art History
Chapter 5	Art of Earliest Times
Chapter 6	Art of East Asia
Chapter 7	Pre-Columbian Art of Latin America
Chapter 8	Native Art of North America
Chapter 9	Art of Greece and Rome
Chapter 10	Art of India and Islam
Chapter 11	Art of Africa and Oceania
Chapter 12	Art of the Middle Ages
Chapter 13	Art of the Renaissance
Chapter 14	Art of the 17th and 18th Centuries
Chapter 15	Art of the 19th Century
Chapter 16	Art of the 20th Century
Chapter 17	Art of Today

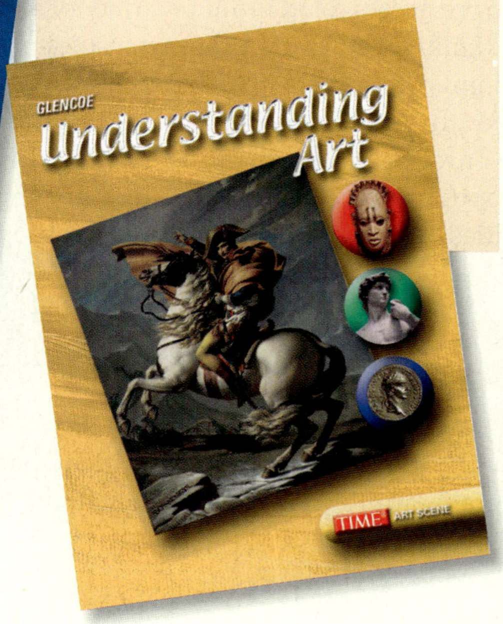

Student Edition

Promoting Visual and Cultural Literacy

The *Introducing Art* student text introduces students to a theme-based program, laying the foundation for lifelong art appreciation and art-production skills. Students will explore the ways in which artists from various cultures and eras have interpreted such subjects as nature, animals, people, places, objects, events, stories, celebrations, and fantasy. They will learn about the elements and principles of art as well as the media and techniques used to create art.

QUICK WRITE This feature, which connects to the artist's quote in the chapter opener, will help students to start thinking about the creative process of producing art, from idea to finished artwork.

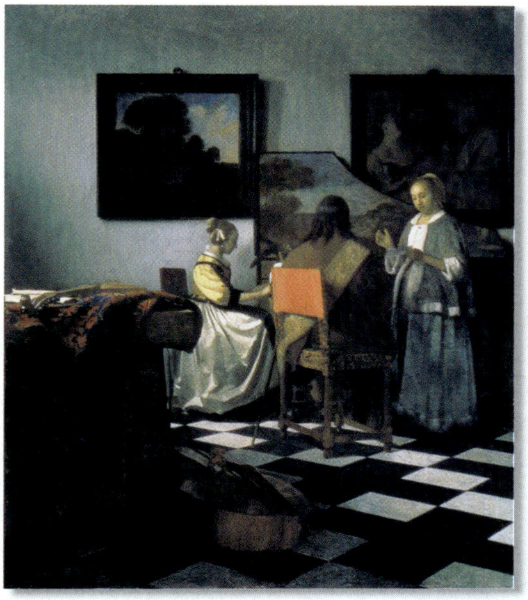

Focus On ◆ Figure 5–1 This painting brings you right into a Dutch home of the 1600s. Notice the young woman playing the virginal, an early kind of piano, and her two companions.

Jan Vermeer. *The Concert*. c. 1665–66. Oil on canvas. 61 × 71.1 cm (24 × 28″). Isabella Stewart Gardner Museum, Boston, Massachusetts.

80

Chapter 5

Art Through the Ages

"All art is an individual's expression of a culture. Cultures differ, so art looks different."

—Henry Glassie, art scholar

Walk into this chapter as if you were walking through time. Try to imagine yourself in ancient Egypt, Greece, or Rome. Travel to the Far East or to Africa, and let the art tell you about the people of each period. Move on to the nineteenth and twentieth centuries, and see how the advancement of science opened new ideas to the artists. This chapter will help you understand people of all ages through their art.

After completing this chapter, you will able to:

- Explain why art history is important.
- Compare specific artworks from a variety of cultures.
- Understand the goals of different cultures and art movements.
- Create artworks of different cultures and times.

Quick Write

Interpreting the Quote Read the quote, and then look again at **Figure 5–1.** Write a descriptive paragraph about what life might have been like in Holland in the 1600s.

KEY TERMS

- art historians
- applied art
- fine art
- bust
- hieroglyphic
- symbol
- contours
- painted screen
- architecture
- Renaissance
- diorama
- art movement

81

CHAPTER OPENER Each chapter opens with a full-color reproduction of a work of art related to the chapter's contents. This motivational artwork and brief introduction with bulleted objectives helps focus students on the knowledge and skills presented in the chapter. Vocabulary terms are also listed so students can preview key words in the chapter.

Student Edition

Promoting Creative Expression

Narrative Lessons

Art concepts are presented and reinforced in accessible, easy-to-understand language. Students study artworks representing a variety of historical periods and cultures. Check Your Understanding provides a short review for each lesson.

STUDIO ACTIVITY Creative expression activities found in narrative lessons explore ways for students to quickly grasp ideas presented in the lessons. Each one gives students the opportunity to demonstrate technical skills, using a variety of art media and materials to produce original artworks.

Studio Lessons

These lessons give students opportunities to create original artworks by elaborating on direct observation, personal experience, and their imaginations. Students are challenged to create visual solutions, using a variety of art media, tools, and techniques including digital media. The lessons are illustrated by examples of fine art and exemplary student artwork is also included.

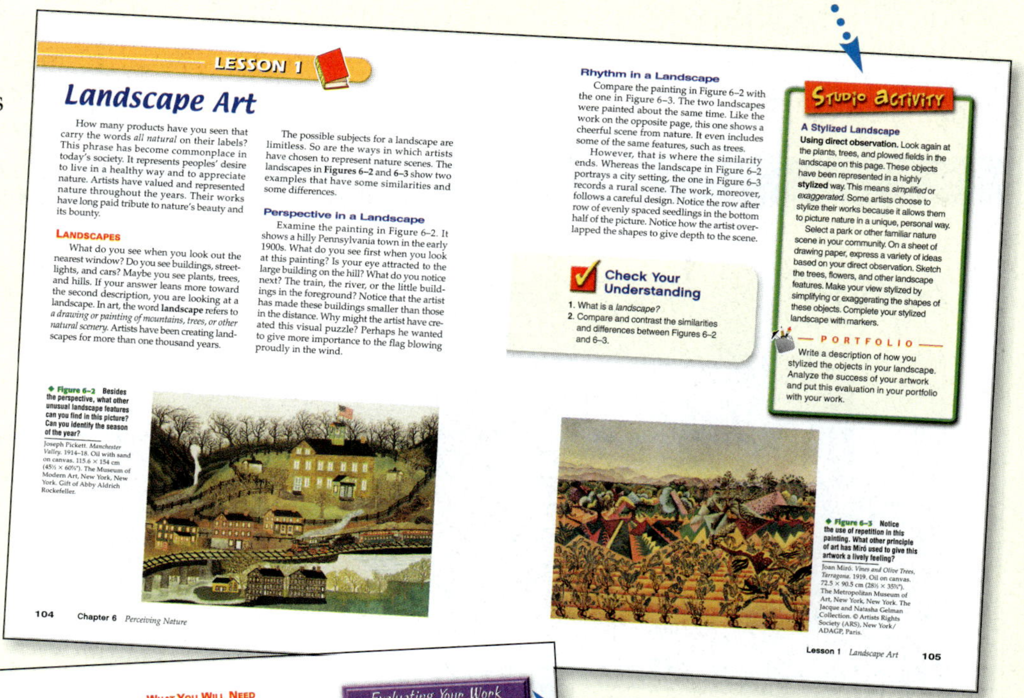

LESSON 1

Landscape Art

How many products have you seen that carry the words *all natural* on their labels? This phrase has become commonplace in today's society. It represents peoples' desire to live in a healthy way and to appreciate nature. Artists have valued and represented nature throughout the years. Their works have long paid tribute to nature's beauty and its bounty.

Landscapes

What do you see when you look out the nearest window? Do you see buildings, streetlights, and cars? Maybe you see plants, trees, and hills. If your answer leans more toward the second description, you are looking at a landscape. In art, the word **landscape** refers to *a drawing or painting of mountains, trees, or other natural scenery.* Artists have been creating landscapes for more than one thousand years.

The possible subjects for a landscape are limitless. So are the ways in which artists have chosen to represent nature scenes. The landscapes in **Figures 6–2** and **6–3** show two examples that have some similarities and some differences.

Perspective in a Landscape

Examine the painting in Figure 6–2. It shows a hilly Pennsylvania town in the early 1900s. What do you see first when you look at this painting? Is your eye attracted to the large building on the hill? What do you notice next? The train, the river, or the little buildings in the foreground? Notice that the artist has made these buildings smaller than those in the distance. Why might the artist have created this visual puzzle? Perhaps he wanted to give more importance to the flag blowing proudly in the wind.

Rhythm in a Landscape

Compare the painting in Figure 6–2 with the one in Figure 6–3. The two landscapes were painted about the same time. Like the work on the opposite page, this one shows a cheerful scene from nature. It even includes some of the same features, such as trees.

However, that is where the similarity ends. Whereas the landscape in Figure 6–2 portrays a city setting, the one in Figure 6–3 records a rural scene. The work, moreover, follows a careful design. Notice the row after row of evenly spaced seedlings in the bottom half of the picture. Notice how the artist overlapped the shapes to give depth to the scene.

Check Your Understanding

1. What is a *landscape*?
2. Compare and contrast the similarities and differences between Figures 6–2 and 6–3.

Studio Activity

A Stylized Landscape

Using direct observation. Look again at the plants, trees, and plowed fields in the landscape on this page. These objects have been represented in a highly **stylized** way. This means *simplified* or *exaggerated.* Some artists choose to stylize their works because it allows them to picture nature in a unique, personal way.

Select a park or other familiar nature scene in your community. On a sheet of drawing paper, express a variety of ideas based on your direct observation. Sketch the trees, flowers, and other landscape features. Make your view stylized by simplifying or exaggerating the shapes of these objects. Complete your stylized landscape with markers.

PORTFOLIO

Write a description of how you stylized the objects in your landscape. Analyze the success of your artwork and put this evaluation in your portfolio with your work.

◆ **Figure 6–2** Besides the perspective, what other unusual landscape features can you find in this picture? Can you identify the season of the year?

Joseph Pickett. *Manchester Valley.* 1914–18. Oil with sand on canvas. 115.6 × 154 cm (45½ × 60⅞"). The Museum of Modern Art, New York, New York. Gift of Abby Aldrich Rockefeller.

◆ **Figure 6–3** Notice the use of repetition in this painting. What other principle of art has Miró used to give this artwork a lively feeling?

Joan Miró. *Vines and Olive Trees, Tarragona.* 1919. Oil on canvas. 72.5 × 90.5 cm (28½ × 35⅝"). The Metropolitan Museum of Art, New York, New York. The Jacque and Natasha Gelman Collection. © Artists Rights Society (ARS), New York/ADAGP, Paris.

104 Chapter 6 *Perceiving Nature*

Lesson 1 *Landscape Art* 105

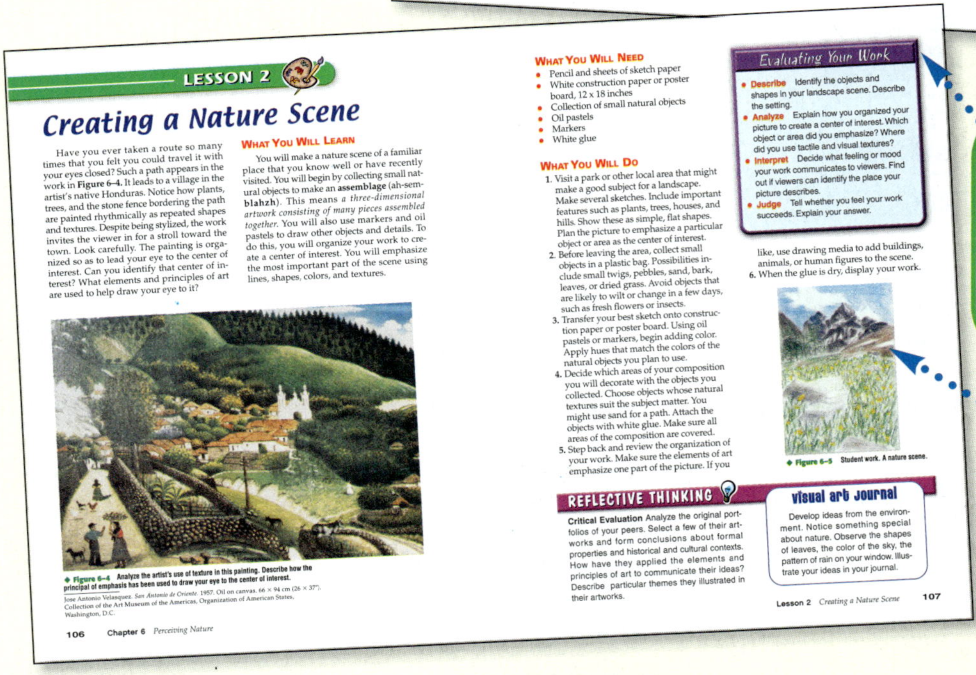

LESSON 2

Creating a Nature Scene

Have you ever taken a route so many times that you felt you could travel it with your eyes closed? Such a path appears in the work in **Figure 6–4**. It leads to a village in the artist's native Honduras. Notice how plants, trees, and the stone fence bordering the path are painted rhythmically as repeated shapes and textures. Despite being stylized, the work invites the viewer in for a stroll toward the town. Look carefully. The painting is organized so as to lead your eye to the center of interest. Can you identify that center of interest? What elements and principles of art are used to help draw your eye to it?

What You Will Learn

You will make a nature scene of a familiar place that you know well or have recently visited. You will begin by collecting small natural objects to make an **assemblage** (ah-sem-blahzh). This means *a three-dimensional artwork consisting of many pieces assembled together.* You will also use markers and oil pastels to draw other objects and details. To do this, you will organize your work to create a center of interest. You will emphasize the most important part of the scene using lines, shapes, colors, and textures.

What You Will Need

- Pencil and sheets of sketch paper
- White construction paper or poster board, 12 x 18 inches
- Collection of small natural objects
- Oil pastels
- Markers
- White glue

What You Will Do

1. Visit a park or other local area that might make a good subject for a landscape. Make several sketches. Include important features such as plants, trees, houses, and hills. Show these as simple, flat shapes. Plan the picture to emphasize a particular object or area as the center of interest.
2. Before leaving the area, collect small objects in a plastic bag. Possibilities include small twigs, pebbles, sand, bark, leaves, or dried grass. Avoid objects that are likely to wilt or change in a few days, such as fresh flowers or insects.
3. Transfer your best sketch onto construction paper or poster board. Using oil pastels or markers, begin adding color. Apply hues that match the colors of the natural objects you plan to use.
4. Decide which areas of your composition you will decorate with the objects you collected. Choose objects whose natural textures suit the subject matter. You might use sand for a path. Attach the objects with white glue. Make sure all areas of the composition are covered.
5. Step back and review the organization of your work. Make sure the elements of art emphasize one part of the picture. If you like, use drawing media to add buildings, animals, or human figures to the scene.
6. When the glue is dry, display your work.

Evaluating Your Work

- **Describe** Identify the objects and shapes in your landscape scene. Describe the setting.
- **Analyze** Explain how you organized your picture to create a center of interest. Which object or area did you emphasize? Where did you use tactile and visual textures?
- **Interpret** Decide what feeling or mood your work communicates to viewers. Find out if viewers can identify the place your picture describes.
- **Judge** Tell whether you feel your work succeeds. Explain your answer.

REFLECTIVE THINKING

Critical Evaluation Analyze the original portfolios of your peers. Select a few of their artworks and form conclusions about formal properties and historical and cultural contexts. How have they applied the elements and principles of art to communicate their ideas? Describe particular themes they illustrated in their artworks.

Visual Art Journal

Develop ideas from the environment. Notice something special about nature. Observe the shapes of leaves, the color of the sky, the pattern of rain on your window. Illustrate your ideas in your journal.

◆ **Figure 6–4** Analyze the artist's use of texture in this painting. Describe how the principal of emphasis has been used to draw your eye to the center of interest.

José Antonio Velasquez. *San Antonio de Oriente.* 1957. Oil on canvas. 66 × 94 cm (26 × 37"). Collection of the Art Museum of the Americas, Organization of American States, Washington, D.C.

◆ **Figure 6–5** Student work. A nature scene.

106 Chapter 6 *Perceiving Nature*

Lesson 2 *Creating a Nature Scene* 107

EVALUATING YOUR WORK This section helps students build important self-assessment skills as they conduct in-progress critiques of their personal artworks.

STUDENT ART Exemplary student artwork of middle school students is displayed within the text to motivate your students.

Offering Current News from the World of Art

TIME ART SCENE

Written in an engaging magazine style, this colorful new feature closes every chapter with an update from the real world of art. Students will read about various artists and discover how art is a part of the world outside their classroom. Each feature is tailored to fit the content of a particular chapter and contains a cross-curriculum activity to help students apply what they have learned.

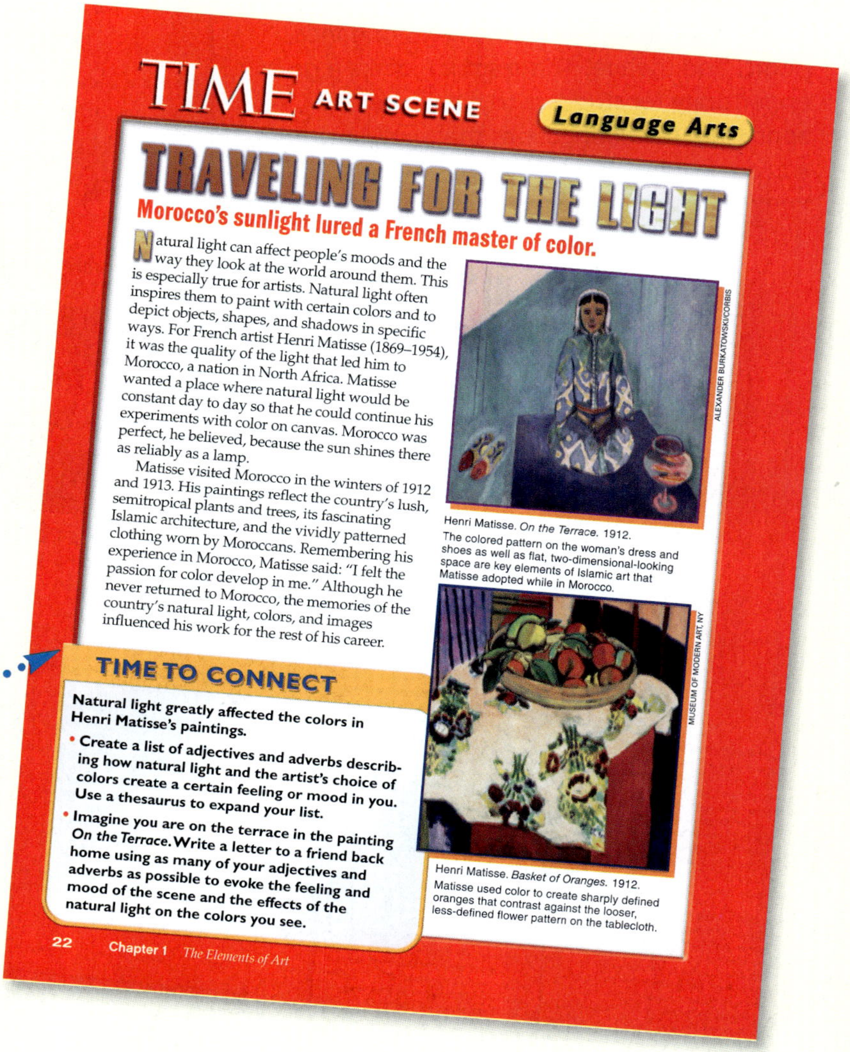
TIME ART SCENE

Language Arts

TRAVELING FOR THE LIGHT

Morocco's sunlight lured a French master of color.

Natural light can affect people's moods and the way they look at the world around them. This is especially true for artists. Natural light often inspires them to paint with certain colors and to depict objects, shapes, and shadows in specific ways. For French artist Henri Matisse (1869–1954), it was the quality of the light that led him to Morocco, a nation in North Africa. Matisse wanted a place where natural light would be constant day to day so that he could continue his experiments with color on canvas. Morocco was perfect, he believed, because the sun shines there as reliably as a lamp.

Matisse visited Morocco in the winters of 1912 and 1913. His paintings reflect the country's lush, semitropical plants and trees, its fascinating Islamic architecture, and the vividly patterned clothing worn by Moroccans. Remembering his experience in Morocco, Matisse said: "I felt the passion for color develop in me." Although he never returned to Morocco, the memories of the country's natural light, colors, and images influenced his work for the rest of his career.

ALEXANDER BURKATOWSKI/CORBIS

Henri Matisse. *On the Terrace.* 1912.
The colored pattern on the woman's dress and shoes as well as flat, two-dimensional-looking space are key elements of Islamic art that Matisse adopted while in Morocco.

MUSEUM OF MODERN ART, NY

Henri Matisse. *Basket of Oranges.* 1912.
Matisse used color to create sharply defined oranges that contrast against the looser, less-defined flower pattern on the tablecloth.

TIME TO CONNECT

Natural light greatly affected the colors in Henri Matisse's paintings.

- **Create a list of adjectives and adverbs describing how natural light and the artist's choice of colors create a certain feeling or mood in you. Use a thesaurus to expand your list.**
- **Imagine you are on the terrace in the painting *On the Terrace*. Write a letter to a friend back home using as many of your adjectives and adverbs as possible to evoke the feeling and mood of the scene and the effects of the natural light on the colors you see.**

22 Chapter 1 *The Elements of Art*

"TIME TO CONNECT" ACTIVITY

These concluding activities link the study of visual art with that of language arts.

Other Chapter Features

Meet the Artist Artist profiles are featured to encourage student understanding of the historical and cultural heritage of the artists featured.

Time & Place This feature makes a historical connection to artworks that appear in the text. It provides students with a window into the historical and cultural context of artists and their works.

Student Edition

Integrating the Performing Arts and Technology

PERFORMING ARTS HANDBOOK Features 15 artists or groups from the fields of dance, music, and theatre. This resource offers a great opportunity for students to recognize and appreciate the connections that exist between arts disciplines.

ARTSOURCE

Dance Ballet Folklórico de Mexico

For over 25 years, Ballet Folklórico de Mexico has presented authentic folk dances from different ethnic groups within Mexico. Amalia Hernández, the Artistic Director of the company...

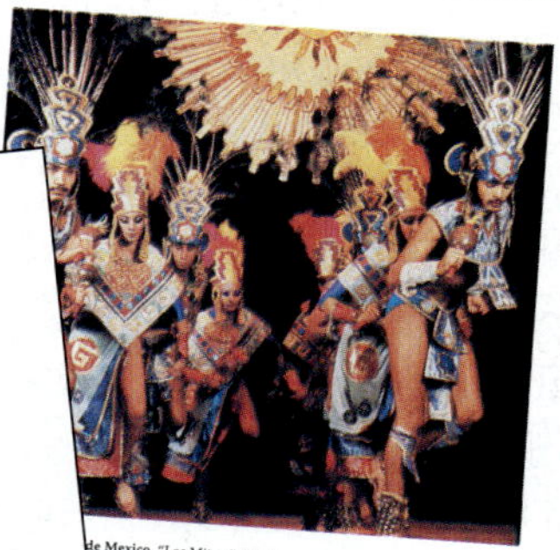

...de Mexico. "Los Mitos." Amalia ...Director. Photo courtesy of Friedson

Creative Expression Activities

Dance Stand in an open area with six to eight students and organize yourselves into three different geometric shapes, selecting from a circle, square, triangle, or the letter X. After your designs are organized, choose two that you like and walk or skip from one figure into another using eight counts to travel.

Language Arts Write a personal reflection of your impressions and feelings about either the images you see in the illustration or of the dance in the video.

ARTSOURCE

Music Vocalworks

Vocalworks has brought the music of the 1930s and 1940s to modern audiences since 1983. Singing the music of the swing era, they note that their group has lasted longer than the swing era itself. In their show, "Vocalworks Radio Hour," they re-create a live radio broadcast from the period when home entertainment meant having the family gather around the radio in the living room to hear news, music, dramas, or comedy programs. Since no production would be authentic without a commercial, Vocalworks also includes singing commercials advertising toothpowder and dish soap. It is hard to believe, but there was no TV during that time—only phonographs, radios, and movies. The Great Depression and World War II were very difficult times for the American people. Concerned about their future and how they and their families would survive, they worried about retaining democracy and freedom as well as the economic and social stability of their country. Swing music was a wonderful escape that helped them forget their troubles for a while, just as music does for people today.

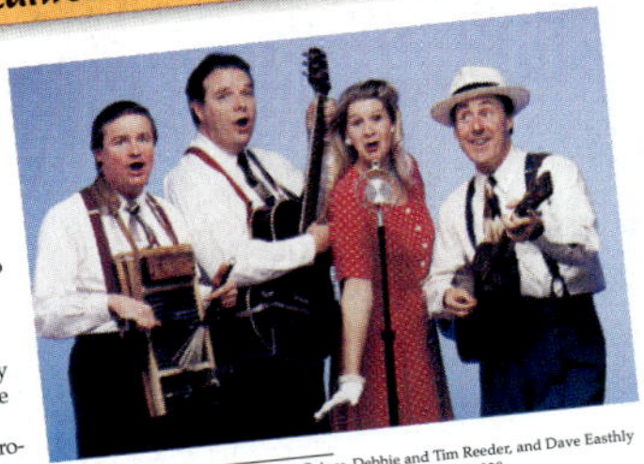

Vocalworks. Bruce Cooper, Michael Geiger, Debbie and Tim Reeder, and Dave Easthly perform "Vocalworks Radio Hour." Photo: Richard Hines. © 1998.

Discussion Questions

1. Improvisation is one of the characteristics of swing jazz. Look at the photo on this page and identify the instruments. Which ones do you think would be the ones most likely to be featured in the improvisation sections?
2. Swing music was characterized by its positive messages and upbeat rhythms during the Great Depression in the 1930s and World War II in the 1940s. Swing music and dance has gained a new popularity today. What do you think the reasons for this might be?
3. What type of popular music today raises your spirits and gives you renewed hope?

Creative Expression Activities

Social Studies Read about the Harlem Renaissance, 1919 to the early thirties. It was a time when African American life and experiences were dealt with from the perspective of African American artists, musicians, and writers. Much of it was inspired by life in Harlem, a small African American community in New York. Read about the Harlem Renaissance and its influence on jazz musicians, writers, poets and visual artists. Working in groups, present a choral verse reading of one of the following Langston Hughes poems to show how he was influenced by jazz: "The Weary Blues," or "Afro-American Fragment."

320 *Artsource: Performing Arts Handbook*

Paint Software

Using Paint Software

Paint software programs offer new conveniences and capabilities to artists. Digital paints do not require any drying time. Not only is there no drying necessary, but paint mixing is a mathematical process. A digital artist has millions of colors in his or her palette. Previously used colors can be duplicated with ease and precision. Also, as with all art software, a painting can be easily erased and altered.

Paint Software Basics

In digital paint programs, images are created and stored as *bitmaps.* These are files made up of tiny dots called *pixels.* Since photographs downloaded to the computer have a similar format, paint programs do double duty as photo editors. A paint program can be used to brighten a dark photo, enhance its contrast, and so forth.

The main features of a paint program are:

- **A menu bar.** The menu bar contains file management commands (such as Open and Save), edit commands (such as Undo and Redo), and view commands (for example, Zoom).
- **The toolbox.** The toolbox contains art tools, such as brushes and pens, and image manipulation tools. These allow you to flip or rotate an image among many other options.
- **Palettes.** These are separate windows that allow you to control colors, brush tip sizes, line thickness, and the like.

Most paint programs also come with a variety of filters. These add special effects to an image or photo. One example is "feathering," which gives an image a wispy, cloudlike look.

Technology Notes

Bitmap File Formats

One important aspect of working with paint programs is understanding file formats. There are many bitmap formats including JPEG, GIF, and PNG. It is worth noting that each of these formats has its own characteristics. JPEG images, for example, are compressed—stored in a smaller size. This means they take up less space on your computer's hard drive. GIF files are used for on-screen images. This format supports up to 256 colors and is often used for Web graphics. GIFs, however do not support print work. Finally, PNG images are increasingly turning up on Web sites and other environments shared by multiple computers and networks.

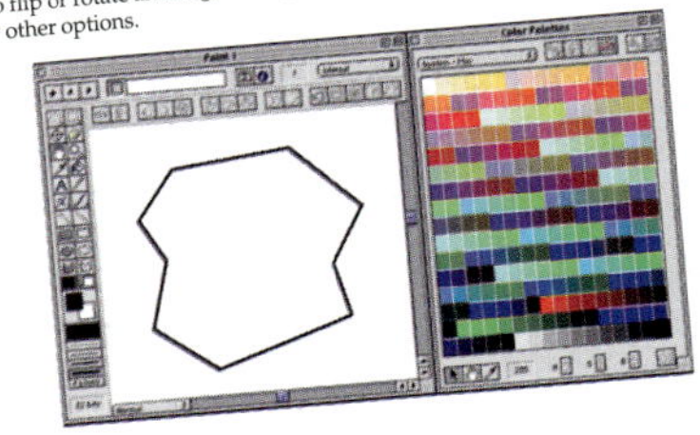

296 *Digital Media Guide*

DIGITAL MEDIA GUIDE Presents simplified information on digital hardware and software used in current art classrooms. A Technology Notes box for each topic provides practical advice that students can apply as they master digital media.

Support for the Art Teacher

The Teacher Wraparound Edition provides complete lesson plans, teaching suggestions, supplemental information, cross-references, and more—all conveniently "wrapped" around every page of the reduced student text. You will discover that the easy-to-follow lesson plan format gives a variety of teaching strategies to motivate students; introduces, teaches, and reinforces concepts; and provides inclusion strategies for adapting the program to the individual learning styles of your students.

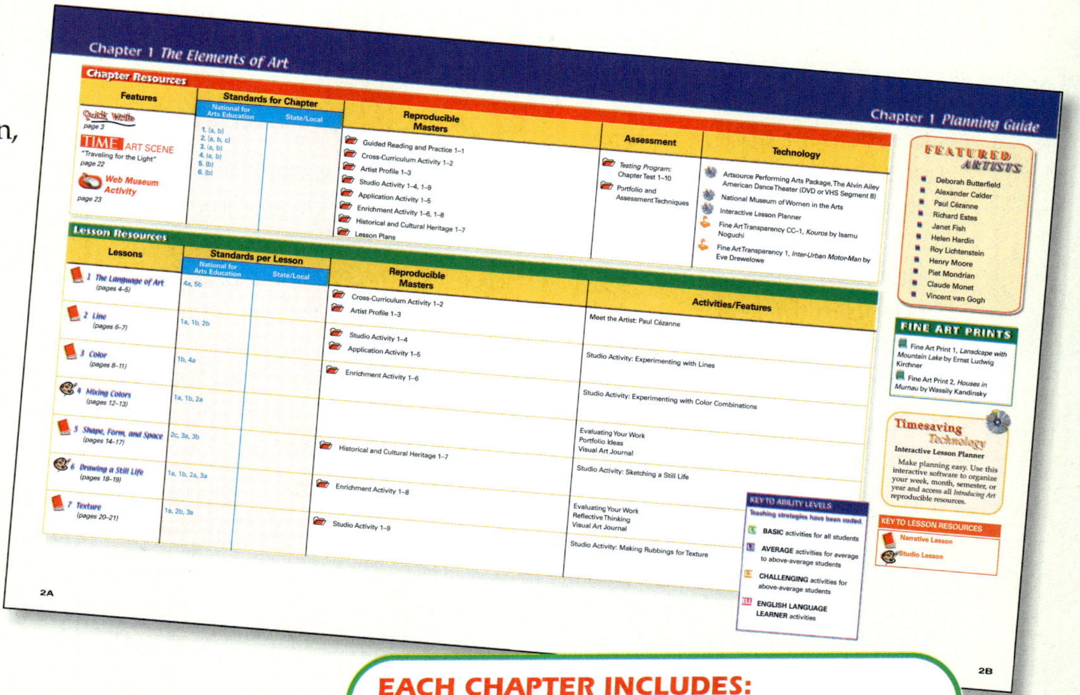

Chapter Planning Guides

To identify how the lessons and activities in each chapter of *Introducing Art* meet the national standards, the Scope and Sequence on pages TM 16–TM22 and each Chapter Planning Guide of the Teacher Wraparound Edition provide a correlation to the National Standards for Arts Education.

EACH CHAPTER INCLUDES:

- A chapter planning guide, which allows teachers to see chapter- and lesson-related resources at a glance, reduce planning time, and get the most from the program.
- Convenient lesson plans with a variety of teaching strategies.
- Features that introduce students to career opportunities and the performing arts.

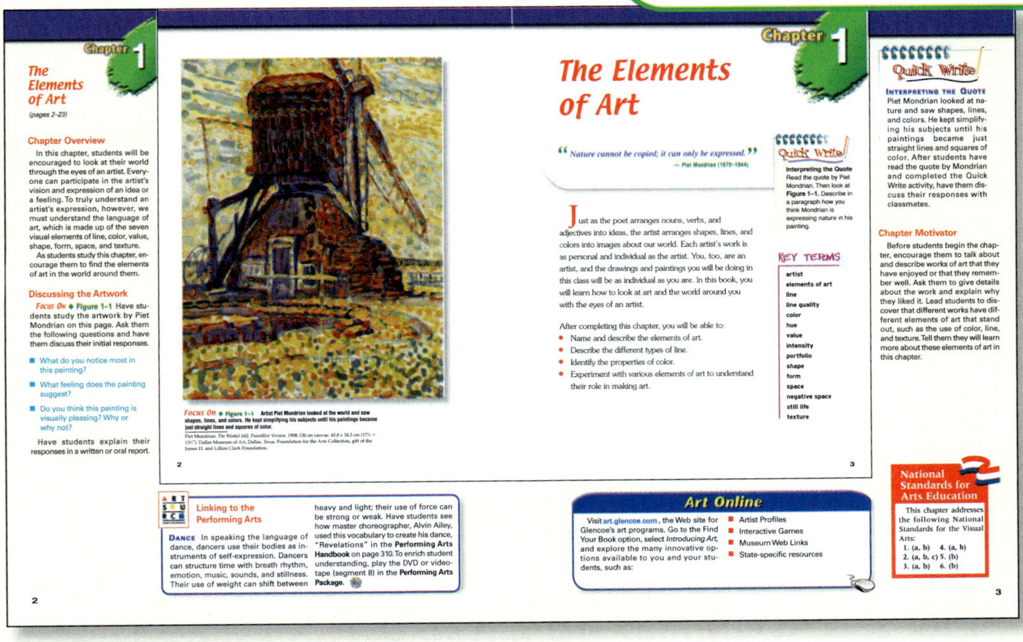

Organized for the Art Teacher

Lesson Plans The teaching material follows a consistent, easy-to-use pattern. The complete lesson cycle—Focus, Teach, Assess, Close—makes it easy to plan a lesson.

1. Focus

- Objectives list student learning goals
- Supplies conveniently indexed for the lesson
- Motivator activity to involve students in the lesson
- Vocabulary strategies to help students build vocabulary skills

2. Teach

Offers a variety of teaching strategies that promote critical thinking, problem solving, creative expression, and historical and cultural knowledge.

3. Assess

- Peer- and Self-Assessment techniques to help students monitor their mastery of lesson content and activities.
- Enrichment activities designed for students who are able and willing to explore the content further.

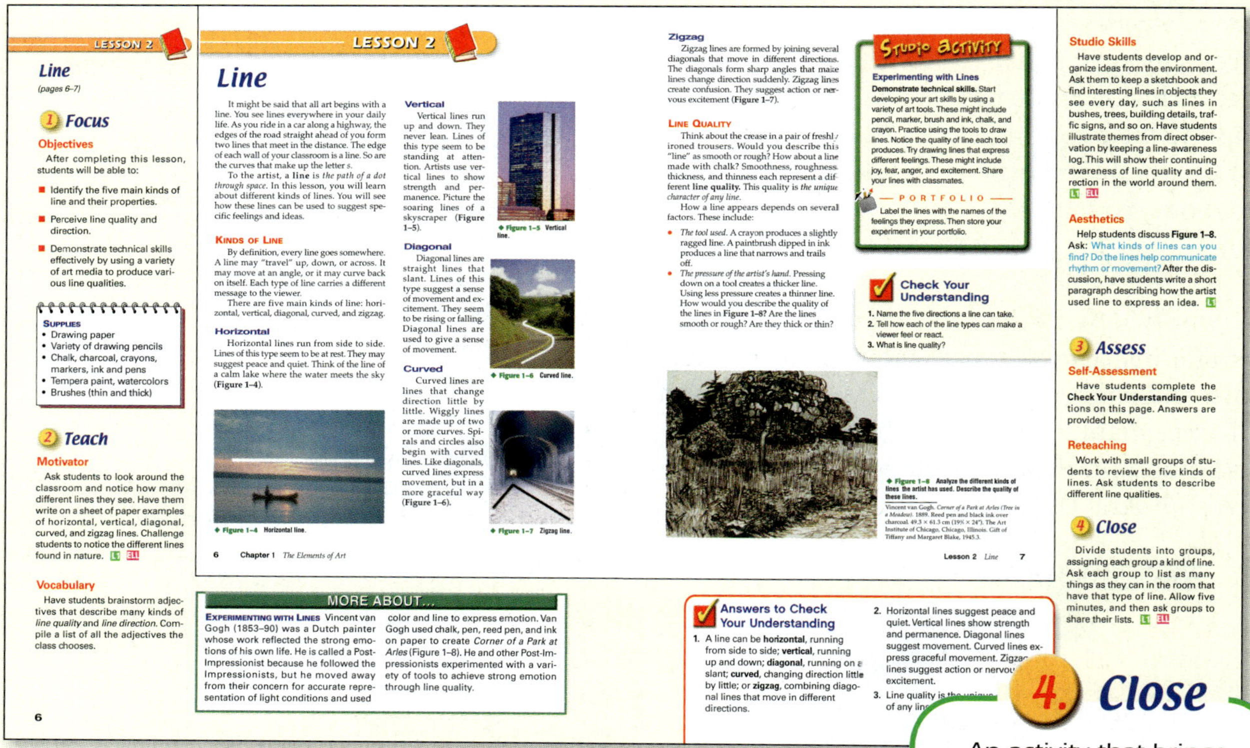
LESSON 2

Line
(pages 6–7)

1 Focus

Objectives

After completing this lesson, students will be able to:

- Identify the five main kinds of line and their properties.
- Perceive line quality and direction.
- Demonstrate technical skills effectively by using a variety of art media to produce various line qualities.

Supplies
- Drawing paper
- Variety of drawing pencils
- Chalk, charcoal, crayons, markers, ink and pens
- Tempera paint, watercolors
- Brushes (thin and thick)

2 Teach

Motivator

Ask students to look around the classroom and notice how many different lines they see. Have them write on a sheet of paper examples of horizontal, vertical, diagonal, curved, and zigzag lines. Challenge students to notice the different lines found in nature.

Vocabulary

Have students brainstorm adjectives that describe many kinds of *line quality* and *line direction*. Compile a list of the adjectives the class chooses.

6

LESSON 2

Line

It might be said that all art begins with a line. You see lines everywhere in your daily life. As you ride in a car along a highway, the edges of the road straight ahead of you form two lines that meet in the distance. The edge of each wall of your classroom is a line. So are the curves that make up the letter *s*.

To the artist, a **line** is *the path of a dot through space*. In this lesson, you will learn about different kinds of lines. You will see how these lines can be used to suggest specific feelings and ideas.

Kinds of Line

By definition, every line goes somewhere. A line may "travel" up, down, or across. It may move at an angle, or it may curve back on itself. Each type of line carries a different message to the viewer.

There are five main kinds of line: horizontal, vertical, diagonal, curved, and zigzag.

Horizontal

Horizontal lines run from side to side. Lines of this type seem to be at rest. They may suggest peace and quiet. Think of the line of a calm lake where the water meets the sky (Figure 1–4).

Figure 1–4 Horizontal line.

Vertical

Vertical lines run up and down. They never lean. Lines of this type seem to be standing at attention. Artists use vertical lines to show strength and permanence. Picture the soaring lines of a skyscraper (Figure 1–5).

Figure 1–5 Vertical line.

Diagonal

Diagonal lines are straight lines that slant. Lines of this type suggest a sense of movement and excitement. They seem to be rising or falling. Diagonal lines are used to give a sense of movement.

Figure 1–6 Curved line.

Curved

Curved lines are lines that change direction little by little. Wiggly lines are made up of two or more curves. Spirals and circles also begin with curved lines. Like diagonals, curved lines express movement, but in a more graceful way (Figure 1–6).

Figure 1–7 Zigzag line.

6 Chapter 1 *The Elements of Art*

Zigzag

Zigzag lines are formed by joining several diagonals that move in different directions. The diagonals form sharp angles that make lines change direction suddenly. Zigzag lines create confusion. They suggest action or nervous excitement (Figure 1–7).

Line Quality

Think about the crease in a pair of freshly ironed trousers. Would you describe this "line" as smooth or rough? How about a line made with chalk? Smoothness, roughness, thickness, and thinness each represent a different **line quality**. This quality is *the unique character of any line*.

How a line appears depends on several factors. These include:

- *The tool used.* A crayon produces a slightly ragged line. A paintbrush dipped in ink produces a line that narrows and trails off.
- *The pressure of the artist's hand.* Pressing down on a tool creates a thicker line. Using less pressure creates a thinner line.

How would you describe the quality of the lines in Figure 1–8? Are the lines smooth or rough? Are they thick or thin?

Studio Activity

Experimenting with Lines

Demonstrate technical skills. Start developing your art skills by using a variety of art tools. These might include pencil, marker, brush and ink, chalk, and crayon. Practice using the tools to draw lines. Notice the quality of line each tool produces. Try drawing lines that express different feelings. These might include joy, fear, anger, and excitement. Share your lines with classmates.

PORTFOLIO

Label the lines with the names of the feelings they express. Then store your experiment in your portfolio.

Check Your Understanding

1. Name the five directions a line can take.
2. Tell how each of the line types can make a viewer feel or react.
3. What is line quality?

Figure 1–8 Analyze the different kinds of lines the artist has used. Describe the quality of these lines.

Vincent van Gogh. *Corner of a Park at Arles (Tree in a Meadow).* 1889. Reed pen and black ink over charcoal. 49.3 × 61.3 cm (19⅜ × 24"). The Art Institute of Chicago, Chicago, Illinois. Gift of Tiffany and Margaret Blake, 1945.3.

Lesson 2 *Line* 7

Studio Skills

Have students develop and organize ideas from the environment. Ask them to keep a sketchbook and find interesting lines in objects they see every day, such as lines in bushes, trees, building details, traffic signs, and so on. Have students illustrate themes from direct observation by keeping a line-awareness log. This will show their continuing awareness of line quality and direction in the world around them.

Aesthetics

Help students discuss **Figure 1–8**. Ask: What kinds of lines can you find? Do the lines help communicate rhythm or movement? After the discussion, have students write a short paragraph describing how the artist used line to express an idea.

3 Assess

Self-Assessment

Have students complete the **Check Your Understanding** questions on this page. Answers are provided below.

Reteaching

Work with small groups of students to review the five kinds of lines. Ask students to describe different line qualities.

4 Close

Divide students into groups, assigning each group a kind of line. Ask each group to list as many things as they can in the room that have that type of line. Allow five minutes, and then ask groups to share their lists.

MORE ABOUT...

Experimenting with Lines Vincent van Gogh (1853–90) was a Dutch painter whose work reflected the strong emotions of his own life. He is called a Post-Impressionist because he followed the Impressionists, but he moved away from their concern for accurate representation of light conditions and used color and line to express emotion. Van Gogh used chalk, pen, reed pen, and ink on paper to create *Corner of a Park at Arles* (Figure 1–8). He and other Post-Impressionists experimented with a variety of tools to achieve strong emotion through line quality.

Answers to Check Your Understanding

1. A line can be **horizontal**, running from side to side; **vertical**, running up and down; **diagonal**, running on a slant; **curved**, changing direction little by little; or **zigzag**, combining diagonal lines that move in different directions.
2. Horizontal lines suggest peace and quiet. Vertical lines show strength and permanence. Diagonal lines suggest movement. Curved lines express graceful movement. Zigzag lines suggest action or nervous excitement.
3. Line quality is the unique ... of any line.

4. Close

An activity that brings closure to the lesson and recaps important concepts from the lesson.

Bottom Column Annotations

Boxes at the bottom of the page offer additional information. Categories include:

- Answers to Check Your Understanding
- Community Connection
- Curriculum Connections
- Technology Strategies in the Art Classroom
- Inclusion Strategies
- More About…
- Teacher to Teacher
- Resources Beyond the Classroom
- Safety Tip
- Story Behind the Artwork
- Developing a Portfolio
- Career Opportunities in Art

Teacher Classroom Resources

Teacher Resource Binder

Teacher Resource Binder provides the following teaching materials for each chapter.

- Guided Reading and Practice
- Cross-Curriculum Activity
- Artist Profile
- Studio Activity
- Historical and Cultural Heritage
- Application Activity
- Enrichment Activity
- Chapter Test
- Reproducible Lesson Plans are also included in the Teacher Resource Binder. They provide a checklist format for lesson objectives, strategies, and resource materials.

Portfolio and Assessment Techniques

This booklet is newly updated to address basic information used in portfolio assessment for the visual arts. It includes worksheets for teachers and students in addition to samples of useful rubrics.

Fine Art Transparencies

The ready-to-use overhead color transparency package contains 28 full-color Fine Art overhead transparencies—14 of which have a cross-curricular focus. Accompanying the transparencies is an Instructor Guide with background information and student activity sheets, all in a convenient three-ring binder.

Fine Art Prints

Twenty quality art masterpieces are printed on sturdy self-supporting stock to supplement the artwork appearing in the student text. The laminated prints are resistant to wear and are presented in a durable portfolio with an Instructor Guide for convenient classroom use and storage. Discussion questions are printed on the back of each print in English and Spanish.

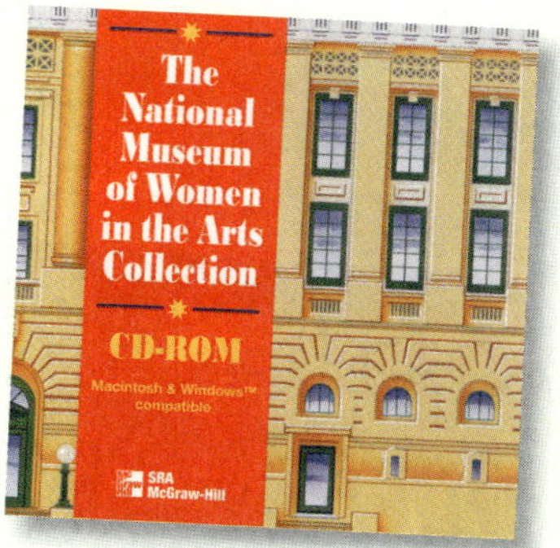

National Museum of Women in the Arts CD-ROM

This easy-to-navigate CD-ROM provides unique access to 200 artworks from the collection of the National Museum of Women in the Arts. Biographies of these renowned artists are also included as well as a quiz feature that offers a multiple choice assessment of your students' knowledge of the artists, times, locations, media, and subjects.

Artsource®: Performing Arts Package

This new performing arts package provides a multimedia resource for further exploration of dance, music, and theatre. This exciting media package includes an Instructor Guide, a DVD and videotape, a CD, and features performances by diverse artists, such as:

- Alvin Ailey American Dance Theater
- Ballet Folklorico de Mexico
- "Cello Man" Eugene Friesen
- Pilobolus Dance Theatre

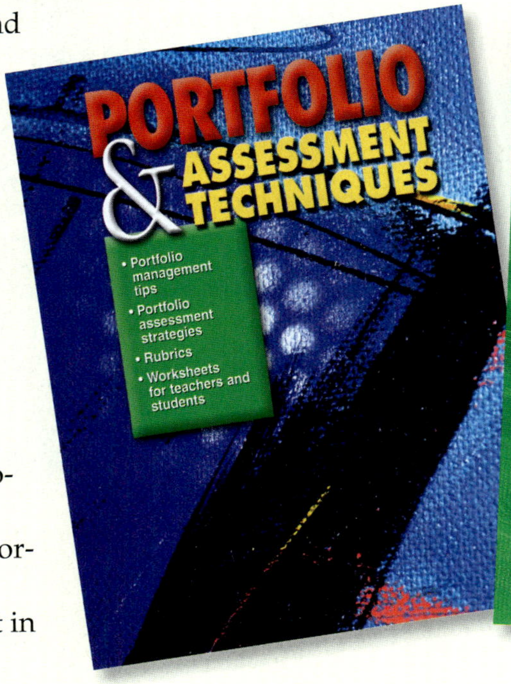

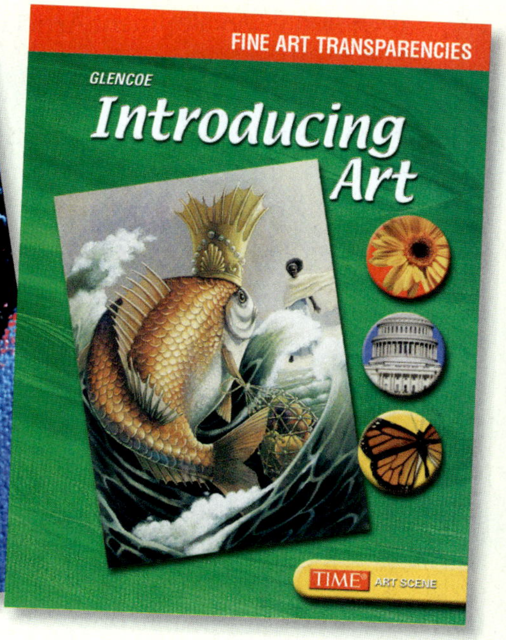

Media and Technology Support

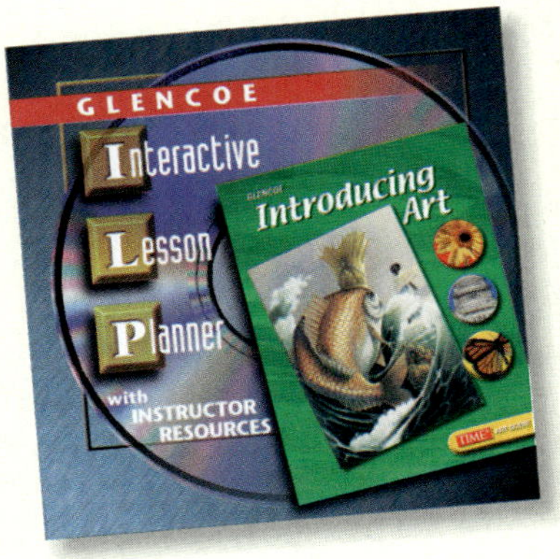

Interactive Lesson Planner

Custom-design your lesson plan with this easy-to-use CD-ROM. The electronic format allows teachers to select a preset plan or create their own—either way, it offers access to electronic files of all reproducible resources at the click of a button. You can print all the blackline master worksheets and activities available in the Teacher Resource Binder.

Visit Introducing Art online at: art.glencoe.com

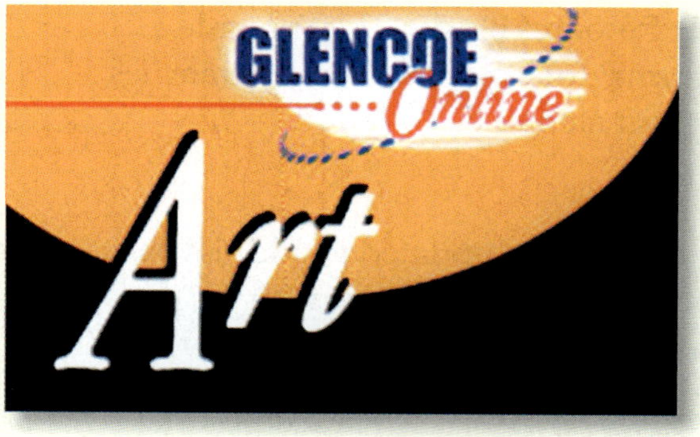

The Glencoe Art Online home page on the Internet provides up-to-date resources and activities to complement Glencoe's comprehensive art program. After selecting the Find Your Book option from the menu, you can explore the customized Web site for *Introducing Art*. Glencoe Art Online and the specific *Introducing Art* site offer many alternative options for enriching your students' art education.

For Teachers

- Correlations to National and State Standards for Arts Education
- Professional Development Articles
- Art Education Links

For Students and Teachers

- Web Museum Tours
- Interactive Games
- Career Corner
- Internet Activities
- Studio Activities and Projects
- Student and Teacher Web Links
- Museum Web Links
- Student Art Gallery
- Artist Profiles
- National Standards

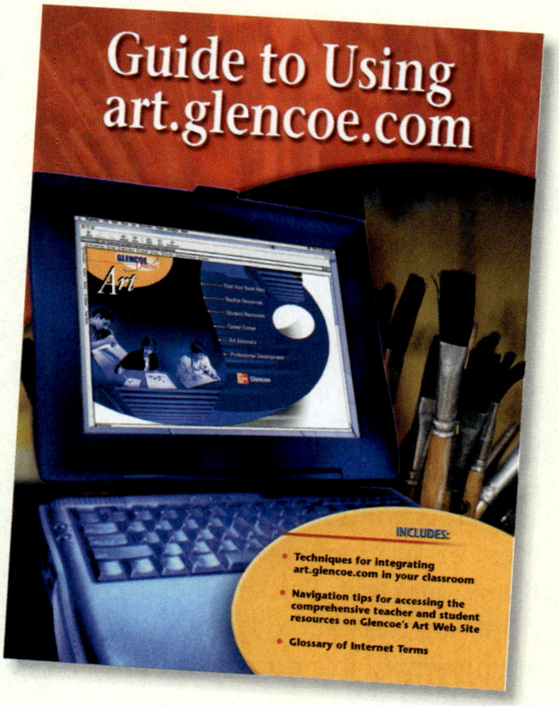

Guide to Using art.glencoe.com

This inclusive guide provides general strategies for incorporating Internet activities into the art classroom. Also, let this booklet be your guide to the many interactive and educational options available at the Glencoe Art Web site.

Introducing Art is for All Students

The *Introducing Art* program incorporates a wealth of resources specifically designed to help students of every learning style and ability level succeed in the visual arts. This table shows how components for the Student Edition, Teacher Wraparound Edition, and Teacher Resource Binder can be used for inclusion.

ADDRESSING STUDENT NEEDS	STUDENT EDITION	TEACHER WRAPAROUND EDITION (TWE)	TEACHER RESOURCE BINDER
Different Learning Styles	Fine art illustration program rich in variety and diversity, and clearly labeled with figure numbers Figure captions point out key concepts illustrated in fine art and provide credit information Vocabulary terms set in boldface for easy identification in text Clearly marked heads, subheads, and bulleted lists Studio Activities actively engage students of all learning styles	Inclusion Strategies throughout, specifically written and labeled for Multiple Intelligences, English Language Learners, Special Learning Needs, Behavioral Problems, At-Risk, Gifted, Physically Impaired, Visually Impaired, and Hearing Impaired Teaching Strategies coded Level 1, Level 2, and Level 3 for students of all ability levels Motivators presented to help teachers jump-start the whole classroom Peer- and Self-Assessment to include students of different learning styles in the assessment process	Guided Reading and Practice Activities Application Activities Artsource: Performing Arts Package Cross-Curriculum Activities Fine Art Prints Fine Art Transparencies Studio Activities Portfolio and Assessment Techniques booklet
Physically and Mentally Challenged Students	Chapter Opener includes bulleted objectives to get students thinking about the chapter content before they begin Fine art illustrations focus on important content	Teaching Strategies coded with Level 1 provide options for teacher-directed activities Inclusion Strategies provide tips on teaching physically and mentally challenged students	Artsource: Performing Arts Package Fine Art Prints Fine Art Transparencies Guided Reading and Practice
Gifted Students	Time & Place feature provides additional historical information on artworks appearing in the text Cross-Curriculum Connections engage students to connect the visual arts with other disciplines	Teaching Strategies coded L3 for students able and willing to work independently Enrichment Activities Art in Everyday Life provides expanded ideas and activities for the self-directed learner	Additional Studio Activities Application Activities Enrichment Activities Artist Profiles Cross-Curriculum Activities Historical and Cultural Heritage Activities

ADDRESSING STUDENT NEEDS	STUDENT EDITION	TEACHER WRAPAROUND EDITION (TWE)	TEACHER RESOURCE BINDER
English Language Learners	Vocabulary terms set in boldface for easy identification in text Vocabulary review for each lesson in Check Your Understanding questions Spanish Glosario for each vocabulary term	Teaching Strategies coded ELL for English Language Learners	Guided Reading and Practice provides visual organizers to allow students to better master concepts Portfolio and Assessment Techniques booklet
Reluctant Readers and Writers	Quick Write encourages students to write about art Meet the Artist captures student interest and engages them in reading about artists' lives Vocabulary terms set in boldface for easy identification in text Figure captions point out key concepts illustrated in fine art and provide credit information Clearly marked heads, subheads, and bulleted lists outline content	Vocabulary strategies for each lesson Reteaching strategies reinforce lesson content before moving on	Application Activities Artist Profiles Fine Art Prints Fine Art Transparencies Historical and Cultural Heritage Activities Studio Activities
Behavioral Disorders (Includes ADD/ ADHD students)	Short, focused lessons hold students' attention Fine art illustration program rich in variety and cultural diversity, and clearly labeled with figure numbers Figure captions provide focus for students and frequently test their understanding of core concepts Clearly marked heads, subheads, and bulleted lists outline content	Team Building Activities foster teamwork and assign specific roles to students who need focus Inclusion Strategies provide ideas for special-needs students	Fine Art Prints Fine Art Transparencies Studio Activities Guided Reading and Practice
At-Risk Students	Short, focused lessons hold students' attention Fine art illustration program rich in variety and cultural diversity	Community Connection provides ideas for involving students in community art projects Linking to the Performing Arts connects content to theatre, music, and dance to enrich the learning experience and inspire students	Artsource: Performing Arts Package Fine Art Prints Fine Art Transparencies Guided Reading and Practice

National Standards for the Visual Arts

The National Standards for Arts Education represents, in part, the results of a two-year effort by the Consortium of National Arts Education Associations to set standards for arts education in the United States. These six standards listed below are designed specifically for students in grades 5–8.

NATIONAL STANDARDS

This chapter addresses the following National Standards for the Visual Arts:

1. (a, b) **3.** (a, b) **5.** (a, b, c)
2. (a, b, c) **4.** (a, b, c) **6.** (a, b)

1. **Content Standard:** Understanding and applying media, techniques, and processes
   Achievement Standard:
   Students
   a. select media, techniques, and processes; analyze what makes them effective or not effective in communicating ideas; and reflect upon the effectiveness of their choices
   b. intentionally take advantage of the qualities and characteristics of art media, techniques, and processes to enhance communication of their experiences and ideas

2. **Content Standard:** Using knowledge of structures and functions
   Achievement Standard:
   Students
   a. generalize about the effects of visual structures and functions and reflect upon these effects in their own work
   b. employ organizational structures and analyze what makes them effective or not effective in the communication of ideas
   c. select and use the qualities of structures and functions of art to improve communication of their ideas

3. **Content Standard:** Choosing and evaluating a range of subject matter, symbols and ideas
   Achievement Standard:
   Students
   a. integrate visual, spatial, and temporal concepts with content to communicate intended meaning in their artworks
   b. use subjects, themes, and symbols that demonstrate knowledge of contexts, values, and aesthetics that communicate intended meaning in artworks

4. **Content Standard:** Understanding the visual arts in relation to history and cultures
   Achievement Standard:
   Students
   a. know and compare the characteristics of artworks in various eras and cultures
   b. describe and place a variety of art objects in historical and cultural contexts
   c. analyze, describe, and demonstrate how factors of time and place (such as climate, resources, ideas, and technology) influence visual characteristics that give meaning and value to a work of art

5. **Content Standard:** Reflecting upon and assessing the characteristics and merits of their work and the work of others
   Achievement Standard:
   Students
   a. compare multiple purposes for creating works of art
   b. analyze contemporary and historic meanings in specific artworks through cultural and aesthetic inquiry
   c. describe and compare a variety of individual responses to their own artworks and to artworks from various eras and cultures

6. **Content Standard:** Making connections between visual arts and other disciplines
   Achievement Standard:
   Students
   a. compare the characteristics of works in two or more art forms that share similar subject matter, historical periods, or cultural context
   b. describe ways in which the principles and subject matter of other disciplines taught in the school are interrelated with the visual arts

Scope and Sequence

KEY
(1), (2), (3) etc. = Lessons
(R) = Chapter Review

	Chapter 1 The Elements of Art	Chapter 2 The Principles of Art
NATIONAL STANDARDS FOR THE VISUAL ARTS	1. (a, b) 3. (a, b) 5. (b) 2. (a, b, c) 4. (a, b) 6. (b)	1. (a, b) 3. (a, b) 5. (b, c) 2. (a, b, c) 4. (a, b, c)
ARTISTIC PERCEPTION	Perceiving color (3) Visual Art Journal (4, 6) Studying uses of color in paintings (6)	Identifying movement and rhythm (4) Visual Art Journal (5) Recognizing unity (6)
CREATIVE EXPRESSION	Experimenting with lines (2) Experimenting with color combinations (3) Mixing colors (4) Sketching a still life (5) Drawing a still life (6) Making rubbings for texture (7)	Sketching shapes with balance (1) Making a mask with formal balance (2) Making a tessellation (5) Computer Option (5)
HISTORICAL/CULTURAL CONTEXT	Artist defined (1) Identifying cultural influence in artworks (1) Van Gogh's use of line (2) Hardin's art (3) Monet's use of color (4) Use of negative space (5) Texture in Guardian Figure (7)	Description of African mask (2) Identifying cultural influence in artworks (3) Identifying in artworks the influence of historical events (4)
AESTHETIC VALUING	Evaluating Your Work (4, 6) Reflective Thinking (6)	Evaluating Your Work (2, 5) Reflective Thinking (2) Identifying unity (6)
ELEMENTS AND PRINCIPLES OF ART	Using the artist's vocabulary (1) Line defined (2) Color and value defined (3) Properties of color; Combining colors (3) Shape, form, space defined (5) Texture defined (7) Web Museum Activity (R)	Balance defined (1) Variety, harmony, emphasis, proportion defined (3) Movement, rhythm defined (4) Unity defined (6)
ART FORMS	Drawing (2, 5, 6) Painting (3, 5, 6, 7) Sculpture (5)	Drawing (2, 5) Painting (3) Sculpture (5)
MEDIA, TOOLS, TECHNIQUES, AND PROCESSES	Tools and processes for creating lines (2) Impressionist color techniques (4) Space techniques (5)	Making a mask with clay (2) Making a Tessellation (5)
CURRICULUM AND PERFORMING ARTS CONNECTIONS	Cross-Curriculum Connections (R) Identifying cultural influence in artworks (TIME Art Scene)	Cross-Curriculum Connections (R) Identify in artworks the influence of historical events (TIME Art Scene)
CAREERS/PORTFOLIOS	Portfolio Ideas (4) Portfolios (2, 3, 5, 7)	Portfolios (1, 6)

Chapter 3 Art Media and Techniques	Chapter 4 Looking at Art	Chapter 5 Art Through the Ages
1. (a, b) 3. (a) 5. (a, b) 2. (a, b, c) 4. (a, c) 6. (a, b)	1. (a, b) 3. (a) 5. (a, b, c) 2. (a, b, c) 4. (a, b) 6. (b)	1. (a, b) 3. (a, b) 5. (b, c) 2. (a, b) 4. (a, b, c) 6. (a, b)
Why artists draw (1) Perception defined (1)	Describing artworks (3) Point-of-view defined (4) Visual Art Journal (4)	Symbol defined (1) Studying abstraction in art (8)
Keeping a sketchbook (1) Making a gesture drawing (2) Experimenting with watercolor (3) Creating a portrait (4) Studio Option (4) Making a relief block print (5) Making a collage (7)	Experimenting with nonobjective art (3) Creating a realistic painting (4) Studio Option (4) Creating an expressive word design (5) Creating an abstract figure (6)	Creating an Egyptian tomb painting (2) Creating a Japanese Drawing (3) Making a relief sculpture (4) Making a stained-glass window (5) Creating a diorama (6) Using abstraction in art (8)
History of painting media (3, 8) History of printmaking techniques (5) Recordings of historical events (6)	Artworks as recordings of historical events (1, 3) History of nonobjective art (3) Web Museum Activity (R)	Art of ancient Egypt, Greece, and Rome (1) Pericles and Exekias (1) Art of ancient India and Japan (3) History of Hinduism and Buddhism (3) African sculpture (4) Art of the Renaissance (5) Art of the 19/20th century (7) Impressionists and Surrealists defined (7)
Evaluating Your Work (2, 4, 7) Reflective Thinking (2)	Aesthetics and aesthetic views (1) Subject, composition, content defined (1) Art criticism (2) Critiquing nonobjective art (3) Evaluating Your Work (4, 6) Reflective Thinking (5) Visual Art Journal (6)	Evaluating Your Work (2, 4, 6, 8) Reflective Thinking (2) Analyzing an abstract artwork (8)
Comparing portraits (4)	Elements and principles as composition (2)	Rules of Egyptian art (1) Elements and principles in Greek art (1) Symbol defined (2) Line perspective defined (6) Using color to create space (6)
Drawing (1, 2) Painting (3, 4) Printing (5) Sculpture (6) Digital Art (8)	Painting (1, 2, 3, 4, 5, 6) Sculpture (3)	Sculpture (1, 2, 3, 4, 6) Pottery (1) Painting (2, 5, 7, 8) Painted screen (3) Architecture (5)
Art media defined (1) Drawing media (1, 2) Shading techniques (1) Gesture drawing defined (2) Painting media (3) Pigments, binders, and solvents defined (3) Printmaking (5) Sculpture (6) Collage defined (7) Digital art media (8)	Nonobjective techniques (3) Expressive techniques (5) Abstract techniques (6)	Bust defined (1) Contour defined (2) Relief sculpture techniques (4) Architecture techniques (5)
Cross-Curriculum Connections (R) Identify in artworks the influence of historical events (TIME Art Scene)	Cross-Curriculum Connections (R)	Cross-Curriculum Connections (R) Artworks as recordings of historical events (TIME Art Scene)
Portfolio Ideas (7) Portfolios (1, 3, 5, 8) Avocational opportunities in art (4)	Portfolios (1, 2, 3) Art Critic (2) Portfolio Ideas (6)	Portfolio Ideas (8) Portfolios (3, 5) Compare career opportunities in art (8)

KEY (1), (2), (3) etc. = Lessons (R) = Chapter Review	Chapter 6 Perceiving Nature	Chapter 7 Observing Animals
NATIONAL STANDARDS FOR THE VISUAL ARTS	1. (a, b) 2. (a, b, c) 3. (a, b) 4. (a, c) 5. (a, b, c) 6. (a, b)	1. (a, b) 2. (a, b) 3. (a, b) 4. (a, b, c) 5. (a, b, c) 6. (a, b)
ARTISTIC PERCEPTION	Landscape defined (1) Nature study defined (3) Point-of-view described (3, 4) Studying seasonal artworks (5)	Illumination defined (5) Tapestry defined (7)
CREATIVE EXPRESSION	Making a stylized landscape (1) Creating a nature scene (1) Experimenting with point-of-view (3) Drawing from a bird's-eye view (4) Creating seasonal colors (5) Painting a seasonal event (6) Making a monoprint (7) Painting a storm (8)	Inventing a mascot (1) Creating a totem (2) Making an animal sculpture (6) Creating an imaginary animal (7) Creating a fantasy creature (8)
HISTORICAL/CULTURAL CONTEXT	Compare artworks from a variety of cultures (3, 5)	Prehistoric art (1) Australian aboriginal art (2) Early Chinese art (3) Compare artworks from a variety of cultures (3) Modern Japanese art (3) Identifying cultural influence in artworks (5) Persian art (5)
AESTHETIC VALUING	Evaluating Your Work (2, 4, 8) Expressive art (8)	Evaluating Your Work (2, 6, 8) Reflective Thinking (2)
ELEMENTS AND PRINCIPLES OF ART	Perspective in an artwork (1) Rhythm in an artwork (1, 2) Using elements and principles in an artwork (2) Size and placement in an artwork (5)	Using line (4) Line in illuminations (5) Identifying elements and principles in sculpture (6) Color in Expressionism (7)
ART FORMS	Painting (1, 2, 3, 4, 5, 6, 7) Assemblage (2) Drawing (3) Printmaking (7)	Sculpture (1, 6, 8) Painting (1, 5, 7) Pottery (3) Printmaking (4) Weaving (7)
MEDIA, TOOLS, TECHNIQUES, AND PROCESSES	Monoprint techniques (7)	Tools of early painters (1) Porcelain defined (2) Appliqué technique (3) Calligraphy defined (5) Tapestry defined (7) Overlapping technique (7) Folk art defined (8) Folk art media (8)
CURRICULUM AND PERFORMING ARTS CONNECTIONS	Art & Reading (6) Cross-Curriculum Connections (R)	Art & Reading (4) Cross-Curriculum Connections (R)
CAREERS/PORTFOLIOS	Portfolio Ideas (4) Portfolios (1, 7) Avocational opportunities in art (8)	Portfolio Ideas (8) Compare career opportunities in art (8)

Chapter 8 Portraying People	Chapter 9 Visiting Places	Chapter 10 Examining Objects
1. (a, b) 3. (a, b) 5. (a, b, c) 2. (a, c) 4. (a, b, c) 6. (b)	1. (a, b) 3. (a) 5. (a, b, c) 2. (a, b) 4. (a, c) 6. (a, b)	1. (a, b) 3. (a) 5. (b, c) 2. (a, b, c) 4. (a, b, c) 6. (b)
Figure study defined (3) Self-portrait defined (2)	Cities in art (5) Sketching details of shapes and objects Panorama defined (7)	Perceive defined (1) Nature studies described (1)
Creating an expressive face (2) Drawing a figure in action (4) Experimenting with abstract designs (5) Making a hero exhibit (7) Creating a mixed-media banner (8)	Creating a fanciful exterior (4) Drawing a building detail (5) Creating a mixed-media cityscape (6) Creating a seasonal panorama (8)	Experimenting with form and value (3) Painting a watercolor still life (4) Creating an object design (5) Building a clay instrument (6) Creating a pendant (8)
Portraits as historical records (1) Painting in the 1500s (1) Compare artworks from a variety of cultures (1) Japanese warrior masks (2) Identify in artworks the influence of historical events (5) Renaissance sculpture (5) Michelangelo (5) African ancestor figures (5) Art & Social Studies (6) Folk legends in art (7)	Vincent van Gogh (1) Comparing artworks from a variety of cultures (1) Homes of the past and present (3) Frank Lloyd Wright (3) Identify in artworks the influence of historical events (3) Russian architecture of the 1500s (4) Victorian architecture (4) Louis H. Sullivan (5) John Sloan and the Eight (6) Identifying cultural influence in artworks (7)	Georgia O'Keeffe (1) Compare artworks from a variety of cultures (1) Japanese still life (3) Persian applied art (5) Roman goldwork (5) Jewelry from the 1500s (7) Jewelry from the 1700s (7) Compare artworks from a variety of cultures (7) Southwestern art (8)
Visual Art Journal (2) Reflective Thinking (4) Evaluating Your Work (2, 4, 8)	Evaluating Your Work (4, 6, 8) Reflective Thinking (6)	Evaluating Your Work (4, 6, 8) Reflective Thinking (6)
Style defined (1) Elements and principles used to suggest movement (3, 4)	Using rhythm in architectural design (4) Analyze art elements and principles (4) Organization of elements and principles in an artwork (5) Using color to suggest season (8)	Using elements and principles in still lifes (3) Using shape to create interest (8)
Painting (1, 3, 4) Sculpture (2, 5, 7) Mixed media (8)	Painting (1, 7) Photography (1) Architecture (3, 4, 5) Mixed media (6) Sculpture (6)	Painting (1, 3, 4) Drawing (1) Sculpture (5) Jewelry making (5, 7, 8) Pottery (6) Pottery defined (6)
Portraiture defined (5) Murals defined (7)	Staged photography defined (1) Architectural techniques defined (4) Cityscape defined (5) Seascape defined (7)	Still life described (3) Fluting defined (5) Slip defined (6) Kiln described (6)
Art & Social Studies (6) Cross-Curriculum Connections (R) Identify in artworks the influence of historical events (TIME Art Scene)	Art & Reading (2) Cross-Curriculum Connections (R) Identify in artworks the influence of political events (TIME Art Scene)	Art & Math (2) Cross-Curriculum Connections (R)
Portfolio Ideas (8) Portfolio (7)	Portfolio Ideas (8) Portfolios (5)	Portfolio Ideas (4) Portfolios (3, 5)

KEY (1), (2), (3) etc. = Lessons (R) = Chapter Review	Chapter 11 Recording Events	Chapter 12 Telling a Story
NATIONAL STANDARDS FOR THE VISUAL ARTS	1. (a, b) 2. (a, b, c) 3. (a, b) 4. (a, b, c) 5. (a, b, c) 6. (a, b)	1. (a, b) 2. (a, b) 4. (a, b) 5. (a, b) 6. (a, b)
ARTISTIC PERCEPTION	Visual reporting and recording (10 Check Your Understanding (1, 3, 5, 7)	Visual stories (1, 2, 5) Using myths and legends in art (3)
CREATIVE EXPRESSION	Composing a photograph (1) Drawing a sporting event (2) Recording a historical event (3) Drawing a cartoon (4) Planning a mosaic (5) Planning a story board (7) Making a video documentary (8)	Designing a cartouche (1) Making a visual autobiography (2) Creating a mythical creature (4) Creating a book cover (8)
HISTORICAL/CULTURAL CONTEXT	Artist as reporter (1) Identify in artworks the influence of historical events (1, 5) Artist as historian (3) Art & Social Studies (6)	Chinese picture writing (1) Native American picture writing (1) Chinese mythical art (3) Hindu mythical art (3) Identify cultural influence in artworks (3) Kachina defined (4) History of book illustration (5) Identify in artworks the influence of historical events (5)
AESTHETIC VALUING	Evaluating Your Work (2, 4, 8) Reflective Thinking (4)	Evaluating Your Work (2, 4, 8) Reflective Thinking (8)
ELEMENTS AND PRINCIPLES OF ART	Using elements and principles to create movement (2)	Using color and pattern to create formal balance and rhythm (4)
ART FORMS	Photography (1, 5) Painting (1, 3) Drawing (2, 4) Mosaic (5) Motion pictures and videos (7)	Picture writing (1, 2) Mixed media (1) Drawing (3) Sculpture (3, 4) Painting (5, 6, 8) Textiles (5) Illumination (7)
MEDIA, TOOLS, TECHNIQUES, AND PROCESSES	Gouache defined (1) Caricature defined (4) Frieze defined (5) Kinetoscope defined (7) Motion picture media (7)	Pictograms described (1) Cartouche defined (1) Petroglyph defined (1) Fresco defined (5) Font (8)
CURRICULUM AND PERFORMING ARTS CONNECTIONS	Art & Social Studies (6) Cross-Curriculum Connections (R)	Art & Social Studies (6) Cross-Curriculum Connections (R)
CAREERS/PORTFOLIOS	Portfolio Ideas (2) Portfolios (3, 7) Videographer (8)	Portfolio Ideas (4) Portfolios (1, 7) Compare avocational opportunities in art (8)

Chapter 13 Celebrations	Chapter 14 Creating Fantasy
1. (a, b) 2. (a) 3. (a, b) 4. (a, b, c) 5. (a, b) 6. (a, b)	1. (a, b) 2. (a, b) 3. (a, b) 4. (a, c) 5. (b) 6. (a, b)
Interpreting celebrations (1, 3, 5, 7)	Juxtaposition described (3, 5)
Making a tricolor (1) Creating an event quilt (2) Creating kinetic "festival" art (4) Making a hat (5) Celebrating a role model (8)	Drawing in the Surrealist style (1) Creating a fantasy bird collage (2) Extending an image (3) Creating a puzzle picture (4)
Artwork celebrating American Independence (1) Artwork celebrating Mexican Independence (1) Hopi celebrations (3) Identify cultural influence in artworks (3) Chinese rite of passage object (5) African rite of passage object (5) Intuit art (7) Identify cultural influence in artworks (7)	Surrealism defined (1) History of fantasy art (1) René Magritte (2) History of juxtaposition in painting (3) Compare artworks from a variety of cultures (5)
Evaluating Your Work (2, 4, 8) Reflective Thinking (8)	Evaluating Your Work (2, 4) Reflective Thinking (2)
Using variety in an artwork (2) Using repetition to create rhythm (4)	Using color and texture (2) Using emphasis (4)
Painting (1, 3, 4, 7) Textile (2) Mixed media (5, 8)	Painting (1, 3, 4) Drawing (1, 6) Mixed media (2) Lithography (5)
Shadow puppet described (4) Kinetic art defined (4) Adenla defined (5)	Architectural rendering defined (5) Belvedere defined (5)
Art & Social Studies (6) Cross-Curriculum Connections (R)	Art & Social Studies (6) Cross-Curriculum Connections (R)
Portfolio Ideas (4) Portfolios (1, 5) Compare career opportunities in art (8)	Portfolio Ideas (4) Portfolios (1, 3, 5)

KEY (1), (2), (3) etc. = Lessons (R) = Chapter Review	Handbooks
NATIONAL STANDARDS FOR THE VISUAL ARTS	
ARTISTIC PERCEPTION	Discussion Questions (pp. 310–324)
CREATIVE EXPRESSION	Creative Expression Activities (pp. 310–324)
HISTORICAL/CULTURAL CONTEXT	Discussion Questions (pp. 310–311, 314–315, 317, 320, 322)
ELEMENTS AND PRINCIPLES OF ART	Discussion Questions (p. 317)
MEDIA, TOOLS, TECHNIQUES, AND PROCESSES	Technique Tips (pp. 281–291) Digital Media Guide (pp. 293–301)
CURRICULUM AND PERFORMING ARTS CONNECTIONS	Theatre (pp. 312, 318, 319) Dance (pp. 310, 313–315, 317, 319, 321, 323) Music (pp. 311, 316, 320, 322, 324) Creative Expression Activities: Dance (pp. 310, 314, 317) Geography (p. 322) Language Arts (pp. 310, 311, 313–319, 321–324) Mime (p. 321) Pantomime (p. 312) Playwriting (p. 312) Social Studies (pp. 315, 320) Science (p. 316, 323) Theatre (p. 310) Visual Arts (p. 324)
CAREERS/PORTFOLIOS	Career Spotlights (pp.302–308) Advertising Artist Architect Art Director Art Teacher Artist Graphic Artist Illustrator Industrial Designer Interior Designer Landscape Architect Museum Curator Photographer Textile Designer Web Designer

SAFETY in the Art Classroom

Art teachers and their students are often in contact with potentially harmful materials, although many may be totally unaware of the danger. Lead poisoning, cancer, nervous system disorders, anemia, silicosis, chemical pneumonia, asthma, dermatitis—all of these as well as others are recognized as industrial diseases caused by hazardous chemicals. However, many fail to recognize that these same diseases are found among artists, craftspeople, theater technicians, teachers, and students using art and craft materials without adequate precautions.

Labeling of Art Materials

The labeling of art materials continues to be limited in many ways. Ingredients that cause laboratory animals to perish within two weeks after a single dose is administered are identified as "acutely toxic" and must bear a warning label. However, if fewer than half the animals die, the product may be labeled "nontoxic." In addition, when products are imported or repackaged, the hazards may not be listed or properly described on the label.

Teachers should be aware of the fact that the Federal Hazardous Substances Act and other legislation introduced at the federal level have not been entirely successful at rectifying problems of this kind. Some worrisome inadequacies persist.

Industry Safety Standards

Not to be overlooked is the fact that the art-materials industry has, for many years, supported the use of voluntary safety standards. These standards have been developed with the cooperation and input of various manufacturers. The Arts and Crafts Materials Institute (ACMI) has for some time adhered to a voluntary program designed to ensure the safety of younger students working with art materials. Most art teachers are familiar with the two ACMI safety labels—AP, indicating "Approved Product," and CL, specifying that the product is certified to be properly labeled. These labels certify that the products on which they are placed have been found to contain no ingredients in sufficient quantities to be toxic or harmful to users. In addition, products bearing the AP label with Performance Certification or the older CP label abide by certain quality standards pertaining to workmanship, working qualities, and color.

The CL seal on a label indicates that the product's ingredients have been examined by toxicologists. The label lists any safety precautions required by law and by labeling standards developed by the American Society of Testing and Materials. Teachers are advised to read and adhere to the safety precautions listed on these labels.

Material Safety Data Sheets and Their Use

Teachers should realize that they can request a Material Safety Data Sheet (MSDS) from manufacturers pertaining to any art products of which they are unsure. Among the items included on the MSDS are a listing of all the ingredients for which industrial standards exist, health-hazard information, fire-hazard data, and the chemicals with which the product might react dangerously.

In most school systems, central ordering procedures are—or should be—developed as a means of ensuring that all art materials entering the school are approved by appropriate authorities (for example, the Health Department or Board of Education). Requiring Material Safety Data Sheets from suppliers as a condition of purchase should effectively eliminate many of the toxic materials that might otherwise be brought into the classrooms by unsuspecting teachers.

Protection from Exposure

Considerable protection from exposure to toxic materials can be achieved by promoting good hygiene in the classroom. Safe storage and proper labeling of art and craft supplies, keeping dust to a minimum by damp mopping rather than sweeping, and thorough cleanup after use of art and craft materials will help prevent toxic exposures. Personal hygiene also plays a role in the prevention of potentially harmful exposures. Students should refrain from eating or drinking while engaged in art projects, and they should wash their hands thoroughly when finished. Another general safety practice is to ensure proper ventilation in the art classroom so that contaminants will be diluted and eventually removed from the air. Exposure to hazardous dusts and fumes will be minimized if the instructor premixes dry materials with water (for example, tempera, wheat paste, and so forth) and fires ceramic products when students are away from the kiln area. If an art material has been transferred to an unlabeled container and its identity is unknown, it should be disposed of. For specific information on the proper disposal of art and craft materials, please contact your local county health department. (From the California Department of Education Program Advisory No. CIL: 94[95-01]).

Safety Precautions for Students

In order for a chemical in an art material to harm a student, it must first come into contact with or enter the body. Teachers should be aware of the following three ways in which this can occur.

SKIN CONTACT. Some chemicals, such as those used in etching, or solvents like lacquer and paint thinners, can irritate the skin on contact and result in a variety of skin problems. Other chemicals, known as sensitizers, can cause skin allergies. Examples of these sensitizers include formaldehyde found in some color photography solutions, turpentine, epoxy glues and resins, nickel and chromium compounds, and many tropical woods.

However, the danger with regard to skin contact does not end here. Many toxic chemicals do not just damage the skin itself. They can also be absorbed through the skin into the bloodstream where they can affect other organs. Examples include methyl alcohol found in some shellacs, toluene found in lacquer thinners and silk-screen inks, and glycol ethers found in photo-etching materials.

INHALATION. Dusts, powders, vapors, gases, aerosols, and other airborne substances may be readily inhaled and, therefore, represent a health hazard. Examples include solvent vapors from paints, inks, and thinners; spray mists from air-brush or aerosol spray cans; gases from photographic baths; pottery kiln firing; metal fumes from soldering, welding, and metal casting; and dusts from dyes and pigments, pottery glazes, and woodworking. Some of the chemicals in these materials can result in lung damage from inhalation while others can be absorbed into the bloodstream, where they can lead to a variety of problems including lead poisoning, nerve damage, and kidney damage.

INGESTION. Ingestion is of particular concern with younger students who are inclined to experiment and put things in their mouths. However, ingestion of hazardous substances can occur in the case of older students as well. These students can be affected if they eat, drink, or apply makeup in a classroom where art materials can contaminate these items.

Precautions in Selecting and Using Art Materials

Although some products on the market are labeled "nontoxic," they should not be purchased for use by students in grades K–6 unless assurance is obtained from the manufacturer. A major reason for this is that the product may have been tested for acute toxicity only. Chronic hazards, cancer-causing potential, and other sensitivities are not included in acute toxicity testing. The "nontoxic" label can thus be misleading, and products identified with such labels should not always be regarded as safe for use by children.

There are certain safety precautions that all teachers should take when selecting art materials for use in their classrooms. Included in these precautions are the following:

- Make certain that the materials obtained for younger students (age 12 or under) have an AP seal of approval.

- Incorporate into the art curriculum written information on the potential hazards of art materials and techniques; students should be tested on this information just as they are tested with regard to other aspects of curriculum content. Documentation of this type of instruction should be made and filed.
- Carefully supervise students in the classroom, making certain that safety rules are understood and observed. Teachers must also remember to obey these safety rules themselves in order to impress upon their students the seriousness of these regulations. Students should never be allowed to work in the classroom, during or after school hours, without direct teacher supervision.
- Avoid using solvents or products containing solvents in the art room. These include turpentine, lacquer, shellac, paint thinner, rubber cement and rubber cement thinner, permanent markers, and solvent-based inks such as silkscreen printing ink.
- Do not use acids, alkalies, or bleaches.
- Do not use aerosol spray cans in the classroom, because the inhalation of the spray mist can cause injury to lung tissue.
- Use dust-causing products with care in a well-ventilated area. This precaution applies to the use of pastels, chalks, plaster and clays in dry form, copper enamels, glazes, papier-mâché mixtures, and powdered tempera paints.
- Place kilns in a separate room, outdoors, or if this is not possible, in an out-of-the-way part of the room where students are not likely to come into contact with them when they are in operation. In addition, all kilns should have local exhaust ventilation.
- Remember that good ventilation is an absolute necessity whenever using any art or craft material.
- Be prepared for emergencies by having written emergency procedures prepared, posted, and explained to students. This includes fire-drill procedures and the use of fire extinguishers.
- Report all accidents, even minor ones such as a small cut. Illnesses suspected of being related to art materials should be reported in writing to the school principal or other designated authority at once so that an investigation can be conducted and corrective action determined.

A 1992 bulletin from the Consumer Product Safety Commission stated that art materials with any warning labels whatever are not suitable for use by students in grade 6 and under. These students cannot be expected to understand the hazards of toxic substances or to carry out precautions effectively or consistently. A teacher must "childproof" the art room to prevent either intentional or unintentional access to toxic materials or dangerous machinery.

At the beginning of each school year or new term, teachers are urged to determine if any of their students are asthmatic, visually impaired, hearing impaired, or on prescribed medication. If asthmatic students are enrolled in the art class, they should not be exposed to dusts, fumes, or vapors because of their breathing difficulties. Visually impaired students understandably operate very close to their artwork and, as a consequence, are more likely to inhale harmful dusts, vapors, and fumes. Students with hearing impairments should not be exposed to activities requiring loud hammering or noisy machinery, because this can aggravate their condition. If students are found to be on medication, the teacher should seek their physicians' advice regarding the potentially harmful interaction between their prescribed medicine and the art materials they might use in class.

Similar precautions are recommended in situations involving students who are physically handicapped in other ways or who may be learning disabled or emotionally disturbed. These students are at an even greater risk from toxic materials and require special care and attention. In some instances, they might not be able to use the same materials and processes as other students. Careful evaluation is needed in each case to determine what special precautions might be necessary.

Clearly, the need to direct time and effort to safeguarding the health and safety of students in the art classroom is essential. Art teachers, aware of their responsibilities in this regard, recognize that assistance may be needed. In order to properly inform and train their students, teachers need specially tailored hazard communication (HAZCOM) training. The curriculum must include formal health and safety training at levels far above the basic information required by the law. This is not only proper, it provides an opportunity for the school to develop training materials for which there is a demand.

Steps to Incorporate Training into Your Program

First find out which law applies to you. There are state and federal HAZCOM laws and they differ somewhat in their requirements. Ask your employer, but do not stop there! Call your Department of Labor's Occupational Safety and Health Administration (OSHA) office to be absolutely sure whose jurisdiction you are under. Ask for a copy of the law and any additional free materials they may have.

Learning the Rules

1. Spend a few moments looking at the HAZCOM file. If you do not know where this file is kept, ask your school administrator. OSHA requires employers to include the file's location in HAZCOM training.
2. Look at the condition of the file. OSHA requires that it is organized and easy to read. Included in the file should be:
   a. A written program telling how the school will comply (including names of parties responsible for each compliance activity).
   b. A survey of all the potentially toxic substances in the school and their locations.
   c. An organized collection of Material Safety Data Sheets on these substances.
   d. A record of training sessions, which usually includes dates of training, lists of participants, qualifications of trainers, results of quizzes given, and so on.
3. Check your classroom/shop.
   a. See if there any containers that do not have the following information:
      - identity of the substance (must be the same as on the MSDS)
      - hazard warnings, if needed
      - name and address of the manufacturer (required for transport)
   b. Be sure you have a dilution ventilation system separate from the ventilation in the rest of the school if you work with solvents or solvent-containing products, black-and-white photo developing, resin casting, or any other process requiring separate ventilation.
   c. Be sure you have local ventilation systems (for example, a spray booth and flexible ducts) for any process that puts substances into the air such as spraying, air brushing, machine sawing, sanding, soldering, welding, mixing clay or glazes, and so on.

REMEMBER: If you cannot demonstrate a process with all proper precautions, safety equipment, and ventilation, eliminate the project from the curriculum. Don't ever let students see you violate safety rules or the law.

Contents

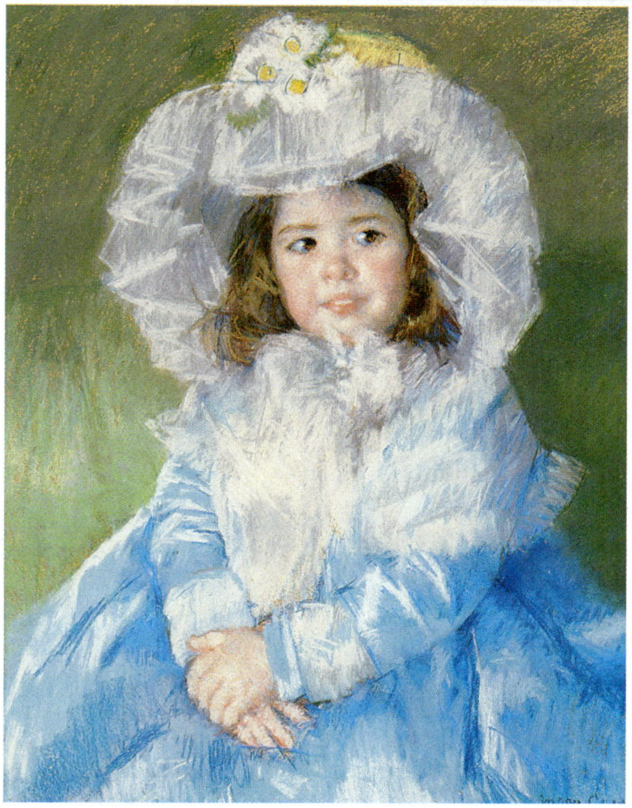

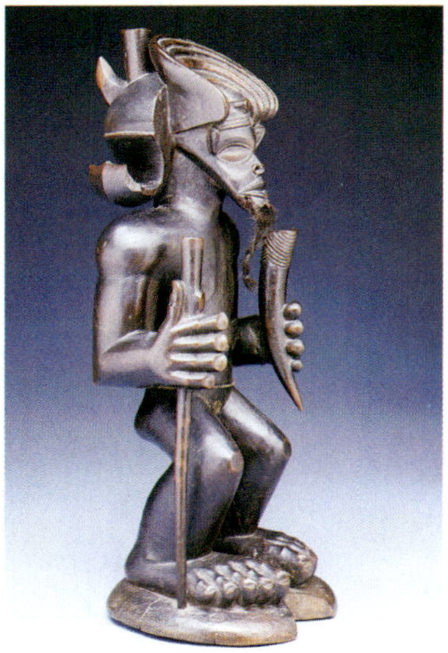

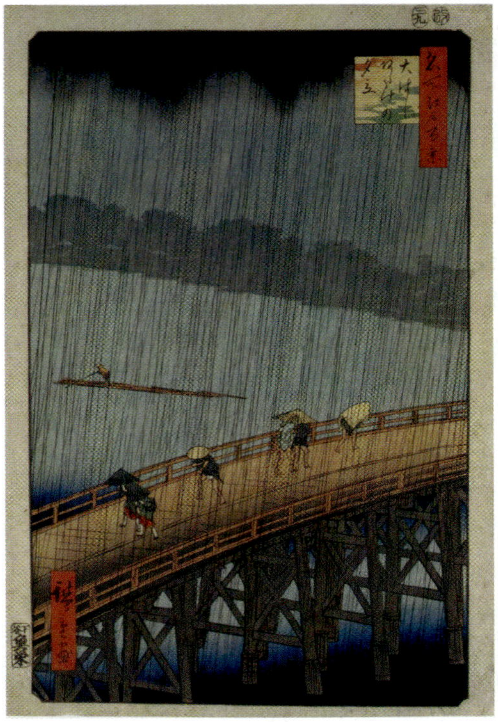

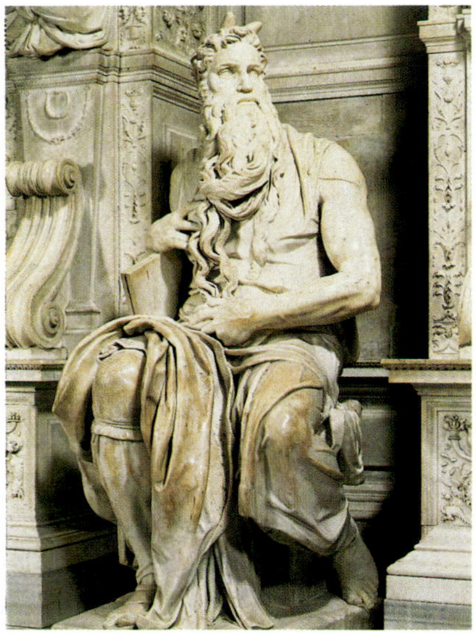

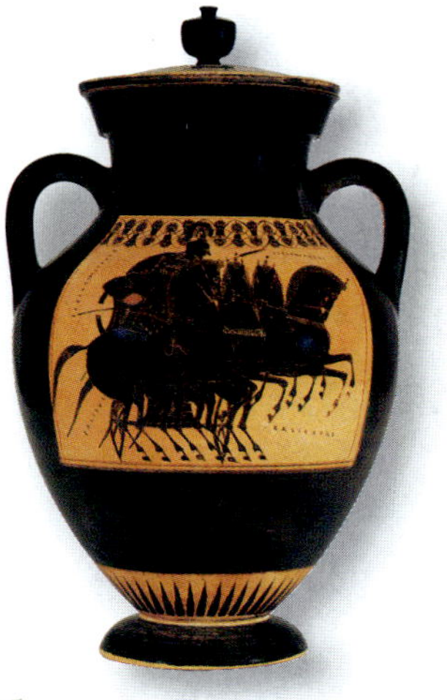

Chapter 5

Chapter 6

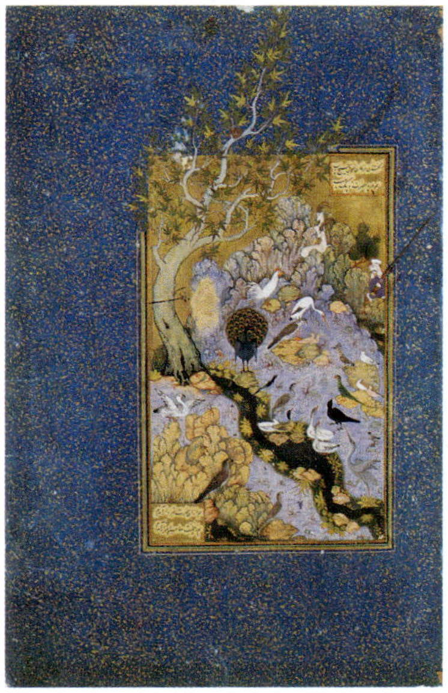

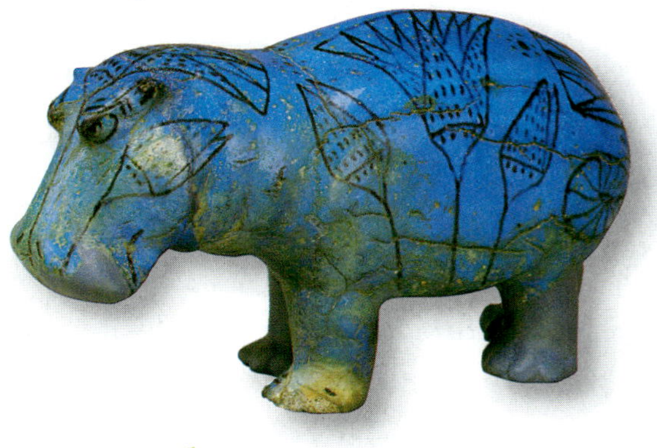

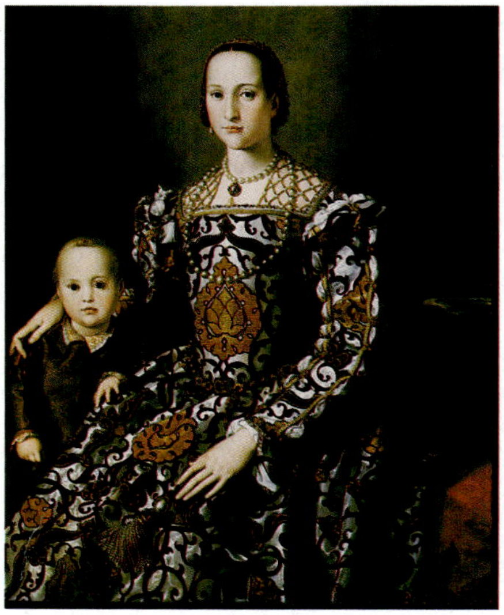

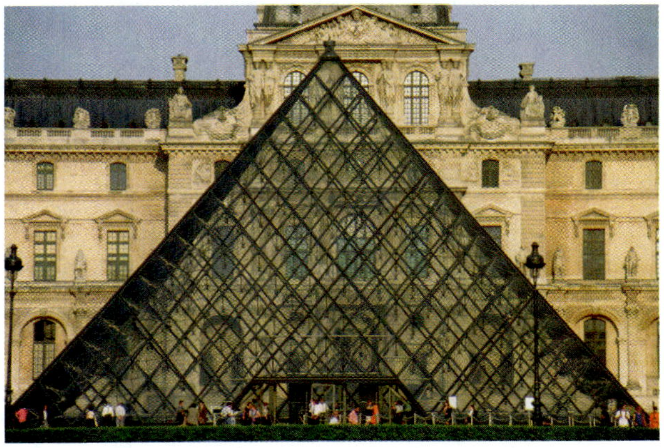

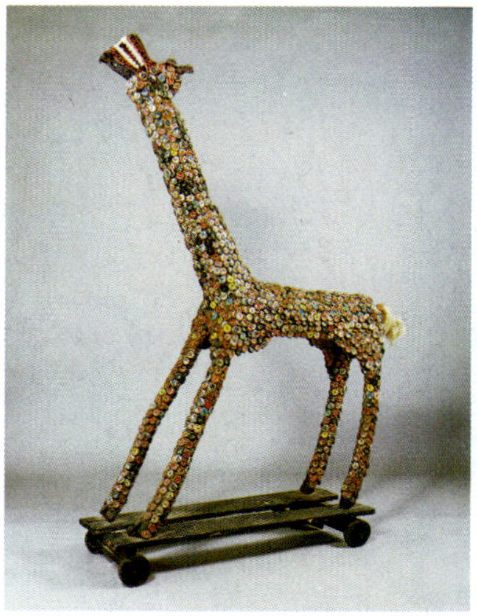

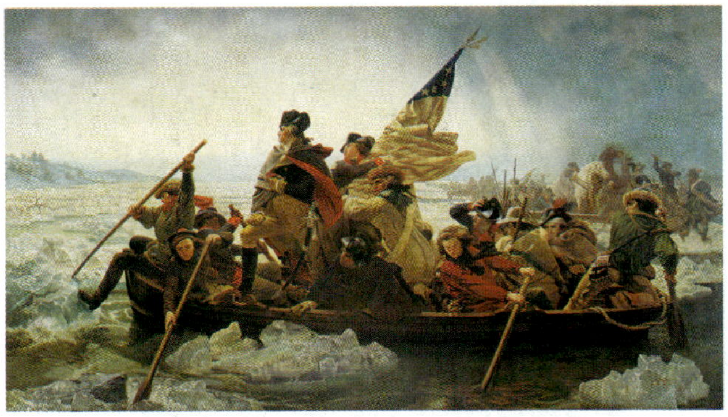

Chapter 11

Chapter 12

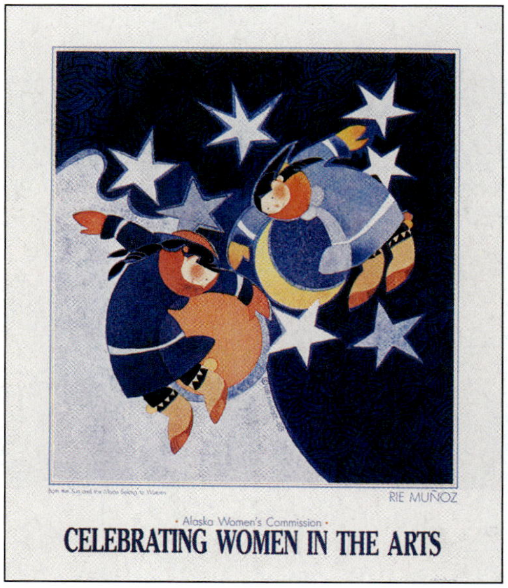

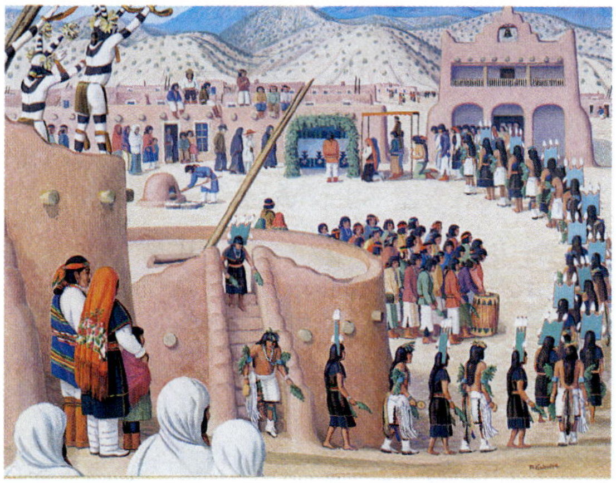

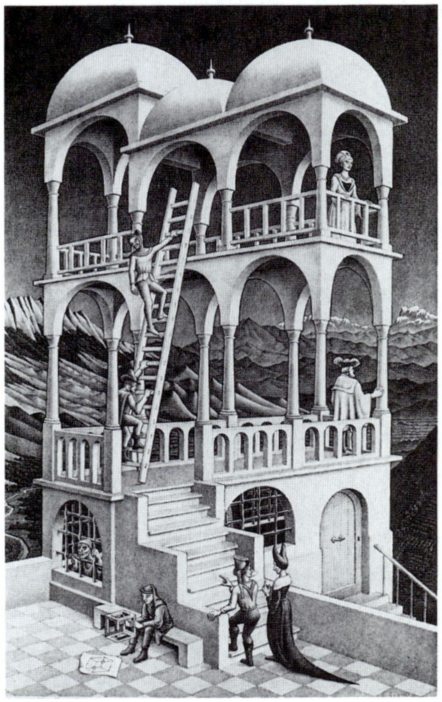

Handbook

Studio Lessons by Media

How to Use Your Textbook

You are about to enter an exciting world. This is a world of creative ideas and imaginations. The images and objects you encounter will stir your curiosity and make you wonder. This is the world of art. *Introducing Art* will lay the foundation for art appreciation and help you develop your technical skills as an artist. This textbook presents you with the tools and skills to learn about the elements and principles of art, apply techniques using various art media, appreciate art history, and develop art criticism skills.

Preview the Chapter

A brief introduction helps you focus on the chapter. Chapter objectives are also listed as well as Key Terms that will be in the chapter.

Quick Write

This feature, which connects to the artist's quote in the chapter opener, will help you start thinking about the process of creating art, from idea to finished artwork.

Narrative Lessons

Art concepts are presented and reinforced in easy-to-understand language. These lessons use relevant examples from daily life or from history. Check Your Understanding provides you with a short review for each lesson.

Studio Lessons

Studio Lessons give you the opportunity to use various media and techniques. The lessons are illustrated by examples of fine art and include student artwork.

Meet the Artist

This feature profiles artists whose works appear in the text. It presents you with biographical information and a brief history of the artist's work.

Time & Place

This feature makes a historical connection to artworks that appear in the text. It provides you with a window into the historical and cultural context of artists and their works.

Studio Activity

This feature includes hands-on activities where you explore ways using various art media to quickly grasp ideas presented in the lessons.

TIME Art Scene

This colorful new feature closes every chapter with an update from the real world of art. You will read about various artists and discover how art is a part of the world outside your classroom.

Chapter Review

Completing the chapter reviews can help you see how well you know the material you have just studied. It also gives you a chance to apply what you've learned in the Web Museum Activity. This feature transports you to a museum where you look at and study different artworks by various artists.

Chapter Resources

Features	Standards for Chapter: National	Standards for Chapter: State/Local	Reproducible Masters
Quick Write *page 3* TIME ART SCENE "Traveling for the Light" *page 22* ***Web Museum Activity*** *page 23*	**1.** (a, b) **2.** (a, b, c) **3.** (a, b) **4.** (a, b) **5.** (b) **6.** (b)		Guided Reading and Practice 1–1 Cross-Curriculum Activity 1–2 Artist Profile 1–3 Studio Activity 1–4, 1–9 Application Activity 1–5 Enrichment Activity 1–6, 1–8 Historical and Cultural Heritage 1–7 Lesson Plans

Lesson Resources

Lessons	Standards per Lesson: National	Standards per Lesson: State/Local	Reproducible Masters
1 *The Language of Art* *(pages 4–5)*	4a, 5b		Cross-Curriculum Activity 1–2 Artist Profile 1–3
2 *Line* *(pages 6–7)*	1a, 1b, 2b		Studio Activity 1–4 Application Activity 1–5
3 *Color* *(pages 8–11)*	1b, 4a		Enrichment Activity 1–6
4 *Mixing Colors* *(pages 12–13)*	1a, 1b, 2a		
5 *Shape, Form, and Space* *(pages 14–17)*	2c, 3a, 3b		Historical and Cultural Heritage 1–7
6 *Drawing a Still Life* *(pages 18–19)*	1a, 1b, 2a, 3a		Enrichment Activity 1–8
7 *Texture* *(pages 20–21)*	1a, 2b, 3a		Studio Activity 1–9

Assessment	Technology
Testing Program: Chapter Test 1–10 Portfolio and Assessment Techniques	Artsource Performing Arts Package, The Alvin Ailey American Dance Theater (DVD or VHS Segment 8) National Museum of Women in the Arts Interactive Lesson Planner Fine Art Transparency CC–1, *Kouros* by Isamu Noguchi Fine Art Transparency 1, *Inter-Urban Motor-Man* by Eve Drewelowe

Activities/Features
Meet the Artist: Paul Cézanne
Studio Activity: Experimenting with Lines
Studio Activity: Experimenting with Color Combinations
Evaluating Your Work Portfolio Ideas Visual Art Journal
Studio Activity: Sketching a Still Life
Evaluating Your Work Reflective Thinking Visual Art Journal
Studio Activity: Making Rubbings for Texture

KEY TO ABILITY LEVELS

Teaching strategies have been coded.

- **L1** Activities for all students; teacher direction required
- **L2** Activities for average to above-average students; some teacher direction needed
- **L3** Activities for students able and willing to work independently
- **ELL** English Language Learner activities

FEATURED ARTISTS

- Deborah Butterfield
- Alexander Calder
- Paul Cézanne
- Richard Estes
- Janet Fish
- Helen Hardin
- Roy Lichtenstein
- Henry Moore
- Piet Mondrian
- Claude Monet
- Vincent van Gogh

FINE ART PRINTS

Fine Art Print 1, *Lansdcape with Mountain Lake* by Ernst Ludwig Kirchner

Fine Art Print 2, *Houses in Murnau* by Wassily Kandinsky

Timesaving Technology

Interactive Lesson Planner

Make planning easy. Use this interactive software to organize your week, month, semester, or year and access all *Introducing Art* reproducible resources.

KEY TO LESSON RESOURCES

Narrative Lesson

Studio Lesson

Chapter 1

The Elements of Art

(pages 2–23)

Chapter Overview

In this chapter, students will be encouraged to look at their world through the eyes of an artist. Everyone can participate in the artist's vision and expression of an idea or a feeling. To truly understand an artist's expression, however, we must understand the language of art, which is made up of the seven visual elements of line, color, value, shape, form, space, and texture.

As students study this chapter, encourage them to find the elements of art in the world around them.

Discussing the Artwork

Focus On ◆ **Figure 1–1** Have students study the artwork by Piet Mondrian on this page. Ask them the following questions and have them discuss their initial responses.

- What do you notice most in this painting?
- What feeling does the painting suggest?
- Do you think this painting is visually pleasing? Why or why not?

Have students explain their responses in a written or oral report.

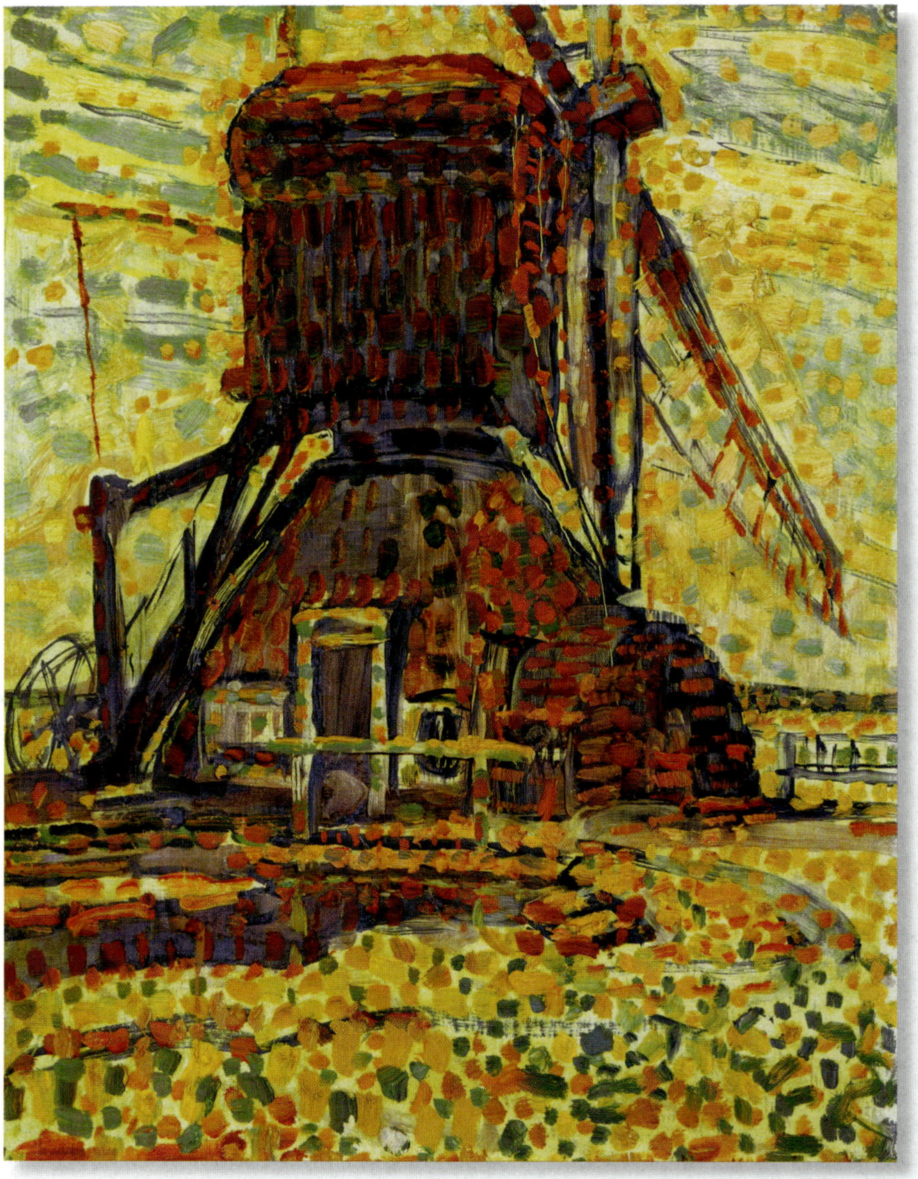

Focus On ◆ **Figure 1–1** **Artist Piet Mondrian looked at the world and saw shapes, lines, and colors. He kept simplifying his subjects until his paintings became just straight lines and squares of color.**

Piet Mondrian. *The Winkel Mil, Pointillist Version.* 1908. Oil on canvas. 43.8 x 34.3 cm (17¼ × 13½"). Dallas Museum of Art, Dallas, Texas. Foundation for the Arts Collection, gift of the James H. and Lillian Clark Foundation.

ART SOURCE

Linking to the Performing Arts

DANCE In speaking the language of dance, dancers use their bodies as instruments of self-expression. Dancers can structure time with breath rhythm, emotion, music, sounds, and stillness. Their use of weight can shift between heavy and light; their use of force can be strong or weak. Have students see how master choreographer, Alvin Ailey, used this vocabulary to create his dance, "Revelations" in the **Performing Arts Handbook** on page 310. To enrich student understanding, play the DVD or videotape (segment 8) in the **Performing Arts Package**.

Chapter 1

The Elements of Art

“Nature cannot be copied; it can only be expressed.”
— Piet Mondrian (1872–1944)

Just as the poet arranges nouns, verbs, and adjectives into ideas, the artist arranges shapes, lines, and colors into images about our world. Each artist’s work is as personal and individual as the artist. You, too, are an artist, and the drawings and paintings you will be doing in this class will be as individual as you are. In this book, you will learn how to look at art and the world around you with the eyes of an artist.

After completing this chapter, you will be able to:

- Name and describe the elements of art.
- Describe the different types of line.
- Identify the properties of color.
- Experiment with various elements of art to understand their role in making art.

Quick Write

Interpreting the Quote
Read the quote by Piet Mondrian. Then look at **Figure 1–1.** Describe in a paragraph how you think Mondrian is expressing nature in his painting.

Key Terms

artist
elements of art
line
line quality
color
hue
value
intensity
portfolio
shape
form
space
negative space
still life
texture

Quick Write

Interpreting the Quote
Piet Mondrian looked at nature and saw shapes, lines, and colors. He kept simplifying his subjects until his paintings became just straight lines and squares of color. After students have read the quote by Mondrian and completed the Quick Write activity, have them discuss their responses with classmates.

Chapter Motivator

Before students begin the chapter, encourage them to talk about and describe works of art that they have enjoyed or that they remember well. Ask them to give details about the work and explain why they liked it. Lead students to discover that different works have different elements of art that stand out, such as the use of color, line, and texture. Tell them they will learn more about these elements of art in this chapter.

Art Online

Visit **art.glencoe.com**, the Web site for Glencoe’s art programs. Go to the Find Your Book option, select *Introducing Art*, and explore the many innovative options available to you and your students, such as:

- Artist Profiles
- Interactive Games
- Museum Web Links
- State-specific resources

National Standards for Arts Education

This chapter addresses the following National Standards for the Visual Arts:

1. (a, b) **4.** (a, b)
2. (a, b, c) **5.** (b)
3. (a, b) **6.** (b)

The Language of Art

(pages 4–5)

1 Focus

Objectives

After completing this lesson, students will be able to:

- Define what an artist is.
- Name the elements of art: line, color, value, shape, form, space, and texture.

2 Teach

Motivator

Ask students to define what art means to them. Have them explain what an artist does. Ask if they find art difficult to relate to or understand. Explain that art can sometimes be challenging to understand, but learning the elements of art will help students better understand how art and artists communicate.

Vocabulary

Write the seven elements of art terms on the board. Ask students to read these terms out loud. Then ask students to define the word *element.*

The Language of Art

Have you ever heard a person described as "wearing many hats"? Saying a person wears many hats means he or she is good at a number of things. An **artist**—*a person who uses imagination and skill to communicate ideas in visual form*—wears many hats. Among the hats artists wear is one labeled "scientist." Wearing this hat, artists experiment with the effects of light on objects. Wearing the mathematician's hat, they carefully measure distances between objects. Wearing the hat of writer, they tell stories and record events.

In this book, you will learn about the different ways in which artists have used these skills over the centuries. You will also meet specific artists and learn about their creations.

The Artist's Language

Like other professionals, artists "speak" a language all their own. Just as the mathematician uses numbers, so the artist uses *line.* Much in the way musicians communicate through notes and sounds, artists speak in *color, value,* and *shape.* The writer relies on words, sentences, and paragraphs; the artist on *form, space,* and *texture.*

These seven terms—line, color, value, shape, form, space, and texture—make up the artist's vocabulary. The terms are grouped together under the heading **elements of art.** These are *the basic visual symbols an artist uses to create works of art.* An artist's success depends on how well he or she uses these elements.

Using the Artist's Vocabulary

When you look at an artwork, it is not always clear where one element ends and another begins. Study the artworks in **Figures 1–2** and **1–3.** You do not see the elements of form and color in the first or the element of line in the second. Instead, you see the works as a whole. As you examine each work, your eye

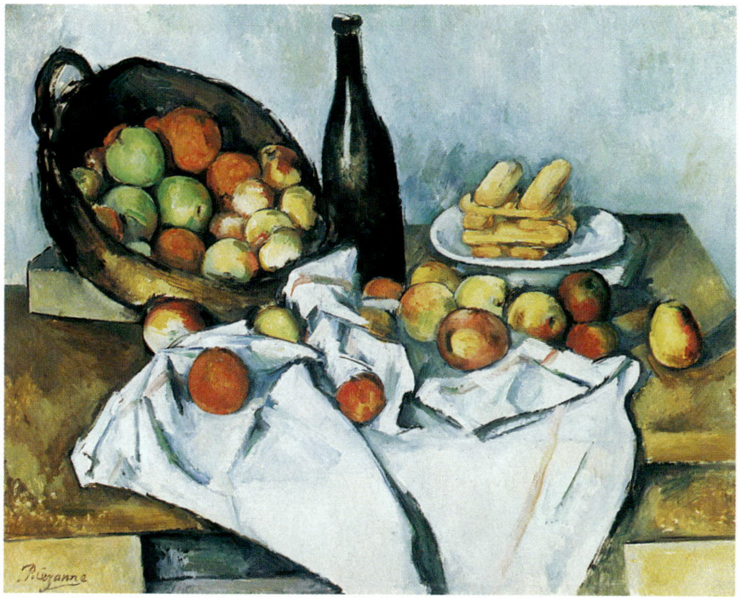

◆ **Figure 1–2** Does the artist use a single color to show an object? Do the objects look real? What does this artwork "say" to you?

Paul Cézanne. *The Basket of Apples.* c. 1895. Oil on canvas. 65.4 cm × 81.3 cm (25¾ × 32″). The Art Institute of Chicago, Chicago, Illinois. Helen Birch Bartlett Memorial Collection.

MORE ABOUT...

The Skills of Art The Egyptians used their remarkable mathematical skills to build the Pyramids. The Greeks devised the Golden Rectangle, the basis of proportion for their temples and sculptures of human figures. Renaissance artists dissected cadavers to study human anatomy. One artist, Leone Battista Alberti, wrote a treatise in 1435 that helped to develop the mathematics of perspective. Today, artists need skills and knowledge in many fields in order to express ideas and work in the varied media of the arts.

"reads" all the elements together. In fact, it is the careful blending of elements that allows you to see an artwork as the artist meant it to be seen. Taken together, the elements in Figure 1–2 "add up" to a basket of apples and a bottle. The lines in Figure 1–3 cleverly suggest a familiar farm animal. Can you identify it?

"Reading" the Artist's Vocabulary

Think back to when you first learned to read. You did not start with a book. Rather, you began by reading a word at a time. This is how you will learn the vocabulary of art. You will learn about the elements of art one at a time.

Each of the remaining lessons in this chapter treats one or more elements. In later chapters, you will learn about other terms that are central to the practice and study of art.

Check Your Understanding

1. Define *artist.*
2. Name the seven elements of art.

Meet the Artist

Paul Cézanne (1839–1906)

Cultural connection. Although he is sometimes associated with the French Impressionist painters, Paul Cézanne was a leader in the movement toward abstraction in painting that became known as Post-Impressionism.

Born in Aix-en-Provence, France, in 1839, Cézanne exhibited a few times with Claude Monet, Auguste Renoir, and Camille Pissarro. It soon became apparent, however, that Cézanne's style and vision were clearly unique.

While the Impressionists were concerned with the effects of light on objects, Cézanne was more interested in showing the basic form and structure of objects. He once said, "Everything in nature is modeled after the sphere, the cone, and the cylinder. One must learn to paint from these simple figures." Look at **Figure 1–2.** How did Cézanne use these "simple figures" in his still life?

To learn more about Cézanne and his work, click on Artist Profiles at **art.glencoe.com**.

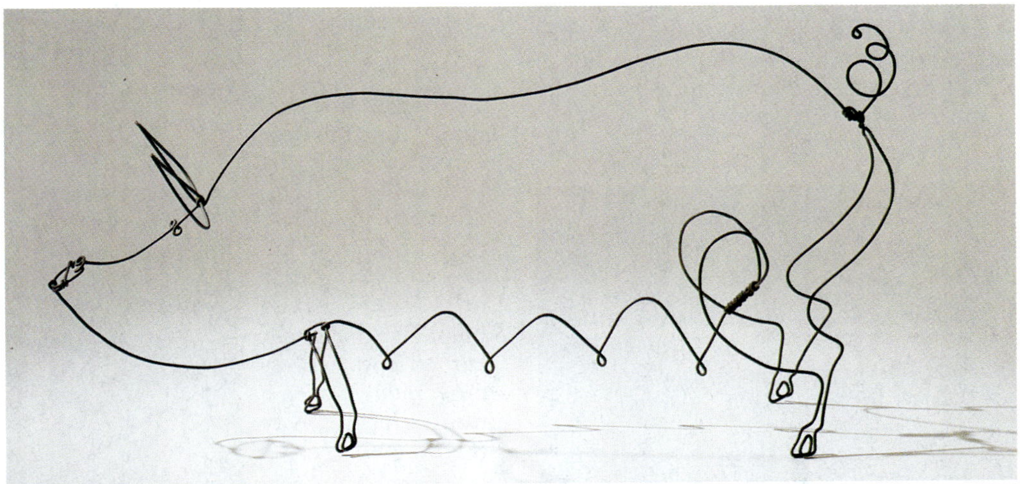

◆ **Figure 1–3** **What are some of the questions you think the artist asked himself while he was creating this work?**

Alexander Calder. *Sow.* 1928. Wire. 43.2 × 76.2 × 19.5 cm (17 × 30 × 7⅔"). The Museum of Modern Art, New York, New York. Gift of the artist. © 1997 Artists Rights Society (ARS), New York/ADAGP, Paris.

Meet the Artist

Paul Cézanne

Have students look closely at **Figure 1–2.** Ask them to pay attention to how Cézanne used and placed the apples in this still life. He repeated the round and angular shape of the apples. Cézanne animated the objects in the painting by placing the basket of apples on one of his characteristically tilted tables.

3 Assess

Self-Assessment

Have students complete the **Check Your Understanding** questions on this page. Answers are provided below.

Reteaching

Have students study Figure 1–2 and discuss what the artist was trying to communicate. L1

Enrichment

IMAGINATION Have students work in small groups to discuss the following statement by Albert Einstein: "Imagination is more important than knowledge." Invite students to share their reactions and give reasons for their opinions. L2

4 Close

Ask each student to name the elements of art.

Answers to Check Your Understanding

1. An artist is a person who uses imagination and skill to communicate ideas in visual form.
2. The seven elements of art are line, color, value, shape, form, space, and texture.

Line

(pages 6–7)

1 Focus

Objectives

After completing this lesson, students will be able to:

- Identify the five main kinds of line and their properties.
- Perceive line quality and direction.
- Demonstrate technical skills effectively by using a variety of art media to produce various line qualities.

Supplies

- Drawing paper
- Variety of drawing pencils
- Chalk, charcoal, crayons, markers, ink and pens
- Tempera paint, watercolors
- Brushes (thin and thick)

2 Teach

Motivator

Ask students to look around the classroom and notice how many different lines they see. Have them write on a sheet of paper examples of horizontal, vertical, diagonal, curved, and zigzag lines. Challenge students to notice the different lines found in nature. L1 ELL

Vocabulary

Have students brainstorm adjectives that describe many kinds of *line quality* and *line direction*. Compile a list of all the adjectives the class chooses.

Line

It might be said that all art begins with a line. You see lines everywhere in your daily life. As you ride in a car along a highway, the edges of the road straight ahead of you form two lines that meet in the distance. The edge of each wall of your classroom is a line. So are the curves that make up the letter *s*.

To the artist, a **line** is *the path of a dot through space.* In this lesson, you will learn about different kinds of lines. You will see how these lines can be used to suggest specific feelings and ideas.

Kinds of Line

By definition, every line goes somewhere. A line may "travel" up, down, or across. It may move at an angle, or it may curve back on itself. Each type of line carries a different message to the viewer.

There are five main kinds of line: horizontal, vertical, diagonal, curved, and zigzag.

Horizontal

Horizontal lines run from side to side. Lines of this type seem to be at rest. They may suggest peace and quiet. Think of the line of a calm lake where the water meets the sky (**Figure 1–4**).

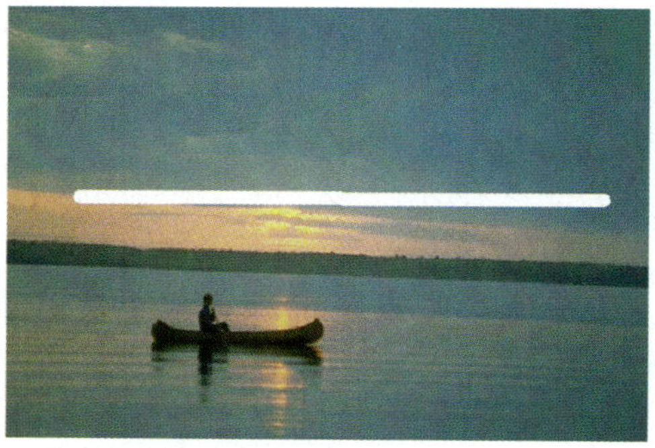

◆ **Figure 1–4** Horizontal line.

Vertical

Vertical lines run up and down. They never lean. Lines of this type seem to be standing at attention. Artists use vertical lines to show strength and permanence. Picture the soaring lines of a skyscraper (**Figure 1–5**).

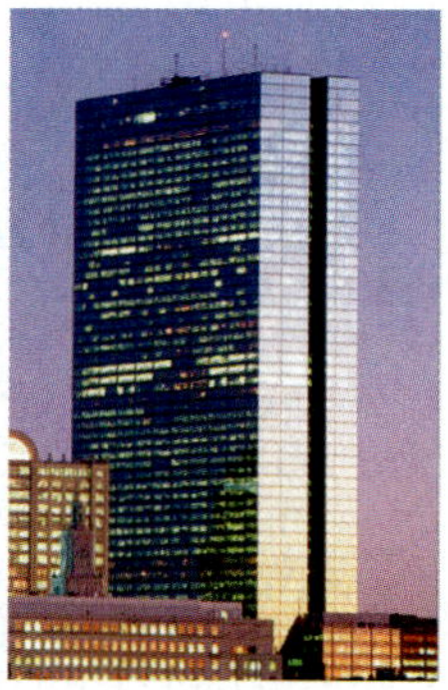

◆ **Figure 1–5** Vertical line.

Diagonal

Diagonal lines are straight lines that slant. Lines of this type suggest a sense of movement and excitement. They seem to be rising or falling. Diagonal lines are used to give a sense of movement.

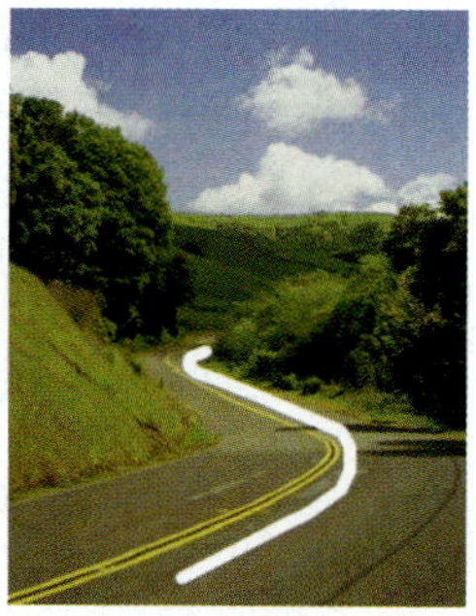

◆ **Figure 1–6** Curved line.

Curved

Curved lines are lines that change direction little by little. Wiggly lines are made up of two or more curves. Spirals and circles also begin with curved lines. Like diagonals, curved lines express movement, but in a more graceful way (**Figure 1–6**).

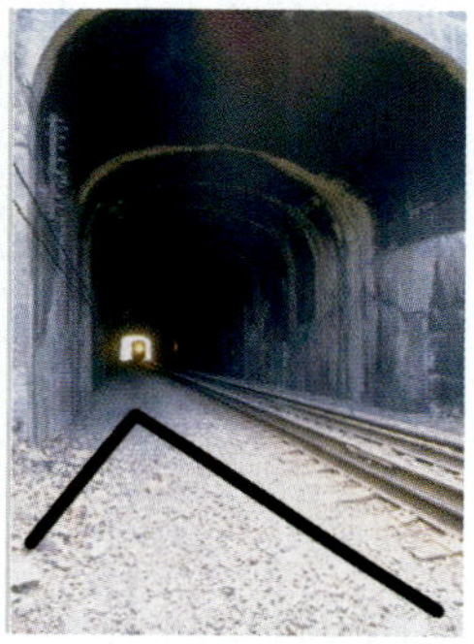

◆ **Figure 1–7** Zigzag line.

MORE ABOUT...

Experimenting with Lines Vincent van Gogh (1853–90) was a Dutch painter whose work reflected the strong emotions of his own life. He is called a Post-Impressionist because he followed the Impressionists, but he moved away from their concern for accurate representation of light conditions and used color and line to express emotion. Van Gogh used chalk, pen, reed pen, and ink on paper to create *Corner of a Park at Arles* (Figure 1–8). He and other Post-Impressionists experimented with a variety of tools to achieve strong emotion through line quality.

Zigzag

Zigzag lines are formed by joining several diagonals that move in different directions. The diagonals form sharp angles that make lines change direction suddenly. Zigzag lines create confusion. They suggest action or nervous excitement (**Figure 1–7**).

Line Quality

Think about the crease in a pair of freshly ironed trousers. Would you describe this "line" as smooth or rough? How about a line made with chalk? Smoothness, roughness, thickness, and thinness each represent a different **line quality.** This quality is *the unique character of any line.*

How a line appears depends on several factors. These include:

- *The tool used.* A crayon produces a slightly ragged line. A paintbrush dipped in ink produces a line that narrows and trails off.
- *The pressure of the artist's hand.* Pressing down on a tool creates a thicker line. Using less pressure creates a thinner line. How would you describe the quality of the lines in **Figure 1–8?** Are the lines smooth or rough? Are they thick or thin?

Studio Activity

Experimenting with Lines

Demonstrate technical skills. Start developing your art skills by using a variety of art tools. These might include pencil, marker, brush and ink, chalk, and crayon. Practice using the tools to draw lines. Notice the quality of line each tool produces. Try drawing lines that express different feelings. These might include joy, fear, anger, and excitement. Share your lines with classmates.

PORTFOLIO

Label the lines with the names of the feelings they express. Then store your experiment in your portfolio.

Check Your Understanding

1. Name the five directions a line can take.
2. Tell how each of the line types can make a viewer feel or react.
3. What is *line quality?*

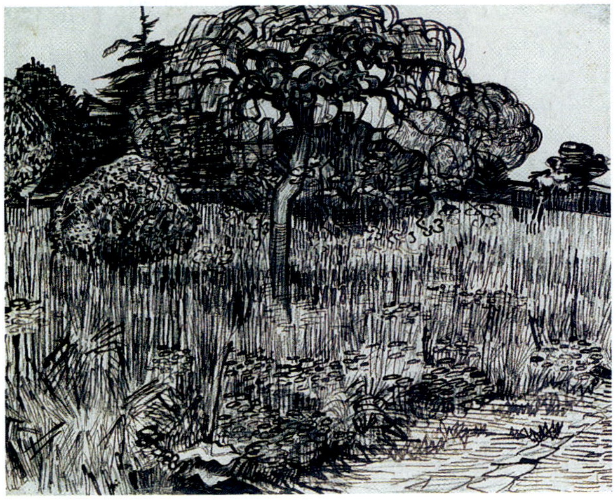

◆ **Figure 1–8** Analyze the different kinds of lines the artist has used. Describe the quality of these lines.

Vincent van Gogh. *Corner of a Park at Arles (Tree in a Meadow).* 1889. Reed pen and black ink over charcoal. 49.3 × 61.3 cm (19⅜ × 24″). The Art Institute of Chicago, Chicago, Illinois. Gift of Tiffany and Margaret Blake, 1945.3.

Studio Skills

Have students develop and organize ideas from the environment. Ask them to keep a sketchbook and find interesting lines in objects they see every day, such as lines in bushes, trees, building details, traffic signs, and so on. Have students illustrate themes from direct observation by keeping a line-awareness log. This will show their continuing awareness of line quality and direction in the world around them. L1 ELL

Aesthetics

Help students discuss **Figure 1–8.** Ask: What kinds of lines can you find? Do the lines help communicate rhythm or movement? After the discussion, have students write a short paragraph describing how the artist used line to express an idea. L1

3 Assess

Self-Assessment

Have students complete the **Check Your Understanding** questions on this page. Answers are provided below.

Reteaching

Work with small groups of students to review the five kinds of lines. Ask students to describe different line qualities.

4 Close

Divide students into groups, assigning each group a kind of line. Ask each group to list as many things as they can in the room that have that type of line. Allow five minutes, and then ask groups to share their lists. L1 ELL

Answers to Check Your Understanding

1. A line can be **horizontal**, running from side to side; **vertical**, running up and down; **diagonal**, running on a slant; **curved**, changing direction little by little; or **zigzag**, combining diagonal lines that move in different directions.
2. Horizontal lines suggest peace and quiet. Vertical lines show strength and permanence. Diagonal lines suggest movement. Curved lines express graceful movement. Zigzag lines suggest action or nervous excitement.
3. Line quality is the unique character of any line.

Color

(pages 8–11)

1 Focus

Objectives

After completing this lesson, students will be able to:

- Define *color*.
- Identify the three main properties of color: hue, value, and intensity.
- Define and identify monochromatic, analogous, and complementary color schemes.
- Describe in detail a variety of practical applications for creating color combinations.

SUPPLIES
- Clear plastic page protectors
- Colored cellophanes and/or gels
- Scissors, transparent tape
- Overhead projector

2 Teach

Motivator

Invite students to imagine what their world would be like without color. Explore with them ways in which color affects their moods and feelings about their clothes, their rooms, and other aspects of their daily lives.

Vocabulary

Discuss with students the meaning of *hue*. Help them distinguish among primary, secondary, and intermediate colors of the color wheel. Ask students to use a dictionary to find the meaning of *analogous, complementary* (as opposed to *complimentary*), and *monochromatic*. L1

LESSON 3

Color

Imagine a world without color. Like lines, color surrounds us. It is in the reds and purples of the sky at sunset. It is in the lush green of a well-tended lawn. Our moods even have "color." We describe someone who is angry as "seeing red." A happy, carefree person is said to be "in the pink."

In this lesson, you will learn about the way color is used in art. In the next lesson, you will practice using color yourself.

PROPERTIES OF COLOR

Have you ever tried to find a pair of matching socks on a dark winter morning? It is not easy. Without light, all colors look the same. Scientists and artists have long understood this. Both know that **color** is *what the eye sees when light is reflected off an object.*

Some artists use color boldly. Others use it softly. To get these results, artists need to understand the three main properties of color. These are hue, value, and intensity.

Hue

Hue is *a color's name.* Orange, green, and violet are all hues. The relationship among hues is shown in the color wheel in **Figure 1–9.** Three of the hues in the wheel—red, yellow, and blue—are known as the primary, or pure, hues. They are called primary because

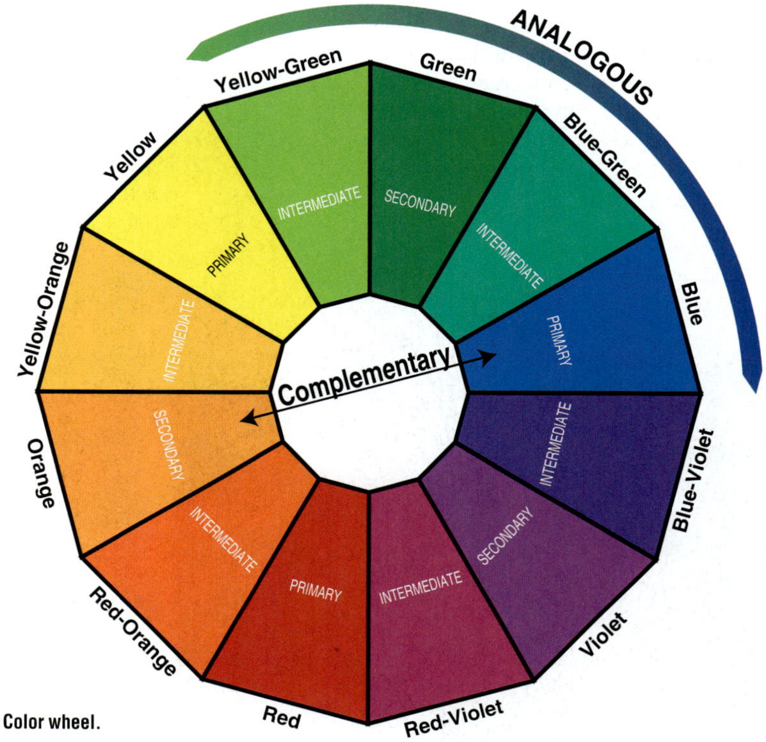

◆ **Figure 1–9** Color wheel.

TECHNOLOGY STRATEGIES IN THE ART CLASSROOM

VALUE Have students make a value scale using computer software. Students should first choose a color, and then draw a square with this color, placing it in the center of the scale. Have them explore the menus and tools to gradually create lighter and darker values sequentially. Students should show at least seven different values. Some colors can be chosen from the color wheel or palettes, but others can be made by changing the opacity of the color or by mixing colors. L1 ELL

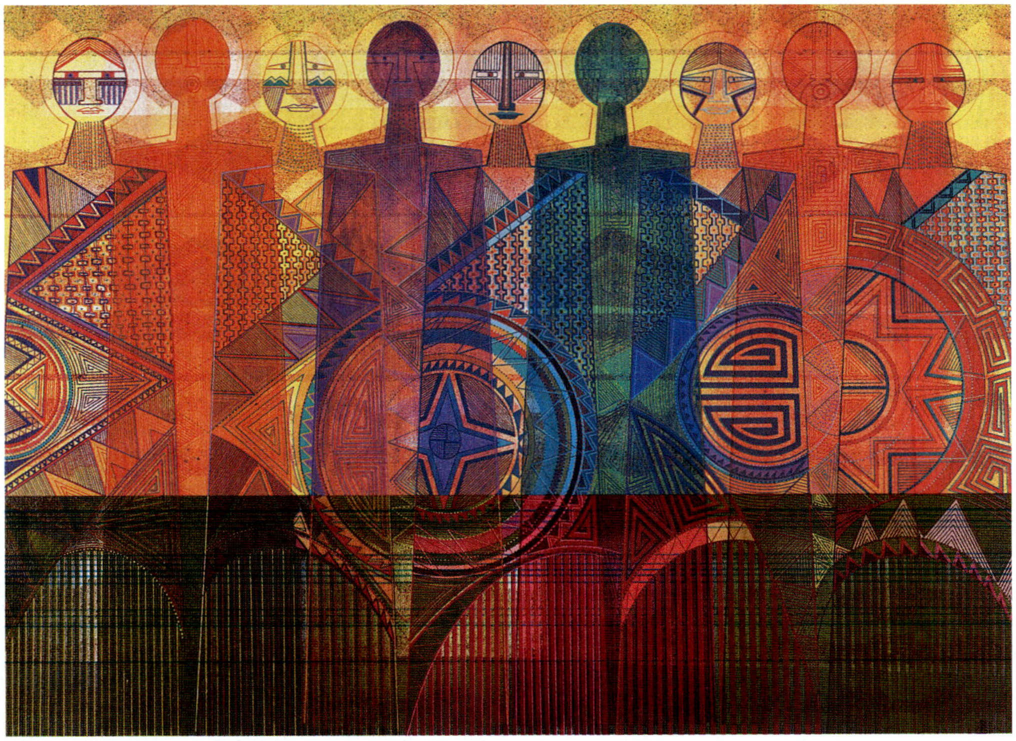

◆ **Figure 1–10** **How did the artist use line and color to portray the figures in this painting?**

Helen Hardin. *Robed Journey of the Rainbow Clan.* 1976. Acrylic. 47 × 76.2 cm (18½ × 30″). © 1996 Helen Hardin, © 1999 Cradoc Bagshaw.

these three are mixed to create all the other hues. Mixing the two primary colors of yellow and blue gives green, a *secondary* color. Mixing a primary color like red with a secondary color like orange gives red-orange, an *intermediate* color. Look at the painting in **Figure 1–10.** The artist has overlapped hues to capture all the colors of the rainbow. Match the hues in the painting with those on the color wheel. Has the artist used any primary hues? Which secondary hues has she used? Which intermediate hues has she used?

Value

The art element, **value,** is *the lightness or darkness of a hue.* Value is also considered as a property of color. You can change a hue's value by mixing in white or black. When white is added to a hue, the resulting color is said to be a *tint.* When black is added, the result is called a *shade.* Pink is a tint of red. Maroon is a dark shade of red. These and other values of red appear in the value scale in **Figure 1–11a.**

◆ **Figure 1–11a** **Value scale.**

Historical/Cultural Heritage

Use of Color in Cultures Ask students to share what they know about the importance of color in various cultures. For example, in Mexico, bright colors are used to decorate the festive piñata. Chinese silks are vibrant with color; red signifies good luck. Encourage students to research attitudes toward and uses of color in our culturally diverse world. Have them bring to class copies of artworks from a variety of cultures and study their use of color. L2

Team Building Activity

Have students work in small groups to identify and analyze some of the color schemes used in some of the art reproduced in this book. Ask each group of students to discuss what they found and what effect the various color schemes achieved. L1

ART IN EVERYDAY LIFE

Idioms Point out to students that color is also part of our everyday language. Such expressions as "seeing red" or being "in the pink" are called *idioms*. Ask students if they know of any other idioms that refer to color (green with envy, feeling blue, etc.). Discuss the meaning of each.

RESOURCES BEYOND THE CLASSROOM

Art Galleries Art galleries provide an important component of art education for students, especially those interested in pursuing art as a career. Galleries have the advantage of showing works by relatively unknown and new artists. Many cities have artists' "co-ops" or shared galleries where the works of local artists are exhibited. Often these works can be purchased for reasonable sums. You might arrange for the class to raise money to purchase a work by a local artist for display in the classroom or the school.

2 Teach *(continued)*

Art Criticism

Have students examine the Helen Hardin painting in **Figure 1–10.** Have them name all the colors in it. Ask students:

- What effect does the artist's choice of colors have on the viewer?
- What mood or feeling do the colors create?
- How would the result be different if the artist had used different colors? Why? L1

Studio Skills

Have students design a simple outline for a school flag or banner. Then have them reproduce the banner five times. On the first version, have students use only black and white to color their banner. On the second, only primary colors, and on the third, only complementary colors. For the fourth banner, students should use intermediate colors. On the final version, invite students to use colors from all parts of the color wheel. Display all the banners and encourage students to discuss their color choices and designs. L1 ELL

◆ **Figure 1–11b** Intensity scale.

Intensity

Some colors appear lively and brilliant. Others look murky or dull. The difference is called the color's **intensity.** This is the *brightness or dullness of a hue.* A strong, bright hue is said to be "high-intensity." Pure green is such a hue. A faint, dull hue is said to be "low-intensity." Olive green is a hue that fits this description. The intensity scale in **Figure 1–11b** shows some intensities of green.

One way of lowering a hue's intensity is by mixing it with its *complementary,* or opposite, hue on the color wheel. Look once again at the color wheel on page 8. Find the hues at either end of the double-headed arrow. If you mix these hues, you get a neutral color such as gray or brown. The same is true if you mix any other complementary hues.

Combining Colors

You may have heard the term *loud* used to describe outfits of clothing. The term also refers to a combination of colors that clash. Art, like clothing, makes use of color combinations, or *schemes.* Different color schemes give different effects. Some color schemes are quiet. Others are exciting.

Some common color schemes used by trained artists are monochromatic, analogous, and complementary.

Monochromatic

A monochromatic (**mah**-noh-kroh-**mat**-ik) color scheme uses different tints or shades of a single hue. Such a combination can help bring together the parts of a work. Monochromatic color schemes must be used with caution, however, because they can produce a dull, uninteresting effect. See an example of a monochromatic color scheme in **Figure 1–11c.**

Analogous

An analogous (uh-**nal**-uh-gus) color scheme uses hues that are side by side on the color wheel and share a hue. (See **Figure 1–11d.**) Analogous color schemes relate objects in a work. Look at the color wheel shown in **Figure 1–9** on page 8 and find the colors analogous to yellow. What hues would be included in an analogous color scheme based on red?

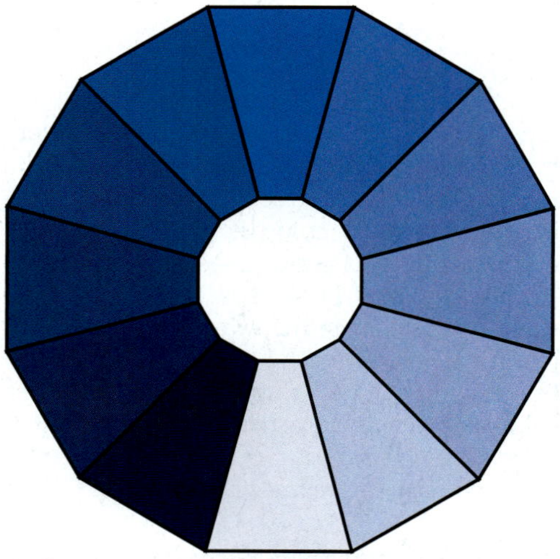

◆ **Figure 1–11c** Monochromatic color scheme.

INCLUSION STRATEGIES

Visually Impaired Some students may not be able to identify colors correctly. If you feel the condition is not just a subjective misdetermination, you might have the school nurse check or mention it to the parents that the student might have color-blindness. The inability to distinguish blue and green hues is the most common kind of color-blindness, and the condition affects more males than females.

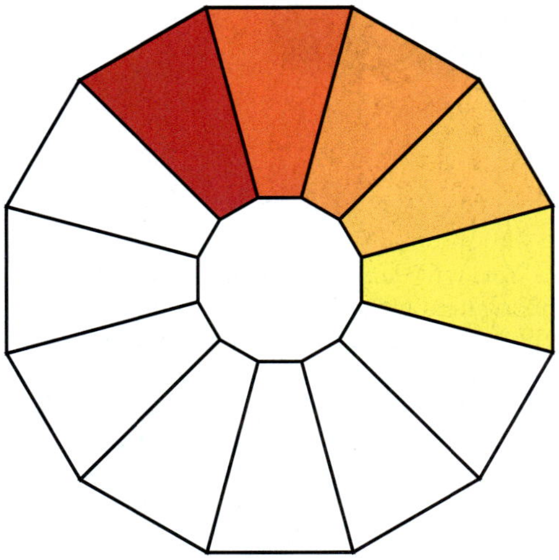

◆ **Figure 1–11d** Analogous color scheme.

Complementary

As its name suggests, the complementary color scheme (**Figure 1–11e**) uses opposite hues on the color wheel. It makes for the most striking color combinations. As with monochromatic colors, care must be taken when combining complementary colors. Placing high-intensity complementary colors close together in an artwork can create an unusual flickering effect.

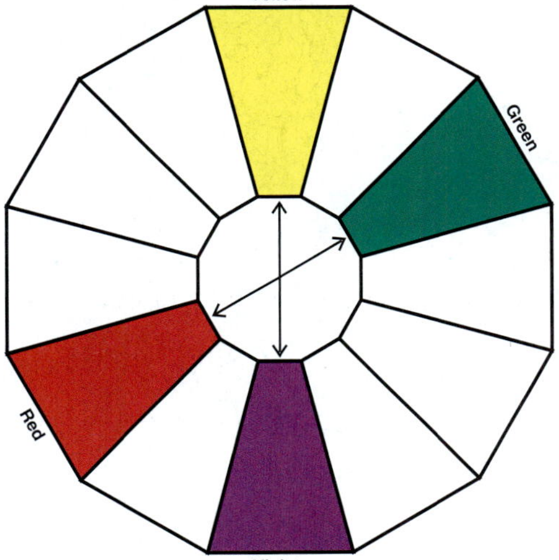

◆ **Figure 1–11e** Complementary color schemes.

Studio Activity

Experimenting with Color Combinations

Practical applications. Gather sheets of colored cellophane. Cut circles or other shapes from each sheet. Experiment with different color combinations by overlapping the shapes in a clear plastic folder. Secure the edges of the folder. Then hold it up to the light. In your sketchbook, note combinations that are especially pleasing to your eye. Repeat the experiment, this time overlapping more colors. Try more than one layer of a single color to deepen it. Last, try making combinations of *warm colors*—red, yellow, and orange—and of *cool colors*—blue, green, and violet. Think about scenes in which you might be likely to use a warm color scheme. How might you use a cool color scheme?

PORTFOLIO

On a separate piece of paper, describe some design ideas where you might use warm and cool color combinations.

Check Your Understanding

1. Define the term *hue.*
2. What are the three properties of color?
3. Where do you find complementary colors on the color wheel?

Studio Activity

Experimenting with Color Combinations

To prepare for the studio activity, place the supply of materials on a table, or distribute quantities of them on desks arranged in groups. Begin by demonstrating the effect of overlays of color on the overhead. As students experiment for themselves, encourage them to talk about the effects they achieve and their reactions to them.

3 Assess

Self-Assessment

Have students complete the **Check Your Understanding** questions on this page. Answers are provided below.

Reteaching

Work with small groups of students to review the concepts of primary, secondary, and intermediate colors.

4 Close

Review with students the differences between value and intensity. Discuss the differences between monochromatic and complementary color schemes.

Answers to Check Your Understanding

1. Hue is a color's name. Orange, red, and green, for example, are all hues.
2. The three properties of color are **hue, value,** and **intensity.** The hue is the color's name, the value is the lightness or darkness of a hue, and the intensity is the brightness or dullness of a hue.
3. Complementary colors are found directly opposite each other on the color wheel.

Mixing Colors

(pages 12–13)
Lesson Time: 45 minutes

1 Focus

Objectives

After completing this lesson, students will be able to:

- Understand color mixing.
- Be able to mix pure hues, tints, and varied intensities.
- Use brushes and paint.
- Demonstrate technical skills effectively by mixing tempera paint colors to produce a painting.

Supplies
Refer to **What You Will Need** in the Student Edition and also include plastic plates to use as palettes.

2 Teach

Motivator

Divide the class into three groups. Give each group two primary colors. Explain that they will be able to paint all full intensity colors by only using two primaries.

Vocabulary

Have students review the terms from Lesson 3: *hue, value, intensity, primary, secondary, complementary, analogous,* and *monochromatic.*

LESSON 4

Mixing Colors

Artists look at the world around them and see far more than a blue sky and green grass. Claude Monet was called an *Impressionist* painter because he looked at the landscape at different times of day and saw every color of the rainbow. At dawn he found purples, pinks, and blues in the farmer's wheat stacks. At noon these stacks appeared to be blazing oranges and yellows. He painted "impressions" of the wheat stack in **Figure 1–12** by laying strokes of many colors on his canvas.

What You Will Learn

You will demonstrate technical skills by mixing tempera paints to discover colors. You will use two *primary* colors and white. Each time you add a stroke of one of these colors and blend it on your paper, you can make a new color. When you have filled your paper, you will have a rich painting. Try to mix as many variations of your two colors as possible.

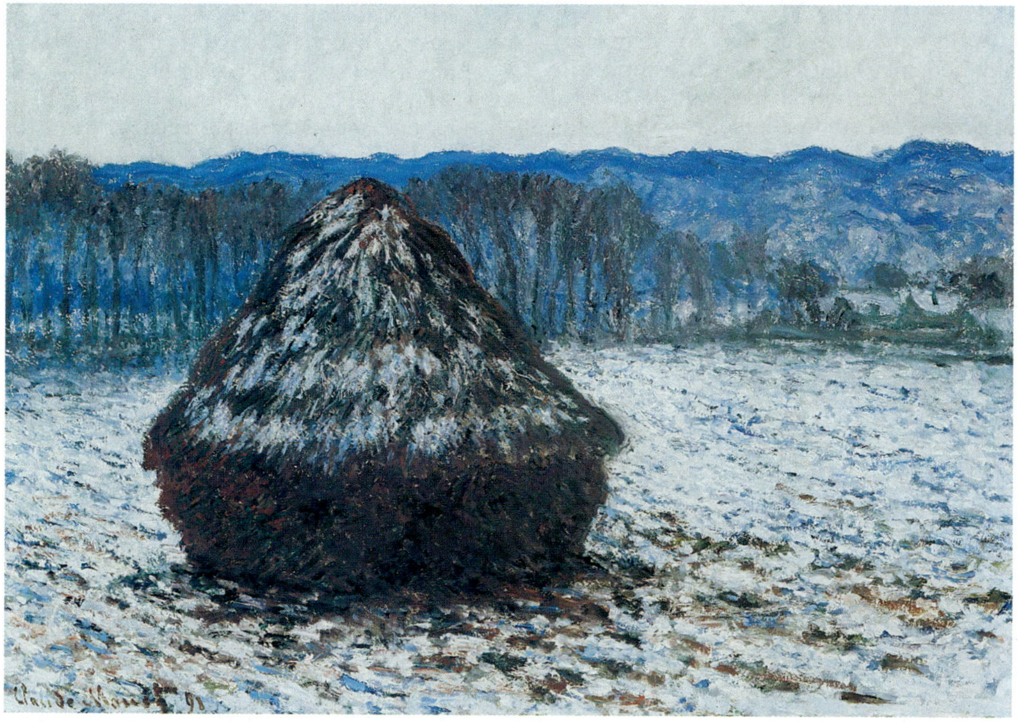

◆ **Figure 1–12** **Analyze the color scheme the artist used in this painting. How would you describe the intensity of the colors?**

Claude Monet. *Stack of Wheat.* 1891. Oil on canvas. 65.6 × 92 cm (25¹³⁄₁₆ × 36½″). The Art Institute of Chicago, Chicago, Illinois. Restricted gift of the Searle Family Trust; Major Acquisitions Centennial Endowment; through prior acquisitions of the Mr. and Mrs. Martin A. Ryerson and Potter Palmer Collections; through prior bequest of Jerome Friedman, 1983.29.

TEACHER TO TEACHER

Tempera Paint Remind students that tempera paint is used because colors are thick or opaque, while watercolors are thinner and colors are transparent. When painting with tempera, water should only be used to rinse a brush between color changes, then blotted with a paper towel. A brush should be moist enough so colors easily coat the paper. Encourage students to blend colors to make new ones, turning the paper as they work. Challenge them to make at least five different color blends by varying amounts of the two primary colors. Remind students to thoroughly clean brushes and store with the handles down, bristles up.

What You Will Need

- White drawing paper, 9 x 12 inches
- Tempera paints—two primary colors and white
- Wash or bristle brush
- Cup of water, paper towels

What You Will Do

1. On a plastic plate, take spoonfuls of two primary colors and white tempera paint. Your teacher will divide the class into three groups and give red and yellow to one, red and blue to another, and yellow and blue to the third.
2. Wet your brush, squeeze the water out of it with your fingers, and dip it into one primary color. Paint an area on your paper. Rinse your brush and dry it with the towel before you start using a new color.
3. Dip into the second primary and begin blending the two colors on your paper until you get the *secondary color*—green or orange or purple.
4. Continue adding more of each primary color as you fill your paper, trying to make new colors each time. Blend the colors into each other.
5. When you have mixed many new colors, begin adding white to all of your colors to get *tints*.

Evaluating Your Work

- **Describe** Point out in your painting the secondary color you mixed and the many variations you blended. Locate the tints you made by mixing white with your colors.
- **Analyze** Discuss the experience of discovering new colors. What happened when you blended the colors longer with your brush?

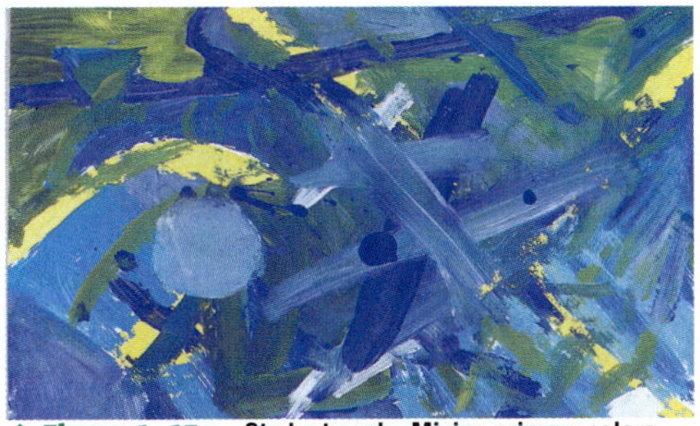

◆ **Figure 1–13a** Student work. Mixing primary colors.

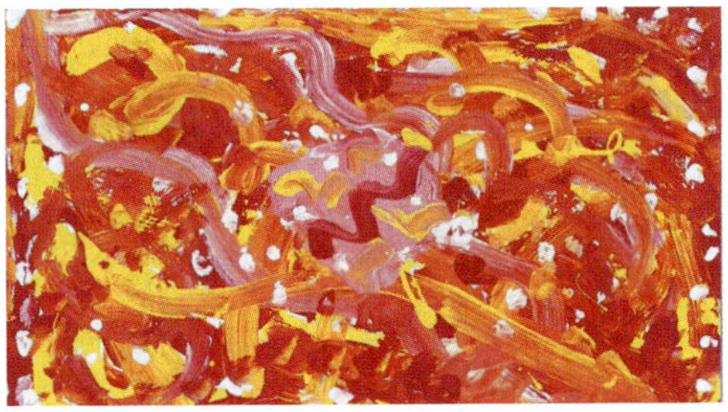

◆ **Figure 1–13b** Student work. Mixing primary colors.

Portfolio Ideas

A **portfolio** is *a carefully selected collection of artwork kept by students and professionals.* As you keep your art projects in a portfolio, it will give you the opportunity to:

- Store your artwork in one place and in good condition.
- Show that you can apply art concepts, techniques, and skills.
- Demonstrate your growth as an artist.

Visual Art Journal

Walk through the produce section of a supermarket. List in your journal all the colors you find in fruits and vegetables. Add adjectives to each one to describe the color and the texture of each.

Studio Skills

Learning to mix colors is an important skill. Discuss the colors students achieved and how they got them. Care of the brushes—not "scrubbing" with them for example—is also an important studio skill.

3 Assess

Self-Assessment

Have students use **Evaluating Your Work** to conduct an in-progress critique of the paintings they created in this Studio Lesson.

Reteaching

Help students recall the three properties of color. Discuss ways in which they were used in the students' paintings.

Visual Art Journal

Have students share their list with the class and compare the adjectives they used to describe the colors. L1 ELL

4 Close

Ask students to make up names for the colors they mixed and to identify the color schemes they used.

Developing a Portfolio

Types of Portfolios There are two main types of portfolio assessment: Authentic Portfolio (Process Portfolio) and Performance Portfolio (Showcase Portfolio). Authentic Portfolio provides evidence of student learning over time and includes self-reflection. Performance Portfolio features a formal presentation of the student's most outstanding works without reflective comments. For specific ideas and guidelines, refer to the booklet, *Portfolio and Assessment Techniques*, that accompanies the *Introducing Art* program.

Shape, Form, and Space

(pages 14–17)

1 Focus

Objectives

After completing this lesson, students will be able to:

- Explain the difference between shape and form.
- Distinguish between geometric and free-form shapes or forms.
- Define space and negative space.
- Identify at least three techniques used to suggest space in two-dimensional art.
- Form generalizations about the art elements of shape, form, and space in artworks.

SUPPLIES
- White drawing paper
- Pencils for sketching
- Several classroom objects including books

2 Teach

Motivator

Divide the class into pairs. Ask each pair to trace the outline of a book on a piece of paper. Then have them measure the height and width of their outlines. Explain that these outlined drawings have two dimensions, height and width. Then have students measure the third dimension of their books, depth. Ask students to discuss the difference between two-dimensional and three-dimensional objects.

Shape, Form, and Space

Here is a riddle. What do *you,* a stop sign, and a rubber ball have in common? You all exist in—and are set off by—space. This is true of all objects. Some objects are recognizable because of their shape or form alone. Even without seeing the letters or the red color, you could identify a stop sign. You would recognize its octagonal shape. Even in the dark, you could identify a rubber ball. You would feel its round form.

Shape, form, and space are closely related. In this lesson, you will learn about these elements and their special place in art.

SHAPE

To an artist, a **shape** is *an area clearly set off by one or more of the other six visual elements of art.* Shapes exist in two dimensions. They have height and width but not depth. Shapes are flat.

All shapes are one of two types:

- **Geometric shapes.** Geometric shapes are precise, mathematical shapes. They look as though they were made with a ruler, compass, or other special tool. The square, circle, and triangle are among the most common geometric shapes. The rectangle and oval are others. Geometric shapes are mostly, though not always, made by people. Examine the painting in **Figure 1–14.** Which geometric shapes has the artist used? How many of each of these shapes can you find in the work?
- **Free-form or organic shapes.** Free-form shapes are not regular or even. Such shapes are found throughout nature.

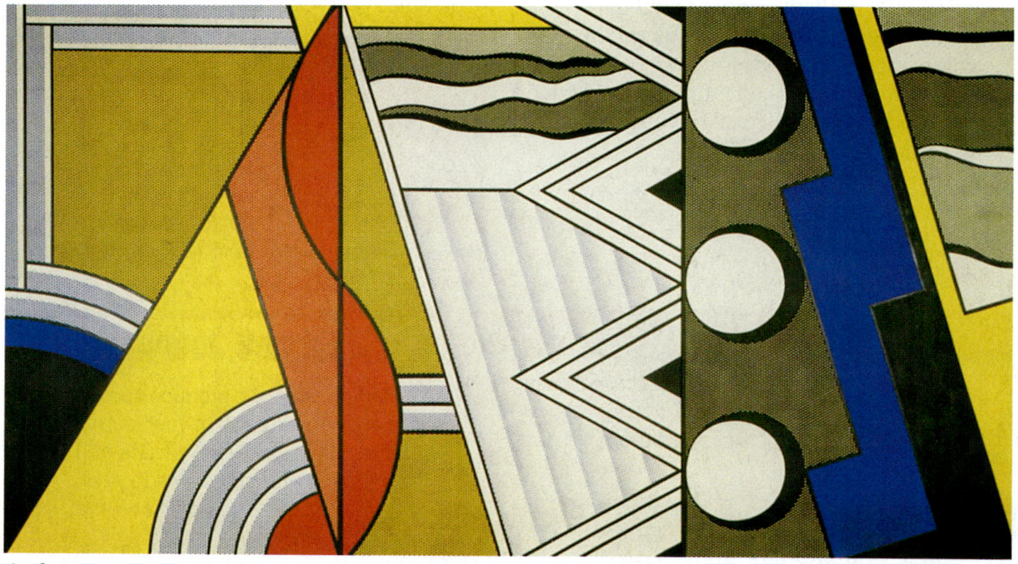

◆ **Figure 1–14** The title of this work mentions a free-form shape from music. Can you find this shape?

Roy Lichtenstein. *Modern Painting with Clef.* 1967. Oil and synthetic polymer and pencil on canvas. 254.3 × 458.2 (100⅛ × 180⅜"). Hirschhorn Museum and Sculpture Garden, Smithsonian Institution, Washington, D.C. Gift of Joseph H. Hirshhorn, 1972.

INCLUSION STRATEGIES

ENGLISH LANGUAGE LEARNERS Students who have difficulty reading text material or directions for the Studio Activities may benefit from being paired with a reading buddy. Choose a reading partner based on the student's level of reading comprehension and the maturity and relationship of the two students. Encourage the two partners to work through written directions together whenever the student needing help feels it necessary. Urge students to take note of key vocabulary words and to number any steps in a process. ELL

The outline of a lake is a free-form shape. So is the outline of your hand. The artwork in Figure 1–3 on page 5 is made up of a number of free-form shapes. How many different shapes can you find?

Form

Like shapes, forms have height and width. Unlike shapes, they also have a third dimension: depth. **Form** is *an element of art that refers to an object with three dimensions.* When you hold a book in your hand, you are experiencing its form in three dimensions: height, width, and depth.

Forms are grouped as geometric or free-form, much as shapes are. An aluminum can is an example of the geometric form called *cylinder.* Rocks and clouds, by contrast, are free-form.

In art, a close relationship exists between shapes and forms. A two-dimensional circle and three-dimensional sphere have the same round outline. A two-dimensional square can be "stretched" into a third dimension to become a cube. These and other shape/form relations are shown in **Figure 1–15.**

Space

All objects take up space. **Space** is *the distance or area between, around, above, below, and within things.* Space is empty until shapes or forms fill it.

In some works of art, space is real. In others, it is only suggested. Compare the artworks in **Figures 1–16** and **1–17** on pages 16–17. The first is an example of sculpture. It exists in three dimensions. If you were viewing this work in person, you could walk around it. You could enter its space and appreciate its form.

The second work of art is a painting. The scene looks very realistic and lifelike. If you tried to move forward into it, however, you would bump into a flat surface.

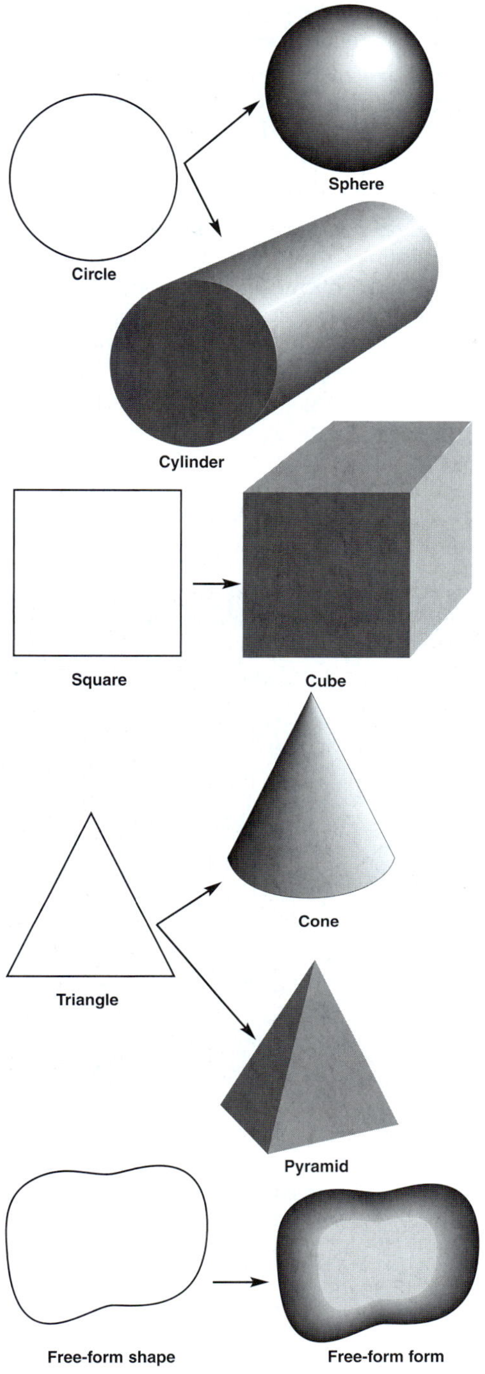

◆ **Figure 1–15** Shape/Form relationships.

Vocabulary

List the new terms found in this lesson. Ask pairs of students to take one term, letter it on a strip of paper, and draw an example of its meaning. Design a bulletin board with these strips. L1 ELL

Aesthetics

Have students compare the Lichtenstein painting in this lesson with the Helen Hardin on page 9 and the Claude Monet on page 12. Ask: How does each artist use color and shape? Note that Monet almost loses the shape in his brushstrokes, while Lichtenstein defines his shapes with strong contrasts. Monet is searching for color; Helen Hardin's shapes and colors are used as symbols. Lichtenstein is simplifying shapes as design. Ask students to write a short paragraph about the use of color and shape in one of these paintings. Students should use adjectives appropriately to write a vivid description of the painting. L1

Team Building Activity

Divide students into small groups. Ask each group to find and identify objects in the classroom that represent the geometric shapes and forms shown in **Figure 1–15.** Allow the groups five to ten minutes to find as many examples as they can, then share with the class their list of identified objects. L1 ELL

ART IN EVERYDAY LIFE

Dimension Ask students to think about ways in which we perceive dimension as we watch television. Encourage them to discuss other forms of entertainment that involve "3D." Responses may be written or oral.

MORE ABOUT...

Perspective The Romans were using perspective in their paintings in ancient times. Remains of wall paintings in Pompeii show remarkable examples. From about A.D. 400 to about A.D. 1000, however, all painting was flat, often with backgrounds of blue or gold. The Renaissance, beginning in the fifteenth century, was a period of rediscovery of Greek and Roman knowledge and art. An Italian architect, Filippo Brunelleschi, studied the ancient Roman buildings and drawings, and in the early 1400s he reinvented linear perspective.

2 Teach (continued)

Art Criticism

As students study and discuss *Paris Street Scene* by Richard Estes, ask them to point to specific techniques the artist has used to achieve a feeling of depth and space. Encourage students to find additional examples of such techniques in other reproductions in this book. L1

Team Building Activity

Have students work in groups to find magazine clippings showing the receding lines of perspective. Those with cameras can take pictures down the hallway or down streets to illustrate perspective. Have each group use tracing paper overlaid on the photographs and trace the perspective lines. Also, try using a washable marker directly on the window glass to draw an outside view down a street. Direct students to close one eye in order to focus on a line. Ask groups to share their drawings to see how the eye sees space. L1 ELL

Studio Skills

Students often feel unskilled in their first attempts at using linear perspective in their own drawings. Help them practice this skill by sketching a familiar classroom object, preferably one with a cubic form. Show them how to draw slanted parallel lines first by observing the example of a cube in Figure 1–15. As students get the hang of sketching cubes, they can apply the same understanding of dimension to other objects they draw. L1 ELL

Space Techniques in Two-Dimensional Art

The artist who painted the street scene in Figure 1–17 used several techniques to capture the feeling of deep space. Artists have developed a number of such techniques. These include the following:

- **Linear perspective.** The lines of buildings, roads, and similar objects are slanted. This makes them appear to come together or meet in the distance.
- **Size.** Distant objects are made smaller than objects that are close up.
- **Overlapping.** Nearer shapes and forms overlap, or partly cover, those meant to appear farther away.
- **Placement.** Distant objects are placed higher up in the picture. Closer ones are placed lower down.
- **Intensity and value.** The colors of objects meant to appear in the distance are lower in intensity than objects meant to appear nearer. They are also lighter in value.
- **Detail.** More detail is added to closer objects and less detail is added to those in the distance.

Which of these techniques was used in Figure 1–17? What other steps has the artist taken to make forms seem to stand out in space?

Negative Space

When it comes to the element of space, there is one question every artist must answer. That is the question of how much negative space to build into a work. **Negative space** is *the empty spaces between the shapes or forms in two- and three-dimensional art.*

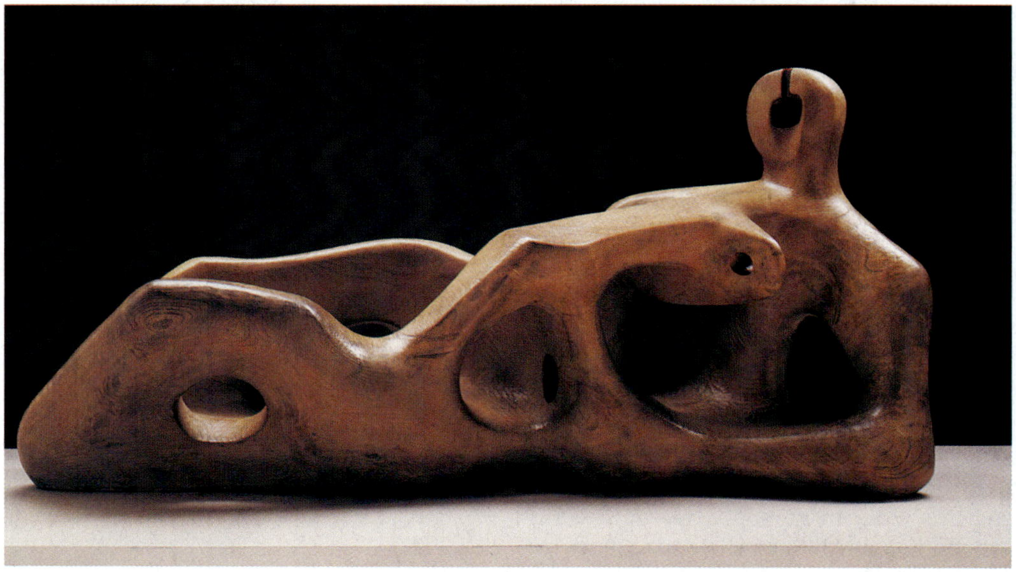

◆ **Figure 1–16** What makes this work a form rather than a shape? Has the artist used real or suggested space?

Henry Moore. *Reclining Figure.* 1939. Elmwood. 94 × 200.7 × 76.2 cm (37 × 79 × 30″). Detroit Institute of the Arts, Detroit, Michigan. Founders Society Purchase with funds from the Dexter M. Ferry, Jr. Trustee Corporation.

CURRICULUM CONNECTIONS

SCIENCE Ask students to think about ways in which they use size, overlapping, and placement in their drawings. Have them find pictures of the wild growth on the "floor" of a forest or rainforest. What is the relationship of tall plants to short ones? Of vines to bushes? Of trees to ground cover? Have students discuss the natural overlapping and positioning of plant life on the forest floor and analyze how nature uses color, shape, line, and form to create its own "still life." L3

How the artist answers the question about negative space will affect the viewer's reaction to the work. Look back at the artwork in Figure 1–3 on page 5. There is far more negative space than form to this work. The abundance of negative space gives it a light, airy feel. Contrast this with the negative space in Figure 1–16. This sculpture seems heavier and more compact because there is less negative space.

Little negative space in a painting or drawing makes the work look busy. A lot of negative space can express calm, peace, or even loneliness.

Check Your Understanding

1. What is *shape?*
2. Define *form.* What forms are closely related to the circle?
3. Identify and describe at least three techniques artists use to suggest space in two-dimensional art.

Studio Activity

Sketching a Still Life

Illustrate themes from direct observation. Look back at the painting of apples in Figure 1–2 on page 4. This work is an example of a type of art called *still life.* A **still life** is *a painting or drawing of nonmoving objects.* What nonmoving objects besides fruit did the artist choose for this still life? What techniques did he use to achieve a sense of space?

Plan a still life of your own by gathering several familiar objects. Illustrate a theme from direct observation using books, pencils, and other materials found in the classroom. Arrange these on a table. Study the arrangement from different angles. Make pencil sketches from several different views. Be sure to use techniques such as overlapping to capture a feeling of space.

PORTFOLIO

Save your best sketch for your portfolio.

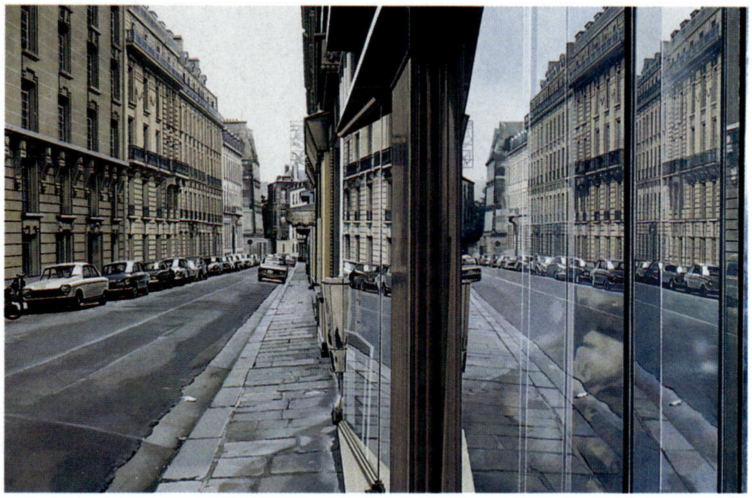

◆ **Figure 1–17** **What techniques has the artist used to give a feeling of space?**

Richard Estes. *Paris Street Scene.* 1972. Oil on canvas. 101.6 × 152.4 cm (40 × 60″). Virginia Museum of Fine Arts, Richmond, Virginia. Gift of Sydney and Frances Lewis. © 1998 Richard Estes/Licensed by VAGA, New York, NY/Courtesy Marlborough Gallery, NY.

Studio Activity

Sketching a Still Life

Encourage students to walk around their still-life arrangement to see it from all sides. Point out that viewing the materials from a standing position and from a seated position changes the shapes. They should start their sketches with the forms in the foreground and then draw those behind them as they overlap.

3 Assess

Self-Assessment

Have students complete the **Check Your Understanding** questions on this page. Answers are provided below.

Enrichment

Have students work in pairs or small groups to compare and contrast **Figures 1–14** and **1–17.** Ask: What similarities and differences do you see between these two paintings? What kinds of lines are used in each? What types of shapes do you find in each (geometric or organic)? Have each group write a short summary of their responses. L1

4 Close

Have students describe the use of shape, form, and space in one of the artworks shown in this lesson.

Answers to Check Your Understanding

1. Shape is an area clearly set off by one or more of the other six visual elements of art. Shape exists in two dimensions, height and width. Shapes can be geometric or free-form.
2. Form is an element of art that refers to an object with three dimensions. Forms can be geometric or free-form. Forms closely related to the circle are spheres and cylinders.
3. The techniques include the following and the descriptions should be accurate: linear perspective, size, overlapping, placement, intensity, detail.

Drawing a Still Life

(pages 18–19)
Lesson Time: 90 minutes

1 Focus

Objectives

After completing this lesson, students will be able to:

- Use color properties to define objects and space.
- Use space techniques to arrange objects in a composition.
- Demonstrate technical skills effectively by using a variety of art media and materials to produce a still-life drawing.

SUPPLIES
Refer to **What You Will Need** in the Student Edition.

2 Teach

Motivator

Direct students' attention to **Figure 1–18**, a painting by Janet Fish. Ask students to notice all the interesting colors and shapes she found in ordinary objects.

Have students look at their still-life sketches and find highlights and shadows. You might place a lamp near the still-life arrangement in order to create shadow effects. Ask students to draw very lightly with pencil and then begin building oil pastel color lightly. This will allow them to combine colors within shapes. Have students fill in the entire paper with color. L1 ELL

Drawing a Still Life

Ordinary objects can become exciting shapes and forms when an artist sees them. Janet Fish arranged these glasses in front of a window and painted *Spring Evening* (**Figure 1–18**). Look at all the colors and shapes she found in the reflections. Notice how she used lines, colors, shapes, forms, and space to provide realism.

WHAT YOU WILL LEARN

Select the best of the still-life sketches you did in Lesson 5. Do an oil pastel drawing of it. You will use the space techniques you learned in Lesson 5 as you draw the objects and choose the colors. Look back at page 12 and study the way Claude Monet mixed colors in his painting *Stack of Wheat*.

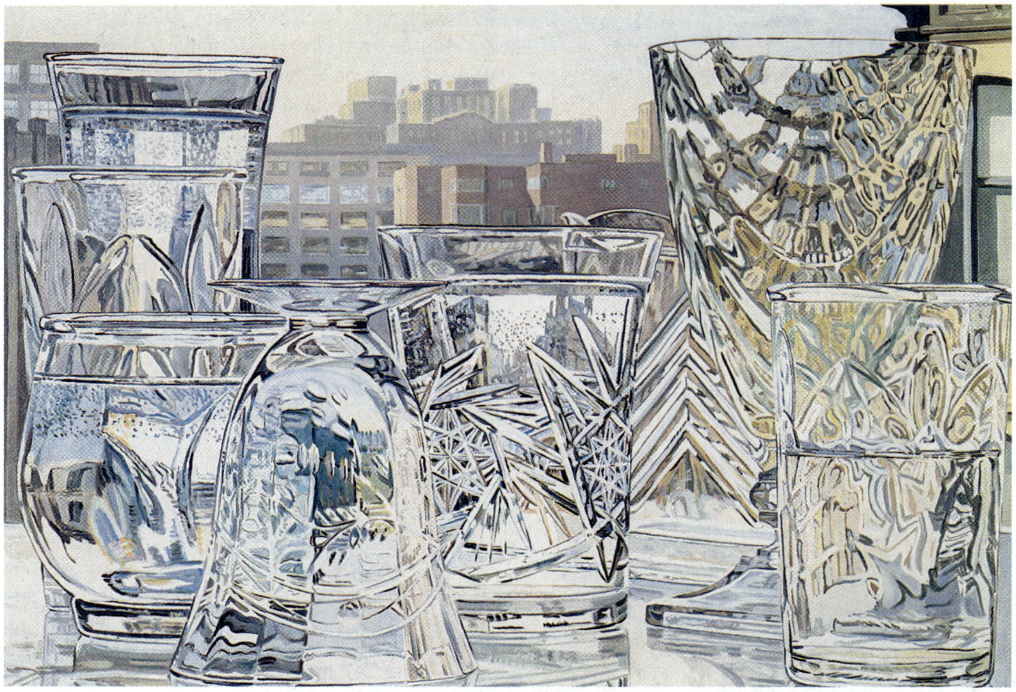

◆ **Figure 1–18** Notice how the artist has overlapped the objects in this still life to show distance. Which objects are farthest from the viewer?

Janet Fish. *Spring Evening*. 1977. Oil on canvas. 111.8 × 162.6 cm (44 × 64″). Rose Art Museum, Brandeis University, Waltham, Massachusetts. Herbert W. Plimpton Collection.

TEACHER TO TEACHER

USING OIL PASTELS Pressing firmly on oil pastels creates more vivid colors. Oil pastels mix and blend colors smoothly and layer colors so they gradually change in value, making objects look three-dimensional. Have students practice on simple forms: a cylinder, cube, cone, or sphere. Determine the light source. Side lighting is easier for beginners. Begin in the middle of a cylindrical shape with the local, or "real," color of the object. Have students use strokes that follow the contour of the form. Blend colors so they subtly become darker or lighter depending on the light source. Apply dark and light hues as well as black and white.

What You Will Need

- Pencil, sketch paper, eraser
- White or colored drawing paper, 12 x 18 inches
- Oil pastels

What You Will Do

1. You will demonstrate technical skills effectively using a variety of art media and materials to produce a still life drawing. Study your sketches and choose the one you like best. Notice that drawings from different angles will show different arrangements of the same objects.
2. On your drawing paper, draw the objects lightly with pencil.
3. Begin applying colors lightly with the oil pastels, building up color as you go. Look for reflections, shadows, and changes in color on your objects.
4. Choose background colors that will set off the objects in the foreground.
5. Fill the entire surface of your paper with color.

Evaluating Your Work

- **Describe** Point out the ways in which you used size, overlapping, and placement in your drawing. Show the way you used intensity and value in coloring your objects in the foreground and background.
- **Explain** Tell what effect you were trying to create as you chose which colors to use. How did you use color to set off the objects in the foreground?

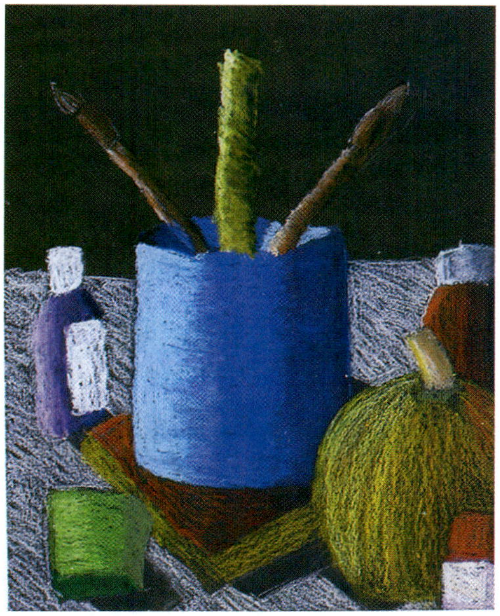

◆ **Figure 1–19** Student work. A still life.

Reflective Thinking

Critical Evaluation. Analyze the original artworks of your peers. Examine the still lifes they drew and form conclusions about formal properties. For example, how did they use color and space in their still lifes?

Visual Art Journal

Take notice of the curved lines of a telephone cord, the shapes of ice cubes in a glass of water, the colors in an oil slick on a rainy day. Draw your observations in your journal. Write notes to remember something special that you see. All this can be part of your next painting or drawing.

Studio Skills

Encourage students to experiment with the oil pastels to blend colors. Oil pastels are much softer than crayons and can be blended much more easily. Fingers can be used to rub colors together. L1 ELL

3 Assess

Peer Assessment

Have students analyze their peers' still-life drawings to form conclusions about formal properties—the elements and principles of art. Responses may be written or oral.

Reteaching

Display the still-life drawings and discuss the use of space and color in them. Ask students to find examples of the techniques of showing space.

Visual Art Journal

Have students develop and organize ideas from the environment. Encourage them to illustrate themes from direct observation by noticing the different shapes and colors found in everyday life. L1 ELL

4 Close

Have students summarize how they used color properties to define objects and space in their still lifes.

Community Connection

Display Student Artworks Partner up with a local business or community hall to create a display area for students' artworks. Have students prepare artworks using the elements of art they learned throughout this chapter. You may also use the still lifes they created in this Studio Lesson. This is a great way to educate the public about the value of arts education. Notify students beforehand that their artworks will be publicly displayed. Students will feel encouraged as artists to have their artwork exhibited.

LESSON 7

Texture

(pages 20–21)

1 Focus

Objectives

After completing this lesson, students will be able to:

- Explain what texture is and how we experience it.
- Demonstrate technical skills effectively by using a variety of materials to create a design with an emphasis on texture.

SUPPLIES

- Several sheets per student of white bond paper
- Textural surfaces such as rough sandpaper, corrugated cardboard, rough boards, woven fabric
- Crayons with paper removed
- Masking tape, scissors, glue
- Colored construction paper for background, 12 x 18 inches

2 Teach

Motivator

Have student partners lead each other on a blind walk around the room, with the blindfolded student touching and trying to identify surfaces. Tell students they will reproduce textures in a much easier way—by doing rubbings of them.

LESSON 7

Texture

His beard was *rough as sandpaper.* The lake was smooth as glass. You have probably read and maybe even written descriptions like these. The descriptions are effective because they bring to mind the sense of touch. They remind us of familiar textures. As an art element, **texture** is *how things feel, or look as though they might feel if touched.*

Like space, texture in art can be *tactile,* texture that can be touched, or *visual.* In this lesson, you will learn about the double role of texture as an element.

TEXTURE

Imagine the smoothness of mashed potatoes, the brittleness of a wheat cracker. Our sense of touch is always alert to the things around us. It helps us identify them and enjoy their feel. It also helps us avoid unpleasant touch sensations. Such an unpleasant sensation is suggested by the sentence that opens this lesson.

Artists take advantage of our experience with textures to enrich their works. How an artist uses texture depends on whether he or she is working in two or three dimensions.

Tactile Texture

Sculptors, you may recall, work in real space. They also work in real texture. Refer back to the sculpture in Figure 1–16 on page 16. How do you think this work would feel to the touch? Contrast that sensation to the one you might get touching the work in **Figure 1–20.** This sculpture of a horse is life-size. It is made of mud and tree branches. What words would you use to describe its texture? What do you think it would be like to ride this horse?

Sometimes artists use texture to capture visual designs in three dimensions. The sculpture in **Figure 1–21** is such a work. Have you ever touched a raised design in fabric? Do you think the "clothing" worn by this guardian would feel smooth or rough to the touch?

Visual Texture

Artists are aware that we experience texture not only through our sense of touch, but also through our sense of vision. Look back at the painting in Figure 1–18 on page 18. The glassware has been painted in a very lifelike fashion. Each facet, or cut design in the glass,

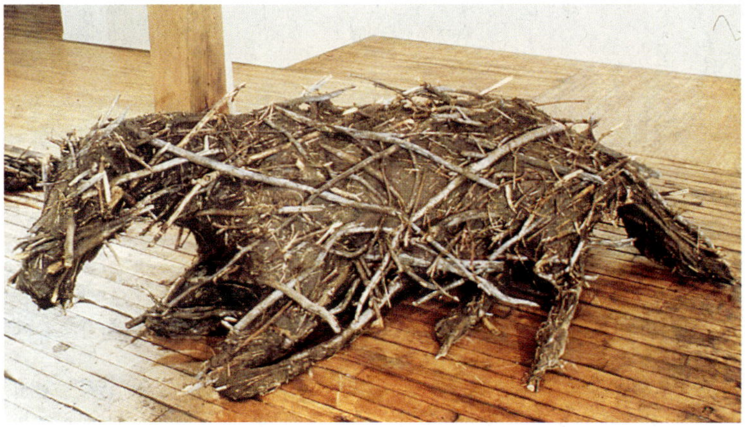

◆ **Figure 1–20** Analyze the use of form and texture to create this sculpture.

Deborah Butterfield. *Horse.* 1977. Mud and sticks. Life-size. Zolla/Lieberman Gallery, Chicago, Illinois.

MORE ABOUT...

LIFELIKE TEXTURE Early Greek painters are believed to have painted very lifelike textures. One painting of grapes was said to be so realistic that birds came and pecked at it. Another artist showed his painting and was asked to remove the drape covering it. That was the painting! When oil painting was invented in the 1400s, artists could blend colors until they achieved remarkably realistic textural surfaces, like gleaming metal and glistening fruit.

looks real enough to touch. Yet, a viewer touching the surface would feel no such facets. The surface instead would feel flat. It would also feel slightly grainy rather than smooth. This is because the work was done on canvas, a coarse material.

This painting makes use of *visual texture.* We "feel" the texture with our eyes. Look back at the realistic street scene in Figure 1–17 on page 17. How many different textures has the artist recorded? Which of these would feel smooth?

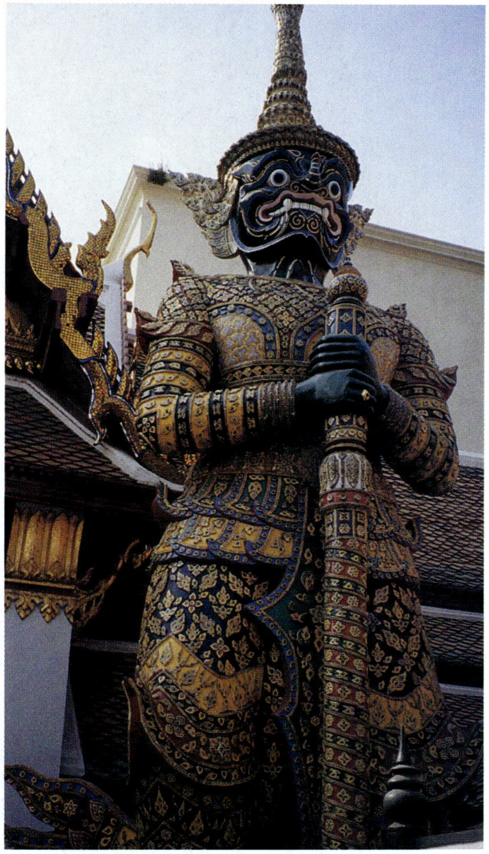

◆ **Figure 1–21** **Analyze the use of color and texture in this work. Notice the work's title and size. Why might the artist have made the sculpture so large?**

Thailand. *Guardian Figure.*

Studio Activity

Making Rubbings for Texture

Practical applications. Explore your classroom and the school grounds for objects with uneven, hard textures. These might include coarse stones and grainy wood. Gather several different surfaces. Place a sheet of drawing paper over each. Using the side of an unwrapped crayon, do a rubbing of each surface. Press down just hard enough to capture the texture.

Use the best of your rubbings as the basis for a still life. Refer to the sketch you did in Lesson 6. For this still life, however, cut the shape of each object from one of your rubbings. Try several arrangements of visual textures before you glue the pieces in place. Decide whether you need areas of solid color. If so, add these.

PORTFOLIO

Write a short paragraph describing in detail a variety of practical applications for design ideas. Which rubbings made for better texture? For what else can you use these textures? Put this paragraph in your portfolio with the still life.

Check Your Understanding

1. What is *texture?*
2. Which of our senses experience texture?
3. What are the two kinds of texture used in art?

Studio Activity

Making Rubbings for Texture

Encourage students to use textures found at hand (sidewalk cement, bricks, etc.). After they fasten paper to a surface, they should rub evenly with a crayon, then gradually intensify the color. When each student has ten or twelve rubbings, they can begin their compositions. L1 ELL

Historical/Cultural Heritage

Discuss with students the use of texture in **Figures 1–20** and **1–21**. Then, encourage students to share their knowledge of how artists from other cultures make use of and express texture in their artwork. Bring in books showing a variety of works from different cultures and time periods and have students compare these artworks.

3 Assess

Self-Assessment

Have students complete the **Check Your Understanding** questions on this page. Answers are provided below.

Reteaching

Review with students the difference between tactile texture and visual texture. Have students give examples of each.

4 Close

Ask students to explain the double role of texture as an element of art.

Answers to Check Your Understanding

1. Texture is the element of art that refers to the way things feel, or look as though they might feel if touched.
2. Our sense of touch and our sense of sight experience texture.
3. The two kinds of texture used in art are tactile and visual.

Traveling for the Light

1 Focus

Objectives

After completing this lesson, students will be able to:

- Plan and write a letter describing the feeling and mood of a specific scene.
- Use watercolors to paint a brightly lit outdoor scene.

2 Teach

Teaching the Feature

1. Let volunteers read aloud the title of the feature, "Traveling for the Light," and describe their impressions of the two artworks shown. Ask: What makes the light an important feature of each painting?
2. Have students read the article to find out where and why Matisse traveled "for the light." Guide students in discussing some of the differences between Paris, where Matisse spent most of his time, and Morocco. Ask: How do you think the weather and the light in Morocco affected Matisse's artworks?

Activity

Have students close their eyes and remember, or imagine, a specific outdoor scene in bright sunlight. Let students use watercolors to paint that scene. Encourage students to focus on depicting the bright light in their selected scenes. L1 ELL

TRAVELING FOR THE LIGHT

Morocco's sunlight lured a French master of color.

Natural light can affect people's moods and the way they look at the world around them. This is especially true for artists. Natural light often inspires them to paint with certain colors and to depict objects, shapes, and shadows in specific ways. For French artist Henri Matisse (1869–1954), it was the quality of the light that led him to Morocco, a nation in North Africa. Matisse wanted a place where natural light would be constant day to day so that he could continue his experiments with color on canvas. Morocco was perfect, he believed, because the sun shines there as reliably as a lamp.

Matisse visited Morocco in the winters of 1912 and 1913. His paintings reflect the country's lush, semitropical plants and trees, its fascinating Islamic architecture, and the vividly patterned clothing worn by Moroccans. Remembering his experience in Morocco, Matisse said: "I felt the passion for color develop in me." Although he never returned to Morocco, the memories of the country's natural light, colors, and images influenced his work for the rest of his career.

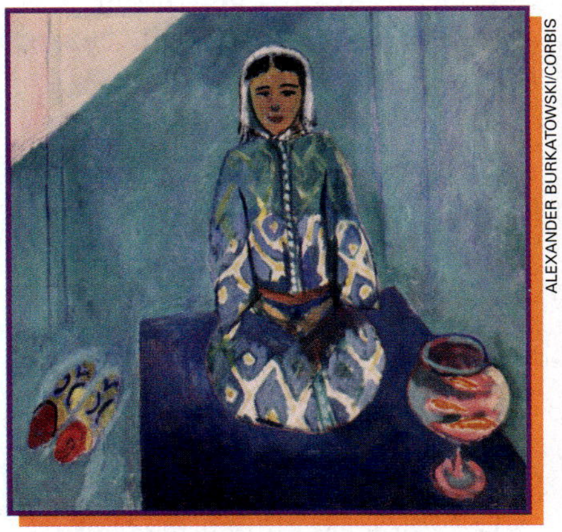
ALEXANDER BURKATOWSKI/CORBIS

Henri Matisse. *On the Terrace.* 1912.
The colored pattern on the woman's dress and shoes as well as flat, two-dimensional-looking space are key elements of Islamic art that Matisse adopted while in Morocco.

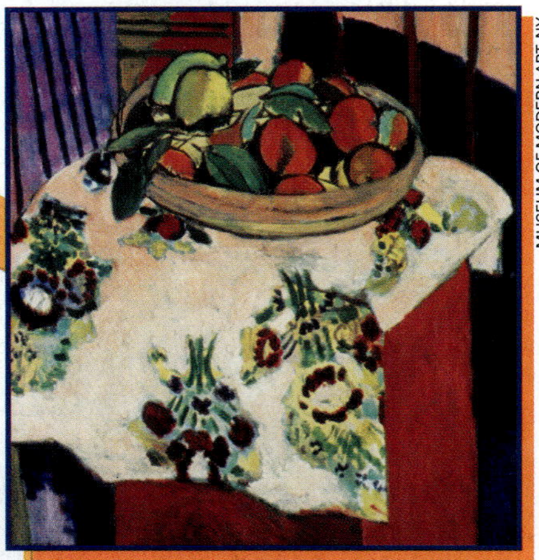
MUSEUM OF MODERN ART, NY

Henri Matisse. *Basket of Oranges.* 1912.
Matisse used color to create sharply defined oranges that contrast against the looser, less-defined flower pattern on the tablecloth.

TIME TO CONNECT

Natural light greatly affected the colors in Henri Matisse's paintings.

- **Create a list of adjectives and adverbs describing how natural light and the artist's choice of colors create a certain feeling or mood in you. Use a thesaurus to expand your list.**
- **Imagine you are on the terrace in the painting *On the Terrace.* Write a letter to a friend back home using as many of your adjectives and adverbs as possible to evoke the feeling and mood of the scene and the effects of the natural light on the colors you see.**

TIME TO CONNECT

Have students work with partners to list vivid adjectives and adverbs. Then ask them to work independently in composing their letters. Ask them to keep these questions in mind as they work:

- Which adjectives and adverbs help make this description clear?
- What other details can I add to make my description more vivid?
- Which parts of my letter do not contribute to a precise description?

Chapter 1 Review

BUILDING VOCABULARY

Number a sheet of paper from 1 to 10. After each number, write the term from the list that matches each description below.

color	shape
elements of art	space
form	still life
line	texture
negative space	value

1. The path of a dot through space.
2. A painting or drawing of nonmoving objects.
3. The basic visual symbols an artist uses to create works of art.
4. An area clearly set off by one or more of the other six visual elements of art.
5. The lightness or darkness of a hue.
6. The distance or area between, around, above, below, and within things.
7. An element of art that refers to an object with three dimensions.
8. Empty spaces between the shapes or forms in two- and three-dimensional art.
9. What the eye sees when light is reflected off an object.
10. How things feel, or look as though they might feel if touched.

REVIEWING ART FACTS

Number a sheet of paper from 11 to 15. Answer each question in a complete sentence.

11. What emotion or feeling is suggested by horizontal lines? What feeling do diagonal lines communicate to the viewer?
12. What is the relationship between primary and secondary colors?
13. Under what circumstances might an artist choose to use complementary colors in a work?
14. In what ways are shape and form alike? In what ways are they different?
15. Name and explain three techniques artists use to achieve a feeling of space.

CROSS-CURRICULUM CONNECTIONS

16. **Language Arts.** Imagine that you were asked to design the cover for a book about a sports legend. What kind of color scheme would you choose for the cover? What kind of lines would you use for the illustration? Write a descriptive paragraph explaining your choices.
17. **Music.** Music, like art, suggests moods and sensations. Listen to fast music and (in your mind) imagine lines, shapes, and colors that look like the music sounds. Now listen to slow, serious music and imagine its lines, shapes, and colors. Which type of music sounded like sharp diagonal lines and bright colors? List some of your favorite types of music and describe each one in visual forms.

Web Museum Activity

The Minneapolis Institute of Arts, Minneapolis, Minnesota

You don't have to travel to Minnesota to sample multimedia offerings at The Minneapolis Institute of Arts. Simply click on the museum's link at **art.glencoe.com**. You will explore the different elements artists use to create their works of art. After you've explored the elements described, look at the artwork depicted throughout this chapter.

Study the different types of elements shown. How many art elements can you identify in each piece? Write a list of these elements and describe how the artist applied them to express a feeling or communicate an idea.

Web Museum Activity

Before you have students go online, visit the Web site to preview the museum's online content, collection, and any online exhibit that might be of interest. Have students identify the different types of elements shown. They should review the artworks shown in this chapter and explain how each artist has applied the elements to express a feeling or communicate an idea. Answers should reveal an understanding of the art elements.

Answers to Chapter 1 Review

Building Vocabulary

1. line
2. still life
3. elements of art
4. shape
5. value
6. space
7. form
8. negative space
9. color
10. texture

Reviewing Art Facts

11. Horizontal lines suggest peace and quiet. Diagonal lines suggest movement.
12. Secondary colors are made from two primaries and are spaced equally between them on a color wheel.
13. He or she might do so to create a striking effect.
14. They can both be geometric or free-form. Shapes are two-dimensional, while forms are three-dimensional.
15. Possibilities include: linear perspective—the slanting of lines to make them appear to come together or meet in the distance; size—making distant objects smaller and close-up objects larger; overlapping—having nearer shapes and forms overlap, or partly cover those meant to appear farther away.

Cross-Curriculum Connections

16. Responses will vary, but should include detailed examples.
17. Students' lists will vary.

Chapter Resources

Features	Standards for Chapter		Reproducible Masters
	National	State/Local	
Quick Write *page 25* TIME ART SCENE "Bottled Up" *page 38* ***Web Museum Activity*** *page 39*	**1.** (a, b) **2.** (a, b, c) **3.** (a, b) **4.** (a, b, c) **5.** (b, c)		Guided Reading and Practice 2–1 Application Activity 2–2, 2–4, 2–8 Historical and Cultural Heritage 2–3 Enrichment Activity 2–5 Studio Activity 2–6 Artist Profile 2–7 Lesson Plans

Lesson Resources

Lessons	Standards per Lesson		Reproducible Masters
	National	State/Local	
1 ***The Language of Design*** *(pages 26–27)*	1a, 2b, 3b		
2 ***Making a Mask with Formal Balance*** *(pages 28–29)*	1a, 1b, 2a, 4a, 5c		Application Activity 2–2 Historical and Cultural Heritage 2–3
3 ***Variety, Harmony, Emphasis, and Proportion*** *(pages 30–31)*	2b, 2c		Application Activity 2–4
4 ***Movement, Rhythm, and Pattern*** *(pages 32–33)*	2b, 4a, 4b, 4c		Enrichment Activity 2–5
5 ***Making a Tessalation*** *(pages 34–35)*	1a, 1b, 2a, 3a		Studio Activity 2–6 Artist Profile 2–7
6 ***Unity in Art*** *(pages 36–37)*	2b, 2c		Application Activity 2–8

Assessment	Technology
Testing Program: Chapter Test 2–9 Portfolio and Assessment Techniques	Artsource: Performing Arts Package, The Alley Cats (Audio CD Track 5) National Museum of Women in the Arts Interactive Lesson Planner Fine Art Transparency CC-2 *Liberty '76* by Robert Indiana Fine Art Transparency 2 *The Stone Cutter* by Diego Rivera

Activities/Features
Studio Activity: Sketching Shapes with Balance
Evaluating Your Work Reflective Thinking Art Online
Meet the Artist: Miriam Schapiro
Time & Place: Japan's Edo Period
Evaluating Your Work Computer Option Visual Art Journal
Studio Activity: Identifying Unity

FEATURED ARTISTS

- M. C. Escher
- Sondra Freckelton
- Katsushika Hokusai
- Lois Mailou Jones
- Ramon José Lopez
- Annie M. Peachey Swarey
- James Rosenquist
- Miriam Schapiro
- Joseph M. W. Turner

FINE ART PRINTS

Fine Art Print 3, *Still Life with Watermelon, Pears, and Grapes* by Lilly Martin Spencer

Fine Art Print 4, *Broadway* by William Conger

Timesaving *Technology*

Interactive Lesson Planner

Make planning easy. Use this interactive software to organize your week, month, semester, or year and access all *Introducing Art* reproducible resources.

KEY TO ABILITY LEVELS

Teaching strategies have been coded.

L1 Activities for all students; teacher direction required

L2 Activities for average to above-average students; some teacher direction needed

L3 Activities for students able and willing to work independently

ELL English Language Learner activities

KEY TO LESSON RESOURCES

Narrative Lesson

Studio Lesson

Chapter 2

The Principles of Art

(pages 24–39)

Chapter Overview

In mathematics, there are rules and principles. When students follow them, they will usually get a correct answer. The principles of art are not that exact. Each work is a new problem, a puzzle to be solved. You cannot measure how much balance is correct, for example. You have to rely on how it looks. How do artists plan their work and solve the puzzle? They use the principles of art to organize the elements of art.

Explain to students that in this chapter they will explore the principles that guide artists as they strive for unity in their work.

Discussing the Artwork

Focus On ◆ **Figure 2–1** Have students analyze the use of color in Lois Mailou Jones's artwork. Ask:

- What color scheme did the artist use?
- What do you think the figures in the painting symbolize? Explain your answer.

Lois Mailou Jones's *Magic of Nigeria* is a two-dimensional, vibrantly colored painting. The colors range from simple browns to vivid reds and blues. She created an image that captures her African American origins and history. The artwork celebrates the Nigerian tradition of masks as spiritual and ritualistic expressions by incorporating many African patterns.

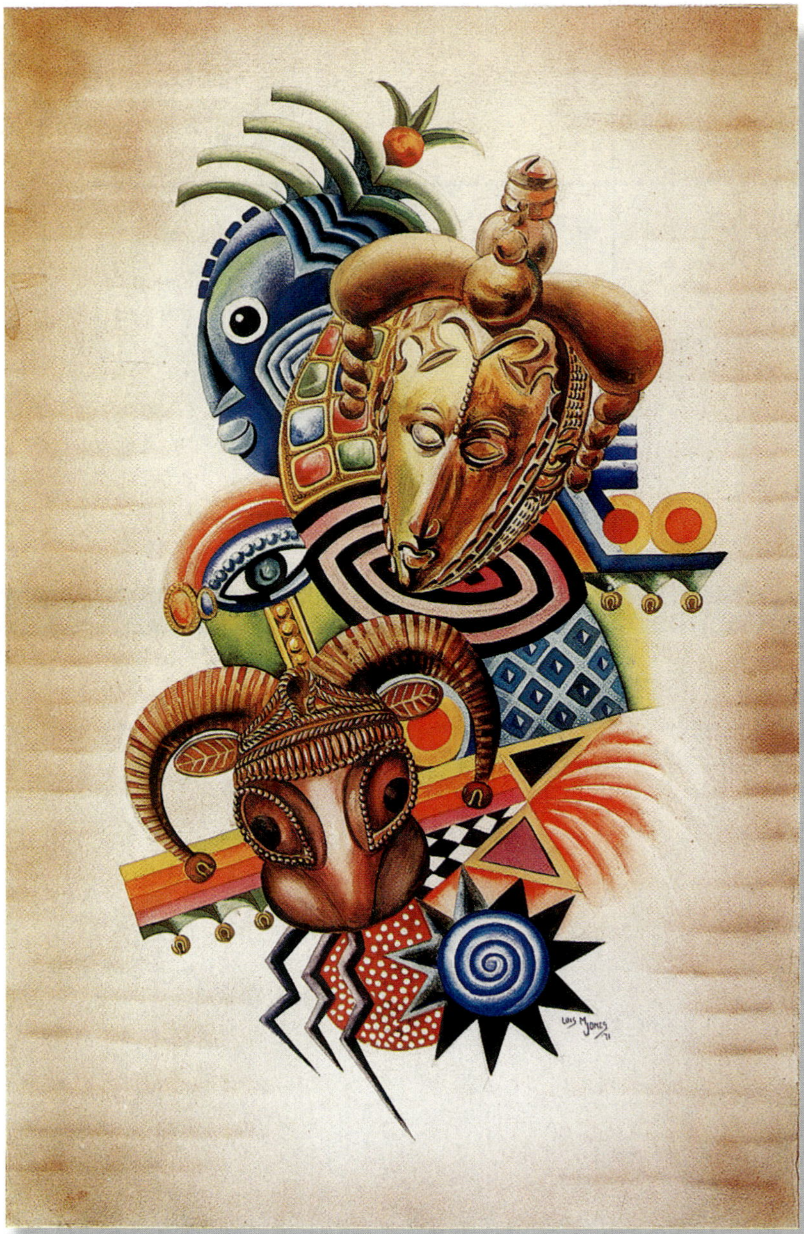

Focus On ◆ **Figure 2–1** **Notice the way the artist has organized her painting to create rhythm that seems to sing and dance. Find repeated colors, lines, and shapes.**

Lois Mailou Jones. *Magic of Nigeria.* 1971. Watercolor. 86.4 x 55.9 cm (34 × 22″). Collection of Dr. Tritobia Hayes Benjamin.

ART SOURCE ARTSOURCE

Linking to the Performing Arts

Music Harmony in music is the combination of two or more tones that sound good to the listener. The music composer manipulates harmony just as the visual artist does, only the musician works with sound and the artist with visual images. The voices of The Alley Cats, an a capella "Doo Wop" quartet, illustrate the element of harmony as they sing "Sh-boom," a popular song from the 1950s. Have students read about The Alley Cats in the **Performing Arts Handbook** on page 311. To enrich student understanding, play the audio CD (track 7) in the **Performing Arts Package.**

Chapter 2

The Principles of Art

"I am always weaving together my research and my feelings—taking from textiles, carvings, and color—to press on canvas what I see and feel."

—Lois Mailou Jones (1905–1998)

In music you can hear the beat of a drum, the wail of a saxophone, and the melody of a piano all working together to make a great sound. An artist also "orchestrates" colors, shapes, spaces, and textures to create a painting, a sculpture, or maybe a quilt. When you understand the rules—or principles—that the artist uses to create a finished piece, you can enjoy looking at art even more.

After completing this chapter, you will be able to:

- Define the term *principles of art.*
- Explain the three kinds of balance.
- Tell how artists use the principles of variety, harmony, emphasis, proportion, movement, rhythm, and pattern.
- Explain how a work achieves unity.
- Analyze how the elements and principles of art are used in original artworks.

Quick Write

Interpreting the Quote Lois Mailou Jones combines her research and feelings to express herself as an artist. Read the quote and look at **Figure 2–1.** Write about what experiences and emotions you might "weave together" to create a work of art.

KEY TERMS

principles of art
balance
variety
harmony
picture plane
emphasis
proportion
movement
rhythm
pattern
motif
unity

Quick Write

Interpreting the Quote Jones communicated her thoughts, feelings, and ideas by expressing them in her artworks. Encourage students to write creatively about experiences and feelings they wish to express in their artworks.

Chapter Motivator

Take time to discuss how the principles that govern art, music, dance, and other arts can be applied to one's own life. Ask students to think about how they achieve balance in their own choice of activities, of friends, of clothes, and so on. Ask students to discuss the principles that shape and guide their own lives.

In this chapter, students will learn that there is a language of art. This language is a visual one, and communication is accomplished through the successful use of the elements and principles of art.

Art Online

Visit art.glencoe.com, the Web site for Glencoe's art programs. This site is designed to help you prepare for your classes and learn about the various opportunities in the art community. Explore the many teacher resources the site has to offer, such as:

- Arts Education Resources
- Galleries and Cultural Resources
- Professional Development Articles
- Teacher's Lounge

National Standards for Arts Education

This chapter addresses the following National Standards for the Visual Arts:

1. (a, b) **4. (a, b, c)**
2. (a, b, c) **5. (b, c)**
3. (a, b)

The Language of Design

(pages 26–27)

1 Focus

Objectives

After completing this lesson, students will be able to:

- Define the term *principle of art.*
- Tell how artists use the principle of balance.
- Explain the three kinds of balance.

Supplies

- Pencils and sketchpads

2 Teach

Motivator

Ask students to stand on one leg. As they do so, point out how they shifted their weight to achieve balance. Lead a discussion of why balance is important or meaningful. Have students brainstorm ways in which we use or value balance in everyday activities, such as adjusting the bass and treble on the stereo, balancing a checkbook, and so on.

Vocabulary

Introduce the terms *formal* balance, *informal* balance, and *radial* balance. Use simple diagrams to illustrate each concept. Ask student volunteers to draw additional examples on the board.

LESSON 1

The Language of Design

Have you ever tried to learn another language? To do so, you need to know more than vocabulary. You also need to know the rules of grammar. These rules govern how words go together.

The language of art has its own set of rules. These rules are called **principles of art.** They are *guidelines that govern the way artists organize the elements of art.* In all there are eight such principles. They are: balance, variety, harmony, emphasis, proportion, movement, rhythm, and pattern. In this lesson, you will meet the first of these principles, balance.

The Principle of Balance

You have probably lost your balance at one time or another. Maybe it was when you were riding your bicycle.

In art, as in life, balance is important. To an artist, **balance** is *a principle of art concerned with arranging the elements so that no one part of the work overpowers, or seems heavier than, any other part.* Artists speak of three types of balance:

- **Formal balance.** In art that has formal balance, one half of a work is a mirror image of the other half. Formal balance can give a feeling of dignity to a work of art. Notice the decorated screen in **Figure 2–2.** With your finger, trace a vertical line that divides the work in half and compare the two halves. Notice how they are alike. Can you find other examples of formal balance within this same work?
- **Informal balance.** Imagine yourself on a seesaw with a much heavier person. To balance the two sides, you might ask the heavier person to move closer to the center. In art, the problem of balance is solved through the use of color and other

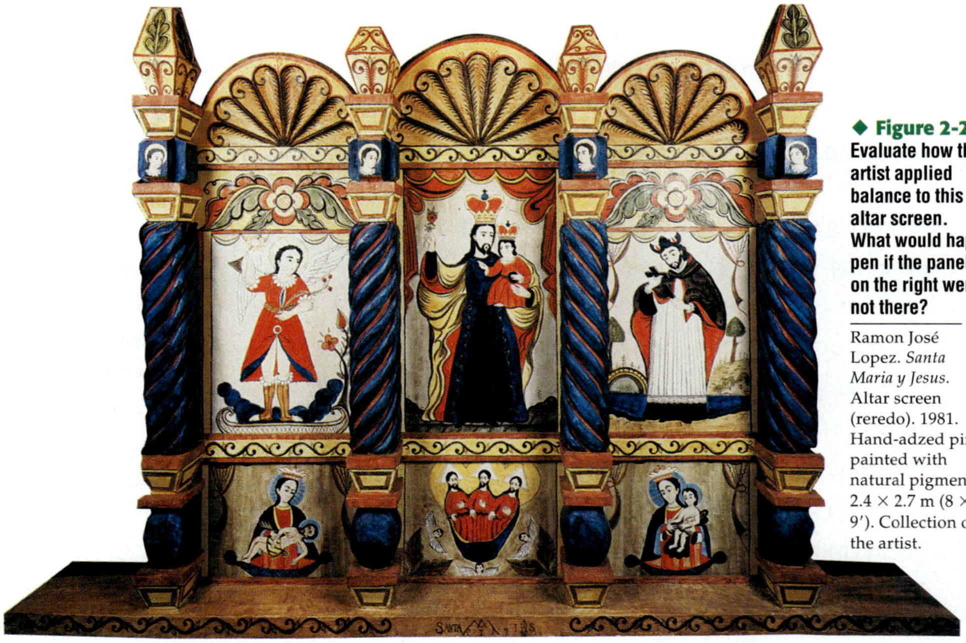

◆ **Figure 2-2** Evaluate how the artist applied balance to this altar screen. What would happen if the panel on the right were not there?

Ramon José Lopez. *Santa Maria y Jesus.* Altar screen (reredo). 1981. Hand-adzed pine painted with natural pigments. 2.4 × 2.7 m (8 × 9′). Collection of the artist.

COMMUNITY CONNECTION

Create Ad Designs Take a field trip to local businesses so students can learn about the graphic design techniques businesses use in day-to-day operations. With partners, have students prepare and present their ideas for posters on product information or designs for advertisements. Allow the class to choose the design that they think will do the best job. Students will then complete the finished product. Students will learn the important skill of marketing a product, giving a quality presentation, and how to use the design techniques learned in this chapter.

elements. A small, brightly colored shape or form in one area of a work will balance a larger, dull one elsewhere. The two shapes carry the same "visual weight." Works of this type are said to have informal balance. Look at the painting in **Figure 2–3**. What single large form is your eye drawn to? What smaller, brighter forms command the same attention?

- **Radial balance.** In art with radial balance, shapes or forms are arranged around a central point. Snowflakes exhibit radial balance. So do bicycle tires. For an example of radial balance in art, look again at Figure 2–2. Notice the half circles at the top of each panel. See how the gold-colored teardrop shapes in each seem to extend outward from an invisible point.

Studio Activity

Sketching Shapes with Balance

Creative expression. Express a variety of ideas based on your direct observation. Look around your home, school, and community for objects with formal, informal, and radial balance. Be creative in your search. With pencil and a sketch pad, make sketches of at least three items. Share your sketches with classmates. Challenge them to identify the type of balance in each sketch.

PORTFOLIO

Label and date your sketches of formal, informal, and radial balance. Put the sketches in your portfolio for future reference.

Check Your Understanding

1. Define *principles of art.*
2. List the principles of art.
3. Describe the three kinds of balance.

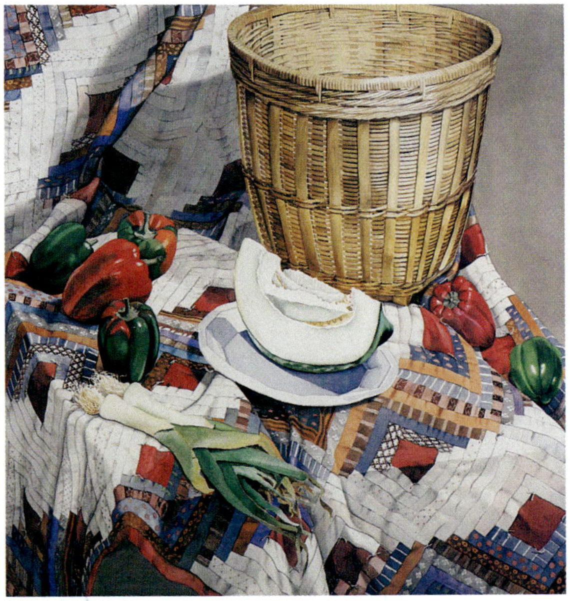

◆ **Figure 2–3** Where does your eye travel first in this painting? Where does it look next? Why is this so?

Sondra Freckelton. *Winter Melon with Quilt and Basket.* 1977. Watercolor on paper. 117.2 × 111.9 cm (46⅛ × 44¹⁄₁₆"). Virginia Museum of Fine Arts, Richmond, Virginia. Gift of Sydney and Frances Lewis.

Team Building Activity

Divide the class into groups and assign a kind of balance to each group. Using their bodies, have them arrange themselves into a composition in their kind of balance. When the groups have decided on their arrangement, ask one group at a time to present their composition. Ask others to identify the kind of balance being demonstrated. Discuss how the groups achieved their balance. L1 ELL

Historical/Cultural Heritage

Ethnic Art Ask students to find, in artifacts from their own family background or other cultural backgrounds, examples of formal, informal, or radial balance. Plan a display of the examples. Have students compare these artworks from a variety of cultures. Discuss the kind of balance in each. (Note: Be sure students have family permission to bring in personal possessions.) L1

3 Assess

Self-Assessment

Have students complete the **Check Your Understanding** questions on this page. Answers are provided below.

Enrichment

Mathematics Have students work with compasses and other tools of mathematics to design examples of all three kinds of balance. Discuss the connections between mathematics and art. L1

4 Close

Ask students: How is the language of art similar to other languages? *(Each has rules and principles to follow.)*

Answers to Check Your Understanding

1. The principles of art are guidelines that govern the way artists organize the elements of art.
2. The principles of art are balance, variety, harmony, emphasis, proportion, movement, rhythm, and pattern.
3. In formal balance, one half of a work is a mirror image of the other half. In informal balance, two different shapes carry the same visual weight. In radial balance, shapes or forms radiate from a central point.

Making a Mask with Formal Balance

(pages 28–29)
Lesson Time: 4 hours

1 Focus

Objectives

After completing this lesson, students will be able to:

- Design a mask using formal balance and geometric form.
- Demonstrate technical skills effectively by using a variety of art media and materials to produce a sculpture of a clay mask.

SUPPLIES

Refer to **What You Will Need** in the Student Edition.

2 Teach

Motivator

Show the Yaware mask and any other photographs of masks you can bring to class. Note the many different geometric forms used by various groups. Begin the project with sketches, but these will be only a start. The real form will develop from experimentation.

Aesthetics

CUBISM The beauty and geometry of African masks was the source of inspiration for Pablo Picasso's Cubism. He saw the geometric shapes in African sculpture as a way of understanding the human form as well as the basic form of objects. Send students online or to the library to research African sculpture and Cubism. L3

LESSON 2

Making a Mask with Formal Balance

Think about masks you have seen or worn. What kind of balance does the mask in **Figure 2–4** show? In many cultures, masks are made from available materials and have formal balance to express the idea, mood, and purpose of the mask. The Yaware people of Africa created the mask shown in Figure 2–4. It was carved from wood that was polished to a high sheen. Notice the arrangement, textures, and kinds of shapes the artist used for facial features and details on the mask. Some shapes are geometric while others are free-form. Can you find examples of each?

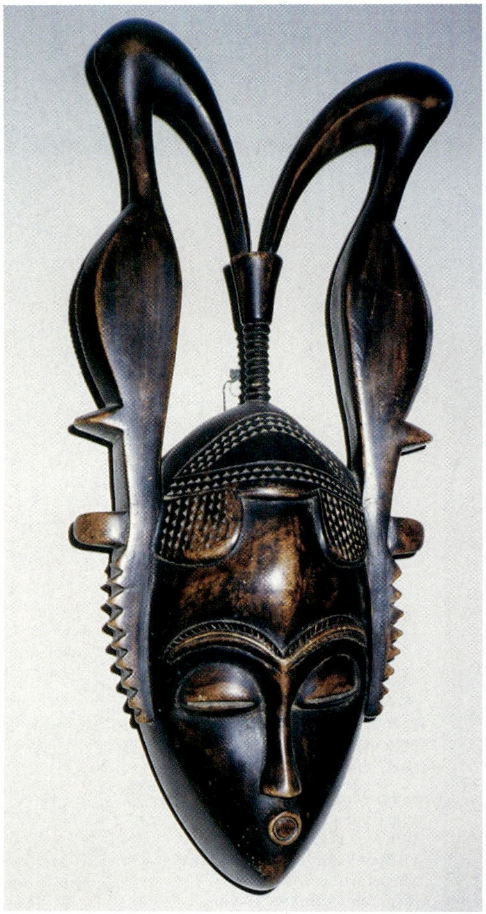

◆ **Figure 2–4** **Analyze the use of geometric and free-form shapes in this mask. How do these shapes create balance?**

Africa. Yaware People. Face Mask. Early twentieth century. Wood. 50.8 3 22.8 cm (20 × 9"). Private Collection.

WHAT YOU WILL LEARN

You will demonstrate technical skills using a variety of art media and materials to produce a sculpture of a clay mask. You will design a personal mask that has formal balance. Select geometric shapes and textures that add interest and express the idea of your mask. Then create a three-dimensional mask in clay. (See Technique Tips 16 and 17 in the Handbook on page 285.)

WHAT YOU WILL NEED

- Pencil and 9 x 12-inch sketching paper
- Clay mat or newspaper
- Rolling pins
- Scissors
- Clay, low-fire or other clay body
- Assortment of common texture tools: paper clips, pencils, skewers, toothbrushes, combs, etc.
- Tempera or acrylic paints and brushes

TEACHER TO TEACHER

USING PAINT AND CLAY Two media that students enjoy most are paint and clay. Combining both in one project motivates students to produce quality results. To prevent breakage, clay objects can be placed in a kiln or oven while still moist. Turn the kiln on and set it at the lowest temperature with the lid open to dry forms overnight. When the objects feel warm, they are ready to complete the firing cycle. Glazes can be used on the bisque-fired clay, but students usually prefer vivid colors. When paint is thoroughly dry, brush on a sealant such as an acrylic polymer gloss or matte medium; or spray the objects outside.

What You Will Do

1. Fold the paper. Cut several symmetrical shapes for a mask. Choose one.
2. Use your imagination to design a mask with formal balance. Choose geometric shapes for facial features and other details. Add pattern or texture to add interest.
3. On a clay mat or newspaper, roll out the clay so that it is about 1/4 of an inch thick and large enough for the drawing. Lay the paper sketch on top of the clay. Lightly trace features and details. Use a fettling knife or open paper clip to cut out the mask shape and small openings, if desired. Be careful, too many openings will weaken the clay mask.
4. Build out some features with clay coils and cut out shapes. Score, slip, and smooth edges to attach.
5. Apply rows of pattern and texture using found objects such as pens, paper clips, cardboard strips, toothbrushes, combs, and so on.
6. When finished, crumple up paper towels or newspaper. Shape the clay over the pillow to softly round the mask shape. Air dry. Bisque fire. Follow directions for clay body.
7. Apply tempera or acrylic paints. Choose a color scheme that emphasizes the mood or idea of the mask and maintains formal balance. Seal water-based paints with medium or spray varnish.

Evaluating Your Work

- **Describe** Identify the shapes used in your mask. What tools were used to apply texture? Explain the color scheme.
- **Analyze** How have you produced formal balance in the mask? What mood or idea does it express? Is this different from your original idea?

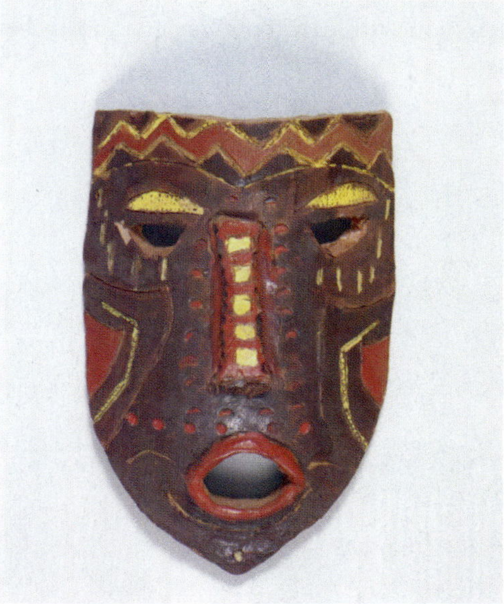

◆ **Figure 2–5** Student work.

Reflective Thinking

Critical Evaluation. Analyze the original artworks of your peers. Examine the mask they created and form conclusions about formal properties—the elements and principles of art. For example, how did they use geometric shapes to create balance?

Art Online

For additional activities, check out our Web site at **art.glencoe.com**. There you will also find:

- Artist Profiles
- Interactive Games
- Museum Web Links
- Student Art Gallery

3 Assess

Peer Assessment

Have students analyze their peers' original artworks created in this Studio Lesson to form conclusions about formal properties—the elements and principles of art. Responses may be written or oral.

Reteaching

Set up a display of the finished clay masks. Have students critique masks for symmetry, geometric detail, and craftsmanship.

Enrichment

Masks Have students research and compare masks from other cultures. Native American masks, particularly those from the Tlinglit tribe in the Northwest, are often asymmetrical. This tribe also carves totem poles, which have mask forms symbolizing whole families. Ask students to find a mask they like and write a paragraph describing its use of balance and geometric form. L2

4 Close

Call on students to summarize how they achieved formal balance and geometric form in their masks. L1

Curriculum Connections

Social Studies Have students read the book *Masks Tell Stories* by Carol Gelber (Brookfield, Conn.: Millbrook, 1993), *Joshua's Masai Mask* by Dakari Hru (New York: Lee and Low, 1996), or another book of your choice about how masks are used and how they can seem to transform the wearer. Have students design a mask based on the material they have read. You may also want to ask students to find out more about how masks are used in a particular culture and report back to the class. L2

Variety, Harmony, Emphasis, and Proportion

(pages 30–31)

1 Focus

Objectives

After completing this lesson, students will be able to:

- Define the four principles of variety, harmony, emphasis, and proportion.
- Find these principles as they are applied in works of art.

2 Teach

Motivator

Discuss with your students what these principles mean in their own lives. How do they achieve variety, harmony, emphasis, and the proper proportion in choosing their clothes, friends, activities, and how their time is spent? These principles are the same as they are applied in works of art. Enjoy with students the various works shown in this lesson. Note the personal statements by Schapiro and Rosenquist and the way they used variety, harmony (or contrast), emphasis, and proportion to organize their works and to communicate their statements.

Vocabulary

These four terms, *variety, harmony, emphasis,* and *proportion* have many applications. Ask students to look each of them up in a thesaurus and discuss the synonyms they find. Discuss these terms in class.

LESSON 3

Variety, Harmony, Emphasis, and Proportion

"Variety is the spice of life." This saying means that a break from humdrum routines makes life more interesting.

This saying also applies to art. In this lesson, you will learn how variety and three other principles—harmony, emphasis, and proportion—add interest to artworks.

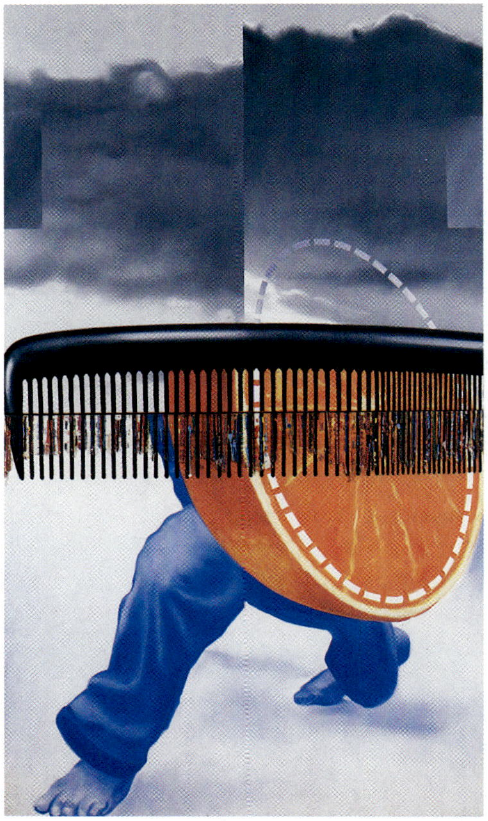

◆ **Figure 2–6 How did the artist create variety and harmony in this painting?**

James Rosenquist. *Early in the Morning.* 1963. Oil on canvas. 241.3 × 142.2 cm (95 × 56″). Virginia Museum of Fine Arts, Richmond, Virginia. Gift of Sydney and Frances Lewis.

The Principle of Variety

In art, **variety** is *combining one or more elements of art to create interest.* A splash of brilliant color will add zest to a painting that has mostly dull tones. A free-form shape adds pep to a work done with mostly geometric shapes. Study the unusual painting in **Figure 2–6.** What has the artist done to add variety?

The Principle of Harmony

Just as you can have too little of a good thing, you can also have too much. In art, an excess of variety can be offset by using the principle of harmony. **Harmony** means *combining the elements of art to accent their similarities.* Look again at the painting in Figure 2–6. This time, study its **picture plane.** This is *the flat surface of a painting or drawing.* Find the horizontal line that divides the upper and lower halves of the picture plane. It runs through the center of the comb. Do you recall from Chapter 1, Lesson 2, the effect horizontal lines have on the viewer? What other lines has the artist used to bring harmony to this active painting?

The Principle of Emphasis

To attract a viewer's attention to an important part of a work, artists use emphasis. **Emphasis** is *making an element or an object in a work stand out.* One way artists create emphasis is through contrast. Examine the sculpture in **Figure 2–7.** Notice how the artist uses contrasting bold colors to draw the viewer's eye into and around the dancing

INCLUSION STRATEGIES

Multiple Intelligence (Kinesthetic) For the more kinesthetic learners, or for English Language Learners, try to find ways to present the concepts of variety, harmony, emphasis, and proportion in physical terms. For example, use related classroom items such as books as examples of varied sizes, shapes, and colors to explain *variety.* Have students hold the items and compare them. For *harmony,* have volunteers play instruments first in harmony, then in discord. Ask students to come up with other physical examples of the four terms. L1 ELL figures. What object or element is emphasized in the work in Figure 2–6?

The Principle of Proportion

As an art principle, **proportion** is *how parts of a work relate to each other and to the whole.* A large shape in a picture filled with smaller shapes would stand out because of the different proportions in size. Look once more at the sculpture in Figure 2–7. Notice how the larger-than-life size of the figures adds to their importance and interest.

Check Your Understanding

1. Name two ways artists can achieve variety in their work.
2. How do artists achieve harmony?
3. Explain the principle of proportion.

Meet the Artist

Miriam Schapiro (b. 1923)

Cultural connection. Born in Canada in 1923, Miriam Schapiro grew up in New York City. Since beginning her art career in the 1950s, Schapiro has worked in a variety of formats, including painting, collage, and sculpture (see **Figure 2–7**). In the 1970s, she became a leader for women in the arts.

Schapiro's work celebrated the traditional roles of women as homemakers and mothers. She coined the term *Femmage* to describe her unique collages in which she combined traditionally "female" household items such as scraps of fabric, lace, and buttons.

To learn more about Shapiro and her work, click on Artist Profiles at art.glencoe.com.

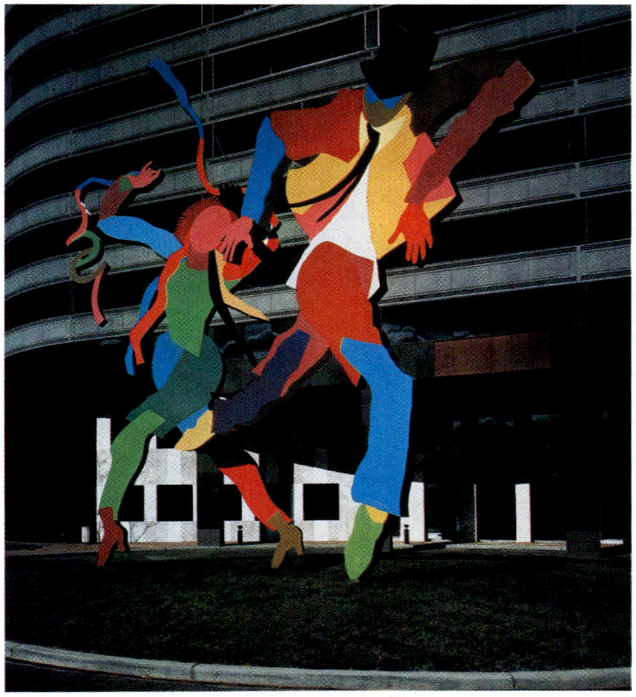

◆ **Figure 2–7** Why do you suppose the artist chose to use emphasis and proportion the way she did in this sculpture?

Miriam Schapiro. *Anna and David.* 1987. Painted stainless steel and aluminum. 10.6 × 9.4 × .23 m (35′ × 31′ × 9″). Steinbaum-Krauss Gallery, New York, New York.

Answers to Check Your Understanding

1. Artists can achieve variety by varying colors, textures, or any of the other elements.
2. Artists achieve harmony by combining any of the elements—line, color, value, shape, form, space, and texture—to accent their similarities.
3. Proportion is how parts of a work relate to each other and to the whole.

Meet the Artist

Miriam Schapiro

For her unique collages called *Femmage,* she used pieces of embroidered, appliquéd, and crocheted fabrics that were created by women to add real textures to her work. In this way she connected her work to traditional women's arts of the past.

Aesthetics

Ask students to express their personal responses to the works in this lesson. Discuss the wide range of subjects that art can have. Ask: Does the harmony and proportion in art, architecture, and music have an effect on people? Lead students to understand that seeing with the eyes of an artist can change the way we see the world. L1

3 Assess

Self-Assessment

Have students complete the **Check Your Understanding** questions on this page. Answers are provided below.

Reteaching

Ask students to form generalizations about the interdependence of the art elements and principles in one of the two artworks in this lesson. Have them identify ways in which the artist achieved variety, harmony, emphasis, and proportion. L1 ELL

4 Close

Ask students to choose one of the works in this lesson and describe how it uses the principles learned in Lessons 1 and 3.

LESSON 4

Movement, Rhythm, and Pattern

(pages 32–33)

1 Focus

Objectives

After completing this lesson, students will be able to:

- Define *movement, rhythm,* and *pattern* in art.
- Explain how artists use these principles in their work.

2 Teach

Motivator

Ask a student to think of a rhythmic sequence and tap it on his or her desk. The others will identify it as **1**23, **1**23 or 12**3**4, 12**3**4, and so on. Listen to music and find the rhythmic pattern.

Vocabulary

Distinguish between *rhythm* meaning repetition and *movement* meaning action or the path of the eye through a work. Ask students to brainstorm simple examples of each.

Aesthetics

Have students analyze the interdependence of the art elements and principles in **Figures 2–8** and **2–9.** Ask:

- How is movement achieved in Hokusai's painting?
- What shapes and colors did the artist use in Figure 2–9 to create pattern?

LESSON 4

Movement, Rhythm, and Pattern

Some works of art permit you to see vivid, fast-paced action as though it were happening before your eyes. Through the careful use of elements such as line, shape, and color, the artist captures movement.

In this lesson, you will learn about movement as a principle of art. You will also learn about two companion principles, rhythm, and pattern.

The Principle of Movement

When you meet a person for the first time, you usually notice the eyes first. Then your gaze moves outward to take in the shape of the person's face.

The same thing happens when you look at a work of art. Your eyes focus on one part. Then they move to the next. This visual journey takes place thanks to **movement**. This is

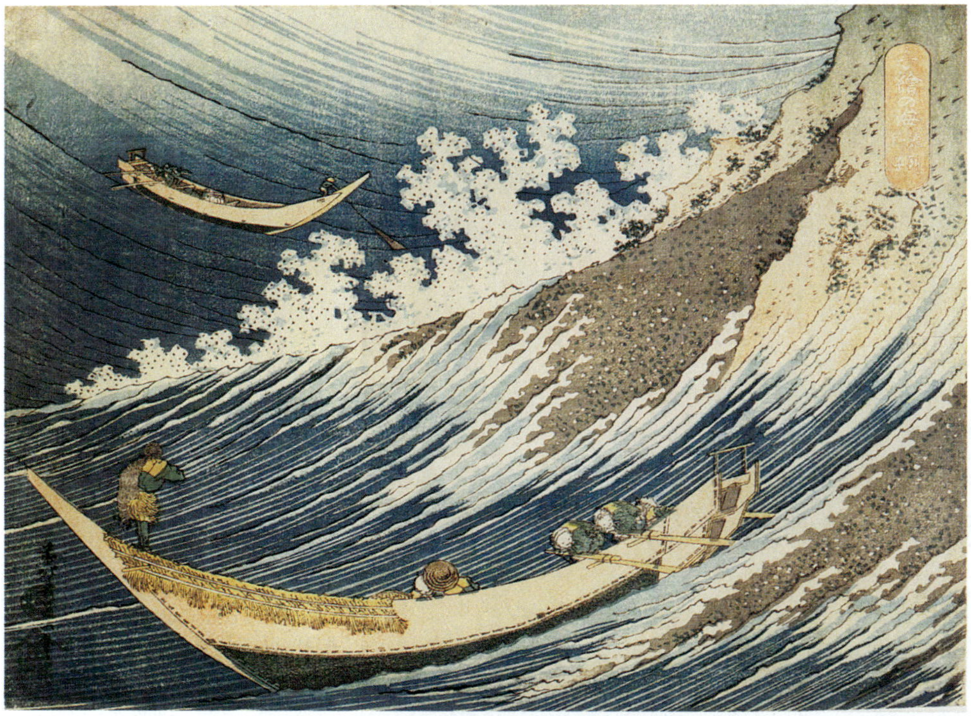

◆ **Figure 2–8** **Analyze the sense of movement this painting suggests. What elements of art did the artist use to create this sense of motion?**

Katsushika Hokusai. *Fishing Boats at Choshi in Shoshu.* c. 1833. Woodblock print. 19.1 × 26.7 cm (7½ × 10½"). The Art Institute of Chicago, Chicago, Illinois. The Kate Buckingham Fund, 1983.583.

INCLUSION STRATEGIES

Hearing Impaired Students with a hearing impairment may be helped by listening to musical selections using an earpiece or headphones, so that the volume can be turned as loud as personally needed by the student. A wooden floor that vibrates to the beat of the music can help students with hearing impairments feel the rhythm. Painting to music is a rewarding activity for students with disabilities, because the requirement for visually accurate representation is minimal or nonexistent.

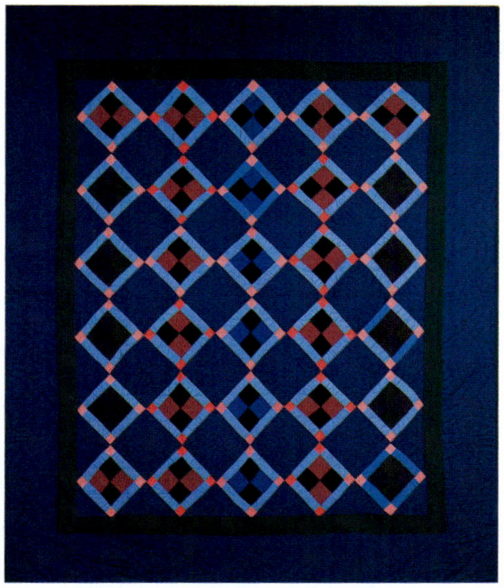

◆ **Figure 2–9** There are two major motifs in this design. One is a solid blue square set on its point. The alternating motif is bordered with a light blue band and divided in the center into four smaller squares.

Annie M. Peachey Swarey. *Four in Block Work Quilt.* Yellow Topper Amish, Byler Group Mifflin County, Pennsylvania. 1925–35. Cotton, rayon, and synthetics. 216 × 184 cm (85 × 72½″). Collection of the Museum of American Folk Art, New York, New York. Gift of Mr. and Mrs. William B. Wigton. 1984.25.10. Photo by Schecter Lee.

Time & Place

Japan's Edo Period (1603-1868)

Historical connection. The Edo period, was a time of peace, isolation, and economic growth. During the 1700s, Edo (now Tokyo) grew into one of the world's largest cities, where entertainment and the arts thrived. Merchants and samurai were entertained by *kabuki*, a type of Japanese theatre.

The entertainment districts in Edo were called *ukiyo*, which means "the floating world." Kabuki actors and other performers became the subjects of a new Japanese art style known as *ukiyo-e*, or "pictures of the floating world." Ukiyo-e became one of the most notable artistic styles of the Edo period.

Katsushika Hokusai—considered one of the greatest ukiyo-e masters—created woodblock prints in this style. Hokusai also created many landscape and seascape prints, including the one shown in **Figure 2–8**. Can you identify any cultural influences in this painting?

the principle of art that leads the viewer to sense action in a work, or it can be the path the viewer's eye follows through the work.

The Principle of Rhythm

Rhythm is *the principle of art that indicates movement through the repetition of elements and objects.* In **Figure 2–8,** the repetition of white curved lines on the blue wave sweep your eyes up to the top of the wave. The foam, which is represented by curved free-form shapes, seems to be in motion. The many small, repeated, free-form shapes that are repeated on the edges of the foam seem to be escaping from the larger mass of white.

The Principle of Pattern

Pattern is *a two-dimensional, decorative visual repetition.* The *unit of repetition in a visual pattern* is called a **motif** (moh-**teef**). The quilt in **Figure 2–9** is decorated with a pattern that has two motifs. Both motifs have the same shape, a square on its point, but one is a solid blue color and the second has several colors. Sometimes a motif can be made up of a complex combination of shapes and colors, such as the curved black lines and dark-orange flowers on the dress of the woman in Figure 8–2 on page 144.

Check Your Understanding

1. What is movement in art?
2. Define *rhythm* in art.
3. How do artists create movement and rhythm?

Time & Place

Japan's Edo Period

The cultural influences in this painting include the distinctly Japanese fishing boats, the fishermen's attire, and the sea as the main theme. *Ukiyo-e,* a distinct Japanese art style, which means "pictures of the floating world," is the dominant style of this painting.

3 Assess

Self-Assessment

Have students complete the **Check Your Understanding** questions on this page. Answers are provided below.

Enrichment

POETRY In poetry, **meter** is the rhythmic pattern used. A line of poetry has a given number of **feet.** An **iambic** foot is two syllables with the second accented. Shakespearian verse, for example, is written in **iambic pentameter**—five iambic feet to a line. Ask students to write a poem in iambic meter. L3

4 Close

Go around the class asking students to point out an example of movement, rhythm, or pattern in artworks in this textbook. L1 ELL

Answers to Check Your Understanding

1. Movement is the principle of art that leads the viewer to sense action in a work, or it can be the path the viewer's eye follows through a work.
2. Rhythm is the repetition of an element or object to make a work seem active.
3. Artists create movement by blending elements in a way that causes the viewer's eye to move from one part of the work to another. Artists create rhythm by repeating an element of art or an object to make a work seem active.

Making a Tessellation

(pages 34–35)
Lesson Time: 2 hours

1 Focus

Objectives

After completing this lesson, students will be able to:

- Design a motif to be used in a tessellation.
- Demonstrate technical skills effectively by using a variety of art media and materials to produce a tessellation design.

Supplies
Refer to **What You Will Need** in the Student Edition.

2 Teach

Motivator

Ask students to find tessellated patterns in the school, such as floor tiles. Hand out the oak-tag squares. Have students cut a shape from one side, cutting no farther than half way into the square. Position the piece by sliding it to the opposite side and taping it in the corresponding position. Do this same procedure on the remaining two sides of the square, resulting in a puzzle-like shape. Allow students to cut more than one until they are satisfied. Tracing must be done very accurately, nesting the next shape into to the previous one, allowing no space between shapes. Tracings will fill the paper. Creating an imaginary form is the next step, carried out with markers. L1 ELL

LESSON 5

Making a Tessellation

Patterns, as you know, are made up of repeating shapes or forms. In some patterns, the same shape or form repeats over and over. In others, it varies.

The interesting artwork shown in **Figure 2–10** contains an example of a type of pattern called *tessellation.* This is a pattern of shapes that fit together in a way that leaves no space in between. The term comes from the Latin word *tessella,* meaning "tile." Perhaps you have seen floors surfaced with tiles. Look closely at Figure 2–10. On the right side of the work, white birds fly over a small town surrounded by farmlands and a river. On the left side, black birds fly over a mirror image of the same scene. Together, the two flocks form a tessellation. The white birds serve as background for the black birds, and the black birds become a background for the white birds.

What You Will Learn

You will design a motif to be used in a tessellation. You will repeat the motif to fill an entire page. Using your imagination, you will add details to your motif. These details will change the shape into a fantasy creature. You will complete your design by using colored markers.

What You Will Need

- Scissors
- Squares of 3-inch oak tag
- Transparent tape, ruler
- Sketch paper
- Pencil
- Drawing or construction paper, 12 x 18 inches
- Colored markers

What You Will Do

1. Cut a shape from one side of an oak tag square. Carefully tape the shape to the opposite side of the square in the same position (see **Figure 2–11**).
2. Cut a shape from a third side. Tape it to its opposite side. You will have a shape that looks something like a jigsaw puzzle piece. This is called a template. Turn the shape you have created. Examine it from different sides and angles. Picture fantasy creatures that might be formed by adding details. Draw around the template on sketch paper,

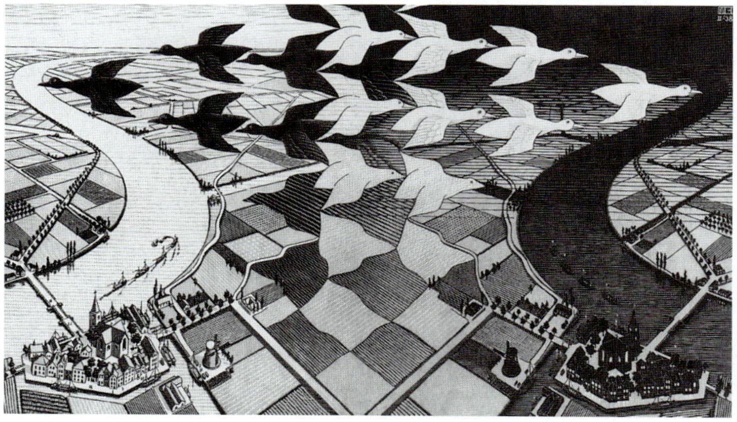

◆ **Figure 2–10** **Describe the pattern in this woodcut. How did the artist create rhythm?**

M. C. Escher. *Day and Night.* 1938. Woodcut in black and gray printed from two blocks. 39.1 × 67.7 cm (15⅖ × 26⅔″). © 1996 Cordon Art, Baarn, Holland. All rights reserved.

MORE ABOUT...

Tessellations Artist Maurits Cornelis Escher, known as M. C. Escher, (1898–1972) was born in Leewarden, Holland. He studied at the School of Architecture and Ornamental Design in Haarlem, Holland, where he learned graphic techniques. Years spent in Italy and many study-travel tours exposed him to the rich patterns and designs of history. However, his own inventions went far beyond the uniform designs he saw. His unique tessellations are now printed on scarves, ties, and many other items.

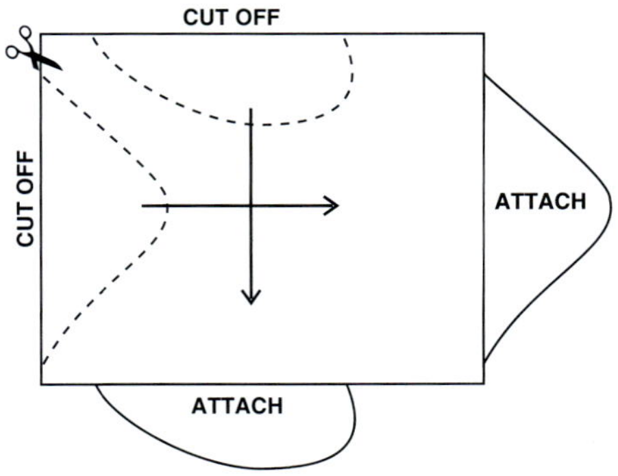

◆ **Figure 2–11** Cut off shape and attach to opposite side.

and record some of your ideas in pencil. You may have to experiment with several squares until you have a shape you like.

3. Place your template so that it lines up with the upper left-hand corner of the paper. Using a pencil, carefully draw around all edges. Move the shape to the right. The cutout on the left side of the cardboard should line up with the bulge on the right of the first shape drawn. Draw around it again until you have completed one row.
4. Move the template underneath the first shape you made. (See **Figure 2–12**). Draw around the edges with the pencil. Continue in this fashion until you have completed a second row. Keep making rows until you have covered the entire paper.
5. Refer to your sketches. Choose details for your fantasy creature. Transfer these features to each of the motifs with colored markers.

Evaluating Your Work

- **Describe** Explain how you made your motif.
- **Analyze** Tell what details you added to make a fantasy creature.

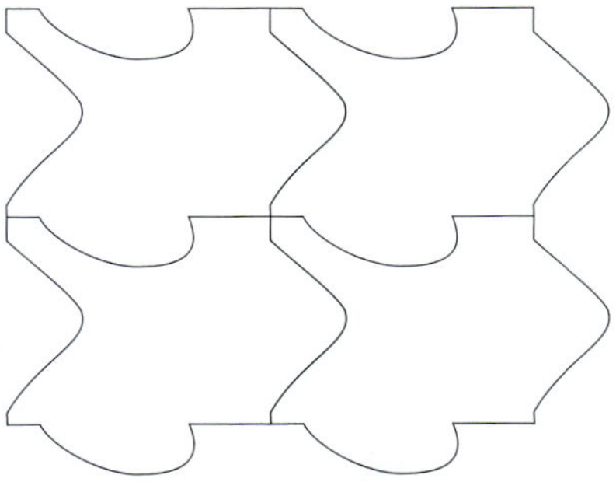

◆ **Figure 2–12** A design using tessellation.

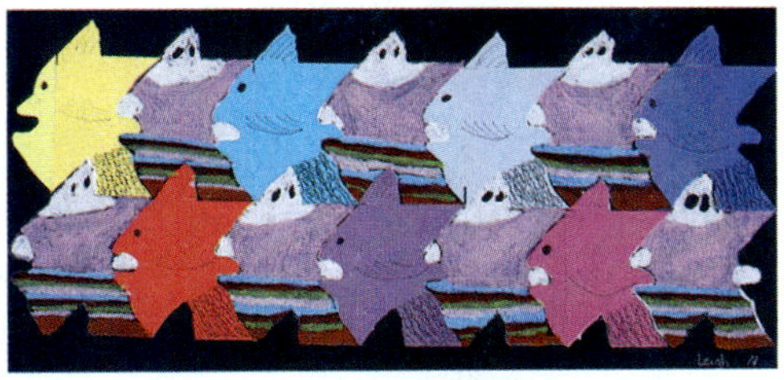

◆ **Figure 2–13** Student work. A tessellation.

COMPUTER OPTION

Select a Shape tool and draw an open shape. With the Pencil tool, draw a varied line from the top corner of one side of the shape to its bottom corner. Select the side with the Lasso tool. Copy and paste it on the opposite side of the shape. This makes a slide translation. Make a second slide translation. Add details, texture, and color to the object. Title and save. Copy, paste, and arrange multiple copies next to each other. Retitle, save, and print.

Visual art Journal

Illustrate themes from direct observation. Find examples of tesselated forms in ceramic bathroom tiles, even in the treads of your sneakers. Do rubbings of several of these patterns and keep them in your journal for future ideas.

ART IN EVERYDAY LIFE

Ask students to find more examples of tile patterns in school, at the mall, at home. Invite them to research mosques, temples, and churches to find other exquisite patterns.

Understanding Art History

Geometry in Art Discuss mathematics in recent design history. Have students research Minimal artists, whose work is often pure geometry; or Cubism, based on basic geometric shapes. L2

3 Assess

Self-Assessment

Have students conduct an in-progress critique of the tessalation they created in this Studio Lesson. Responses may be written or oral.

Reteaching

Review the concept of tessellations and how repeated patterns can be used to make art.

Visual art Journal

Encourage students to develop ideas from the environment. Have them look for different styles of patterns and illustrate these designs in their journal. L1 ELL

4 Close

Display the tessellations in the classroom. Talk about the importance of accurate rendering in such artworks.

TECHNOLOGY STRATEGIES IN THE ART CLASSROOM

Designing Tessellations When students understand the concept of a slide translation as described in the Computer Option, they can more easily create them on the computer. Remind students to use the Undo command immediately when they make an error and to save frequently. To take advantage of multiple solutions, tell students to use the Save As command and retitle work with a number. This saves work in a series, allowing students to return to an earlier point and try a different solution.

Unity in Art

(pages 36-37)

1 Focus

Objectives

After completing this lesson, students will be able to:

- Define unity and all the principles of art.
- Look for these principles in a work of art.
- Analyze the interdependence of the art elements and principles in artworks.

SUPPLIES

- 30 to 40-foot length of thick cord

2 Teach

Motivator

As a way of demonstrating unity, ask students to stand in a group and take hold of the cord. First ask them to let the cord wind around and through the group in a random way. Feel the chaos. Then "orchestrate" the group to create shapes and movement with the cord and evaluate the unity in their designs. Spend time studying the Turner painting in **Figure 2–14.** Go back to other works in this chapter and discuss unity in them. Use this as an opportunity to review the elements and principles of art. Look for each of the elements and principles in the artworks.

Vocabulary

Ask students to find related forms of the word *unity* and write their definitions. Lead students to see the common root word, meaning "one."

Unity in Art

You have probably witnessed the pluses of teamwork. When members of the school basketball team play as one, they usually win. When members of the marching band are "in sync," they put on a great performance.

This idea of acting as one is important in art, too. When you look at a successful work of art, you do not see parts. You see a well-designed whole that has **unity.** This is *the arrangement of elements and principles of art to create a feeling of completeness or wholeness.*

UNITY

You have probably had toys or other possessions that were broken. Sometimes, a broken object can be glued back together so that the cracks are invisible. In an artwork with unity, the "cracks" are likewise invisible. You cannot point to unity as you can to an element or principle. You can sense it, however. You can also sense its absence.

Examine the painting in **Figure 2–14.** This powerful work shows a fierce storm. Much

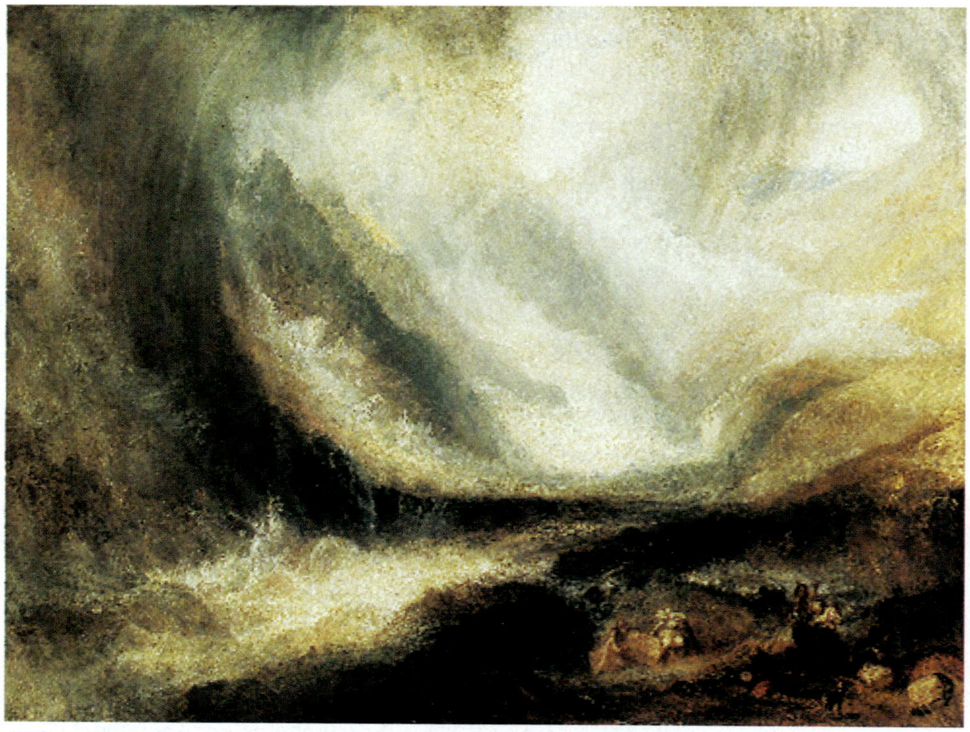

◆ **Figure 2–14** **How would you describe the feeling conveyed by this painting? Analyze the principles and elements of art that have been used to create this feeling.**

Joseph M. W. Turner. *Valley of Aosta: Snowstorm, Avalanche, and Thunderstorm.* 1836–37. Oil on canvas. 92.2 × 122 cm (36⅓ × 48″). The Art Institute of Chicago, Chicago, Illinois. Frederick T. Haskell Collection, 1947.513.

RESOURCES BEYOND THE CLASSROOM

MEDIA SUPPLY HOUSES Students rarely need to obtain art supplies beyond the minimum, such as acrylic paints and inexpensive brushes. Yet, by introducing them to media supply houses, you can help them feel more confident in understanding and using various media, in analyzing cost, and understanding the care of materials and supplies. Visits to such sources can also stimulate the imagination. Some examples are crafts and hobby shops and bead shops. Fabric stores are equally interesting, as are architectural supply stores, print shops, photo shops, and even hardware stores.

of the picture is given over to a sweeping curve of wind and snow. Can you find the people in this picture? Their tiny forms, along with that of a small animal, appear huddled in the lower-right corner. The artist achieves unity in this work in the following ways. He:

- uses *proportion* to contrast the vast fury of the storm with the small people.
- captures vivid *movement* through the careful use of line and color.
- adds excitement and suspense through informal *balance.*
- draws the viewer's eye from one part of the work to another through *variety* in shape, form, and color.

In most cases, the art elements are interdependent of the art principles. *Interdependent* means being dependent of one another. For example, the art principle of movement is dependent on the element of line to create a sense of motion.

Recognizing Unity

One way of recognizing unity in an artwork is by using a checklist like the one in **Figure 2–15.** For each element used, you would make a check mark in the box under the principles the artist has used to organize each element.

Studio Activity

Identifying Unity

Analyze art principles. Copy the checklist in Figure 2–15 onto a blank sheet of paper. Look back at Figure 2–8 on page 32. Go through the checklist one element at a time. For each element found, identify the principle or principles used. Remember that not all artworks use all elements and principles.

PORTFOLIO

Make another copy of the checklist and use it to analyze your artworks.

Check Your Understanding

1. Define *unity.*
2. Explain how an understanding of unity is important to an understanding of art.

DESIGN CHART		PRINCIPLES OF ART								
		Balance	Variety	Harmony	Emphasis	Proportion	Movement	Rhythm	Pattern	
ELEMENTS OF ART	Line									UNITY
	Color									
	Value									
	Shape									
	Form									
	Space									
	Texture									

◆ **Figure 2–15** Unity checklist.

Understanding Art History

Joseph Mallord William Turner (1775–1851) began painting in the Academic tradition of English landscapes. However, his fascination with nature—he once had himself tied to the mast of a sailing ship during a storm on the English Channel so that he could experience the violence of the winds and rain—brought him to break from defined shapes and paint in pure color. Many of his paintings are almost abstractions. Turner opened the way to the Impressionists of the later nineteenth century. Invite students to find out more about Turner and his influence on his contemporaries.

3 Assess

Self-Assessment

Have students complete the **Check Your Understanding** questions on this page. Answers are provided below.

Reteaching

Ask students to identify the principles of art and point to some examples of each from artworks in Chapter 1 or 2.

4 Close

Review the concept of unity as it applies to life situations and to artworks.

Answers to Check Your Understanding

1. Unity is the arrangement of elements and principles of art to create a feeling of completeness or wholeness.
2. In an artwork with unity, you do not see parts. You see a well-defined whole. Understanding the elements and principles of art helps to evaluate how and whether the artist has achieved a unified whole.

Bottled Up!

1 Focus

Objectives

After completing this lesson, students will be able to:

- Read about and discuss the sculptures of Oldenburg and van Bruggen.
- Plan and describe ideas for a common-object sculpture for their school.
- Create a miniature clay sculpture.

2 Teach

Teaching the Feature

1. Let students meet in cooperative groups to describe and discuss *Bottle of Notes,* shown in the photograph.
2. Have group members read and discuss the article. Ask: Does the information about Oldenburg and van Bruggen change your reaction to their artwork? If so, how? What would you tell the citizens of Middlesbrough who ask what the oversized sculpture means?

Activity

Ask students: How does changing the expected size of an object change the viewer's understanding of it? Point out that Oldenburg and van Bruggen make giant-size sculptures of relatively small objects. Have students reverse the process, using clay to make tiny figures of relatively large objects. L1 ELL

Bottled Up!

An oversized sculpture honors a famous explorer.

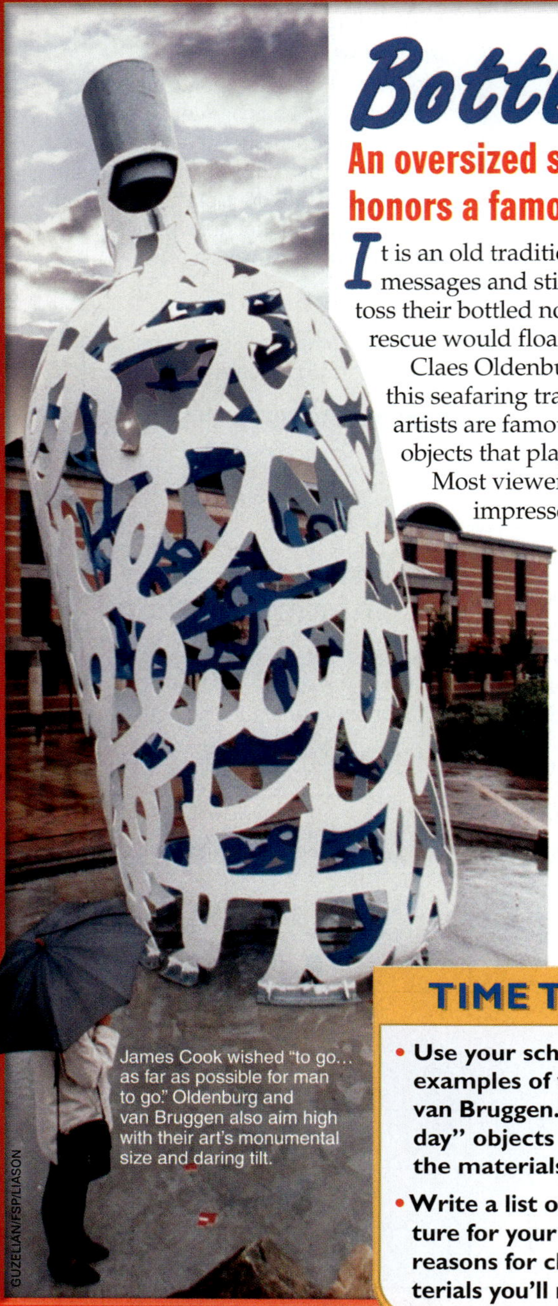

James Cook wished "to go... as far as possible for man to go." Oldenburg and van Bruggen also aim high with their art's monumental size and daring tilt.

GUZELIAN/FSP/LIASON

It is an old tradition that shipwrecked sailors would write messages and stick them into corked bottles. They would toss their bottled notes into the water, hoping their calls for rescue would float ashore and bring help.

Claes Oldenburg and Coosje van Bruggen have turned this seafaring tradition into a BIG work of art. These two artists are famous for their huge sculptures of everyday objects that play with our expected sense of proportion. Most viewers are at first surprised—and then impressed—by the team's oversized artworks, such as their 40-foot-high sculpture of a bottle. The looming, tilted artwork lightheartedly honors James Cook (1728–1779). He was the British sailor and explorer who sailed around the world twice.

The 40-foot-tall *Bottle of Notes* is located in Cook's birthplace, Middlesbrough, England. The bottle is made of giant steel script. The words form a quote from Cook's journals. Oldenburg says the bottle should look as if it were "stuck in the sand by a wave." Yes, but is there a note inside that reads "Help"?

TIME TO CONNECT

- **Use your school's media resource center to look at examples of work by Claes Oldenburg and Coosje van Bruggen. From your research, identify the "everyday" objects they have enlarged into sculptures and the materials needed to produce these works of art.**
- **Write a list of your ideas for a common-object sculpture for your school. Explain in a written report your reasons for choosing that object. Describe the materials you'll need to create your enlarged sculpture.**

TIME TO CONNECT

In a class discussion, have students share their ideas for a common-object sculpture. As students write their reports, emphasize that they write in complete sentences and use correct spelling to communicate clearly and effectively.

Chapter 2 Review

BUILDING VOCABULARY

Number a sheet of paper from 1 to 12. After each number, write the term from the list that matches each description below.

balance	picture plane
emphasis	principles of art
harmony	proportion
motif	rhythm
movement	unity
pattern	variety

1. How parts of a work relate to each other and to the whole.
2. Combining one or more elements of art to create interest.
3. The arrangement of elements and principles of art to create a feeling of completeness or wholeness.
4. The principle of art that leads the viewer to sense action in a work, or it can be the path the viewer's eye follows through the work.
5. Making an element or an object in a work stand out.
6. A principle of art concerned with arranging the elements so that no one part of the work overpowers, or seems heavier than, any other part.
7. Guidelines that govern the way artists organize the elements of art.
8. The principle of art that indicates movement through the repetition of elements and objects.
9. The flat surface of a painting or drawing.
10. Combining the elements of art to accent their similarities.
11. Two-dimensional, decorative visual repetition.
12. The unit of repetition in a visual pattern.

REVIEWING ART FACTS

Number a sheet of paper from 13 to 17. Answer each question in a complete sentence.

13. What kind of balance does a hubcap have?
14. What happens when there is too much harmony in a work of art? What can be done to correct this problem?
15. What are some ways of achieving proportion in an artwork?
16. What principle might be used to organize a work of art that contains a motif?
17. What is a tessellation?

CROSS-CURRICULUM CONNECTIONS

18. **Language Arts.** Emphasis occurs in literature as well as in art. In stories, words are *italicized* to show they receive stress or emphasis. With a group of classmates, write a short story in which words are emphasized. Read your story in front of the class. Challenge classmates to identify examples of emphasis.
19. **Mathematics.** The principles of art, such as balance and proportion, are based on math skills. What math skills do you think you need to work with balance and proportion? Explain.

Web Museum Activity

Indianapolis Museum of Art, Indianapolis, Indiana

What do geometry and art have to do with each other? Visit the Indianapolis Museum of Art by clicking on its link at **art.glencoe.com**, and explore how geometry is used as a creative tool in the work of many artists. Discover how artists have used geometry to create their artworks.

Write a description of the ways in which geometry is applied to the works of art.

Answers to Chapter 2 Review

Building Vocabulary

1. proportion
2. variety
3. unity
4. movement
5. emphasis
6. balance
7. principles of art
8. rhythm
9. picture plane
10. harmony
11. pattern
12. motif

Reviewing Art Facts

13. It would have radial balance.
14. The work can become boring or monotonous. This problem can be remedied by using variety, emphasis, or proportion.
15. It can be achieved by varying the size of objects or the amounts of color used in different objects.
16. The principle would be pattern.
17. It is a pattern of shapes that fit together in a way that leaves no space in between.

Cross-Curriculum Connections

18. Students' stories will vary, but should include examples of the principle of art emphasis. Stories should reflect a clear understanding of emphasis and how it is applied in writing.
19. Answers will vary, but should include the use of geometry to create balance and proportion in artworks.

Web Museum Activity

Before you have students go online, visit the Web site to preview the museum's online content, collection, and any online exhibit that may be of interest.

Have students learn the different ways geometry is used in art. Students' descriptions should reveal an understanding of how the artists used math in their artworks.

Chapter Resources

Features	Standards for Chapter: National	Standards for Chapter: State/Local	Reproducible Masters
Quick Write *page 41* TIME ART SCENE "Every Stitch Tells a Story" *page 60* ***Web Museum Activity*** *page 61*	**1.** (a, b) **2.** (a, b, c) **3.** (a) **4.** (a, c) **5.** (a, b, c) **6.** (a, b)		Guided Reading and Practice 3–1 Historical and Cultural Heritage 3–2, 3–7 Application Activity 3–3, 3–9 Studio Activity 3–4, 3–5 Enrichment Activity 3–6 Cross-Curriculum Activity 3–8 Lesson Plans

Lesson Resources

Lessons	Standards per Lesson: National	Standards per Lesson: State/Local	Reproducible Masters
1 ***Drawing*** *(pages 42–43)*	1b, 2b, 2c, 3a		
2 ***Gesture Drawing*** *(pages 44–45)*	1a, 1b, 2a, 5c		
3 ***Painting*** *(pages 46–47)*	1b, 2a, 2b		Historical and Cultural Heritage 3–2
4 ***Creating a Portrait*** *(pages 48–49)*	1a, 1b, 2a, 2c		Application Activity 3-3
5 ***Printmaking*** *(pages 50–51)*	1a, 2b		Studio Activity 3-4, 3-5 Enrichment Activity 3–6 Historical and Cultural Heritage 3-7
6 ***Sculpture*** *(pages 52–53)*	4a, 5b		Cross-Curriculum Activity 3-8 Application Activity 3-9
7 ***Making a Collage*** *(pages 54–55)*	1a, 1b, 2a, 2b, 3a		
8 ***Digital Art*** *(pages 56–59)*	4c, 6a, 6b		

Assessment	Technology
Testing Program: Chapter Test 3–10 *Portfolio and Assessment Techniques*	Artsource Performing Arts Package, The Chameleons (DVD or VHS Segment 12) National Museum of Women in the Arts Interactive Lesson Planner Fine Art Transparency CC-3, *Tinglit Effigy Pipe Bowl* Fine Art Transparency 3, *Anemones in a Blue Vase,* by Emil Nolde

Activities/Features
Studio Activity: Keeping a Sketchbook
Evaluating Your Work Reflective Thinking Visual Art Journal
Studio Activity: Experimenting with Watercolor
Evaluating Your Work Studio Option Visual Art Journal
Studio Activity: Making a Relief Block Print
Time & Place: Rome c. 50 B.C.
Evaluating Your Work Portfolio Ideas Art Online
Studio Activity: Exploring Tools of Art Software

KEY TO ABILITY LEVELS

Teaching strategies have been coded.

- L1 Activities for all students; teacher direction required
- L2 Activities for average to above-average students; some teacher direction needed
- L3 Activities for students able and willing to work independently
- ELL English Language Learner activities

FEATURED ARTISTS

- Romare Bearden
- Mary Cassatt
- Honoré Daumier
- Francisco de Goya
- Rhoda Grossman
- Gustav Klimt
- Jeannette Leroy
- Shiko Munakata
- Emil Nolde
- Erol Otis
- Nam June Paik
- John Wilson

FINE ART PRINTS

Fine Art Print 5, *Mother with Child* by Elizabeth Catlett

Fine Art Print 6, *Personal Appearance* by Miriam Schapiro

Timesaving Technology

Interactive Lesson Planner

Make planning easy. Use this interactive software to organize your week, month, semester, or year and access all *Introducing Art* reproducible resources.

KEY TO LESSON RESOURCES

Narrative Lesson

Studio Lesson

Chapter 3

Art Media and Techniques

(pages 40–61)

Chapter Overview

In this chapter, students will begin to explore the characteristics of various art media—the tools of the artist. They will learn about the media used in drawing, painting, printmaking, and sculpture. Students will have an opportunity to develop their technical skills and experiment with a variety of art media to create their own artworks.

Discussing the Artwork

Focus On ◆ **Figure 3–1** Have students study *Hamlet Robot* by Nam June Paik. Paik's portrait of Hamlet is a video sculpture programmed with contemporary visual technology. In this artwork, 13 video screens play scenes from stage, screen, and fine art representations of Shakespeare's *Hamlet.* Nam June Paik's *Hamlet Robot* demonstrates the ways in which artists are further pushing the limits of artistic form and media, using found materials (old radio and TV cabinets) as well as digital electronic media (video images). Ask students how well they think this artwork illustrates *Hamlet.*

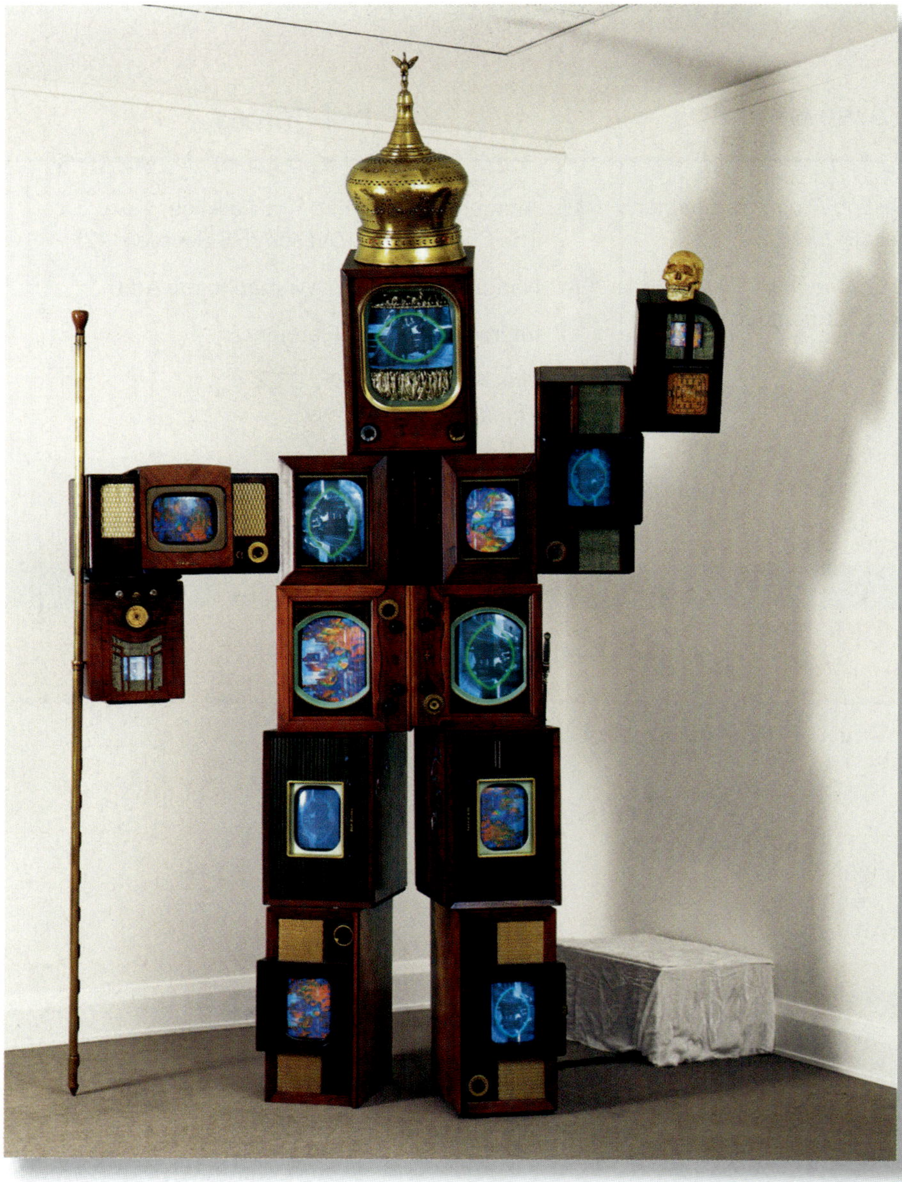

Focus On ◆ **Figure 3–1** **In this artwork, artist Nam June Paik programs televisions with patterns, images, and audio sounds to get you to think about his subject.**

Nam June Paik. *Hamlet Robot.* 1996. Video installation. 365.8 × 223.5 × 81.3 cm. (144 × 88 × 32"). The Chrysler Museum of Art, Norfolk, Virginia. Museum purchase and gift of Joan Dalis Martone, Fran and Lenox Baker, Mr. and Mrs. Macon F. Brock, Jr., Susan and Paul Hirschbiel, Dr. and Mrs. Paul Mansheim, Robert McLanahan Smith III.

40

ART SOURCE ARTSOURCE

Linking to the Performing Arts

Theatre Mime is an art form that captures the essence of specific gestures and postures. *Life Cycle,* created by Keith Berger and Sharon Disken, who are known as The Chameleons, illustrates the life cycle using only physical adjustments and no words. Have students learn how The Chameleons portray the gamut of human experience through mime in the **Performing Arts Handbook** on page 312. To enrich student understanding, play the DVD or videotape (segment 12) in the **Performing Arts Package.**

Chapter 3

Art Media and Techniques

"Technology has become the body's new membrane of existence."

— Nam June Paik (b. 1932)

Every musical instrument has its own voice, or characteristic. You can identify a guitar by its twang, a flute by its fine clear line of sound. The materials of art, called art *media,* also have their own characteristics. Wood can be carved. Clay is pliable. Watercolor is transparent and thin. Tempera, acrylics, and oils are opaque and thick. This chapter will teach you about the tools and materials artists use. You will learn to appreciate the special characteristics of each *medium.*

After completing this chapter, you will be able to:

- Define the term *medium of art.*
- Identify the different kinds of media used in drawing, painting, printmaking, and sculpture.
- Demonstrate technical skills effectively using a variety of art media.
- Use mixed media to create an original work of art.

Quick Write

Interpreting the Quote Look at **Figure 3–1** and read the quote by Nam June Paik. Think of how technology influences your life. What are your daily rituals that involve technology?

KEY TERMS

art medium
perception
gesture drawing
pigment
binder
solvent
portrait
printmaking
intaglio
sculpture

Quick Write

Interpreting the Quote Have students read the quote and complete the Quick Write activity. Ask students to write a description of the role technology plays in their daily lives. Student responses will vary, but may include how the Internet has influenced the way we communicate, shop, and research. Students should include examples of daily rituals involving their use of technology.

Chapter Motivator

Before students begin the chapter, encourage them to talk about and describe works of art that they have enjoyed or that they remember well. Ask them to give details about the work and explain why they liked it. Lead students to discover that different works exhibit different media and techniques that make the works stand out in a viewer's mind. Tell them they will learn more about these media, techniques, and technology in this chapter.

Art Online

Visit **art.glencoe.com**, the Web site for Glencoe's art programs. This site offers general student resources to help guide your students as they learn about art and artists. Encourage your students to visit this site and explore the various resources and activities, such as:

- Artist Profiles
- Career Corner
- Student Art Gallery
- Web Links to museums, art techniques, art history, and cross-curricular activities.

National Standards for Arts Education

This chapter addresses the following National Standards for the Visual Arts:

1. (a, b)	**4. (a, c)**
2. (a, b, c)	**5. (a, b)**
3. (a)	**6. (a, b)**

Drawing
(pages 42–43)

1 Focus

Objectives

After completing this lesson, students will be able to:

- Define *perception*.
- Recognize blending and cross-hatching as methods of achieving depth in drawing.
- Draw with their eyes on the object.

Supplies
- Newsprint or drawing paper
- Pencils or crayons
- Objects to draw

2 Teach

Motivator

Discuss the importance of drawing for every person. Perceptual drawing can be done by everyone. Emphasize looking at the object while drawing. This is a means of getting "right brain" control of the drawing. The hand will follow the path of the eye. Remind students that this takes much practice.

Vocabulary

Encourage students to brainstorm other words they may know that have an irregular plural form like medium, media *(stadium, stadia; datum, data; and so on)*. Have students research the word history of *medium*.

LESSON 1

Drawing

To most people, a pencil is a writing tool. To artists, it is a key. As an art medium, this familiar object opens the door to endless creative possibilities. An **art medium** is *a material used to create a work of art.* When we speak of more than one medium, we use the word *media.* Artists rely on a wide variety of media in their work, such as pencils, paints, charcoal, and pastels.

In this lesson, you will learn about media used in drawing. In later lessons, you will learn about media used to create other kinds of art.

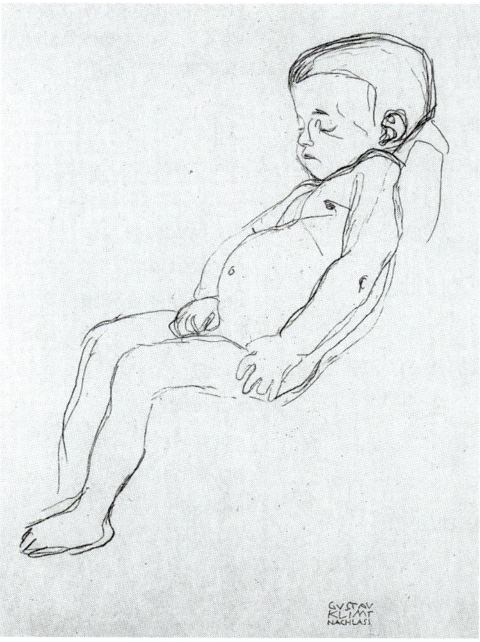

◆ **Figure 3–2** What drawing medium was used for this sketch? How would you describe the characteristics of this art tool?

Gustav Klimt. *Sleeping Boy.* 1905–07. Graphite pencil on cream wove paper. 55.2 × 34.9 cm (21¾ × 13¾"). Detroit Institute of Arts, Detroit, Michigan. Founders Society Purchase, John S. Newberry Fund.

Why Artists Draw

In baseball, a pitcher takes warm-up throws before facing a batter. Musicians warm up before a performance. Artists follow a similar approach by drawing. Drawing "limbers" up the artist's eye. It helps develop visual **perception** (pur-**sep**-shun). This is *an awareness of the elements of an environment by means of the senses.* Perception is more than looking at an object. It is really "seeing" the object. It is studying how lines, shapes, forms, and colors blend to form the whole.

Some drawings are used to plan paintings or other large projects. **Figure 3–2** shows this type of drawing, or "study." Other drawings are done as finished works of art. Such a drawing appears in **Figure 3–3.**

Drawing Media

Do you recall scribbling with a crayon when you were small? You didn't realize it at the time, but you were using a drawing medium. Crayons, colored markers, pencils, pens, and chalk are all drawing media.

Each drawing medium has its own characteristics. Chalk and crayon, for example, produce rough lines. Pens, by contrast, make smooth lines. **Figure 3–4** shows lines made with three different drawing media. Notice the line quality of each.

Shading Techniques

Look once more at the drawing in Figure 3–3. The scarf in this picture looks so real you can almost feel the texture in the fabric. The artist accomplishes this through shading. *Shading* is the use of light and shadow to give a feeling of depth and texture. There are four main shading techniques. (See **Figure 3–5.**)

- **Hatching.** This is drawing thin lines all running in the same direction.

Teacher to Teacher

Drawing Skills Build confident drawing skills by having students select and carefully observe the lines, shapes, and textures of a natural object such as a leaf, piece of bark, or shell. Tell them to notice any marks or details that make it unique. After spending a few minutes inspecting the form, students will draw the object. Have them position the object close to the paper. Ask them to visualize how it will occupy the space on the drawing paper. How large will the drawing be? Will any parts touch the edges of the paper? Remind them to look at the object and draw with continuous flowing lines. L1 ELL

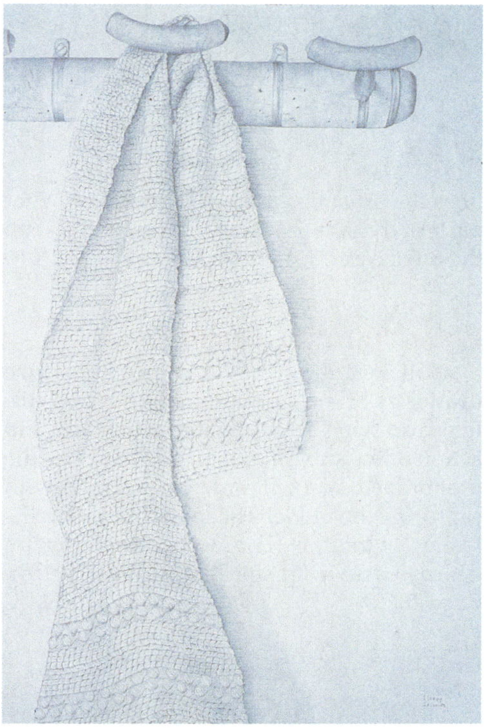

◆ **Figure 3–3** Notice the attention to detail in this pencil drawing. What art principles have been used to organize the work?

Jeanette Leroy. *Scarf on a Coat Rack.* 1976. Pencil on paper. 55.9 × 38.1 cm (22 × 15″). National Museum of Women in the Arts, Washington, D.C. Gift of Wallace and Wilhelmina Holladay.

- **Crosshatching.** This is drawing criss-crossing lines.
- **Blending.** This is changing color value little by little.
- **Stippling.** This is creating dark values by means of a dot pattern.

Which of these shading techniques was used in Figure 3–3?

◆ **Figure 3–4** Drawing media.

Studio Activity

Keeping a Sketchbook

Develop perception. One way in which artists develop perception is by keeping a sketchbook. Many artists carry a sketchbook to record interesting scenes and objects.

Begin a sketchbook of your own to illustrate themes from direct observation, personal experience, and traditional events. Use your sketchbook to sharpen your drawing skills and perception. The more you draw, the better you will "see" objects.

PORTFOLIO

Put your best sketch in your portfolio. Remember to date, sign, and write a self-reflection.

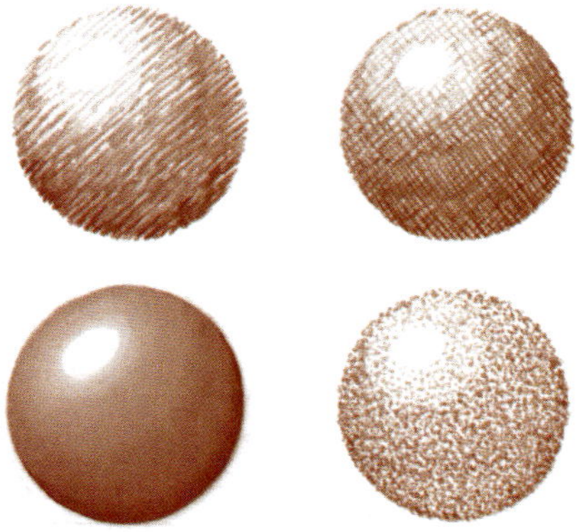

◆ **Figure 3–5** Shading techniques.

Check Your Understanding

1. What is *perception?* Why is developing perception important?
2. Name four drawing tools.
3. Demonstrate the four shading techniques.

Art Criticism

Display student drawings of their natural objects. Have students analyze the original artworks of their peers to form conclusions about formal properties—the elements and principles of art. Encourage positive critique to sharpen perception and prepare for the next drawing. It is essential that students develop this kind of attitude toward learning from their work.

Art on a Shoestring

Check with local printers, paper distributors, and similar suppliers to see if they would be willing to donate paper products to the school, especially overruns, unclaimed orders, and so on.

3 Assess

Self-Assessment

Have students complete the **Check Your Understanding** questions on this page. Answers are provided below.

Reteaching

Have students review the four kinds of shading techniques. Ask volunteers to demonstrate each.

4 Close

Have students define visual perception and explain how drawing and sketching can help develop one's perception.

Answers to Check Your Understanding

1. Perception is an awareness of the elements of an environment by means of the senses. It is important to develop one's perception in order to fully "see" an object.
2. Answers will vary. Possibilities include: pencils, crayons, colored pencils, chalk, pens, and colored markers.
3. Students should demonstrate hatching, crosshatching, blending, and stippling.

LESSON 2

Gesture Drawing

(pages 44–45)
Lesson Time: 2 hours

1 Focus

Objectives

After completing this lesson, students will be able to:

- Demonstrate technical skills effectively using a variety of drawing media.
- Capture the form and actions of a subject.
- Conduct an in-progress critique of their personal artwork.

SUPPLIES

Refer to **What You Will Need** in the Student Edition and include drawing boards if possible (so students can position themselves around the model).

2 Teach

Motivator

You will probably find students who are apprehensive about drawing figures. Tell them not to expect their first drawings to be perfect. This takes practice and careful observation. It is important to teach students the value of trying and failing. Explain that they will learn from each effort. Tell students that their drawing styles will be as unique as their handwriting.

Vocabulary

Ask students to discuss the meaning and history of the word *gesture*. Help them discover that gestures emphasize an idea, a feeling, or a movement.

LESSON 2

Gesture Drawing

Examine the drawing of the figures in **Figure 3–6.** From an art standpoint, the most important thing about the work is not *who* it shows, but *what* it shows. This drawing is of the human form. Capturing the human form has been a goal of artists through the ages. Notice the loose, scribbly quality of most of the lines. The artist used a technique called **gesture drawing.** This means *drawing lines quickly and loosely to capture the form and actions of a subject.* In gesture drawing you draw with your whole arm, not just your hand. Some gesture drawings are merely quick scribbles. Others are done with greater precision and care. How would you describe the lines the artist has used in Figure 3–6? What parts of the subjects have been recorded with the most care?

WHAT YOU WILL LEARN

You will make several quick gesture drawings of a classmate using several different drawing media. Focus on the form and action of the subject, not on one part, like the foot or face. You will not be concerned with capturing the model's likeness, but rather the feeling of motion. (For more information on gesture drawing, see Technique Tip 1 on page 281.)

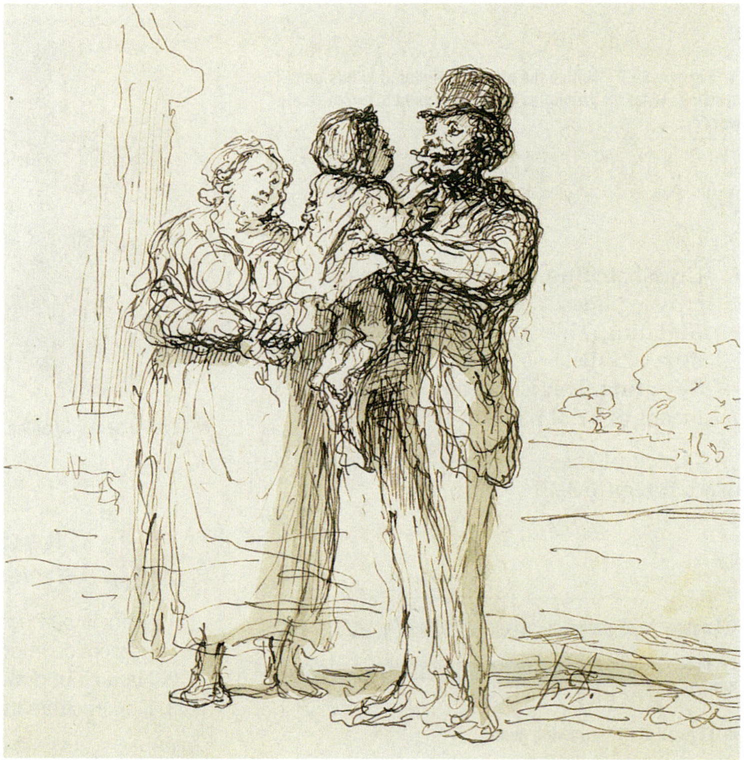

◆ **Figure 3–6** Do you think the artist captured the appearance of the human forms? Where is line used to show details?

Honoré Daumier. *Family Scene.* c. 1867–70. Pen and black ink, and brush and gray wash, on ivory wove paper (discolored cream). 21.6 × 20.3 cm (8½ × 8″). The Art Institute of Chicago, Chicago, Illinois. Helen Regenstein Collection, 1965.633.

INCLUSION STRATEGIES

SPECIAL LEARNING NEEDS Some students with limited mental capacity may not be able to conceive of the human figure in action as a continuous gesture. They may be able to conceive of it as sticks or as a circle, perhaps with stick arms and legs, or simply as a scribble. Allow for such variations in your expectations. Students with special learning disabilities may be able to draw with a finger in white salt spread evenly onto a piece of black paper to suggest the figure's motion. L1 ELL

What You Will Need

- Assorted drawing media, such as sticks of charcoal, soft graphite, unwrapped crayons, and markers
- Sheets of white paper, 12 x 18 inches
- Sharpened pencil

What You Will Do

1. You will demonstrate technical skills effectively using a variety of art media to produce a gesture drawing. You and your classmates will take turns modeling. Models should pretend to be frozen in the middle of an activity. This may be an everyday action, such as jogging, lifting, or dancing.
2. Make at least four gesture drawings. Use a different medium for each drawing. Make your figures at least eight or ten inches tall. Begin by drawing the head. Sketch loose, free lines. Draw quickly to capture the overall form of the subject. Build up the shape of the figure little by little.
3. Switching to the pencil, make a slower gesture drawing of a seated model. Fill an entire sheet of paper. Select one area of the figure to emphasize as the artist has done in Figure 3–6. Emphasize this area with details and shading.
4. Display your finished gesture drawings along with those of your classmates. Compare the different styles used to capture the form and actions of the subjects.

Evaluating Your Work

- **Describe** Did you include all the body parts in each of your rapid gesture drawings? Identify the medium used for each drawing.
- **Analyze** Point to and describe the different kinds of lines in your gesture drawings. Is the area you chose to emphasize clearly identified with shading?

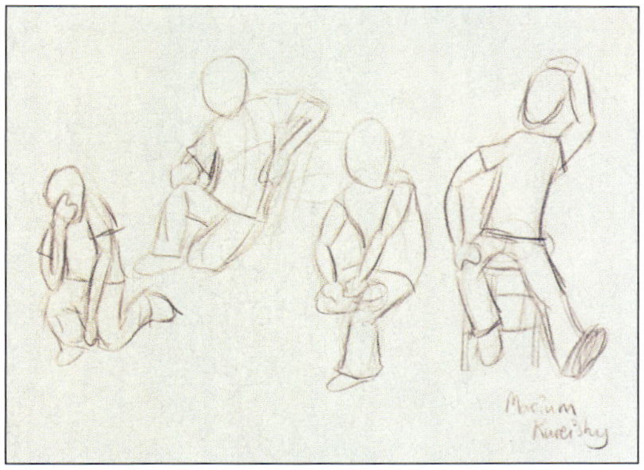

◆ **Figure 3–7** Student work. Gesture drawings.

Reflective Thinking

Critical Evaluation. Analyze the original artworks of your peers. Examine their gesture drawing and form conclusions about formal properties. For example, what kinds of lines did they use? Were they able to catch a feeling of motion?

Visual Art Journal

Look through fitness and sports magazines. Notice the different action poses, such as a person mountain biking, jogging, or demonstrating some exercise positions. Select three different poses and use these as your models. Draw these action poses in your journal.

Curriculum Connections

Language Arts Have students work in small groups to write a short skit about an event at school or in the community. The skit must rely mostly on gestures, rather than words, to communicate the actions and feelings of the actors. Invite students to rehearse their ideas as they write out the scene. Assign a role to each person in the group, then have them perform their skit for the class. As students plan their skits, work with each group to provide ideas about effective gestures that convey meaning with physical movement and expression rather than words. L1 ELL

Art Criticism

Invite students to study the effects of various media on the drawings. Students should develop a sensitivity to media so that they can make a deliberate choice when they begin a drawing. When students are ready, encourage shading and use of hatching, crosshatching, or stippling to show volume and shadows.

Visual Art Journal

Encourage students to practice their drawing skills. Based on direct observation, students should draw their action poses using a variety of art media with appropriate skill. L1 ELL

3 Assess

Peer Assessment

Have students analyze the original artworks of their peers to form conclusions about formal properties—the elements and principles of art.

Reteaching

Have students do frequent sketches from posed models to build confidence. Review what students learned about the media they used. Ask for words to describe the quality of each. Students should demonstrate their technical skills effectively using their choice of drawing media to produce their sketches. L1

4 Close

Have students explain why they chose the media they selected.

Painting

(pages 46–47)

1 Focus

Objectives

After completing this lesson, students will be able to:

- Define the three main ingredients of paint.
- Understand the difference between oil-based and water-soluble paints.
- Demonstrate technical skills effectively to make a painting with watercolors on paper, experimenting with varying amounts of water.

SUPPLIES

- Watercolor sets, large brush and small brush for each student
- Watercolor paper
- Trays or boards for paper
- Cups for water; sponges; paper towels
- Pencils

2 Teach

Motivator

Ask students what their previous experiences with paints have been. In earlier grades, what kinds of painting media did they use? Which ones did they enjoy? Why? List on the board the kinds of paints the students' name.

Vocabulary

Review definitions of *pigment, binder,* and *solvent.* Ask students to give examples of each.

Painting

When they hear the term *art,* many people think of paintings. This is not unreasonable when you consider that the first artists were painters. They produced their "artworks" on the walls of caves some 15,000 years ago. They made paint from crushed rocks mixed with animal fat or blood.

Since that time, many new painting media have appeared. In this lesson, you will learn about some of these.

PAINT

Although paints have changed over the centuries, the way of making them has not. Like paints used by early cave artists, those today contain three main ingredients:

- **Pigment.** Pigment is *a finely ground powder that gives paint its color.* The pigment that cave artists relied on came from minerals in rocks. Through the mid-1800s, artists continued to grind their own pigments.

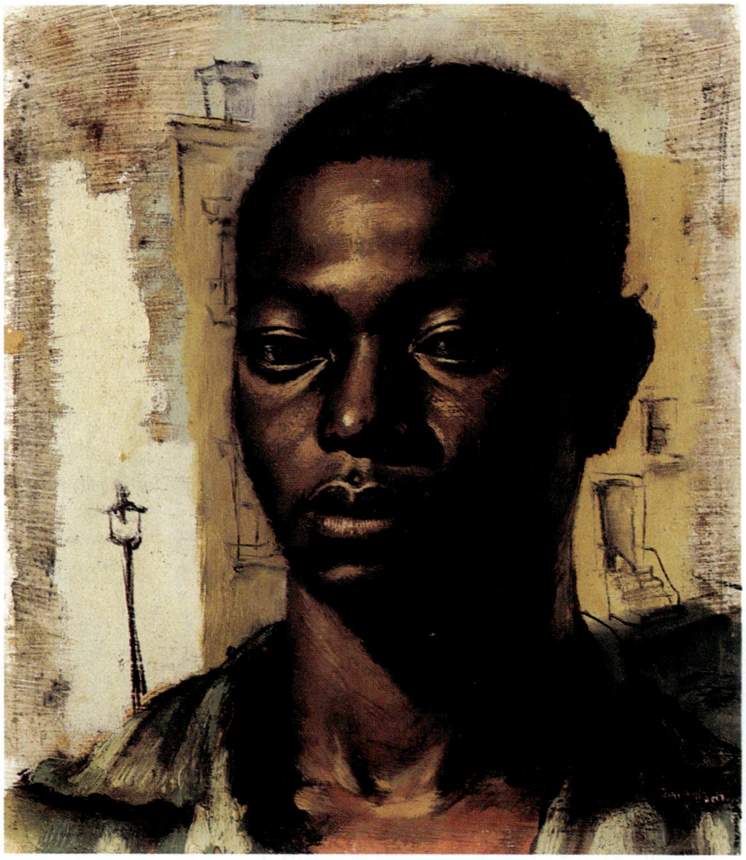

◆ **Figure 3–8** **Notice this artist's attention to detail. What shading technique did he use?**

John Wilson. *My Brother.* 1942. Oil on panel. 30.5 × 27 cm (12 × 10⅝"). Smith College Museum of Art, Northampton, Massachusetts. Purchased 1943.

SAFETY TIP

SAFETY LABELS When using tempera paint or other materials, make certain that the container or package bears one of the following safety labels: *AP* (Approved Product) or *CL* (product is certified to be properly labeled). The AP and CL labels certify that the product contains no material in sufficient amounts to be toxic or dangerous to the user. The AP label with Performance Certification also indicates that the product meets specific quality standards.

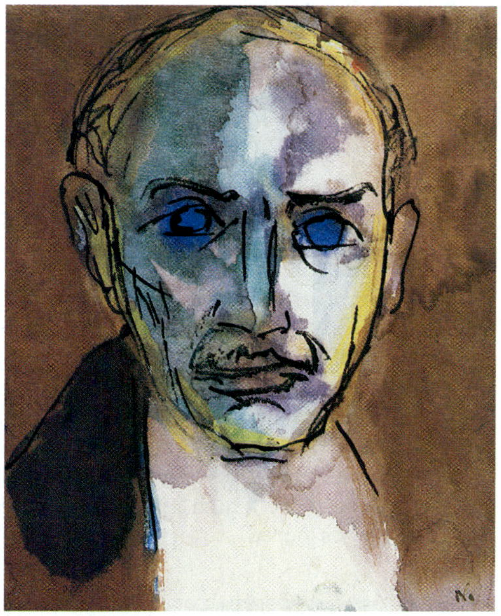

◆ **Figure 3–9** **When watercolors are applied to wet paper, the colors flow and blend.**

Emil Nolde. *Self-Portrait.* 1917. Watercolor, reed pen, and black ink. 21.6 × 16.5 cm (8½ × 6½″). Detroit Institute of Arts, Detroit, Michigan. Bequest of John S. Newberry.

- **Binder.** A binder is *a liquid that holds together the grains of pigment.* The binder allows the pigment to stick to the surface. The liquid parts of eggs have long been used as a paint binder.
- **Solvent.** A painter may also choose to use a **solvent** when working with paints. This is *a liquid used to control the thickness or thinness of the paint.* Solvents are also used to clean paintbrushes and other applicators.

Painting Media

As with drawing media, there are many different kinds of paint. Each has its own personality. Some paints that artists use are oil-based. Others are made with plain water.

Oil-Based Paint

First used in the 1400s, oil paint remains a popular medium today. True to its name, oil paint uses linseed oil as its binder. Its solvent is turpentine.

Studio Activity

Experimenting with Watercolor

Practical applications. Using a primary hue of watercolor, draw several shapes on a dry sheet of watercolor paper. Repeat the process, this time using paper that has been brushed thoroughly on both sides with water. Share and compare your results with those of classmates.

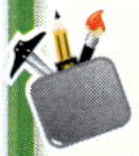

PORTFOLIO

Note the properties of watercolor on a piece of paper. Put this in your portfolio with your painting.

One advantage of oil paint is that it dries slowly. This allows the artist to blend colors right on the canvas. The work in **Figure 3–8** is an oil painting. Notice how smoothly the colors blend together.

Water-Based Paint

The most popular of water-based painting media, watercolor, takes its name from its solvent, water. The binder is gum arabic. Watercolors give a transparent quality to paintings. Compare the watercolor in **Figure 3–9** with the oil painting in Figure 3–8. What differences do you see?

Tempera, another water-based paint, comes in both powder and liquid form. Because tempera is not oil-based, it dries more quickly than oil paint. It is also more opaque than watercolor.

✓ Check Your Understanding

1. What are the three main ingredients of paint?
2. What is the main difference between oil paint and tempera?

Art Criticism

Have students compare the two paintings in this lesson. Wilson's portrait uses the fluidity of oil paint to blend skin tones. Nolde's work allows the watercolor to flow on the face and uses non-skin tones of green and purple. Black brush lines define the features. Ask students to comment on the effects of these two techniques. L1

Studio Skills

Take this opportunity to explain how to clean and care for brushes and palette knives and the differences between cleaning up oil paint and water-soluble paint. See Technique Tip 10 in the *Handbook* on page 283.

3 Assess

Self-Assessment

Have students complete the **Check Your Understanding** questions on this page. Answers are provided below.

Reteaching

Review the ingredients of paint and the function of solvents. Discuss the differences between oil paint and water-soluble paints.

4 Close

Have volunteers summarize the three main ingredients of paint and explain the different characteristics of oil paints and water-soluble paints. L1

✓ Answers to Check Your Understanding

1. The main ingredients of paint are the pigment, which gives paint its color; the binder, which holds the grains of pigment together; and solvents, which are used to control the thickness or thinness of the paint.
2. Oil paint dries slowly. Tempera paint, which is water-soluble, dries more quickly.

Creating a Portrait

(pages 48–49)
Lesson Time: 90 minutes

1 Focus

Objectives

After completing this lesson, students will be able to:

- Demonstrate technical skills effectively by using a variety of art media to produce a portrait drawing.
- Add shading and highlighting using oil pastels to create an expressive portrait.

SUPPLIES

Refer to **What You Will Need** in the Student Edition, and also include mirrors, watercolors, brushes, cups for water, and paper towels.

2 Teach

Motivator

Ask students to explore their faces with their fingers. Then have them use mirrors to draw and paint a life-size face, neck, and shoulder image on paper using watercolors. Encourage control of the wetness of the paper by using paper towels.

Vocabulary

Have students create a word portrait of the model before they begin drawing. Ask how a word portrait is different from an artist's portrait.

Creating a Portrait

Look once more at the paintings in Figures 3–8 and 3–9 on pages 46 and 47. Both are examples of a type of artwork called *portrait.* A **portrait** *is a visual representation of a person at rest.* Compare these two portraits with the one in **Figure 3–10.** This artwork was done with oil pastels. This is a medium with properties of both drawing and painting media. Notice the delicate lines and soft tones in this work. See also how the artist used dark values to shade some areas of the subject and light values to highlight others.

WHAT YOU WILL LEARN

You and a partner will take turns serving as model and artist. As artist, you will create a portrait of the other person's face. You will make certain to place each feature of the face in its proper place. You will add shading and highlighting using oil pastels, as in Figure 3–10. Your portrait will express a mood or feeling, as do the portraits in Figures 3–8 and 3–9. To do this, you will have to capture the model's expression, which might be happy or sad, angry or bored.

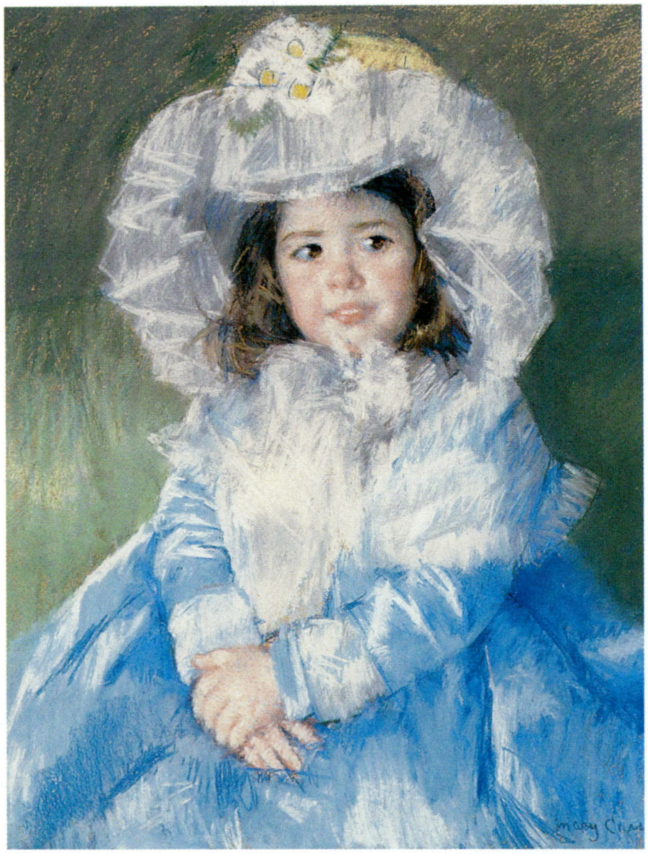

◆ **Figure 3–10** What mood or feeling has the artist captured? What shading technique has she used to create depth?

Mary Cassatt. *Margot in Blue.* 1902. Pastel. 61 × 49.9 cm (24 × 19⅝"). The Walters Art Gallery, Baltimore, Maryland.

INCLUSION STRATEGIES

PHYSICALLY IMPAIRED Students who are physically impaired may have difficulty dipping paint brushes to the right level, knocking off the excess, and rinsing brushes without spilling paint containers. A holder for the containers can be fashioned and attached to the table with a C-clamp. Plastic paint jars should only be filled with three-fourths of an inch of paint. Blocks of dry paint can be used with water on a brush. To make another type of paint, colored chalk can be dipped into buttermilk and applied to paper. Deodorant bottles with roller-ball tops can be filled with paint for still another painting adaptation. L1 ELL

What You Will Need

- Pencil and sketch paper
- Sheet of white paper, 9 x 12 inches
- Black colored marker
- Oil pastels

What You Will Do

1. Have your model sit facing you head-on. This means that you are looking squarely at the person's face. Ask the model to express a mood with his or her facial expression. Make several quick gesture drawings of the person's face. Add eyes, nose, mouth, ears, and hair. Your goal is not to create an exact likeness. Rather, it is to capture the shape of the person's head and facial features. You are also to capture a mood or feeling as seen in your model's expression.
2. Transfer your best sketch to the sheet of paper.
3. Using the black marker, go over the outline of the head and facial features. Work quickly, as you did in the gesture drawings. The lines should have a sketchy quality, as in Figure 3–9 on page 47.
4. Decide which areas of your portrait you will shade. Decide which you will highlight. Use a dark value of a single color of pastel for the shaded areas. Use a light value of the same color for highlighted areas.
5. Display your completed work along with those of classmates. Challenge students to identify the mood or feeling your portrait expresses.

Evaluating Your Work

- **Describe** Identify the type of artwork you created. Did you include all of the facial features? Were these in the proper places on your portrait?
- **Analyze** What value did you use to shade areas of the portrait? What value did you use to highlight areas?

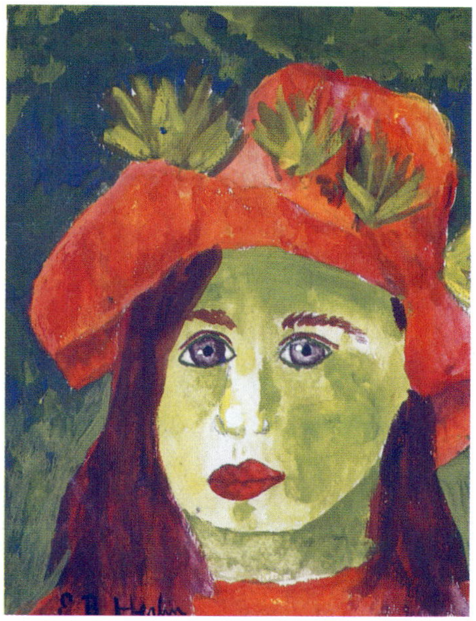

◆ **Figure 3–11** Student work. A portrait.

Studio Option

Do a second portrait based on the same sketch. This time, substitute watercolors for the oil pastels. Moisten cakes of watercolor with a few drops of water. This will soften them. Use a fairly large brush to apply the paint. Compare the results of your two portraits.

Visual Art Journal

In your journal, list the rewards of creating art as a hobby. Compare various avocational—not related to a job or career—opportunities in art. Describe how these opportunities can add interest to your life.

Studio Skills

Review with students the techniques for using oil pastels. (See Technique Tip 3 on page 281.) Remind students that they can use layers to create tint variations.

Sparking Creativity

Invite students to add interest to their portraits by giving a unique mood or expression to their model. Remind them that using emphasis is one way to create a center of interest in their subject.

Visual Art Journal

In pairs, have students share their lists. They should describe each avocational opportunity and discuss how they can enrich one's life.

3 Assess

Self-Assessment

Have students use **Evaluating Your Work** to conduct an in-progress critique of their portraits.

Reteaching

Ask students to discuss their portraits and how they captured the model's expression. L1

4 Close

Have students share their opinions of the portraits they painted.

Teacher to Teacher

Art as Avocation Encourage students to explore the many avocational opportunities in art. Explain that avocational means not related to a job or career. Studying or creating art as a hobby can provide many rewards. Learning about art in school or at museums can be very enriching. Students will gain knowledge and appreciation that they can share with others. Tell students that making art projects, such as paintings or pottery can be fun and relaxing. Students will feel pride and satisfaction in creating artworks and developing their art skills.

LESSON 5

Printmaking

(pages 50–51)

1 Focus

Objectives

After completing this lesson, students will be able to:

- Define *relief* and *intaglio* printmaking.
- Make and print a relief plate.

SUPPLIES

- Cardboard cut into 4 x 5-inch pieces
- String, glue, scissors, spoons
- Two or more 4-inch brayers
- Waterbase black block-printing ink and spatula
- Two or more palettes (water-resistant surfaces)
- 8½ x 11-inch bond paper
- Newspaper, paper towels

2 Teach

Motivator

Show students some rubber stamps if you have them. Demonstrate that the image is reversed when it is printed. If students choose to cut their initials for their design, they must glue them top side down and in reverse order. Smooth string (not fuzzy yarn) can be added to the design to make lines. When ready, the design should be glued with strong school glue and allowed to dry before printing.

Vocabulary

Ask students to define *brayer* and *palette.* Encourage volunteers to research intaglio printing and report to the class on methods of etching and engraving. L2

LESSON 5

Printmaking

What comes to mind when you hear the word *printing?* You may think of writing in block letters. You may think of the process used to create books, newspapers, and magazines. To an artist, printing, or **printmaking,** is *transferring an image from an inked surface to another surface.* As in commercial printing, the artist uses a printing press of sorts. As in forming letters, the artist creates by hand the image to be printed.

PRINTMAKING BASICS

While prints may be made with many different media, all use the same basic tools. These are:

- **A printing plate.** This is a surface on which the print is made. The plate carries the mirror image of the finished print. Letters and numbers must be made backward on the plate.
- **Ink.** Ink is applied to the plate. It is responsible for the image appearing on the print.
- **Brayer.** The brayer is a roller with a handle. It is used to "ink"—or apply ink to—the plate.

Editions

Usually, more than one print is made from a single plate. Together, all the prints made from a plate form an *edition.* Each print in an edition is signed and numbered by the artist. The number is made up of two numerals with a slash (/) between them. The first number tells which print you are viewing. The second tells

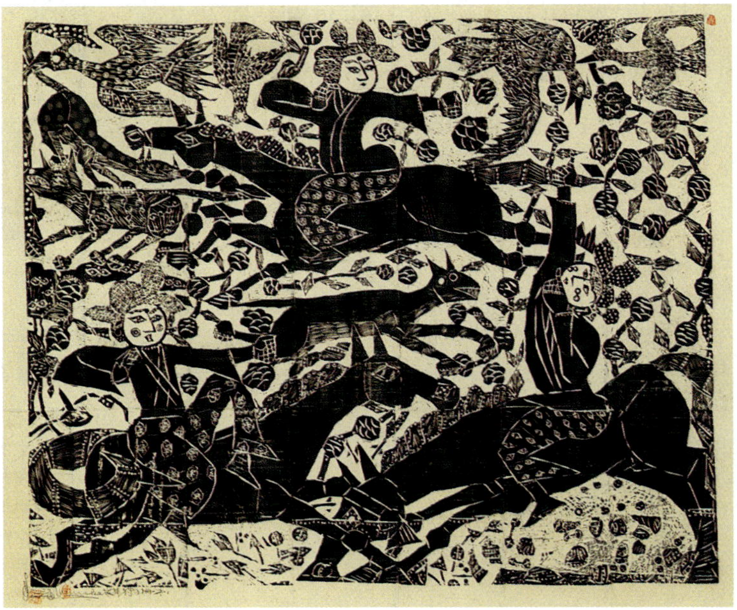

◆ **Figure 3–12** **Analyze the interdependence of the art elements and principles used to organize this work.**

Shiko Munakata. *Floral Hunting Scene.* 1954. Woodcut, printed in black and dark grey. 131.8 × 159.7 cm (51⅞ × 62⅞″). The Museum of Modern Art, New York. Gift of the Felix and Helen Juda Foundation.

TEACHER TO TEACHER

SETTING UP PRINTING STATIONS Determine the number of printing stations by the number of students in the class and printing colors. No more than four students should share a printing station. Set up each station by covering the area with newspaper and placing an inking plate, brayer, and tube of ink on top. Students take turns rolling out the ink and inking their plate evenly. Remind students that the first print requires more time inking the dry plate than later prints. Demonstrate how to lay a sheet of paper on top of the inked plate and how to apply even pressure with the flat side of your hand to achieve a clear print.

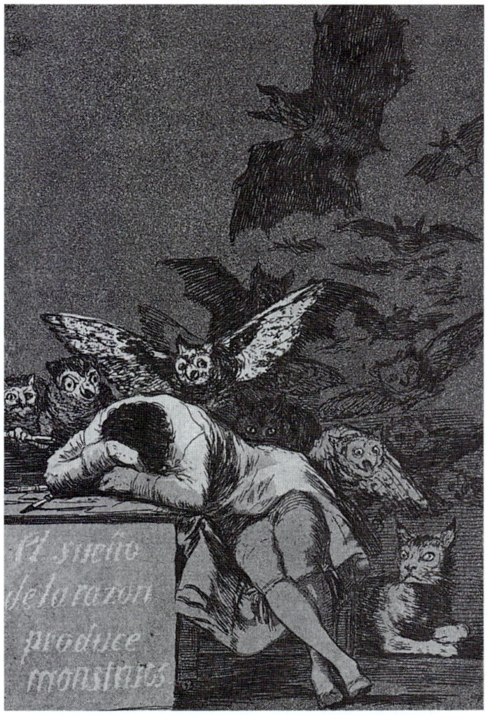

◆ **Figure 3–13** **How does this intaglio print differ from the woodcut in Figure 3–12?**

Francisco de Goya. *Capricho n. 43: The Sleep of Reason Produces Monsters.* 1796–98, published 1799. Etching and aquatint. 21.6 × 15.2 cm (8½ × 6″). Courtesy of The Hispanic Society of America, New York, New York.

how many prints are in the edition. The number 4/50 means "the fourth print in an edition of fifty." How would you read 13/25?

Printmaking Techniques

Imagine touching your finger to a stamp pad and then pressing your finger on paper. In doing so, you would make a *relief* (ruh-**leef**) print. This is an image raised from a background that is inked and printed. The raised ridges on your finger would pick up the ink and then transfer your "fingerprint" to the paper. Relief printing is one of the oldest forms of printmaking. It dates back nearly 2,000 years.

A popular medium used in relief printing is wood. The artist cuts away the areas of the surface not meant to hold ink. **Figure 3–12** shows a woodblock print, or *woodcut.*

Figure 3–13 shows the result of another printing process. This process is known as **intaglio** (in-**tahl**-yoh). It is *a printmaking technique in which the image to be printed is cut or scratched into a surface.* In a way, intaglio is the reverse of relief printing. The image on the plate is transferred when paper is forced into grooves that hold the ink. Study the intaglio print in Figure 3–13. Notice the many fine lines.

Studio Activity

Making a Relief Block Print

Demonstrate technical skills. You can make your own relief printing plate using a variety of found materials. Begin by cutting a 4-inch square from a sheet of cardboard. Cut a variety of smaller geometric shapes from the same sheet. Arrange these on the surface of the square. Form an interesting design.

Glue the shapes in place. Let them dry overnight. Apply printing ink to the surface with a brayer. Lay a sheet of paper over your inked plate. Apply pressure evenly. Carefully peel back the print.

PORTFOLIO

Write an evaluation of what you learned, and put it in your portfolio with your print.

Check Your Understanding

1. Define the term *printmaking.*
2. What are the three tools in printmaking?
3. Name two printmaking techniques.

Studio Activity

Making a Relief Block Print

Explain the procedure before beginning the inking. Desks and hands must stay clean. If used newspaper is removed each time, the area will be ready for each new inking. Put about a tablespoon of ink on the palette; add more as needed. Wash brayers with water when finished, checking the edges and handle for ink traces.

Art Criticism

Display the student prints and discuss the designs in terms of the principles of art. Have students analyze the original artworks of their peers to form conclusions about balance, harmony, variety, emphasis, and proportion. Ask them to find rhythm in repetition and movement. Students should critique prints for unity, neatness, and craftsmanship. L1

3 Assess

Self-Assessment

Have students complete the **Check Your Understanding** questions on this page. Answers are provided below.

Reteaching

Ask students to explain relief and intaglio printmaking. L1

4 Close

Have students describe the process used in making a relief block print.

Answers to Check Your Understanding

1. Printmaking is a process of transferring an inked image from one prepared surface to another.
2. The three tools in printmaking are:
   - **printing plate,** the surface on which the print is made
   - **ink,** which is applied to the plate with a brayer
   - **brayer,** a roller used to apply ink to the plate.
3. Relief and intaglio printing are two printmaking techniques.

Sculpture

(pages 52–53)

1 Focus

Objectives

After completing this lesson, students will be able to:

- Define *sculpture in the round* and *relief sculpture.*
- Describe four sculpting processes.

2 Teach

Motivator

Have three volunteers stand in front of the class and try to arrange themselves in a "sculpture." Ask the class to comment and suggest positions that will create a feeling of movement. When a pose is decided on, give class members poster board to make realistic or abstract shapes that represent the form they see. Have students fasten the pieces into a three-dimensional form, turning the sculpture around as they work to see how it looks from all sides.

Vocabulary

Review terms for sculpture: *in the round, relief, carving, modeling, assembling,* and *sculptor.* Review the term for three-dimensional work: *form.*

LESSON 6

Sculpture

Have you ever built a house of cards? Maybe you have made a project out of modeling clay. Both activities borrow processes from the art of sculpture. **Sculpture** is *a three-dimensional work of art.* Artists who work in sculpture are called sculptors.

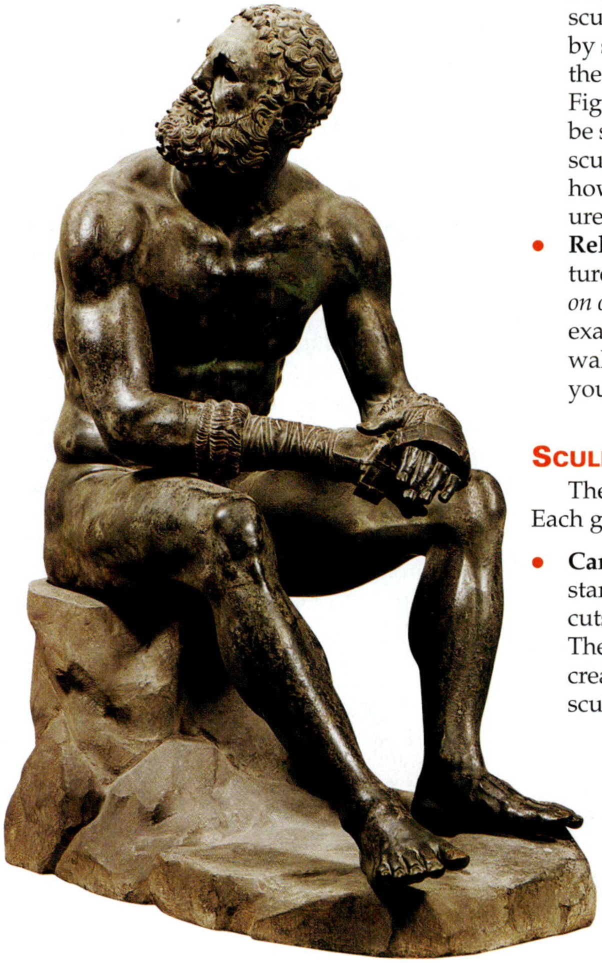

◆ **Figure 3–14** What sculpting process and medium was used for this sculpture? What has the artist done to make this boxer look like a real person?

The Pugilist. c. 50 B.C. Bronze. Museo Nazional Romano delle Ferme, Rome, Italy. Scala/Art Resource, NY.

The Media of Sculpture

Like other artists, sculptors use a wide variety of media in their work. One sculpting medium is marble. Various woods and metals are other sculpting media. What medium was used for the sculpture in **Figure 3–14?**

No matter what medium is used, a work of sculpture will be one of two types:

- **Sculpture in the round.** This is a type of sculpture that is surrounded *on all sides* by space. Another name for sculpture in the round is *freestanding sculpture.* Like Figure 3–14, sculptures in the round can be statues of people. Not all freestanding sculptures have recognizable subjects, however. Examine the sculpture in Figure 1–16 on page 16.
- **Relief sculpture.** This is a type of sculpture in which forms extend into space *on one side* only. **Figure 3–15** shows an example of relief sculpture. If you could walk around to the back of this sculpture, you would find that it is flat.

Sculpting Processes

There are four basic sculpting processes. Each gives a different result. These are:

- **Carving.** In this process, the sculptor starts with a block of material. He or she cuts or chips away pieces of the block. The relief sculpture in Figure 3–15 was created by carving. What medium did the sculptor use?

RESOURCES BEYOND THE CLASSROOM

Art Museums Art museums have much more to offer than just guided tours. In addition to providing brochures, maps, and newsletters about the collection, museums shops often sell inexpensive postcards and slides featuring art reproductions. Museums also offer high-quality reproductions of museum pieces that can be purchased, or, occasionally, borrowed. Many museums now have Web sites that show all or part of the collections, in-depth information that describes the museum and their collections, and interactive activities for students.

- **Casting.** In this process, the sculptor starts by making a mold. He or she then pours in a melted-down metal or other liquid that later hardens. Bronze, the medium used in Figure 3–14, is a common metal used for casting. It is an alloy made of copper and tin. In the 1990s, sculptors began experimenting with different casting media. In 1996, a 9-foot statue was cast from chocolate!
- **Modeling.** Modeling is building up and shaping a soft material to create a sculpture. Clay and fresh plaster can be used for modeling.
- **Assembling.** Also known as *constructing*, assembling is a process in which pieces of material are glued or joined together. As in modeling, assembled sculptures are built up. A house of cards, for example, is made by assembling.

Check Your Understanding

1. Name three media used in sculpture.
2. What is the difference between sculpture in the round and relief sculpture?
3. Name four sculpting processes.

Time & Place

Rome c. 50 B.C.

Historical connection. The world of ancient Rome could be a raw and uncivilized place. On Roman holidays, the public was often treated to free entertainment in amphitheaters, which were outdoor arenas. This entertainment, however, was often very violent. One popular event involved gladiators. These gladiators were often slaves or criminals, fighting each other to the death. During the rule of Julius Caesar, these exhibitions involved 300 pairs of gladiators.

However, not all forms of entertainment were this violent. Watching chariot races was a popular pastime in ancient Rome.

Many Roman citizens also enjoyed going to the theatre to see comedies, dramas, mimes, or pantomimes. **Figure 3–14** shows an ancient Roman sculpture of a boxer. To this day, boxing remains a popular spectator sport.

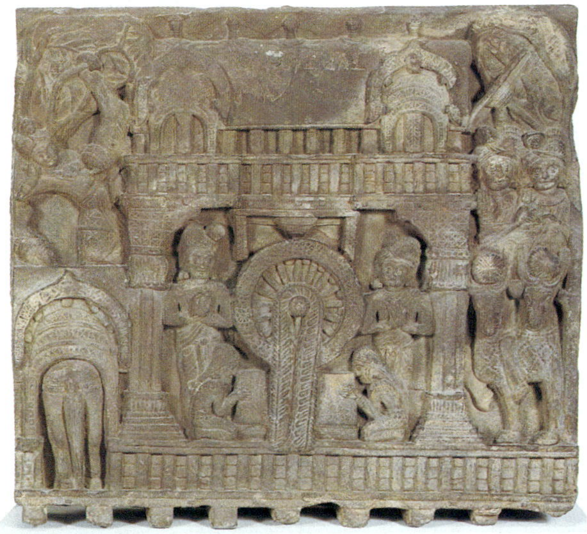

◆ **Figure 3–15** What kind of balance has the artist used? What sculpting medium was used?

King Prasenajit Visits the Buddha. Early second century B.C. Hard, reddish sandstone. 48.3 × 52.7 × 8.9 cm (19 × 20¾ × 3½″). Freer Gallery of Art, Smithsonian Institution, Washington, D.C.

Time & Place

Italian Renaissance

Sculpture has been an important art form through the ages, particularly in ancient Rome. Ask students to research particular forms of sculpture—portrait, religious, mythological, war memorial, and so on. Have them compare sculptures from a variety of cultures. Have them locate the time and place in which they were created and explain the ideas they were meant to represent. L2

3 Assess

Self-Assessment

Have students complete the **Check Your Understanding** questions on this page. Answers are provided below.

Reteaching

Have students explain how a sculpture is different from a painting. L1

Enrichment

SCULPTING MEDIA Encourage students to discuss and explore some contemporary sculpting media used in freestanding or relief sculpture, such as holograms or the mixed media found in assembled pieces. L2

4 Close

Ask volunteers to give examples of different media used in the four sculpting processes.

Answers to Check Your Understanding

1. Answers will vary. Some possibilities include clay, wood, metal, stone, and plaster.
2. Art that you can walk around and see from all sides is called sculpture in the round. Relief sculpture has forms that extend into space on one side only.
3. Four processes of making sculpture are carving, casting, modeling, and assembling (or constructing).

Making a Collage

(pages 54–55)
Lesson Time: 3 days

1 Focus

Objectives

After completing this lesson, students will be able to:

- Define the term *collage.*
- Demonstrate technical skills effectively using a variety of art media and materials to produce a collage that applies the principles of art.

SUPPLIES

Refer to **What You Will Need** in the Student Edition, and also include sheets of oak-tag.

2 Teach

Motivator

Explore with students the Bearden collage in **Figure 3–16** to see how he selected images and combined them to express his idea. Make magazines available to students for cutting. Ask them to select a theme and find several photos that fit it. If students have trouble thinking of a theme, encourage them to brainstorm ideas that have meaning to them.

Vocabulary

Remind students that the word *collage* is derived from the French word for paste. Point out that there are many art terms that come from French, for example, *papier-mâché,* a French word meaning *chewed paper.* Ask volunteers to identify other art terms from the French.

LESSON 7

Making a Collage

Artists are always on the lookout for new ways of creating. One such way is shown in **Figure 3–16.** This work is a *collage* (kuh-**lahzh**). Based on a French word meaning "to glue," a *collage* is an artwork arranged from cut or torn materials that are pasted to a surface. The group of artists who came up with this idea lived and worked in the early 1900s.

Study Figure 3–16. The work contains a rich assortment of objects and materials. These include photographs of African masks and one of a cat. What other familiar images can you find? Notice how the artist used rectangular patches of colored paper to create a window.

WHAT YOU WILL LEARN

You will make a collage out of colored paper that exhibits a variety of shapes and hues. You will use images and, if you like, words clipped from magazines. Your collage will express a theme. The addition of original crayon drawings will help you carry out your theme.

WHAT YOU WILL NEED

- Discarded magazines
- Pencil and sketch paper
- Sheets of white paper, 9 x 12 inches
- Crayons or markers
- Scissors
- Sheets of construction paper in assorted colors
- Sheet of oak tag, 12 x 18 inches
- Glue

WHAT YOU WILL DO

1. Decide on a theme for your collage. Themes to illustrate should come from direct observation, personal experience, and traditional events. Browse through

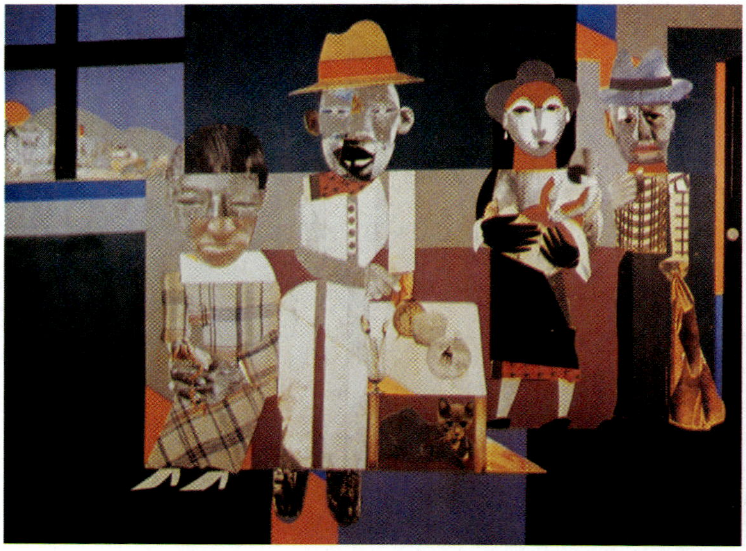

◆ **Figure 3–16** What kinds of shapes has the artist used? How many visual textures do you count? How has the artist introduced variety?

Romare Bearden. *Saturday Morning.* 1969. Collage. 111.8 × 142.2 cm (44 × 56″). © 1998 Romare Bearden Foundation/Licensed by VAGA, New York, NY.

TECHNOLOGY STRATEGIES IN THE ART CLASSROOM

DIGITAL COLLAGE Have students demonstrate technical skills by producing an electronic media-generated collage. Students will combine a variety of images that are captured and imported into the computer art program they are using. Have students choose a theme based on an interest of theirs. They can include pictures scanned from magazines or newspapers. Students can also take pictures with a digital camera and import them, or download a few images from the Internet. Next, have students combine all or parts of these images, adding their own original drawings. Refer students to the **Digital Media Guide.**

old magazines. Look for photos, illustrations, and words that go along with your theme. Carefully remove the pages containing these images.

2. Think of other words or images that support your theme. Make sketches of these images. Transfer your best sketches to white paper. Complete these drawings using crayon or marker.
3. Cut around the images you have selected or created. Arrange these on the oak tag in an interesting way. You may want to alternate your original drawings with your magazine clippings.
4. Next, cut shapes from construction paper. These are to fill the spaces between your images. They are also to serve as background. Add these around and under the images on the oak tag.
5. When you are satisfied with your design, begin gluing the pieces. Start with the construction paper shapes. Work carefully so as not to disturb the unglued portions of your design. Use the glue sparingly. If any glue oozes out from under the pieces, carefully remove it with a slightly damp tissue.
6. When your collage is dry, display it along with those of your classmates. Challenge classmates to identify your theme.

Evaluating Your Work

- **Describe** Identify the images you chose or created for your collage. Explain how these images emphasize your theme.
- **Analyze** Did you use a variety of shapes and hues in your collage? In what way is harmony demonstrated in your work?

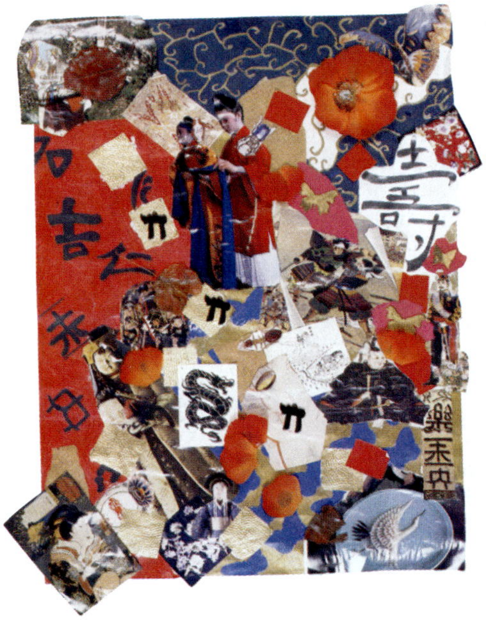

◆ **Figure 3–17** Student work. A collage.

PORTFOLIO IDEAS

Each entry of your portfolio should be marked clearly for identification. As you add to your portfolio, make sure each piece includes:

- Your name and date the artwork was created
- The assignment
- Your comments or self-reflection
- Any additional information requested by your teacher

Art Online

For additional student art, check out our Web site at **art.glencoe.com**. There you will find:

- Artist Profiles
- Interactive Games
- Student Art Gallery
- Museum Web Links

Understanding Art History

It was Pablo Picasso and Georges Braque who introduced collage when they were doing their Cubist works. They were searching for basic geometric shapes in their subjects, so they began cutting the shapes and then moving them, shifting them, and often showing just parts of them. They used newspaper, wallpaper simulating wood grains, and many other materials. Ask your students to research and compare Picasso's and Braque's Cubist period in the library and report on their work. L3

3 Assess

Self-Assessment

Have students use **Evaluating Your Work** to conduct an in-progress critique of their collages.

Reteaching

Discuss with your students their feelings about the process of making a collage. Did it free them to take chances on new ideas? This is an important learning experience, one which the arts can teach well.

4 Close

Have students explain how the images in their collages communicate their theme.

DEVELOPING A PORTFOLIO

Written Summaries Art assessment is an evaluation technique that challenges students to think critically. Through this process, students increase their perceptual and analytical skills. Students need to know how to support their opinions and organize their ideas, based on reasonable rationales. When assessing student responses, you should focus on the quality of the content rather than just the written expression. You may want to develop a rubric, a guide for scoring an assignment. For more information on developing a rubric, refer to the booklet, *Portfolio and Assessment Techniques*.

Digital Art

(pages 56–59)

1 Focus

Objectives

After completing this lesson, students will be able to:

- Understand the advantages of using computer hardware and software to create art.
- Identify what computer paint programs and draw programs can do.
- Use art software to create three different images.

Supplies

- Computer (Mac or IBM)
- A compatible art application or software (such as Illustrator, Elements, or Photoshop)
- Printer (black and white, or color)
- CD to save artwork

2 Teach

Motivator

Ask students to discuss ways in which they already use a computer. Have them share their knowledge of software applications and ways they have used or could use various programs at home or at school.

Vocabulary

Students may already be familiar with some computer terms. Review the terms *application* and *bitmap.*

LESSON 8

Digital Art

Throughout history, advances in technology have shaped the way artists create. The 1930s, for example, saw the arrival of paints made with plastic binders. These paints extended the media choices of painters. They were also less messy than oil paints because they used water as a solvent.

More recent advances have brought about other sweeping changes in the way art can be created. In this lesson, you will learn about an advance that has touched off a new revolution in art. That advance is digital technology.

Electronic Media-Generated Art

Before the mid-1800s, painters had to grind pigments by hand. The appearance of paint in tubes changed all that. It made the painter's life easier. In the same way, technology has been making many art tasks easier.

Digital Art Programs

How many computers do you have in your classroom? How many do you have at home? Even if you have not used computers very much, you are probably aware that they do a number of different tasks. Many tasks

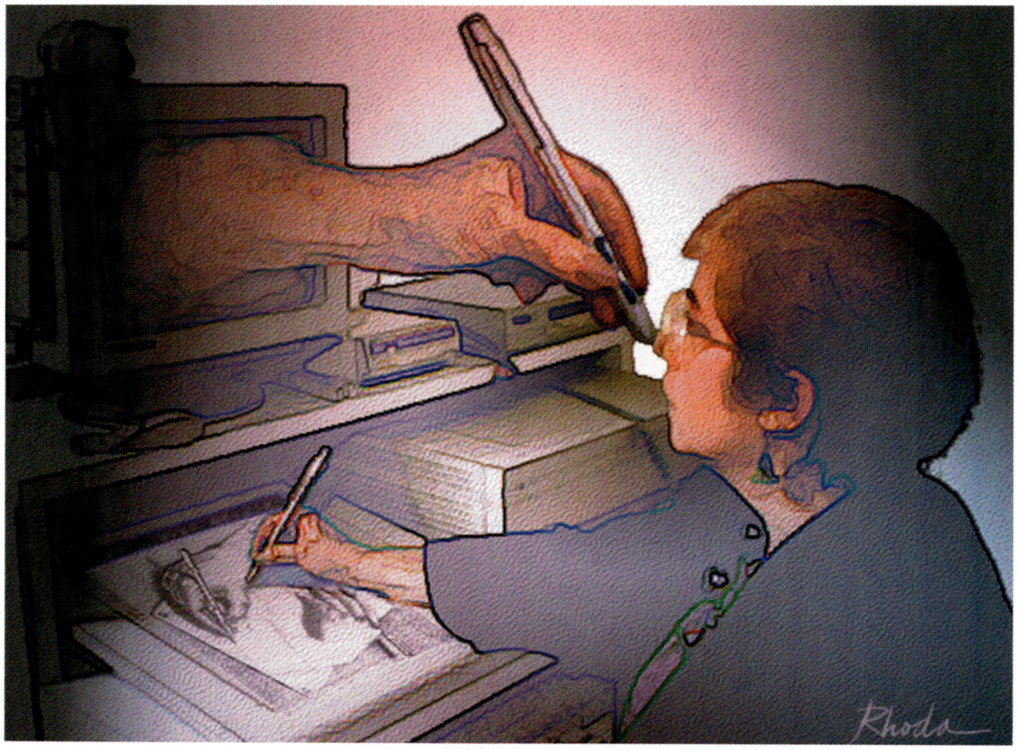

◆ **Figure 3–18** What is happening in this picture? What statement might the artist be making about computer art?

Rhoda Grossman. *Self-Portrait After Escher.* 1992. Digital art. Salzman International, San Francisco, California.

COMMUNITY CONNECTION

Creating Brochures Invite a digital artist to your classroom as a guest speaker. Using the "Tools of the Digital Artist" located in this chapter, have students create an imaginative brochure for their town or city. Using the computer will allow students to experiment with a variety of colors, shapes, and designs. Encourage them to do some research about the sites and features of their city so that they can include these in their brochures. Share these ideas with the City Planning Commission or City Hall. Don't forget to send copies of your brochures along with a thank-you letter to your visiting graphic artist.

are done with one or several programs, or applications. Digital drawings or images are stored as files in the computer's memory. Once saved, they may be opened and reworked.

Most digital art applications are one of two main types:

- **Paint programs.** In paint programs, images are stored as *bitmaps,* which are a series of tiny dots called pixels. It is easy to edit an image pixel by pixel. In general, paint programs have tools to create original images and alter images that are scanned in or captured with a digital camera. **Figures 3–18** and **3–19** were made using paint programs.
- **Draw programs.** In draw programs, images are stored as a series of lines and curves called vectors. Each line or curve used to create a shape results from a mathematical formula. Each shape is known as an *object.* An advantage of draw programs is that objects have sharp, crisp edges and can be resized without distortion. Think of draw programs as a collection of objects or a collage. **Figure 3–20** on the next page shows an image, or "group of objects," created in a draw program.

In the last decade, lines between paint and draw programs have begun to blur. Web design and photo-enhancing programs combine aspects of each, although they mainly remain bitmap-based (Paint) or vector-based (Draw). Web design programs include animation tools for images that are only viewed on a computer monitor or screen.

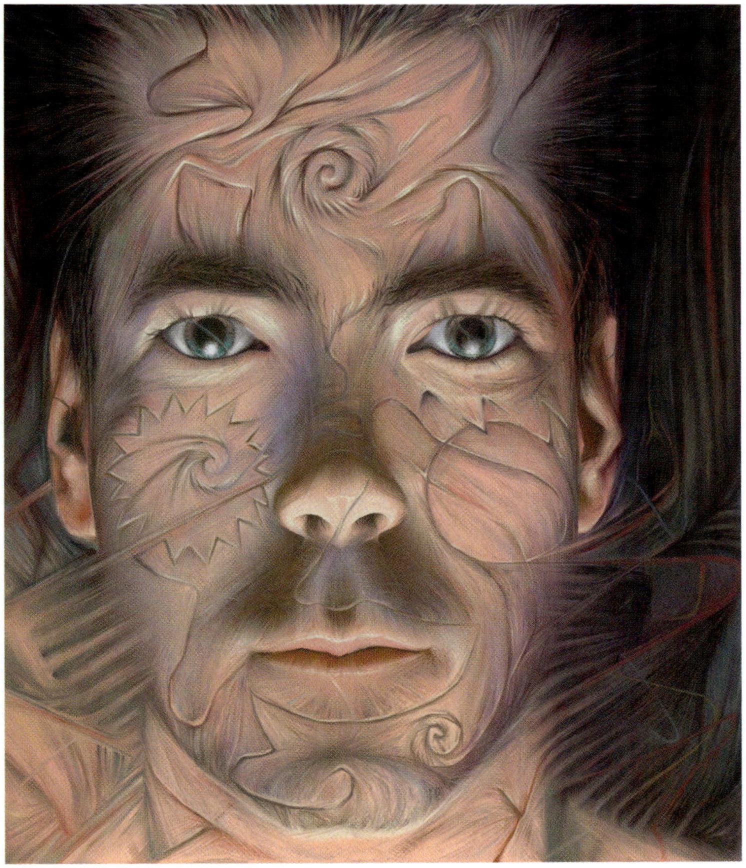

◆ **Figure 3–19** **How does this self-portrait and the one on the facing page differ from the ones in Figures 3–8 and 3–9 on pages 46–47?**

Erol Otis. *Self-Portrait.* 1991. Digital art. Courtesy of the artist.

ART IN EVERYDAY LIFE

Ask students to observe and report on ways in which people in the local community use computers to create graphics and digital art. Encourage them to explore how architects render drawings using computer programs.

Aesthetics

Instruct students to study Rhoda Grossman's self-portrait and speculate what materials were used to create it. Discuss computer scanning techniques. Ask students how much drawing skill was required to make the self-portrait. Direct attention to Erol Otis's portrait and ask what students think of its design. Have them point to the features that support their view. Ask students to imagine that both portraits were painted with oils or acrylics instead of the computer. Ask: Would both artworks still be considered as important or valuable? Why or why not?

Understanding Art History

Bring in a reproduction of M. C. Escher's lithograph *Drawing Hands.* Point out how Rhoda Grossman was inspired by the Escher drawing and adapted the idea for her digital self-portrait. Ask students how she changed his concept and what she did to bring it into the present.

CAREER OPPORTUNITIES IN ART

Researching Art Careers Encourage students to think about art-related careers. Have them read the Career Spotlights section in the Handbook. Have students learn about different careers, such as graphic design, advertising, and other commercial-art applications. Ask students to write a brief report describing three different careers. Have students compare these careers opportunities in art and select which one appeals to them most and explain why.

Teach *(continued)*

Vocabulary

To further explain the terms and tools listed in **Figure 3–21,** share with students the following:

- **Brush tool** paints with current fill color. Menus allow choice of color, shape, and size.
- **Pencil tool** draws in a single pixel line. It can be used for editing with the Zoom-In tool.
- **Eraser** erases marks under the tool. Sizes can be changed. In many programs, you can conveniently double click to erase "visible" screen. You can erase to a white page or fill color. Some programs use a different icon.
- **Paint Bucket** pours the Fill color and/or texture into a space.
- **Rectangle shape tool** captures rectangular or square shapes. When an object is selected it looks as if it has "marching ants" around the perimeter.
- **Selection tool** for a draw or object-oriented program puts "handles," or four small squares, at the corner points. These can be used to alter the image. Clicking in the center and dragging moves the object.

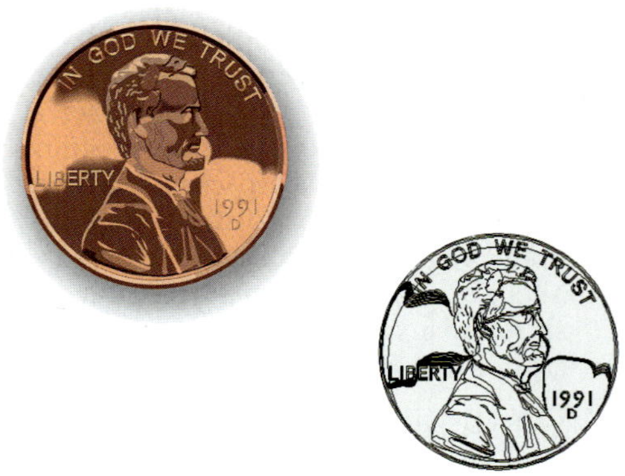

◆ **Figure 3–20** The image in the upper-left was made from the 298 separate "objects" shown in the lower-right. Do you recognize this familiar image?

Tools of the Digital Artist

In digital art, there are tools and menus. The physical tools that digital artists use are called *hardware.* Hardware refers to the equipment, such as the monitor, keyboard, and printer used in computer graphics.

The most important tool to artists is the mouse, the familiar pointing and clicking device. The mouse is used to draw and paint. It is also used to make selections from the menus and toolboxes. Menus are lists of commands appearing in a bar at the top of the screen. The mouse is also used as a drawing or painting device by selecting tool icons from a visual side menu called a toolbox.

Tool	Description	Type of Program
Selection	Selects an object, handles appear	Draw
Selection	Selects a rectangular space around an object	Paint
Lasso Selection	Selects only the object, no background	Paint
Text	Adds letters and words	Paint or Draw
Brush	Paints with varied kinds of lines, patterns, and textures, simulates other media	Paint
Pencil	Draws lines, shapes, and objects using only a single pixel width	Paint (sometimes Draw)
Ellipse or Round Shape	Draws ovals or (Shift key) circles	Paint or Draw
Rectangular Shape	Creates rectangles or (Shift key) squares	Paint or Draw
Bucket Fill	Adds colors, gradients, patterns to enclosed shapes	Paint or Draw
Eyedropper	Selects color, known as color picker	Paint or Draw

◆ **Figure 3–21** Common on-screen tools.

MORE ABOUT...

TECHNOLOGY Many artists and illustrators use digital art applications to quickly combine images and make multiple copies in varying sizes. The computer offers artists advantages over conventional techniques because it can quickly make two-dimensional objects look three-dimensional. Some art applications provide tools or menus to add textures that change the surface quality of the image to imitate textured surfaces of different kinds. Have students explore both paint and draw programs. Ask them to list familiar tools, icons, and menus, but also note differences between both programs.

Other tools used by digital artists include the following:

- **Stylus and graphics tablet.** In simplest terms, a stylus and graphics tablet are electronic answers to the pencil and paper. In recent years, these tools have been improved. The stylus responds to pressure from the hand, much like a real pencil, pen, or brush and includes an eraser. The woman in Figure 3–18 on page 56 is shown using a stylus and graphics tablet.
- **Scanner.** A scanner is a device that "reads" printed images and text. It is then translated into a language the computer— and the digital artist—can use. The work in Figure 3–9 on page 57 began with a photograph that the artist scanned into his computer.
- **Digital camera.** Digital cameras are similar to traditional cameras, but images are saved onto a media card rather than film. Captured images are then imported into art programs where they can be manipulated in many ways.

On-Screen Tools

A second category of tools digital artists work with is "on-screen" tools or desktop tools that mimic hand-held tools used by conventional artists. Desktop tools found in the toolbox include pencils, pens, assorted brushes, and even erasers. Desktop tools vary from program to program. The table in **Figure 3–21** shows a few common tools and the type of program in which each is found. It also shows the icon, or picture symbol, commonly used to indicate each.

Each program or application saves the images and text in a language or script known as a file format. Programs usually offer several file format choices, so you can transfer the saved files to another application to take advantage of its unique features, tools, and menus. Universal or common file formats are: JPEG, GIF, PICT, and PNG.

Studio Activity

Exploring Tools of Art Software

Demonstrate technical skills. Use a variety of art media to produce an electronic media-generated artwork. Begin by launching the art application. Art applications are either based on pixels (Paint), or vector (Draw). To discover how to use the features of your art software, you will draw a tree, a car, and a house. From the tools palette, find the Pencil tool and Shape tool. To select each, click once. Begin drawing by clicking and dragging a shape to the size you want. You can also simply draw a line on the page with the pencil tool.

Explore with different sizes and shapes. Draw the three objects so they do not touch. Fill a pencil-drawn shape with the Fill tool. Use the Selection tool to encircle and select a shape. Move it or make multiples. After an object is selected, choose Copy from the Edit menu, then Paste. Position copies and overlap the objects. Click anywhere outside the object to paste it in place. Most importantly, if you make a mistake or don't like an effect, immediately choose the Undo option from the Edit menu.

PORTFOLIO

Print your image and put it in your portfolio with an evaluation of how you explored tools of art software.

Check Your Understanding

1. What is the difference between a paint program and a draw program?
2. Name two hardware tools and three desktop tools.

Studio Activity

Exploring Tools of Art Software

Encourage all students to use an available paint or draw application to explore the tools and menus of art software. If color printing is not an option, complete the drawing in black and white, print, and then apply color with pencils, pens, or paints. ELL L1

3 Assess

Self-Assessment

Have students complete the **Check Your Understanding** questions on this page. Answers are provided below.

Reteaching

Ask students to review ways of using the computer to create artworks. L1

Enrichment

DIGITAL ART Invite a computer teacher or architectural draftsperson to demonstrate a high-end graphics program. Encourage students to experience firsthand the advantages and disadvantages of using such programs to create art.

4 Close

Have students define the two types of digital art applications. L1

Answers to Check Your Understanding

1. In paint programs, images are stored as bitmaps, a series of tiny dots. In draw programs, images are stored as a series of lines and curves. Objects created in draw programs can be resized without distortion.
2. Hardware tools include the monitor, the keyboard, the mouse, a stylus and graphics tablet, a scanner, and the computer itself. On-screen, or desktop, tools include pencils, pens, brushes, and erasers.

Every Stitch Tells a Story

1 Focus

Objectives

After completing this lesson, students will be able to:

- Draw and color a pattern of geometric shapes.
- Plan, write, and share a short story inspired by an image in a quilt.

2 Teach

Teaching the Feature

1. Ask whether students are familiar with quilts and quilting. Let several students share their experiences with seeing, using, and/or making quilts.
2. Have volunteers describe the quilt shown in the photographs. Ask: What makes this quilt unusual?
3. Let students work with partners to read the article about Faith Ringgold and her work. Ask each pair of students to summarize the article in one or two sentences.

Activity

Guide students in discussing the various geometric patterns shown in traditional patchwork quilts. Then have students use pencils and rulers to draw their own geometric designs; let them use markers or colored pencils to add color to the shapes in their designs.

Every Stitch Tells a Story

Faith Ringgold makes quilts you can read.

Faith Ringgold makes it easy to fall asleep while reading a story. Her fabric quilts have tales and stories right on them. However, Ringgold's quilts are not just blankets. They are works of art.

For centuries, the realm of fine arts was limited to painting and sculpture. Items such as quilts made for the home weren't thought of as art. At best, they qualified as a craft.

No one disputes that Ringgold's fabrics are art. As a child, she learned about fabric from her mother, a clothing designer in New York City's Harlem—a mostly African American neighborhood. In her mother's shop, Ringgold heard customers tell stories, which would later find their way into her work. Ringgold made her first story quilt with her mother. The quilt had 30 painted fabric grids. Each grid had a portrait of a Harlem resident. Since then, Ringgold has continued painting, printing, and writing stories on quilts. She combines historical and fictional characters to create tales about fascinating African American women.

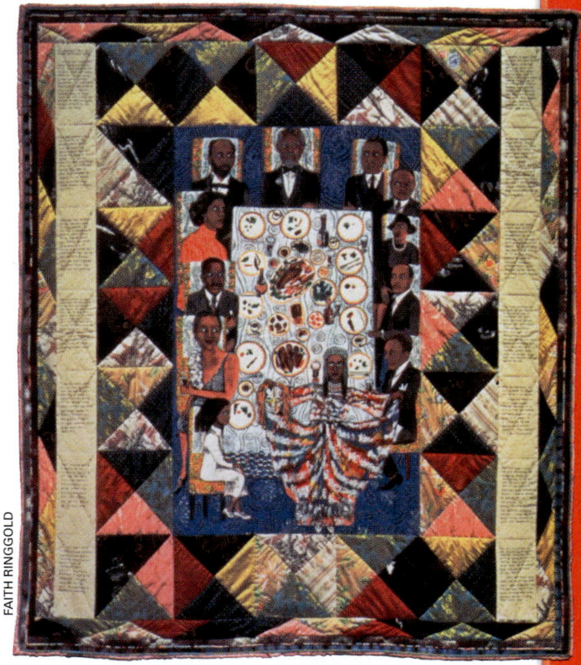

FAITH RINGGOLD

Faith Ringgold. *The Bitter Nest, Part II: The Harlem Renaissance Party.* 1988. "I'm writing little, bitty short stories and putting them on quilts," says Ringgold (BELOW). Her pieces combine acrylic painting on canvas, quilted fabric, and storytelling—often a handwritten text that frames the painted image.

TIME TO CONNECT

Write a tale related to the image from Ringgold's quilt *The Bitter Nest*.

- **What specifically in the quilt inspires you?**
- **Write an outline and draft with distinct character(s) and plot.**
- **Revise your work for correct punctuation, grammar, and spelling and strong story line.**
- **Share your work with the class. Compare and contrast your tale to those of other students.**

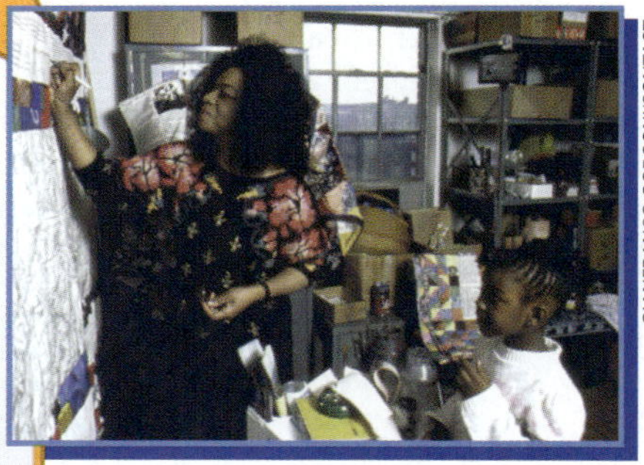

GIANFRANCO GORGONI/CONTACT

TIME TO CONNECT

Encourage students to discuss their story ideas before they outline and draft their work. Once they have finished writing, have them work with partners to proofread each other's work. Have students follow these suggestions:

- Capitalize and punctuate correctly to clarify and enhance meaning.
- Use resources to find correct spellings.

Chapter 3 Review

BUILDING VOCABULARY

Number a sheet of paper from 1 to 10. After each number, write the term from the list that matches each description below.

art medium	pigment
binder	portrait
gesture drawing	printmaking
intaglio	sculpture
perception	solvent

1. Transferring an image from an inked surface to another surface.
2. A liquid that holds together the grains of pigment.
3. A printmaking technique in which the image to be printed is cut or scratched into a surface.
4. An awareness of the elements of an environment by means of the senses.
5. A visual representation of a person at rest.
6. A three-dimensional work of art.
7. A material used to create a work of art.
8. A finely ground powder that gives paint its color.
9. Drawing lines quickly and loosely to capture the form and actions of a subject.
10. A liquid used to control the thickness or thinness of the paint.

REVIEWING ART FACTS

Number a sheet of paper from 11 to 20. Answer each question in a complete sentence.

11. What are three ways in which artists use the art of drawing?
12. Name and describe four shading techniques.
13. What is the binder in oil paint? What is one advantage of using this medium?
14. What is a water-soluble paint?
15. What are the three tools common to printmaking? Name two techniques of printmaking.
16. How does the use of space in sculpting differ from its use in other areas of art?
17. What is relief sculpture?
18. Name and describe four methods of sculpting.
19. Explain the difference between computer paint and draw programs.
20. Identify three pieces of hardware used in digital art.

CROSS-CURRICULUM CONNECTIONS

21. **Language Arts.** Imagine that you are planning a painting. Write a brief report describing factors that might lead you to select a water-soluble paint over an oil paint. What might prompt you to make the opposite choice? Explain.
22. **Language Arts.** Describe the role technology has played in changing the way we see and use art. Locate examples of digital art in magazines and books. Compare and contrast the digital artworks you selected with the artworks on pages 48–51.

Web Museum Activity

The Baltimore Museum of Art, Baltimore, Maryland

Engravings, etchings, and woodcuts are not purely images of black ink on white paper. These images were often painted in the mid-fifteenth and sixteenth centuries.

Learn about the techniques that were applied to these images by clicking on the Baltimore Museum link at **art.glencoe.com**.

Describe the different types of techniques and the reasons for coloring the images. Compare the woodcut and etching in this chapter with the artworks on the museum site. How does color enhance the artworks?

Answers to Chapter 3 Review

Building Vocabulary

1. printmaking
2. binder
3. intaglio
4. perception
5. portrait
6. sculpture
7. art medium
8. pigment
9. gesture drawing
10. solvent

Reviewing Art Facts

11. Drawing limbers up the artist's eye, develops perception, and serves as a plan for a finished artwork.
12. Hatching; crosshatching; blending; and stippling.
13. Linseed oil. Oil paint dries slowly and blends smoothly.
14. It is paint in which water is the solvent.
15. Tools: printing plate, ink brayer. Techniques: relief prints and intaglio.
16. Sculpture is three-dimensional and occupies space.
17. Its forms extend into space on one side only.
18. Carving; casting; modeling; and assembling.
19. In paint programs, images are stored as bitmaps; in draw programs, images are stored as lines and curves.
20. Monitor; mouse; keyboard; scanner; stylus and graphics tablet; and the computer itself.

Cross-Curriculum Connections

21. Reports will vary.
22. Responses will vary, but may include how digital art has provided a new dimension to creating and using art.

Web Museum Activity

Before you have students go online, visit the Web site to preview the museum's online content, collection, and any online exhibit that might be of interest. Have stu-dents study and describe the different techniques of applying color to engravings, etchings, and woodcuts. Have them compare the colored etchings with those that are black and white. Students should write a detailed report describing the differences between the colored and black-and-white etchings. Which do they find more visually appealing and why?

Chapter Resources

Features	Standards for Chapter: National	Standards for Chapter: State/Local	Reproducible Masters
Quick Write *page 63* TIME ART SCENE An Art Critic's View *page 78* ***Web Museum Activity*** *page 79*	**1.** (a, b) **2.** (a, b, c) **3.** (a) **4.** (a, b) **5.** (a, b, c) **6.** (b)		Guided Reading and Practice 4–1 Application Activity 4–2, 4–3, 4–6 Historical and Cultural Heritage 4–4 Enrichment Activity 4–5 Studio Activity 4–7 Cross-Curriculum Activity 4–8 Lesson Plans

Lesson Resources

Lessons	Standards per Lesson: National	Standards per Lesson: State/Local	Reproducible Masters
1 ***Aesthetics*** *(pages 64–65)*	2b, 4a, 5b		Application Activity 4–2
2 ***Art Criticism*** *(pages 66–69)*	2b, 2c, 5c		Application Activity 4–3
3 ***Critiquing Nonobjective Art*** *(pages 70–71)*	2b, 4b, 5a, 5b		Historical and Cultural Heritage 4–4
4 ***Creating a Realistic Painting*** *(pages 72–73)*	1a, 1b, 2a, 4b		Enrichment Activity 4–5
5 ***Creating an Expressive Word Design*** *(pages 74–75)*	1a, 1b, 2a, 2c, 5c		Application Activity 4–6 Studio Activity 4–7
6 ***Creating an Abstract Figure*** *(pages 76–77)*	1a, 1b, 2a, 3a, 5c		Cross-Curriculum Activity 4–8

Assessment	Technology
Testing Program: Chapter Test 4–9 Portfolio and Assessment Techniques	Artsource Performing Arts Package, Pilobolus Dance Theatre (DVD or VHS Segment 11) National Museum of Women in the Arts Interactive Lesson Planner Fine Art Transparency CC-4, *Kastūra* by Frank Stella Fine Art Transparency 4, *Two Children at the Seashore,* by Mary Cassatt

Activities/Features
Time & Place: Picasso's Blue Period
Studio Activity: Reading a Credit Line
Time & Place: Pop Art and Op Art
Evaluating Your Work Studio Option Visual Art Journal
Evaluating Your Work Reflective Thinking Art Online
Evaluating Your Work Portfolio Ideas Visual Art Journal

KEY TO ABILITY LEVELS

Teaching strategies have been coded.

- L1 Activities for all students; teacher direction required
- L2 Activities for average to above-average students; some teacher direction needed
- L3 Activities for students able and willing to work independently
- ELL English Language Learner activities

FEATURED ARTISTS

- Arthur Dove
- Albrecht Dürer
- Naum Gabo
- Winslow Homer
- Pieter de Hooch
- Edward Hopper
- Henri Matisse
- Pablo Picasso

FINE ART PRINTS

Fine Art Print 7, *The Three Umbrellas* by Raoul Dufy

Fine Art Print 8, *The Challenge* by David Alfaro Siqueiros

Timesaving Technology

Interactive Lesson Planner

Make planning easy. Use this interactive software to organize your week, month, semester, or year and access all *Introducing Art* reproducible resources.

KEY TO LESSON RESOURCES

Narrative Lesson

Studio Lesson

Chapter 4

Looking at Art

(pages 62–79)

Chapter Overview

In this chapter, students will explore ways of looking at art that will encourage them to ask and answer questions about why a piece of artwork is successful. By understanding the nature of aesthetics and art criticism, students can better evaluate and understand the art of others as well as their own artworks.

Discussing the Artwork

Focus On ◆ **Figure 4–1** Have students study the painting, *Girl Reading at a Table*, by Pablo Picasso. In this painting, the shapes are distorted in the condensed room. The girl's pale blond hair and blue-white skin make her appear delicate in the dark-colored room. Ask students to:

- Analyze the interdependence of the art elements color and shape and the principle variety in Figure 4–1.
- Describe the feeling the painting communicates.
- Explain why you think this work is sucessful or not.

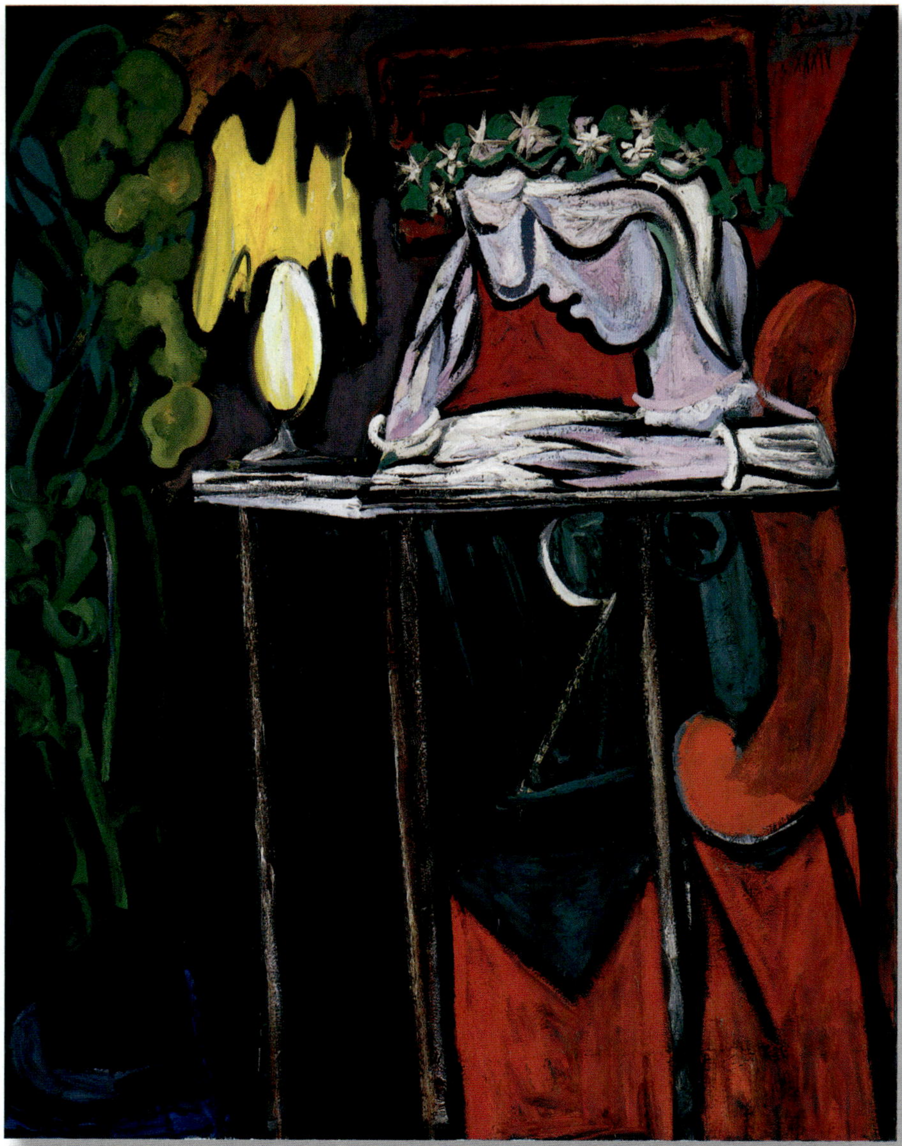

Focus On ◆ **Figure 4–1** **Look at how artist Pablo Picasso used color, shape, and form. Notice the distortions of the objects in the room and the subject's pose. What feeling does this painting express?**

Pablo Picasso. *Girl Reading at a Table.* 1934. Oil and enamel on canvas. 162.2 × 130.5 cm (63⅞ × 51⅜″). The Metropolitan Museum of Art, New York, New York. Bequest of Florence M. Schoenborn, in honor of William Lieberman.

ART SOURCE

Linking to the Performing Arts

DANCE The 1960s were a time of change and experimentation, socially, politically, and artistically. A new invention arose in dance, called "contact improvisation." Skills such as rolling, falling, and being upside down were explored, guiding the body to an awareness of its own natural movement. The work of Pilobolus Dance Theatre grew out of this way of working. Have students see how the Pilobolus Dance Theatre performs this type of dance in the **Performing Arts Handbook** on page 313. To enrich student understanding, play the DVD or videotape (segment 11) in the **Performing Arts Package**.

Chapter 4

Looking at Art

“To draw, you must close your eyes and sing.”

— Pablo Picasso (1881–1973)

To understand some poems and stories, you need to look beyond mere words on the page. You need to “read between the lines.” Only by doing so are you able to see the true meaning. The same may be said of art. Artists open new ideas to us as we look at their work. Each artist’s work is as individual as his or her handwriting. In this chapter, you will learn how to “read” between the lines and ask questions about the form and the content of artworks. You will make discoveries that will change the way you see and respond to art.

After completing this chapter, you will be able to:

- Explain how subject, composition, and content relate to works of art.
- Define *aesthetics.*
- Identify the four steps of art criticism.
- Discuss the different ways in which critics judge works of art.

Quick Write

Interpreting the Quote
Read the quote by Picasso. What do you think Picasso meant by this quote? Look again at his painting in **Figure 4–1.** How do the colors and shapes “sing?”

Key Terms

aesthetics
aesthetic view
subject
composition
content
art critic
credit line
nonobjective
point of view
abstract

Quick Write

Interpreting the Quote
Have students read the quote and complete the Quick Write activity. Tell them Picasso was expressing that an artist must express him or herself freely. After students have written a brief interpretation of the quote in their own words, have them discuss their interpretations with classmates.

Chapter Motivator

Ask students to discuss a toy or other object that, when they first saw it, they were not interested in. Yet, after closer inspection, they found they really liked it. Have students explain what changed their minds. Perhaps they noted details they had not noticed at first. Help students see that, by looking past the obvious, we can often find value we did not know was there.

Art Online

Visit art.glencoe.com, the Web site for Glencoe’s art programs. This site offers helpful general teacher resources, such as educational resources. The following topics are discussed and are a useful guide for your professional development:

- Annual Student Art Contests
- Conferences
- Educational Agencies
- Grants

National Standards for Arts Education

This chapter addresses the following National Standards for the Visual Arts:

1. (a, b) **4.** (a, b)
2. (a, b, c) **5.** (a, b, c)
3. (a) **6.** (b)

Aesthetics

(pages 64–65)

1 Focus

Objectives

After completing this lesson, students will be able to:

- Define *aesthetics.*
- Identify the three aesthetic views of art: subject, composition, and content.
- Form generalizations about the interdependence of the art elements and principles in artworks.

2 Teach

Motivator

Begin this lesson by asking students how they judge a work of art. What do they look for when deciding whether they find an artwork successful? Have students give examples of artworks they like and explain their reasoning. In this lesson, students will learn to identify the three ways by which an artwork can be measured.

Vocabulary

Ask students to look up the term *aesthetics* in the dictionary and trace its word history (from the Greek *aisthetikos* meaning "sense perception").

LESSON 1

Aesthetics

Taste is a personal matter. What is music to one person might be noise to another. In art, differences in taste may be traced to **aesthetics** (es-**thet**-iks). This is *the study of the nature of beauty and art.* Aesthetics raises the question "What makes a work of art successful?"

Over the centuries, thinkers seeking answers to this question have come up with different "aesthetic views" of art. An **aesthetic view** is *an idea or school of thought on what is most important in a work of art.* Historically, the debate among scholars has centered on three competing aesthetic views. These are the *subject view,* the *composition view,* and the *content view.*

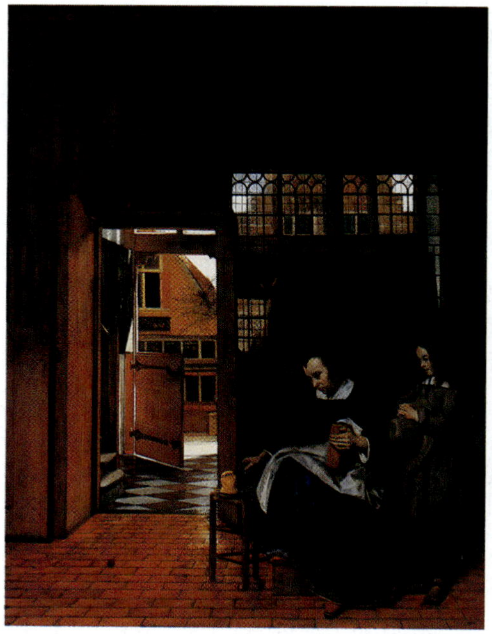

◆ **Figure 4–2** What is the subject of this work? What elements and principles of art has the artist used? What mood or feeling does the work communicate?

Pieter de Hooch. *A Woman Preparing Bread and Butter for a Boy.* 1660–63. Oil on canvas. 68.3 × 53 cm (26⅞ × 20⅞"). The J. Paul Getty Museum, Los Angeles, California.

Subject View

The subject view holds that a successful artwork is one whose subject looks convincing and lifelike. A work's **subject** is *an image viewers can easily identify.* The subject may be a person or people, as in **Figure 4–2.** It may be an object, such as a chair. It may even be an event, such as a holiday celebration. Look again at the painting in Figure 4–2. Notice how realistic the subject is. How do you think a scholar taking the subject view would evaluate this painting?

Composition View

The second aesthetic view—the composition view—maintains that what counts most in an artwork is its **composition.** This is *the way the principles of art are used to organize the elements of art.* Supporters of the composition view attach the most importance to how the parts of a work fit together. They would focus on an artwork's *formal properties,* or the organization of the elements of art by the principles of art. They might look, for example, at

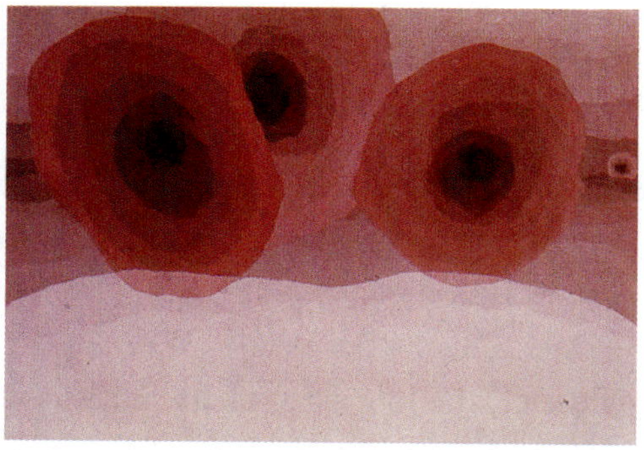

◆ **Figure 4–3** Analyze the use of color and shape in this painting. How do you think this work communicates with the viewer?

Arthur Dove. *Fog Horns.* 1929. Oil on canvas. 45.5 × 66 cm (18 × 26"). Colorado Springs Fine Arts Center, Colorado Springs, Colorado.

STORY BEHIND THE ARTWORK

Fog Horns Where did Arthur Dove find the inspiration for his unusual painting of *Fog Horns?* After an unsuccessful attempt at chicken farming in Connecticut, the artist moved into a houseboat on the Harlem River and wandered from port to port on Long Island Sound. During this period, he began creating abstract paintings of his experiences on the river. One of these paintings captures the waves of sound coming from foghorns in a heavy fog. The circular forms suggest the rims, or funnels, of the horns themselves and their pulsating sound spreading outward over the water.

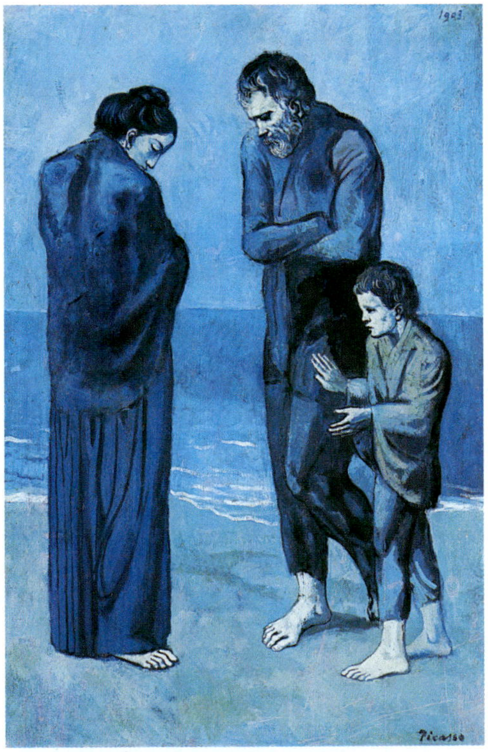

◆ **Figure 4–4** **Examine the body language of the people in this painting. What mood is conveyed? What role does color play?**

Pablo Picasso. *The Tragedy.* 1903. Oil on wood. 105 × 69 cm (41⅓ × 27⅛"). National Gallery of Art, Washington, D.C. Chester Dale Collection.

the way balance is used to control shape or form. Such people would find much to applaud in the painting in **Figure 4–3.** Examine this work yourself. Notice that it lacks any recognizable subject matter. The artist has relied instead on the elements of color and shape to spark visual interest.

Content View

The third and final view states that the most important single ingredient of any artwork is its **content**. This is *the message, idea, or feeling expressed by a work of art.* Scholars who hold the content view place the greatest value on a work's expressive qualities. A painting like the one in **Figure 4–4** would earn high marks from people who hold this view. Notice the downward glances and forlorn expressions. Observe how the man's body language—his arms folded tightly about him—seems to shut out the world around him. You can almost feel this family's pain. Note the work's title. Do you find yourself wondering about the tragedy that befell them?

Time & Place

Picasso's Blue Period (1901–04)

Cultural connection. During Pablo Picasso's Blue Period, the artist painted almost exclusively in shades of blue. The Blue Period started with the suicide of Picasso's close friend. After this tragic event, Picasso began using blue to depict emotions such as sadness, loneliness, and isolation (see **Figure 4–4**).

The Blue Period is considered Picasso's first original artistic style. Shortly before this period, Picasso had traveled to Paris for the first time. There, he experimented with established artistic styles, including Impressionism and Pointillism.

In 1904, he began painting in a new style. This more optimistic style, in which Picasso used shades of rose, became known as the Rose Period. Compare the subjects in Figure 4–4 with those in Figure 4–2.

To learn more about Picasso and his work, click on Artist Profiles at **art.glencoe.com**.

Check Your Understanding

1. What is *aesthetics?*
2. What are the three commonly held aesthetic views?

Time & Place

Pablo Picasso

Have students compare **Figure 4–2** with **Figure 4–4**, which are from two different cultures—Dutch and Spanish. The subjects in both artworks reflect a melancholy mood. The mood communicated in de Hooch's painting seems more severe, while Picasso's painting communicates sadness. L1

Aesthetics

Have students study the artworks reproduced in this lesson. Have them work in pairs to identify and describe the subject matter, composition, and content of each work of art. Help those students who may have trouble differentiating between subject matter and content. Call on volunteers to share their ideas. L1 ELL

3 Assess

Self-Assessment

Have students complete the **Check Your Understanding** questions on this page. Answers are provided below.

Reteaching

Work with small groups of students to review the meaning of aesthetics and the three aesthetic views discussed in the lesson. L1 ELL

4 Close

Have students restate the three aesthetic views.

Answers to Check Your Understanding

1. Aesthetics is the study of the nature of beauty and art.
2. The three views are **subject view, composition view,** and **content view.** The subject view holds that if the subject of a work looks convincing and lifelike, the work is successful. The composition view holds that the way the principles of art are used to organize the elements of art is the most important aspect of an artwork. The content view states that the most important ingredient for a successful work of art is its content—the message, idea, or feeling expressed by the work of art.

Art Criticism

(pages 66–69)

1 Focus

Objectives

After completing this lesson, students will be able to:

- Define *art criticism.*
- Identify and explain the four steps of art criticism.
- Critique artworks by analyzing the interdependence of the art elements and principles.

2 Teach

Motivator

Tell students that in this lesson they will learn about the art-criticism process. It is a strategy that will enable them to focus their attention on each of these aesthetic views in works of art.

Aesthetics

It is important that students realize that each of the first three art-criticism steps focuses on one of the ways of measuring a work's success. Point out that a positive judgment for a work of art can be made in terms of subject matter, composition, or content. In some cases only one of these may apply. In other cases, a judgment might be based on two or all three concerns.

LESSON 2

Art Criticism

Do you enjoy solving mysteries? Maybe you are a fan of brainteasers. In either case, having all the facts at hand is critical to finding a solution. So is arranging the facts in a logical fashion.

These statements apply not only to "whodunits" and puzzles. They also apply to artworks. In getting to the "bottom" of a work of art, you need to follow a series of ordered steps. In this lesson, you will learn about these steps and about the solutions they yield. You will also learn how to apply these steps to your own works of art.

The Art Critic

As an amateur detective, you use evidence and clues to crack a case. In a sense, art critics do the same. An **art critic** is *a person whose job is studying, understanding, and judging works of art.* In getting this job done, critics will use all three aesthetic views.

When studying a work of art, the critic uses a four-step process. These steps are *describing, analyzing, interpreting,* and *judging.* The first three of these steps, as you will see, correspond to the three aesthetic views.

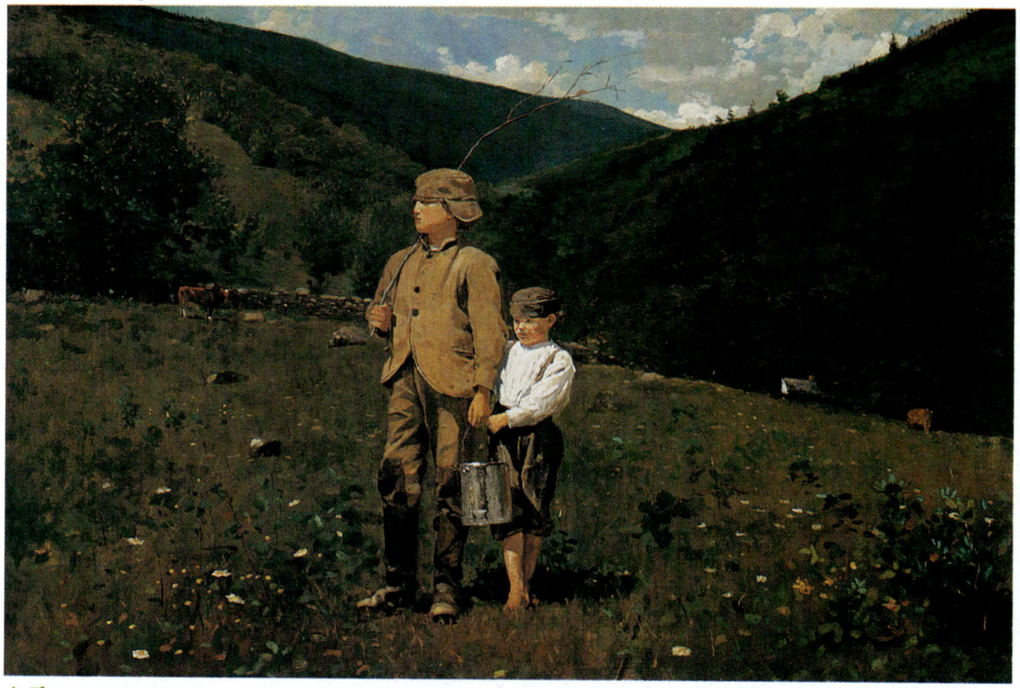

◆ **Figure 4–5** **Does this work succeed because it is lifelike, because of its composition, or because of the mood it expresses?**

Winslow Homer. *Crossing the Pasture.* c. 1872. Oil on canvas. 66.4 × 96.9 cm (26⅛ × 38⅛"). Amon Carter Museum, Fort Worth, Texas.

INCLUSION STRATEGIES

Learning Disabilities Students with disabilities involving speech, hearing, and vision will probably require adaptive consideration when the class views and discusses art prints. Those with visual impairments should be seated close to the artwork and a good light should fall on the artwork. Likewise, those with hearing impairments should be seated up close to the teacher in order to hear the discussion leader. Do not interrupt students with speech disabilities. Encourage them to give in-depth answers. Even students with minimal language skills can participate by holding the art print up for viewing by the entire class.

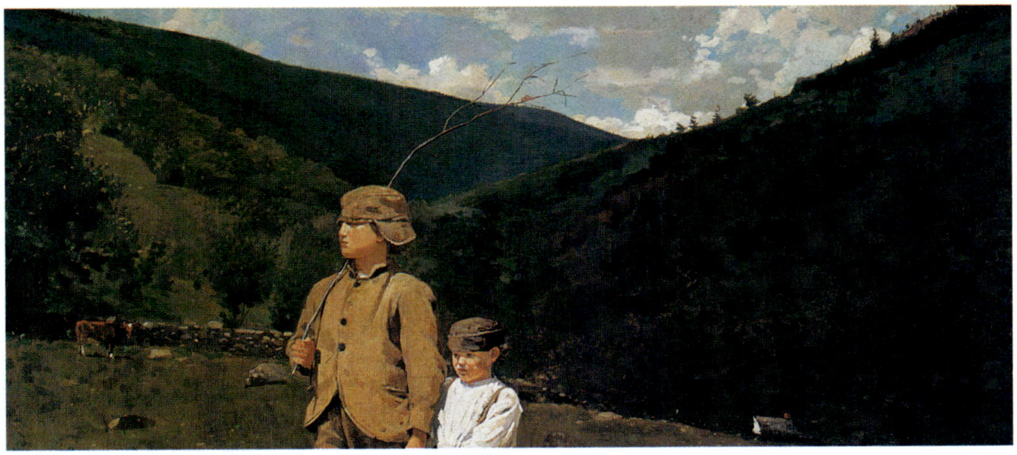

◆ **Figure 4–6a** **What would you say is the subject of this painting?**

Winslow Homer. *Crossing the Pasture.* Detail. c. 1872. Oil on canvas. 66.4 × 96.9 cm (26⅛ × 38⅛″). Amon Carter Museum, Fort Worth, Texas.

Describing

In describing a work, the critic asks the question, "What do I see when I look at this work?" The work's *subject* is the focus of this step. Carefully list all the things you see in the work. Look at the credit line to find out what medium the artist has used and how large the artwork is.

Examine the work shown in **Figure 4–5.**

- How many figures do you see in the picture?
- What object are they both holding? What does the taller boy have over his shoulder?
- What animals do you see in the background?
- How would you describe the surroundings?

In answering these questions, you will be describing the subjects of this artwork.

Analyzing

In analyzing a work, the critic asks, "How is this work of art organized? How are the elements and principles of art used?" The work's *composition* is the focus of this step. Again, look at the detail of the painting in **Figure 4–6a.**

- What forms appear at the center of the composition? Why does the artist place the boys in the center, close to the viewer?
- Can you find any intense or bright colors in this picture?
- Where is the lightest value? What purpose does it serve?
- Notice the diagonal lines formed by the stick in the taller boy's hand and by the downward slope of the hill on the right. These lines converge on, and emphasize, the face of the taller boy. Can you find a third diagonal line that does the same?
- Can you find a more gently sloping diagonal that points to the face of the smaller boy?
- What colors has the artist used? What textures has he included?
- How has the artist used emphasis to make the subjects stand out?
- What role does proportion play in this artwork?

These questions and their answers are examples of the critic's analysis of the composition in the painting *Crossing the Pasture.*

Art Criticism

Provide time for students to prepare written descriptions of the painting by Winslow Homer. Then ask them to present and discuss their descriptions. Follow the same procedure with the remaining art-criticism questions. Here are guidelines for student responses:

- In the descriptions, students should describe the two young boys and note the presence of the bull in the pasture.
- Analysis should reveal the artist's concern for composition. Dabs of bright color that define the wildflowers and highlight the bull, trees, rocks, and house help unify the scene. The light value of the smaller boy's shirt helps draw the viewer's attention to him. The shapes of the two figures, linked by the shiny pail, are emphasized by their placement in the center foreground. Point out how the larger boy's head marks almost exactly the crossing of the two hills behind them.
- During interpretation, students should be able to detect a sense of alertness in the taller boy's protective stance and the stick on his shoulder. The other boy shelters himself close to his side. Ask students if they can identify the subject of his concern. A bull, either the one in the left background or another one out of view may be a danger to the boys.
- Have students express their judgments about the painting and tell why they responded as they did. Ask: Do you think the work is successful because of its subject matter, composition, or content?

CURRICULUM CONNECTIONS

SOCIAL STUDIES The works of Winslow Homer (1836–1910) reflect time and place. His early paintings record rural American scenes of the time—schoolrooms, croquet games, husking bees. His illustrations of Civil War battlefield scenes portrayed the cruel images of war. Eventually Homer focused on the role of the sea in late nineteenth-century America. Have students learn more about Winslow Homer and bring to class more examples of his work. Then, ask students to describe what Homer is expressing about historical or political events in those artworks.

LESSON 2

Teach *(continued)*

Team Building Activity

Divide students into small groups and have them apply the art-criticism steps to Figure 4–2 on page 64. Remind the groups that they do not have to agree, particularly in their interpretations and judgments. When they have completed the process, have a spokesperson for each group share their ideas and explain the various judgments within each group.

Students can learn a great deal about works of art through this kind of collaborative information exchange. Discussions of this kind can help in expanding art vocabulary. L1 ELL

Understanding Art History

After students begin to look at art more critically, their curiosity may be aroused and they may begin to ask such questions as: Who painted this work? When was it done? Where was it done? Explain that these are art-history questions that require research in order to answer them. Appoint two teams of two or three students each to research the lives and careers of both Pieter de Hooch (Figure 4–2) and Winslow Homer (Figure 4–5). Students should present their findings in class and bring in some examples of their artworks. Ask the class to compare both artists' works. How are their works different or similar? L2

ART IN EVERYDAY LIFE

Encourage students to be on the lookout for articles about art in newspapers and periodicals. Have them bring in clippings as they find them and post them on a bulletin board under the heading "Art in the News."

Interpreting

In interpreting a work, the critic asks, "What is the artist saying to me? What moods, feelings, or ideas are expressed?" The work's content is the focus of this step. Look closely at **Figure 4–6b.**

- What emotion is communicated by the look and body language of the taller boy? Would you say that he stands tall and appears sure of himself?
- Contrast these observations with the facial expression and posture of the smaller boy.
- Why has the artist placed the boys against a darker, textured background? Does this focus your attention on their faces and facial expressions? What do you think the artist has accomplished by drawing the viewer's eyes to the boys' expressions and body language?
- What visual clue can you find in the distance off to the left that might explain the boys' behavior?

Interpretation can be the most challenging step in art criticism. It is challenging because you must use your imagination. Do not be afraid to make an interpretation that is different from someone else's. Your interpretation will depend on what you have experienced in life.

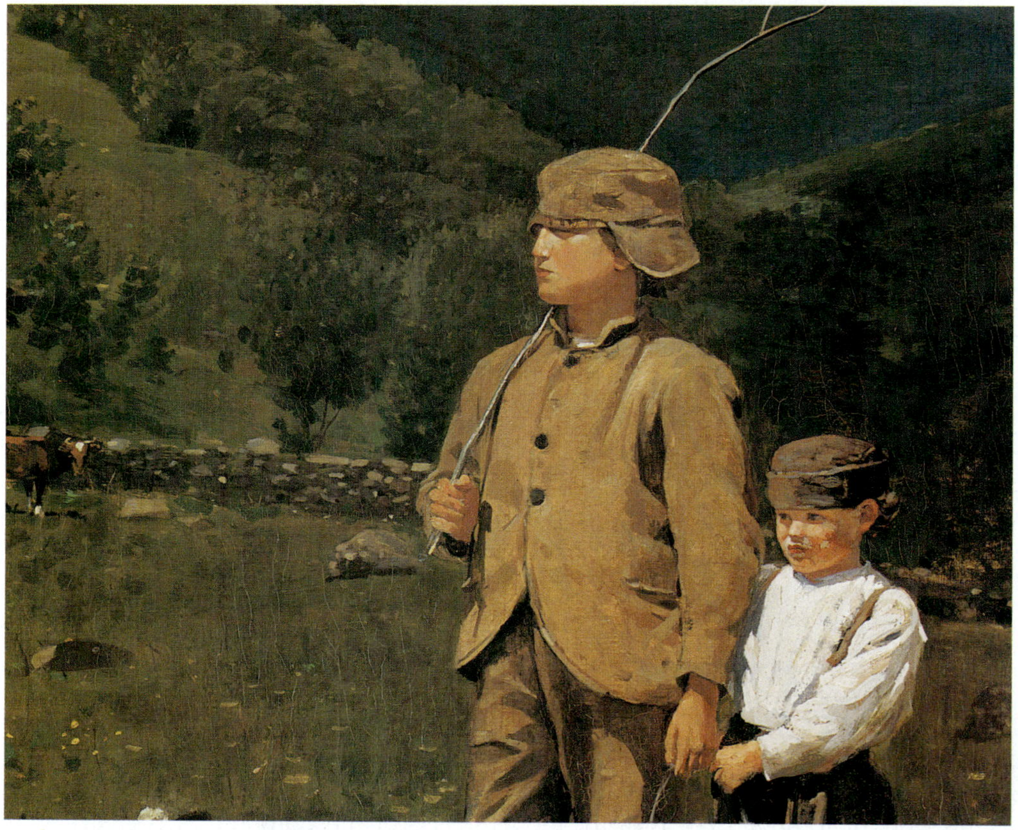

◆ **Figure 4–6b** Notice the feelings conveyed by the boys' expressions. How does this information help you understand the story the painting tells?

Winslow Homer. *Crossing the Pasture.* Detail. c. 1872. Oil on canvas. 66.4 × 96.9 cm (26⅛ × 38⅛"). Amon Carter Museum, Fort Worth, Texas.

COMMUNITY CONNECTION

Art Critics As a community service project, contact a local art museum and have your class become docents for the younger students that visit the museum. Working in groups, students will apply the four art-criticism steps (describing, analyzing, interpreting, and judging) to several pieces of artwork in the museum. After groups have mastered these pieces, plan age-appropriate activities for the younger museum visitors to complete after their tours. Break the groups into a rotating schedule with the museum as they are needed.

Judging

In judging a work, the critic asks, "Is the work successful?" This step depends on the answers to the questions asked during the first three steps. A work may be judged successful on the basis of its subject, composition, content, or some combination of the three. How do you think an art critic would judge the painting in Figure 4–5? Using what you have learned, how would you judge it?

If you have been an alert art sleuth up to this stage, you might have homed in on the story this painting tells. A part of it is revealed in the detail from the work in Figure 4–6b.

The slightly comical narrative centers on two boys, probably brothers. The two are seen crossing a field—taking a shortcut, maybe, after having just completed the morning's milking. Suddenly, each becomes aware of a real and present danger. Did you notice the bull in the background? The two boys certainly did! The younger boy's fear is obvious as he clings to his companion. The older boy, armed with a switch, proceeds fearlessly—or so he would like his younger brother to believe.

Once you have described, analyzed, and interpreted this painting, you will be able to decide for yourself whether or not it is successful. Do you find, now that you have gone through the three steps of art criticism, that you have made a judgment about whether Homer's *Crossing the Pasture* is a successful work of art? What is your opinion?

Check Your Understanding

1. What is art criticism?
2. Name the four steps used by art critics. Explain what is done at each step.

Studio Activity

Reading a Credit Line

Apply your knowledge. Look again at the painting in Figure 4–5 on page 66. You can learn about this work by noting its title, *Crossing the Pasture.*

This information and much else appears in the painting's credit line. A **credit line** is *a listing of important facts about an artwork.* Appearing under or near a work, a credit line has six parts. It begins with the artist's name and the title of the artwork. The year the work was created and the art medium or media appear next. After that comes the size of the artwork. The last piece of information is the name of the museum, gallery, or other place in which the work is located. Referring to the credit line of Figure 4–5, you would learn that the work was painted by Winslow Homer in about 1872. The "c." before the date means "about."

Every artwork in this book has a credit line. Use the credit lines in Figures 4–1 and 4–2 to answer the following:

- Which of the works was painted by artist Pieter de Hooch?
- Which work was painted in the seventeenth century?
- Which of the works is housed at The Metropolitan Museum of Art?

PORTFOLIO

Write a credit line for your next artwork and place it in your portfolio.

Studio Activity

Reading a Credit Line

Direct students' attention to the credit line for Figure 4–5 on page 66. As students discuss the items in a credit line, ask them to think about why such information is important and how it can be used. Invite them to investigate other credit lines in the book.

3 Assess

Self-Assessment

Have students complete the **Check Your Understanding** questions on this page. Answers are provided below.

Reteaching

Have students work in pairs to practice applying the four steps of art criticism to a work of art. L1 ELL

Enrichment

Ask students to write a critical review of a program they have seen on television. Be sure students use the four steps used by art critics. Students should produce coherent written texts by organizing ideas, using effective transitions, and choosing precise wording.

4 Close

Have students retrace the steps used in art criticism.

Answers to Check Your Understanding

1. Art criticism is a process of studying works of art to determine whether they are successful or not.
2. The steps in art criticism are: describing, analyzing, interpreting, and judging. In describing, the critic asks, "What do I see, and what elements of art are predominant?" While analyzing, the critic looks at the composition of the art, asking, "How are the principles of art used to organize the elements of art?" In interpreting the artwork, the critic focuses on the content, asking, "What moods, feelings, or ideas are expressed?" In judging the work, the critic asks, "Is the work successful?" The answer depends on the answers found in the first three steps.

LESSON 3

Critiquing Nonobjective Art

(pages 70–71)

1 Focus

Objectives

After completing this lesson, students will be able to:

- Identify nonobjective art.
- Apply the art-criticism questions to critique nonobjective works of art.

2 Teach

Motivator

Begin this lesson by briefly reviewing the three ways of measuring success in works of art and explaining that this lesson will focus on the second of these: dealing with composition. Explain that in order for a work to be judged successful in terms of composition it must have unity. Ask students to explain what this term means to them. Is unity a quality associated with the visual arts only, or is it desirable in other disciplines? Have students give examples.

Vocabulary

Write the word *unity* on the board. Remind students that if an artwork has unity, the different parts in the work *look* as if they belong together. Artists must carefully organize the elements and principles of art to give their works unity, a feeling of completeness or wholeness.

LESSON 3

Critiquing Nonobjective Art

Describing a work of art, you have learned, means identifying what you see. Sometimes this is easier said than done. Examine the artwork on this page. Compare it with the painting in Figure 4–3 on page 64. How would you describe these works? What do you see when you look at each?

In this lesson, you will learn how to apply the steps of art criticism to works without recognizable subjects.

Nonobjective Art

Artists do not work in isolation. Each generation builds on and refines the ideas of the one that came before. At times, throughout history, this process has led to startling changes. It has provided new answers to the question "What is art?"

One such major breakthrough came in the early 1900s. For several decades, artists had been experimenting with distorting shapes

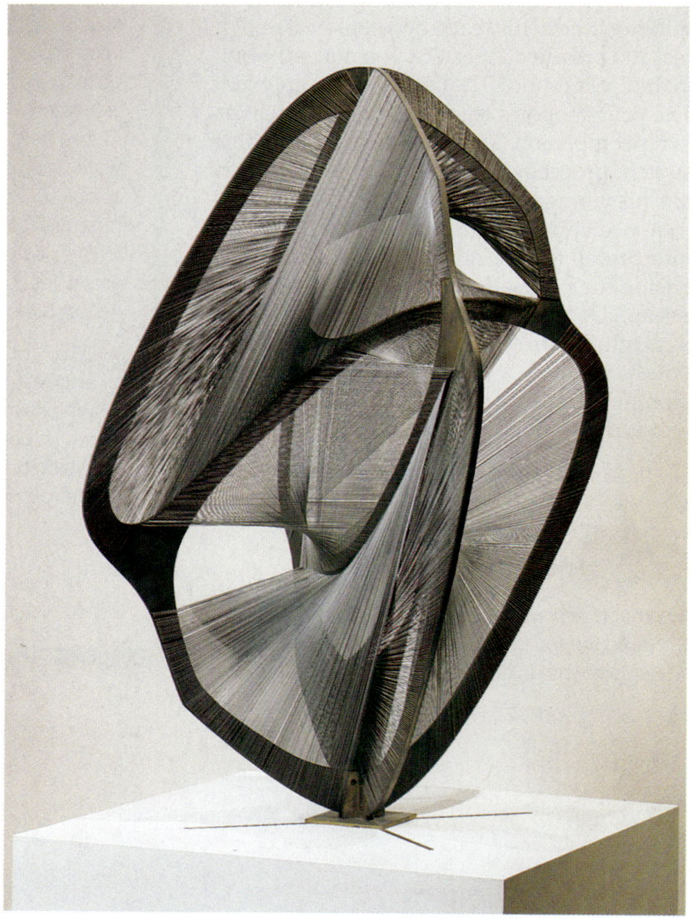

◆ **Figure 4–7** **Analyze the interdependence of the art element shape and principle balance. How is repetition used in this sculpture?**

Naum Gabo. *Linear Construction No. 4.* 1962. Bronze, stainless steel, piano wire. 128.3 × 63.5 × 63.5 cm (50½ × 25 × 25″). Detroit Institute of Arts, Detroit, Michigan. Gift of W. Hawkins Ferry.

RESOURCES BEYOND THE CLASSROOM

Specialized Museums Make use of local specialized museums. Children's museums, historical museums, and even natural history museums can illuminate concepts learned in class. Children's museums house exhibits that appeal to school-age children and often specialize in collectibles, hand-crafted toys, and mechanical objects. Historical museums generally highlight local arts and crafts as well as local history. Natural history museums are a source of natural forms for inspiration. Just looking at the exhibits can stimulate the imagination and spark a creative urge in your students.

and forms. This new group took matters a step further. They abandoned subject matter altogether. They created nonobjective works of art. **Nonobjective** means *having no readily identifiable subjects or objects.*

Critiquing a Nonobjective Artwork

In studying nonobjective works of art, critics apply the same four-step process outlined in the previous lesson. The main difference comes at the description step. To see this, look again at the sculpture in **Figure 4–7.** There is no identifiable subject. Even the title provides little help. In *describing* this work, a critic would, therefore, concentrate first on identifying the elements of art in it. He or she would take note of the different lines and forms that are used. Because the work is a sculpture that exists in three dimensions, the critic would pay special attention to the element of space. How would you describe the sculptor's use of space? How would you describe his use of negative space?

Now it is your turn to be a critic. Using the skills you have learned, try applying each of the following art-criticism steps to this artwork:

- **Describing.** How would you describe this sculpture? How many varieties of line have been used? What kinds of geometric or free-form shapes are visible? Is there any color used? Where are negative spaces apparent?
- **Analyzing.** How would you analyze this sculpture? What principle or principles of art have been used to organize the elements of art?
- **Interpreting.** What ideas, moods, and feelings are suggested by this work? Does the sculpture express an idea of some kind?
- **Judging.** Would you say that this work is successful? Does it have unity? What factors contribute to its success or lack of success?

Time & Place

Pop Art and Op Art

Historical connection. During the late 1950s and early 1960s, many technological changes were taking place in the United States. The advent of television was one. Improvements in communication, transportation, and the media were also changing the way people lived and worked. These changes were reflected in two art movements of the time period: Pop art and Op art.

In Pop art (short for Popular art), everyday objects, such as soup cans, comic strips, and fast food, were used as subjects. Pop artists, including Andy Warhol and Roy Lichtenstein, depicted images from popular culture using the techniques of advertising and mass media. Op art (short for Optical art) was a form of abstract art that presented viewers with an optical illusion. Works in the Op art style often created an illusion of movement.

Look at **Figure 4–7.** Do you think it could be categorized as Pop art or Op art? If so, which one and why?

Check Your Understanding

1. What is meant by nonobjective art?
2. When examining a nonobjective artwork, what is identified during the description step?

Time & Place

Pop Art and Op Art

Ask students to identify in Figure 4–7 the influence of historical events. The political, social, and technological changes during the 1960s influenced how art was created. The sculpture in Figure 4–7 could be categorized as Op art, because it is abstract art that can present an optical illusion of movement.

3 Assess

Self-Assessment

Have students complete the **Check Your Understanding** questions on this page. Answers are provided below.

Reteaching

Review with students what nonobjective art is. Have students point to some examples in the book.

Enrichment

Invite students to research the work of Pablo Picasso. Ask students to choose one of his works of art and write a brief critique of it, using the steps discussed in this lesson.

4 Close

Ask students to summarize the steps used to critique nonobjective art.

Answers to Check Your Understanding

1. Nonobjective art is a term used to describe works with no readily identified subjects or objects.
2. When examining a nonobjective artwork, the elements of art are identified during description and the principles during analysis.

Creating a Realistic Painting

(pages 72–73)
Lesson Time: 3 hours

1 Focus

Objectives

After completing this lesson, students will be able to:

- Demonstrate technical skills effectively by drawing a window and the scene viewed through the window in a realistic style using oil pastels.
- Understand the viewer's point of view.
- Conduct an in-progress analysis of their sketches.

SUPPLIES
Refer to **What You Will Need** in the Student Edition.

2 Teach

Motivator

Ask students to discuss what makes a painting realistic. Have them find examples of realistic art in the text. Then have students examine Hopper's painting *Night Hawks* in **Figure 4–8.** Instruct them to write down a single word that they think best describes this painting. Then ask them how they would describe the *subject* of the work. Is it extraordinary or rather common? Tell them that Hopper was able to take common scenes and transform them through his own unique style of painting.

Creating a Realistic Painting

The emptiness and gloom of a nation fallen on hard times would seem like a strange theme for art. Yet, it is precisely this theme that runs through the works of American artist Edward Hopper. Hopper lived through a period called the Great Depression, a time when there was very little money. Many people in the United States and abroad were left without jobs or homes. Hopper's paintings accurately capture the mood of the era. They show lonely, often desperate people in shabby, rundown rooms.

Figure 4–8 shows one of Hopper's best-known paintings. Notice the **point of view.** This *is the angle from which the viewer sees the scene in an artwork.* Typical of Hopper's work, we do not see the people in this picture head-on. Instead, we are given a glimpse of them through a window.

What You Will Learn

In this lesson, you will use oil pastels to create your own Hopper "window." Like Figure 4–8, your painting will have a realistic subject. Your point of view, like Hopper's, will be outside, looking into a lighted room through a window. It will be nighttime. The room will have no people. The furniture and other contents will overlap to indicate space. These objects will be drawn to show the mood or personality of the person living or working in this room.

What You Will Need

- Pencil and sheets of sketch paper
- Oil pastels
- White drawing paper, 12 × 18 inches

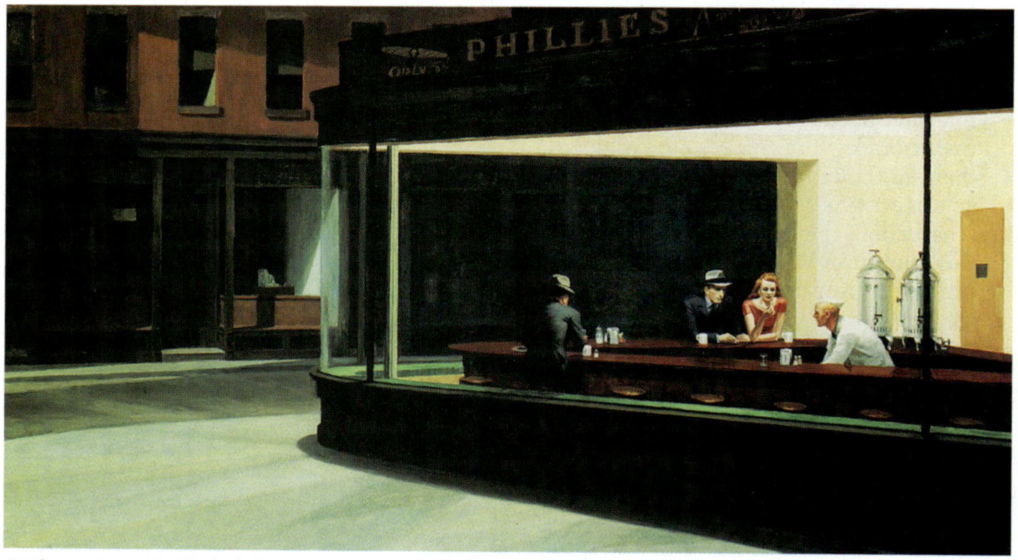

◆ **Figure 4–8** **Identify the influence of historical events in this painting. During what time period was this artwork created?**

Edward Hopper. *Night Hawks.* 1942. Oil on canvas. 83.8 × 152.4 cm (33 × 60″). The Art Institute of Chicago, Chicago, Illinois. Friends of American Art Collection, 1942.51.

MORE ABOUT...

EDWARD HOPPER Hopper (1882–1967) was a twentieth-century American painter. He gained widespread recognition as a realistic painter of the American scene. However, he once said, "I don't think I ever tried to paint the American scene; I'm trying to paint myself." Discuss with students what they think the artist meant by this statement. If he was indeed trying to paint himself, what does *Night Hawks* tell us about him? Hopper was a shy, reserved man who preferred a public image of an uneducated and backward artist working in realistic tradition. His paintings, however, reveal the artist's own sensitive, strongly felt emotions.

What You Will Do

1. Begin by looking closely at the building across from the all-night diner in Figure 4–8. Study the row of dark windows on the second floor. Try to picture the kinds of rooms behind those windows. Decide whether they are fancy apartments, drab hotel rooms, offices, or something else. Think about the outside of the building. What material is it made of?
2. Imagine that the lights were turned on inside one of the rooms. Make several sketches of what your mind "sees." Draw a window frame like the one in Figure 4–8, only larger. As you sketch, continue to imagine the contents of the room. You might include wallpaper, carpeting, and other furniture. As you work, ask yourself, "What kind of person lives or works here?" Decide what clues you can provide in your drawing to tell viewers something about the mood or personality of this person.
3. Transfer your best sketch to the white drawing paper. Work lightly in pencil. Make the outside wall of the building look like brick, stone, or wood.
4. Color your picture using oil pastels. Select colors that will give your room a "personality" to match that of its imaginary occupant.
5. Like Hopper, avoid small, unnecessary details. Lay one color over another to create textures. Overlap shapes and forms to suggest space inside the room.
6. Display your finished drawing in a horizontal row along with those of classmates.

Evaluating Your Work

- **Describe** Are the objects inside the room easy to identify? What texture did you use for the outside of your building?
- **Analyze** Did you show the different values for objects inside the lighted room compared to those in the darkness outside? Did you overlap shapes and forms to suggest space?
- **Interpret** Does your drawing offer clues about the mood or personality of the person who might live or work in the room?
- **Judge** Do you think your drawing is successful? Does it present the subject matter in a realistic way?

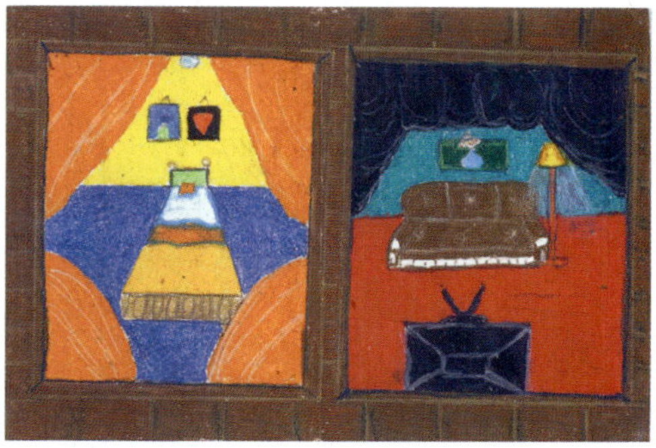

◆ **Figure 4–9** Student work. Hopper windows.

Studio Option

Create another version of your Hopper window. This scene is to be set during the day and is to reflect a mood opposite the one in your first drawing. This time the point of view will be looking through the window to the outside. Use pastels for the window frame and watercolors for the landscape out of doors.

Visual Art Journal

Organize ideas from the environment. At a local park or outside your home, sketch the scene around you in your journal. Notice the people, buildings, and time of day. Your drawing should be realistic and capture the mood of the scene.

Studio Skills

Have students speculate about the rooms behind the windows in *Night Hawks.* Discuss the furniture and other objects that might be in those rooms and how these might reflect the mood of the occupant. Encourage students to brainstorm ideas, and then develop their ideas in sketches. Provide time for them to experiment with the oil pastels before beginning work on their finished drawings. L1 ELL

Visual Art Journal

Encourage students to develop their perceptual skills. As they sketch their scene, have them illustrate themes from direct observation. What do they notice in the scene around them?

3 Assess

Self-Assessment

Have students use **Evaluating Your Work** to conduct an in-progress critique of their realistic paintings. L1

Reteaching

Review with students the four steps in art criticism.

4 Close

Have students summarize why they think Hopper's *Night Hawks* is or is not a successful painting.

Teacher to Teacher

Achieving Dimension and Space Encourage students to include the buildings and scene outside the window. Keep the outside scene simple in order to focus attention on the objects inside the window. Students should also overlap shapes, use more details, increase the size, and apply brighter colors to objects that are close. Have students notice the angles Hopper used that make the composition more interesting: the diner, the building behind the diner, the counter, and lines of the windows. Encourage them to consider their viewpoint and angles they can include.

Creating an Expressive Word Design

(pages 74–75)
Lesson Time: 90 minutes

1 Focus

Objectives

After completing this lesson, students will be able to:

- Create a design using the letters of an expressive word and a background of color bands that all together imply the emotion conveyed by that word.
- Demonstrate technical skills effectively using a variety of art media and materials to produce an expressive word design.
- Describe, analyze, interpret, and judge their design in terms of its success in expressing an emotion.

SUPPLIES
Refer to **What You Will Need** in the Student Edition.

2 Teach

Motivator

Have students examine the engraving by Albrecht Dürer and ask them to describe what they see. Is the feeling or mood of this artwork easily understood? What elements and principles has the artist used to emphasize that feeling or mood?

LESSON 5

Creating an Expressive Word Design

Have you ever had one of those days in which nothing seemed to go right? Maybe, like the young woman in **Figure 4–10,** you felt "blue." Study this fine-art print. Notice that the artist has not shown us much of the woman's face. We are still able to "read" her mood by observing her body language. What details of the woman's posture help us identify how she is feeling? What other moods can you identify from the way a person sits or stands?

What You Will Learn

The artist has taken one approach to capturing a particular mood or feeling. In this lesson, you will take another approach. You will communicate the mood of your choice through a word, written in large block letters, rather than an image. You will use variety of shapes and colors to create a background that emphasizes the emotion suggested by this word.

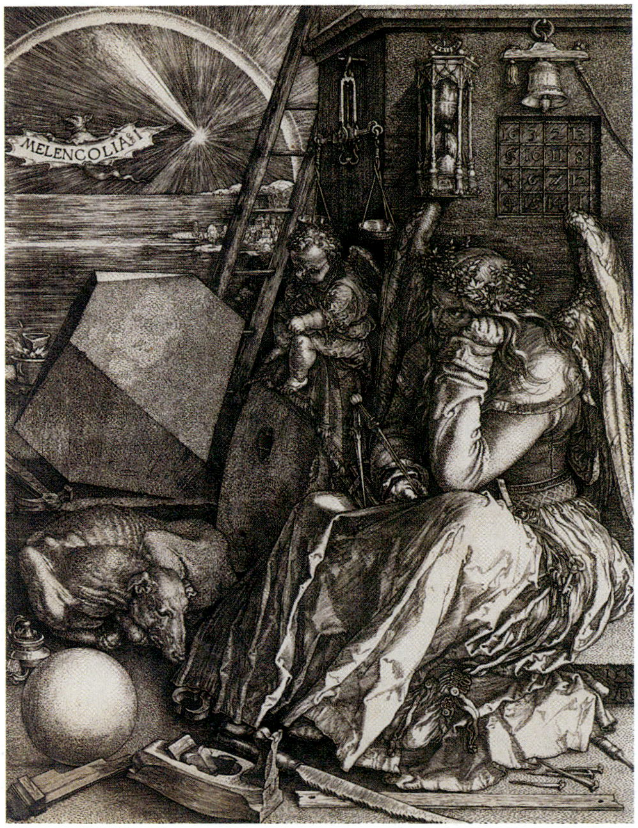

◆ **Figure 4–10** **What does the subject's body language reveal about her mood?**

Albrecht Dürer. *Melancholia 1.* 1514. Engraving. 24.1 × 18.6 cm (9½ × 7⁵⁄₁₆"). The Metropolitan Museum of Art, New York, New York. Harris Brisbane Dick Fund, 1943.

RESOURCES BEYOND THE CLASSROOM

LOCAL MANUFACTURERS AND PRINTERS Tour a local manufacturer of art supplies where students might learn how paint or ink is made, how fabric is woven, or how wood is milled. Such tours can alert students to potential hazards of the materials they use and show them appropriate safety procedures.

If feasible, arrange a tour of a local printer. Ask to see the printing process used. Encourage students to ask lots of questions and to take notes. Ask to have each step demonstrated and find out which processes are used for the fine arts.

What You Will Need

- Pencil and sketch paper
- White drawing paper, 9 × 12 inches
- Tempera paint
- Mixing trays
- Brushes
- Water

What You Will Do

1. With classmates, brainstorm words naming moods and emotions. Possibilities include *happy, tired, worried, angry,* and *bored.*
2. Choose one of the words. On sketch paper, write the word out in large block letters. Experiment with different letter designs that communicate the mood you have chosen. You might, for example, use rounded, overlapping letters for an upbeat mood. Letters with straight edges and sharp points might communicate a negative mood, such as anger. Letters may be all capitals or upper and lower case but should fill the page.
3. Transfer your best design to the sheet of drawing paper. Still working in pencil, create a background design. This is to have the form of thick and thin bands extending horizontally or vertically from one edge of the paper to the other. As with the shape of the letters, the bands should reflect the word you are using. Zigzag lines might be used for the word *tense.* Curved lines signal a more peaceful mood.
4. Select a color scheme that emphasizes the emotion or feeling of your word. Boldly contrasting hues, intensities, and values might be used to express tension. Hues, intensities, and values that are harmonious could express peace.
5. Paint the background bands in the colors you have selected. Do not paint the letters themselves.

Evaluating Your Work

- **Describe** Is the word you selected easily read? Did you use large block letters to write this word?
- **Analyze** Did you create a background made up of bands of color? Did these colors contrast with one another to create variety?
- **Interpret** Does your design reflect the mood or feeling of the word? Do the shapes and colors help emphasize that emotion?
- **Judge** Does your design communicate an emotion with letters, shapes, and colors? Is this a successful work of art?

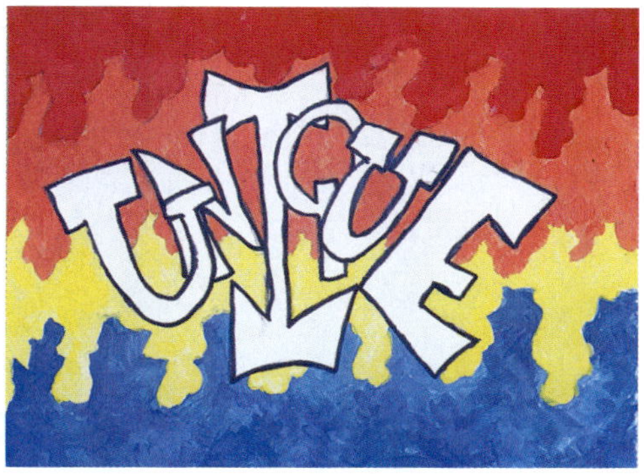

◆ **Figure 4–11** Student work. An expressive word.

Reflective Thinking

Critical Evaluation. As your class displays their artworks, analyze the original exhibition of your peers. Examine the expressive word designs they created and form conclusions about formal properties. For example, how did they use shape and color to emphasize emotion?

Art Online

For additional student art, check out our Web site at **art.glencoe.com**. There you will find:

- Interactive Games
- Student Art Gallery
- Artist Profiles
- Museum Web Links

Art Criticism

Divide the class into three groups of art critics with differing aesthetic points of view. One group feels that subject is the primary concern, another that composition is the determining factor, and the third that content is most important. Have each group critique **Figure 4–10** using the art-criticism steps of description, analysis, interpretation, and judgment. L1 ELL

Studio Skills

Demonstrate ways to create simplified block letters. The letters must be thick and large and may overlap slightly, but where this occurs, erase overlapping lines. Show students how to create different kinds of horizontal and vertical bands that vary in width to go behind the letters. L1 ELL

3 Assess

Peer Assessment

Have students analyze the original exhibition of their peers to form conclusions about formal properties—the elements and principles of art.

Enrichment

Ask students to find examples of expressive word designs found in print advertising. Have them display the examples with the exhibit of the students' word designs. L1 ELL

4 Close

Have students critique their own expressive word designs using the four steps of art criticism.

Technology Strategies in the Art Classroom

Special Effects Most computer software programs include Word Art or font menus that create special effects. Have students explore options that include lettering styles, text wrapping, color fills, alignment, spacing, overlapping, stretching, and rotation. Encourage students to experiment with these effects. Have students select an expressive word, and explore fonts, colors, and textures to match the idea. Encourage students to try options that change size, change direction, and distort. Repeat the word. Overlap and fill the page.

Creating an Abstract Figure

(pages 76–77)
Lesson Time: 1 hour

1 Focus

Objectives

After completing this lesson, students will be able to:

- Define *abstract art.*
- Create a simplified abstract shape using a single, continuous line.
- Describe, analyze, and interpret their designs and judge them on the basis of composition.

Supplies
Refer to **What You Will Need** in the Student Edition.

2 Teach

Motivator

Bring in several examples of paintings by Henri Matisse. Ask students to express their opinions of his style. What elements and principles seemed to appeal to him? Explain that he used shape and color to express joy and beauty. Direct students' attention to **Figure 4–12.** Point out that in an effort to eliminate detail, Matisse often distorted the shapes in his works. Tell students that this particular work was done late in his life. Crippled by arthritis, he had to abandon painting and worked mainly with cut paper, using simple, basic shapes.

Creating an Abstract Figure

Nonobjective art, as you learned in Lesson 3, began in the early 1900s. By avoiding subject matter, nonobjective artists created a new means of self-expression. Since that time, other artists have taken a more middle-of-the-road approach to subject matter. They have produced art that is **abstract.** This means *having a recognizable subject that is shown in an unrealistic manner.*

The work in **Figure 4–12** is an example of abstract art. Its subject is a character from Greek mythology. His name is Icarus. According to legend, Icarus tried to fly using wings held together with wax. Ignoring warnings, Icarus flew too close to the sun. The wax melted, and the youth fell to his death. Study this work of art. Can you recognize it as a falling figure?

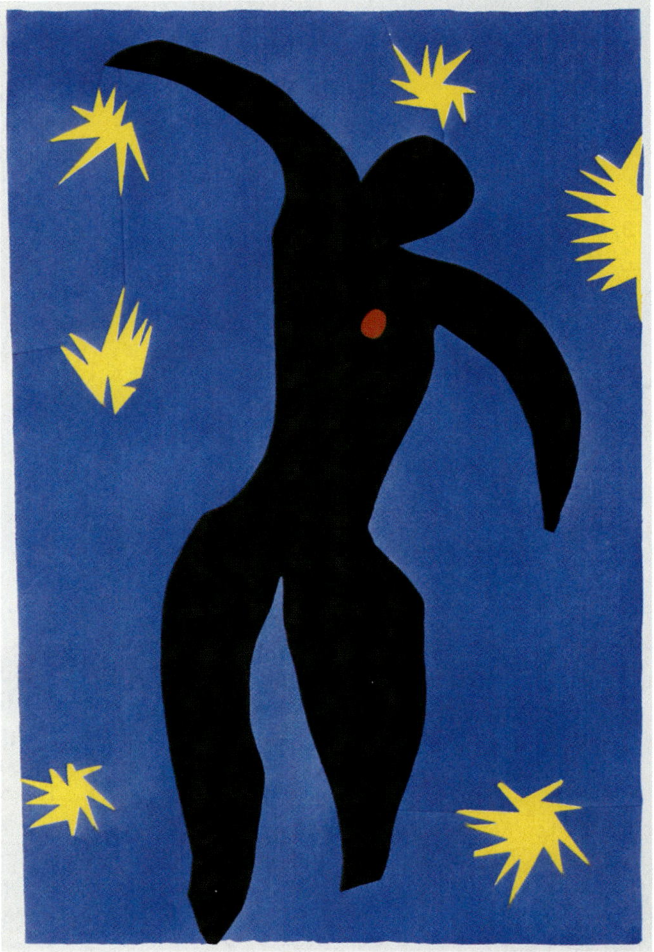

◆ **Figure 4–12** **How would you describe the use of negative space in this work? Why do you think the artist chose to make the figure abstract?**

Henri Matisse. *Icarus.* Plate VIII from *Jazz.* 1947. Pochoir, printed in color. Each single page: 21.1 × 32.6 cm (8⅓ × 12⅞″). The Museum of Modern Art, New York, New York. The Louis E. Stern Collection.

TEACHER TO TEACHER

Working with Glue and Yarn Show students how to follow the lines of the abstract figure with glue and yarn. Notice how the yarn's thickness simplifies the shape. Make several shapes and vary their size and position. To make a mobile, use thick rug yarn. Dip the yarn into thinned white glue and follow the lines of the drawing. Plastic wrap as well as wax paper can be used. If available, use 14-gauge copper or brass wire to follow the design. To strengthen the wire figure, harden the curves by flattening the wire with a metal hammer.

What You Will Learn

You will demonstrate technical skills effectively using yarn to produce fiberart of a simplified abstract shape. The shape will be of a falling figure. The image will be made with a single, continuous line of colored yarn. The same thickness of the line throughout will add harmony to your work.

What You Will Need

- Pencil and sketch paper, 12 × 18 inches
- Waxed paper
- Transparent or masking tape
- Yarn, about 60 inches in length
- Large bowl
- White glue, thinned with water

What You Will Do

1. Study Figure 4–12. Notice the way the artist has captured the sense of a figure falling through space. Trace your finger around the outline of the abstract shape of this figure.
2. Complete several drawings of your version of the falling Icarus. As in Figure 4–12, your work should be abstract. Use a single continuous pencil line to create your figures.
3. Transfer your best drawing to a sheet of sketch paper. Make a heavy line using pencil. Cover the drawing completely with a sheet of waxed paper that is smaller than the page. Secure the waxed paper in place with tape. The drawing should be clearly visible through the waxed paper.
4. Draw a line of white glue over the pencil line. Carefully lay the yarn on the line of glue. Allow time for the yarn to dry.

Evaluating Your Work

- **Describe** Is your work easily recognized as an abstract figure?
- **Analyze** Did you use one continuous line to create the abstract shape? Did the use of a line with the same thickness throughout add harmony to your design?
- **Interpret** Does your figure appear to be falling through space?
- **Judge** Using composition to measure accomplishment, is your work a success? Why or why not?

5. Once the glue is thoroughly dry, the yarn will be stiff and hold its shape. Carefully lift the shape off the waxed paper.

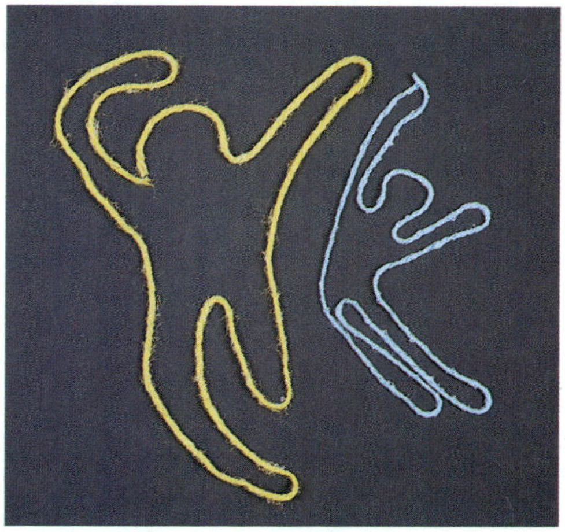

Figure 4–13 Student work. Abstract figures.

Portfolio Ideas

Include some form of written self-reflection with your portfolio entry. In self-reflection, you have the opportunity to critique your own works. You describe what you learned from the assignment. You can also express whether you think the work is a success, and what you liked or didn't like about doing the project.

Visual Art Journal

Conduct in-progress analyses of personal artworks. As you begin Step 3, analyze your work and select your best drawing. Keep the other drawings in your portfolio to show your progression as an artist.

Aesthetics

Ask students to imagine they are describing Matisse's cutout to a friend over the telephone. Ask: Would you spend as much time identifying the elements of art as you would the subject? What does this tell you about how you might go about judging this work?

Historical/Cultural Heritage

Ask students to locate and read myths from other cultures, such as African, Norse, Chinese, or Native American cultures. If possible, have students also locate artworks that deal with mythological characters or creatures from those cultures. Have students compare these artworks and describe the details found in each. L2

3 Assess

Self-Assessment

Have students use **Evaluating Your Work** to conduct an in-progress critique of their abstract figure.

Reteaching

Ask students to explain what makes the image of Icarus abstract.

4 Close

Have students review the concept of abstraction.

Developing a Portfolio

Choosing a Project A portfolio should exhibit strong, confident examples of a student's work. Typically, evaluators would rather see fewer competent works than many that are mediocre. However, a diversity of artistic skill is also critical, so students must learn to balance both objectives. Encourage them to approach each assignment as a potential project for their portfolios as well as a method of isolating their strengths and weaknesses. For more information on choosing projects to include in portfolios, refer to the booklet, *Portfolio and Authentic Assessment* that accompanies the *Introducing Art* program.

An Art Critic's View

1 Focus

Objectives

After completing this lesson, students will be able to:

- Define what an art critic is.
- Plan, write, and edit a critical review of a given artwork.

2 Teach

Teaching the Feature

1. Ask students to share what they know about movie reviews. Who writes and/or broadcasts reviews of movies? What facts do you expect to find in a movie review? Whose opinions are presented?
2. Explain that art critics are like movie critics: They present their own opinions about artworks. They use facts to support their opinions.
3. Have students work in cooperative groups to read and discuss the review. Ask: Do you agree with the reviewer? Why or why not?

Activity

Have students review the description of the pie slices. Then have students write their own review of the two paintings shown on the page. Encourage students to share and compare their critiques.

An Art Critic's View

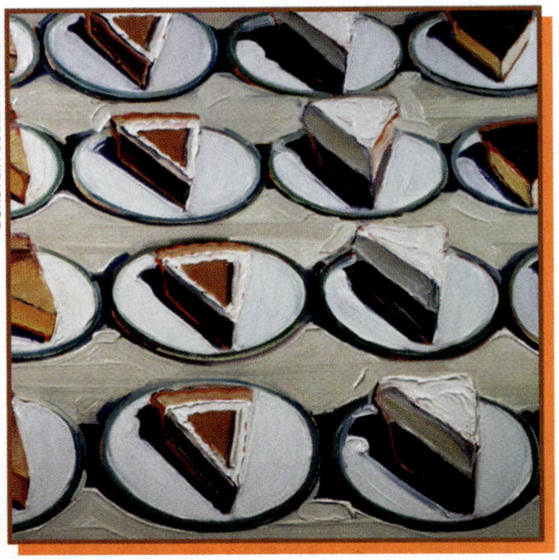

BURSTEIN COLLECTION/CORBIS

Wayne Thiebaud. *Pie Table.* 1963.

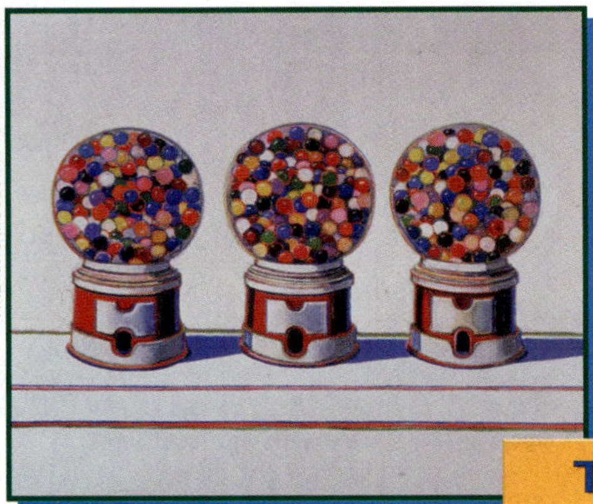

FINE ARTS MUSEUM OF SAN FRANCISCO

Wayne Thiebaud. *Three Machines.* 1963.

Thiebaud's artistic goal is to give pleasure in a serious, intelligent way. His paintings look simple, but there is more to them than at first meets the eye. One point he vividly makes in his work is that nothing is exactly the same as anything else—whether those things are soft wedges of pie or dozens of delicious gumballs.

Not all criticism is negative.

Critics who review work by actors, singers, dancers, and artists may like what they see. They may also have different opinions. Robert Hughes, the art critic for TIME, shares his opinion in this portion of his review of painter Wayne Thiebaud.

Wayne Thiebaud (b. 1920) is a Realist. He loves material objects. More than anything, however, Thiebaud is delighted by the sight of mass-produced American food. Not so much the soup can as the soup itself, or for that matter the sandwich, the cake, or the slices of pie. He is fascinated by tiny variations within many similar-looking objects. So no two of Thiebaud's slices are identical. The small but clear differences in color and shape make an interesting painting. You end up thanking Thiebaud for reminding you how full of variety the world really is.

Thiebaud especially loves the craft of painting. He is a terrific craftsman. Whatever he asks paint to do, it will do, and come up looking effortless after it's done. The surface of his pictures is dense and smooth, and it looks as though he never reworks the paint. Thiebaud's art isn't hit-or-miss, however. All his lines and colors have a purpose. His creamy pie slices and cakes are drawn with a strict, purposeful geometry.

TIME TO CONNECT

- **Now, you are the critic. Review the artworks on this page and write a critical review, making sure to strongly support your thoughts with specific references to the art.**
- **Proofread your work with a partner. Besides checking for spelling, punctuation, and grammar, be sure to express your opinions with supporting details.**

TIME TO CONNECT

Have students revise their drafts for coherence, progression, and logical support of ideas. With a partner, have them discuss these editing questions:

- Which sentences express opinions?
- Do facts and details support those opinions?
- What other facts and details could be added to support each opinion more clearly?

Chapter 4 Review

BUILDING VOCABULARY

Number a sheet of paper from 1 to 10. After each number, write the term from the list that matches each description below.

abstract	content
aesthetics	credit line
aesthetic view	nonobjective
art critic	point of view
composition	subject

1. The message, idea, or feeling expressed by a work of art.
2. A person whose job is studying, understanding, and judging works of art.
3. Art with a recognizable subject that is shown in an unrealistic manner.
4. Art with no readily identifiable subjects or objects.
5. An image viewers can easily identify.
6. The way the principles of art are used to organize the elements of art.
7. The study of the nature of beauty and art.
8. A listing of important facts about an artwork.
9. The angle from which the viewer sees the scene in an artwork.
10. An idea or school of thought on what is most important in a work of art.

REVIEWING ART FACTS

Number a sheet of paper from 11 to 15. Answer each question in a complete sentence.

11. Why do students of art usually accept more than one aesthetic view?
12. What are the four steps of art criticism?
13. What kinds of art criticism questions join an art element with an art principle?
14. Why is it impossible to measure the success of a nonobjective artwork in terms of subject?
15. When examining a nonobjective artwork, what is identified during description?

CROSS-CURRICULUM CONNECTIONS

16. **Language Arts.** Imagine that two critics are examining the same work of art. Each comes up with a different interpretation. Write a paragraph describing the reasons that you think might explain this.
17. **Language Arts.** Review the artworks in this chapter. Select one that might be a good illustration for a short story or poem. Write the story or poem.

Web Museum Activity

The Metropolitan Museum of Art, New York, New York

Take a closer look at the history and techniques behind various artworks. Visit the Metropolitan Museum of Art by clicking on the museum's link at **art.glencoe.com**. Discover the story behind these images.

Write a brief summary of what you learned about two of the artworks. What were the most interesting facts? Knowing this information, do you look at those two artworks differently? Explain your answer.

ANSWERS TO Chapter 4 Review

Building Vocabulary

1. content
2. art critic
3. abstract
4. nonobjective
5. subject
6. composition
7. aesthetics
8. credit line
9. point of view
10. aesthetic view

Reviewing Art Facts

11. All three aesthetic views have merit.
12. Describing, analyzing, interpreting, and judging.
13. Questions involving analysis of a work.
14. Works of this type have no recognizable subject.
15. During this stage, one identifies the art elements used.

Cross-Curriculum Connections

16. Responses will vary, but should include that interpretation is largely a matter of personal experience.
17. Students' short stories or poems should reveal a clear description of the selected artwork.

Web Museum Activity

Before you have students go online, visit the Web site to preview the museum's online content, collection, and any online exhibit that might be of interest. Students should include in their summary a clear description of the two artworks and include facts about those works of art. Summaries should also include a critique of those artworks and explain how they view the artworks after learning the facts behind those works.

Chapter Resources

Features	Standards for Chapter: National	Standards for Chapter: State/Local	Reproducible Masters
Quick Write *page 81* TIME ART SCENE "The Great Restoration" *page 100* ***Web Museum Activity*** *page 79*	**1.** (a, b) **2.** (a, b) **3.** (a, b) **4.** (a, b, c) **5.** (b, c) **6.** (a, b)		Guided Reading and Practice 5–1 Application Activity 5–2, 5–8 Enrichment Activity 5–3, 5–7 Cross-Curriculum Activity 5–4 Studio Activity 5–5, 5–6 Artist Profile 5–9 Historical and Cultural Heritage 5–10, 5–11 Lesson Plans

Lesson Resources

Lessons	Standards per Lesson: National	Standards per Lesson: State/Local	Reproducible Masters
1 ***Art of Long Ago*** *(pages 82–85)*	2b, 4a, 4b, 4c		Application Activity 5–2
2 ***Egyptian Tomb Painting*** *(pages 86–87)*	1a, 1b, 2a, 3b, 5c		Enrichment Activity 5–3
3 ***Eastern Art*** *(pages 88–89)*	1a, 4b, 5b		Cross-Curriculum Activity 5–4 Studio Activity 5–5, 5–6
4 ***Making a Relief Sculpture*** *(pages 90–91)*	1a, 1b, 2a, 5b, 5c		Enrichment Activity 5–7
5 ***Art of the Middle Ages and Renaissance*** *(pages 92–93)*	1a, 2b, 4c		Application Activity 5–8 Artist Profile 5–9
6 ***Creating a Diorama*** *(pages 94–95)*	1a, 1b, 2a, 3a		
7 ***Art of the Nineteenth and Twentieth Centuries*** *(pages 96–97)*	4a, 5b		Historical and Cultural Heritage 5–10
8 ***Using Abstraction in Art*** *(pages 98–99)*	1a, 1b, 2a, 2b, 4c		Historical and Cultural Heritage 5–11

Assessment	Technology
Testing Program: Chapter Test 5–12 Portfolio and Assessment Techniques	Artsource Performing Arts Package, Ballet Folklórico de Mexico (DVD or VHS Segment 1) National Museum of Women in the Arts Interactive Lesson Planner Fine Art Transparency CC-5, Temple at Angkor Wat Fine Art Transparency 5, *Janitor* by Duane Hanson

Activities/Features
Time & Place: Roman Empire A.D. 100–130
Evaluating Your Work Reflective Thinking Visual Art Journal
Studio Activity: Creating a Japanese Drawing
Evaluating Your Work Studio Option Visual Art Journal
Studio Activity: Making a Stained-Glass Window
Evaluating Your Work Studio Option Visual Art Journal
Meet the Artist: Claude Monet
Evaluating Your Work Portfolio Ideas Art Online

KEY TO ABILITY LEVELS

Teaching strategies have been coded.

- L1 Activities for all students; teacher direction required
- L2 Activities for average to above-average students; some teacher direction needed
- L3 Activities for students able and willing to work independently
- ELL English Language Learner activities

FEATURED ARTISTS

- Exekias
- Orazio Gentileschi
- Helen Lundeberg
- Claude Monet
- Elizabeth Murray
- Maruyama Okyo
- Jan Steen
- Jan Vermeer

FINE ART PRINTS

Fine Art Print 9, *Portrait of Theresa, Countess Kinsky* by Marie-Louise Elisabeth Vigée-Lebrun

Timesaving Technology

Interactive Lesson Planner

Make planning easy. Use this interactive software to organize your week, month, semester, or year and access all *Introducing Art* reproducible resources.

KEY TO LESSON RESOURCES

- Narrative Lesson
- Studio Lesson

Chapter 5

Art Through the Ages

(pages 80–101)

Chapter Overview

Having a general understanding of art history is fundamental to students' appreciation of art. In this chapter, students will look at the effects of time and place on artists and their works. They will begin to see the changes and similarities among artworks, cultures, and art movements through the ages.

Discussing the Artwork

Focus On ◆ **Figure 5–1** Most of Jan Vermeer's paintings portray people in interior settings. This painting brings you right into a Dutch home of the seventeenth century. All his works are admired for the sensitivity with which he depicted the effects of light and color in his images. Have students look for the light streaming through the window, the foreground shapes, and the shadowed areas. His use of light and color creates a poetic quality to the scene illustrated. Ask students:

- What mood is the painting trying to communicate?
- Describe the scene in your own words.

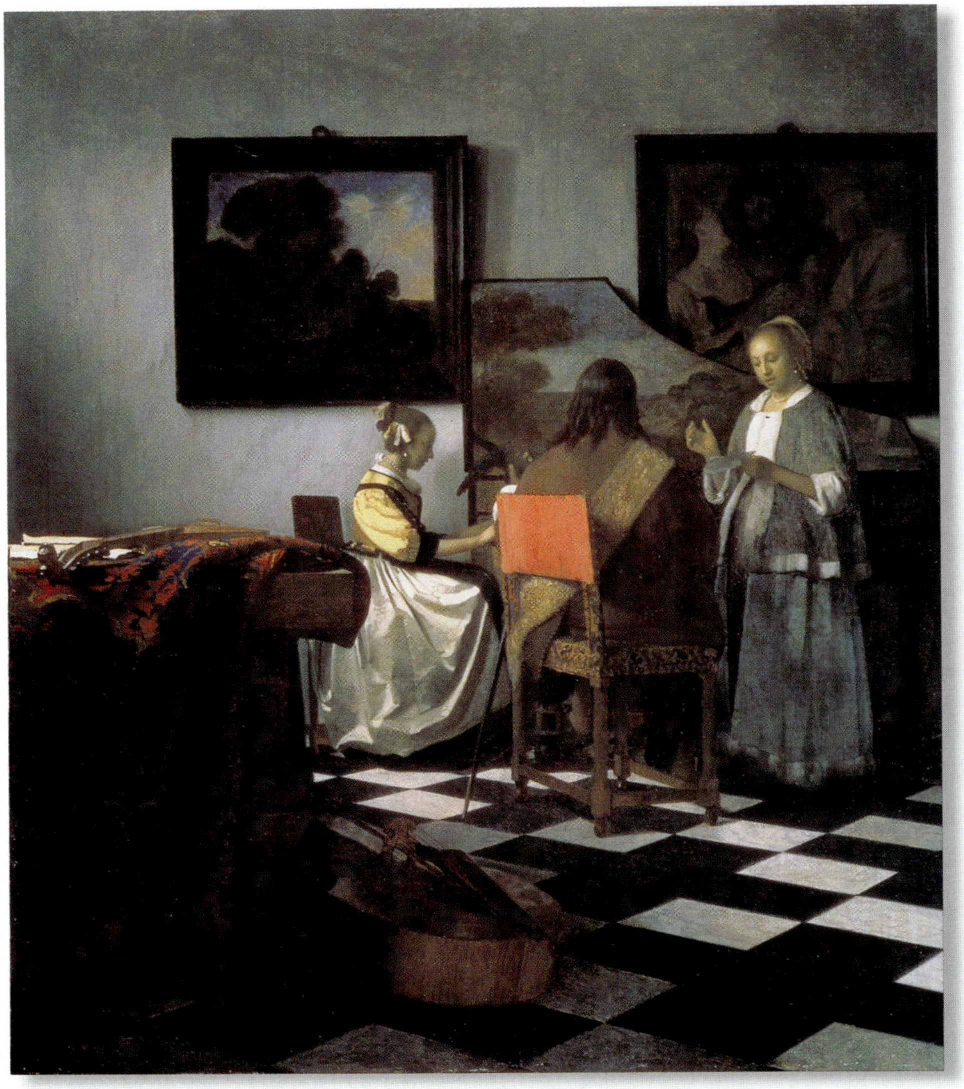

Focus On ◆ **Figure 5–1** **This painting brings you right into a Dutch home of the 1600s. Notice the young woman playing the virginal, an early kind of piano, and her two companions.**

Jan Vermeer. *The Concert.* c. 1665–66. Oil on canvas. 61 × 71.1 cm (24 × 28″). Isabella Stewart Gardner Museum, Boston, Massachusetts.

ART SOURCE

Linking to the Performing Arts

Dance Choreographer Amalia Hernández researches the dances and music of the various cultural groups that have contributed to Mexican culture. "Los Mitos," part of a suite of dances from *Los Concheros,* grew out of ancient Aztec myths. Have students explore how dance can express ancient traditions and beliefs in the **Performing Arts Handbook** on page 314. To enrich student understanding, play the DVD or videotape (segment 1) and audio CD (track 1) in the **Performing Arts Package.**

Chapter 5

Art Through the Ages

"All art is an individual's expression of a culture. Cultures differ, so art looks different."

—Henry Glassie, art scholar

Walk into this chapter as if you were walking through time. Try to imagine yourself in ancient Egypt, Greece, or Rome. Travel to the Far East or to Africa, and let the art tell you about the people of each period. Move on to the nineteenth and twentieth centuries, and see how the advancement of science opened new ideas to the artists. This chapter will help you understand people of all ages through their art.

After completing this chapter, you will able to:

- Explain why art history is important.
- Compare specific artworks from a variety of cultures.
- Understand the goals of different cultures and art movements.
- Create artworks of different cultures and times.

Quick Write

Interpreting the Quote
Read the quote, and then look again at **Figure 5–1.** Write a descriptive paragraph about what life might have been like in Holland in the 1600s.

KEY TERMS

- **art historians**
- **applied art**
- **fine art**
- **bust**
- **hieroglyphic**
- **symbol**
- **contours**
- **painted screen**
- **architecture**
- **Renaissance**
- **diorama**
- **art movement**

Quick Write

INTERPRETING THE QUOTE Have students read the quote and complete the Quick Write activity. Students should write a paragraph describing life in Holland in the 1600s. They should also include information about the Dutch culture at that time and its influence on daily life.

Chapter Motivator

Tell students that in this chapter they will have an opportunity to get a behind-the-scenes view of art—the story behind much of the art created over many centuries and all over the world. As they take this journey, encourage students to ask questions about art, artists, and their time and place.

Art Online

Visit **art.glencoe.com**, the Web site for Glencoe's art programs. This site offers insightful resources for you and your students. Explore the many resources this site has to offer, such as:

- Art Advocacy
- Career Corner
- General Student Resources
- Professional Development

National Standards for Arts Education

This chapter addresses the following National Standards for the Visual Arts:

1. (a, b) **4.** (a, b, c)
2. (a, b) **5.** (b, c)
3. (a, b) **6.** (a, b)

Art of Long Ago

(pages 82–85)

1 Focus

Objectives

After completing this lesson, students will be able to:

- Understand the work of an art historian.
- Describe and compare the styles of ancient Egyptian, Greek, and Roman art.
- Differentiate between fine art and applied art.

2 Teach

Motivator

Write the word *civilization* on the board and ask students to explain what this means. Tell students that civilization is a stage of development in which people gather to form towns, conduct trade, and generally try to make life safer and more productive. Some historians believe that civilization and recorded history began between 4000 and 3000 B.C. in several areas including the Near East, India, and China. Have students find these locations on a world map.

LESSON 1

Art of Long Ago

No artist works completely alone. Artists of each age, rather, study and learn from works created in ages past. The same may be said of **art historians.** These are *people who study art of different ages and cultures.* Like art critics, art historians examine and analyze art. Unlike critics, art historians are not content to look only at artworks. Their job is to look beyond them. They record milestones in art and changes in the way artists work.

In this chapter, you will journey back through the ages. You will learn about some of these milestones and changes. Your journey will begin with a look at art of earlier times.

Art of Ancient Egypt

Have you ever followed a brook or stream to its source? If we follow the long, twisting "stream" of art history to its source, we end up on the banks of an actual river. That river is the Nile. The time is 5,000 years ago. The place is Egypt. Powerful kings called pharaohs ruled. Farming and trade thrived. So did art.

Rules of the Egyptian Artist

The Egyptians built mighty temples and monuments. It was with an eye toward decorating these structures that much of their art was created. Study the relief carving in **Figure 5–2.** This work probably once graced a pharaoh's tomb. The subject is the Egyptian god of learning. The figure has a human body and the head of a bird, specifically an ibis.

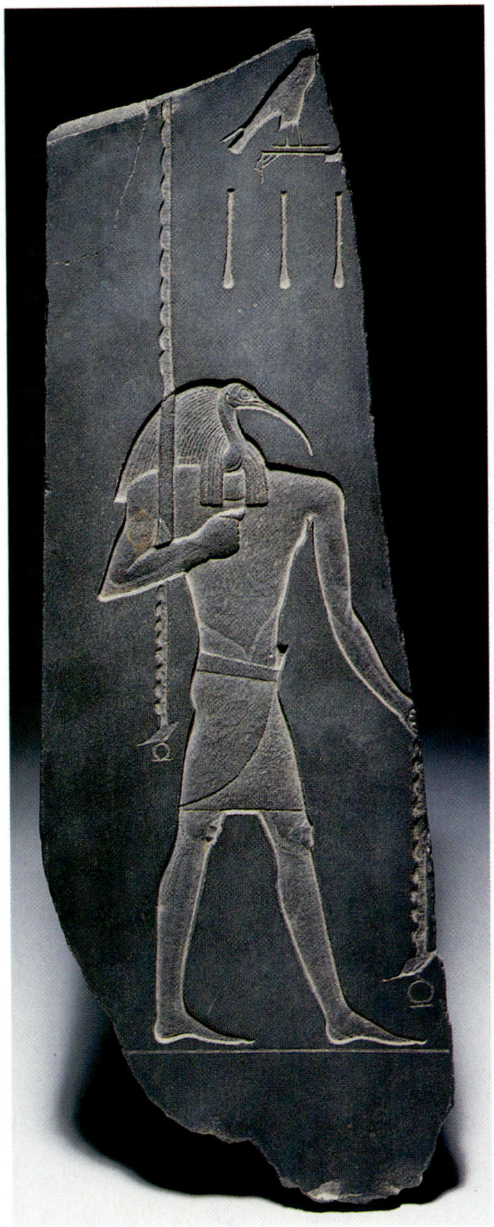

◆ **Figure 5–2** **Look at the subject of this sculpture. What does it reveal about the Egyptians' system of beliefs?**

Egyptian. *Thoth, God of Learning and Patron of Scribes.* 26th Dynasty, 663–525 B.C. (Late period). Slate relief. 36.5 × 12 × 1 cm (14⅜ × 4¾ × 7/16"). Dallas Museum of Art, Dallas, Texas. Gift of Elsa von Seggern.

CURRICULUM CONNECTIONS

Social Studies Many students think about the pyramids when asked about Egypt. Explain that the pyramids are just one aspect of the ancient Egyptian culture. Building these huge structures required the efforts of 100,000 men for thirty years. Workers labored to stack 2.3 million blocks of stone to heights of 480 feet. The stone blocks, each averaging 2.5 tons, were fitted precisely together and covered with a smooth layer of polished white limestone. Explain that the pyramids were built to house the dead bodies of the pharaoh, the queen, and their immediate family, the most important people in Egyptian society.

This long-beaked creature was one of many animals the Egyptians worshiped. They believed the ibis possessed special powers.

Did you notice anything unusual about the way the figure is shown? Some body parts, including the head and arms, appear as they would if they were viewed from the side. Others, such as the shoulders, are shown as if they are seen from the front. This odd mix-and-match might seem at first to be a mistake. In fact, it is common to Egyptian art. It reflects certain strict rules Egyptian artists were forced to follow. The rules required that each body part be shown from its most familiar angle. What parts besides those mentioned above are shown as side views? Which are treated as views from the front?

Art of Ancient Greece

While Egypt was still at its peak, another great empire took root some 500 miles to the north. This was Greece. Greece reached its peak during the fifth and fourth centuries B.C. This was a time known as the Golden Age. It was called the Golden Age because it produced influential writers and thinkers. It produced important political leaders. It also produced great artists.

Greek Vases

One of the most powerful leaders and influential thinkers of the Golden Age was a man named Pericles (**pehr**-ih-kleez). Pericles loved beauty and preached its importance. The aesthetic ideals Pericles held sacred may be seen in everything the Greeks created. Beauty can be found in the perfectly proportioned temples of the period. It is reflected in the idealized sculptures of gods and athletes. It also appears in carefully designed vases such as the one in **Figure 5–3.**

Examine this art object. Vases like this are examples of **applied art.** This is *art made to be useful as well as visually pleasing.* Applied art is usually seen in contrast with **fine art,** or *art made to be enjoyed visually, not used.* In this program, you will see many examples of each type of art.

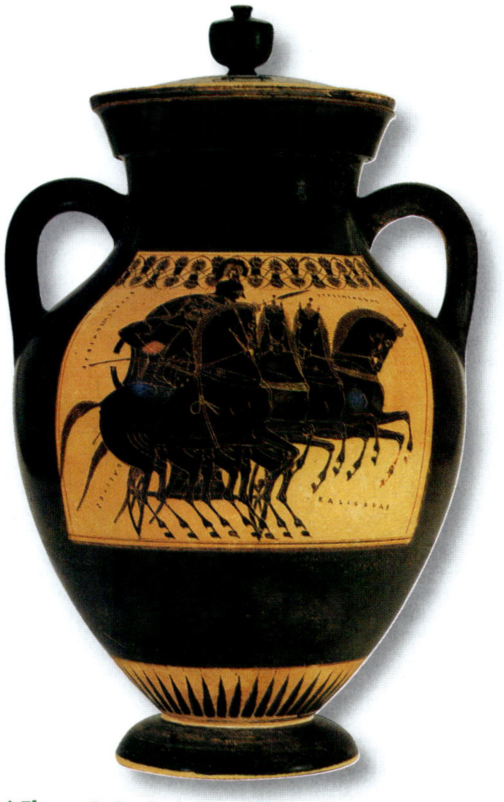

◆Figure 5–3 **Analyze the interdependence of the art element line and the principle movement in this vase painting.**

Greek. Exekias. *Quadriga Wheeling Right.* Slip-decorated earthenware. 46.2 cm (18 3/16″). Toledo Museum of Art, Toledo, Ohio.

Like other Greek vases, this one is remarkable for the beauty of its form. It is equally noteworthy for the quality of the painting that decorates it. The painting was done by Exekias (ex-**zee**-kee-uhs), the most famous of Greek vase painters. It shows a chariot led by a team of four spirited horses. Notice the air of excitement in the work. What art elements contribute to this feeling? What principles of art are used to organize them?

Aesthetics

Have students draw a human figure and compare it to the relief carving in **Figure 5–2.** How does their figure differ from the Egyptian figure? Have a student pose like the Egyptian figure; point out how such a pose reveals all major parts of the body. Explain that Egyptian paintings and sculptures were created as substitutes for the body; no major parts could be hidden from view. Ask students: Do you think this should be taken into account when judging Egyptian paintings and sculptures of the human figure? Explain. L1 ELL

Understanding Art History

Review with students the four art-criticism questions. Tell them that examining works of art from an art history point of view requires a similar series of questions. However, these questions are asked to gain information *about* the work of art and the artist who created it. They are:

- Who created the artwork, and when and where?
- Are there stylistic features in this work that are similar to features found in other works?
- How was the artist influenced by time and place?
- Does the artwork have historical importance?

Have students use these art-history questions to examine and compare the three artworks represented in this lesson. Provide examples of other ancient Egyptian, Greek, and Roman art for comparison. L1

TEACHER TO TEACHER

Art History Help students use detailed questions to gain information about the history of a specific artwork. For example, use the following art-history questions to lead a class discussion of the Greek vase by Exekias shown in **Figure 5–3.**

- Where was this work created?
- What style of vase painting is represented? Was this an early or a late style of vase painting?
- What does this vase tell you about the artists who perfected this art form?
- Why are works like these historically important?

LESSON 1

2 Teach *(continued)*

Historical/Cultural Heritage

Explain to students that the painted vessels of ancient Greece are generally called vases, but they were intended to hold more than just flowers. The Greeks designed each vase to serve a specific purpose, creating shapes to fill every possible need, from large storage jars to delicate drinking cups. Ask students to research the design and purpose of vases and similar vessels in other cultures. Have students compare artworks from a variety of cultures. Bring in photocopies of examples from China, Australia, Native American cultures, and African cultures. L2

Understanding Art History

Point out the locations of Greece and Rome on a map. Tell students that the Western world owes much to the ancient Greeks and Romans. The Greeks made the first recorded contribution to Western philosophy, science, and art. The Romans' interest in engineering, law, and government built on the Greeks' contributions. Ask students to discuss how such areas of interest and expertise could influence artists and their works. L1

Art Criticism

Ask students to explain how any examination of a Greek vase painting is really an examination of two works at the same time. Would it be possible to judge one of these works a success and the other a failure? If so, how would students judge the complete work of art? Students should recognize that a thorough critique of a Greek vase must take into account the vase itself as well as the painting on it. L1

Art of Ancient Rome

Despite its greatness, Greece suffered from fighting within the empire. As a nation divided, it was doomed. After 1,300 years of almost continuous strife, Greece fell. The people who conquered it were the Romans.

Although Greek power came to an end as Rome grew in strength, Greek influence continued on. The Romans admired Greek art. Following their conquest of Greece in 146 B.C., they shipped many Greek art treasures to their homeland. They also hired many Greek artists to work for them.

Roman Portrait Sculpture

Roman artists were skilled at creating lifelike sculptures. Like the Greeks, they made statues of important people such as rulers. Unlike the Greeks, who always showed the entire figure in their sculptures, Roman artists

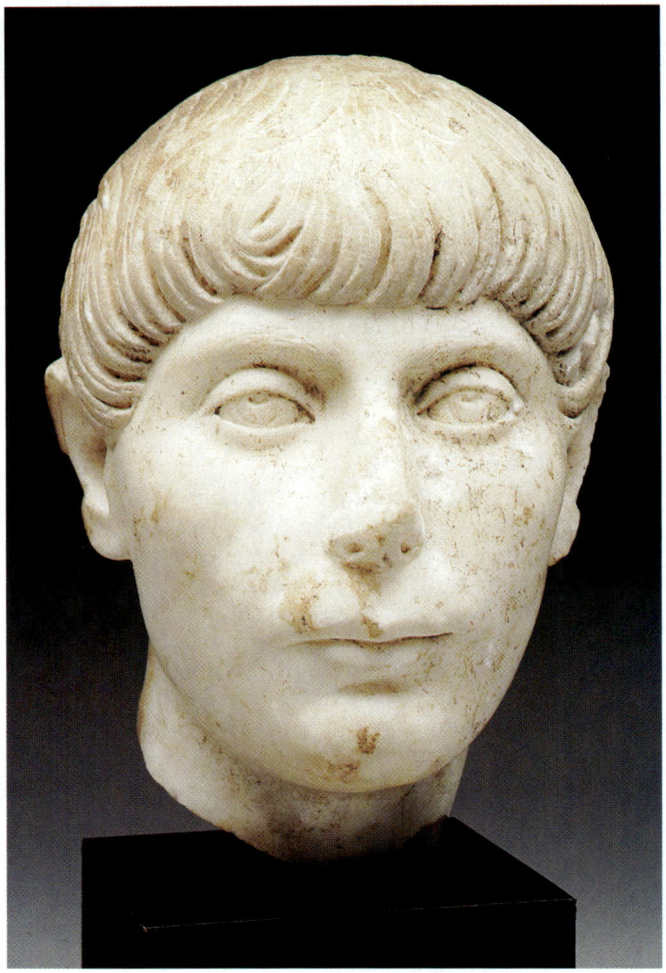

◆ **Figure 5–4** **Describe the details in this sculpture. What qualities attribute to its lifelike features?**

Roman. Head of a Young Man. A.D. 100–130. Marble. 22.5 × 16.5 cm (8⅞ × 6½″). Dallas Museum of Art, Dallas, Texas. Anonymous gift in memory of Edward Marcus.

MORE ABOUT...

Greek Vase Painting Unfortunately, no examples of Greek painting still exist. However, we can get an idea of what they may have looked like by examining images found on Greek vases that have survived. Early Greek vase paintings of people and the Greek gods were little more than stick figures. The style evolved until the figures became more lifelike and lively.

instead focused on heads and busts. A **bust** is *a sculpture that shows a person's head, shoulders, and upper chest.*

Many wealthy Romans had busts made of themselves and their families. These were placed in the subject's home. One such portrait sculpture appears in **Figure 5–4.** It is a marble head of a young man. Clearly, the artist made no effort to flatter the sitter. Rather, the sculpture captures in great detail the likeness of a real person. Inspect this work. In what ways is it similar to other portrait sculptures you have seen? In what ways is it different? Would a critic taking the content view praise this work? Why or why not?

Check Your Understanding

1. What is the job of an art historian?
2. Why did Egyptian artists always show the human figure in the same unusual way?
3. When did ancient Greece reach its peak? When and by whom was it conquered?
4. Compare Roman sculptures of people with Greek sculptures of people? How do they differ?
5. What is the difference between applied art and fine art?

Time & Place

Roman Empire A.D. 100–130

Historical connection. In the long and fascinating history of ancient Rome, the years between A.D. 100 and 130 fall in the middle of the period known as the Early Roman Empire. This was a time of peace and prosperity. This period also saw a great expansion of the Roman Empire. During this time, Rome was ruled by a series of emperors.

The first of these emperors was Trajan, who ruled from 98 to 117. During Trajan's rule, many new public buildings were constructed and the empire was expanded. Following Trajan was the emperor Hadrian, who ruled the Roman Empire from 117 to 138. Hadrian also undertook many building projects, including completion of the Pantheon and the construction of Hadrian's Wall—a stone wall in northern Britain.

During this period, Roman art was influenced by the styles and techniques used by the ancient Greeks. Roman art was concerned primarily with showing man and his achievements. Important events, such as military victories, were commemorated in paintings and sculptures. Portrait sculptures, such as the one in **Figure 5–4,** were also common.

Compare Figure 5–4 with the Greek vase painting in Figure 5–3. What cultural differences do you notice in these artworks?

Time & Place

Roman Empire A.D. 100–130

Figure 5–4 is typical of Roman art; it is a bust that captures the likeness of a real person. The vase in **Figure 5–3** is noted for the beauty of its form and of the figures painted on it, which is characteristic of Greek art.

3 Assess

Self-Assessment

Have students complete the **Check Your Understanding** questions on this page. Answers are provided below.

Reteaching

Ask students to give examples of the differences between fine art and applied art. L1

Enrichment

GREEK ART Invite students to respond to a classmate's comment that Greek vase paintings lacked interest and excitement. Ask them what they would point to in Exekias's artwork; for example, to convince others that Greek vase paintings are worthy of close examination. L2

4 Close

Have students explain what an art historian does.

Answers to Check Your Understanding

1. An art historian studies art of different ages and cultures.
2. Ancient Egyptian artists were required to follow certain strict rules in portraying the human form.
3. The ancient Greek civilization reached its peak during the fourth and fifth centuries. It was conquered by the Romans in 146 B.C.
4. Greek artists always showed the entire human figure, but Roman artists often created portrait heads and busts.
5. Applied art is art made to be useful as well as visually pleasing. Fine art is art made to be enjoyed visually, not used.

LESSON 2

Egyptian Tomb Painting

(pages 86–87)
Lesson Time: 2 hours

1 Focus

Objectives

After completing this lesson, students will be able to:

- Express a variety of design ideas for an Egyptian tomb painting.
- Demonstrate technical skills effectively by using a variety of art media and materials to produce an Egyptian tomb painting.
- Conduct an in-progress analysis of their artwork.

Supplies

Refer to **What You Will Need** in the Student Edition.

2 Teach

Motivator

Bring in or create a simple example of pictographic writing to share with students. Ask them to try writing a few sentences using mostly simple pictures. Have them try to read each other's sentences. Point out that the ancient Egyptians also used symbols and pictures in their writing called hieroglyphics.

LESSON 2

Egyptian Tomb Painting

Look back at the Egyptian relief sculpture in Figure 5–2 on page 82. This work teaches us about the ancient Egyptian system of beliefs. The same may be said of the painting in **Figure 5–5.** The work is from the tomb of an Egyptian pharaoh named Sethos. He is the figure pictured on the right. With him is the goddess Hathor. According to Egyptian myth, Hathor was the goddess of the sky. She was also queen of heaven. It appears that Hathor is about to take the pharaoh's hand, as if to lead him somewhere. Where might she be preparing to lead the fallen pharaoh?

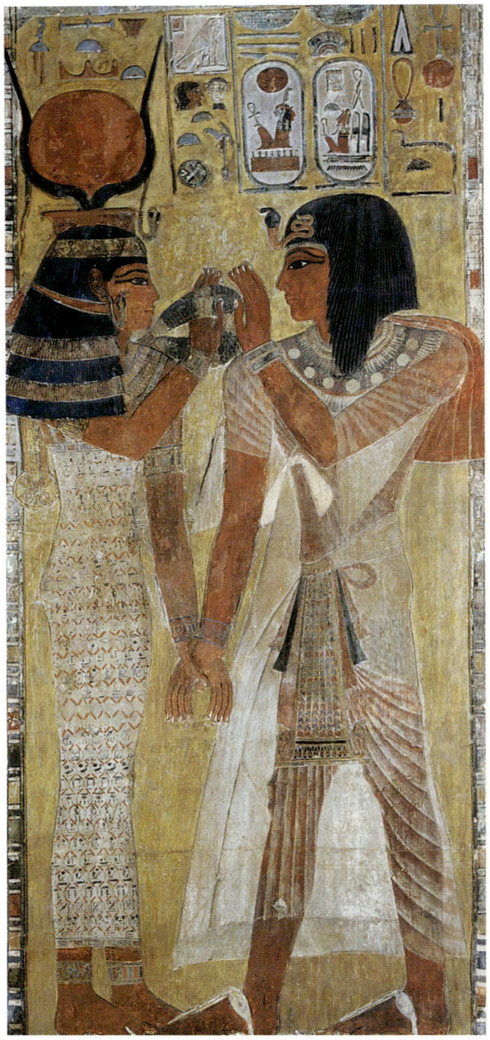

◆ **Figure 5–5** **Analyze the use of balance and texture in this work. What makes you think these figures are important?**

Egyptian. *The Goddess Hathor Places the Magic Collar on Sethos I.* Thebes, 19th Dynasty. c. 1303–1290 B.C. Painted bas-relief. 226.5 cm (89⅛"). The Louvre, Paris, France.

Look more closely at this painting. Did you notice the abstract shapes in the rounded boxes? They appear in the picture above the head of Sethos. These are examples of **hieroglyphic** (hy-ruh-**glif**-ik). This is *an early form of picture writing.* Perhaps these "words" identified the object that the goddess is handing to the pharaoh.

What You Will Learn

In this lesson, you will design and create an Egyptian tomb painting. The subject will be a well-known figure from American or world history. In portraying this figure, you will try to show his or her character. You will also follow the rules of Egyptian art. You will use a repeating pattern for the figure's clothing, as in Figure 5–5. In the background, you will include hieroglyphics. These will be made up of objects that help define the person's identity. You will complete your tomb painting using tempera paints.

What You Will Need

- Pencil and sheets of sketch paper
- White drawing paper, 12 x 18 inches
- Fine-tipped black marker
- Tempera paints
- Mixing tray
- Medium and fine brushes
- Paper towels

MORE ABOUT...

Egyptian Pyramids The Egyptians thought the huge pyramids they built would protect the mummified bodies of their dead rulers for eternity. However, they were wrong. The fortress-like tombs were often quickly broken into and robbed of its treasures. In fact, a written account exists of eight tomb robbers who were caught, tried, and found guilty. They were imprisoned until the pharaoh chose a suitable punishment; their ultimate fate is unknown. When King Tutankhamen's tomb was discovered undisturbed in 1922, it was a rare find indeed. The tomb had remained intact for more than thirty-two centuries.

What You Will Do

1. With a partner, brainstorm possible historical figures as subjects for your tomb painting. Choose a person you know a lot about. Think about objects and visual symbols that help define the person's identity. A **symbol** is *an image used to stand for a quality or idea.* If you chose George Washington, for example, your symbols might include an ax and a cherry tree. Jot down notes about your subject and symbols.
2. Study the figures in Figure 5–5. Notice the position of the head, shoulders, chest, arms, legs, and feet. Make pencil sketches of your subject. Follow the same formula the ancient Egyptian artist used.
3. Conduct an in-progress analysis of your work. Transfer your best sketch to the drawing paper. Make your figure large enough to fill the page. In the background, draw boxes with rounded corners. These are to contain your hieroglyphics. In the boxes, draw abstract visual symbols based on the notes you made.
4. Complete your painting by mixing tints and shades of tempera paint. Apply the colors to your figure and background objects. Carefully color the motifs in your pattern.
5. Switch to fine-tipped black marker. Lightly retrace the **contours,** or *outlines and surface ridges,* of important shapes, including body parts. Create a pattern on your subject's clothing.
6. When your painting is dry, display it alongside those of fellow students. Challenge classmates to identify the subject of your work.

Evaluating Your Work

- **Describe** Is your painting based on a figure from history? Did you include symbols that would help your viewer pinpoint the person's identity?
- **Analyze** Did you follow the rules of Egyptian art for representing human body parts? Did you use a repeating pattern to decorate the person's clothing?
- **Interpret** Did you capture the character of your figure? Were classmates able to identify your person?
- **Judge** Do you consider your painting successful? Why or why not?

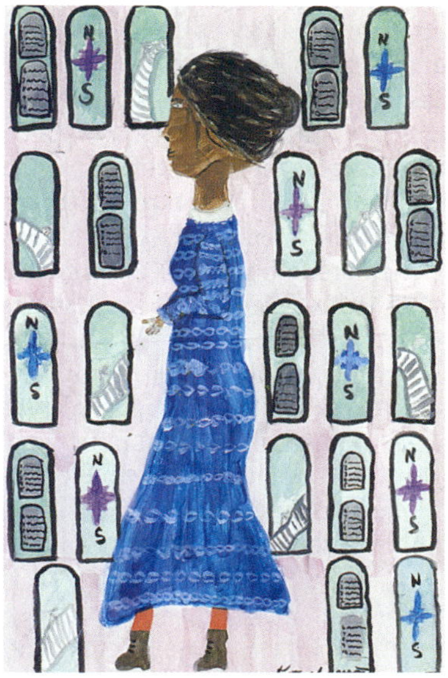

◆ **Figure 5–6** Student work. Egyptian tomb painting.

Reflective Thinking

Critical Response. Analyze the original artworks of your peers. Study the Egyptian tomb painting they created and form conclusions about historical contexts. For example, which historical figure did they use as their subject? What symbols did they use?

Visual Art Journal

Describe the figure you portrayed in your Egyptian tomb painting. Explain why you chose this person. What details did you use to show his or her character?

Studio Skills

To demonstrate rules of Egyptian art, have students draw and cut from colored construction paper 15 simple shapes representing the following:
Seen from the front: upper body
Seen in profile: head, lower body, and two each of upper legs, lower legs, upper arms, lower arms, hands, and feet. Have students cut the shapes to create a figure that will fill a 12 x 18-inch sheet of construction paper. Show how these 15 shapes can be assembled in different ways to show movement by bending the arms at the elbows and the legs at the knees. Once the shapes have been glued in place students may use a combination of crayon and smaller bits of construction paper to add details and Egyptian-style garments. If eyes are added, they must be shown as if viewed from the front. L1 ELL

Visual Art Journal

Ask students to describe in detail a variety of practical applications for design ideas based on their Egyptian tomb painting.

3 Assess

Peer Assessment

Have students analyze the Egyptian tomb painting of their peers to form conclusions about historical and cultural contexts.

4 Close

Guide students in a summary of the ancient Egyptian figure-painting style.

Resources Beyond the Classroom

Festivals and Fairs Festivals and fairs allow fellow artists to explore the arts of other countries and other times. Ethnic and religious festivals, such as Greek Orthodox fairs, Native American powwows, and Latino/Hispanic festivals, show how various cultures create and use art. Some festivals may celebrate the Chinese New Year, while others may host a St. Patrick's Day parade. These events allow students to see artists and craftspeople at work. Other kinds of fairs are also becoming popular, in particular medieval or Renaissance festivals, modeled on societies of centuries ago. Authentic foods and crafts are re-created at these events.

Eastern Art

(pages 88–89)

1 Focus

Objectives

After completing this lesson, students will be able to:

- Appreciate the artistic traditions of ancient Asian civilizations.
- Define *Hinduism* and *Buddhism.*
- Create a drawing of an image from memory.

SUPPLIES
- Drawing paper
- Pencils, colored pencils, oil pastels

2 Teach

Motivator

Ask students to think of a river they have seen or learned about. Ask: What is the river like? How do people use it or benefit from it? Point out that rivers have always played an important part in the development of civilization. For example, fertile river valleys were productive farmland. Rivers also provided a means of transportation. Have students discuss other ways that rivers have affected civilization.

LESSON 3

Eastern Art

No tour of the ancient art world would be complete without a swing through Asia. Here, halfway around the globe from the great temples and pyramids of Egypt, other mighty empires rose and fell. Each left behind an artistic tradition as rich as those of the Greeks and Romans.

In this lesson, you will read about two of those cultures. You will also view some of the art treasures they left behind.

ART OF ANCIENT INDIA

In the mid-1800s, railroad workers digging in the Indus River valley of present-day Pakistan made a remarkable discovery. They unearthed bits and pieces of a lost city. Archaeologists later pieced together this ancient puzzle. Their explorations revealed that the city was once the center of a river civilization that had existed some 4,500 years earlier. It had achieved a splendor at least as great as that of ancient Egypt.

Like the Egyptians, the people of the Indus River valley worshiped animals and the forces of nature. These beliefs were later combined with others to form the foundation of the religion Hinduism (**hin**-doo-iz-uhm). Today, this faith has 700 million followers.

Sculpture

Among the gifts passed down by the Indus River valley civilization was a knowledge of bronze casting. This sculpting method was used by later inhabitants of the region to create the work in **Figure 5–7.** The subject of this sculpture is Hanuman, king of the monkeys. According to Hindu myth, Hanuman helped the god Rama rescue Rama's wife from a demon's evil clutches.

Like other characters in Hindu legend, Hanuman represents a human virtue (**vur**-chew). A *virtue* is a positive quality, in this case loyalty.

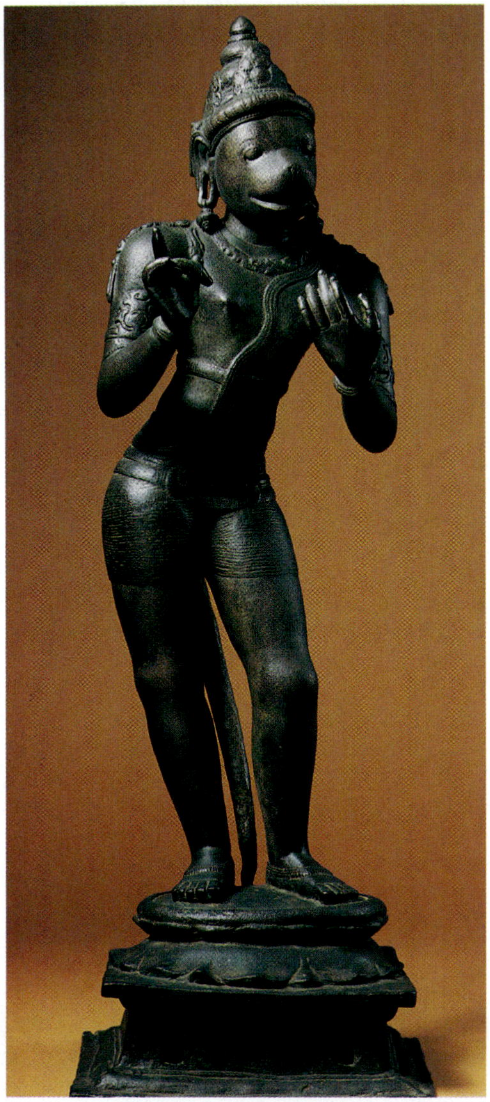

◆ **Figure 5–7** **Notice that the creature has the body of a human but a monkey's head and tail. What does Hanuman's posture tell you about his character?**

Indian, Tamil Nadu. *Standing Hanuman.* Chola Period. Eleventh century. Bronze. 64.5 cm (25⅜"). The Metropolitan Museum of Art, New York, New York. Purchase, funds and bequests from various donors.

CURRICULUM CONNECTIONS

SOCIAL STUDIES All of the early civilizations began in river valleys, where the soil was fertile and the water supply abundant. Among the first was Sumer, located in the lower part of the Tigris-Euphrates Valley (present-day Iraq). Tiny Sumerian farming villages had formed in the valley by about 5000 B.C.; by about 3500 B.C., many villages had grown to the size of small cities. The Sumerians developed the first-known system of written language, called cuneiform writing. They also invented the potter's wheel and produced decorative pottery. They made jewelry, metal ware, musical instruments, and glass items.

Art of Ancient Japan

The civilization of the Indus River valley is among the earliest on record. Evidence of an even older culture has been found on the island nation of Japan. This culture is believed to have sprung to life around 5000 B.C.

As with Indian art, the art of ancient Japan was inspired by religion. Interestingly, one of the religions that shaped much of early Japanese art began in India and then came to Japan through China in A.D. 552. That religion is Buddhism (**boo**-diz-uhm). Buddhism was an outgrowth of Hinduism. It emphasizes physical and spiritual discipline as the means for reaching a state of inner peace.

Screen Painting

One common form of Japanese artistic expression is shown in **Figure 5–8.** Each object is a **painted screen.** This is *an art object used as a wall or room divider.* Do you recall the name for art that is both useful and pleasing to the eye?

Look carefully at these screens. They show two creatures, one real and one mythical. Both have symbolic value. The tiger was believed to chase evil. The dragon was thought to bring luck.

Studio Activity

Creating a Japanese Drawing

Creative expression. Bring an object of nature, such as a leaf or stone. Silently study the object from different angles. Examine its lines, form, texture, and color. Place the object out of sight. Using black or colored pencils, create the image of the object that remains in your mind.

PORTFOLIO

Write a short paragraph explaining whether you think you were successful at creating the image.

Check Your Understanding

1. How was the Indus River valley civilization discovered?
2. For what is this civilization most remembered?

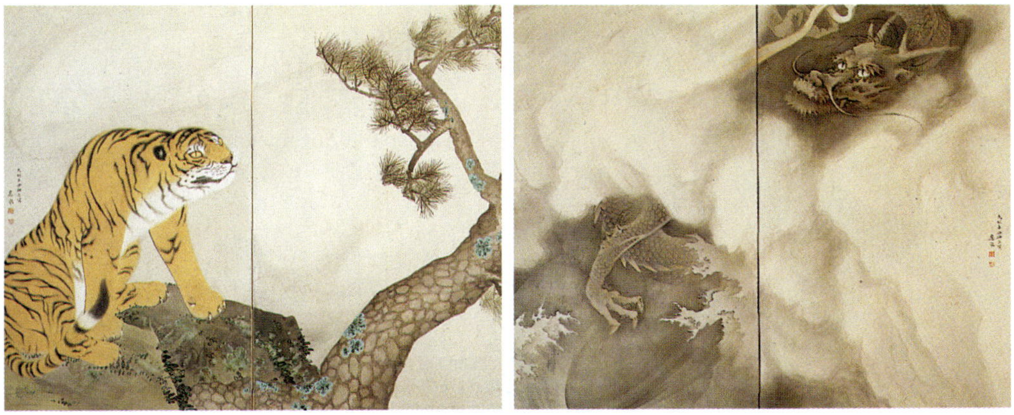

◆ **Figure 5–8** Identify the cultural characteristics in these Japanese screens. What do they reveal?

Maruyama Okyo. *Tiger and Dragon Screens.* 1781. Edo Period. Ink and colors on paper. Each 168.3 × 177.8 cm (66¼ × 70″). Detroit Institute of Arts, Detroit, Michigan. Founders Society Purchase with funds from various contributors.

Understanding Art History

Hinduism and Buddhism have always had a profound influence on the culture and art of Asia. Hindu shrines portray gods and godesses in sculptured images. Hindus believe the gods are present within the images. As a result, the sculptured images are treated with reverence and care. Buddhist sculpture and relief carvings often depict the life and teachings of Buddha. Ask students to compare the Indian and Japanese artworks in this lesson. What cultural characteristics can they identify in each? L2

Team Building Activity

Divide the class into four groups. Assign each group one of the following ancient civilizations to research: Tigris-Euphrates Valley, Nile Valley, Indus Valley, Huang He Valley. In their research, students should identify some of the major cultural, historical, and artistic developments of that time and place. L1 ELL

3 Assess

Self-Assessment

Have students complete the **Check Your Understanding** questions on this page. Answers are provided below.

Enrichment

Bronze Casting Bronze casting was developed in the Indus River Valley, but other early civilizations also used this method of sculpting. Have students research examples of the bronze vessels cast by people of the Shang dynasty. L3

4 Close

Ask students to describe some of the artistic traditions of ancient Asian civilizations.

Answers to Check Your Understanding

1. In the mid-1800s, railroad workers digging in present-day Pakistan discovered a lost city that had flourished 4,500 years earlier.
2. The Indus civilization is remembered as the birthplace of the religion Hinduism.

Making a Relief Sculpture

(pages 90–91)
Lesson Time: 3 hours

1 Focus

Objectives

After completing this lesson, students will be able to:

- Design and create an abstract sculpture modeled after a Kota figure.
- Describe, analyze, interpret, and judge their sculptures.

SUPPLIES
Refer to **What You Will Need** in the Student Edition.

2 Teach

Motivator

Ask students to examine the Kota figure and identify its different parts, pointing out the large oval shape representing the head and the open, diamond shape suggesting the body or legs. Tell them that the shapes at the top and sides of the head may represent a headdress, although some claim these shapes were intended to be wings. Ask students to identify how the figure is balanced. *(They should note that the figure is symmetrically balanced in terms of its overall shape and surface decorations.)*

Aesthetics

Discuss with students why it is necessary to understand the culture from which an African artwork comes before one can understand the artwork. Students should realize that Africa is composed of many different cultures, and that each one is unique.

Making a Relief Sculpture

The history of African art extends over a vast period, beginning as early as 500 B.C. and continuing to the present. Africa has many traditions and a variety of cultures. Examine the work in **Figure 5–9.** It is the product of the Kota people, a culture in central Africa.

The Kota sculpture in the picture is an abstract figure. Works like this were placed over a container. Inside the container were the remains of an honored ancestor. The original purpose of the sculptures remains a mystery. One popular view is that the works were meant to drive away evil spirits. What are some other possibilities?

What You Will Learn

You will demonstrate technical skills effectively using a variety of art media and materials to produce a sculpture. You will create an abstract sculpture modeled after the Kota figure in Figure 5–9. Like that sculpture, your work will have formal balance. It will be decorated with a pattern of lines made from glue. These will suggest facial features and add tactile texture.

What You Will Need

- One large piece of cardboard, about 12 x 8 inches, and several smaller pieces
- Pencil
- Scissors
- White glue
- Heavy twine
- Aluminum foil
- Transparent or masking tape

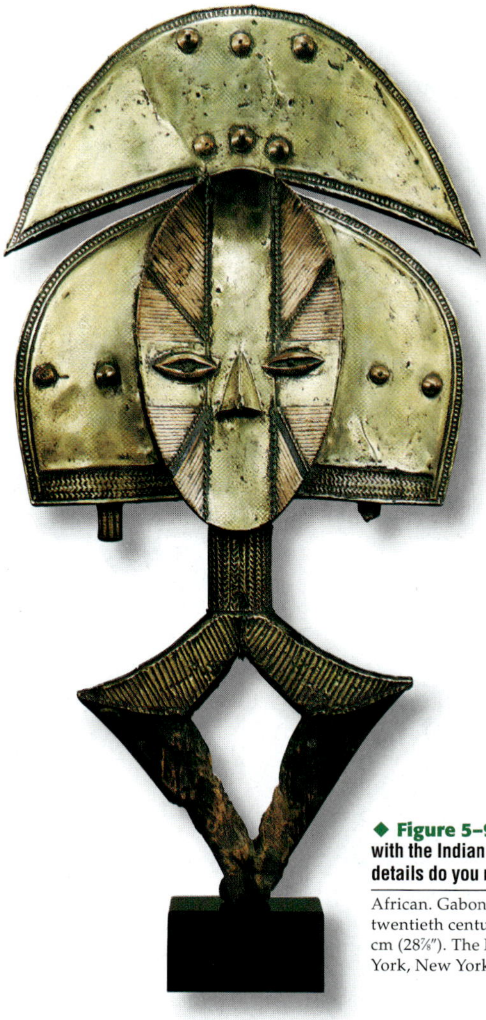

◆ **Figure 5–9** **Compare this African sculpture with the Indian sculpture in Figure 5–7. What details do you notice in each?**

African. Gabon, Kota. *Reliquary Figure.* Nineteenth–twentieth century. Wood, brass, copper, iron. 73.3 cm (28⅞″). The Metropolitan Museum of Art, New York, New York. Purchase 1983.

TEACHER TO TEACHER

WORKING WITH CARDBOARD AND FOIL To create details and simulate layers of metal, use cardboard scraps such as mat board, railroad board, or cereal and cracker boxes. Working from small to large shapes, securely glue cardboard onto corrugated base. Remind students to wipe off excess glue. When complete, press the layered cardboard figure under a heavy book overnight. Coat the cardboard relief with thinned white glue. Encourage students to work from the center of the design to smooth the foil over each edge repeatedly as the glue slowly dries.

What You Will Do

1. Carefully study the Kota figure illustrated in Figure 5–8. Examine the tactile textures in the work. Notice the use of formal balance. On the large piece of cardboard, complete an outline drawing in pencil of a similar figure. Like the one pictured, your figure should be abstract.
2. Cut out your figure. With the pencil, add facial features and decorative lines. Squeeze white glue over the pencil lines. Lay twine over glue lines. Allow the glue to dry before proceeding to the next step.
3. Lay the prepared figure on a sheet of aluminum foil. Place a dull pencil point on the foil about one-half inch from the outer edge of the figure. Following the contour of the figure, make a light outline one-half inch larger.
4. Using the indented outline as a guide, cut out the foil copy of your figure. Beginning on one side, fold the foil over the edge of the cardboard. Gently smooth it down and press it into place.
5. Press the foil securely around the raised glue lines. Use the blunt end of a brush, dull pencil, or your fingers to make these lines stand out clearly. Be careful not to tear the foil.
6. When completed, the foil should be bent under all edges of the figure and smoothed flat everywhere except over the glue lines. Secure the foil to the cardboard with tape.
7. Use the same blunt tool to apply texture—dots and lines.

Evaluating Your Work

- **Describe** Does your figure include all the shapes identified in the original?
- **Analyze** Does your figure have formal balance? Does it show features of the face and decorations as patterns of line on the surface of the sculpture? Do these lines give your work an interesting texture?
- **Interpret** Do you think your figure looks as though it, too, could chase away evil spirits?
- **Judge** Suppose you were to make another Kota figure. What would you do differently to make it better?

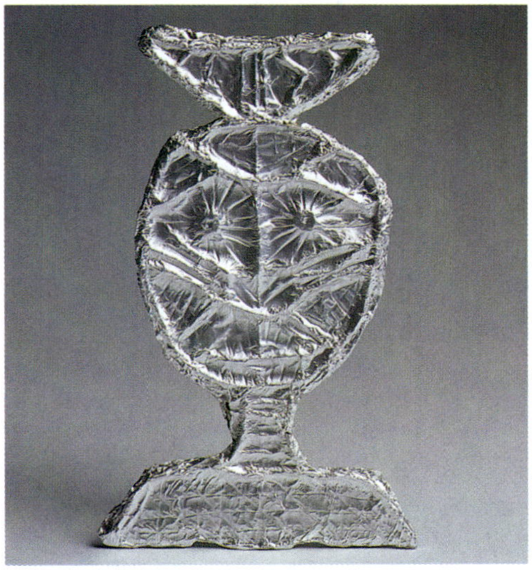

◆ **Figure 5–10** Student work. Relief sculpture.

Studio Option

Accent the decorations on the foil surface of your Kota figure. Do this by painting on a coat of black ink. You may have to apply several coats to penetrate all areas. When the ink has dried, lightly rub steel wool over the design. The raised areas will return to their original metallic finish. The other areas will remain black.

Visual Art Journal

Create another abstract figure of your own design. Before sketching the design, decide on its purpose. Describe in your journal the kind of mood the completed work will express.

Studio Skills

Demonstrate how to complete a symmetrical drawing of the Kota figure on the large piece of cardboard. Some students may need help in cutting out the figure. Show how to use pencil lines for facial features and how to apply white glue and twine over the lines. Demonstrate how to apply the aluminum foil, pressing firmly around the twine and other decorations. L1 ELL

3 Assess

Self-Assessment

Have students use **Evaluating Your Work** to conduct an in-progress critique of their relief sculpture.

Reteaching

In pairs, have students analyze each other's relief sculpture to form conclusions about formal properties—the art elements of line and texture and principles of balance and pattern. L1 ELL

Enrichment

African Art In most African art, the head is large in comparison to the body to show its importance as the center of reason and wisdom. Ask students to find other examples of African art that have this same characteristic. L2

4 Close

Have students explain how their figure is similar to the Kota original.

Safety Tip

Using Scissors Cutting through the thick cardboard can be hazardous. Remind students to be very careful when using any cutting tools such as scissors and knives. They should pick up the tool only by the handle, never by the blade. If handing the tool to another person, students should offer the handle. Have students hold the cardboard away from them as they make their cuts. Tell them to make sure no one is standing nearby. Demonstrate safe cutting procedures and help any student who may be frustrated. Provide sharp scissors. Dull ones can fail to cut materials cleanly and can slip, causing accidents.

Art of the Middle Ages and Renaissance

(pages 92–93)

1 Focus

Objectives

After completing this lesson, students will be able to:

- Understand what the terms *Middle Ages* and *Renaissance* mean.
- Define architecture.
- Identify in works of architecture the influence of historical and political events.
- Demonstrate technical skills effectively by using butcher paper and colored tissue to produce a stained-glass window.

Supplies

- Black butcher paper
- Colored cellophane or tissue paper
- Scissors
- Transparent tape

2 Teach

Motivator

Begin the lesson by asking students to imagine what it must have been like in western Europe after Rome lost its power. What feelings might people experience when hearing that invaders from the north were quickly approaching? Explain that fear of the unknown caused people to destroy grand temples in order to use the stone to build fortresses to keep out the invaders.

Art of the Middle Ages and Renaissance

Empires, as you have learned, come and go. Rome was no exception. In the fifth century, this great empire suffered the fate that had earlier claimed Egypt, Greece, and the Indus River valley civilization.

The period following Rome's collapse was one of chaos. Today we know this time in history as the Middle Ages. It lasted some one thousand years.

Art of the Middle Ages

After Rome fell, some of its great temples and palaces were torn down. The stone was carried off and used to build fortresses. These were built to keep invaders out. In time, structures of this type led to a new form of architecture. **Architecture** is *the art of planning and creating buildings.*

Castle Building

You probably recognize the structure in **Figure 5–11.** It is a castle. This is a fortlike dwelling with high walls and towers. Many castles were further protected by moats and drawbridges.

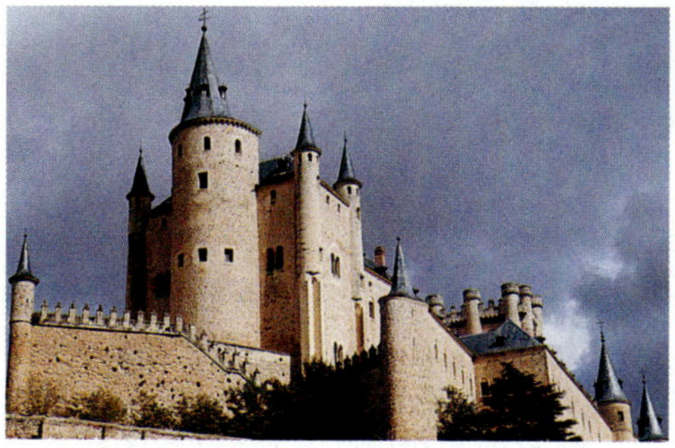

◆ **Figure 5–11** **The architect of this castle avoided windows because the walls would not support them. What other factors might have led to a lack of windows?**

View of castle, Alcazar, Segovia, Spain. Eleventh-fifteenth centuries. SEF/Art Resource, N.Y.

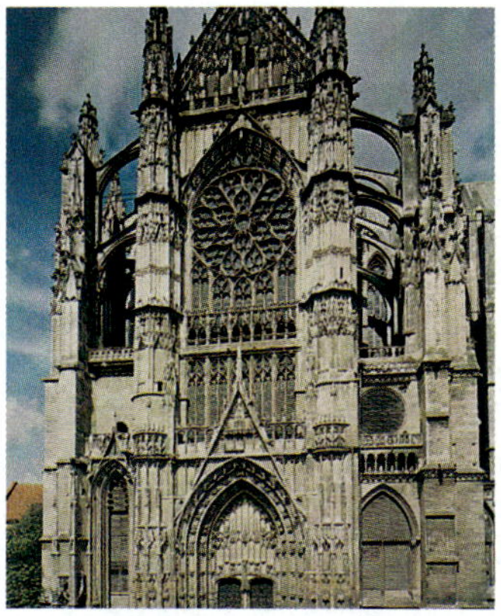

◆ **Figure 5–12** **The cathedral has graceful, upwardly soaring lines and large windows.**

Beauvais Cathedral, West Façade. Beauvais, France.

Guards stationed in the towers would sound the alarm when enemies approached.

Study the castle in Figure 5–11. Do you think the architect's main concern was safety or comfort?

Cathedral Building

Just before Rome fell, Christianity spread throughout much of Europe. During the Middle Ages, the Church remained the single strongest force.

By around 1300, a new type of building began to appear. This type of structure is shown in **Figure 5–12.** It was a special type of church known as a cathedral (kuh-**thee**-druhl).

Compare the cathedral in this picture with the castle in Figure 5–11. The cathedral has graceful, upwardly soaring lines.

Art of the Renaissance

After ten centuries of slumber, Europe awoke in the 1400s to a period of unparalleled

TECHNOLOGY STRATEGIES IN THE ART CLASSROOM

Electronic Media–Generated Art If your art software has a symmetry tool, have students explore its options. Draw with a thick, black line. Design a symmetrical, radial window or rosetta window using simple geometric shapes. Add bright colors to the spaces with the bucket fill tool. If available, have students print on transparency paper intended for the kind of color printer they are using. Remember, if it is ink jet, the ink dissolves in water. Remind students to protect the artwork by sliding it into a plastic cover.

growth. Trade and knowledge spread. New discoveries were made in science. Artists and scholars developed an interest in the art and literature of ancient Greece and Rome. This period is known today as the **Renaissance** (**ren**-uh-sahns), which means *period of rebirth.*

Renaissance Painting

The Renaissance was a time of great discoveries in art as well. Painters achieved a level of realism never before imagined by using perspective to give depth and shading to provide three-dimensionality.

This realism is evident in the painting in **Figure 5–13.** The work was done sometime after the Renaissance. Notice the attention to detail. Every fold in the woman's clothing is faithfully recorded. So is the glint in her eye. Look at her expression. What do you suppose she is thinking about as she pauses from playing her violin?

Check Your Understanding

1. What is meant by the term *Middle Ages?*
2. What changes occurred in art during the Renaissance?

Studio Activity

Making a Stained-Glass Window

Demonstrate technical skills. Cathedrals like the one in Figure 5–12 were fitted with stained-glass windows. These were made of colored glass pieces held together with lead strips. Because of these windows, the insides of the cathedrals were bathed in softly tinted light.

Cut black butcher paper into a circle about 12 inches in diameter. Fold the circle in half three times until you have a cone shape. Cut out geometric and simple shapes from the two folded sides. Vary the sizes of the cuts. Open the circle. Cover each opening with a patch of colored cellophane. Cut the patches so that each slightly overlaps the shape it is meant to cover. Secure the cellophane patches with transparent tape. Place your finished work on a windowsill.

PORTFOLIO

Write a short paragraph explaining how you made your choices of colors and shapes. Keep your description and your artwork together in your portfolio.

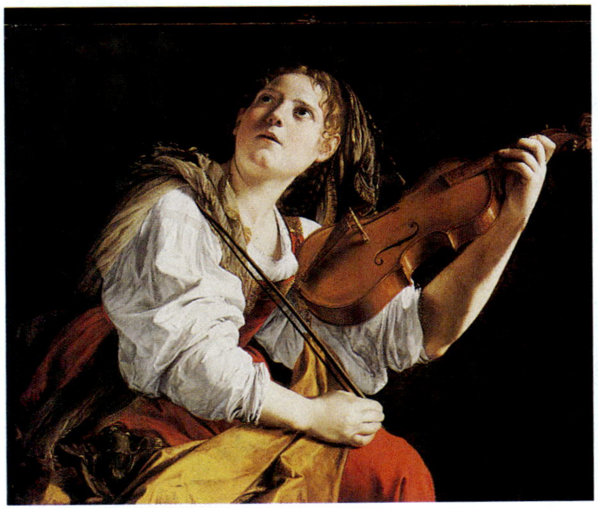

◆ **Figure 5–13** Observe the striking use of value in this painting. How does it add to the lifelike quality of the work?

Orazio Gentileschi. *Young Woman with a Violin.* c. 1612. Oil on canvas. 83.5 × 98 cm (32⅞ × 38⅝″). Detroit Institute of Arts, Detroit, Michigan. Gift of Mrs. Edsel B. Ford.

ART IN EVERYDAY LIFE

Encourage students to find pictures of existing cathedrals in newspapers and old travel or news magazines. Make a bulletin board with the clipped photos.

3 Assess

Self-Assessment

Have students complete the **Check Your Understanding** questions on this page. Answers are provided below.

Reteaching

Have students describe some of the differences between castles and cathedrals. L1

Enrichment

Direct students' attention to **Figure 5–13.** Explain that art historians have speculated that the woman in the painting may have been Orazio Gentileschi's daughter, a successful artist in her own right. Invite students to find out more about the painter of this work and his daughter as well.

4 Close

Ask volunteers to explain major changes in Europe after Rome fell. L2

Answers to Check Your Understanding

1. It was the period of time in history from the fall of Rome in the fifth century until the beginning of the Renaissance in the 1400s.
2. Painters used perspective to give depth and dimension to their artworks. They also strove for realism in their paintings. Artists and writers developed a renewed interest in the art and literature of ancient Greece and Rome.

Creating a Diorama

(pages 94–95)
Lesson Time: 4 hours

1 Focus

Objectives

After completing this lesson, students will be able to:

- Demonstrate technical skills effectively by using a variety of art media and materials to create a diorama of a realistic scene.
- Describe, analyze, interpret, and judge their diorama in terms of its success in showing depth.

Supplies
Refer to **What You Will Need** in the Student Edition.

2 Teach

Motivator

Draw a large rectangle on the board. Ask students how two circles drawn in that rectangle could be made to look as if they are at different distances in space. Have them draw the circles in the rectangle. Their drawings should show how differences in size, overlapping, and placement can suggest depth. Then ask them how changes in hue, intensity, and value can also add to the illusion of space. Have them draw and color another series of circles in the rectangle, this time using changes in color to suggest depth *(brighter and darker circles appear closer than duller, lighter circles).* Ask students to form generalizations about the interdependence of the art elements color and value and principle unity.

LESSON 6

Creating a Diorama

The Renaissance, you have learned, was a time of bold new discoveries. One of these was a technique called *linear perspective.* This technique aided painters in their quest for realism. In linear perspective, the horizontal lines of objects are slanted. This makes them appear to extend back into space. As **Figure 5–14** shows, the lines meet at an imaginary point called the *vanishing point.*

The painting in **Figure 5–15** uses linear perspective. Examine this lifelike work. Find the slanted lines in the vine-covered latticework above the dancers. Try extending these lines with your finger. At what point in the painting do they come together? Where else in the work has the artist used slanted lines? What other techniques has he relied upon to create a sense of depth?

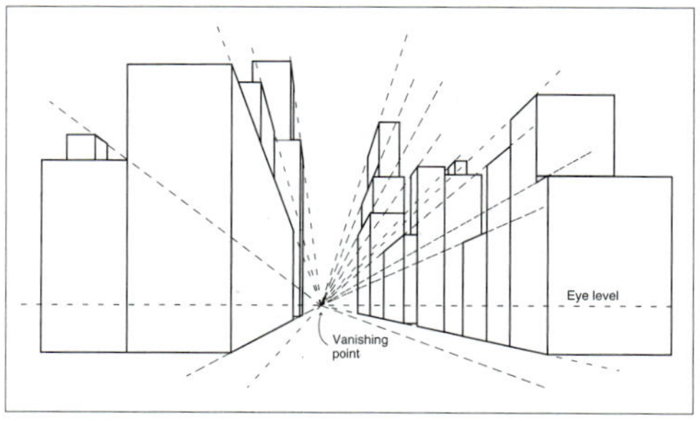

◆ **Figure 5–14** Diagram showing linear perspective.

What You Will Learn

Linear perspective is used to lend a feeling of space to two-dimensional works. In this lesson, you will create a three-dimensional work of art that uses both real and suggested space. You will use a variety of items to create a **diorama** (dy-uh-**ram**-uh). This is *a scenic representation in which miniature sculptures and other objects are displayed against a painted backdrop.* You will create a sense of deep space through changes in hue, value, and intensity.

What You Will Need

- Pencil and sketch paper
- Cardboard box, lid discarded

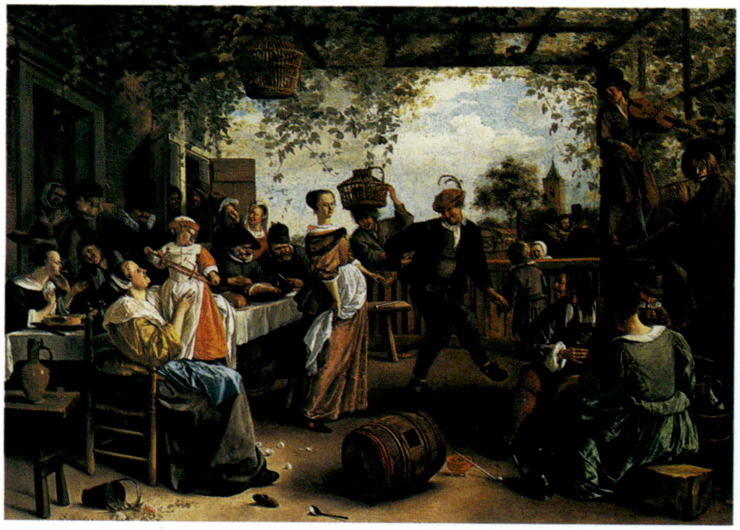

◆ **Figure 5–15** What elements of art did the artist use to create a sense of space?

Jan Steen. *The Dancing Couple.* 1663. Oil on canvas. 102.5 × 142.5 cm (40⅜ × 56⅛"). National Gallery of Art, Washington, D.C. Widener Collection.

Story Behind the Artwork

The Dancing Couple Jan Steen's paintings are famous for portraying warmhearted, often humorous scenes of everyday life in seventeenth-century Holland. Often, Steen used members of his own family as models for his pictures, dressing them in theatrical costumes. In *The Dancing Couple,* Steen also included his own portrait—he is the grinning man at the left touching the chin of a woman drinking from a glass. The setting for this and many of Steen's paintings may have been the inn that he ran to supplement his income. He created about 800 paintings, providing one of the best records of seventeenth-century Dutch life.

- Construction paper in a variety of colors
- White glue
- Chalk or markers
- Tempera paints
- Mixing tray
- Brushes, paper towels
- A variety of found objects

What You Will Do

1. Complete several pencil sketches of an imaginary scene. Include buildings, trees, and other objects. Select a point of view that suggests depth. One possibility might be a view looking down a city street.
2. Turn the box on its side. On the outside of the box, use colored construction paper to decorate the bottom, sides, back, and top. Glue the paper in place. Allow time for the glue to dry.
3. Select your best sketch. Using chalk or markers, transfer the scene to the back wall of the box. Sketch the lines of buildings along the sides of the box. The lines of objects should mirror the natural lines of the box.
4. Choose hues of tempera paint that reflect the colors of objects in your scene. You might use brown for buildings, gray for pavements. Mix duller intensities and lighter values of these hues. These will be used to show objects in the distance. Use a fine brush to add details, such as doors and windows.
5. Use found materials to form free-standing houses, trees, and other objects in your sketch. Gravel might be used for a stone fence, for example. Bark might be used for tree trunks. To give a sense of deep space, glue larger, more colorful objects in the foreground. Smaller, less colorful objects should be placed farther back.
6. Display your finished work

Evaluating Your Work

- **Describe** What have you included in your diorama?
- **Analyze** Did you use changes in hue, value, and intensity to create the feeling of deep space? Did you use placement of objects to help carry out this feeling?
- **Interpret** Would anyone looking at your diorama think it is much deeper than it actually is?
- **Judge** Does your diorama succeed in using real and suggested space?

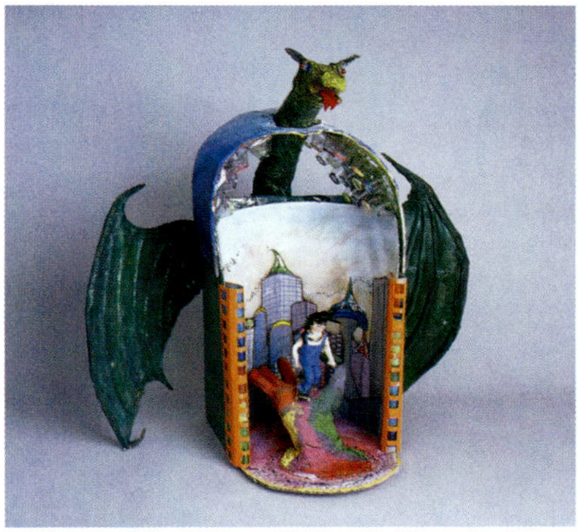

◆ **Figure 5–16** Student work. A diorama.

Studio Option

Do a realistic painting of the scene in your diorama. Your painting should use linear perspective to suggest depth. Refer to Figure 5–15 on page 94 to help you plan this project. Use size, overlapping, and values and intensities of hues to help create a feeling of space.

Visual Art Journal

Learn more about the visual trick *camera obscura* as a way of seeing perspective in an artwork. It was the forerunner of the camera. Look it up on the Internet or in encyclopedias. Write your findings in your journal.

Studio Skills

Help students brainstorm ideas for scenes for their dioramas, and then have them list some of the objects that might be included in such a scene. For example, an underwater scene might include fish, shells, seaweed, stones, shipwrecks, treasure chests. Point out that the more objects they include the better, since it will give them more opportunities to use overlapping and changes in color and size to suggest space. L1 ELL

Art On A Shoestring

Encourage students to be imaginative in identifying found objects to include in their dioramas. The items can be extremely simple and common. It is the composition of the items that requires creative thought.

3 Assess

Self-Assessment

Have students use **Evaluating Your Work** to conduct an in-progress critique of their diorama.

Reteaching

Ask pairs of students to identify each other's scene and point of view in their dioramas. L1 ELL

4 Close

Have students explain how they were able to achieve depth in their dioramas. L1

Inclusion Strategies

Special Learning Needs Students who are developmentally delayed may not be able to grasp the notion of vanishing-point perspective. If the idea that depth can be shown by slanting the horizontal lines of forms diagonally toward one or two points on the horizon is too difficult for some students to grasp, other ways to show depth can be shown. These include using overlapping, placing figures in the background higher on the picture plane, and making distant forms lighter, grayer, and bluer.

Art of the Nineteenth and Twentieth Centuries

(pages 96–97)

1 Focus

Objectives

After completing this lesson, students will be able to:

- Define *art movement.*
- Understand the goals of the Impressionists and of the Surrealists.

2 Teach

Motivator

Tell students to look at the Monet painting. After five seconds, have them close their books and describe what they saw. Have them do the same with the Lundeberg painting. Ask them which painting captures what and how the eye actually sees. Ask:

- Did you notice that the blurred effects of the Monet painting capture the effects of bright sunlight?
- Did the Lundeberg painting cause any confusion?

LESSON 7

Art of the Nineteenth and Twentieth Centuries

Seen against the long tapestry of art history, the last 100 years are but a stitch. Yet, during the twentieth century, more changes have taken place in art than in all the centuries before. In this lesson, you will learn about some of these changes.

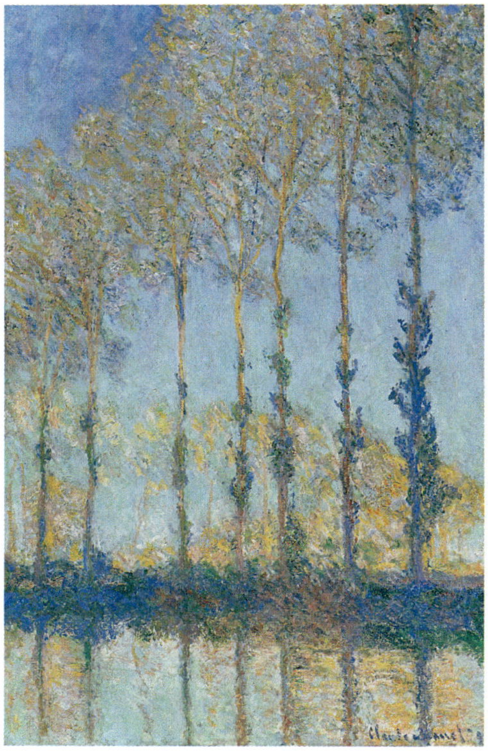

◆ **Figure 5–17** **Compare this painting with the one in Figure 5–15. In what way is this nature scene more "realistic" than the painting of the dancers?**

Claude Monet. *Poplars on the Bank of the Epte River.* 1891. Oil on canvas. 100.3 × 65.2 cm (39½ × 25¹¹⁄₁₆″). Philadelphia Museum of Art, Philadelphia, Pennsylvania. Bequest of Anne Thomson in memory of her father, Frank Thomson, and her mother, Mary Elizabeth Clarke Thomson.

Art of the Nineteenth Century

In the centuries following the Renaissance, the pursuit of realism continued. Artists produced pictures that showed solid figures moving naturally in space. They created works in which sunlight poured through windows, glinting off glass goblets and other shiny surfaces. Their brushes captured the look and feel of warm skin, cold metal, and soft velvet.

Toward the end of the 1800s, the search for realism took a new direction. One group of French painters in particular "saw the light." They left their dark studios and went to paint outdoors. They worked feverishly, using all their energies to capture the fleeting effects of sunlight on objects. This group became known, at first jokingly, as the *Impressionists.*

Painting

The leader of this **art movement**—*a trend formed when a group of artists band together*—was an artist named Claude Monet (**klohd** moh-**nay**). Monet's goal was to record what the eye saw at any given moment. Have you ever noticed how, on a cloudy day, the sun "goes in" and "comes out" again without warning? It was this "reality" that Monet set out to capture.

The work in **Figure 5–17** is one of his paintings. Viewed up close, it looks like a hastily done collection of paint dabs and dashes. When seen from a distance, however, the painting takes on an almost shimmering quality. The dabs and dashes are now brilliant flecks of color and blend together to form a stand of slender trees by the banks of a river. You can almost feel the gentle breeze rustling through the leaves on the trees and rippling the glassy surface of the water.

COMMUNITY CONNECTION

Cultural Diversity Find out about the cultural diversity within your classroom by taking a survey about each student's heritage. Have students use the Internet or visit a local library to research and choose a famous visual artist from a culture other than their own. Students will then create a two-dimensional work of art in that artist's style. Have students display their works around the school. Have students compare artworks representing various cultures. Ask them to describe the cultural characteristics in those artworks.

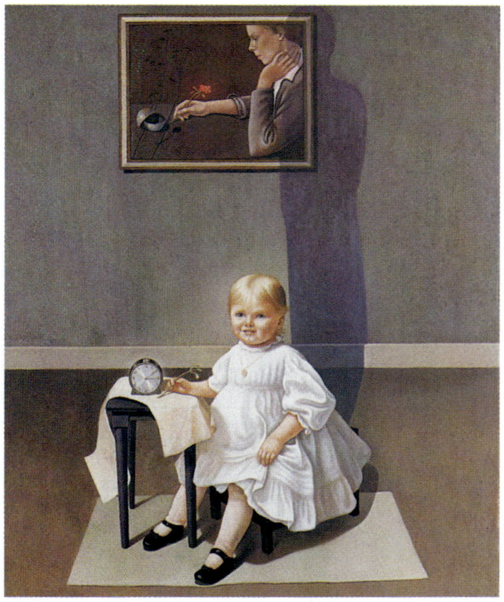

◆ **Figure 5–18** What statement might the artist be making about the passage of time? What clues are provided by the object in the hand of each figure?

Helen Lundeberg. *Double Portrait of the Artist in Time.* 1935. Oil on Masonite. 121.3 × 101.6 cm (47¾ × 40″). National Museum of American Art, Smithsonian Institution, Washington, D.C.

Meet the Artist

Claude Monet (1840–1926)

Cultural connection. Claude Monet was not only the leader of the Impressionists, but his work titled *Impression: Sunrise* also inspired the name of this art movement. The characteristic of the Impressionist style is capturing the impression of light in a scene.

Monet's paintings, including **Figure 5–17,** reflect his interest in the effects of outdoor light and atmosphere. In 1883, Monet settled at a country home in Giverny, France. There, he created a water lily pond that became the subject of many of his paintings. In his later years, Monet's eyesight began to fail. Still, the artist kept on painting, nearly until the time of his death in 1926. Compare the use of light and color in Figures 5–17 and 5–18. What type of feeling do they each express?

To learn more about Monet and his work, click on Artist Profiles at art.glencoe.com.

Art of the Twentieth Century

You have learned that the Impressionists were seeking new ways to capture realistic appearances in their art. However, the search for realism was nothing new. Roman sculptors and Renaissance painters sought the same goal. Strands in the fabric of art history, it seems, loop back on themselves.

One strand that came full circle in the twentieth century is the use of symbolism in art. You learned about symbolism in the lessons on Egyptian art earlier in this chapter. A heavy reliance on symbols became a feature of a twentieth-century art movement known as *Surrealism.*

Painting

In their works, the Surrealists tapped into the mysterious world of dreams. In this nighttime "world," symbols often play important roles. Consider the curious painting in **Figure 5–18.** Notice the work's title. You will probably have no trouble finding the two "portraits" of the artist. One—the artist as a child—appears in the lower half of the picture. The other—the adult artist—appears in the picture on the wall. The long, unnatural shadow cast upward by the child's image helps tie the two portraits together.

Yet, like most Surrealist paintings, this one asks more questions than it answers. What, for example, is the meaning of the clock? What are we to make of the empty container in the painting within a painting? Some critics have detected a sense of sadness or longing in this painting. What feeling does the work communicate to you?

Check Your Understanding

1. What was the aim of the Impressionists? What was the goal of the Surrealists?
2. What is an art movement?

Meet the Artist

Claude Monet

The use of light and color in Monet's painting is very bright and realistic; it expresses a warm and comforting feeling. Lundeberg's use of color and light is dull; the painting expresses an overall feeling of confusion.

Understanding Art History

Impressionism Explain to students that when the artworks of the Impressionists were first exhibited, and for many years thereafter, art critics and the public rejected these works. To most viewers, the Impressionists' artworks looked unfinished. Critics thought the works looked more like sketches than fully developed compositions. Today the art of the Impressionists is among the most admired in history.

3 Assess

Self-Assessment

Have students complete the **Check Your Understanding** questions on this page. Answers are provided below.

Reteaching

Have student partners choose either painting on these two pages to describe the Impressionistic or Surrealistic style of painting. L1 ELL

4 Close

Ask students to describe the qualities of Impressionism. L1

Answers to Check Your Understanding

1. The aim of the Impressionists was to record what their eyes actually saw in one particular moment of time rather than what their minds knew to be there. They attempted to capture realistic appearances, particularly the fleeting effects of sunlight on objects. The Surrealists used symbols in their realistic but dreamlike works.
2. An art movement is a trend formed when a group of artists band together.

Using Abstraction in Art

(pages 98–99)
Lesson Time: 2 hours

1 Focus

Objectives

After completing this lesson, students will be able to:

- Demonstrate technical skills effectively by drawing and painting an abstract or simplified image representing their aspirations for the future.
- Describe, analyze, interpret, and judge their abstract painting.

SUPPLIES
Refer to **What You Will Need** in the Student Edition.

2 Teach

Motivator

Ask students to examine the painting by Elizabeth Murray in **Figure 5–19.** Can they identify the objects depicted in this painting? Call attention to the title, *Painter's Progress.* Ask:

- What meaning do they attach to this title?
- How does the artist exhibit her progress as a painter? *(She does so with the painting itself.)*

Tell students that Murray's work identifies her *aspirations* to succeed as a painter, and she presents her work to show her progress.

LESSON 8

Using Abstraction in Art

While some artists today have borrowed ideas and techniques of the past, others have moved in new directions. One such groundbreaking direction is reflected in the painting in **Figure 5–19.** This work is an example of abstraction in art. As you read in Chapter 4, *abstract* means having a recognizable subject that is shown in an unrealistic or simplified manner. Abstract art straddles the fence between representational—or realistic—art and nonobjective art.

Examine the painting in Figure 5–19. You will probably recognize the fragmented objects in this brightly colored work. The main one is a painter's palette. Protruding from it is an assortment of brushes. Why has the artist chosen to shatter these familiar images? What do the picture's content and title reveal about the changes you read about in the previous lesson?

What You Will Learn

In this studio lesson, you will create your own abstract painting. Through abstraction, you will express your goals and hopes for the future. Your finished work will exhibit a variety of brilliantly colored, angular shapes. As in Figure 5–19, these will be joined together to make a visually pleasing whole.

What You Will Need

- Pencil and sketch paper
- Tempera or acrylic paints

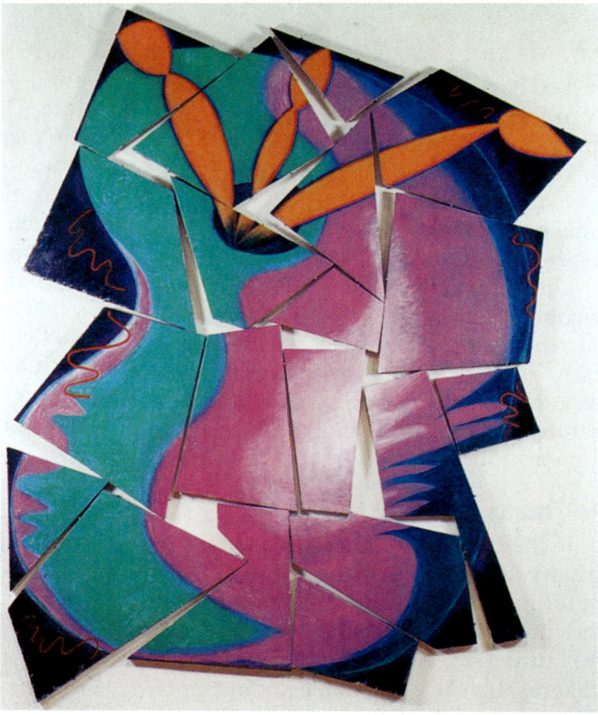

◆ **Figure 5–19** **Analyze and form generalizations about the interdependence of the art element color and principle variety in this painting.**

Elizabeth Murray. *Painter's Progress.* 1981. Oil on canvas in 19 parts. 294.5 × 236.2 cm (9′8″ × 7′9″). The Museum of Modern Art, New York, New York. Acquired through the Bernhill Fund and gift of Agnes Gund.

TEACHER TO TEACHER

Adapting Materials If not enough illustration board is available for each student to use two pieces, this studio can be done with other materials. The original painting can be created on white drawing paper. It is easy to draw lines on the back of the painting and then cut out the shapes. The shapes can then be mounted on illustration board, if it is available, or the pieces can be mounted on a larger piece of colored construction paper or white drawing paper.

- Two sheets of illustration board, one measuring 12 x 18 inches and the other 18 x 24 inches
- Brushes and mixing tray
- Paint cloth
- Ruler or other straight edge
- Scissors, white glue

What You Will Do

1. Everyone has dreams and goals. What is your own life goal? Begin this studio lesson by answering that question. Think of symbols or objects connected with your goal. Draw several sketches of these images. Then abstract, or simplify, the images by eliminating all unnecessary details.
2. Transfer your best sketch to the sheet of illustration board. Fill the board completely with your drawing.
3. Using tempera or acrylic paints, paint your subject. Include a background area by using bright hues.
4. When your work is dry, turn it over. With a ruler or other straight edge, draw straight lines at angles to one another. Include enough lines to divide the painting into at least 15 large and small angular shapes.
5. Use scissors to cut out your shapes. As you work, turn each piece over so its painted side is facing up. Carefully fit the cut-out pieces together so that you know where each one goes.
6. Center the rearranged shapes on the sheet of illustration board. Overlap some pieces. Leave narrow spaces between others. Move the shapes around until you are satisfied with the arrangement. Then glue the pieces in place.

Evaluating Your Work

- **Describe** Did you select images that identify a particular dream or goal? Did you simplify the images?
- **Analyze** Did you use a variety of brightly colored hues? Does your work contain large and small angular shapes?
- **Interpret** Do you think other people could interpret the images in your picture? Would they be able to recognize the idea the images represent?
- **Judge** Do you think the shapes in your composition are joined in a way so as to create a pleasing whole?

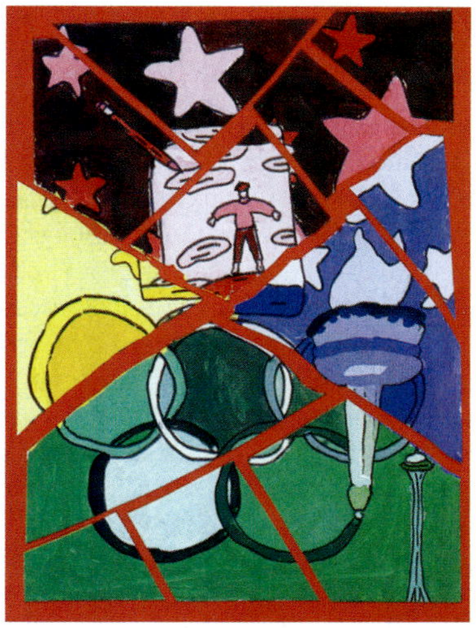

◆ **Figure 5–20** Student work. Abstraction in art.

PORTFOLIO IDEAS

A strong portfolio reflects what you learn about art history as well art techniques. Make sure to include written entries that demonstrate your ability to describe an artwork from the art historian's point of view—by telling who created the work, and when and where it was created. Show that you understand how time and place influence an artist.

Art Online

Careers in art. Visit our Web site at **art.glencoe.com** to learn about different art-related careers. Compare career opportunities in art. Which career is most appealing to you?

Sparking Creativity

Students should have fun with the possibilities offered in this Studio Lesson. Encourage them to look around for unusual items or unconventional ideas that convey their goals and interests. Have them experiment with atypical colors or shapes and express a variety of ideas based on personal experience.

Art Criticism

Tell students that Murray's painting makes effective use of contrast. Explain that contrast is a technique in which differences between objects are stressed. A tall person contrasts with a short one, a dark patch of sky contrasts with a light one. Ask students: Point out two ways that Murray uses contrast in her painting. *(Contrast of red and green; curved painted shapes and angular cut-out shapes.)*

3 Assess

Self-Assessment

Have students use **Evaluating Your Work** to conduct an in-progress critique of their abstract painting.

Reteaching

Have pairs of students interpret the images in each other's work. L1 ELL

4 Close

Have students identify another example of abstract art in this textbook. L1 ELL

DEVELOPING A PORTFOLIO

Parental Review Periodically, you may wish to have parents review the student portfolio entries. This not only gives the student additional feedback and reinforcement, but it also helps communicate the purpose and scope of the art class. Here are some questions for parents to consider:

- What was the goal of the work reviewed?
- What was the student trying to do or say?
- Why did the student choose to include this entry?

The Great Restoration

1 Focus

Objectives

After completing this lesson, students will be able to:

- Draw two versions of a scene, one with dull colors and one with bright, clear colors.
- Research monuments and buildings affected by pollution.
- Plan, write, and share an analysis of erosion and restoration efforts for a specific monument.

2 Teach

Teaching the Feature

1. Let several volunteers describe what seems to be happening in the photograph. Ask: What changes are being made? Then have another volunteer read the photo caption aloud.
2. Guide students in reading and discussing the article. Ask: Why do you think restoration is such a slow process? Why did the Sistine Chapel need restoration? How did the restoration affect Michelangelo's reputation as a colorist?

Activity

Ask students to select a simple scene. Have them use colored pencils to draw two versions of that scene. First, have them use dull colors to show the scene. Then have them use bright clear colors. Ask: How does the difference in color change the drawing's impression?

TIME ART SCENE Language Arts

THE GREAT RESTORATION

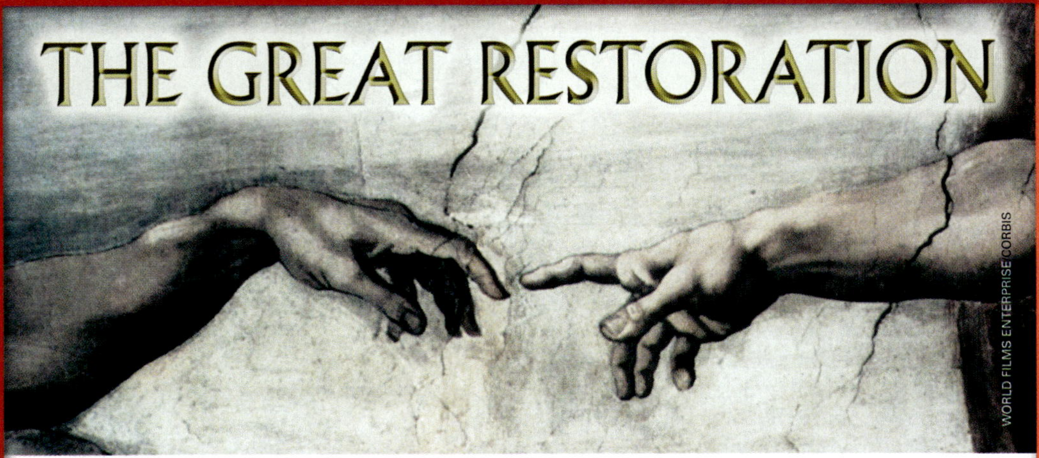

WORLD FILMS ENTERPRISE/CORBIS

A Renaissance masterpiece looks new again.

Imagine working on one project for nearly ten years. That's how long it took for a team of expert art restorers to bring Renaissance master Michelangelo's (1475–1564) famed Sistine Chapel back to its original beauty. The Italian art restorer Gianluigi Colalucci started small, applying a new solvent to a postage-stamp-sized section of one of Michelangelo's frescoes. Colalucci's work ended in 1989 with the careful cleaning of one of Jonah's toes. The toe turned from a gray smudge to a healthy pink. The restorers took twice as long to clean the artwork as it did for the artist to paint it.

Michelangelo began filling Rome's Sistine Chapel with stories and figures from the Bible in 1508, but his gemlike colors didn't last. They quickly dulled from air pollution, dirt, and soot. In the late 1700s, an archaeologist called Michelangelo "the weakest colorist." However, the current restoration of Michelangelo's initial sparkling color removes any doubt about his supreme skill.

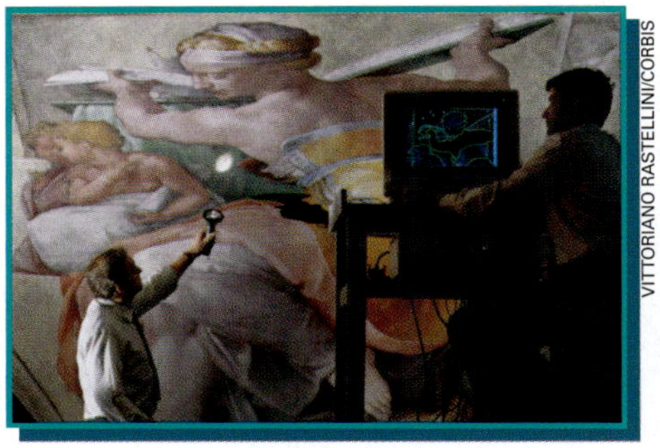

VITTORIANO RASTELLINI/CORBIS

TOP: A detail of the Sistine Chapel (before the restoration) portrays the creation of life. ABOVE: Experts use high-tech equipment to restore Michelangelo's frescoes.

TIME TO CONNECT

- Use the Internet to research monuments and buildings (such as the Taj Mahal or the pyramids in Egypt) that are suffering from the effects of pollution.
- Analyze the causes and the extent of the erosion and efforts under way to save the monument.
- Look at before-and-after drawings or photos, and use descriptive adjectives and adverbs to compare and contrast the images. Share your work with the class.

TIME TO CONNECT

Suggest that students work with partners to select a monument and report on the causes of the erosion and progress of the restoration efforts. Students should draw inferences such as conclusions and support them with text evidence. Before they begin writing, have them respond to these questions:

- What conclusions can we draw from our reading?
- What details support those conclusions?

Chapter 5 Review

BUILDING VOCABULARY

Number a sheet of paper from 1 to 12. After each number, write the term from the list that matches each description below.

applied art	diorama
architecture	fine art
art historians	hieroglyphic
art movement	painted screen
bust	Renaissance
contours	symbol

1. Art made to be enjoyed visually, not used.
2. People who study art of different ages and cultures.
3. An image used to stand for a quality or idea.
4. An early form of picture writing.
5. The art of planning and creating buildings.
6. A sculpture that shows a person's head, shoulders, and upper chest.
7. Period of rebirth.
8. Art made to be useful as well as visually pleasing.
9. Outlines and surface ridges.
10. An art object used as a wall or room divider.
11. A trend formed when a group of artists band together.
12. A scenic representation in which miniature sculptures and other objects are displayed against a painted backdrop.

REVIEWING ART FACTS

Number a sheet of paper from 13 to 17. Answer each question in a complete sentence or two.

13. What are the rules of Egyptian art for showing the human body?
14. Name a difference and a similarity between the way the Greeks and Romans showed the human figure.
15. What religious beliefs guided the art of the Indus River valley?
16. What methods did Renaissance painters use to achieve realism in their works?
17. Compare and contrast the goals of the Impressionists and the goals of the Surrealists.

CROSS-CURRICULUM CONNECTIONS

18. **Music.** Like art, music has undergone changes over the centuries. Working with a group, research the following "movements" in the history of music: Romanticism, Expressionism, Neo-Classicism. For each, identify when the movement occurred and the names of the principal composers. Share your findings with classmates in an oral report.
19. **Social Studies.** This chapter covers art from different cultures. Compare and analyze artwork from three different cultures. What are the important cultural differences and similarities?

Web Museum Activity

The Art Institute of Chicago, Chicago, Illinois

Understanding the meaning and purpose of a certain artwork teaches you about the culture where it originated. To enrich your understanding of various artworks' historical and cultural background, go to **art.glencoe.com** and click on the link for The Art Institute of Chicago.

You will discover artworks from diverse cultures. Select and compare two artworks from separate cultures. What did you learn about those cultures? Write a descriptive report explaining the meaning and history behind the artworks.

Web Museum Activity

Before you have students go online, visit the Web site to preview the museum's online content, collection, and any online exhibit that might be of interest. Student responses will vary. Their descriptions should include a clear understanding of the meaning and history behind their selected artworks. If possible, they can also bring copies of the images they selected to class. Encourage students to learn more about a favorite artist or a particular time in art history.

Answers to Chapter 5 Review

Building Vocabulary

1. fine art
2. art historians
3. symbol
4. hieroglyphic
5. architecture
6. bust
7. Renaissance
8. applied art
9. contours
10. painted screen
11. art movement
12. diorama

Reviewing Art Facts

13. All major body parts are to be shown from their most familiar angle.
14. The Greeks and Romans both made statues of important people and rulers. The Greeks showed the whole figure in their sculptures, whereas the Romans focused on heads and busts.
15. People of the ancient Indus River valley worshiped animals and nature; those beliefs influenced their art.
16. Renaissance painters used linear perspective and lifelike expression to achieve realism in their art.
17. The Impressionists sought to record what the eye saw at any given moment. The Surrealists relied on symbolism and dreamlike images.

Cross-Curriculum Connections

18. Reports will vary, but students should identify the movements, eras, and principle composers.
19. Responses will vary depending on the artwork they selected.

Chapter Resources

Features	Standards for Chapter		Reproducible Masters
	National	State/Local	
Quick Write *page 103* TIME ART SCENE "Horsing Around" *page 120* ***Web Museum Activity*** *page 121*	**1.** (a, b) **2.** (a, b) **3.** (a, b) **4.** (a, b, c) **5.** (a, b, c) **6.** (a, b)		Guided Reading and Practice 6–1 Studio Activity 6–2 Enrichment Activity 6–3, 6–8 Historical and Cultural Heritage 6–4, 6–10 Cross-Curriculum Activity 6–5 Artist Profile 6–6 Application Activity 6–7, 6–9 Lesson Plans

Lesson Resources

Lessons	Standards per Lesson		Reproducible Masters
	National	State/Local	
1 ***Landscape Art*** *(pages 104–105)*	2b, 3a, 3b		Studio Activity 6–2 Enrichment Activity 6–3
2 ***Creating a Nature Scene*** *(pages 106–107)*	1a, 1b, 2a, 2b, 5c		
3 ***Nature Up Close*** *(pages 108–109)*	2b, 2c, 4a		Historical and Cultural Heritage 6–4
4 ***Drawing from a Bird's Eye View*** *(pages 110–111)*	1a, 1b, 2a, 3a		Cross-Curriculum Activity 6–5
5 ***Art and the Seasons*** *(pages 112–113)*	2c, 4a, 4c		Artist Profile 6–6 Application Activity 6–7
6 **ART & READING** *(pages 114-115)*	3b, 6a, 6b		
7 ***The Power of Nature*** *(pages 116–117)*	1a, 2a, 3a, 3b		Enrichment Activity 6–8 Application Activity 6–9
8 ***Painting a Storm*** *(pages 118–119)*	1a, 1b, 2a, 3b		Historical and Cultural Heritage 6–10

Assessment	Technology
Testing Program: Chapter Test 6–11 Portfolio and Assessment Techniques	Artsource Performing Arts Package, African American Dance Ensemble (DVD or VHS Segment 2 and Audio CD Track 2) National Museum of Women in the Arts Interactive Lesson Planner Fine Art Transparency CC-6, *Krishna Lifts Mount Govardhan* Fine Art Transparency 6, *Autumn Oak and Beech* by C.W. Jeffries

Activities/Features
Studio Activity: A Stylized Landscape
Evaluating Your Work Reflective Thinking Visual Art Journal
Meet the Artist: Leonardo da Vinci
Evaluating Your Work Portfolio Ideas Art Online
Time & Place: Sixteenth Century Flemish Art
Make the Connection
Studio Activity: Making a Monoprint
Evaluating Your Work Computer Option Visual Art Journal

KEY TO ABILITY LEVELS

Teaching strategies have been coded.

L1 Activities for all students; teacher direction required

L2 Activities for average to above-average students; some teacher direction needed

L3 Activities for students able and willing to work independently

ELL English Language Learner activities

FEATURED ARTISTS

- Pieter Bruegel
- Charles Burchfield
- Albrecht Dürer
- Marsden Hartley
- Andō Hiroshige
- Katsushika Hokusai
- Leonardo da Vinci
- Joan Miró
- Joseph Pickett
- Tom Thompson
- José Antonio Velasquez
- Frederick Varley
- Andrew Wyeth

FINE ART PRINTS

Fine Art Print 10, *The Cottage Door* by Thomas Gainsborough

Timesaving *Technology*

Interactive Lesson Planner

Make planning easy. Use this interactive software to organize your week, month, semester, or year and access all *Introducing Art* reproducible resources.

KEY TO LESSON RESOURCES

Narrative Lesson

Studio Lesson

Chapter 6

Perceiving Nature

(pages 102–121)

Chapter Overview

Artists continually try to capture the beauty and mystique of the natural world. In this chapter, students will look at nature from an artist's point of view. They will learn the various ways in which artists have been inspired by, and expressed the wonders of nature.

Discussing the Artwork

Focus On ◆ **Figure 6–1** Andō Hiroshige is one the best-known artists of the Japanese landscape print. In this print, *Great Bridge: Sudden Rain at Atake,* Hiroshige illustrates rain pouring down on pedestrians on the bridge at Ohashi in the city of Edo (present-day Tokyo). Lines in the work have a rich black tone that makes the figures, bridge, and umbrellas stand out. The colors in this print are vibrant, particularly the blue sky and water underneath the bridge. The artist used care when making this print. This is evident in the rubbing of the bridge supports and water, where the grain of the woodblock suggests the ripples caused by the falling rain.

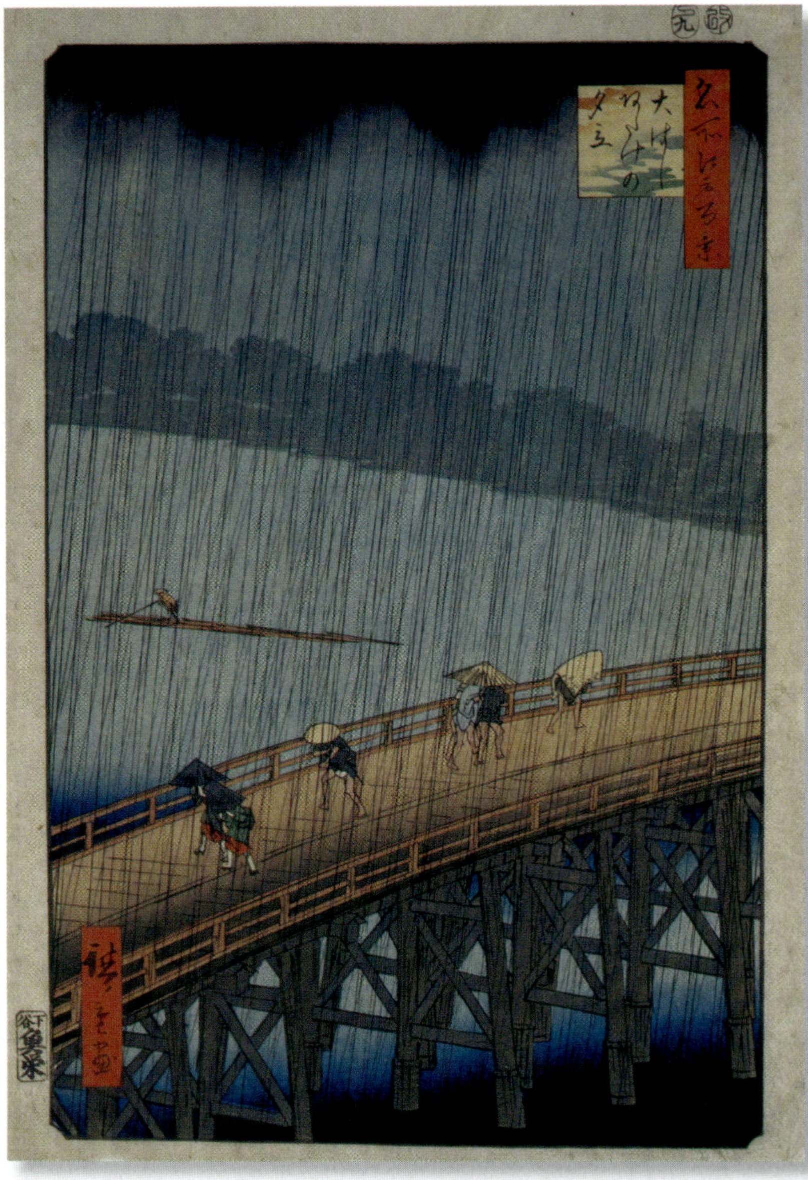

Focus On ◆ **Figure 6–1** **This is a Japanese woodblock print. Notice how the artist cut the lines into the block to represent a heavy rain. How do the colors and shapes add to the feeling of the people walking across the bridge?**

Andō Hiroshige. *Great Bridge: Sudden Rain at Atake (Ohashi, Atake No Yudachi),* from the series "One Hundred Famous Views of Edo." 1857. Woodcut. 36.2 × 21.9 cm (14¼ × 8⅝"). Carnegie Museum of Art, Pittsburgh, Pennsylvania. Bequest of Dr. James B. Austin.

Linking to the Performing Arts

DANCE Dr. Chuck Davis, Artistic Director of the African American Dance Ensemble, travels to West Africa each year to research and experience traditional dances of different groups. "Balante" is a post-initiation dance of the Jolas of the Casamance region of Senegal. Have students see how the African American Dance Ensemble performs this type of dance in the **Performing Arts Handbook** on page 315. To enrich student understanding, play the DVD or videotape (segment 2) and audio CD (track 2) in the **Performing Arts Package.**

Chapter 6

Perceiving Nature

"It is not the language of painters but the language of nature which one should listen to, the feeling for the things themselves, for reality, is more important than the feeling for pictures."

—Vincent van Gogh, (1853–90)

Nature has many different moods ranging from calm to stormy. It also has many colors as it changes seasons, as well as various shapes—from rolling hills to mountain peaks to roaring waterfalls. Artists have always celebrated nature, each in a unique way. Whether it is a majestic landscape or a close-up drawing of a tiny flower, the artist helps us to see nature in a new way. In this chapter, you will learn about the many ways in which artists have expressed the wonders of nature.

After completing this chapter, you will be able to:

- Define the term *landscape.*
- Understand stylization.
- Explain what artists accomplish through nature studies.
- Experiment with two- and three-dimensional forms of self-expression.

Quick Write

Interpreting the Quote
Vincent van Gogh was inspired by Japanese woodblock prints. What do you think he means by "the language of nature?" Describe how Hiroshige used line and color to express a feeling of nature in **Figure 6–1.**

KEY TERMS

landscape
stylized
assemblage
study
nature study
monoprint

Quick Write

Interpreting the Quote
Have students read the quote and complete the Quick Write activity. Explain to students that van Gogh meant that "the language of nature" is depicting nature as it really is and the different feelings nature evokes. In Figure 6–1, Hiroshige expresses nature through a rainfall. The use of vibrant color, such as the blue sky and water under the bridge expresses nature in the middle of a rainstorm as well as evokes a sensation in the viewer.

Chapter Motivator

Ask students to think of a favorite activity or event held outdoors—perhaps a family picnic, a hike in the woods, a sporting event, watching the sun set, or some other regular or occasional outdoor activity. Have them illustrate themes from personal experience and traditional events. What aspect of nature contributed to their enjoyment of that event? In general, what do they enjoy about nature? Explain that nature has long been the focus of artists, and that in this chapter, students will explore ways of their own to capture images of nature that are special to them.

National Standards for Arts Education

This chapter addresses the following National Standards for the Visual Arts:

1. (a, b)	**4. (a, c)**
2. (a, b, c)	**5. (a, b, c)**
3. (a, b)	**6. (a, b)**

Art Online

Visit **art.glencoe.com**, the Web site for Glencoe's art programs. This site is designed to help you advance in your career as an art teacher and learn about the various opportunities in the art community. Explore the many teacher resources the site has to offer, such as:

- Annual Student Art Contests
- Art Conferences
- Educational Agencies
- Grants

LESSON 1

Landscape Art

(pages 104–105)

1 Focus

Objectives

After completing this lesson, students will be able to:

- Define landscape art.
- Understand what it means for a work to be done in a *stylized* way.
- Demonstrate technical skills effectively by using a variety of materials to produce a drawing of a stylized landscape.

SUPPLIES

- Pencil and sheets of sketching paper
- White construction or watercolor paper
- Watercolors, brushes, and water containers
- Colored markers and/or colored pencils

2 Teach

Motivator

Have students cover the title of **Figure 6–2** and imagine where and what type of place it represents. Ask students to describe this place and record their responses. Then, have them view **Figure 6–3** and ask them to respond to the same question, adding new words to the list. Now, tell students they have just won a vacation to the "paradise" of their dreams. Ask students to make a list of words that describe this place.

Vocabulary

Discuss the meaning of *landscape* with students. Compare *landscape* with *cityscape*.

LESSON 1

Landscape Art

How many products have you seen that carry the words *all natural* on their labels? This phrase has become commonplace in today's society. It represents peoples' desire to live in a healthy way and to appreciate nature. Artists have valued and represented nature throughout the years. Their works have long paid tribute to nature's beauty and its bounty.

LANDSCAPES

What do you see when you look out the nearest window? Do you see buildings, streetlights, and cars? Maybe you see plants, trees, and hills. If your answer leans more toward the second description, you are looking at a landscape. In art, the word **landscape** refers to *a drawing or painting of mountains, trees, or other natural scenery.* Artists have been creating landscapes for more than one thousand years.

The possible subjects for a landscape are limitless. So are the ways in which artists have chosen to represent nature scenes. The landscapes in **Figures 6–2** and **6–3** show two examples that have some similarities and some differences.

Perspective in a Landscape

Examine the painting in Figure 6–2. It shows a hilly Pennsylvania town in the early 1900s. What do you see first when you look at this painting? Is your eye attracted to the large building on the hill? What do you notice next? The train, the river, or the little buildings in the foreground? Notice that the artist has made these buildings smaller than those in the distance. Why might the artist have created this visual puzzle? Perhaps he wanted to give more importance to the flag blowing proudly in the wind.

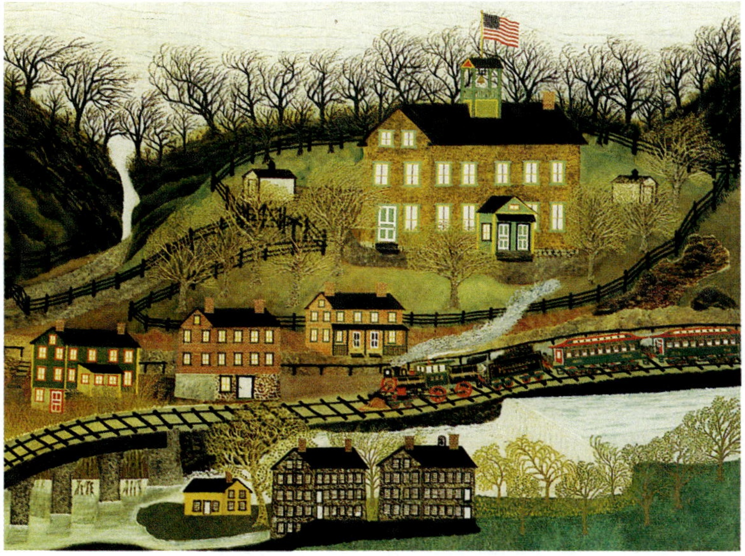

◆ **Figure 6–2** **Besides the perspective, what other unusual landscape features can you find in this picture? Can you identify the season of the year?**

Joseph Pickett. *Manchester Valley.* 1914–18. Oil with sand on canvas. 115.6 × 154 cm (45½ × 60⅝"). The Museum of Modern Art, New York, New York. Gift of Abby Aldrich Rockefeller.

TECHNOLOGY STRATEGIES IN THE ART CLASSROOM

ELECTRONIC MEDIA-GENERATED ART Have students practice perspective techniques in a landscape. First, ask them to draw, scan, or photograph a building or other object. Once the image is in an art application, select it, and copy and paste a second copy on the page. While still selected, change the scale. If the house is large, reduce the size. Repeat steps so sizes of the object vary from large to small. Overlap and arrange it to show depth. Remind students that foreground objects have more details and vivid colors. Ask students to add a setting and complete the picture.

Rhythm in a Landscape

Compare the painting in Figure 6–2 with the one in Figure 6–3. The two landscapes were painted about the same time. Like the work on the opposite page, this one shows a cheerful scene from nature. It even includes some of the same features, such as trees.

However, that is where the similarity ends. Whereas the landscape in Figure 6–2 portrays a city setting, the one in Figure 6–3 records a rural scene. The work, moreover, follows a careful design. Notice the row after row of evenly spaced seedlings in the bottom half of the picture. Notice how the artist overlapped the shapes to give depth to the scene.

Check Your Understanding

1. What is a *landscape?*
2. Compare and contrast the similarities and differences between Figures 6–2 and 6–3.

Studio Activity

A Stylized Landscape

Using direct observation. Look again at the plants, trees, and plowed fields in the landscape on this page. These objects have been represented in a highly **stylized** way. This means *simplified* or *exaggerated.* Some artists choose to stylize their works because it allows them to picture nature in a unique, personal way.

Select a park or other familiar nature scene in your community. On a sheet of drawing paper, express a variety of ideas based on your direct observation. Sketch the trees, flowers, and other landscape features. Make your view stylized by simplifying or exaggerating the shapes of these objects. Complete your stylized landscape with markers.

PORTFOLIO

Write a description of how you stylized the objects in your landscape. Analyze the success of your artwork and put this evaluation in your portfolio with your work.

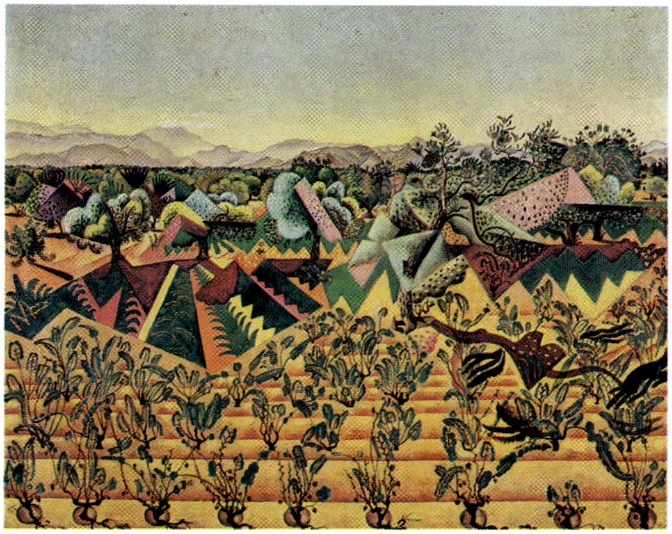

◆ **Figure 6–3** **Notice the use of repetition in this painting. What other principle of art has Miró used to give this artwork a lively feeling?**

Joan Miró. *Vines and Olive Trees, Tarragona.* 1919. Oil on canvas. 72.5 × 90.5 cm (28½ × 35⅝"). The Metropolitan Museum of Art, New York, New York. The Jacque and Natasha Gelman Collection. © Artists Rights Society (ARS), New York/ ADAGP, Paris.

Answers to Check Your Understanding

1. A landscape is a drawing or painting of mountains, trees, or other natural scenery.
2. Similarities: Both show a regional landscape with trees and plants. Differences: One is a realistic painting of a city scene in late fall or early spring; the other is a stylized, rural farming scene in the summer.

Studio Activity

A Stylized Landscape Instruct students to choose their own style of representing this scene. The view should have some recognizable features. Have students make several sketches and explore different media to discover textures and effects they want to use.

Art Criticism

Have students use the four steps of art criticism to critique Pickett's and Miró's paintings. Then have them compare the paintings, listing any commonalities and differences. Ask students: Was each artist's intent the same? Is each painting successful? Why or why not? L1

3 Assess

Self-Assessment

Have students complete the **Check Your Understanding** questions on this page. Answers are provided below.

Reteaching

Have students explain what is stylized about their landscapes. L1

Enrichment

Encourage students to find out more about Pickett's and Miró's unique painting styles. Bring in if you can additional examples of their work. Invite students to draw a landscape imitating the style of each. L1 ELL

4 Close

Ask students to define a stylized landscape.

LESSON 2

Creating a Nature Scene

(pages 106–107)
Lesson Time: 3 hours

1 Focus

Objectives

After completing this lesson, students will be able to:

- Demonstrate technical skills effectively to create an assemblage representing a familiar place combining natural objects and drawing materials.
- Conduct an in-progress analysis of their nature scene.

SUPPLIES
Refer to **What You Will Need** in the Student Edition.

2 Teach

Motivator

Ask students if they have ever walked along a path or route so many times that they felt as though they could go there automatically with their eyes closed. Artists often paint familiar scenes that call attention to things or feelings that may normally be overlooked. Have students recall a familiar landscape scene. Ask them to identify details about the scene others might not notice. Explain that artists sometimes use that special, overlooked detail as the focus of a painting.

LESSON 2

Creating a Nature Scene

Have you ever taken a route so many times that you felt you could travel it with your eyes closed? Such a path appears in the work in **Figure 6–4.** It leads to a village in the artist's native Honduras. Notice how plants, trees, and the stone fence bordering the path are painted rhythmically as repeated shapes and textures. Despite being stylized, the work invites the viewer in for a stroll toward the town. Look carefully. The painting is organized so as to lead your eye to the center of interest. Can you identify that center of interest? What elements and principles of art are used to help draw your eye to it?

WHAT YOU WILL LEARN

You will make a nature scene of a familiar place that you know well or have recently visited. You will begin by collecting small natural objects to make an **assemblage** (ah-sem-**blahzh**). This means *a three-dimensional artwork consisting of many pieces assembled together.* You will also use markers and oil pastels to draw other objects and details. To do this, you will organize your work to create a center of interest. You will emphasize the most important part of the scene using lines, shapes, colors, and textures.

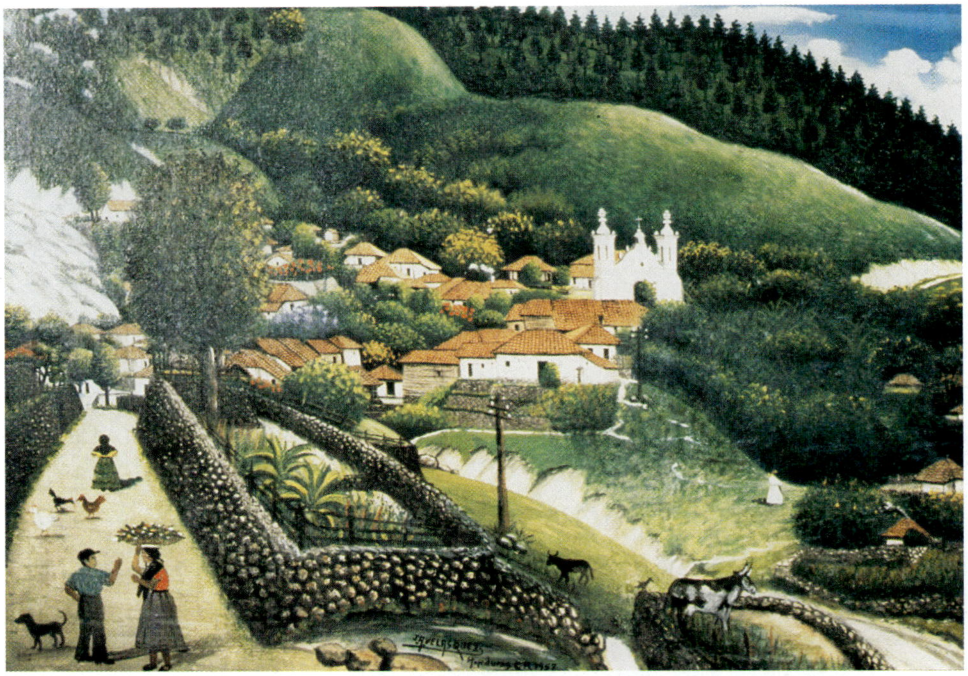

◆ **Figure 6–4** Analyze the artist's use of texture in this painting. Describe how the principal of emphasis has been used to draw your eye to the center of interest.

Jose Antonio Velasquez. *San Antonio de Oriente.* 1957. Oil on canvas. 66 × 94 cm (26 × 37″). Collection of the Art Museum of the Americas, Organization of American States, Washington, D.C.

STORY BEHIND THE ARTIST

JOSÉ ANTONIO VELASQUEZ Velasquez tried several careers before he began to paint in 1933. These professions included mayor of San Antonio de Oriente, which is the subject of his painting in **Figure 6–4,** and barber in the Pan American School of Agriculture. Velasquez is considered to be a folk artist because he is not interested in representing a realistic image but is more interested in communicating an idea or feeling. Folk artists appear to lack interest in using accurate proportion, perspective, shading, and other visual elements that make an artwork look realistic. Their work provides an invaluable visual history of everyday life.

What You Will Need

- Pencil and sheets of sketch paper
- White construction paper or poster board, 12 x 18 inches
- Collection of small natural objects
- Oil pastels
- Markers
- White glue

What You Will Do

1. Visit a park or other local area that might make a good subject for a landscape. Make several sketches. Include important features such as plants, trees, houses, and hills. Show these as simple, flat shapes. Plan the picture to emphasize a particular object or area as the center of interest.
2. Before leaving the area, collect small objects in a plastic bag. Possibilities include small twigs, pebbles, sand, bark, leaves, or dried grass. Avoid objects that are likely to wilt or change in a few days, such as fresh flowers or insects.
3. Transfer your best sketch onto construction paper or poster board. Using oil pastels or markers, begin adding color. Apply hues that match the colors of the natural objects you plan to use.
4. Decide which areas of your composition you will decorate with the objects you collected. Choose objects whose natural textures suit the subject matter. You might use sand for a path. Attach the objects with white glue. Make sure all areas of the composition are covered.
5. Step back and review the organization of your work. Make sure the elements of art emphasize one part of the picture. If you like, use drawing media to add buildings, animals, or human figures to the scene.
6. When the glue is dry, display your work.

Evaluating Your Work

- **Describe** Identify the objects and shapes in your landscape scene. Describe the setting.
- **Analyze** Explain how you organized your picture to create a center of interest. Which object or area did you emphasize? Where did you use tactile and visual textures?
- **Interpret** Decide what feeling or mood your work communicates to viewers. Find out if viewers can identify the place your picture describes.
- **Judge** Tell whether you feel your work succeeds. Explain your answer.

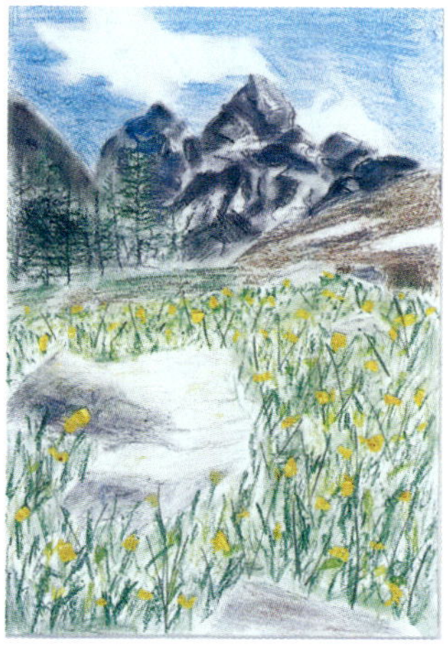

◆ **Figure 6–5** Student work. A nature scene.

Reflective Thinking

Critical Evaluation Analyze the original portfolios of your peers. Select a few of their artworks and form conclusions about formal properties and historical and cultural contexts. How have they applied the elements and principles of art to communicate their ideas? Describe particular themes they illustrated in their artworks.

Visual Art Journal

Develop ideas from the environment. Notice something special about nature. Observe the shapes of leaves, the color of the sky, the pattern of rain on your window. Illustrate your ideas in your journal.

Inclusion Strategies

Special Learning Needs Making an assemblage is a good way to build self-esteem and self-confidence in students who may not view themselves as particularly talented artists. Encourage students to be creative in their search for natural objects, and make practical suggestions for tactile, textured objects that are easily collected. Augment what the students collect with a variety of easy-to-get objects like seeds, leaves, twigs, and so on. As students gather their found natural objects, be sure they do not pick any protected species of wildflower or take anything from private property without prior permission. L1 ELL

Vocabulary

Explain the term *assemblage.* Point out that the word comes from *assemble.* Help students understand the three-dimensional qualities of an assemblage.

Studio Skills

Students should sort the assembled objects to make them easier to use. Then have students make a few preliminary sketches to plan the composition so that it emphasizes a center of interest. Encourage students to add color first to the poster board spaces, and then use a thick, nontoxic white glue to attach materials. L1 ELL

Visual Art Journal

Encourage students to develop their perceptual skills by having them illustrate environmental themes from direct observation.

3 Assess

Peer Assessment

Group students in pairs and have them analyze each other's portfolios. They should select a few artworks from the portfolios to analyze and form conclusions about formal properties (the elements and principles of art), and historical and cultural contexts. Encourage students to assess each other's progress.

4 Close

Have students share their assemblages and identify the center of interest.

LESSON 3

Nature Up Close

(pages 108–109)

1 Focus

Objectives

After completing this lesson, students will be able to:

- Define *study* and *nature study* as the terms relate to art.
- Compare and contrast two nature studies from different artists.

2 Teach

Motivator

Put a sample of soil on a sheet of paper. Have students predict what they could expect to find in the soil. Use a pencil to separate small sticks, stones, and to observe all other soil ingredients. What did they discover in looking closely at the soil that they did not expect to find?

Vocabulary

Review the meaning of *point of view.* Then clarify the meaning of *study* as a noun, and *nature study.*

Understanding Art History

RENAISSANCE In small groups, have students research the Renaissance. List important historical events, famous people in the arts, popular literature, dance forms, music, and other artists and their works. Bring in several copies of artworks from the Renaissance era. Ask students to identify the influence of historical and political events in those artworks. L1 ELL

LESSON 3

Nature Up Close

Have you ever looked at a familiar object under a microscope or magnifying glass? Maybe you have seen the "rivers" that crisscross the surface of human skin. Perhaps you discovered that grains of table salt, far from shapeless forms, are perfect cubes!

When seen up close, the world reveals many surprises. Artists have long known this. Many have recorded insect's-eye views of nature. In this lesson, you will see some of these.

NATURE STUDIES

The art of drawing serves several purposes. One of these is to help artists improve perception—how they "see" objects. Another is to make studies. A **study** is *a drawing used to plan a painting or other large project.* The artwork in **Figure 6–6** was created with both purposes in mind. The work is an example of a **nature study.** This is *a drawing used to help artists sharpen their perception of natural objects.*

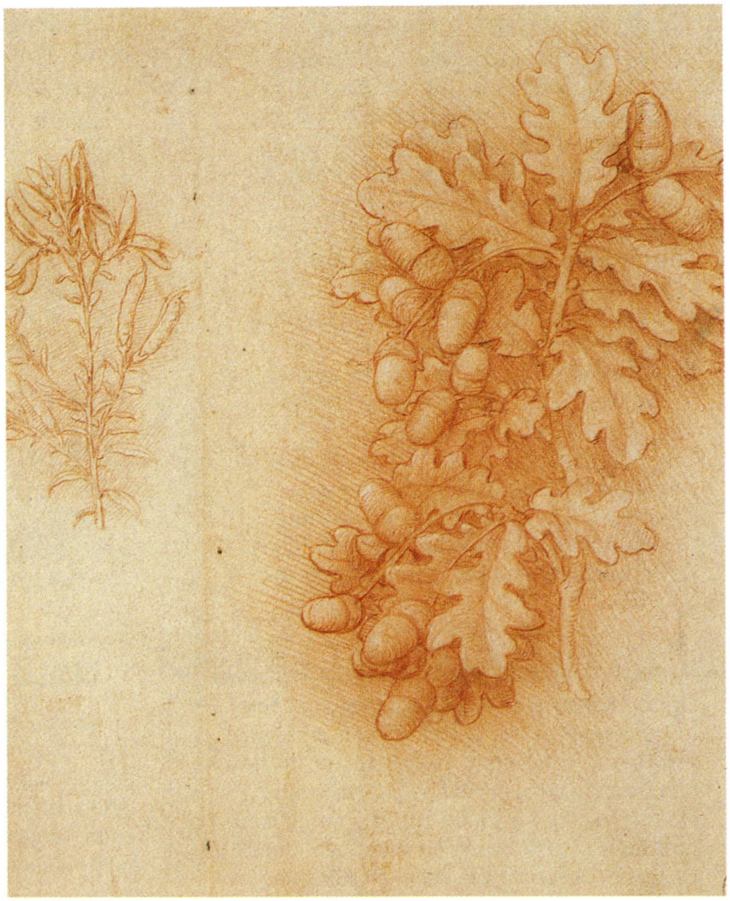

◆ **Figure 6–6** **Which of the works on these two pages is more realistic? What role do you think art materials played in this difference?**

Leonardo da Vinci. *Oak Leafs and a Spray of Greenwood.* c. 1506–08. Red conte pencil. 18.8 × 15.4 cm (7½ × 6″). The Royal Collection © Her Majesty Queen Elizabeth II.

COMMUNITY CONNECTION

PLANTING A GARDEN Check with your local Arboretum or phonebook to see if there is a community garden in your neighborhood. If there isn't one, discuss with the school administration the idea of creating one on your school site. Research what native plants and flowers will grow in your area. Have students take turns tending the garden and invite other grades to contribute to its upkeep. Encourage students to use the garden as inspiration for nature studies and drawings of their favorite plants. Have students use their sketches to create journals that identify the plants.

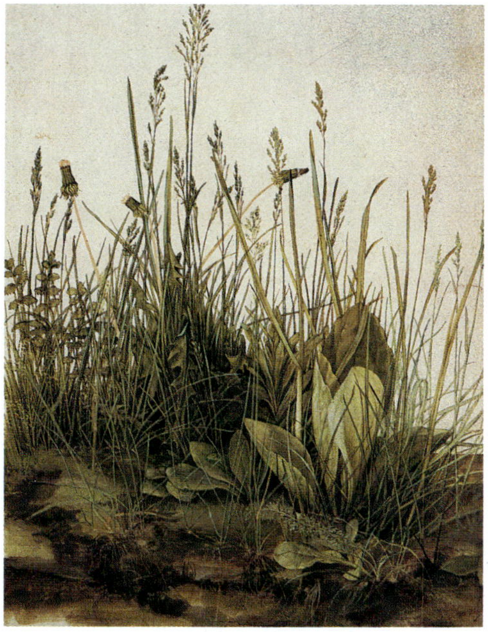

◆ **Figure 6–7** **Examine the way in which the artist used form and texture in this painting.**

Albrecht Dürer. *The Great Piece of Turf.* c. 1503. Watercolor on paper. 41.3 × 31.8 cm (16¼ × 12½″). The Bridgeman Art Library, London. Albertina Graphic Collection, Vienna, Austria.

The artist who made this drawing is Leonardo da Vinci. Leonardo had many talents. He was an architect, a musician, and an inventor. As an artist, he filled many sketchbooks with drawings like the one on this page. He often included detailed written descriptions of what he saw. Study Figure 6–6. Do you recognize the objects hanging between the leaves of the branches? Leonardo called them "oak nuts." You probably know them better as acorns. Notice how the artist has created three dimensions working with pencil. How many different textures can you find in this work?

A Painting of Nature Up Close

Not all studies of nature are drawings. The work in **Figure 6–7** is a painting. It was done around the same time as Leonardo's nature study. Like Figure 6–6, it shows a close-up view of plant life.

Study this painting. In it, the artist focuses mainly on the shapes and patterns of the leaves. He uses different values of green and yellow to capture lines and details. How does he create a sense of depth in this painting? What aesthetic view would you use to judge this work? (See Chapter 4, pages 64–65 for a review of the aesthetic views.)

Meet the Artist

Leonardo da Vinci (1452–1519)

Cultural connection. Although he is probably most famous for his paintings, such as *Mona Lisa* and *The Last Supper*, artist Leonardo da Vinci was one of the greatest scientific minds of the Renaissance. He studied many fields of science, including botany, anatomy, and astronomy. Leonardo filled notebooks with designs and drawings for inventions, such as aircraft and war machines, which were centuries ahead of their time.

Leonardo da Vinci was born in 1452 in the village of Vinci, Italy, not far from Florence. (The name *da Vinci* is Italian for "from Vinci.") He was fascinated by nature and wanted to understand the workings of what he observed. Leonardo used drawings as a way to study nature (see **Figure 6-6**) and as a tool for planning his artistic compositions. Compare the depiction of nature in Figures 6–6 and 6–7. How are they similar? What are their differences?

To learn more about Leonardo da Vinci and his work, click on Artist Profiles at art.glencoe.com.

Check Your Understanding

1. What is a *study?* What is a *nature study?*
2. What were some of Leonardo da Vinci's talents besides art?
3. What is the point of view of the painting in Figure 6–7?

Meet the Artist

Leonardo da Vinci

Have students describe **Figure 6–6** and **6–7.** Ask them to decide if one work shows more texture and represents nature more effectively. What is the message or artists' intent in making the drawing and the painting? Have students judge both works and support their answers.

3 Assess

Self-Assessment

Have students complete the **Check Your Understanding** questions on this page. Answers are provided below.

Reteaching

Ask students to work in pairs to discuss the point of view used in Figures 6–6 and 6–7.

Enrichment

LEONARDO DA VINCI Invite students to research the life of Leonardo da Vinci in more detail. Have students share what they discover about his roles in science, medicine, architecture, and art, for example. L2

4 Close

Ask students to define *nature study* and *point of view.*

Answers to Check Your Understanding

1. A study is a drawing used to plan a painting or other large project. A nature study is a drawing used to help artists sharpen their perception of natural objects.
2. He was an architect, a musician, and an inventor.
3. It is a close-up view from the ground level.

Drawing from a Bird's-Eye View

(pages 110–111)
Lesson Time: 90 minutes

1 Focus

Objectives

After completing this lesson, students will be able to:

- Draw a scene from nature using a bird's-eye point of view.
- Demonstrate technical skills effectively by using chalk and oil pastels to produce designs and express a certain feeling in their drawing.
- Describe, analyze, interpret, and judge their work.

SUPPLIES
Refer to **What You Will Need** in the Student Edition.

2 Teach

Motivator

Ask students if they have ever wanted to climb to a high place to get a better view. Tell them that such a view is called a "bird's-eye view." Have students consider how the perspective of objects changes with added distance. Direct their attention to Wyeth's painting in **Figure 6–8.** Ask: From the colors and details, can you recognize the season and where the scene was painted? Is this painting effective in showing a "bird's-eye view"?

Vocabulary

Explain that *organic* refers to nature. Organic lines or shapes would represent natural shapes and forms such as plants, rocks, animals, and people.

Drawing from a Bird's-Eye View

The painting in Figure 6–8 is done from an interesting point of view. Look carefully at this work. Like those in the previous lesson, this one provides a close-up view of nature. In this case, the subject is a tree. The point of view is from high among the branches. There is more to the work, however. Did you notice the lone human figure in the painting? His red cap stands out vividly against the mostly brown earth tones. He is a hunter. You won't find his prey—a bird—in the picture. That is because the bird sits in the branches, gazing down at the hunter. You are seeing the scene through the bird's eyes!

WHAT YOU WILL LEARN

In this lesson, you will picture a familiar scene as a bird might view it. Depending on where you live, the scene may be in the country or city. You will include natural objects, such as mountains, fields, rivers, and streams, or objects made by people, such as buildings, streets, and trucks. After sketching the scene in chalk, you will add color by blending oil pastels. Use colors that give your picture a certain mood or feeling. As in Figure 6–8, your work will make use of different textures to achieve variety.

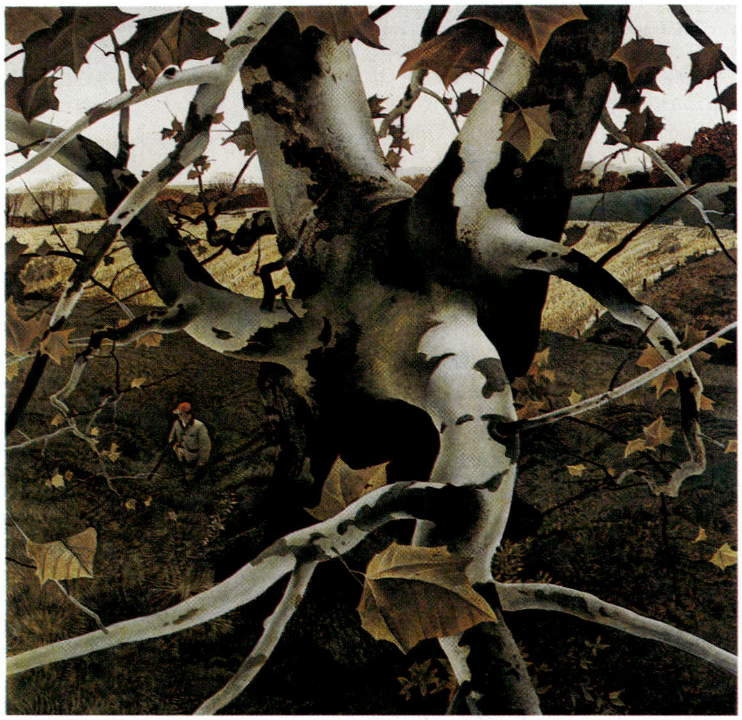

◆ **Figure 6–8** **Notice the attention to detail in this work. How many different visual textures can you find?**

Andrew Wyeth. *The Hunter.* 1943. Tempera on Masonite. 83.8 × 86 cm (33 × 33⅞"). Toledo Museum of Art, Toledo, Ohio. Elizabeth C. Mau Bequest Fund.

TEACHER TO TEACHER

DIRECT OBSERVATION SKILLS To improve drawing skills, students need to become keen observers. If objects they draw are too familiar, students do not look carefully enough to record them accurately. Begin a collection of uncommon objects from nature such as fossils, shells, bark, or plants. Ask students to find and bring unique objects to draw. These should be small items that can be stored in baskets and be displayed in an area of the room. You should also include magnifying glasses. Students will be curious and observe them more intently. Students' drawings will improve along with their observation skills.

What You Will Need

- Pencil and sketch paper
- Construction paper, 12 x 18 inches
- Chalk
- Oil pastels

What You Will Do

1. Select the place you will draw. Complete several sketches of this location from a bird's-eye view. Include natural or other objects found in the setting.
2. Decide which is your best sketch. Redraw it lightly in chalk on construction paper. Erase any unwanted lines.
3. Choose hues of oil pastels that fit your subject. Blend some colors. Include different textures, as in Figure 6–8, to add variety to your work. Color in all of the areas of your picture.

Evaluating Your Work

- **Describe** Tell what your work shows. Point to natural objects or those objects in the work that were made by people.
- **Analyze** Identify the hues in your work. Which hues were created by blending oil pastels? Explain how you added variety using different textures.
- **Interpret** Tell what mood your drawing captures. Did you record a stressful moment, as in Figure 6–8?
- **Judge** Tell whether you are satisfied with your drawing. Identify areas of the work that especially pleased you. Address what you would do differently next time.

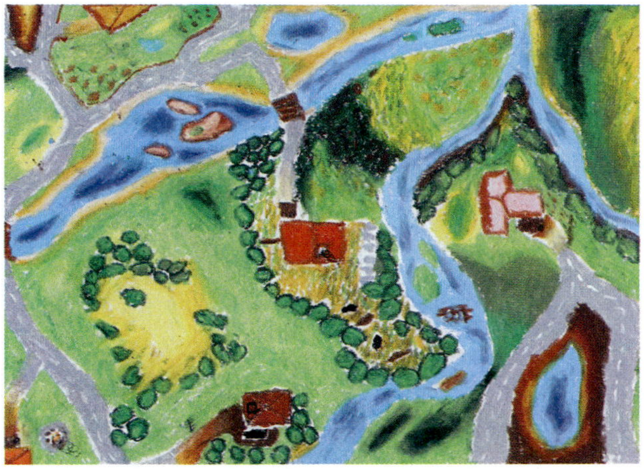

◆ **Figure 6–9** Student work. A bird's eye view.

Portfolio Ideas

A strong portfolio contains samples of work created with a variety of media, techniques, and processes. Your entries might include preliminary sketches as well as finished works. By including self-reflections and written evaluations, you will learn more about yourself as an artist.

Art Online

For additional student art and other activities, check out our Web site at art.glencoe.com. There you will also find:

- Artist Profiles
- Interactive Games
- Museum Web Links
- Studio Activities

Team Building Activity

Students may have difficulty imagining a familiar scene from a bird's-eye point of view. Encourage students to work in small groups to come up with a list of ideas to draw from. Then have them fine-tune their choice and proceed with the studio lesson. L1 ELL

3 Assess

Self-Assessment

Have students use **Evaluating Your Work** to conduct an in-progress critique of their drawing from a bird's-eye view.

Reteaching

Ask students to explain how they attempted to achieve texture and mood in their drawings. L1

Enrichment

Andrew Wyeth The Wyeth family is famous for several generations of talented artists. Invite students to find out about the Wyeths and share that information with the class, bringing in examples of their work. Have a one-day Wyeth festival to discuss the variety and scope of this family's talent. L2

4 Close

Have students differentiate the natural and human-made objects in their drawings, and explain the mood they tried to achieve.

Developing a Portfolio

Establishing Expectations Knowing what can go into a portfolio helps both the teacher and student. Written observations, verbal responses, records, sketches, and final products are recognized as the basic contributions. Try to include students in the development of what is expected in the portfolio. Asking questions like, "What do you think would be useful for me to see in your art portfolio?" immediately involves them in the learning and helps them see the rationale for the assignments they do. It also sets a pattern for self-reflection. For other ideas, refer to the booklet, *Portfolio and Assessment Techniques.*

Art and the Seasons

(pages 112–113)

1 Focus

Objectives

After completing this lesson, students will be able to:

- Understand that certain images and colors are linked to different seasons.
- Compare and analyze artworks depicting a season.

2 Teach

Motivator

Have students look closely at the winter landscape in **Figure 6–11.** From the details, can they identify the time and place where it was painted? Have students make a list of all the tasks they observe people doing in the painting and list features that show how everyday life then was different from today.

Vocabulary

Have students look up the word *season.* What parts of speech is this word? *(Noun and verb.)*

LESSON 5

Art and the Seasons

The seasons showcase nature's many faces. Think of the changing leaves in autumn. Think of winter, with its icy chill. Imagine the beauty of spring with its new buds and shoots.

The seasons and their colors have appealed to artists throughout the ages. Many artists have used their art to share special views of one season or another.

A Work Showing Autumn

From falling stars to rainbows to picture-perfect sunsets, nature stages many remarkable shows. One spectacular view is depicted in the painting in **Figure 6–10.** Study this work. It was done early in the twentieth century by a Canadian artist. The painting records the changing of the leaves in autumn. Have you ever heard autumn colors described as *fiery?* It is precisely this aspect of the leaves that the artist has captured. See how the sweeping brushstrokes and bright hues have been combined to suggest flames. As you study the painting, in which direction is your eye drawn? What principles have been used to organize the work?

A Work Showing Winter

Another seasonal event recorded by an artist is shown in **Figure 6–11.** The artist has

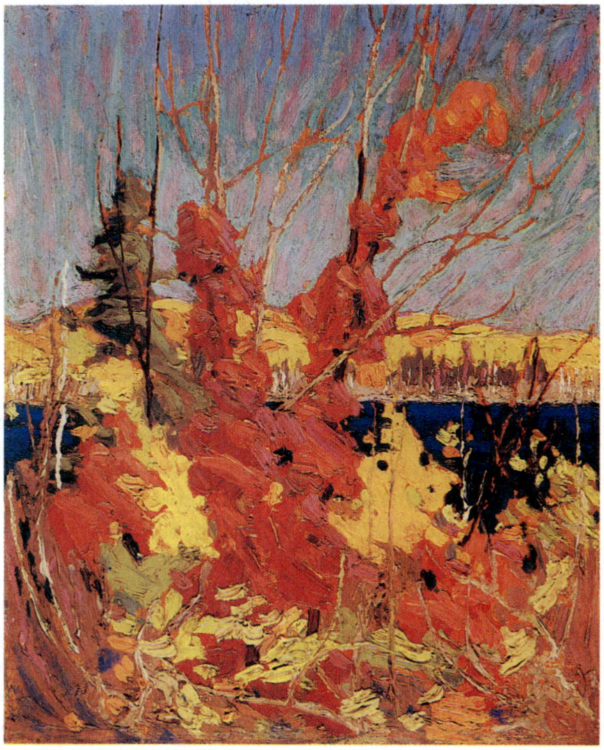

◆ **Figure 6–10** **Where is this landscape set? What aspects of scenery has the artist included to define this setting?**

Tom Thompson. *Autumn Foliage.* 1916. Oil on wood. 26.7 × 21.5 cm (10½ × 8½″). National Gallery of Canada, Ottawa.

CURRICULUM CONNECTIONS

Music Locate a CD of Vivaldi's concertos, *The Four Seasons.* Before you play the music for students, ask them to get paper and pencil out to take notes. As you play segments of the music, invite students to imagine what season the music seems to suggest. Explain that they may or may not "hear" all four seasons, but encourage them to describe any seasonal images that do come to mind. In their word descriptions, students should use colorful, vivid language such as adjectives and adverbs, to create a seasonal word picture.

offered a glimpse not only of an event but of a season. This winter scene has been preserved for over four centuries.

Examine the work. It shows a party of hunters and their dogs. They are returning home after a cold outing in the woods. A trio of birds huddle in the bare branches of the trees above the hunters. Still farther overhead is a bleak sky that promises more snow. Yet, the scene is not gloomy. In fact, it is almost cheerful. Down below the hunters, on a frozen lake, townspeople merrily skate.

Notice the suggestion of distance in the painting. The artist has used several of the techniques for capturing space covered on page 16 in Chapter 1. Two of these are *size* and *placement.* Observe how the trees in the background are smaller and placed higher up in the picture plane than the hunters are. What other techniques for suggesting space can you find?

Check Your Understanding

1. What images and colors are linked with different seasons?
2. Which of these colors and images appear in the two works in this lesson?

Time & Place

Sixteenth Century Flemish Art

Historical connection. You may be familiar with the Italian Renaissance of the fifteenth and sixteenth centuries. Other parts of Europe also experienced a Renaissance during this time period. In northern Europe, the cultural center was located in Flanders—an area found in modern-day France, Belgium, and the Netherlands. People who lived in this area were known as Flemish.

Some of the most celebrated Flemish painters include Jan van Eyck, Peter Paul Rubens, and Pieter Bruegel. These artists were masters of oil painting. They painted scenes of the world around them using precise, realistic detail and paying attention to light and atmosphere. **Figure 6-11** is an example of Pieter Bruegel's work. Although his impressive talent was not fully appreciated during his lifetime, Bruegel is now considered the greatest Flemish painter of the sixteenth century. Compare Figure 6–10 with Bruegel's painting. Which one do you think is more realistic at illustrating a season?

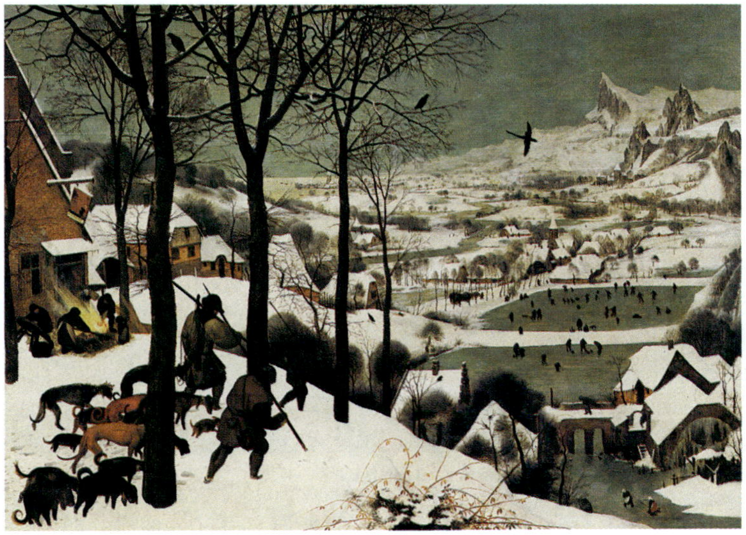

◆ **Figure 6–11** **This work by Pieter Bruegel shows winter activities in the 1500s. How has the artist used color to portray a winter landscape?**

Pieter Bruegel. *Hunters in the Snow.* 1565. Oil on wood. 117 × 162 cm (46 × 63¾"). Kunsthistorisches Museum, Vienna, Austria. Erich Lessing/Art Resource, NY.

Time & Place

Answers will vary. Both artworks are successful at depicting a season, but some students may answer that Bruegel's painting is more realistic than Thompson's because the subjects are representational.

Art Criticism

Have students describe both works reproduced in the lesson and analyze the interdependence of the art elements and principles. Ask: Which work uses the elements and principles of art to emphasize perspective? Does one work show more movement? Which work is more expressive? In small groups, have students write a paragraph interpreting each painting and explaining the meaning or mood communicated in each work. L1 ELL

3 Assess

Self-Assessment

Have students complete the **Check Your Understanding** questions on this page. Answers are provided below.

Reteaching

Invite students to brainstorm colors and images they associate with different seasons. L1 ELL

4 Close

Have students explain how certain colors are linked to specific seasons.

Answers to Check Your Understanding

1. Answers will vary. The changing colors of the leaves and vibrant reds, browns, and yellows are linked with autumn. Gray skies, blue-white snow, barren land and trees, ice skating, and snow are linked with winter. Spring carries images of budding trees and flowers, light green shoots, rich black or red earth, blue skies, and spring rains. Summer suggests cloudless, sun-filled skies, bees and insects buzzing, heat waves rising from the pavement, green lawns, and yellow corn.
2. Autumn leaves and fiery colors appear in Thompson's work. Bruegel's painting has winter images of snow, skaters, and gray skies.

The Ocean's Tide
(pages 114–115)

1 Focus

Objectives

After completing this lesson students will be able to:

- Compare how nature is depicted in artworks and poetry.
- Explain the literary device of *personification.*
- Write a poem that describes the sea.

2 Teach

Motivator

On the board write the phrase *the angry sea.* Explain that it describes one of the "moods" of the sea. Ask students to name some of the sea's other moods. Note that two of these are reflected in the poem they are about to read, as well as in the painting they are about to view.

Active Reading

Have volunteers read each of the two stanzas of the poem. Then divide the class into small groups. Ask each group if they can name the literary device used in line 1, in which the sea is said to awaken from sleep. *(It is personification.)* Ask them to define this term. *(It is assigning human properties to nonhuman things.)* L2

The Ocean's Tide

So far, you've learned how nature can be illustrated in various ways, such as landscapes, nature studies, and depicting seasonal events. Another way of demonstrating nature is depicting the ocean.

Think about the many states or moods the ocean shows. The sea can be calm or choppy. It can be majestic or angry. Sometimes, the ocean can be downright menacing. How would you describe the mood of the sea in the painting shown in **Figure 6-12?** This work is by twentieth-century American artist Marsden Hartley. Notice the precise moment Hartley has captured. An enormous wave has just broken over a rocky coastline. You can almost hear the loud cymbal-like crash of the water against the shore. Contrast the white foam of the wave with the steel-blue sea beyond or the moody gray sky overhead. This is more than just a painting of the ocean. It is a painting of the raw power and force of nature.

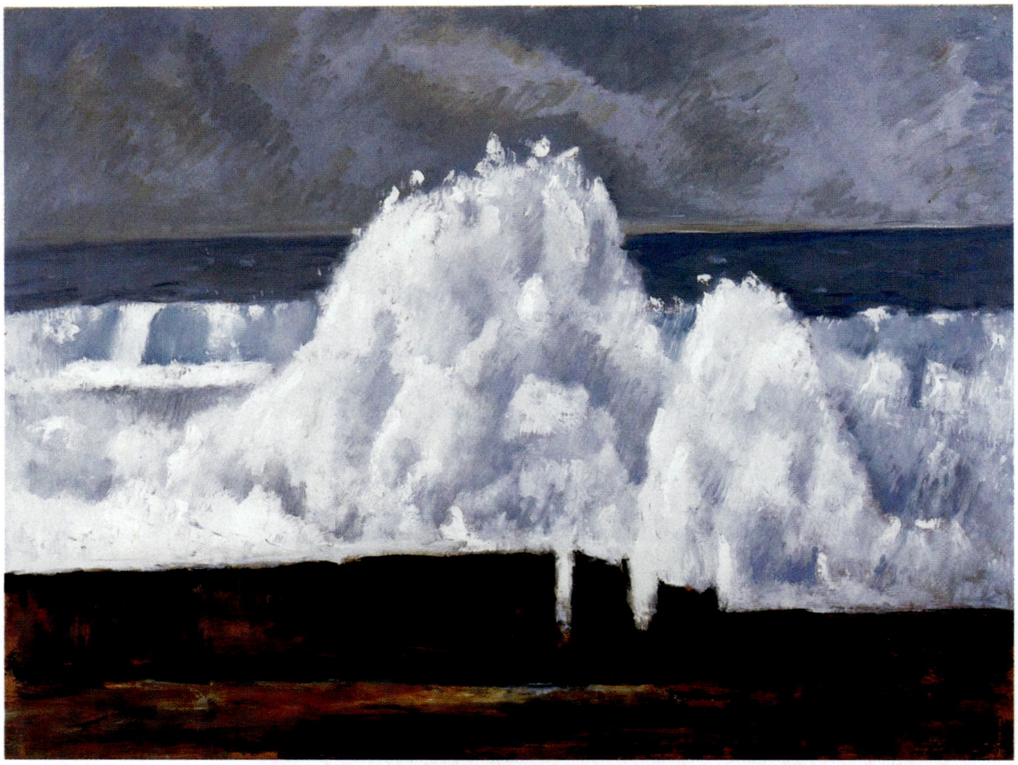

◆ **Figure 6–12** **How does this painting reveal the raw power and force of nature?**

Marsden Hartley. *The Wave.* 1940–41. Oil on masonite. 76.8 × 103.8 cm (30¼″ × 40⅞″). Worcester Museum of Art. Worcester, Massachusetts.

MORE ABOUT...

Marsden Hartley (1877–1943) A native of Lewiston, Maine, Hartley earned a scholarship to the Cleveland School of Art at the age of 15. He continued his studies in New York, where he met the photographer and art promoter Alfred Stieglitz. Hartley became part of Stieglitz's inner circle of artists, writers, and critics. While a member of this circle, Hartley was exposed to works by modern masters, including Paul Cézanne, Henri Matisse, and Auguste Rodin. In 1913, Hartley relocated to Berlin, where he joined a group of progressive, abstract artists. It was during this period that he painted what critics today regard as his finest work.

Describing the Ocean

Clearly, art can be a powerful visual medium in capturing the mood of the sea. Another way to illustrate this mood is through words, especially when they are combined into a poem.

The poem in **Figure 6–13** describes the changing moods of the sea. It was written by the nineteenth-century poet Henry Wadsworth Longfellow. It is the first two stanzas of his sonnet "The Sound of the Sea." From calmness to an onset of waves, the sea can change its mood instantly. Read Longfellow's poem and think of the other ways the ocean reveals its different states.

From "The Sound of the Sea"

"The sea awoke at midnight from its sleep,
And round the pebbly beaches far and wide
I heard the first wave of the rising tide
Rush onward with uninterrupted sweep;
A voice out of the silence of the deep,
A sound mysteriously multiplied
As of a cataract from the mountain's side,
Or roar of winds upon a wooded steep."

◆ **Figure 6–13** From "The Sound of the Sea" by Henry Wadsworth Longfellow.

MAKE THE CONNECTION

Take Another Look

1. Like artist Marsden Hartley, poet Longfellow captures a very precise moment in his verbal seascape. In your own words, describe what is happening at this moment. What time of day is it?
2. Is the natural event Longfellow describing similar to the one in Hartley's painting? If not, explain the differences.

ART & READING

Writing a Poem. Choose a partner. Together, brainstorm a list of words that describe aspects of the sea. Some possibilities include *tide, crest, foam, surf,* and *brine.* Use these words and others to write your own original poem about the sea. Choose a moment other than the one chosen in Figure 6–13. Your poem can rhyme or not rhyme as you choose.

Art Criticism

Note that the artist uses the element of line to emphasize the size and power of the wave. Illustrate this by having students locate all the horizontal lines in the painting. *(These may be found at the horizon, along the top of the breaking wave in the middle ground, and implied by the shoreline.)* L1 ELL

Understanding Art History

Direct students' attention to another artwork that depicts the ocean: Figure 9–16 on page 177. Have students compare and contrast Hartley's depiction of the sea with Homer's. What similarities and differences in style can they identify? L1 ELL

3 Assess

Self-Assessment

Have students complete the **Take Another Look** questions on this page. Answers are provided below.

Reteaching

Ask students to summarize the description in the first four lines of the poem. L1

4 Close

Have students think about other aspects of nature that could be reflected in poems and in paintings. L1 ELL

MAKE THE CONNECTION

Take Another Look Student answers will vary, but may include the following:

1. Presumably it is afternoon. A large wave has just crashed on the shore.
2. Both works depict very similar events. The difference between the two works is the reference in the poem to the sea "waking up."

The Power of Nature

(pages 116–117)

1 Focus

Objectives

After completing this lesson, students will be able to:

- Recognize how the use of expressive color schemes and diagonal lines can communicate nature's power.
- Define the term *monoprint.*
- Demonstrate technical skills effectively by using a variety of materials to create a monoprint.

SUPPLIES
Refer to **What You Will Need** in the Student Edition.

2 Teach

Motivator

Have a group of students demonstrate the position of their bodies as they struggle and strain against a powerful and imaginary wind. Point out the diagonal body lines. Ask students to list all the different ways the artists show the action of the wind in **Figures 6–14** and **6–15**.

Vocabulary

Have students look up the combining form *mono-* in the dictionary, then list some words that begin with *mono-*.

LESSON 7

The Power of Nature

"March comes in like a lion and goes out like a lamb." You have probably heard this saying. It describes two of nature's personalities. The second of them is nature's gentle side. This can be seen on a mild spring day when there is sunshine, a soft breeze, and the season's first flowers.

The first—nature's rough and sometimes frightening side—is another personality. With floods, earthquakes, and tornadoes, we experience the power of nature. In this lesson, you will see and learn about artworks that relate to nature's power.

CAPTURING A STORM IN A PAINTING

Sometimes nature's fury makes the headlines. The threat of a hurricane sends coastal residents packing. A blizzard dumping three feet of snow closes schools for days.

Weather conditions command the attention of the news media and artists. The painting in **Figure 6–14** shows the raw power of nature. Look closely at this work. You can almost feel the force of the wind that tears at the struggling tree in the foreground. You can almost hear the sound of the foaming waves crashing against the rocks.

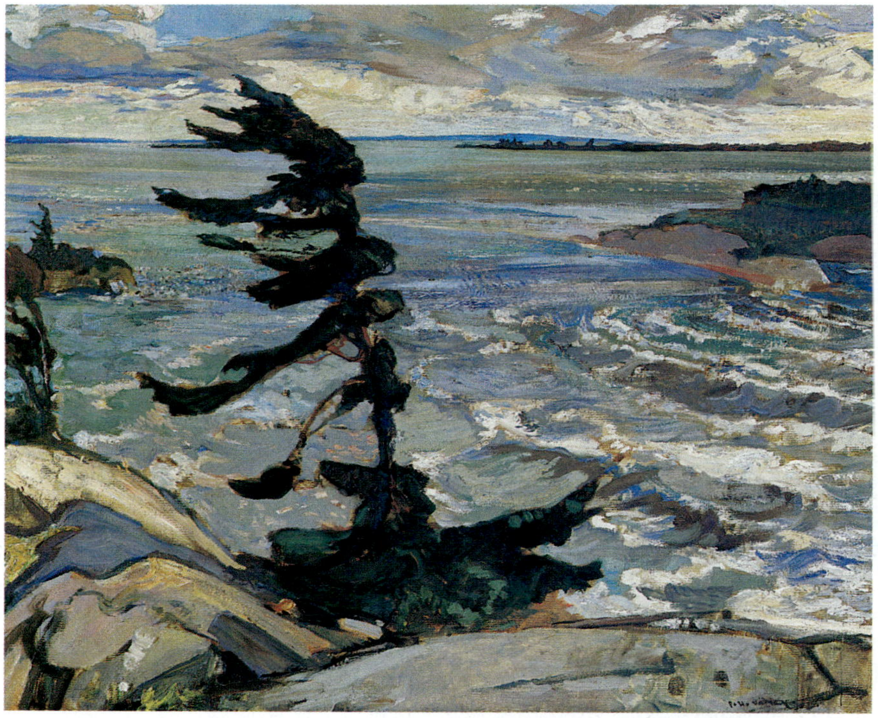

◆ **Figure 6–14** **Study this painting and form generalizations about the interdependence of the art element shape and the principle movement. Explain how these are used to depict blowing wind.**

Frederick Varley. *Stormy Weather, Georgian Bay.* 1920. Oil on canvas. 132.6 × 162.8 cm (52⅕ × 64″). National Gallery of Canada, Ottawa.

CAREER OPPORTUNITIES IN ART

SHADOWING Students can learn about art careers by "shadowing" adults who work in art-related fields. The adults allow students to follow—shadow—them in the workplace for a few hours. Students get a chance for one-on-one discussions of art careers, and adults have the opportunity to mentor a young person. Ask students to write a list of different art-related careers. Have them compare these career opportunities and select those in which they are most interested. Arrange to have professionals in those fields pair up with students.

Expressive Color Schemes

The creator of the painting in Figure 6–14 achieved this powerful effect using a cool color scheme. The limited use of color in this painting emphasizes the idea that the wind is everywhere. There is no escape or shelter from it. Its fierce gusts overpower the trees, land, the water, and even the sky. What basic hues are used in this painting? Where do you find light values of those hues? Where are darker values used?

Capturing a Storm in a Print

You will find a similar theme running through **Figure 6–15.** This work is a woodblock print. Notice the work's title. Ejiri is a place in the artist's homeland of Japan. Examine the use of line and color in the work. In what ways is this "view" of the wind similar to the one in Figure 6–14? What differences can you find between the two works?

Check Your Understanding

1. Describe the type of color schemes you would use to show nature's seasons.
2. What is a *monoprint?* Why can only a single image be created using this printmaking technique?

Studio Activity

Making a Monoprint

Demonstrate technical skills. Develop your printmaking skills by making a **monoprint**. This is *a print made by applying ink or paint to a plate and then transferring the image by hand-rubbing.*

Begin by drawing a simple landscape in crayon on a sheet of gray or pale blue construction paper. Use mostly dark values of the colors you choose.

Place a drop of liquid starch the size of half a dollar on a table top. Sprinkle a small amount of white powdered tempera onto the starch. With one bare hand, mix the starch and paint. Spread the mixture out until it is the size of your drawing. Make diagonal lines and swirls in the paint with your hand. Wash and dry your hands. Carefully lay your drawing face-down on the "plate" you have created. Press all over the surface with your other hand. Lift your print by pulling it up from one side. Lay it on newspapers to dry.

PORTFOLIO

Examine your monoprint and evaluate the success of your technique.

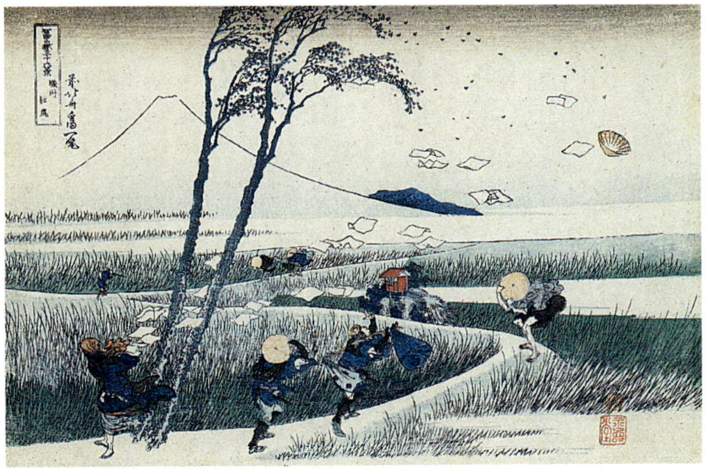

◆ **Figure 6–15** How would you have been able to identify a gust of wind as the subject of this painting without the aid of the title?

Katsushika Hokusai. *A Gust of Wind at Ejiri, from the series The Thirty-Six Views of Fuji.* 1831–33. Woodblock print. 24.5 × 37.5 cm (9⅝ × 14¾"). The Metropolitan Museum of Art, New York, New York. Rogers Fund, 1936.

Studio Activity

Making a Monoprint

Emphasize that using color heavily assures that shapes will not disappear later under the monoprint. Demonstrate the printing process. Remind students to use only one hand to mix the starch and paints. Have them explore different kinds of action lines with the side or palm of their hand. Since the printing process removes most of the fingerpaint, more starch and tempera need to be added for the next student, and it cleans up very easily.

3 Assess

Self-Assessment

Have students complete the **Check Your Understanding** questions on this page. Answers are provided below.

Reteaching

Have students practice using monochromatic colors and diagonal lines to sketch a stormy scene. L1 ELL

4 Close

In pairs, have students analyze each other's monoprint. Was their technique successful?

Answers to Check Your Understanding

1. Dark or bright, monochromatic color schemes can be used to show nature's seasons.
2. A monoprint is a print made by applying ink or paint to a plate and then transferring the image by hand-rubbing. This printing technique produces only a single image and the plate can be used only once, because the transferred image absorbs all the ink.

Painting a Storm

(pages 118–119)
Lesson Time: 2 hours

1 Focus

Objectives

After completing this lesson, students will be able to:

- Identify the kinds of lines, colors, and brushstrokes that create movement and action in a painting.
- Plan an informally balanced composition that includes repeating lines, shapes, and colors to create harmony and emphasize movement and mood.
- Demonstrate technical skills effectively by painting a stormy scene mixing three hues plus white and black to make tints and shades and using brushstrokes that enhance the mood and action.
- Describe, analyze, interpret, and judge their work.

SUPPLIES
Refer to **What You Will Need** in the Student Edition.

2 Teach

Motivator

Have students identify the feelings and moods they associate with dramatic weather changes and storms. Have students identify the lines and brushstrokes that help create movement and action in Burchfield's painting.

LESSON 8

Painting A Storm

Have you ever had days when things just didn't seem to go right? So, it seems, does nature. Such a day is the subject of **Figure 6–16.** The work pictures a bleak, rainy afternoon. Unlike the works you studied in the previous lesson, there is no fury in the storm depicted here—just gloom. Notice the churning gray clouds overhead. See the rippling puddles underfoot of anyone unlucky enough to be out on such a day. The monochromatic tones of clouds and buildings make you glad to be inside, where it is safe and dry. That is, in fact, where you are as you look at this scene. Did you notice the blurred lines on the window at the left? The distortion is caused by the rain on your own window—the one you are gazing through. Can you find the single raindrop that has beaded on the glass?

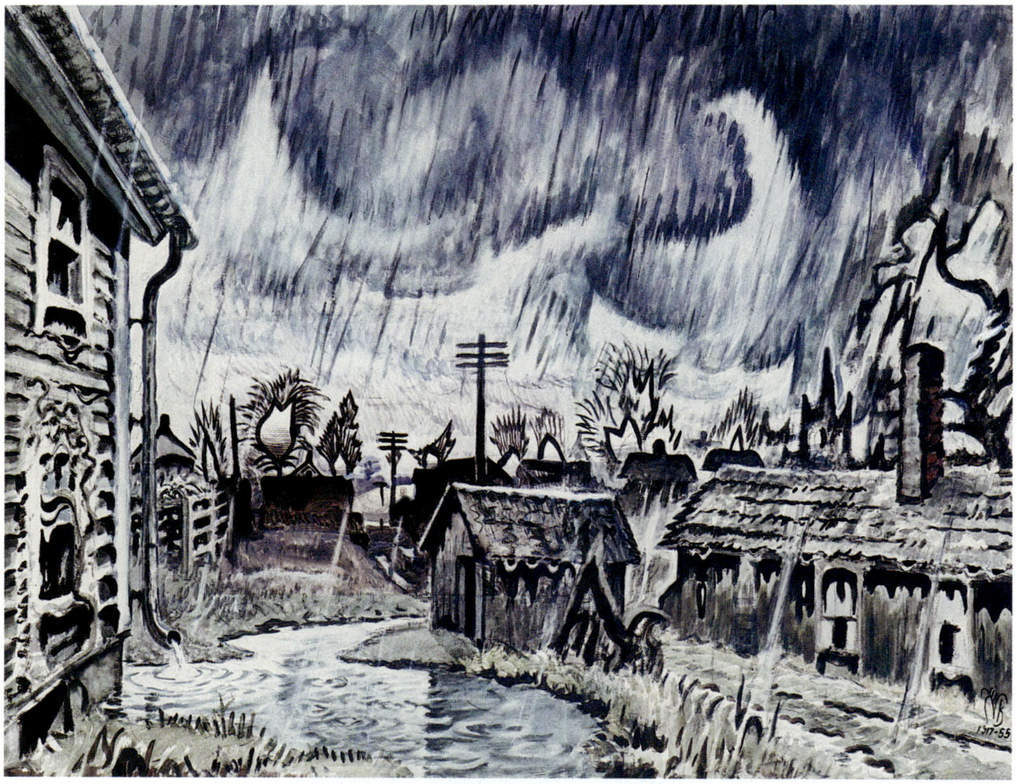

◆ **Figure 6–16** **The artist uses slanted lines to represent the falling rain. What type of line does he use to capture the clouds? How does he use color and value to create mood?**

Charles Burchfield. *Night of the Equinox.* 1917–55. Watercolor, brush, and ink, gouache and charcoal on paper. 102 × 132.5 cm ($40\frac{1}{8} \times 52\frac{3}{16}$″). The National Museum of American Art, Smithsonian Institution, Washington, D.C. Gift of the Sara Roby Foundation/Art Resource, NY.

CURRICULUM CONNECTIONS

BEHAVIORIAL PROBLEMS Painting a stormy scene provides an excellent opportunity for anyone to talk about disturbing things through the veiled language of art. Some students with behavior disorders may show evidence of problems in their actions and in their artwork. Classroom teachers may be among the first to see clues in an emotionally upset student's artwork suggesting a corroboration of an unhappy or upsetting life situation. Of course, untrained people should certainly not attempt to diagnose from artwork, but artwork can provide specialists with corroborating clues to conditions.

What You Will Learn

You will paint an expressive bad-weather scene. You will begin by selecting a season, time of day, and place. You will include trees, plants, and objects that help to describe the setting and the weather conditions. You will use tints and shades of a single hue of tempera paint. Various tints and shades of blue, for example, might be used to suggest a landscape with falling snow. You will use a variety of lines to help express movement.

What You Will Need

- Pencil and sketch paper
- Poster board or heavy construction paper, 12 x 18 inches
- Tempera paint
- Paper plate and brushes
- Water container and paper towels

What You Will Do

1. With classmates, brainstorm examples of bad weather. Choose a particular image. Decide on the time of year and place.
2. Working by yourself, complete several sketches of your bad weather scene. Sketch plants, trees, and other objects quickly. Use a variety of lines that suggest movement, as in Figure 6–16. Repeat some of the lines to create rhythm.
3. Transfer your scene onto poster board or construction paper. Choose a color of tempera that best fits your scene. On the paper plate, mix white and black tempera with the color you selected to create different tints and shades. Paint your scene.
4. Paint all of the spaces. Switch to a small brush with fine bristles to paint small shapes and details. Use black or white tempera to outline any important areas.
5. Choose a title for your work that reflects the mood and weather. See if other students can identify the season, time of day, and place in your painting.

Evaluating Your Work

- **Describe** Identify the season in your painting. Identify the time of day and place.
- **Analyze** Explain how you organized your work. Identify the different tints and shades you used. Where did you repeat lines or shapes to show movement?
- **Interpret** Tell what mood or feeling your work communicates. What is the title of your painting? Does it capture this mood or feeling?
- **Judge** State whether your artwork is successful. What details help make your painting expressive?

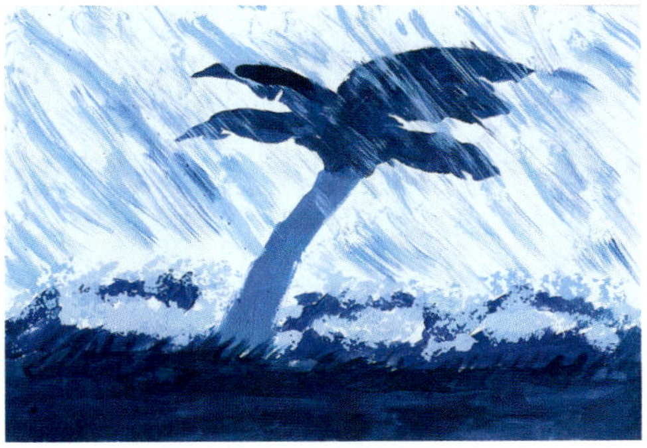

◆ **Figure 6–17** Student work. Rain in spring.

Computer Option

Use your program's Shape and Fill tools to create a simple landscape. Shapes should be flat. Choose dark shades of colors. If the software you are using has a Blend or Smear brush, select and use it. Paint objects with diagonal lines. Make some lines longer than others. Describe the effect you have achieved.

Visual Art Journal

In your journal, list the rewards of studying or creating art as a hobby. Compare these avocational opportunities in art, such as visiting museums and making art projects.

Team Building Activity

Divide the class into groups of three. Have each group scan old newspapers and magazine articles and photos related to severe weather. Have them share their findings with the whole class. L1 ELL

Studio Skills

Review mixing tints and shades by adding white and black to the hues. Have students use different brushes and strokes to represent the kinds of lines and weather conditions in their painting, and use pure hues of black or white to outline any important shapes or features. L1 ELL

3 Assess

Self-Assessment

Have students use **Evaluating Your Work** to conduct an in-progress critique of their stormy-weather scenes.

Reteaching

Have students analyze the original artworks of their peers to form conclusions about formal properties—the elements and principles of art. Ask them to identify the season and the mood in each other's work and how the work is organized. L1 ELL

4 Close

Have students evaluate their paintings in terms of the concept "storm."

Teacher to Teacher

Arts as avocation. Encourage students to explore the many opportunities in art. Explain that avocational means not related to a job or career. Studying or creating art as a hobby can provide many rewards. Pursuing art for personal enjoyment can teach students life skills, by strengthening their problem-solving skills. Explain that when they create art projects, they experiment with different tools, materials, and techniques. Students can then make an informed decision about what is the best design solution for the project. Emphasize to students that this kind of problem-solving skill will help them in other areas of their lives.

Horsing Around

1 Focus

Objectives

After completing this lesson, students will be able to:

- Sculpt a small animal figure out of clay or mud.
- Plan, write, and edit a proposal for a natural-media artwork.

2 Teach

Teaching the Feature

1. Encourage students to describe and discuss the horse sculpture shown in the photo. Ask: What makes this sculpture look like a real horse? What materials do you think the sculptor used?
2. Have students work with partners to read the article and determine the article's main ideas. Suggest they read to find answers to these questions: Why does Butterfield sculpt horses? What materials does she use? Why does she choose those materials?

Activity

Have each student choose a favorite animal. Let students use clay to sculpt figures of their chosen animals. If natural materials are readily available, have students experiment with using mud or a combination of mud, grass, and twigs to form their sculptures. L1 ELL

HORSING AROUND

An artist's ties to nature

Much of Deborah Butterfield's life is tied to the outdoors. Butterfield's sculptures are about natural objects, and she uses natural objects to create them. She especially likes sculpting horses. In fact, her life-size horses don't just stand outdoors in the mud—they're often made of mud!

Butterfield first constructed horses from mud and sticks in 1976. She has also created horses from old auto parts, farm equipment, and bits and pieces of metal buildings. In Butterfield's hands, even her metallic horses appear to have been created from natural materials.

Most people recognize Butterfield's sculptures as horses. But if you look closely, her horses aren't completely realistic. She uses materials to suggest animals rather than describe them in minute detail. Butterfield leaves viewers with a strong sense of a horse's anatomy and even its specific personality. Each piece, like the horses themselves, is unique.

Butterfield has loved horses since her California childhood. Today, she and her husband live on a ranch in Montana, where they own real horses. To Butterfield, living in the country is an advantage. This closeness to her subject matter is apparent in the lifelike quality of her sculpture.

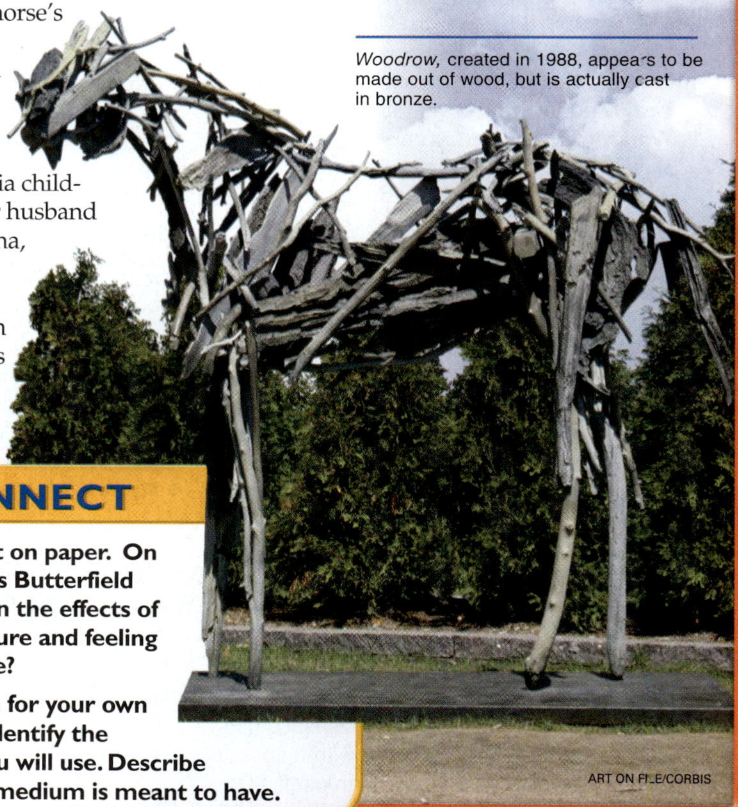

Woodrow, created in 1988, appears to be made out of wood, but is actually cast in bronze.

ART ON FILE/CORBIS

TIME TO CONNECT

- **Make a two-column chart on paper. On one side, list the materials Butterfield uses. On the other, explain the effects of each material. What texture and feeling does each material create?**
- **Write and edit a proposal for your own natural-media artwork. Identify the subject and the media you will use. Describe what effect each natural medium is meant to have.**

TIME TO CONNECT

Have students work with partners to write their two-columned charts. Ask partners to discuss their plans for artwork proposals and then work independently to write their ideas. Suggest that they keep these questions in mind as they write and review their proposals:

- How do my chosen media relate to the subject of this artwork?
- What reasons support my choice of media?
- Which other details can be added to make my reasons more clear?

Chapter 6 Review

BUILDING VOCABULARY

Number a sheet of paper from 1 to 6. After each number, write the term from the list that matches each description below.

assemblage	nature study
landscape	study
monoprint	stylized

1. A drawing or painting of mountains, trees, or other natural scenery.
2. A three-dimensional artwork consisting of many pieces assembled together.
3. Simplified or exaggerated.
4. A drawing used to plan a painting or other large project.
5. A drawing used to help artists sharpen their perception of natural objects.
6. A print made by applying ink or paint to a plate and then transferring the image by hand-rubbing.

REVIEWING ART FACTS

Number a sheet of paper from 7 to 11. Answer each question in a complete sentence.

7. Give two reasons why artists might stylize works of art.
8. What were Leonardo da Vinci's two purposes in creating the drawing in Figure 6–6?
9. What is point of view?
10. What are some hues associated with spring? What colors are associated with winter?
11. What season is shown in Figure 6–10? How did the artist convey this time of year?

CROSS-CURRICULUM CONNECTIONS

12. **Language Arts.** Look at Figure 6–4 on page 106. Write a short story about the scene. Describe the village and the people in the painting. Explain who they are and what they are doing. Illustrate the image with words.
13. **Music.** Storms have been the subject not only for visual artworks, but have also been depicted in numerous musical compositions. Speak with a music teacher in your school or community to learn about musical works that "describe" storms. Listen to one of these compositions. Write a paragraph describing how the music captures some of the images shown throughout the chapter.

Web Museum Activity

National Gallery of Art, Washington, D.C.

In this chapter, you explored the different ways artists have depicted nature. Visit the National Gallery of Art and study Henri Rousseau's painting *Tropical Forest with Monkeys.* Go to **art.glencoe.com** and click on the National Gallery of Art link.

Describe what is illustrated in the painting. How is nature depicted? How has the artist used colors to show it is a tropical forest? Is it an imaginary or realistic scene? Explain your answer.

Answers to Chapter 6 Review

Building Vocabulary

1. landscape
2. assemblage
3. stylized
4. study
5. nature study
6. monoprint

Reviewing Art Facts

7. This is done to fit the design rules of a specific culture and to personalize a work of art.
8. He did this to improve perception and as a study for a larger project.
9. The angle from which the viewer sees the scene in an artwork.
10. Spring colors include green and yellow. Winter colors include blue and white.
11. The season is autumn. This is clear from the red and yellow leaves and the bare tree branches.

Cross-Curriculum Connections

12. Answers will vary. Students' compositions should be imaginative and descriptive and reflect the scene in Figure 6–4.
13. Student responses will vary according to the musical composition they have selected. Their paragraph should include details as to how the music captures seasonal images seen in this chapter.

Web Museum Activity

Before you have students go online, visit the Web site to preview the museum's online content, collection, and any online exhibit that may be of interest. Have students study the painting by Henri Rousseau and describe how he depicted nature. Rousseau used green as the dominant color to depict the tropical forest. The scene can be viewed as more imaginary in its portrayal of the animals and jungle. Students' descriptions should reflect these answers.

Chapter Resources

Features	Standards for Chapter: National	Standards for Chapter: State/Local	Reproducible Masters
Quick Write page 123 TIME ART SCENE "The Ultimate Moo-seum" page 140 Web Museum Activity page 141	**1.** (a, b) **2.** (a, b) **3.** (a, b) **4.** (a, b, c) **5.** (a, b, c) **6.** (a, b)		Guided Reading and Practice 7–1 Enrichment Activity 7–2, 7–9, 7–12 Historical and Cultural Heritage 7–3, 7–6, 7–7 Cross-Curriculum Activity 7–4, 7–8 Studio Activity 7–5 Application Activity 7–10 Artist Profile 7–11 Lesson Plans

Lesson Resources

Lessons	Standards per Lesson: National	Standards per Lesson: State/Local	Reproducible Masters
1 *Animals in Earliest Art* (pages 124–125)	1a, 1b, 2a, 4a, 4c		Enrichment Activity 7–2 Historical and Cultural Heritage 7–3 Cross-Curriculum Activity 7–4
2 *Creating a Totem* (pages 126–127)	1a, 1b, 2a, 3b, 5b, 5c		Studio Activity 7–5 Historical and Cultural Heritage 7–6
3 *Sea Creatures* (pages 128–129)	2b, 4a, 4b, 5b		Historical and Cultural Heritage 7–7
4 ART & READING (pages 130–131)	4a, 6a, 6b		
5 *Birds in Art* (pages 132–133)	4a, 4b, 5b		Cross-Curriculum Activity 7–8 Enrichment Activity 7–9
6 *Making an Animal Sculpture* (pages 134–135)	1a, 1b, 2a, 2b		Application Activity 7–10
7 *Fantasy Animals* (pages 136–137)	1a, 1b, 4a, 4c		Artist Profile 7–11 Enrichment Activity 7–12
8 *Creating a Fantasy Animal* (pages 138–139)	1a, 1b, 2a, 3a		

Assessment	Technology
Testing Program: Chapter Test 7–13 Portfolio and Assessment Techniques	Artsource Performing Arts Package, Eugene Friesen (DVD or VHS Segment 4) National Museum of Women in the Arts Interactive Lesson Planner Fine Art Transparency CC-7, *Howling Coyote* Fine Art Transparency 7, *Bactrian Camel with Packsaddle*

Activities/Features
Studio Activity: Inventing a Mascot
Evaluating Your Work Reflective Thinking Visual Art Journal
Time & Place: Yuan Dynasty in China
Make the Connection
Time & Place: Ancient Persian Art
Evaluating Your Work Studio Option Visual Art Journal
Studio Activity: Creating an Imaginary Animal
Evaluating Your Work Portfolio Ideas Art Online

KEY TO ABILITY LEVELS

Teaching strategies have been coded.

- **L1** Activities for all students; teacher direction required
- **L2** Activities for average to above-average students; some teacher direction needed
- **L3** Activities for students able and willing to work independently
- **ELL** English Language Learner activities

FEATURED ARTISTS

- Habib Allah
- Constantin Brancusi
- Helen Hardin
- Martin Johnson Heade
- Franz Marc
- Ayako Miyawaki
- Spider Nabunu
- Frans Snyders

FINE ART PRINTS

Fine Art Print 11, *Daniel in the Lion's Den* by Peter Paul Rubens

Timesaving Technology

Interactive Lesson Planner

Make planning easy. Use this interactive software to organize your week, month, semester, or year and access all *Introducing Art* reproducible resources.

KEY TO LESSON RESOURCES

- Narrative Lesson
- Studio Lesson

Chapter 7

Observing Animals

(pages 122–141)

Chapter Overview

Understanding and appreciating the symbolic nature of animals in artworks is the focus of this chapter. Students will explore ancient artworks of animals as well as contemporary works. They will see how animals of the air, the land, and the sea have inspired artists, and they will tap their individual imaginations to create animal artworks of their own.

Discussing the Artwork

Focus On ◆ **Figure 7–1** Helen Hardin was a Native American artist of the Santa Clara Pueblo tribe in New Mexico. Early in her career, Hardin's paintings reflected more of a traditional realism. She later broke free from the traditional style after experiencing an artistic revolution. Her work became strongly geometric and increasingly abstract. Much of her work incorporates Mimbres figures, as in Figure 7–1. The rabbits pictured in this painting were an important food source for the Mimbres people. The Mimbres people were prehistoric Native Americans who lived from around A.D. 200 to 1350 in present-day southwestern New Mexico. In Native American tradition, the circle symbolizes the people's connection to the earth. It signifies how people, nature, and the earth are interconnected and how their connection completes a full circle.

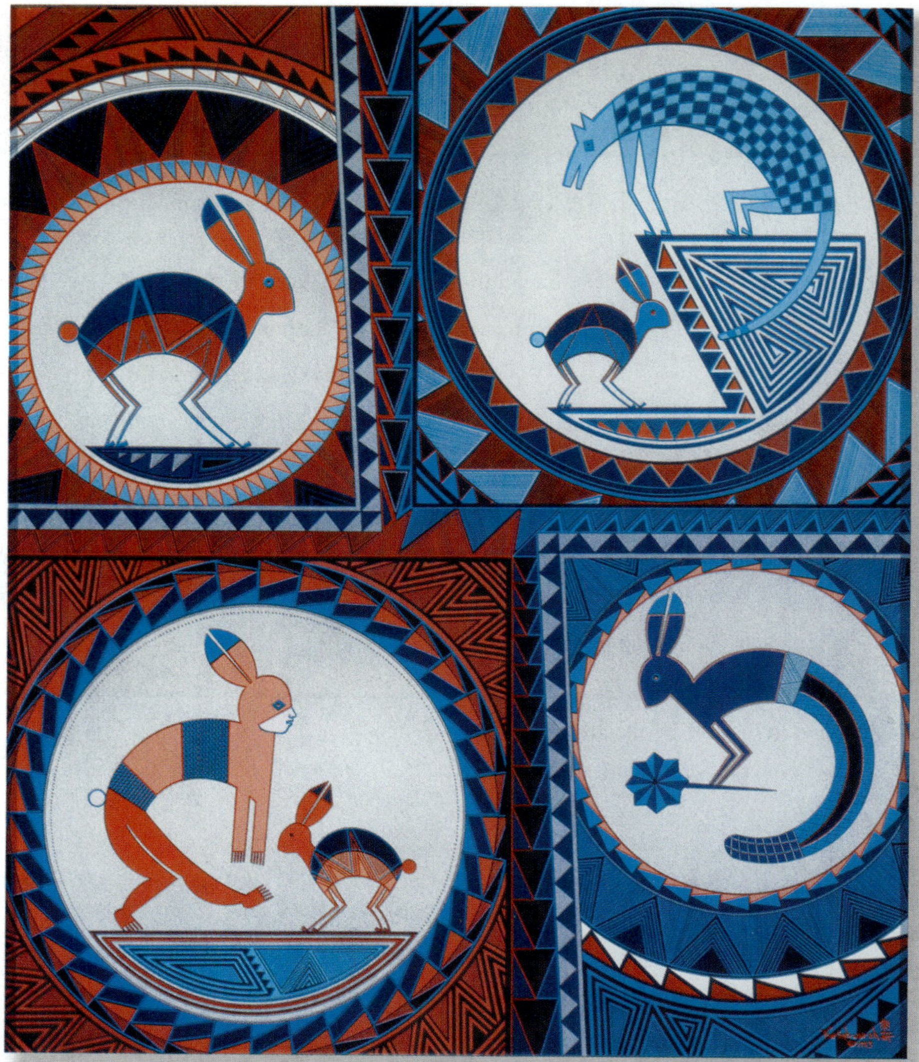

Focus On ◆ **Figure 7–1** Helen Hardin was a Native American artist of the Santa Clara Pueblo tribe. Her inspiration for these lively rabbits comes from the ancient Mimbres culture of the Southwest. Notice how she has used a repetition of pattern.

Helen Hardin. *Mimbres Rabbit Ceremonies.* 1983. Acrylic on board. © Helen Hardin 1983. Photo © Cradoc Bagshaw 2003.

ART SOURCE

Linking to the Performing Arts

Music Telling stories and playing his cello, Eugene Friesen, creates spellbinding performances. By wearing different masks throughout his performance, he transforms himself into various characters that connect to the specific music he plays. Have students see how "Cello Man" Eugene Friesen performs music wearing animal masks in the **Performing Arts Handbook** on page 316. To enrich student understanding, play the DVD or videotape (segment 4) in the **Performing Arts Package.**

Chapter 7

Observing Animals

"[My paintings] are almost abstract; I really like abstract painting, but I like the spiritual element too. I think all my paintings have to have something alive in them."

—Helen Hardin (1943–84)

From the prehistoric cave paintings of animals to Deborah Butterfield's horse sculpture made of mud and sticks (see page 20), animals have always been the subject of art. Sometimes they are symbols of power, such as a lion representing a king, or an eagle representing the United States; but often it is just the animals—their shape and their action—that fascinate artists. This chapter will demonstrate the many different ways in which artists have depicted animals in their work.

After completing this chapter, you will be able to:

- Recognize the ways in which artists use the environment for subject matter.
- Identify in artworks the influence of historical and cultural events.
- Define the term *symbol,* and tell how symbols are used in art.
- Create art featuring real and imaginary animals.

Quick Write

Interpreting the Quote
Read the quote by Hardin. Then look at **Figure 7–1.** People have often expressed the meaning of their lives through art and symbols. Write about how an animal could symbolize something in your life.

KEY TERMS

environment
Old Stone Age
mascot
trait
totem
porcelain
appliqué
illumination
calligraphy
symbol
tapestry
folk art

Quick Write

Interpreting the Quote
Have students read the quote and complete the Quick Write activity. Students should describe how an animal can be used to symbolize something in their own life. To help guide students, ask the following questions:

- What is your favorite animal?
- What does this animal represent to you?
- Describe some personal qualities that can also be recognized in this animal.

Chapter Motivator

Invite students to imagine that they could transform themselves into an animal. What creature would it be? Why? What characteristics does that animal have that are admirable or beautiful? Have students discuss any artworks of animals they have seen. Explain that in this chapter, students will observe how different animals have been portrayed in artworks.

Art Online

Visit **art.glencoe.com**, the Web site for Glencoe's art programs. This site offers general student resources to help guide your students as they learn about art and artists. Encourage your students to visit this site and explore the various resources and activities. The general student resources include the following:

- Artist Profiles
- Interactive Games
- Student Art Gallery
- Web Links

National Standards for Arts Education

This chapter addresses the following National Standards for the Visual Arts:

1. (a, b)	4. (a, b, c)
2. (a, b)	5. (a, b, c)
3. (a, b)	6. (a, b)

Animals in Earliest Art

(pages 124–125)

1 Focus

Objectives

After completing this lesson, students will be able to:

- Understand the role of animals in the lives and art of prehistoric people.
- Draw an animal mascot that conveys an animal trait.

SUPPLIES

- Pencils and sketch paper
- Magazines and books with photos of animals
- White drawing paper
- Markers

2 Teach

Motivator

Bring in a favorite stuffed animal or a photo of an animal that is special to you. Share with students your experiences with the animal. Invite students to share anecdotes about animals in their lives. Discuss ways in which animals are important to us.

Vocabulary

Ask students to describe the Old Stone Age and discuss any discoveries that were made at that time.

LESSON 1

Animals in Earliest Art

Does your family have a cat or dog? Maybe you own a bird or horse. Perhaps you know someone else who does. Animals, whether they are pets or roam wild, share our **environment,** or *surroundings.* Like other objects in the environment, animals have long been a favorite subject of artists.

In the following lessons, you will learn about different ways artists have portrayed animals. This lesson will focus on the role of animals in earliest art.

Animals as Subjects

Using animals as art subjects is as old as art itself. For proof, look at the painting of a horse in **Figure 7–2.** This picture is on the wall of a cave in the Dordogne region of France. Two boys came upon the cave while playing ball. The boys made their discovery in 1941. The picture, however, is tens of thousands of years old. It dates back to the **Old Stone Age.** This is *the historical period that occurred between 30,000 and 10,000 B.C.*

Experts regard this painting as one of the earliest artworks on record. Why did the first artists make pictures of animals? The experts have come up with likely answers to this question by looking closely at the role animals played in the environment of people long ago.

To people of the Old Stone Age, animals meant life. Their main source of food was the animals around them. They wore the animals' pelts, or furs, to protect them from the cold. For these reasons, a successful hunt was important; and the paintings may have been used in a ritual, or ceremony, to bring luck.

Tools of the Early Painter

The environment of early artists not only answers the question of *why* they made cave paintings. It also answers the question of *how.* Like artists today, they started with pigment, which often came from clay. Iron deposits in the clay may account for the heavy presence of red, yellow, and brown. The pigment was then mixed with animal fat, vegetable juice,

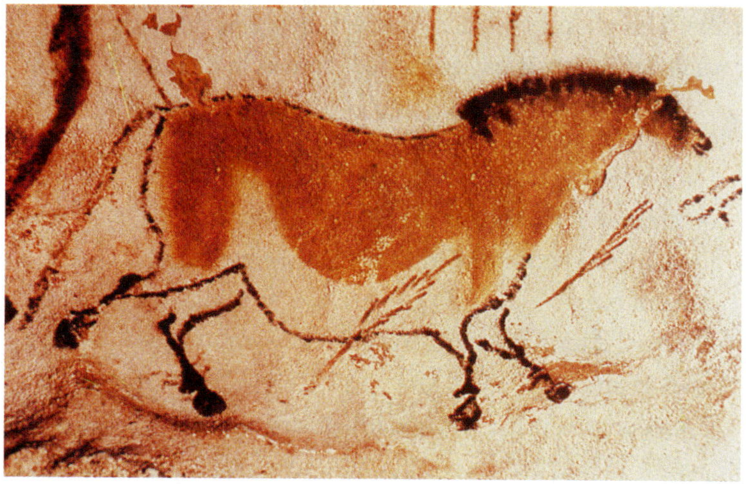

◆ Figure 7–2 This prehistoric cave painting is sometimes called ***The Chinese Horse.*** Animals shaped like this one appear in later Chinese art.

Cave Painting. Lascaux, Dordogne, France. *Chinese Horse* (The Yellow Horse). c. 15,000–10,000 B.C.

CURRICULUM CONNECTIONS

SCIENCE The Stone Age is the period of human culture in which people used stone, bone, wood, and ivory—rather than metal—to make tools. Stone Age art consisted of rock paintings, clay figures, pottery, and engravings and carvings of bone, stone, antlers, ivory, teeth, and shells. Paint pigments were four basic colors: black from charcoal, clay, and ground-up oxide of manganese; yellow and red from ocher, mashed berries and seeds, and animal blood; and white from clay and lime mud. Cave paintings and stone engravings still in existence provide scientific evidence about animals and humans during the Stone Age.

or egg white as binders. The paint may have been brushed on with fingers, leaves, or animal hide. It may also have been blown onto the wall through a hollow reed.

Early Animal Sculptures

After the Old Stone Age, animal art was not limited to painting. Some early artists worked in three dimensions. The miniature hippopotamus shown in **Figure 7–3** comes from ancient Egypt. This sculpture is nearly 4,000 years old. It was found in the tomb of an important member of Egyptian society. The hippo was meant to protect the body after death. It is believed that this hippo was placed in the tomb as a good luck charm to protect the tomb from intruders.

There is another way in which the hippo in this artwork relates to its environment. The creature's head, back, and sides are decorated with features of the lotus plant. This plant grows in the marshes where hippos live. The sculptor painted a "record" of the hippo's environment on its body.

Check Your Understanding

1. Why may early cave dwellers have made pictures of the animals in their environment?
2. Explain the purpose of the hippo to ancient Egyptian society.

Studio Activity

Inventing a Mascot

Describe practical applications for design ideas. Look again at the hippo in Figure 7–3. Its form is so appealing that it has become the unofficial mascot of the Metropolitan Museum of Art in New York City. A **mascot** is *an animal or person used by a group as a sign of luck.* Your school sports teams may have mascots.

Make a mascot for your class or for yourself. Begin by thinking about popular animal sayings. *Sly* as a *fox* and *strong as a bull* are two such sayings. Decide on the **trait**, or *personal characteristic,* your mascot will show. Write the trait down on a sheet of paper. Next, study the shapes of animals in pictures found in books or magazines. Select an animal to draw. If possible, your choice should relate to the trait you wrote down. Notice the outline of the animal's body. Practice by making some rough sketches. Then, using markers, draw the shape of the animal on white paper. Add the head, legs, tail, and other details.

PORTFOLIO

Write a short paragraph telling how you used the elements of art to draw your animal. Put it in your portfolio with your artwork.

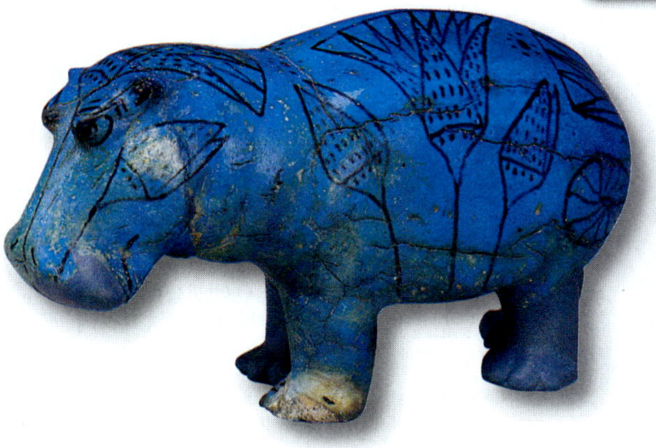

◆ **Figure 7–3** **The artist has given clues to the hippo's environment by decorating its body with lotus plants. These grow in the marshes where hippos live.**

Egyptian. Meir, Tomb of Senbi. *Figure of Hippopotamus.* Twelfth Dynasty (1991–1786 B.C.). Ceramics-Faience. 11 × 20 cm (4⅓ × 7⁹⁄₁₀"). The Metropolitan Museum of Art, New York, New York. Gift of Edward S. Harkness, 1917.

Answers to Check Your Understanding

1. Animals were a very important part of their lives. They provided food and clothing. The paintings may also have been used in a ritual to bring luck in the hunt.
2. The hippo was believed to be a good luck charm and was placed in tombs of important members of Egyptian society to protect their bodies after death.

Studio Activity

Encourage students to study animals and to view other animal art and artists' techniques. Bring in books or show slides to provide animal models. Point out that mascots may be realistic but are often stylized or humorous. Encourage students to use an imaginative approach.

3 Assess

Self-Assessment

Have students complete the **Check Your Understanding** questions on this page. Answers are provided below.

Reteaching

In pairs, have students read their paragraphs telling how they used the elements of art in their drawings. Ask them to analyze the interdependence of the art elements and principles in their drawings. L1 ELL

Enrichment

Team Mascots Students may enjoy researching team mascots used by various professional sports clubs or other organizations. Have them bring in magazine clippings or other artifacts displaying team mascots. L1

4 Close

Ask students to give examples of how Stone Age people created artwork. L1 ELL

Creating a Totem

(pages 126–127)
Lesson Time: 90 min.

1 Focus

Objectives

After completing this lesson, students will be able to:

- Understand the importance of a totem to aboriginal people.
- Demonstrate technical skills effectively by using a variety of materials to create a totem that relates to their character and personality.
- Conduct an in-progress analysis of their artwork.

SUPPLIES
Refer to **What You Will Need** in the Student Edition.

2 Teach

Motivator

Explain how a totem is different from a mascot. Point out that a totem serves as an emblem, a respected symbol.

Vocabulary

Have students look up synonyms for the word *aboriginal (native, first, indigenous).*

Studio Skills

Encourage students to think of unique animals during the brainstorming session. For their patterns, suggest using related colors such as analogous or warm colors. Then help them think of contrasting colors for their watercolor resist. L1 ELL

Creating a Totem

Study the painting in **Figure 7–4.** It shows a long-necked tortoise. It is the work of an Australian Aborigine (ab-uh-rij-ih-nee). The term *Aborigine* comes from two word parts. The first part, *ab,* means "from." The main part, *origine,* means "the beginning." Aborigines are called as such because their ancestors were the first humans to settle in a given area. The traditions of Australian Aboriginal art go back 50,000 years. This fact was proven by researchers who discovered and dated rock engravings and paintings similar to those being done today.

The tortoise in this picture was the artist's totem. The word **totem** means *an object that serves as an emblem or respected symbol.* This totem may have been used to protect the artist's family from harm.

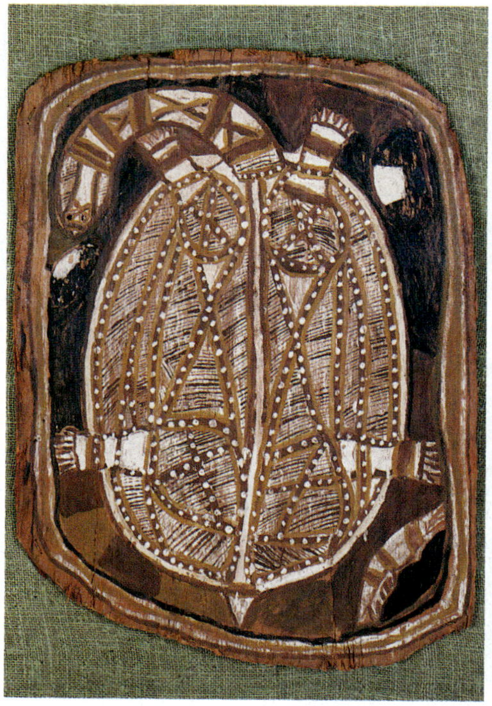

WHAT YOU WILL LEARN

You will design and create a totem of your own. As in Figure 7–4, your totem will be an animal. Select as your totem an animal that you believe symbolizes the kind of person you think you are. Begin by drawing the outline of the animal of your choice. Then fill in the outline with a pattern. Next, color the lines of the pattern with oil pastels or crayons. Finally, use a contrasting color of watercolor paint to fill in the animal shape and complete your totem.

WHAT YOU WILL NEED

- Sketch paper and pencil
- White drawing paper, 12 x 18 inches
- Oil pastels or crayons
- Watercolor paints
- Large, soft brushes

WHAT YOU WILL DO

1. With a partner, brainstorm a list of animals that would make good subjects for a totem. Share your ideas with the class.
2. From all the ideas presented, choose an animal as the subject of your totem. Select an animal that you believe symbolizes the kind of person you think you are. Study photographs of that animal and make several sketches. Focus mainly on the animal's outline. Choose your best drawing. Decide on a name for your totem. Write this name on the sketch you have chosen.

◆ **Figure 7–4** **Analyze the use of line in this painting and how the artist created variety in this artwork.**

Spider Nabunu. *Long-Necked Tortoise.* 1956–1960. Bark painting. 57.2 × 43.2 cm (22½ × 17"). The Art Gallery of New South Wales, Sydney, Australia. Aboriginal and Torres Strait Islander Collection. Gift of Stuart Scougall.

MORE ABOUT...

ABORIGINAL ART The Aborigines have inhabited Australia for over 40,000 years. Art was the core of their life, an expression of knowledge that gave them strength and power. Their arts and crafts were varied and rich and are carried on by their ancestors today. They carved wood and stone figures, and then painted them. They also carved intricate designs on the surfaces of rocks, on wooden grave posts, spear handles, canoe paddles, and boomerangs. Their cave paintings and paintings on eucalyptus bark and on stone are world renowned. Their best-known paintings include the white *wondjina,* or ancestor spirit figures.

3. Using a light pencil line, transfer your line drawing to a sheet of white paper. Fill the page, as the Aboriginal artist has done in Figure 7–4. Letter a name for your totem somewhere in your design.
4. Next, study the pattern of lines and dots the Aboriginal artist has used. Notice how this pattern adds texture to the painting. Think of a pattern that would go well with the animal you have selected. Practice making this pattern. Then fill in the animal's body using this pattern.
5. With oil pastels or crayons, go over all the lines in your picture. This includes the lines that make up your pattern. Use pressure to make the lines bold so the oil pastels will resist the watercolor.
6. Finally, select contrasting colors of watercolor paint. Choose colors that will make your design stand out and emphasize your pattern. Using a large brush, apply these colors to the entire surface of your paper. Do not worry about painting over the lines you made. The natural oils in the oil pastels or crayons will resist the paint.

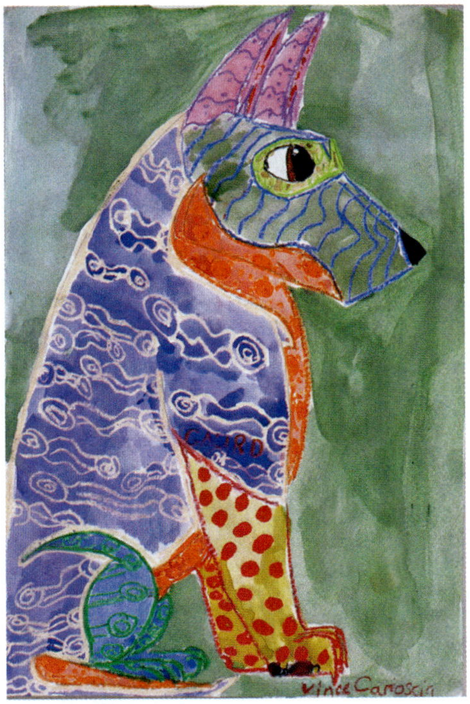

◆ **Figure 7–5** Student work. A totem.

Evaluating Your Work

- **Describe** Explain what animal appears in your totem. Tell what name you chose for your totem and where it appears in the design.
- **Analyze** Identify the pattern you used to fill the shape of your animal. Tell what colors of oil pastel you used and which colors of watercolor you selected. Explain whether the colors emphasize your pattern.
- **Interpret** Write a brief paragraph explaining what this animal symbolizes. Explain why it makes a good totem.
- **Judge** Tell whether you think your work is successful. Explain what you would do differently if you had a chance to do the project over again.

REFLECTIVE THINKING

Critical Response. Analyze the original artworks of your peers. Study the totem they painted. Form conclusions about historical and cultural contexts, such as the symbols they used and their meaning. Does it reveal anything about their culture?

Visual art Journal

Often, the figures in totems are animals that symbolize certain qualities. In your journal, write a list of special qualities you would like to have. Then, draw a contemporary totem mask that illustrates those qualities.

Team Building Activity

As an alternative approach to the lesson, divide the class into groups of three or four. Ask each group to choose an animal that would best symbolize the personality of their group. After the group has chosen its totem, have each student proceed individually with the studio lesson. L1 ELL

Historical/Cultural Heritage

Several Native American tribes of the Pacific Northwest are known for their beautiful carvings of totem poles. Ask students to research some of these tribes and compare the different totem poles. L2

3 Assess

Peer Assessment

Have students analyze the totem created by their peers in this Studio Lesson to form conclusions about historical and cultural contexts.

Enrichment

Aboriginal Art Ask students to find out more about present day Australian Aborigines and bring in additional examples of their art. L2

4 Close

Have students explain what their totems symbolize and why they chose this particular animal as their totem.

TEACHER TO TEACHER

Expanding Media Remember that students get bored if they often use the same art materials. If your budget and media are limited, vary the kinds of tools, papers, and surfaces you use. Many early cultures used natural materials found in their environment and drew with sticks, reeds, rocks, and feathers. Bark cloth was also a popular material. For totems or other artworks, use brown grocery bags or recycled paper to make the work stand out. Try wrinkling the paper; crumple it up several times. Flatten and draw on it with pen, pastel, crayon, or paint. Add a brown watercolor wash on top to simulate bark or leather.

Sea Creatures

(pages 128–129)

1 Focus

Objectives

After completing this lesson, students will be able to:

- Recognize porcelain as a high quality form of pottery
- Understand the technique of appliqué as a fiber-art form.
- Compare early and present-day art of sea animals.

2 Teach

Motivator

Ask students if they have ever looked at a goldfish or other aquarium fish up close. What details did they notice? *(Bright color, large eyes, gaping mouth.)* Have students share what they know and like about different sea creatures: shellfish, finned fish, and so on.

Vocabulary

Explain to students that porcelain is a kind of ceramic ware. It is made of kaolin (a kind of clay), feldspar, and quartz or flint. Porcelain is often referred to as china or chinaware because it was first made in China.

Aesthetics

Ask students to compare the depiction of fish in **Figures 7–6** and **7–7.** The attention to detail is more apparent in Figure 7–6. The artist took great care in illustrating the fish and representing its environment. The artist whose work is shown in Figure 7–7 represented various kinds of fish, using different shapes and fabrics.

LESSON 3

Sea Creatures

The word *earth* has two meanings. It is the name of the planet we live on and also another word for "land." Yet, land accounts for only 30 percent of Earth's surface. The rest is given over to a mysterious world with its own special population, the world of water—the rivers, lakes, and oceans.

Like creatures of the land, the animals of this special environment have long held a fascination for artists.

Early Art of Sea Animals

Ancient Egypt, which you learned about in Lesson 1, was one of the first great civilizations to create many kinds of art. Another early people who invented numerous art forms were the Chinese.

The jar shown in **Figure 7–6** is described as "blue-and-white ware." It is made of **porcelain** (**por**-suh-lihn), a *fine-grained, high-quality form of pottery.* Porcelain is very hard to work with because it is a very stiff clay. The Chinese perfected work in this medium during the 1300s. It was around that time that this jar was made.

The jar is notable not only for its craft. It is also important because of the design on its surface. The design shows a fish in its natural environment.

Notice the attention to detail shown in this jar. You can easily find the fish's mouth, eye, gills, and other body features. The fish is shown surrounded by water lilies and other water plants. The artist appears to have been quite familiar with these freshwater plants.

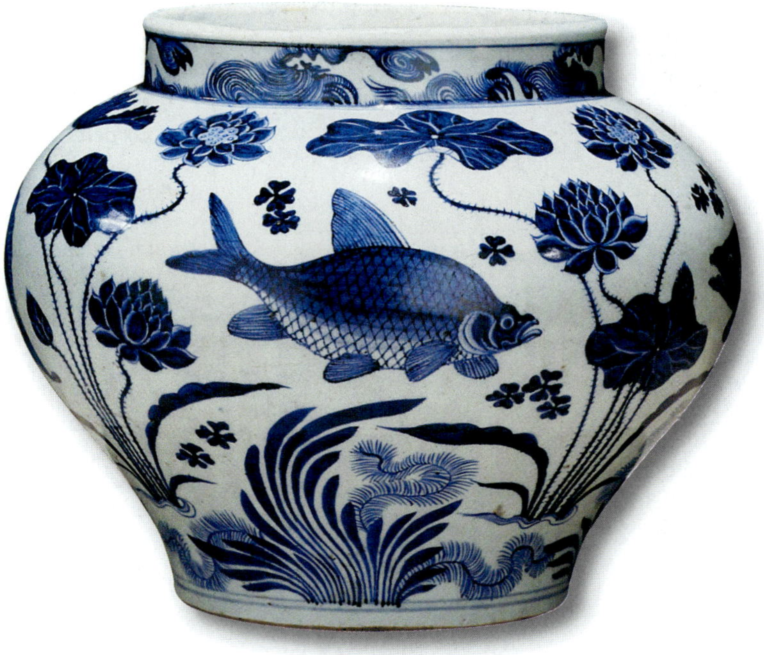

◆ **Figure 7–6** Notice how the shape of the flower petals has been repeated to create the full blossom. Where have lines been repeated to create other forms?

China. Yuan Dynasty. *Blue and White Jar with a Design of Fish and Water Plants.* Early 1300s. Porcelain with underglaze decoration. 29.8 × 34.9 cm (11¾ × 13¾"). Brooklyn Museum of Art, Brooklyn, New York. Gift of the Executors of Augustus S. Hutchins.

COMMUNITY CONNECTION

Reaching Out Contact the children's ward at your local hospital to see if your class can put up a display of artworks for the sick or injured children to enjoy. Students can use calendars, posters, or art prints as inspiration for their artwork. Have students use oil pastel, tempera, or acrylic paint to create bright and cheerful images. Use poster board to frame each artwork. If there is not enough space to display all the student art, you can rotate your students' artworks every other week.

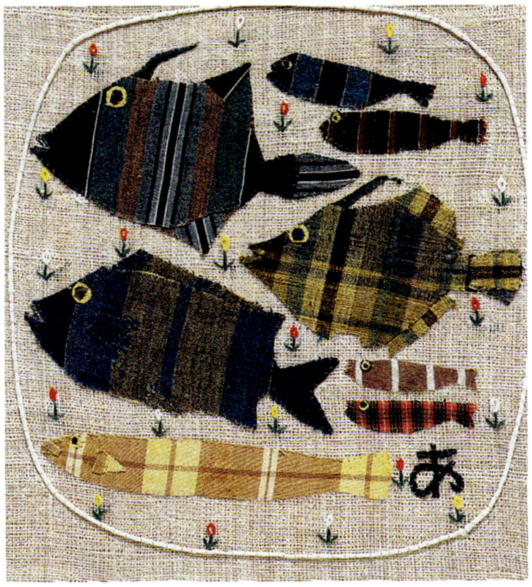

◆ **Figure 7–7** **Analyze how the artist used line in this work. Where has she used repetition to create harmony?**

Ayako Miyawaki. *Various Fish.* 1967. Cotton collage on burlap. 33 × 29.9 cm (13 × 11¾"). National Museum of Women in the Arts, Washington, D.C. Gift of the artist.

Present-Day Art of Sea Animals

Ancient Chinese ways of making art were shared with China's neighbors. One of those neighbors is the island nation of Japan. The artwork in **Figure 7–7** was done by a Japanese artist in the 1960s. Her name is Ayako Miyawaki.

Many people, when they think of art, think of paintings. Artists, as you have learned, are forever looking for new ways of creating. The work of art in Figure 7–7 was created with fabrics and fibers. It is an example of a technique called **appliqué** (ap-lih-**kay**). This is *an art form in which cutout shapes are attached to a larger surface.* They can be stitched or glued in place.

Miyawaki cuts her fabrics freehand. In this artwork, she has carefully cut out fabrics to represent various kinds of fish. Observe how the shapes of the fish differ, and how their mouths, fins, and tails vary in shape. Look at the striped and plaid fabrics the artist has used. Can you tell where she has overlapped fabrics to add gills and eyes? The symbol in the lower right corner is the artist's signature. It appears in every one of her works.

Time & Place

Yuan Dynasty in China (1279–1368)

Historical connection. The Yuan dynasty was the shortest-lived major dynasty in the history of China. Genghis Khan, a Mongol conqueror, originally established the dynasty when he invaded and occupied North China. Genghis Khan's grandson Kublai Khan later captured South China, establishing control over all of China.

The arts were not encouraged during the Yuan dynasty. Nonetheless, several important developments in ceramics did occur during this time of Mongol rule. These developments included new forms, ornamentation, and glazes. The introduction of underglaze blue-and-white ware ceramics, such as the jar in **Figure 7–6,** received special notice. These ceramics went on to become very popular. The Yuan dynasty was overthrown in the mid-fourteenth century. Compare the Chinese vase in Figure 7–6 with the Greek vase in Figure 5–3 on page 83. How are they different?

Check Your Understanding

1. In what century and by whom was the technique for blue-and-white ware invented?
2. Explain the term *appliqué.*

Time & Place

Yuan Dynasty in China (1279–1368)

Both artworks are equally noteworthy for the beauty of their form. In Figure 7–6, the artwork surrounds the entire Chinese vase. In Figure 5–3, the Greek vase is decorated with a single painting.

3 Assess

Self-Assessment

Have students complete the **Check Your Understanding** questions on this page. Answers are provided below.

Reteaching

Ask students to explain the fiber-art technique of appliqué.

Enrichment

Tell students to imagine they have been invited to travel with a famous oceanographer like Jacques Cousteau to explore the South Pacific Ocean. Have them draw the colorful sea creatures they would see on their journey. L1 ELL

4 Close

Have students explain why blue-and-white ware porcelain is a notable art form.

Answers to Check Your Understanding

1. The Chinese are credited with perfecting the technique of making blue-and-white ware in the fourteenth century.
2. Appliqué is an art form in which cutout shapes are fastened to a larger surface to create a new design.

Animals in Literature and Art

(pages 130–131)

1 Focus

Objectives

After completing this lesson, students will be able to:

- Recognize character traits in works of fiction.
- Compare and analyze subjects in artworks and in literature.
- Write and illustrate a fable.

2 Teach

Motivator

Share with students a real or invented news story that teaches a lesson. You might, for example, narrate the events of a foiled robbery that made the local news. Ask students to identify the "moral" of the story you share. In the case of the foiled robbery, the moral might be that crime does not pay. Tell students that they are about to read and view a literary form known for its morals.

Active Reading

Ask students to read the fable. Have them analyze the two main characters, including each of their traits and motivations. Ask students to interpret the symbolism in this fable.

Animals in Literature and Art

Since earliest times, animals have been used as symbols in a variety of cultures. As noted earlier, ancient cave dwellers made symbolic pictures of animals they planned to hunt. Animals also can be used to represent concepts and ideals. For example, the concept of peace is often symbolized by the dove. Animals are also used to exemplify human characteristics.

In literature, animals are often portrayed in fables. A *fable* is a tale that teaches a moral or lesson. In fables, animals symbolize character traits of people. Greed, dishonesty, and bravery are just a few of these traits. Read the fable in **Figure 7–8.** It was written two thousand years ago by the famous Greek writer Aesop. Its title is *The Fox and the Crane.*

The Fox and the Crane

Once upon a time, a Fox invited a Crane to supper. When the Crane arrived, a delicious scent hung in the air. It was soup. The Fox poured his guest's soup into a broad flat stone dish. The hungry Crane eagerly sipped a mouthful. To her dismay, the soup ran out the sides of her long bill. She sipped again, and the same thing happened.

The Fox, unable to conceal his merriment, howled with laughter. When the Fox had eaten his fill, he asked whether the Crane had enjoyed her meal. "Indeed," she replied innocently. "Please do me the honor of dining with me tomorrow. I wish to return your hospitality." The Fox agreed.

The next day, the Fox arrived at the Crane's home. His appetite was sharp. No sooner was he seated at the table, than the Crane served the evening meal. An assortment of fish was presented in a bottle with a slender neck. When the Fox attempted to eat, he encountered a problem. His snout was too wide to fit through the narrow bottle neck. The Crane's slender beak fit perfectly. She ate to her heart's content.

◆ **Figure 7-8** Fables, as you know, always have a moral, or lesson. What would you say is the moral of *The Fox and the Crane?*

MORE ABOUT...

FRANS SNYDERS (1579–1657) Flemish painter Frans Snyders was born and raised in the city of Antwerp, Belgium. While an art student, he became friends with Peter Paul Rubens, with whom he frequently collaborated. Rubens's influence may be seen in the simple and clear composition of Snyders's still lifes and in the liveliness with which he rendered animals. *The Fable of the Fox and the Stork* illustrates Snyders's sharp eye for animal anatomy as well as his ability to teach through art. The work is masterful in balance between light and dark colors and its painstaking brushwork.

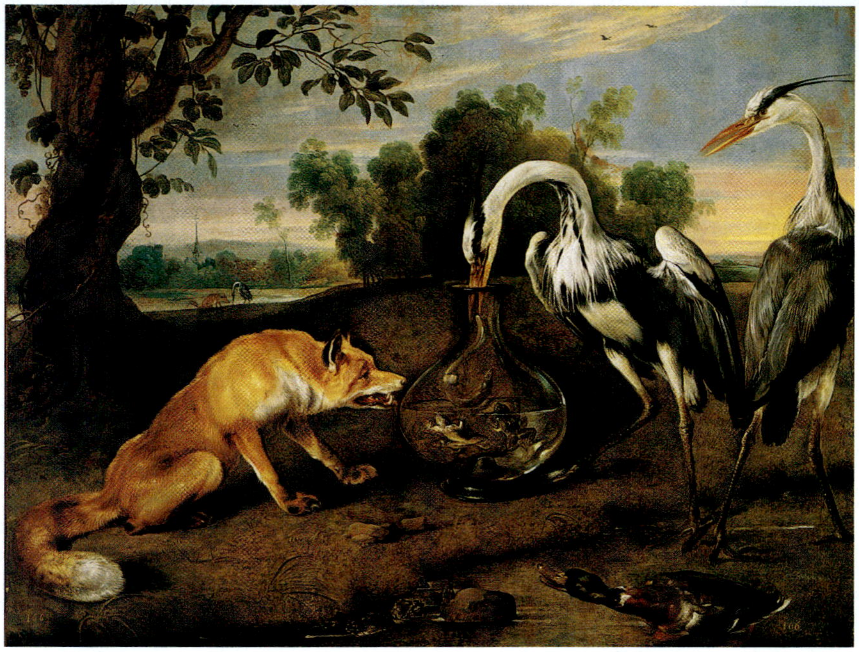

◆ **Figure 7–9** **How would you describe the style of this painting? What details has the artist included that are not in the fable?**

Frans Snyders. *The Fable of the Fox and the Stork.* c. 1630–40. Oil on canvas. 116.8 cm × 152.4 cm (46 × 60″). Memorial Art Gallery of the University of Rochester, New York. Gift of Dr. and Mrs. James V. Aquavella.

The animals in this fable possess human traits and each displays a distinct personality. Notice the character traits shown by the animals' behaviors. Which traits are being depicted in this fable? What is the lesson or moral of the fable?

Fables in Art

Look at **Figure 7–9.** This painting is by a seventeenth-century Flemish artist named Frans Snyders. This painting illustrates a particular scene from the fable *The Fox and the Crane.* Notice, in particular, the expression Snyders has depicted on the faces of the animals. The painting captures a significant moment in the fable. What moment is illustrated in this scene? Do you think the artist successfully captured this moment?

MAKE THE CONNECTION

Take Another Look

1. Look once more at the painting in Figure 7–9. The painting captures a frozen moment in the fable. Which moment has the artist depicted?
2. What character traits can you associate with the fox and the crane?

ART & READING

Writing and illustrating a fable. Now it is your turn to write and illustrate a fable of your own:

- Begin by brainstorming well-known morals or lessons. Select a moral for your fable.
- Write your fable describing the moral you selected.
- Next, do visual illustrations of one or more scenes from your fable. Remember, to select animals as "actors" that represent character traits reflected in your fable.
- When you have finished, share your fable with classmates. See if they can identify the moral and scene(s) depicted in your illustrations.

Critical Thinking

Have small groups of students each analyze the moral objective of the fable. Allow time for groups to share and compare their responses with the class. L1 ELL

3 Assess

Self-Assessment

Have students complete the **Take Another Look** questions on this page. Answers are provided below.

Reteaching

In pairs, have students write five factual questions about the fable or painting. Possibilities might include "Which creature gets the last laugh?" Partners are then to swap questions and answer those in the list received. L1

Enrichment

Point out that fables and other works of literature have long been a favorite source of subject matter among artists. Have students explore the art-literature tradition using print or online resources. Allow time for students to share their findings with the class in brief oral reports. L2

4 Close

Emphasize the character traits illustrated in this and other fables by having students complete similes such as the following: "Sly as a _____," "Wise as a(n) _____," and so on.

MAKE THE CONNECTION

Take Another Look Student answers will vary, but may include the following:

1. It is the moment of truth for the fox—the instant when the creature realizes he has been vanquished by the crane.
2. The fox might be described as tricky, devious, and sly. The crane might be described as trusting and clever.

Birds in Art

(pages 132–133)

1 Focus

Objectives

After completing this lesson, students will be able to:

- Understand the history and purpose of illumination.
- Define and identify calligraphy.
- Analyze the interdependence of the art elements line and color and principle unity in two different artworks.

2 Teach

Motivator

Direct students' attention to **Figure 7–10.** Ask them to describe the setting shown. Encourage them to hunt for details in what they see. Explain that the purpose of miniature paintings was to "shed light on," or illuminate, a story or poem. Some illuminations were meant to explain a portion of a story, others nearly all of the story. As a result, the small painting had to provide lots of intricate detail.

Vocabulary

Ask students to think of other words that are made with the Greek combining form of *-graph* or *-graphy.* What do those words mean? Encourage students to look at word parts to help unlock the meaning of unfamiliar words.

LESSON 5

Birds in Art

Have you ever wondered what it would be like to soar like a bird? If you have, you are not alone. Since earliest times, humans have dreamed of flying. This dream became a reality in 1903. That year the Wright Brothers conquered the air in the first "flying machine."

The desire to capture the grace and majesty of birds has not been limited to inventors. Artists, too, have long been inspired by the beauty of flight and of creatures that fly.

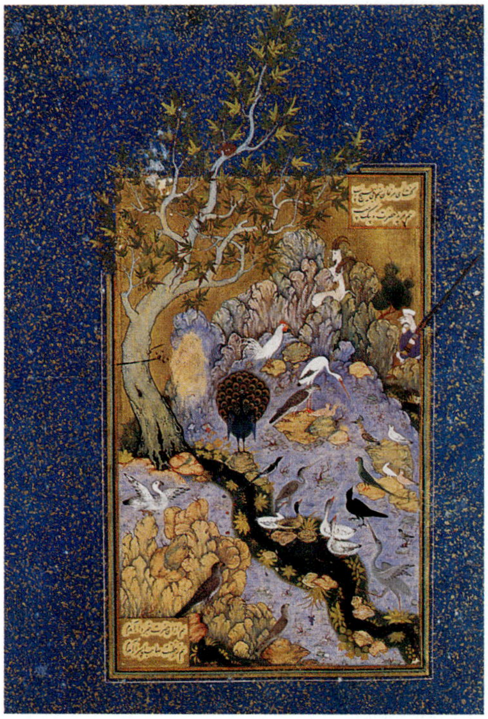

◆ **Figure 7–10** Notice that some birds appear higher in the picture. This was the artist's way of adding depth. What are some other ways of suggesting space?

Habib Allah. *Mantiq al-tair (The Language of the Birds).* c. 1600. Illustrated manuscript (Ink, opaque colors, gold, and silver on paper). 25.4 × 11.4 cm (10 × 4½"). The Metropolitan Museum of Art, New York, New York. The Fletcher fund.

Early Bird Illumination

You have probably heard the saying, "A picture is worth a thousand words." Artists have understood the truth of this saying for more than eleven centuries. Since about A.D. 850, artists have been making pictures to illustrate books. The picture in **Figure 7–10** is from ancient Persia. It is a type of *hand-painted book illustration* known as an **illumination.** The word *illuminate* means "to light up." These miniature paintings were so named because they "shed light on" the words, or made them easier to understand. Imagine that the book you are reading right now contained no pictures. Think how hard it would be to "see" the artworks from descriptions of them alone.

The illumination in Figure 7–10 tells a story. It is about thirty birds that set out on a long journey. Their goal is to find the king of birds.

Notice the many different types of birds in this picture. How many can you identify? What other animals are in the scene?

Illuminations and the Element of Line

Like most Persian paintings, this one makes strong use of the element of line. With your finger, trace the flowing curves that make up the birds, tree, and landscape. These lines suggest graceful movement. The tree is made to look as if it is growing beyond the picture's frame.

You may have noticed the curves in the two corner boxes. These are more than just decoration. They are an example of **calligraphy** (kuh-**lig**-ruh-fee). This word is from two Greek words meaning "beautiful" and "writing." Calligraphy is *the art of beautiful writing.* These curves are letters of the Persian alphabet. Notice that the thickness of these lines varies from curve to curve.

TECHNOLOGY STRATEGIES IN THE ART CLASSROOM

Digital Calligraphy Encourage students to explore the tools and menus on the word processing program they use. In addition to choices of font, size, style, and color, they can choose special effects such as emboss, engrave, twist, stretch, and many more. Elaborate frames and borders can be added and clip art or photos can be imported. Ask students to design the opening paragraph of a favorite story, illuminating the first letter. Remind them to explore text wrap and other options. Display student artworks in class.

Bird Art

Although we think of birds as creatures of flight, the sky is only one environment in which birds live. The nature study in **Figure 7–11** shows another. This is the Brazilian rain forest in South America. The brightly colored winged creatures in the work are hummingbirds. Hummingbirds are special because of their ability to fly backward and their great speed. They are also the smallest of all birds. Some are less than 3 inches long!

Here the artist has provided a close-up of three of these unusual birds in their natural environment. They hover near an orchid, a type of flower. The birds may have fed moments earlier on the flower's nectar. What principle of art has the artist used to draw the viewer's attention to the birds and flower?

Check Your Understanding

1. What is an illumination? For what were illuminations used?
2. In what way is a line of calligraphy different from other kinds of lines?
3. What is the environment of the birds in Figure 7–11?

Time & Place

Ancient Persian Art

Historical connection. Islam is one of the largest religions in the world. Followers of Islam are known as Muslims. Countries in the Middle East, including Saudi Arabia, Iraq, and Iran, have large Muslim populations. Islam began in the early seventh century by the Prophet Muhammad, an Arab born in 570. The teachings of Muhammad are written down in the Muslim holy book, called the Koran.

Before the twentieth century, the country of Iran was known as Persia to the Western world. In ancient Persia, the advent of Islam created a need for copies of the Koran. The ancient Persian arts of calligraphy and book illumination developed out of this need. Because the Koran forbids the worship of idols, artists were not allowed to include representations of human or animal figures in their work. Instead, they focused on creating beautiful calligraphy that was in itself a work of art. In some nonreligious books, however, representations of living beings were allowed (see **Figure 7-10**). Can you identify any cultural influences in Figure 7–10?

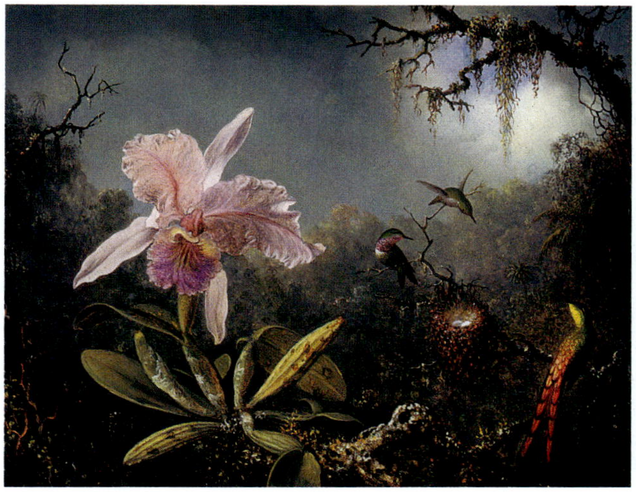

◆ **Figure 7–11** How many different textures and shapes can you find in this rich painting?

Martin Johnson Heade. *Cattleya Orchid and Three Brazilian Hummingbirds.* 1871. Oil on wood. 34.8 × 45.6 cm (13¾ × 18″). National Gallery of Art, Washington, D.C. Gift of Morris and Gwendolyn Cafritz Foundation.

Answers to Check Your Understanding

1. An illumination is a hand-painted book illustration. Illuminations were used to help readers understand what they were reading.
2. In a line of calligraphy, the thickness of the line varies from curve to curve.
3. The environment of these birds is a tropical rain forest in Brazil.

Time & Place

Ancient Persian Art Typical of Islamic art, the illustration maintains a decorative quality. It possesses a strong romantic, poetic quality that depicts an ideal setting rather than a real one.

ART IN EVERYDAY LIFE

Calligraphy is often used on greeting cards and invitations. Ask students to look for examples of calligraphy that they find in advertising or on book jackets. Have students describe in detail a variety of practical applications for design ideas based on calligraphy.

3 Assess

Self-Assessment

Have students complete the **Check Your Understanding** questions on this page. Answers are provided below.

Reteaching

Have students explain the purpose for illumination paintings. L1

Enrichment

Birds have long been a source of inspiration for all the fine arts. Play a portion of a recording of either Stravinsky's *The Firebird* or Tchaikovsky's *Swan Lake.* Ask students to make a drawing based on what they hear in the ballet.

4 Close

Ask students to explain which element of art was most important to their calligraphy.

Making an Animal Sculpture

(pages 134–135)
Lesson Time: 90 min.

1 Focus

Objectives

After completing this lesson, students will be able to:

- Demonstrate technical skills effectively by using clay to create a sculpture of an animal at rest.
- Describe, analyze, interpret, and judge their artwork.

SUPPLIES
Refer to **What You Will Need** in the Student Edition.

2 Teach

Motivator

Engage students in a discussion of their favorite animals. What does the animal look like when at rest? Ask students to discuss ways of observing animals to learn more about them. Explain that they will create a clay sculpture of an animal at rest. Like Brancusi, they should keep their image simple.

Vocabulary

Review with students the meaning of the word *abstract.* Ask them what makes the animal in **Figure 7–12** abstract. *(Recognizable but not realistic image of a bird.)*

LESSON 6

Making an Animal Sculpture

Around the time the Wright Brothers were experimenting with flight, a Romanian artist was doing the same. His name was Constantin Brancusi (**kon**-stan-teen bran-koos-ee). The sculpture shown in **Figure 7–12** is the result of one of Brancusi's more successful experiments. Study the artwork. In it, the artist has captured the essence of a soaring bird. What elements of art contribute to this feeling? What principle has been used to arrange the elements of art?

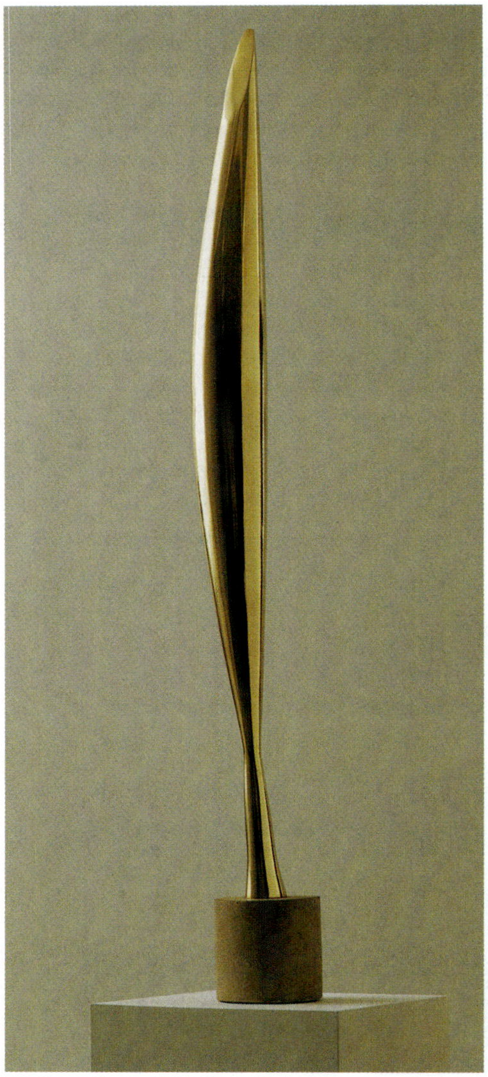

◆ **Figure 7–12** How would you describe the artist's use of line? What idea or feeling does this sculpture communicate?

Constantin Brancusi. *Bird in Space.* 1928. Bronze (unique cast). 137.2 × 21.6 × 16.5 cm (54 × 8½ × 6½"). The Museum of Modern Art, New York, New York. Given anonymously.

WHAT YOU WILL LEARN

Notice how Brancusi has simplified the bird into a solid form. Using the method of modeling, you will create an abstract sculpture of a real or imaginary creature at rest. You will begin by molding the basic form of this creature with clay. When the clay has turned leather hard, you will create a texture or polish the animal to give harmony to your sculpture.

WHAT YOU WILL NEED

- Pencil and sketch paper
- Wooden board
- Ball of clay (about the size of an orange)
- Clay modeling tools
- Watercolors

WHAT YOU WILL DO

1. You will demonstrate technical skills effectively using a variety of art materials to produce an animal sculpture. Look at Figure 7–12. Observe how the artist has simplified the shape of the bird. Draw several sketches of an animal at rest. Simplify the shape of your animal, keeping the legs, tail, and head close to the body. Choose your best sketch.

STORY BEHIND THE ARTWORK

BIRD IN SPACE When Constantin Brancusi sent his sculpture *Bird in Space* to the United States for an exhibition in 1928, custom officials reacted with confusion. It did not look like a bird to them, and so they felt it could not be allowed to enter the country duty-free as a work of art. They finally put it on a scale and taxed it by the pound as a piece of metal. Brancusi sued, lawyers argued, and expert witnesses testified. Finally, the judge gave his verdict—he declared *Bird in Space* a work of art. It was the first piece of abstract sculpture shown in the United States.

2. Knead your ball of clay on the board to rid it of air bubbles. Begin to form the ball into the general shape of the animal in your sketch. Use your fingers or clay modeling tools to make shallow indentations that indicate the position of the head, legs, and tail. Keep turning your sculpture as you work to make sure it looks good from all angles.
3. If you intend to fire the piece in a kiln, use a pencil to push holes into the bottom, when the clay is firm but not dry, to keep it from exploding in the kiln.
4. Finish your sculpture by using clay modeling tools to add texture to part or all of the surface. A comb or toothbrush pulled across the surface will create the look of fur. You can use the back of a spoon to polish the surface for a shiny look. This is called burnishing. You can also use watercolors to add color to your animal.

Evaluating Your Work

- **Describe** What kind of a creature did you create? What surface texture did you use?
- **Analyze** Name the most important element and principle of art you used in creating your animal. Tell how you used them to give your animal harmony.
- **Interpret** Were you able to create the impression that your animal was at rest? Describe how you created this feeling.
- **Judge** Which aesthetic view would you use to judge this work? Tell whether you think your work is successful.

5. Display your finished work with that of your classmates to make an abstract

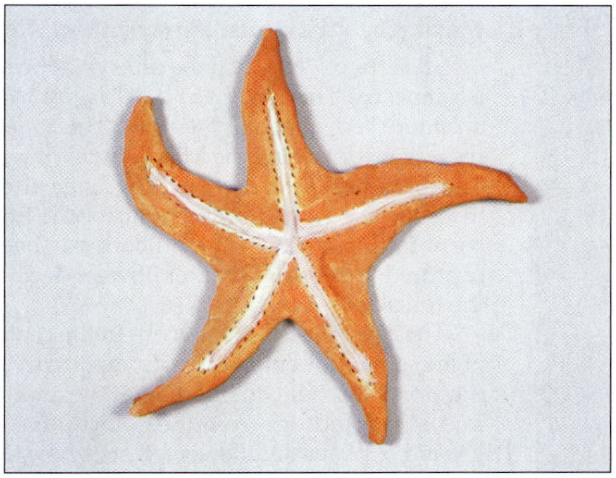

◆ **Figure 7–13** Student work. A creature at rest.

STUDIO OPTION

Do a second clay sculpture, this time creating an imaginary creature. Exaggerate the features of this animal, making it look fierce and active. Use many textures to provide a varied surface. Give your creature a name that fits its personality. Photograph this sculpture for your portfolio.

Visual Art Journal

Look for different company logos that are designs of birds, fish, or other animals. Think about what these animals might signify. In your journal, make a list of these logos and their possible meanings.

Studio Skills

Before beginning the lesson, give each student a ball of clay to hold and squeeze. Ask them to notice how it feels. Demonstrate how to use clay-modeling tools to mold the clay. Instruct students to be careful as they use pencils to puncture the bottom of the clay prior to firing. L1 ELL

Art on a Shoestring

If you don't have clay-modeling tools, improvise with a variety of housewares and craft items. Silverware, vegetable brushes, spatulas, small rolling pins, paper clips, wire, nails, combs, and old paintbrush handles are some examples.

3 Assess

Self-Assessment

Have students use **Evaluating Your Work** to conduct an in-progress critique of their animal sculpture.

Reteaching

Ask students to explain what makes their creature abstract.

4 Close

Have students identify their creatures and tell what techniques they used to create texture and harmony in the work. L1

INCLUSION STRATEGIES

Physically Impaired Some students may find the clay too hard to form with the strength in their hands. Their clay might be softened ahead of time with additional water or torn into pieces, which they would then be able to press together. You will need to check students' pieces so that attachments are firmly secured to the main form and a hollow is made in the thickest part, especially if the pieces are to be fired. Students with visual impairments will especially enjoy using a piece of clay at least as large as a grapefruit so they can freely manipulate it and show details.

LESSON 7

Fantasy Animals

(pages 136–137)

1 Focus

Objectives

After completing this lesson, students will be able to:

- Recognize the use of symbolism in art.
- Define *tapestry*.
- Understand that Expressionism is an art style in which artists express strong inner feelings.
- Analyze the interdependence of the art elements color and shape and principle unity in an artwork.

SUPPLIES

- Pencils and sketch paper
- Magazines and books with pictures of various animals
- White drawing paper
- Watercolors, brushes, trays

2 Teach

Motivator

Have students study the reproduction of the tapestry in **Figure 7–14.** Ask if they can identify the animal. Some may know this creature from TV and literature. Explain that myths and legends from many cultures feature such imaginary creatures.

Vocabulary

Students may be unfamiliar with fiber-art forms such as tapestry. Tell them that a tapestry is usually a heavy cloth woven by hand or machine that has decorative designs or pictures woven into it.

LESSON 7

Fantasy Animals

Land, sea, and air are the only true environments of animals. Yet, artists sometimes turn to another special environment when creating animal art. This is the environment of the imagination.

Some imaginary animals in art are inspired by myths, legends, or beliefs. Others reflect an artist's personal style or taste. Still others are made up of the body parts of many animals. You may have read Dr. Seuss books when you were small. If you did, you are probably familiar with such animals.

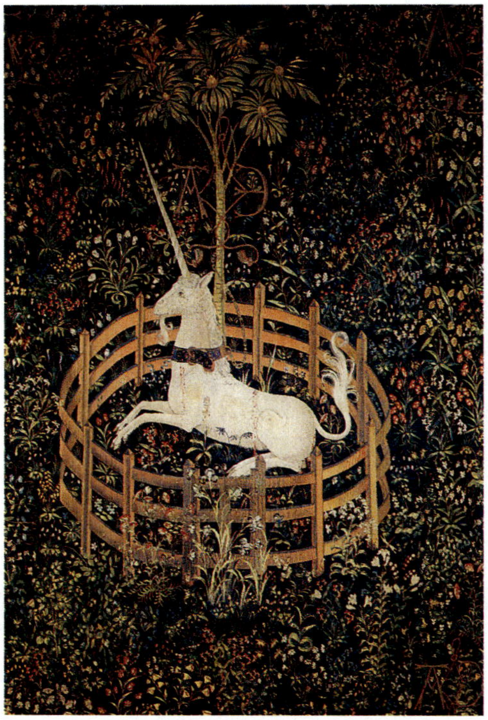

◆ **Figure 7–14** **What techniques has the artist used to give a feeling of depth in this tapestry?**

The Unicorn Tapestries, VII: The Unicorn in Captivity. c. 1500. Silk, wool, silver and silver-gilt threads. 3.7 × 2.5 m (12′ 1″ × 8′3″). The Metropolitan Museum of Art, New York, New York. Gift of John D. Rockefeller, Jr., The Cloisters Collection.

Fantasy Animals from Myth

The ancient Egyptians, you may recall, viewed animals as symbols. A **symbol** is *an image used to stand for a quality or an idea.* The hippopotamus was a symbol of strength.

Another animal symbol from long ago appears in **Figure 7–14.** This fantasy animal is a unicorn. The name blends the word parts *uni,* meaning "one," and *corn,* meaning "horn." It comes from the single twisted horn on the creature's forehead. White in color, the unicorn was a symbol of purity. Its horn was thought to have many magical powers. One power was the ability to restore health to someone who has been poisoned.

Fantasy Animals in Applied Art

The artwork in which the unicorn appears is a **tapestry.** This is *a woven wall hanging with decorative designs or colorful scenes.* This tapestry was made during the Middle Ages. It was one of a series of seven. Together they recorded the legend of the hunt for the unicorn. In this tapestry, the unicorn has been captured. It rests on a bed of flowers deep in the forest.

The artist placed the unicorn in the center of the scene. This emphasizes its importance in the story. The light color value of the animal makes it stand out from the colorful background of plants and flowers. Notice how the artist has used the fence to create a sense of depth. This technique is called *overlapping.* The front half of the fence overlaps, or covers, the unicorn's back legs. Where else is overlapping used in the work?

Fantasy Animals that Reflect Style

In art and the surrounding world, colors are sometimes used as symbols. A person who is scared is called "yellow." Someone who is

RESOURCES BEYOND THE CLASSROOM

ILLUSTRATED BOOKS Children's picture books can provide excellent examples of the art of manuscript illumination. Just as medieval artists enhanced a manuscript with ornate images that explained the text, children's book illustrators also capture the essence of the story in their drawings and paintings. Exemplary children's book illustrations convey a sense of character, setting, action, and time. Although their choice of subject matter and other elements might be restricted, children's book artists often create masterpieces of art. Explore editions of *Aesop's Fables* and *Grimm's Fairy Tales* as well as the Caldecott Medal books.

sad is said to feel "blue." During the early 1900s, a group of artists in Europe developed a new way of making art, called *Expressionism*. It was called this because it expressed inner feelings. Color was very important to the Expressionists. It was especially important to one of their leaders, Franz Marc.

An Expressionist Fantasy Painting

Yellow Cow, the painting in **Figure 7–15,** is one of Marc's most famous. To Franz Marc, yellow meant "gentle" and "cheerful." This leaping cow is so cheerful it seems as though it is about to jump off the canvas. Trace the sweeping curve that starts at the cow's tail. It pulls your eye through the painting.

Check Your Understanding

1. What is a *symbol?*
2. What was the unicorn's color? What did that color symbolize?

Studio Activity

Creating an Imaginary Animal

Use your imagination. Create a fantasy animal by combining body parts from different animals.

Begin by brainstorming animals famous for their unusual body parts. The giraffe, for example, has a long neck. The elephant has a trunk. Working independently, select body parts you want to use to create your creature. Make some rough sketches. Choose your best idea and draw your animal in pencil. Using watercolors, complete your fantasy animal. Select colors that suggest a mood. Use contrasting colors to create its environment. Name your creature.

PORTFOLIO

Write down your ideas for animals with unusual body parts. Use the list as an idea bank for creating other fantasy animals.

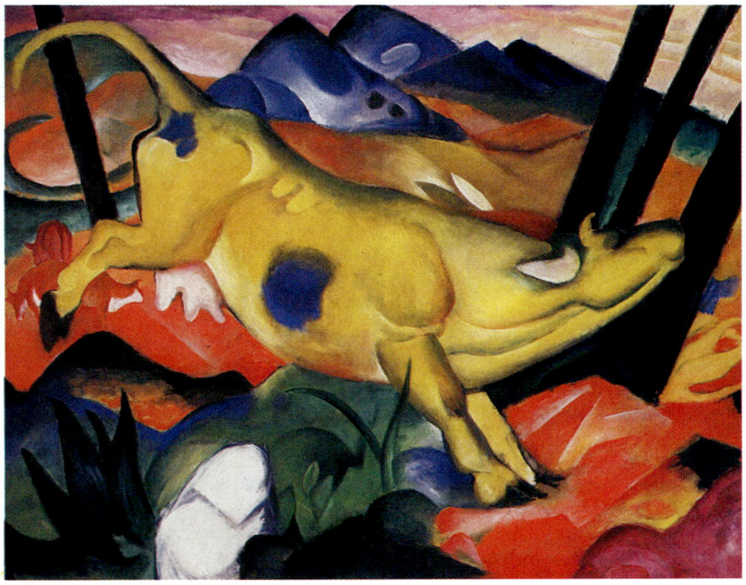

◆ **Figure 7–15** Analyze the use of color and shape in this painting. What message do you think the artist is trying to communicate?

Franz Marc. *Yellow Cow.* 1911. Oil on canvas. 141 × 189 cm (55⅜ × 74½″). Solomon R. Guggenheim Museum, New York, New York.

Answers to Check Your Understanding

1. A symbol is an image used to stand for a quality or idea.
2. The unicorn was white in color. White symbolized purity.

Studio Activity

Creating an Imaginary Animal

As an alternative, have students try using chalk on dark colors of construction paper, instead of using watercolors. The dark construction paper will reveal the texture of the chalk strokes.

Aesthetics

The Expressionist movement originated in Germany in the early 1900s. The Expressionists ignored the "rules" of contemporary art. They delighted in experimenting with exaggeration, proportion, and color to express strong inner feeling. Ask students to look at **Figure 7–15.** How has the artist experimented with color? How has he used shape?

3 Assess

Self-Assessment

Have students complete the **Check Your Understanding** questions on this page. Answers are provided below.

Reteaching

Ask students to work in pairs to find and explain examples of symbolism used by artists in this chapter. L1 ELL

4 Close

Call on students to explain how they used color in their artwork to express a mood and feeling.

LESSON 8

Creating a Fantasy Animal

(pages 138–139)
Lesson Time: 90 min.

1 Focus

Objectives

After completing this lesson, students will be able to:

- Demonstrate technical skills effectively by using recyclable materials and found objects to create a three-dimensional animal sculpture.
- Write a story about the creature's life and environment.
- Describe, analyze, interpret, and judge their fantasy creature.

SUPPLIES
Refer to **What You Will Need** in the Student Edition.

2 Teach

Vocabulary

Ask students to think about expressions that share the word folk—folk art, folk music, folktales, folk dance, folklore. Explain that these are all aspects of culture shared and usually handed down among the common people.

Art Criticism

Have students use the four steps of art criticism to discuss **Figure 7–16.** Discuss how the work is organized. Ask: What art elements are most important in this work? Is this artwork successful? Explain.

LESSON 8

Creating a Fantasy Animal

Look at the artwork in **Figure 7–16.** This is an example of folk art. **Folk art** is *art made by artists who have had no formal training.* In some cases, the name of the folk artist is not known.

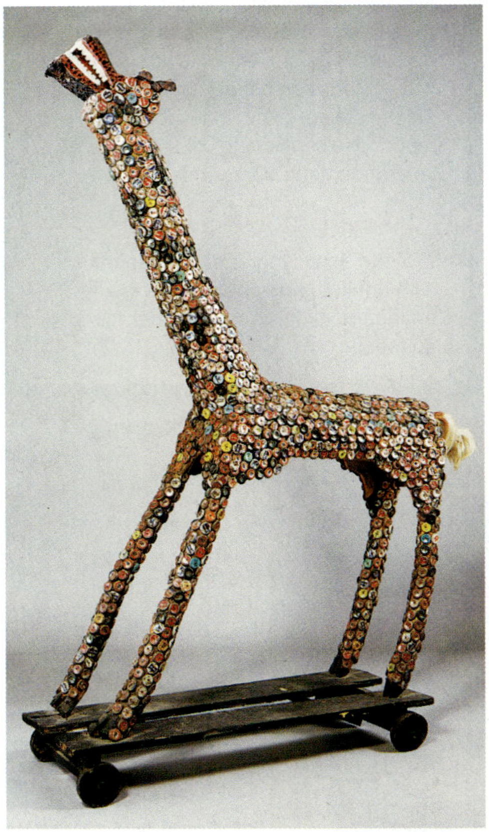

◆ **Figure 7–16** **What unusual material has the artist used to create this giraffe? What is the main principle of art in this sculpture?**

Unknown American Artist. *Bottlecap Giraffe.* c. 1966. Carved and painted wood, bottlecaps, rubber, glass, animal hair and fur. 184.2 × 137.2 × 44.5 cm (72½ × 54 × 17½″). The National Museum of American Art, Smithsonian Institution, Washington, D.C. Gift of Herbert Waide Hemphill, Jr. and museum purchase made possible by Ralph Cross Johnson.

The main medium in this example of folk art is bottle caps. The type used, called a crown cap, was first produced in 1891. Some bottlers today still use crown caps. These metal caps add an unusual surface texture to the giraffe. The work contains many other found objects as well. These include tree branches and a fur tail. All are attached to a metal body. How many different found media can you see?

Notice how the giraffe seems as though it is about to move. The diagonal slant of its legs and its neck help create that feeling.

What You Will Learn

You will create a three-dimensional fantasy animal using recyclable materials and other found objects. Your creature will have a head, a body, legs, and a tail. Depending on the materials you collect, you may create other parts. These might include wings, ears, horns, spikes, hair, or fur. To add color, you will finish your creature by painting it or covering it with interesting buttons, fabric scraps, papers, foils, and so on. Give your creature a name. You will also write a story about its life and environment. Finally, present your creature to the class by telling your story.

What You Will Need

- Assorted recyclable packing materials (yogurt cups, tubes, or other containers)
- White glue or masking tape
- Masking or transparent tape
- Newsprint for papier-mâché
- Cellulose wallpaper paste and water
- School tempera paints
- Assorted brushes
- Buttons, fabric scraps, pieces of broken toys, and other found materials
- Sheets of corrugated cardboard, poster board, or colored construction paper

CAREER OPPORTUNITIES IN ART

COMPARING CAREERS IN ART Have students write a list of some art careers they are interested in learning more about. Have students research the particular art careers. They should answer questions such as, "What is the job description?" "What are the requirements" "What are some additional skills needed for this type of work?" Students can refer to the Web site at **art.glencoe.com** or the Career Spotlights section in the *Handbook* for information. Have students share their findings with the class, and then ask students to compare the different career opportunities in art. Their responses may be written or oral.

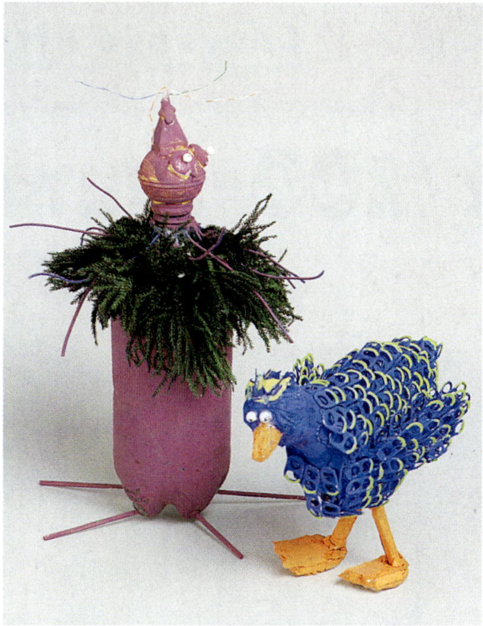

◆ **Figure 7–17** Student work. Fantasy creatures.

What You Will Do

1. Collect a variety of recyclable packing materials. You might gather boxes, plastic containers, or tubes. Study these items. Practice placing them together to create the form of an imaginary creature. The form should include a head, a body, and legs.
2. When you have decided on an arrangement, attach the objects with masking tape. Apply papier-mâché strips to strengthen the joints and cover the body.

Evaluating Your Work

- **Describe** List the materials used to create your animal. Describe the materials used for ears, eyes, and so on.
- **Analyze** Describe the form you created. What surface texture did you use? What colors did you select?
- **Interpret** What kind of mood or feeling does your creature express? Was your story funny or serious?
- **Judge** Which aesthetic view would you use to describe your work? If you were to do this project again, what, if anything, would you change?

3. Choose colors of tempera paint. Decide whether your creature will have a smooth or rough surface texture. Apply the paint using brushes that will give the desired texture. Use large-bristled brushes for a rough texture. Use fine-bristled brushes for a smooth texture.
4. Add a tail, ears, eyes, and other parts. Use buttons, felt, trims, fabric, and other found objects. If you prefer, substitute pieces of cardboard, poster board, or colored construction paper.
5. Give your creature a name. Write a brief story about the creature and its environment. Present your fantasy creature to the class by reading your story aloud.

PORTFOLIO IDEAS

Make sure each entry remains separate and protected in your portfolio. You may want to separate artworks with a piece of tissue paper or newsprint. Mount and label photographs for clear identification. All entries should be easy to identify or read.

Art Online

Careers in art. If you're thinking about pursuing a career in art, visit our Web site at **art.glencoe.com** to compare different career opportunities in art. Which do you find most interesting?

Studio Skills

As students work to construct their creatures, instruct them to spread the glue thinly so that the surfaces will stick quickly. They may need to use tape to temporarily hold the glued segments together until the glue has dried. Students might want to use ribbon or thread to string items together before fastening them. L1 ELL

3 Assess

Self-Assessment

Have students use **Evaluating Your Work** to conduct an in-progress critique of their artwork.

Reteaching

Have students describe how they tried to achieve texture and dimension in their artwork. L1

Enrichment

An American artist made the fantasy creature in **Figure 7–16.** Invite students to find examples of fantasy creatures created by artists of other cultures. Make photocopies to make an international display. Ask students to compare these artworks from a variety of cultures. L1 ELL

4 Close

In a class discussion, have students explain how their fantasy creatures are examples of folk art.

DEVELOPING A PORTFOLIO

Presentation When making decisions about the appearance of artworks in a portfolio, encourage students to pay attention to important concerns such as the mounting for paintings and using protective jackets for pastels and chalk drawings. Remind them to label individual pieces to avoid loss. Use slides for projects too large to include and show multiple viewpoints of three-dimensional artworks. When photographing a work of art, encourage the use of quality film and careful lighting, as it will enhance the finished slide. For more information, refer to the booklet, *Portfolio and Assessment Techniques.*

The Ultimate Moo-seum

1 Focus

Objectives

After completing this lesson, students will be able to:

- Draw original ideas for decorating a fiberglass cow.
- Plan and write a persuasive essay about a specific approach to using art as a fundraiser.

2 Teach

Teaching the Feature

1. Let several volunteers share their responses to the cows in the photograph. Ask: What makes these cows special? How do you think they are being used?
2. Guide students in reading and discussing the article. Ask: Why do you think artists participate in a project like the Cow Parade? What do you think motivates people to buy cows from this kind of project? How would you feel about your school participating in a Cow Parade fundraising project?

Activity

Ask students to imagine that your school will be decorating a cow for a Cow Parade fundraiser. Have students use colored pencils and/or markers to draw their ideas for the best way to decorate the school's fiberglass cow. Schedule class time for students to share and discuss their drawings.

The Ultimate MOO-seum

In "Cow Parade," some cows look like art, and others look like . . . cows!

Students at Poe School in Houston, Texas, didn't have a beef sharing their classroom with a cow. In fact, they loved it! The cow in this case was made of fiberglass. The students decorated the donated critter with 700 hearts and named it Cupid. "The whole school worked on it," says Harry Perkins, a student at Poe.

Unlike the classroom cow, most of the 300 cow sculptures for Houston's "Cow Parade" were created by professional artists. The cows were later sold at auction, raising more than one million dollars for charity. Today, each individually designed cow lives in Houston. Some are in private homes, some grace city parks, and others milk the attention of passersby outside office buildings.

The "Cow Parade" idea started with Swiss-born artist Pascal Knapp. He first sculpted a cow for a public art event in Switzerland in 1998. Since then, several cities have held "Cow Parades," including New York, Kansas City, Portland, and Sydney, Australia.

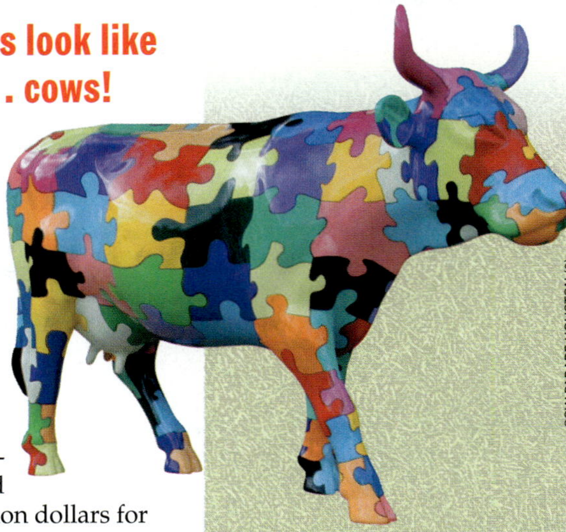

COW PARADE HOUSTON (2)

Cowabunga! This bovine beauty looks as if it were made by a jigsaw-puzzle artist.

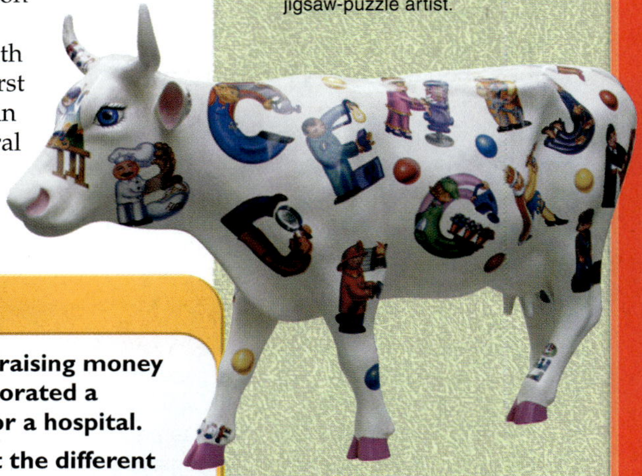

Letter-Perfect Art: Here's a cow that knows its alphabet!

TIME TO CONNECT

Schools around the United States are raising money for good causes. The students who decorated a fiberglass cow sold it to raise money for a hospital.

- **Discuss various ideas as a class about the different ways art can serve to raise funds.**
- **Write a persuasive essay explaining your ideas on whether art should be used as a fundraiser. Support it with a logical argument. Share your work with the class.**

TIME TO CONNECT

Let students work in cooperative groups to brainstorm a list of ideas for using art to raise money for good causes. Then have students work independently to plan, write, and revise their persuasive essays. Ask students to keep these suggestions in mind as they write:

- Use an interesting first sentence to capture your readers' interest.
- State your main idea clearly.
- Support that idea with specific, detailed reasons.

Chapter 7 Review

BUILDING VOCABULARY

Number a sheet of paper from 1 to 12. After each number, write the term from the list that matches each description below.

appliqué	Old Stone Age
calligraphy	porcelain
environment	symbol
folk art	tapestry
illumination	totem
mascot	trait

1. The historical period that occurred between 30,000 and 10,000 B.C.
2. Surroundings.
3. A fine-grained, high-quality form of pottery.
4. A woven wall hanging with decorative designs or colorful scenes.
5. An art form in which cutout shapes are attached to a larger surface.
6. Art made by artists who have had no formal training.
7. The art of beautiful writing.
8. An image used to stand for a quality or an idea.
9. A hand-painted book illustration.
10. An animal or person used by a group as a sign of luck.
11. Personal characteristic.
12. An object that serves as an emblem or respected symbol.

REVIEWING ART FACTS

Number a sheet of paper from 13 to 18. Answer each question in a complete sentence.

13. What do experts believe was the purpose of the cave paintings?
14. Explain why experts believe a sculpture of a hippo was placed in the tomb of Senbi.
15. Name two ways in which an appliqué can be fastened to a background surface.
16. What art element was emphasized most in Persian painting?
17. What effects are achieved through the use of this element in the illumination in Figure 7–10?
18. What did the color yellow symbolize for Franz Marc?

CROSS-CURRICULUM CONNECTIONS

19. **Language Arts.** Select an artwork in this chapter with symbolic meaning. Explain the symbol. Write a brief paragraph describing how it adds to your appreciation of the work.
20. **Science.** Learn about carbon-14 dating. This is a technique scientists have used to prove that cave paintings were really done thousands of years ago. Use an encyclopedia or online resource. Share your findings with your class.

Web Museum Activity

National Museum of Wildlife Art, Jackson Hole, Wyoming

Create a wildlife and landscape composition using the art principles. Experience the artistic process online by visiting the National Museum of Wildlife Art. Go to **art.glencoe.com** and click on the museum's link.

Begin your composition by selecting a landscape photograph, crop it, and then drag an assortment of animals to create your wildlife artwork.

Evaluate your composition. What principles of art did you use? What is the overall theme? Describe the animals in your painting.

Web Museum Activity

Before you have students go online, visit the Web site to preview the museum's online content, collection, and any online exhibit that may be of interest. Students' compositions will vary.

Students should be able to identify how they used the principles of art and explain the overall theme of their artwork.

ANSWERS TO Chapter 7 Review

Building Vocabulary

1. Stone Age
2. environment
3. porcelain
4. tapestry
5. appliqué
6. folk art
7. calligraphy
8. symbol
9. illumination
10. mascot
11. trait
12. totem

Reviewing Art Facts

13. They believe the paintings may have been used in a ritual to bring luck.
14. The hippo was believed to protect the body after death.
15. It can be stitched or glued into place.
16. The element of line.
17. The flowing curved lines suggest graceful movement.
18. Yellow symbolized peace.

Cross-Curriculum Connections

1. Student paragraphs will vary. Students should support their descriptions with specific details.
2. Responses should include that carbon-14 dating is a technique used for obtaining age estimates on organic materials. This method has been used to date samples as old as 700,000 years.

Chapter Resources

Features	Standards for Chapter: National	Standards for Chapter: State/Local	Reproducible Masters
Quick Write *page 143* TIME ART SCENE "Faces of Ground Zero," *page 160* ***Web Museum Activity*** *page 161*	**1.** (a, b) **2.** (a, c) **3.** (a, b) **4.** (a, b, c) **5.** (a, b, c) **6.** (a, b)		Guided Reading and Practice 8–1 Studio Activity 8–2 Historical and Cultural Heritage 8–3 Application Activity 8–4 Enrichment Activity 8–5, 8–6 Cross-Curriculum Activity 8–7 Lesson Plans

Lesson Resources

Lessons	Standards per Lesson: National	Standards per Lesson: State/Local	Reproducible Masters
1 ***Portraits*** *(pages 144–145)*	4a, 4b, 5c		Guided Reading and Practice 8–1
2 ***Creating an Expressive Face*** *(pages 146–147)*	1a, 1b, 2a, 2c, 3a		
3 ***Figures in Action*** *(pages 148–149)*	4a, 4c		Studio Activity 8–2
4 ***Drawing a Figure in Action*** *(pages 150–151)*	1a, 1b, 2a		
5 ***Portraits in the Round*** *(pages 152–153)*	4a, 4c, 5a		Historical and Cultural Heritage 8–3
6 **ART & SOCIAL STUDIES** *(pages 154–155)*	4b, 5a, 6b		Application Activity 8–4
7 ***Heroes in Art*** *(pages 156–157)*	1a, 1b, 5a, 5b		Enrichment Activity 8–5, 8–6 Cross-Curriculum Activity 8–7
8 ***Creating a Mixed-Media Banner*** *(pages 158–159)*	1a, 1b, 2a, 3b		

Assessment	Technology
Testing Program: Chapter Test 8–8 Portfolio and Assessment Techniques	Artsource Performing Arts Package, Donald McKayle (DVD or VHS Segment 9) National Museum of Women in the Arts Fine Art Transparency CC-8 *A Meeting* by Marie Bashikirsteff Fine Art Transparency 8 *Senora Sabasa Garcia* by Francisco Goya Interactive Lesson Planner

Activities/Features
Time & Place: Italian Renaissance
Evaluating Your Work Studio Option Visual Art Journal
Meet the Artist: Edgar Degas
Evaluating Your Work Reflective Thinking Visual Art Journal
Meet the Artist: Michelangelo
Make the Connection
Studio Activity: Making a Hero Exhibit
Evaluating Your Work Portfolio Ideas Art Online

KEY TO ABILITY LEVELS

Teaching strategies have been coded.

- L1 Activities for all students; teacher direction required
- L2 Activities for average to above-average students; some teacher direction needed
- L3 Activities for students able and willing to work independently
- ELL English Language Learner activities

FEATURED ARTISTS

- Agnolo Bronzino
- Franck Craig
- Honoré Daumier
- Edgar Degas
- Jean Dubuffet
- Frida Kahlo
- Vincent van Gogh
- Michelangelo
- Jerry Pinkney

FINE ART PRINTS

Fine Art Print 12, Seated Bodhisattva: *Guanyin*

Timesaving *Technology*

Interactive Lesson Planner

Make planning easy. Use this interactive software to organize your week, month, semester, or year and access all *Introducing Art* reproducible resources.

KEY TO LESSON RESOURCES

- Narrative Lesson
- Studio Lesson

Chapter 8

Portraying People

(pages 142–161)

Chapter Overview

Capturing the individuality of a person is the essence of the portrait. In this chapter, students will explore the various ways in which artists have tried to capture their subject's unique qualities. They will learn about various styles in art. They will learn too, that human subjects have been portrayed differently, depending on time, place, and cultural influence.

Discussing the Artwork

Focus On ◆ **Figure 8–1** Have students analyze the interdependence of the art element color and the principle of balance in Frida Kahlo's painting. Ask:

- Why do you think the artist chose bright colors for this painting?
- What type of balance is used?
- What is Frida expressing in this portrait?

Have students discuss the feeling they get from this painting. Explain to students that the type of balance used in a work of art affects the feeling expressed by that work. The use of formal balance in this painting suggests a sense of dignity and importance.

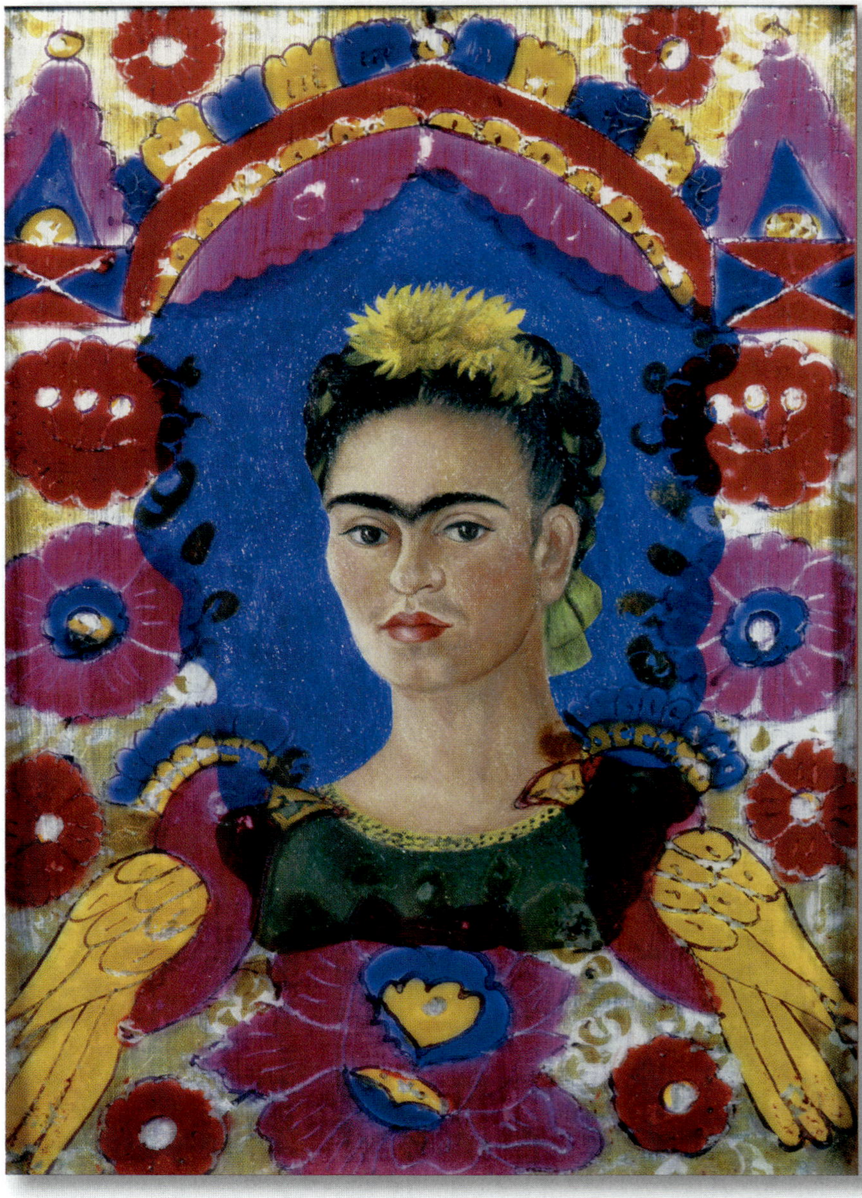

Focus On ◆ **Figure 8–1** **Notice the birds, the flowers, and the use of brilliant colors in this painting. What message or feeling do you think this self-portrait communicates?**

Frida Kahlo. *The Frame, Self Portrait.* c. 1937–38. Oil on aluminum, under glass and painted wood. 28.5 × 20.5 cm (11.2 × 8.1″). Musée National d'Art Moderne, Centre Georges Pompidou, Paris, France. © Banco de Mexico Trust.

Linking to the Performing Arts

Dance In the dance "Rainbow 'Round My Shoulder," dancers representing prisoners perform sharp, repeated rhythmic patterns that convey their tedious quality of life. The motion and words, selected by choreographer Donald McKayle, communicate that these men no longer have control over their own lives. Have students learn how choreographer Donald McKayle expressed these qualities in the **Performing Arts Handbook** on page 317. To enrich student understanding, play the DVD or videotape (segment 9) in the **Performing Arts Package.**

Chapter 8

Portraying People

"I paint self-portraits because I am so often alone, because I am the person I know best."

— Frida Kahlo (1907–1954)

Like snowflakes, no two people are exactly alike. Each person has his or her own likes, dislikes, thoughts, feelings, and dreams. It is this unique quality that has made people a favorite subject of artists. This chapter will help you learn how to "read" artworks that depict people. It will also teach you about the different styles of portraits.

After completing this chapter, you will be able to:

- Explain what is meant by having a *style* in art.
- Identify the differences in ways people have been portrayed throughout history and in a variety of cultures.
- Create artworks with people as subjects.

Quick Write

Interpreting the Quote
Read the quote by Kahlo and look at **Figure 8–1.** How well do you know yourself? Write about yourself and how you might depict yourself in a self-portrait.

Key Terms

- style
- self-portrait
- figure study
- portraiture
- ancestor figure
- public art
- murals

Quick Write

Interpreting the Quote
Have students read the quote by Frida Kahlo and complete the Quick Write activity. Ask students to write a brief interpretation of the quote in their own words. Ask students: Why do you think knowing yourself well is important when creating a self-portrait? Discuss their responses in class.

Chapter Motivator

Ask students to bring a snapshot of themselves from an earlier grade and a recent photo as well. Have them compare the two pictures. Ask students the following questions:

- How are the pictures similar?
- How are they different?
- If you were to draw a picture of yourself combining the best qualities of each photo, what would the drawing look like?
- What would the drawing reveal about your personal style?

Tell students that in this chapter they will study ways in which artists have shown the human figure. They will also learn about the styles of art.

National Standards for Arts Education

This chapter addresses the following National Standards for the Visual Arts:

1. (a, b)
2. (a, c)
3. (a, b)
4. (a, b, c)
5. (a, b, c)
6. (b)

Art Online

Visit **art.glencoe.com**, the Web site for Glencoe's art programs. This site is designed to help you prepare for your classes and learn about the various opportunities in the art community. Explore the many teacher resources the site has to offer, such as:

- Arts Education Resources
- Galleries and Cultural Resources
- Professional Development Articles
- Teacher's Lounge

Portraits

(pages 144–145)

1 Focus

Objectives

After completing this lesson, students will be able to:

- Define *style.*
- Describe the style differences between Mannerism and Expressionism.

2 Teach

Vocabulary

Point out to students that the words *portrait* and *portray* come from a Latin word meaning "to draw." Ask students to discuss the ways a person can be portrayed: in a picture or painting, in a sculpture, in words, in a play, and so on. Have students write a brief word portrait of themselves.

Understanding Art History

Mannerism Explain that *Mannerism* is a style of art that developed in Rome and Florence between 1520 and 1600. It was a style that rejected Renaissance balance and harmony in favor of emotion and distortion. Bring in some examples of artworks in the Mannerist style and ask students to identify the influence of historical and political events in those artworks. Works of art done in this style reflected the tension that marked Europe at that time in history.

Portraits

Ever since the first cave dwellers roamed the earth, the world's population has been steadily growing. So has the number of ways of portraying people in art. Each age has given rise to new art styles. A **style** is *an artist's personal way of using the elements and principles of art to express feelings and ideas.*

In this chapter, you will see examples of different styles artists have used to depict people through the ages.

Portraits as Historical Records

Today, we know what our leaders and other celebrities look like. It wasn't always so. Imagine for a moment that you live in an age before television, newspapers, and magazines. Such a time existed in the not-too-distant past. As recently as the early 1800s, people who wanted to see important figures had to rely largely on painted *portraits* of them.

Portraits from the 1500s

Figure 8–2 shows a portrait from the 1500s. Bronzino was an Italian painter who was the outstanding artist of the Tuscan High Mannerist Style. His work is cold, refined, aristocratic and technically brilliant in the rendering of surface details and color. As the credit line reveals, the subjects are a woman and her son. What can you tell about the two people from

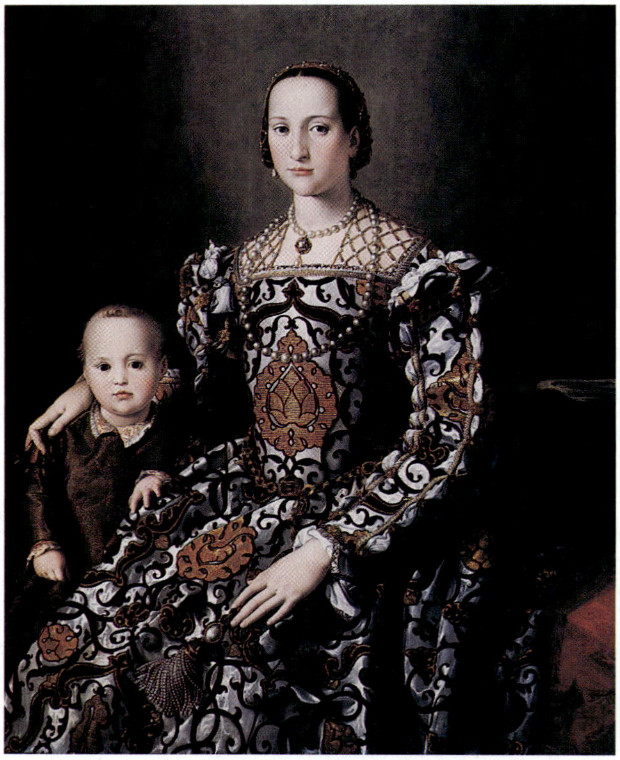

◆ **Figure 8–2** Compare this work with the Roman portrait sculpture on page 84 (Figure 5–4). Which of the works do you think is truer to life? Why?

Agnolo Bronzino. *Eleonora of Toledo and Her Son.* c. 1550. Oil on panel. 1.2 × 1 m (48 × 39⅜"). Detroit Institute of Arts, Detroit, Michigan. Gift of Mrs. Ralph Harmon Booth in memory of her husband Ralph Harmon Booth.

STORY BEHIND THE ARTWORK

Portraiture Portrait painting became popular in the fourteenth century with the appearance of "donor portraits." These were works of religious art in which a wealthy churchgoer was included in pictures with his or her favorite religious figures. Eventually these kinds of religious paintings gave way to portraits with natural settings. Portraits were used to commemorate marriages, to show off family, and to capture the likeness of the sitter just as he or she actually appeared.

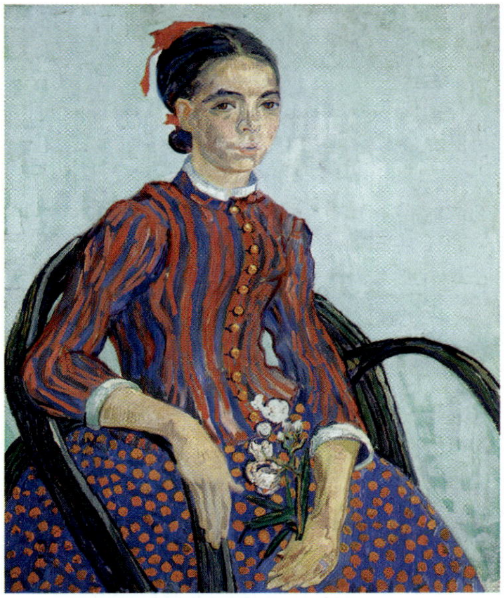

◆ **Figure 8–3** Compare and contrast the eyes in this portrait to the eyes in Figure 8–2. Both women are looking directly at the viewer, but their eyes reveal different expressions. Describe what they reveal.

Vincent Van Gogh. *La Mousmée.* 1888. Oil on canvas. 73.3 × 60.3 cm (28⅞ × 23¾″). National Gallery of Art, Washington D.C. Chester Dale Collection. Image © 2003 Board of Trustees.

looking at this painting? Look at the face and hands of Eleonora. How old does she seem to be? How old does her son look? Look at the size of his head and the size of his hands. Notice how carefully the pearls around Eleonora's neck are placed. Notice the elaborate brocade design woven into the fabric of her dress and the shine of the boy's jacket. What do the clothing and jewelry tell you about the social status of these two? This portrait was commissioned to show the wealth and beauty of this woman. Do you think the artist depicted these people as they really looked or as they preferred to be shown?

Expressive Portraits

The portrait in **Figure 8–3** was painted over 300 years after Bronzino's portrait by Vincent van Gogh. The style van Gogh used is called *Expressionism*. He painted to express his personal feelings about a subject. No one paid van Gogh to paint this work. He chose the young woman, and asked her to pose for him because he saw something in her that he wanted to express. Did he try to depict the surface details and colors accurately? Compare the quality of her skin to that of Eleonora's. Notice the brushstrokes. Look at the girl's face. With which of these two women would you feel most comfortable? Which is the most realistic? Which is the most appealing?

Time & Place

Italian Renaissance

Historical connection. Look at **Figure 8–2**, an example of a portrait commissioned by the Medici family during the Italian Renaissance. The Renaissance was a period of great awakening. It began in Italy around 1400 and lasted for over a century. During this time, the arts flourished, trade spread, and advancements in science were made.

The Medici family played an important role in the Italian Renaissance. This family ruled Florence and much of Italy from 1537 to 1631. Through trade and banking, the family became one of the wealthiest in fifteenth-century Italy.

The Medicis were important patrons of the arts. In fact, they commissioned many paintings, sculptures, and tapestries from artists such as Agnolo Bronzino and Michelangelo.

Compare this portrait with Figure 8–3. What do the subjects' clothing tell you about their status?

Check Your Understanding

1. What is an artist's style?
2. Explain how portrait painting changed from the 1500s to the 1800s.

Time & Place

Italian Renaissance

Have students look closely at **Figure 8–2.** They should notice that the dress style, fabric, and detail reveal that she is wealthy. The subject's rigid pose and serious expression also show that she is of a higher stature.

3 Assess

Self-Assessment

Have students complete the **Check Your Understanding** questions on this page. Answers are provided below.

Reteaching

Have students compare the artists' styles in **Figures 8–2** and **8–3.** L1

Enrichment

Artistic Style Ask a local portrait photographer to come in to discuss his or her style. Encourage students to ask questions about how a photographer can develop an artistic style. Ask the photographer to show slides of his or her work showing different approaches and styles.

4 Close

Ask students to write a paragraph describing the style they used in their self-portraits. L1

Answers to Check Your Understanding

1. Style is an artist's personal way of using the elements and principles of art to express feelings and ideas.
2. In the 1500s, portrait painting appeared stiff and formal, and people were portrayed as they wanted to be shown, not as they really were. In the portraits of the 1800s, figures were shown with more realistic expressions.

Creating an Expressive Face

(pages 146–147)
Lesson Time: 90 min.

1 Focus

Objectives

After completing this lesson, students will be able to:

- Demonstrate technical skills effectively by creating an expressive face from torn pieces of colored construction paper.
- Describe, analyze, interpret, and judge their pictures of expressive faces.

Supplies
Refer to **What You Will Need** in the Student Edition.

2 Teach

Motivator

Direct attention to the Japanese mask in **Figure 8–4** and ask students to express their opinions about it. On the board, compile a list of adjectives used by students to describe the mask. Ask: What do you think masks like this might be used for? Discuss the various occasions on which masks are used today.

Historical/Cultural Heritage

Have students conduct a library search for examples of masks used in other cultures and bring these examples to class. Compare the masks from a variety of cultures and discuss the purpose of each. Ask: How is color and shape used in these masks? Which masks do you think are the most impressive as works of art? Why? Discuss their responses in class. L2

LESSON 2

Creating an Expressive Face

Have you ever heard the expression "whistling in the dark?" It refers to efforts to look and sound brave in the face of danger. The iron mask in **Figure 8–4** was created for much the same purpose. It was worn by a fifteenth-century Japanese warrior—making him look fierce and frightening to enemies, while adding to his own confidence in battle. Take a closer look at this art object. Notice the furrowed brow, the wide-open eyes, and the angry scowl. Does the expression on this mask succeed in frightening you?

What You Will Learn

In this lesson, you will create a masklike, expressive face. You will use a variety of large and small shapes in contrasting colors torn from colored construction paper. These will be assembled and glued to a sheet of black construction paper. To make the face as expressive as possible, you will exaggerate and distort the features and use contrasting colors. Then arrange the shapes in layers to give your picture a bold, expressive look.

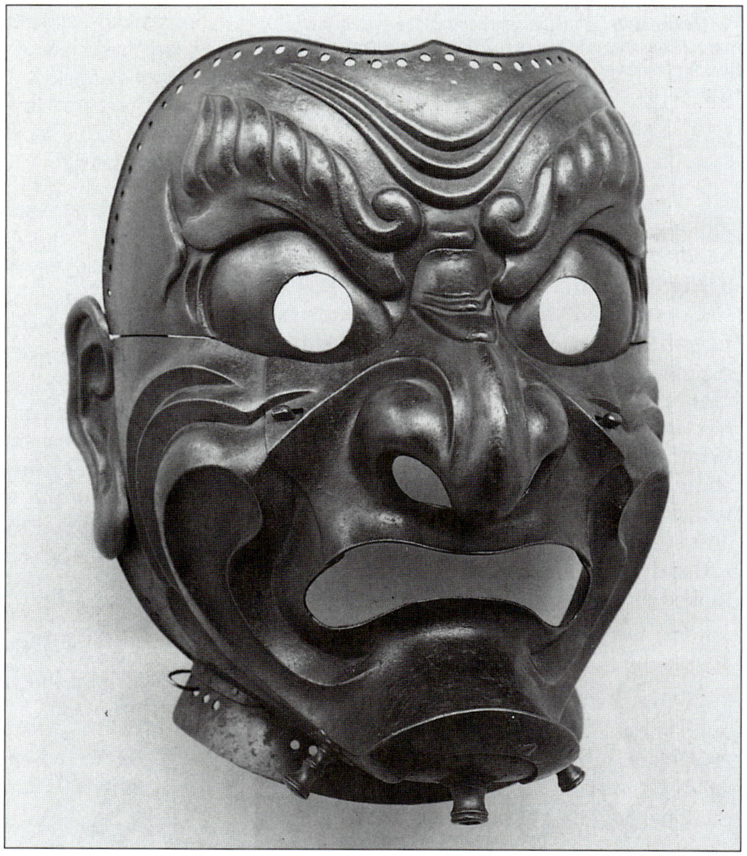

◆ **Figure 8–4** What expression do you "read" on this mask? What features give it such an expression?

Japan. *Mask.* 1716. Iron repoussé. 19.7 × 17.1 cm (7¾ × 6¾"). The Metropolitan Museum of Art, New York, New York. Rogers Fund, 1913.

Curriculum Connections

Social Studies As early as the thirteenth century, masks similar to the one illustrated in **Figure 8–4** were worn in Japan during war. At that time, the Mongols under Kublai Khan took control of China. Hearing of Japan's wealth, Khan decided to extend his rule to Japan. Over 100,000 warriors and 3,500 warships were readied for the assault. Nature, however, played a decisive role. The invasion was launched in 1281, but a storm, which came to be known as "the Great Wind," scattered the ships of the Mongol invaders. Thousands of men perished or were captured as slaves.

What You Will Need

- Pencil and sheets of sketch paper
- Colored construction paper 9 x 12 inches
- White glue or glue sticks
- Cardboard cut into ½-inch squares
- Scissors

What You Will Do

1. Begin by studying the Japanese mask in Figure 8–4. Note the way the artist distorted the features and expression of the face to make it appear more frightening.
2. Complete several sketches of faces. Experiment with different ways of exaggerating and distorting the facial features. Notice the different moods and feelings suggested by the sketches.
3. Using your best sketch as a guide, tear a wide oval or round shape from a piece of construction paper. *Do not use scissors for this task.* Glue the shape to a sheet of construction paper.
4. Tear other shapes from the construction paper to form the eyes, eyebrows, nose, and mouth. For each feature, tear out *six or more* shapes. Layer them from large to small. Keep in mind that the more shapes you use for a single feature, the more sculpted it will look. To make your work more expressive, distort the shapes. Be sure to use bright, contrasting colors.
5. Assemble the various features on the face shape. For each feature, glue the largest piece in place first. Continue stacking smaller shapes in this fashion. The result will be a layered effect.

Evaluating Your Work

- **Describe** Are all the features of the face included in your mask? Are these features distorted?
- **Analyze** Did you use a variety of large and small shapes? Point out places on your mask where contrasting colors are used.
- **Interpret** Would viewers agree that your mask is expressive? If asked to describe your mask with a single word, what word would you choose?
- **Judge** Do you think you succeeded in creating an expressive face? If you were to do another, what would you change to make the work more effective?

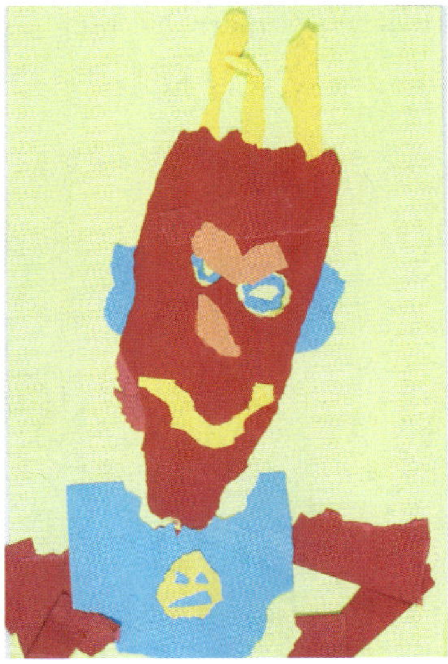

◆ **Figure 8–5** Student work. Expressive face.

Studio Option

Create a **self-portrait**, a *painting or drawing of an artist's own image.* Study your face in the mirror. Using charcoal, draw a large oval to represent the outline of your face. Try to capture your expression. Use white chalk to highlight eyes, cheeks, and so on. Complete your self-portrait by adding details and shading.

Visual Art Journal

Using descriptive adjectives, write a paragraph in your journal describing the expression you were trying to capture in your portrait and whether you were successful.

Studio Skills

As students sketch, remind them to exaggerate facial features and expressions. Demonstrate how to achieve a layered effect with the construction paper, gluing down larger shapes first and then progressively smaller shapes on top. Point out how eyes that are wide open differ from those that are squinted, or how turning the mouth up or down at the corner alters the expression. L1 ELL

Visual Art Journal

Have students share their entries with the class. Ask the class to determine whether each mask successfully captured the intended expression.

3 Assess

Self-Assessment

Have students use **Evaluating Your Work** to conduct an in-progress critique of their expressive face.

Reteaching

Ask students to describe how the Japanese mask is successful in being expressive.

4 Close

Have students analyze the origional artworks of their peers, pointing out successful use of distortion and contrast to achieve an expressive face.

Inclusion Strategies

Behavioral Problems Before students start to assemble their masks, write a list of emotions on the board, such as sad, angry, scared, surprised, and so on. Have them identify situations where they felt those emotions. As students assemble and create their masks, encourage them to express one of those feelings in their masks. Ask students to describe that feeling and how it is represented in their masks. Responses may be written or oral.

Figures in Action

(pages 148–149)

1 Focus

Objectives

After completing this lesson, students will be able to:

- Define *figure study.*
- Demonstrate body language.

2 Teach

Motivator

Begin by asking a student to serve as a model in an action pose, and then instruct the class to complete a quick gesture drawing of the model. Place the finished drawings on display and ask the class to discuss them in terms of their success at capturing a figure in action. Explain that in this lesson they will study two artworks showing figures in action.

Vocabulary

Take a few minutes to discuss *body language* with the class. Explain that body language can be large, expansive physical motions, small gestures, or even subtle facial movements.

Aesthetics

After they have had an opportunity to examine Daumier's action figure **(Figure 8–6)**, ask students to express their opinions about it. Write the word action on the board and ask students if they think the artist convincingly captures the action of the messenger in flight. Have them provide reasons for their answers. L1

LESSON 3

Figures in Action

One of the hardest parts of a barber's or hairstylist's job is working on a customer who won't sit still. Even the slightest movement presents a real challenge to the stylist's sure hand.

This observation holds true not only for haircutters but also for artists. For the artist, however, the challenge provided by the human body in motion is a *welcome* one. It is an opportunity to present people as they often appear—in the midst of one activity or another.

In this lesson, you will learn about artworks that show figures in action.

Figure Studies

As emphasized in Chapter 6, the Renaissance artist Leonardo da Vinci filled many sketchbooks with drawings. Among the sketches he made were hundreds of figure studies. A **figure study** is *a drawing that focuses on the human form.* Leonardo observed and faithfully recorded in great detail the workings of the arms and legs in motion.

The studies Leonardo made set the stage for generations of artists to follow. Take a moment to study the drawing in **Figure 8–6**. Notice the way in which Daumier captures the movement of a running messenger.

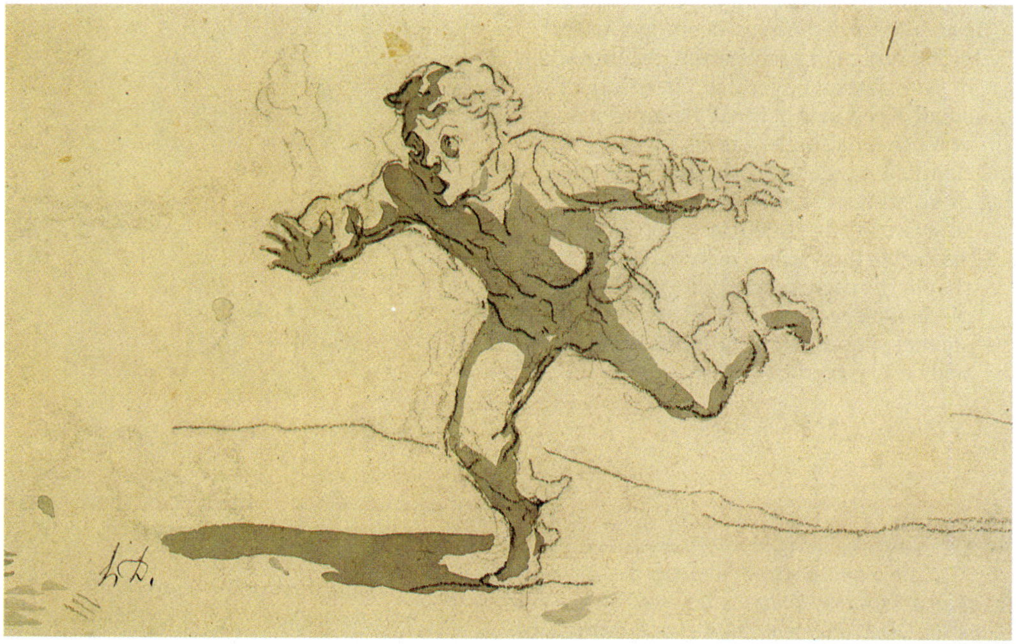

◆ **Figure 8–6** **Do you detect a sense of urgency? How has value and line been used to convey this feeling?**

Honoré Daumier. *The Young Courier.* Black chalk and gray wash on laid paper. 15.5 × 23.2 cm (6⅛ 9⅛"). © 1997 Board of Trustees, National Gallery of Art, Washington, D.C. The Rosenwald Collection.

CAREER OPPORTUNITIES IN ART

Researching Art Careers Encourage students to think about art-related careers. Have them read the Career Spotlights section in the Handbook. Ask students to learn about different careers, such as graphic design, advertising, and other commercial-art applications. Have them write a brief report describing three different careers. Ask students to compare these career opportunities in art, select which one appeals to them most, and explain why.

Figure Painting

The recording of figures in action is not limited to drawing. Many painters try to capture action in their work.

Edgar Degas often depicted his subjects in natural, active poses. In **Figure 8–7** you see a backstage ballet scene. Notice how he has used diagonal movement to depict the arms, legs, and torsos of the dancers. No one is standing straight and stiff. Everyone looks alive and ready to dance off the background. In this work, his technique of leaving the strokes of the pastel unblended adds to the movement and excitement.

Check Your Understanding

1. What is a figure study?
2. Describe the body language of the figures in motion on these two pages.

Meet the Artist

Edgar Degas (1834–1917)

Cultural connection. You may know that Degas is famous for his paintings of ballet dancers, but did you also know that he studied to be a lawyer? Born in Paris to a wealthy family in 1834, Degas studied law for a short time before discovering his interest in painting.

To pursue a career in art, he trained at the École des Beaux-Arts in Paris and traveled widely to find inspiration. Influenced by photography and Japanese prints, Degas used many innovative compositions in his artwork. His themes dealt with people and city life, especially ballet dancers at the theater (see **Figure 8–7**).

After 1909, Degas turned to sculpture due to failing eyesight. He left many wax models of dancers and horses that were cast into bronze after his death.

◆ **Figure 8–7** Notice the simple shapes the artist has used. Explain how the artist has used color to create movement.

Edgar Degas. *Ballet Scene.* c. 1907. Pastel on cardboard. 76.8 × 111.2 cm (30¼ × 43¾″). National Gallery of Art, Washington D.C. Chester Dale Collection. Image © 2003 Board of Trustees.

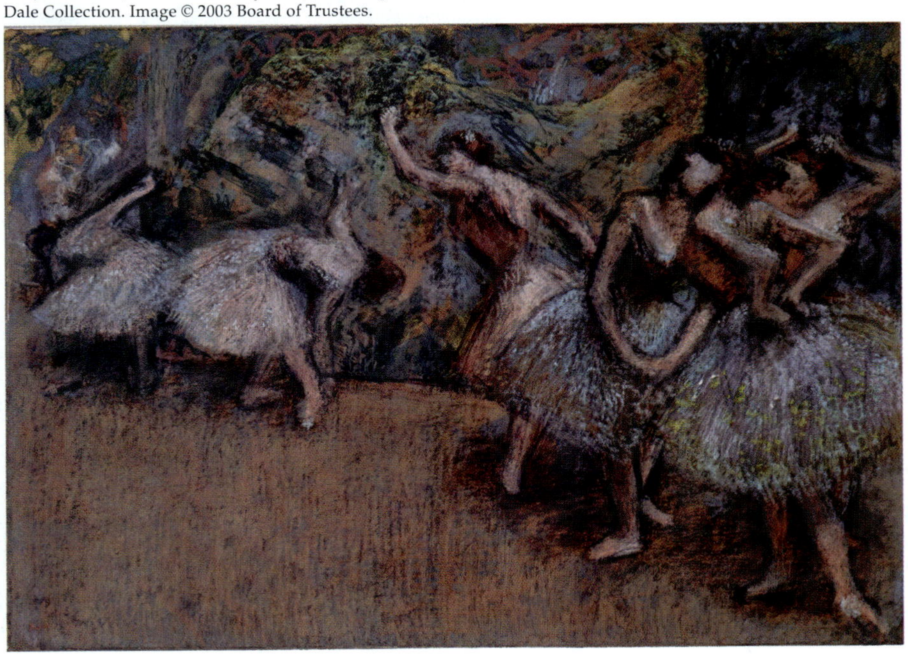

Meet the Artist

Edgar Degas (1834–1917)

Tell students that while Degas was influenced by the Impressionists' use of light and in their depiction of nature, he was more interested in capturing figures in natural and spontaneous movements. He is best known for his study of ballet dancers.

ART IN EVERYDAY LIFE

People in Action Remind students that action figures are all around them. Ask them to observe and pay close attention to all the walkers and joggers they see everyday. Encourage students to try and capture such actions in their visual art journals.

3 Assess

Self-Assessment

Have students complete the **Check Your Understanding** questions on this page. Answers are provided below.

Enrichment

Figure Drawing Invite students to locate examples of Leonardo da Vinci's drawings of human anatomy or his sketches of faces and facial expressions. Point out the variations in line thickness, the shading techniques, and the use of shadow. L1

4 Close

Invite students to bring to class examples of artist's figure drawings for discussion.

Answers to Check Your Understanding

1. A figure study is a drawing that focuses on the human form. Da Vinci observed and recorded in great detail the actions of muscles and muscle groups. He studied arms and legs in motion, and he examined and drew the minute differences between facial expressions like a frown and a scowl.
2. In Figure 8–6, the runner is leaning forward as he races to deliver his message. In Figure 8–7, the dancers look alert and ready to dance with bodies flexed.

Drawing a Figure in Action

(pages 150–151)
Lesson Time: 60 min.

1 Focus

Objectives

After completing this lesson, students will be able to:

- Demonstrate technical skills effectively by using a variety of art materials to produce a drawing of an abstract figure in action.
- Use a variety of lines, shapes, colors, and textures to add visual interest and a sense of movement to their compositions.
- Conduct an in-progress critique of their abstract figures.

Supplies

Refer to **What You Will Need** in the Student Edition.

2 Teach

Motivator

Instruct students to examine **Figure 8–8**. Ask students:

- Does the artist's technique of using small shapes remind you of anything? *(pieces of a puzzle)*
- What does this indicate? *(puzzles appeal to children)*
- Is there anything else that suggests children? *(manner in which the work is created appears to be childlike)*

Explain that Dubuffet tried to capture in his work the freedom and joy he observed in children's drawings.

Drawing a Figure in Action

The painting in Figure 8–7, as you saw, has an energetic quality. Its mood is achieved, moreover, through a union of natural, active poses.

Both those comments apply equally to the work in **Figure 8–8.** Take a moment to examine this painting closely. Do the playful shapes in it remind you of the interlocking pieces of a jigsaw puzzle? If so, your thinking is in line with the artist's. All of his art was meant to be playful. Notice the work's title. The word *reveler* means merrymaker. Can you find the head, arms, and legs of this merrymaker?

What You Will Learn

In this studio lesson, you will paint an abstract figure in action. You will not worry about making your subject look real. Instead, you will concentrate on using a variety of lines, shapes, bright colors, and textures to suggest a moving figure. These art elements will add up to a cheerful design.

What You Will Need

- Pencil and sheets of sketch paper
- White drawing paper, 12 x 18 inches
- Black marker with a medium point

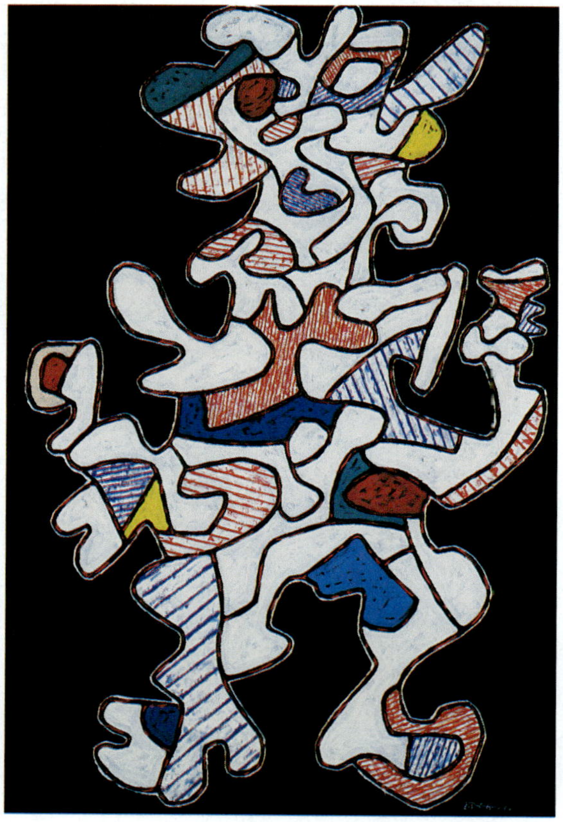

◆ **Figure 8–8** Analyze the variety of lines and shapes in this painting. How has the artist tied these elements together to form a human figure?

Jean Dubuffet. *The Reveler.* 1964. Oil on canvas. 195 × 130.2 cm (76¾ × 51¼"). Dallas Museum of Art, Dallas, Texas. Gift of Mr. and Mrs. James H. Clark.

Technology Strategies in the Art Classroom

Electronic Media-Generated Art
Have students look through sports and recreational magazines. Ask them to find images that show body positions and actions that clearly demonstrate a sport, dance or other activity. Scan the images. Use the tools on the photo-imaging program to isolate the figure. Remove any background. Then have students analyze the motion of the figure. For more information on using a scanner, refer to page 293 of the Digital Media Guide.

- Several brushes
- Tempera paints, mixing tray
- Scissors
- White glue
- Black construction paper

What You Will Do

1. Begin by looking again at Figure 8–8. Concentrate on the lines of the figure. Observe how the artist has used a variety of lines, shapes, colors, and textures, within the overall shape. See how these add action to the work's composition.
2. Complete several pencil sketches of a student model in an action pose. In your sketches, focus on capturing the lines of action in the figure. Draw only the outline of the figure.
3. Working lightly with a continuous pencil line, transfer your best sketch to the sheet of white drawing paper. Make your drawing large enough to fill most of the paper. Go over the pencil line with a black marker.
4. Still working with the marker, divide your figure into a variety of large and small shapes.
5. Switching to tempera and brush, paint the smaller shapes within the large figure shape. Select bright, cheerful colors that contrast with one another. You do not have to paint all the shapes. You may also want to add painted lines or lines made with the marker to some of the shapes. Notice that the artist has done this in Figure 8–8 to create different textures.
6. With scissors, cut out your drawing. Use white glue to mount the drawing on a sheet of black construction paper.

Evaluating Your Work

- **Describe** Can you easily identify the head, arms, and legs in your figure? Does the figure appear to be moving?
- **Analyze** Did you break up your figure with a variety of large and small shapes? Did you also use a variety of colors and textures?
- **Interpret** Do you think most viewers will recognize your work as an abstract figure in action?
- **Judge** What do you consider to be the best part of your composition?

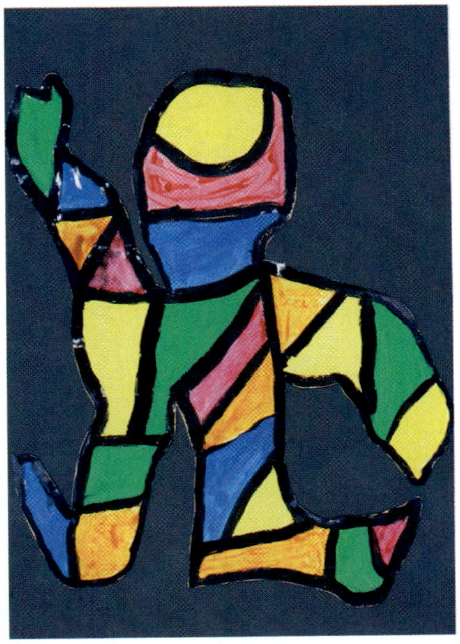

◆ **Figure 8–9** Student work. Abstract figure in action.

REFLECTIVE THINKING

Critical Evaluation. Select and display a variety of your artworks in the classroom. Analyze the original exhibition of your peers to form conclusions about formal properties and historical and cultural contexts.

Visual Art Journal

Take notice of the various shapes found in nature. Explore these shapes and forms by illustrating them in your journal. Try different colors, shapes, and sizes.

Team Building Activity

Divide the class into small groups. Ask students to analyze the interdependence of the art elements and principles in Figure 8–8. Have each group answer the following questions:

- Which art principles are demonstrated? *(movement and variety)*
- Why is this painting called *The Reveler?* *(it has a sense of cheerfulness and revelry)* L2

Visual Art Journal

Have students illustrate ideas from the environment. Encourage them to observe the different shapes found in nature.

3 Assess

Peer Assessment

Have students analyze their peers' drawings to form conclusions about formal properties—the elements and principles of art. How did they achieve a sense of movement?.

Reteaching

Have students discuss the varied use of line and color in Figure 8–8. L1

4 Close

Have students evaluate their work and discuss how they used variety and color.

TEACHER TO TEACHER

Contour Drawing Remind students that contour drawing requires moving the eye and hand in tandem, looking constantly at the model and not at the paper. By practicing their contour drawing, students will improve their perceptual skills of direct observation. Reinforce students' efforts, and tell them not to worry if their drawings appear awkward at first. For additional help in developing the skill of contour drawing, refer students to the Technique Tip 2 on page 281 in the Handbook section.

Portraits in the Round

(pages 152–153)

1 Focus

Objectives

After completing this lesson, students will be able to:

- Define *portraiture.*
- Explain what an ancestor figure is.

2 Teach

Motivator

Begin by having students examine **Figure 8–10**. Ask if they can identify the subject. What details do they notice most? Ask students to point out realistic details in this sculpture.

Art Criticism

Ask students to identify some of the details that make Michelangelo's *Moses* (Figure 8–10) look lifelike. Then ask them to discuss the ancestor figure:

- What details tell the viewer that this figure is based on a real person? *(the details of his body, such as the veins across his hands and arms)*
- Compare both artworks. Which sculpture seems to portray more emotion?*(Moses)*
- Does a portrait sculpture have to be completely realistic to be successful? Why or why not? L1 ELL

LESSON 5

Portraits in the Round

Are you familiar with the phrase *in the flesh?* It is a colorful way of saying "in person." This phrase also calls to mind a property of people that can never be fully captured in two-dimensional paintings or drawings. That is the three-dimensionality of the human form. What better way to show this property than in art that has three dimensions?

In this lesson, you will explore another approach to **portraiture** (**pohr**-tray-chur)—*the art of making portraits*—that highlights this property. You will learn about and see examples of portraits "in the round."

Sculpture

Many artists through the ages have striven for realism in their works. Look back at the Ancient Roman sculpture in Figure 3–14 on page 52. Notice how the artist has captured the feeling of the athlete through the accurate proportions of his body and the careful depiction of muscles. Look at the careful attention to details such as the toenails and hair.

Renaissance Portrait Sculpture

During the Renaissance ancient works from the Greeks and Romans were rediscovered

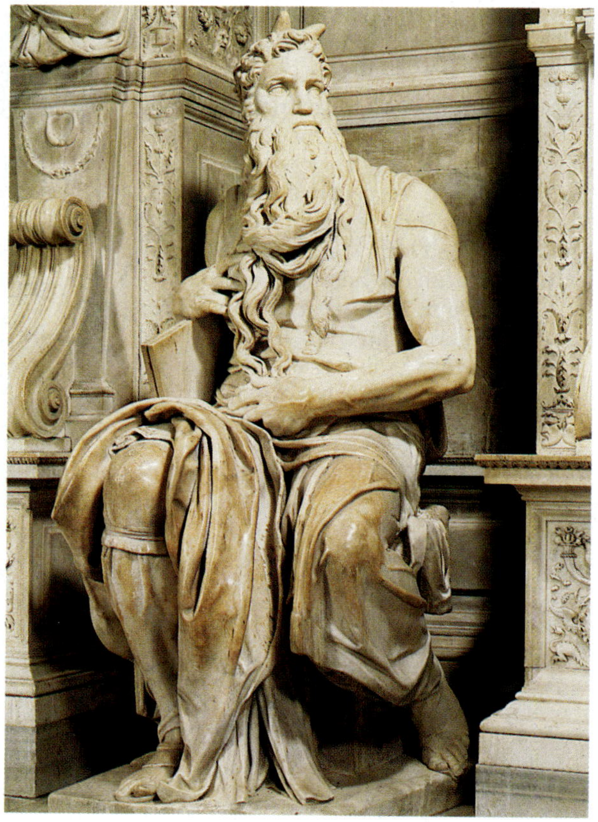

◆ **Figure 8–10** Does this figure appear calm and relaxed? If not, how would you describe it?

Michelangelo. *Moses.* c. 1513–15. Marble. Approx. 244 cm (8′) high. San Pietro in Vincoli, Rome. Scala/Art Resource, NY.

RESOURCES BEYOND THE CLASSROOM

Community Patrons Community groups sponsor art education in many ways. Some specifically promote the arts, such as the Texas Visual Arts Association. These groups can identify local resources, and provide guest speakers in such diverse areas as art careers, art history, and art criticism. Community groups can sponsor art events, exhibit student and professional artwork, and otherwise support and encourage the appreciation of art.

and appreciated. Artists like Michelangelo and Leonardo da Vinci secretly studied anatomy so that they could create anatomically accurate paintings and statues of people. **Figure 8–10** is a sculpture that was created by Michelangelo that represents Moses. Michelangelo has depicted Moses with heroic proportions. Notice the athletic muscles and veins of his arms.

Michelangelo paid careful attention to detail. Notice the lifelike quality of his hair and beard and the graceful folds of the fabric. His right arm is resting on the stone tablets that represent the Ten Commandments.

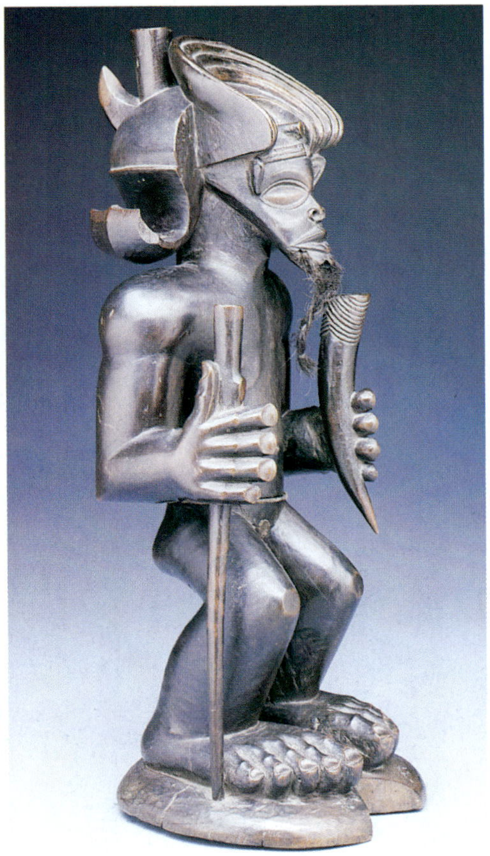

◆ **Figure 8–11** **What clues can you find that this figure was a great leader and hunter?**

Africa. Angola. Chokwe. *Chibinda (The Hunter), Ilunga Katele.* Mid-nineteenth century. Wood, hair, hide. Height: 40.6 cm (16″). Kimbell Art Museum, Fort Worth, Texas.

Meet the Artist

Michelangelo (1475–1564)

Cultural connection. Born in a small village near Florence, Italy in 1475, Michelangelo Buonarroti was the creator of some of the greatest masterpieces in the history of art. Not only was he a brilliant sculptor, but also a talented painter, architect, and poet.

Figure 8–10 illustrates Michelangelo's genius as a sculptor of marble. He also created the awe-inspiring paintings on the ceiling of the Sistine Chapel. This monumental task took four years. He depicted intricate Biblical scenes on a ceiling that was almost ten thousand square feet in area, while lying on a scaffold erected high above the chapel floor.

To learn more about Michelangelo, click on Artist Profiles at art.glencoe.com.

African Ancestor Figure

The work in **Figure 8–11** is typical of the style of art of the Chokwe (**choh**-kway) people of Africa. The work is an example of an **ancestor figure.** This is *an image carved in wood that was used as the resting place of a spirit.* This particular ancestor figure is based on a great leader and hunter.

Like most African figures, this carving was created for two reasons. One was respect for the dead and the other was a fear of angry spirits of the dead. Notice that the proportions are different from the statue of Moses. The head and the hands are very large. These proportions are found in much African art.

Check Your Understanding

1. Which of the sculptures in this lesson served as an example for artists who created realistic art later on? Explain your answer.
2. What is an ancestor figure?

Meet the Artist

Michelangelo (1475–1564)

Michelangelo was greatly influenced by the classical statues and buildings that were being discovered in Rome. He studied their formal qualities and proportions. Ask students to look again at **Figure 8–10.** Moses seems about to come alive and rise up from his marble seat. Have students notice the proportions of Moses' body.

Historical/Cultural Heritage

Portrait Sculptures Portrait sculptures are as varied and diverse as the cultures in which they are created. Invite students to research examples of portrait sculptures across time and place. Working in pairs, have them compare portrait sculptures from a variety of cultures and present their research to the class.

3 Assess

Self-Assessment

Have students complete the **Check Your Understanding** questions on this page. Answers are provided below.

Reteaching

Ask students to explain the reasons for which African ancestor figures are created.

4 Close

Have students discuss artists' pursuit of realism in art.

Answers to Check Your Understanding

1. Michelangelo's Moses served as a model of realistic art. This sculpture comes to life through careful attention to detail. Each muscle and vein stands out in vivid relief.
2. An ancestor figure is a carved image that was used as the resting place of a spirit. It was created out of respect for the dead and out of fear of angry spirits of the dead.

Sculpted Soldiers

(pages 154–155)

1 Focus

Objectives

After completing this lesson, students will be able to:

- Describe the purpose of the life-size soldiers discovered in the tomb of the first emperor of Qin.
- Explain the historical significance of these sculpted soldiers.

2 Teach

Motivator

On the board, write the statement "Art is made to be viewed." Ask students whether this statement is ever false. After allowing time for discussion of this question, reveal that students are about to examine an artwork that was deliberately buried soon after it was created. Explain that the lesson students are about to read will explain this purpose for creating art.

Aesthetics

Have students examine **Figure 8–12** and ask them to comment on ways the three-dimensional soldiers appear. Have them identify the similarities and differences among the figures. L1 ELL

Understanding Art History

Tell students that this sculpted army, arranged in precise military formation, has been buried since 210 B.C. Ask students what this undertaking tells us about the emperor who commissioned it. Have students draw comparisons between this emperor and the pharaohs in Egypt. L2

Sculpted Soldiers

Look at the clay soldiers shown in **Figure 8–12.** These life-size sculptures were created in China around 221 B.C. This "spirit army" was intended to protect Qin Shi Huang, the first emperor of Qin (**chin**) in the afterlife. Notice the differences in the soldiers' facial expressions. What clues give you an idea about the soldiers' rank or position? How do the figures differ from each other? What are their similarities?

Unearthing the Soldiers

For 2,000 years, these clay figures remained buried in the tomb of Emperor Qin Shi Huang, the founder of the Qin dynasty. The sunken soldiers were discovered in 1974 by farmers digging a well in the city of Xi'an in the Shaanxi province (see **Figure 8–13)**, home of Qin's burial site. For the next two years, archeologists unearthed more than 8,000 of these sculpted clay warriors, each with an actual likeness to Qin's army. After the excavation of the site, measurements were taken of the giant burial site. One of the tombs is roughly 18 feet deep and over 350 yards long. That's bigger than three football fields!

The figures now appear gray and colorless, but were originally painted in vivid colors. Each figure

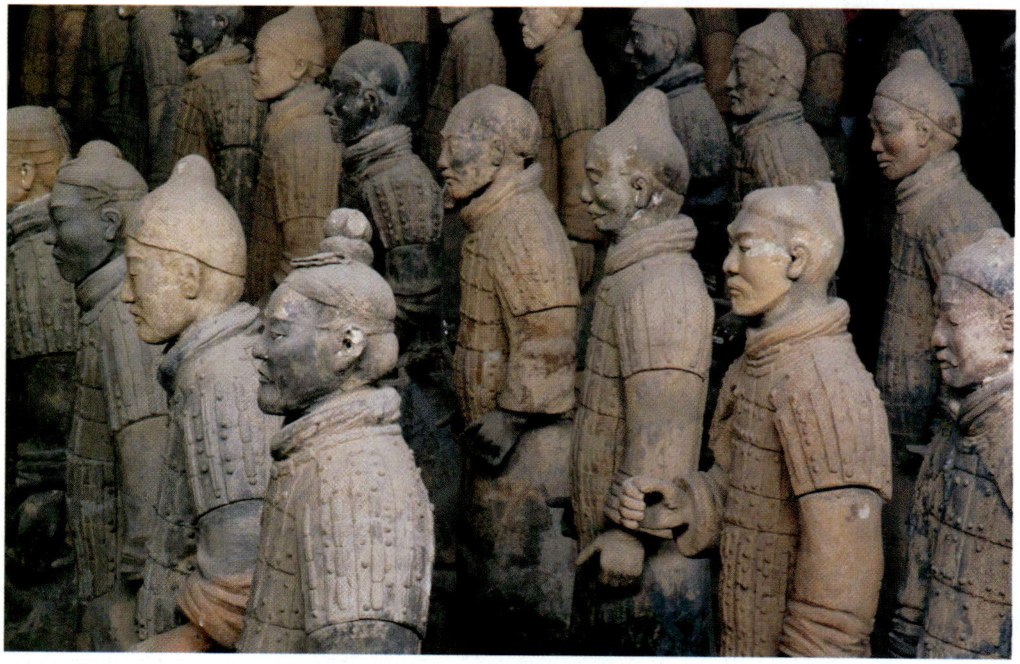

◆ **Figure 8–12** Life-size clay soldiers created as a "spirit army" for the first emperor of Qin.

MORE ABOUT...

Clay Soldiers The clay soldiers shown in this photograph are located in the Shaanxi province in China. For 2,000 years, these clay figures were buried in the tomb of the first emperor of Qin (**chin**). They were discovered accidentally by archaeologists. Their bodies stand erect, with hand gestures and postures giving a lifelike appearance. Each face was made with unique features and expressions, giving personality to the soldiers guarding the emperor's tomb.

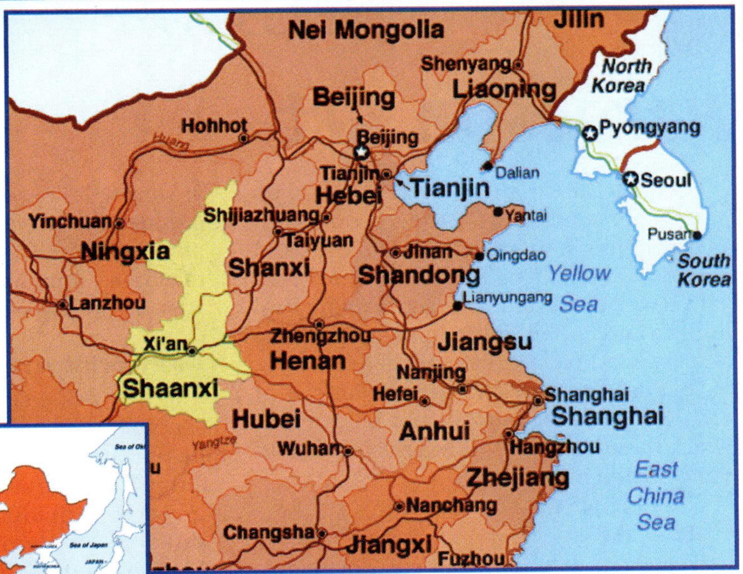

◆ **Figure 8–13** Shaanxi province of China.

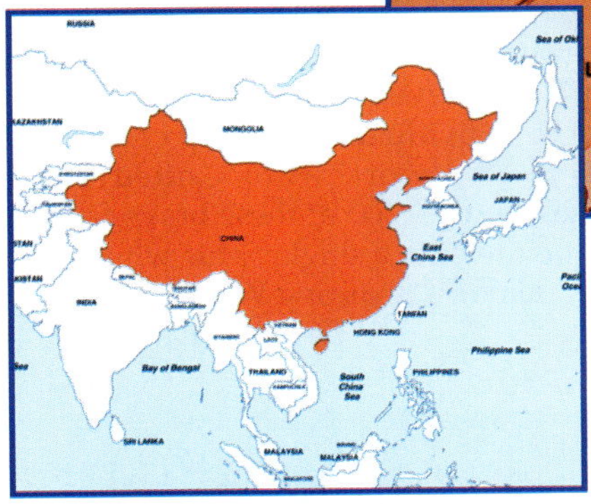

has a distinct expression, posture and hairstyle. Some appear to gaze straight ahead while others lower their heads, as if worried or troubled. Standing erect, these haunting soldiers were depicted with hand gestures that make them seem almost alive.

You've seen portraits in the round created from marble and wood, but these were crafted out of *terra-cotta,* which means "baked earth" in Italian. This material was used because the clay in the region was heavy enough to support the life-size figures. Once formed, the sculptures were fired in large brick kilns at high temperatures. They were then colored with vegetable dyes.

MAKE THE CONNECTION

Take Another Look

1. Look again at Figure 8–12. What do you notice about the soldiers' expressions?
2. Why do you think it was important for the emperor of Qin to have these soldiers built and buried?
3. What might historians learn about studying this burial site?

ART & SOCIAL STUDIES

Create a time capsule. Art such as Emperor Qin Shi Huang's "spirit army" provides a glimpse of an ancient culture. It reveals information on the emperor's beliefs and tells us about the time in which he lived. Imagine that you are planning a time capsule to give future generations a glimpse of your culture. What would you include? What would these objects reveal about the culture of the early twenty-first century?

Critical Thinking

Emphasize that these portrait sculptures were originally painted but now appear colorless. Ask small groups of students to think about aspects of environment that might cause this change. Invite volunteers to explore possible explanations for changes to the sculptures using on-line resources. L2

Using Map Skills

Direct students' attention to the map in Figure **8–13** which shows the location of China. Point out the size comparison of China to an island, such as Japan.

3 Assess

Self-Assessment

Have students complete the **Take Another Look** questions on this page. Answers are provided below.

Reteaching

Challenge students to think about how they would create their sculpture. After they have discussed their options, have them prepare a sketch of their design.

Enrichment

Encourage students to learn more about the Qin dynasty. Have them conduct an Internet or library search and write a report of significant facts, such as the duration of the Qin dynasty. Ask students to present their findings to the class.

4 Close

Ask students to explain the historical significance of these sculpted soldiers.

MAKE THE CONNECTION

Take Another Look Student answers will vary, but may include the following:

1. Some soldiers appear to be confident, while others have a worried facial expression.
2. It was important for the emperor to build this "spirit army" to protect him in the afterlife.
3. Historians might learn about the Qin dynasty and the Chinese culture during that period.

Heroes in Art

(pages 156–157)

1 Focus

Objectives

After completing this lesson, students will be able to:

- Define *public art.*
- Define *mural.*
- Understand what heroes and folk heroes are.
- Demonstrate technical skills effectively by using a variety of art materials to produce a hero exhibit.

Supplies

- Old newspapers and magazines
- Colored construction paper in strips about 4 x 11 inches
- Markers
- White glue or glue sticks; scissors
- Poster board 12 x 18 inches or larger

2 Teach

Motivator

Write the word *hero* on the board. Ask students to identify people they regard as heroes. Distinguish between real heroes and fictional ones. Next, discuss the qualities and actions common to folk heroes. Explain that *folk heroes* often take on a "larger-than-life" quality—their strengths and achievements are exaggerated and enlarged as the stories about them pass from generation to generation. Some folk heroes are based on real people; others are composites of people who may or may not have lived.

Heroes in Art

Every culture and generation has its heroes. Some heroes are living people such as firefighters, law enforcement officers, and doctors. Other heroes are lasting symbols of values we hold dear. The larger-than-life Paul Bunyan and his faithful companion, Babe the blue ox, are a pair of such folk heroes.

In this lesson, you will meet examples of each type of hero. You will also see ways in which these heroes have been celebrated and remembered in art.

Public Art

Are there statues in your city or community? Perhaps there is a statue of your city's founder in a local park or square. Such works are examples of **public art,** which is *art to be displayed in and enjoyed by a community.* Usually, public art is found outdoors in the form of statues, fountains, or murals. **Murals** are *large two-dimensional works painted on walls.*

Memorial Art

The work displayed in **Figure 8–14** is a special type of public art. Called *memorial art,* its purpose is to help people remember the singular achievement or dedication of a group or individual. The group commemorated in this work were United States Marines. Some 6,000 of these brave fighters gave their lives in a single battle while fighting for democracy during World War II.

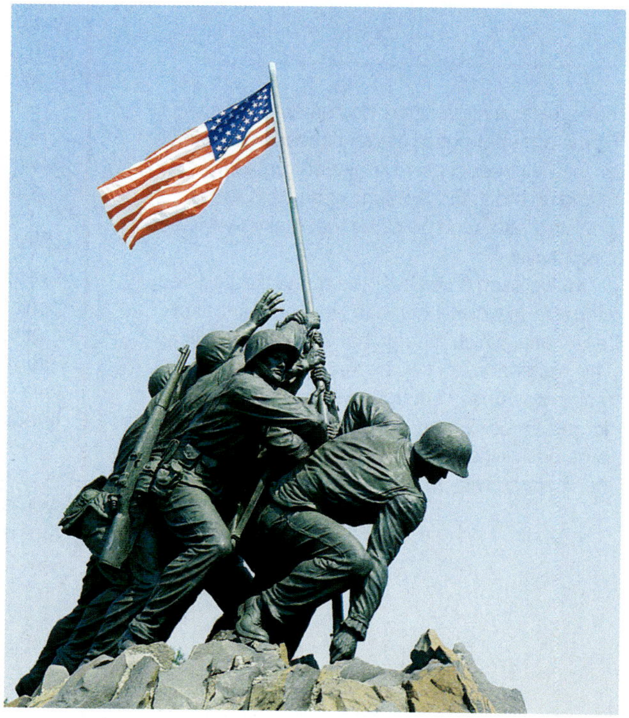

◆ **Figure 8–14** This artwork is displayed, appropriately, in Arlington National Cemetery outside Washington, D.C. Explain how World War II influenced this sculpture.

Raising the Flag on Iwo Jima. Arlington Cemetery, Arlington, Virginia.

COMMUNITY CONNECTION

Developing Advocacy Involving others in your art program is invaluable to its success. Just as sports programs often have booster clubs, art programs can benefit from community assistance, too. Work with journalism instructors to create newsletters designed by students notifying the community about upcoming art shows, award programs, scholarship opportunities, and general student progress in your program.

Human Legends in Art

Figure 8–15 shows a hero of a different sort. He is the folk legend John Henry. A mythical railroad worker of the 1800s, he has been the subject of countless songs and poems. John Henry symbolizes the "sweat and tears" of hardworking people during our nation's time of growth. In this painting, he raises two hammers above his head as he gazes out on future generations of settlers heading west. How has the artist captured the inner—and outer—strength of this hero? What meaning can you attach to the rainbow that appears in the distance? Notice how the muscles of the figure's forearms glisten. What sculpture from this chapter does this attention to detail call to mind?

Check Your Understanding

1. What is public art? What are murals?
2. What folk hero appears in Figure 8–15?

Studio Activity

Making a Hero Exhibit

Practical applications for design ideas. With several classmates, plan a "Heroes in the News" exhibition. Search newspapers and magazines for illustrations of heroes of the moment. Cut out the images. Work together to think of words that help convey the heroism of the people in the pictures. Write these words in decorative fashion on strips of colored construction paper. With white glue, paste the images and words to a sheet of poster board.

PORTFOLIO

Take photographs of the poster so that each member of your workgroup has a copy. Attach your photo to a self-reflection and add it to your portfolio.

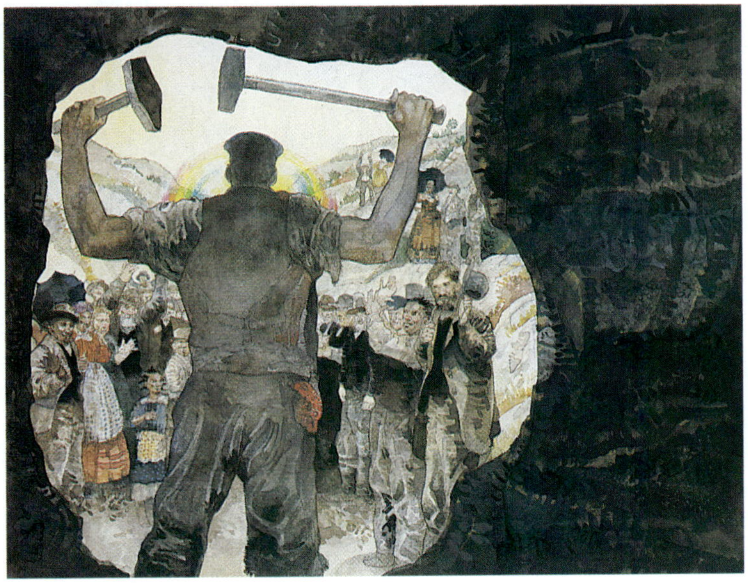

◆ **Figure 8–15** Notice that the artist has chosen not to show John Henry's face. Why do you suppose this is so?

Jerry Pinkney. *John Henry*. 1994. Pencil, colored pencils, and watercolor on paper. 32.4 × 40.6 cm (12¾ × 16"). From *John Henry* by Julius Lester, published by Dial Books, 1994.

Answers to Check Your Understanding

1. Public art is art that is displayed in and enjoyed by a community. Murals are large two-dimensional works painted on walls.
2. John Henry is the folk hero depicted in Figure 8–15.

Studio Activity

Making a Hero Exhibit

Have groups of students work together to plan the mural for the main corridor or other wall in the school.

Historical/Cultural Heritage

Heroic Influence Have students write a report on one hero describing that person's heroic qualities. Ask them to explain what this person achieved. Have students also share any artworks they find about their hero. L1

3 Assess

Self-Assessment

Have students complete the **Check Your Understanding** questions on this page. Answers are provided below.

Enrichment

Local Heroes The sculpture of the Marines in **Figure 8–14** is located in Arlington National Cemetery in Virginia. Ask students to identify statues or memorials in cemeteries or parks, or in books, and bring in pictures or drawings of them to create an exhibit of monuments honoring local heroes. Have them identify the historical or political events represented by the artworks. L2

4 Close

Have students summarize how heroes and folk heroes are celebrated in public art.

Creating a Mixed-Media Banner

(pages 158–159)
Lesson Time: 45 min.

1 Focus

Objectives

After completing this lesson, students will be able to:

- Demonstrate technical skills effectively by using a variety of art media and materials to create a mixed-media banner honoring a hero.
- Describe, analyze, interpret, and judge their banners.

Supplies

Refer to **What You Will Need** in the Student Edition.

2 Teach

Motivator

Direct students' attention to **Figure 8–16.** Tell them that Joan of Arc was a French peasant girl born in about 1412. In a vision, she saw herself helping King Charles VII of France drive the English from France. At first the king doubted Joan, but finally he gave her armor and weapons, a banner, and the command of many troops. She was successful in several battles, but Joan was captured in 1431 and burned at the stake. She became an admired folk heroine of legendary proportions.

Vocabulary

Review the word *texture.* Have students explain the difference between visual texture and actual (tactile) texture.

LESSON 8

Creating a Mixed-Media Banner

In the previous lesson, you viewed art based on several heroes. **Figure 8–16** contains yet another such work. Do you recognize the hero in this painting? It is Joan of Arc. Joan of Arc lived in France in the 1400s. She was not much older than you when she bravely led an army of French troops against the English.

Look closely at Figure 8–16. The picture is filled with figures and action. Even so, Joan is easily identified. She is mounted on a white charger and carries a huge banner.

What You Will Learn

In this lesson, you will create your own banner honoring a hero. Your banner, which will use mixed media, may focus on a real-life or made-up hero. The work will be divided into three sections. In each section you will use different media to create images and symbols associated with your hero. Using different media will allow you to create a variety of visual textures. These in turn will add interest to your banner.

What You Will Need

- Pencil and sheets of sketch paper
- Ruler or other straight edge
- Butcher paper, 18 x 24 inches
- Scissors
- Tissue paper in assorted colors
- White glue
- Pen

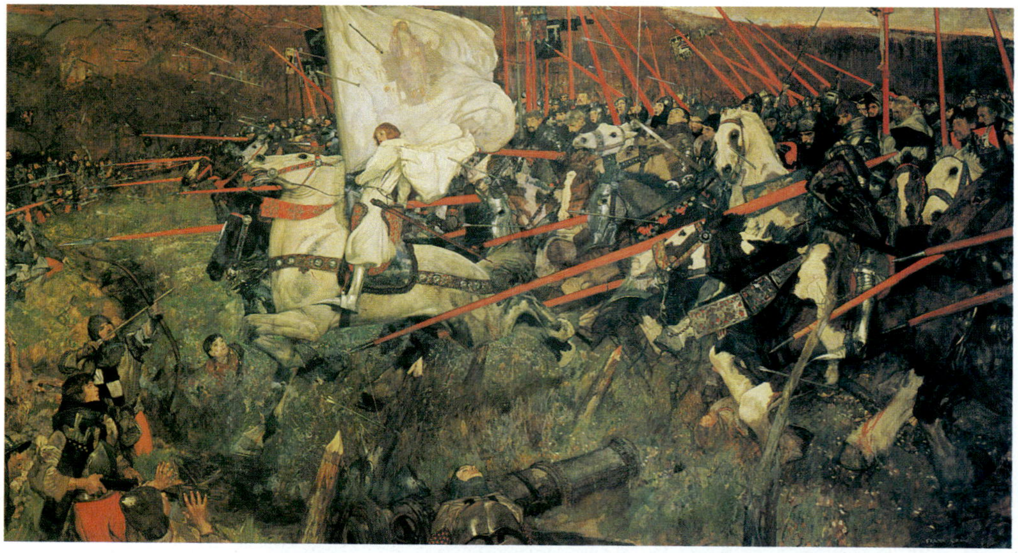

◆ **Figure 8–16** **Do you sense movement when you look at this artwork? What element of art contributes to this strong feeling?**

Franck Craig. *"La Pucelle": Jeanne d'Arc Leads Her Army.* 1907. Oil on canvas. 190 × 341.5 cm (74¾ × 134⅖"). Musée d'Orsay, Paris, France. Erich Lessing/Art Resource, NY.

Curriculum Connections

Social Studies Find books and resources about the history and use of banners. Make photocopies of the images and exhibit them in the classroom. Ask students to select and analyze the banners for historical and cultural contexts. Have students answer the following questions:

- How was the artist influenced by time and place? Identify the influence of historical events.
- What visual elements in the banner are clues to the history and culture of the artist? L2

- Magazines
- Colored markers

What You Will Do

1. Select a hero. Sketch several designs for banners to honor your hero. Use straight or curved lines to divide each banner design into three sections.
2. In each of the three sections, create images or symbols that tell something about your hero. For example, a banner honoring Paul Bunyan might include trees, an ax, and a blue ox. Make your drawings large. Avoid small details.
3. Using a ruler or other straight edge, transfer your best banner design to a sheet of butcher paper. Fill the paper with your design. With scissors, trim away the portions of the paper beyond the banner's outline. Divide the banner into three sections with straight or curved pencil lines. Using your sketch as a model, lightly draw the images and symbols for each section.
4. Cut or tear shapes from sheets of colored tissue paper. Overlap and glue these down to complete one section. Define shapes and details with pen. Cut or tear pictures and words cut from magazines to complete another section. Complete the third section using colored markers. Make certain to fill each section of your banner with color. Take care not to cross the lines between sections.
5. Place your banner on display. Ask classmates if they can identify your hero.

Evaluating Your Work

- **Describe** Identify the images and symbols in each of the three sections of your banner.
- **Analyze** Does your banner show a variety of visual textures? In which section of your banner do you think texture is best demonstrated?
- **Interpret** Could classmates identify the hero your banner honors? What image or symbol was most helpful to them in making this identification?
- **Judge** What is the best feature of your design?

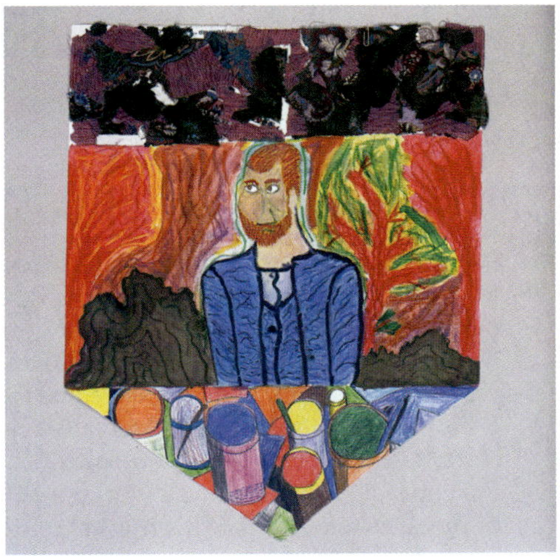

◆ **Figure 8–17** Student work. Mixed-media banner.

Portfolio Ideas

There are different ways to choose what to put into your portfolio. You might select an artwork because:

- It shows your best example of composition.
- It demonstrates your growth in using a specific medium.
- It shows the skill you exhibited in making an artwork.

Art Online

For additional activities, check out our Web site at **art.glencoe.com**. There you will also find:

- Artist Profiles
- Interactive Games
- Museum Web Links
- Student Art Gallery

Studio Skills

Urge students not to cross the lines dividing their banners into sections; they can emphasize the dividing lines by using a black marker. Advise them to use a brush to apply the glue to make bonding smoother and neater; show how the stick or dowel is inserted into the folded-over "tunnel" to provide a frame to support and hang the banner. L1 ELL

3 Assess

Peer Assessment

Have students analyze their peers mixed-media banners to form conclusions about historical and cultural contexts. Responses may be written or oral.

Reteaching

Have students work in pairs to create "texture boards." That is, divide a sheet of mat board into a number of angular shapes and fill each with a different visual or actual texture. L1 ELL

Enrichment

Have students describe in detail a variety of practical applications for creating banners, such as for sporting events, fundraiser activities, or church events. Have them make a sketch of the banner and describe other design ideas.

4 Close

After completing the lesson, ask students to evaluate their understanding of visual texture.

Developing a Portfolio

Organizing the Portfolio Providing students with an outline or checklist of the assignments that have been given in the grading period helps them keep track of what should be completed and can go into the portfolio. This outline can be posted, but students should have their own copies. They can easily record assignments themselves and reflect on where they are with the assignments as they check the list. Throughout the grading period it is a good idea to set aside time for students to update and reorganize their portfolios. Peer reviews and written reflection can occur at these times, too.

Faces of Ground Zero

1 Focus

Objectives

After completing this lesson, students will be able to:

- Sketch the face of a rescue worker.
- Plan, write, and share a paragraph describing themselves.
- Identify in artworks the influence of historical events.

2 Teach

Teaching the Feature

1. Guide students in recalling the events of September 11, 2001. Ask: What rushed to help the victims that day? How have the rescue workers of September 11th been honored?
2. Have students meet in small cooperative groups to read and discuss the article. Ask: What historical event inspired McNally to photograph rescue workers on such a large scale? What makes McNally's camera unusual? Why did he use that camera to photograph New York City rescue workers after September 11, 2001?

Activity

Ask students to recall or imagine the face of a firefighter, police officer, or other rescue worker. What emotions might show on that person's face? Why? Have each student draw a pencil sketch of one rescue worker's face.

FACES OF GROUND ZERO

The largest camera on Earth captures faces and feelings of twenty-first-century heroes.

A unique camera sits in a studio in New York City. It is a 12-foot-wide by 16-foot-high Polaroid. In 90 seconds, it takes color pictures that are 40 inches wide by 106 inches high. That's as high as an average room's ceiling.

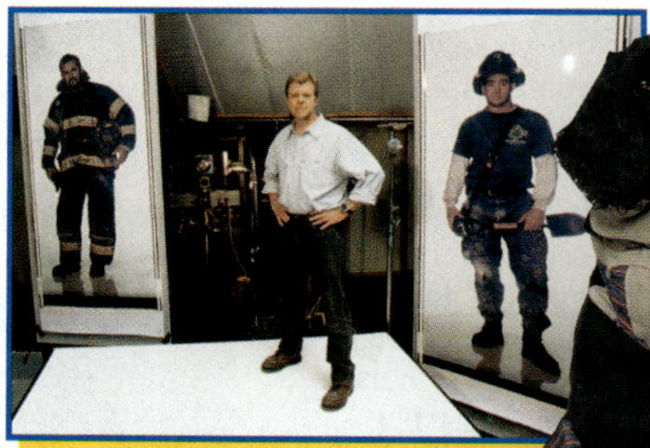

ABOVE: McNally in his studio. The camera is behind him. RIGHT: An animal rescue worker photographed by McNally.

The camera was put to use days after September 11, 2001, when terrorists destroyed New York City's World Trade Center towers. Photographer Joe McNally used the Polaroid to take pictures of rescue workers. He photographed firefighters, police officers, doctors, and nurses. The portraits show the workers' emotions and feelings since that fateful day.

At the end of the project, McNally was exhausted. He was certain, however, that his photos would stand as a tribute to the courage and heroism of workers at Ground Zero—the site of the disaster. "I think this might be the one significant thing I will do as a photographer," said McNally.

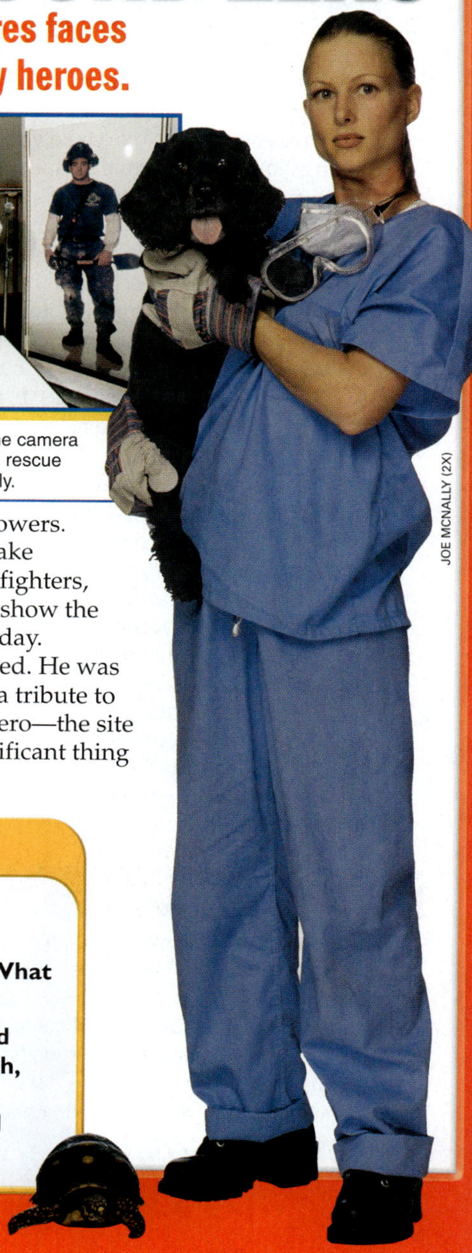

JOE MCNALLY (2X)

TIME TO CONNECT

- **How has technology changed the look of art and the way it is produced? Give examples.**
- **Analyze the photo of the animal rescue worker. What do her face, uniform, and body language express?**
- **If you were posing for a life-size photo, how would you want the world to see you? Write a paragraph, using descriptive adjectives, to let the people know who you are. Write about the clothes you'd wear, your pose, and so on.**

TIME TO CONNECT

Have students write their descriptions. Then, suggest that they meet in groups to proofread their writing and share ideas for corrections and improvements. Have them use these questions to guide their discussion:

- Does the paragraph begin with a clear topic sentence?
- Are all words spelled correctly?
- Are capital letters and punctuation marks used correctly?

Chapter 8 Review

BUILDING VOCABULARY

Number a sheet of paper from 1 to 7. After each number, write the term from the list that best matches each description below.

ancestor figure	public art
figure study	self-portrait
murals	style
portraiture	

1. Art to be displayed in and enjoyed by a community.
2. A drawing that focuses on the human form.
3. A painting or drawing of an artist's own image.
4. The art of making portraits.
5. An image carved in wood that was used as the resting place of a spirit.
6. Large two-dimensional works painted on walls.
7. An artist's personal way of using the elements and principles of art to express feelings and ideas.

REVIEWING ART FACTS

Number a sheet of paper from 8 to 12. Answer each question in a complete sentence.

8. In what artistic style did Agnolo Bronzino paint the portrait in Figure 8–2?
9. What features gave the Japanese mask a fierce look?
10. What types of lines are emphasized in the figure in action drawing in this chapter? Why are they emphasized?
11. What are some of the ways in which Michelangelo made his figures lifelike?
12. What are two reasons why the Chokwe of Africa made figure carvings?

CROSS-CURRICULUM CONNECTIONS

On a sheet of paper, answer each question in a sentence or two.

13. **Language Arts.** Explain the following statement: "Art styles change over time and from place to place." Restate this in your own words. Use examples from the chapter that illustrate the truth of this statement.
14. **Language Arts.** Locate a book of poems that includes "The Ballad of John Henry." Practice reading the poem aloud. Share it with classmates as they look at Figure 8–15. Discuss the qualities of this fictional character that the artist pinpoints in his work.

Web Museum Activity

Smithsonian National Portrait Gallery, Washington, D.C.

In this chapter, you have learned about portraits and the way people, heroes, and legends from different cultures are depicted in art.

Go to **art.glencoe.com** and take a historic tour by clicking on the Smithsonian National Portrait Gallery link. You will learn about America's first president, George Washington. You will study artist Gilbert Stuart's original portrait of Washington.

Describe the symbolic, biographical, and artistic elements. How did the artist depict these in the painting? What techniques did the artist use?

Answers to Chapter 8 Review

Building Vocabulary

1. public art
2. figure study
3. self-portrait
4. portraiture
5. ancestor figure
6. murals
7. style

Reviewing Art Facts

8. The portrait is painted in the Mannerist style.
9. The fierce expression was due to the furrowed brow, the wide open eyes, and the angry scowl.
10. Diagonal lines are emphasized. This is because they suggest tension and movement.
11. He recorded details, such as muscles and veins, faithfully. He also gave lifelike postures to his figures.
12. These include respect for the dead and a fear of angry spirits of the dead.

Cross-Curriculum Connections

13. Responses will vary. Art styles change from one generation to the next and from one culture to another. For example, the changes seen in portrait sculpture in ancient Rome, and the differences in the way figure sculptures are done in Japan and in European and African countries.
14. Students' responses will vary.

Web Museum Activity

Before you have students go online, visit the Web site to preview the museum's online collection and to check out any online exhibit that might be of interest. Have students study the portrait of George Washington. Suggest these questions as students view the portrait.

- In what type of style is this portrait?
- Would you consider this portrait to be expressive? Explain.
- What did you like most about this portrait?

Chapter Resources

Features	Standards for Chapter		Reproducible Masters
	National	State/Local	
Quick Write page 163 TIME ART SCENE "Aschcan Artists Paint the Town" page 180 *Web Museum Activity* page 181	**1.** (a, b) **2.** (a, b) **3.** (a) **4.** (a, c) **5.** (a, b, c) **6.** (a, b)		Guided Reading and Practice 9–1 Enrichment Activity 9–2, 9–6, 9–7 Artist Profile 9–3 Historical and Cultural Heritage 9–4, 9–8, 9–9 Studio Activity 9–5 Lesson Plans

Lesson Resources

Lessons	Standards per Lesson		Reproducible Masters
	National	State/Local	
1 *Personal Places* (pages 164–165)	4a, 5b, 6a		Enrichment Activity 9–2 Artist Profile 9–3 Historical and Cultural Heritage 9–4
2 ART & READING (pages 166–167)	6a, 6b		
3 *Architectural Design* (pages 168–169)	4a, 4c, 5a, 5c		Studio Activity 9–5 Enrichment Activity 9–6
4 *Creating a Fanciful Exterior* (pages 170–171)	1a, 1b, 2a, 4a		Enrichment Activity 9–7
5 *Cityscapes* (pages 172–173)	1a, 1b, 2b		Historical and Cultural Heritage 9–8
6 *Creating a Mixed-Media Cityscape* (pages 174–175)	1a, 1b, 2a, 3a, 5c		
7 *The Outdoors* (pages 176–177)	2a, 2b, 5b		Historical and Cultural Heritage 9–9
8 *Creating a Seasonal Panorama* (pages 178–179)	1a, 1b, 2a, 5b		

Assessment	Technology
Testing Program: Chapter Test 9–10 Portfolio and Assessment Techniques	Artsource Performing Arts Package, Blue Palm (DVD or VHS Segment 7) National Museum of Women in the Arts Interactive Lesson Planner Fine Art Transparency CC-9, *The Blind Girl* by Sir John Everett Millais Fine Art Transparency 9, *Venice, the Quay of the Piazzetta* by Canaletto

Activities/Features
Meet the Artist: Vincent van Gogh
Make the Connection
Time & Place: Prairie-Style Architecture
Evaluating Your Work Studio Option Visual Art Journal
Studio Activity: Drawing a Building Detail
Evaluating Your Work Reflective Thinking Visual Art Journal
Meet the Artist: Winslow Homer
Evaluating Your Work Portfolio Ideas Art Online

KEY TO ABILITY LEVELS

Teaching strategies have been coded.

- L1 Activities for all students; teacher direction required
- L2 Activities for average to above-average students; some teacher direction needed
- L3 Activities for students able and willing to work independently
- ELL English Language Learner activities

FEATURED ARTISTS

- Jean-Baptiste-Camille Corot
- David Hockney
- Winslow Homer
- Philip Johnson and Associates
- Louis Le Vau and Jules Hardouin-Mansart
- I. M. Pei
- Charles Sheeler
- Sandy Skoglund
- John Sloan
- Vincent van Gogh
- Grant Wood
- Frank Lloyd Wright

FINE ART PRINTS

- Fine Art Print 13, *The Dovecote* by Francois Boucher
- Fine Art Print 14, *The Old Bridge* by Hubert Robert
- Fine Art Print 15, *The Farm* by Joan Miró

Timesaving *Technology*

Interactive Lesson Planner

Make planning easy. Use this interactive software to organize your week, month, semester, or year and access all *Introducing Art* reproducible resources.

KEY TO LESSON RESOURCES

- Narrative Lesson
- Studio Lesson

Chapter 9

Visiting Places

(pages 162–181)

Chapter Overview

Artists help us discover new places and help us rediscover familiar places. In this chapter, students will learn about the different approaches artists take to re-create a scene or favorite place. Whether the place is home, a scene of the city, or an image of the sea, the artist tries to convey a personal feeling about it using the elements and principles of art in his or her own unique way.

Discussing the Artwork

Focus On ◆ **Figure 9–1** Architect I. M. Pei had a new idea—to build a glass pyramid in the courtyard of the elegant Renaissance buildings that house the Louvre. The Louvre is a centuries old art museum in Paris, France. Pei's "new idea" was strongly resisted, because it is extremely different from the Renaissance buildings around the museum. Traditionalists were shocked when Pei designed this glass pyramid at the entrance to the Louvre. The Paris art museum was a Renaissance masterpiece, and Pei's design consisted of unusual arrangements of geometric shapes. Despite the initial resistance, today the 71-foot high pyramid is celebrated both for its beauty and its "harmony" with the old structure. Pei was awarded the prestigious Pritzker Prize for his creative use of space and materials.

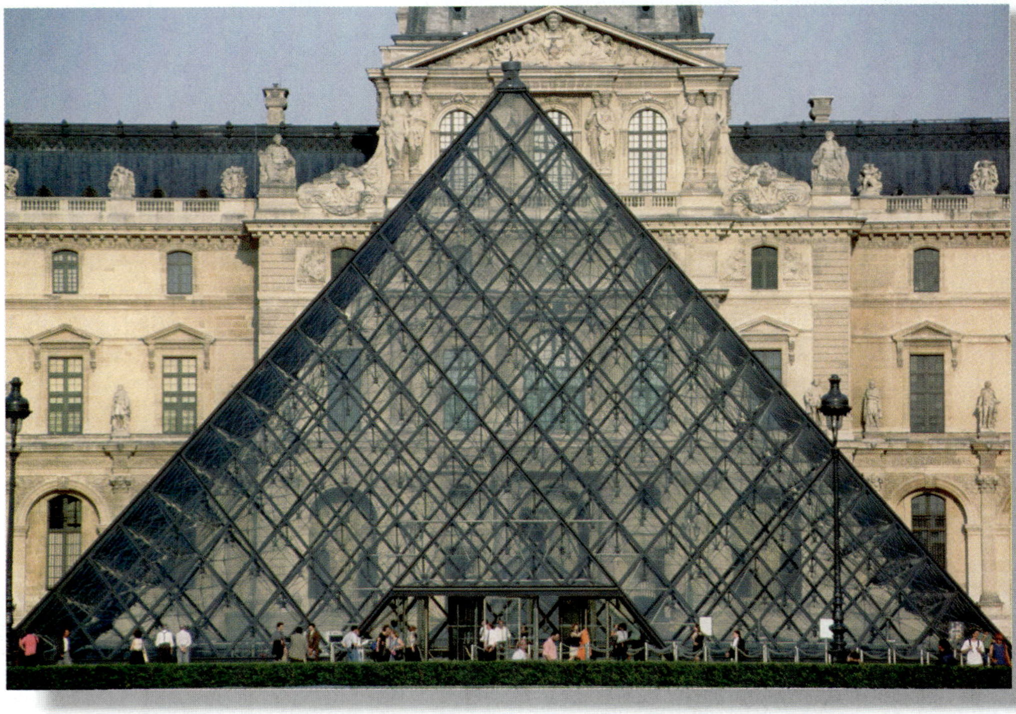

Focus On ◆ **Figure 9–1** **Serving as an entrance to the Louvre, the pyramid's glass encasement gives a feeling of space that architect I.M. Pei wanted to show.**

I. M. Pei. Pyramid at the Louvre. 1983–89. Paris, France.

162

Linking to the Performing Arts

THEATRE Most of us have a favorite place where we played as children. Theatre artists, Tom Crocker and Jackie Planeix of Blue Palm, portray two childhood friends who spent years playing in a vacant lot. After he has grown up, one of the characters returns to this special place and is surprised to see that his friend is still there clinging to her childhood. Have students read how Blue Palm performs the scene from the play "Childhood" in the **Performing Arts Handbook** on page 318. To enrich student understanding, play the DVD or videotape (segment 7) in the **Performing Arts Package.**

Chapter 9

Visiting Places

"Let us all be attentive to new ideas, [. . .] so that we may achieve, beyond architectural originality, a harmony of spirit in the service of man."

—I. M. Pei (b. 1917)

Our world is filled with wonders. There are natural wonders, like waterfalls, forests, lakes, and flowers. There are also wonders that people have created, such as art, architecture, parks, and gardens.

In this chapter, you will see many ways in which artists express their ideas about places. You will travel with each artist to see a building, a city, a seascape, or a room that holds special meaning. You will also learn how each artist expressed that meaning.

After completing this chapter, you will be able to:

- Understand approaches artists have taken in using places as subjects for their work.
- Recognize how the idea of *home* has changed over time.
- Define *cityscape* and *seascape*.
- Create two- and three-dimensional works that show space.

Quick Write

Interpreting the Quote
Read the quote by I. M. Pei and then look at **Figure 9–1.** Explain what he means about being "attentive to new ideas." Write about some of your ideas you'd like to realize.

KEY TERMS

- **staged photograph**
- **architects**
- **Rococo**
- **elevation**
- **façade**
- **columns**
- **cityscape**
- **The Eight**
- **panorama**
- **seascape**

Quick Write

INTERPRETING THE QUOTE
Have students read the quote and complete the Quick Write activity. Have students explain what Pei means by "being attentive to new ideas." What kind of new ideas are students thinking about? Their ideas can range from art to science. Encourage students to be creative and imaginative as they think and write about new ideas they'd like to realize.

Chapter Motivator

Ask students what they enjoy doing when they visit new and exciting places. What places have they visited that were memorable to them? Invite students to discuss some of their favorite haunts, whether they are near or far, and to bring in snapshots of those places if they like. As students talk about why some places are special to them, encourage them to think about how artists communicate their feelings about a place through their artwork.

Art Online

Visit **art.glencoe.com**, the Web site for Glencoe's art programs. This site offers general student resources to help guide your students as they learn about art and artists. Encourage your students to visit this site and explore the various resources and activities, such as:

- Artists Profiles
- Career Corner
- Student Art Gallery
- Web Links to museums, art techniques, art history, and cross-curricular activities.

National Standards for Arts Education

This chapter addresses the following National Standards for the Visual Arts:

1. (a, b)	4. (a, c)
2. (a, b)	5. (a, b, c)
3. (a)	6. (a, b)

LESSON 1

Personal Places

(pages 165–166)

1 Focus

Objectives

After completing this lesson, students will be able to:

- Explain why van Gogh's decision to paint his bedroom was so unusual.
- Describe how van Gogh used vivid colors and distortion to communicate his personal feelings about places.
- Define a *staged photograph* as an art medium.

2 Teach

Motivator

Tell students to write these words down: "My own special place is . . ." Have them complete the thought in a detailed description of this special place. Ask how many students identified their bedrooms as their own special place. Discuss their reasons. Ask how many selected a place other than their bedrooms. What made those places special?

Art Criticism

Have students study van Gogh's painting in **Figure 9–2.** Ask students: What techniques did van Gogh used to suggest space? How has the artist used diagonal lines to draw the viewer in? Ask students to identify with a single word the mood or feeling associated with this painting. Tell students to make a judgment about the work's success or lack of success and give reasons for their judgment. L1

LESSON 1

Personal Places

Rooms come in all sizes and shapes. Some are large and airy. Others are small and cramped. How would you describe your room at home? Regardless of your answer to that question, this much is clear: your room, whether or not it is shared, is one of a kind. It contains your personal things, and there is no other place exactly like it.

Perhaps it is this unique quality that has made rooms a popular subject for art.

Painting of a Room

Possibly the first artist ever to make a picture of his room was Vincent van Gogh (van **goh**). You may have heard of him. Books, movies, and even a song have been devoted to his dark, troubled life. Before van Gogh, few artists thought a room without people could be a subject worthy of art. Yet, the artist found peace and safety in his simple room that he could find nowhere else. He wanted to express his personal feelings in his art.

Look closely at van Gogh's painting of his room in **Figure 9–2.** What do you think he was trying to say about this safe haven in a stormy world? What objects did he emphasize? Did you notice that the window shutters are closed? What meaning, if any, do you attach to this? Carefully study each of the items in the room. Do these items tell you anything about the artist's feelings or mood?

Staged Photograph of a Room

A room of a very different kind appears in **Figure 9–3.** This room is different from van Gogh's not only in its content but also in the medium the artist chose. This work is a **staged photograph.** Far from an ordinary

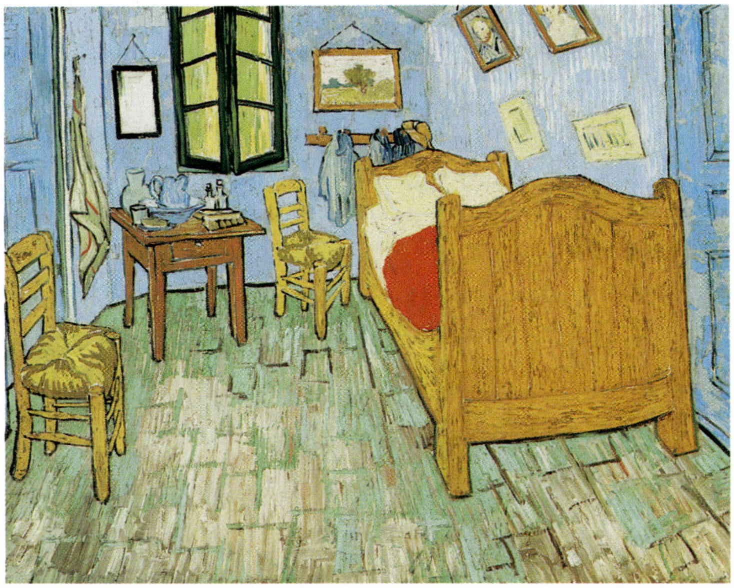

◆ **Figure 9–2** What personal "stamp" has the artist placed on his room? In what ways is this room similar to yours? How is it different?

Vincent van Gogh. *Bedroom at Arles.* 1888. Oil on canvas. 73.6 × 92.3 cm (29 × 36 3/10"). The Art Institute of Chicago, Chicago, Illinois. Helen Birch Bartlett Memorial Collection.

INCLUSION STRATEGIES

At-Risk Some students may be reluctant to verbally or visually share the details of their less-than-ideal sleeping rooms at home. To overcome this, discuss how some famous people have had only a living room couch or pad on the floor, shared with others in a succession of different houses or boarding houses, with next-to-no possessions, to call "their room." Provide emotional assurance that "good people" have lived in such rooms and created productive lives and good artworks out of the experience.

snapshot, this is *a photographic composition that makes use of artificial images or processes.* In this case, Sandy Skoglund sculpted each of the goldfish from clay. She also painted the room to look like an underwater environment. Then she used models to pose while she photographed the room.

Examine the strange world the artist has created. Notice the title. Can you think of other creatures who, like goldfish, live in a "controlled environment"? Maybe you keep such creatures as pets. Imagine waking up in a room like this one!

Check Your Understanding

1. Why did van Gogh choose to paint a picture of his room? What did he hope to communicate through his painting?
2. Describe the process Sandy Skoglund used to create her staged photograph.

Meet the Artist

Vincent van Gogh (1853-90)

Cultural connection. Vincent van Gogh is considered one of history's greatest painters, and his work had an enormous influence on modern art. After his death, van Gogh's paintings became extremely popular and sold for extraordinary amounts of money. Surprisingly, though, the artist sold only one painting during his lifetime.

Born in the Netherlands in 1853, Vincent van Gogh was the oldest child of a minister. In 1880, he decided to focus on painting as a career. He lived in Paris and later moved to Arles in southern France. In Arles, van Gogh created some of his most famous works, such as the painting in **Figure 9–2.** Although he painted for only ten years, he produced more than 800 paintings and 700 drawings. After a lifelong struggle with mental illness, van Gogh committed suicide at the age of 37.

To learn more about van Gogh and his work, click on Artist Profiles at **art.glencoe.com**.

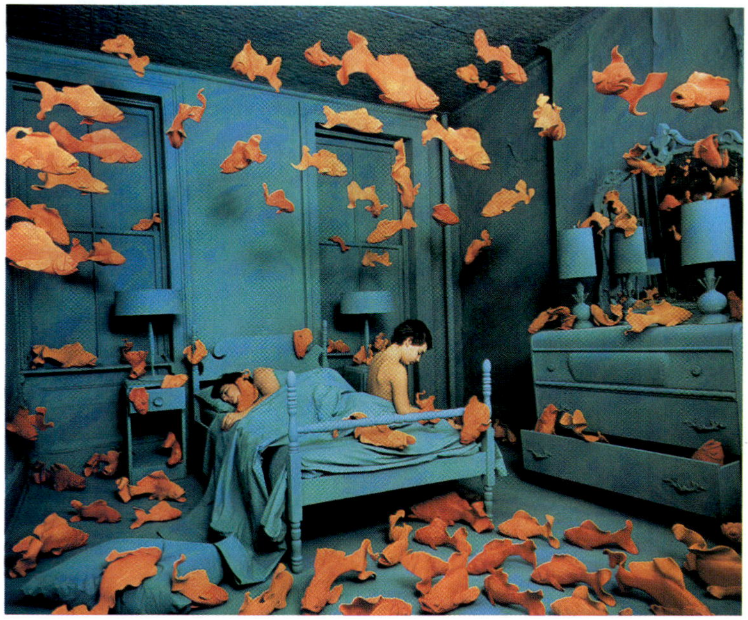

◆ **Figure 9–3** Compare how the room in this staged photograph is different from the painting in Figure 9–2. What kind of color scheme did the artist use?

Sandy Skoglund. *Revenge of the Goldfish.* 1981. Staged photograph. Lorence Monk Gallery, New York, New York.

Answers to Check Your Understanding

1. The artist found peace and safety in his simple room that he could find nowhere else. He wanted to communicate his personal feelings in his art.
2. Skoglund sculpted each of the goldfish from clay. She also painted the room to look like an underwater environment and used models to pose while she photographed the room.

Meet the Artist

Vincent van Gogh

Ask students if they noted the unrealistic distortion in van Gogh's painting of his room. Did they think these distortions were intentional or the result of a lack of skill? What quality in the artwork compensates for its lack of realism?

3 Assess

Self-Assessment

Have students complete the **Check Your Understanding** questions on this page. Answers are provided below.

Reteaching

In pairs, have students identify and analyze the interdependence of the art element color and principle harmony in Figure 9–3. Students should use art vocabulary appropriately. L1 ELL

Enrichment

PHOTOGRAPHY Have students create a variation of a staged photograph. Have them begin with an enlarged photo of the classroom (8 x 10 inches or larger, if possible). Then have them cut out drawn images to add to the photo to create a unique version of a familiar place. L1 ELL

4 Close

Ask students to explain why rooms are a popular subject for artists.

Getting from Place to Place

(pages 166–167)

1 Focus

Objectives

After completing this lesson, students will be able to:

- Compare and contrast fine art and literature in terms of style.
- Understand the use of symbolism in works of literature.
- Draw and write a poem describing a road.

2 Teach

Motivator

Bring to class and display a road map. Ask students to explain the purpose of a road map. *(It is a means of finding your way from one place to another.)* If the map has a legend, ask students to explain its function. *(It symbolizes various features on the map, such as types of routes, capital cities, bodies of water, etc.)* Explain to students that they will compare the concept of road maps in both an artwork and literature piece.

Art Criticism

Have students note the style of the painting. Ask whether they would describe the style as realistic or not, and have them explain their responses. L1

Getting from Place to Place

Whether a place is outdoors or inside, public or private, one thing is sure: To reach it requires following a road or path. Roads and paths are not only a means to an end. They can be an adventure all to themselves. Consider as an example the country lane in the picture in **Figure 9–4.** Notice that the main road shown stretches as far as the eye can see. Let your mind wander as you glimpse this enchanting rural scene. Where does this road lead? What will be waiting there when you arrive? Where will you end up if you turn left? If you turn right? The artist used his imagination in creating this picture. He leaves it to viewers to use their own imagination to answer questions like these.

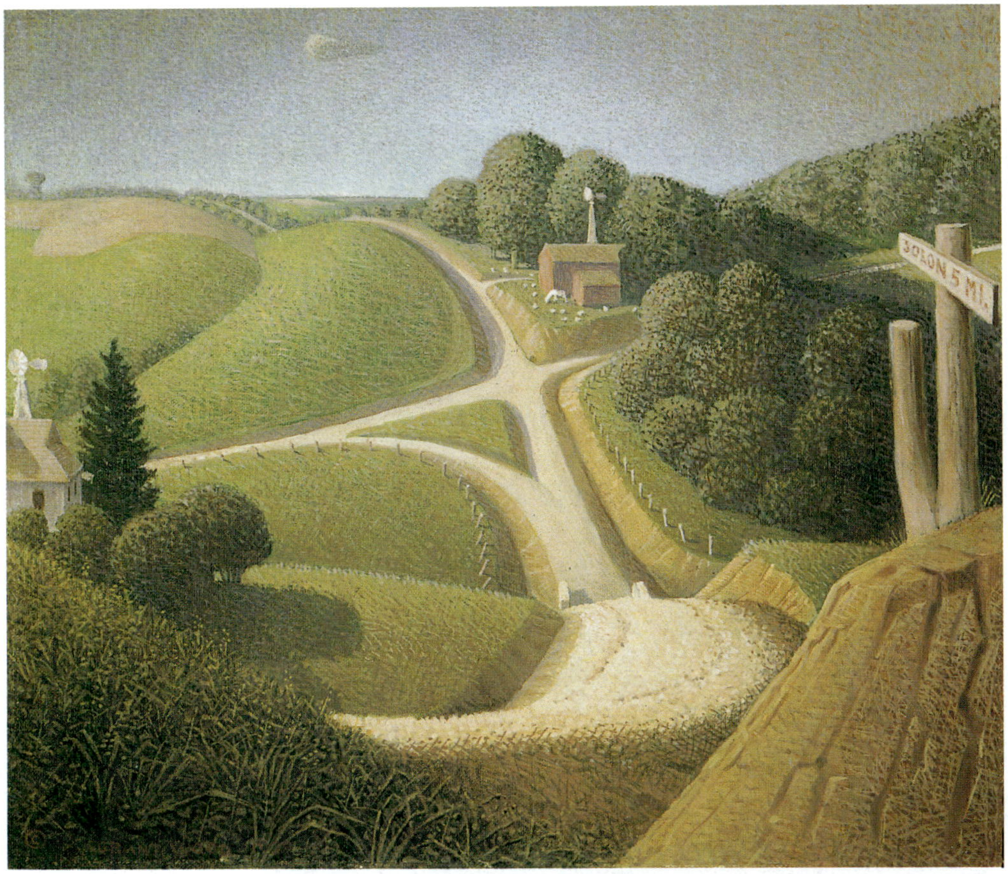

◆ **Figure 9–4** Grant Wood painted using an art style known as Regionalism. This is art that draws upon local scenes from specific parts of the country. Can you tell what part of the country this picture represents?

Grant Wood. *New Road.* 1939. Oil on canvas on paperboard mounted on hardboard. 33 × 37.8 cm (13 × 14⅞″). National Gallery of Art, Washington, D.C. Gift of Mr. and Mrs. Irwin Strasburger. Image © 2003 Board of Trustees.

MORE ABOUT...

Grant Wood (1892–1942) American painter Grant Wood was born in Anamosa, Iowa. He is best known for his depictions of scenes and people of his native Iowa. A leader in the Regionalist school, Wood was strongly influenced by the subject matter and technique of German and Flemish painters of the Renaissance. He introduced his own unique take on their stylized formality, however, by adding satirical elements to his paintings. The best example of this whimsical treatment may be seen in his most famous work, *American Gothic.*

"The Road Not Taken"

Two roads diverged in a yellow wood,
And sorry I could not travel both
And be one traveler, long I stood
And looked down one as far as I could
To where it bent in the undergrowth;

Then took the other, as just as fair,
And having perhaps the better claim,
Because it was grassy and wanted wear;
Though as for that, the passing there
Had worn them really about the same,

And both that morning equally lay
In leaves no step had trodden black.
Oh, I kept the first for another day!
Yet knowing how way leads to way,
I doubted if I should ever come back.

I shall be telling this with a sigh
Somewhere ages and ages hence:
Two roads diverged in a wood, and I—
I took the one less traveled by,
And that has made all the difference.

◆ **Figure 9–5** "The Road Not Taken" by Robert Frost.

Roads in Literature

Roads are not only a subject in artworks. They are also a subject in works of literature. One of these appears above in **Figure 9–5.** It is a poem by the twentieth-century American poet Robert Frost. As in the painting, Frost describes a point where two roads meet. The speaker of the poem is faced with a big decision. Read the poem. Then decide what you would do if you were in the speaker's place.

MAKE THE CONNECTION

Take Another Look

1. Which of the two roads does the speaker of the poem take? Why does the speaker choose that road?
2. Roads are used as a symbol in this poem. What do roads stand for?
3. The poem, like the painting, offers visual details about the two roads. The painting, like the poem, shows a fork in the road. What other similarities can you find between the roads depicted in the poem and artwork?

ART & READING

Creating a road picture. Think of an unusual or interesting road in your own community or that you have seen. It might be a very winding road or one that leads to a fun location. Create a drawing of this road. Then write a poem describing what waits at the end of the road.

Active Reading

Have students note that the poem in **Figure 9–5** is divided into four parts. Ask what these parts are called. *(Stanzas)* Ask whether students notice a pattern in the rhyming of words within a stanza. Have four students each read one stanza aloud. Ask the class to make note of the rhyming words.

Critical Thinking

Have students read line 16 of the poem. Ask: Why do you think the speaker will be telling his decision "with a sigh?" What does this reveal about the choice he made? L2

3 Assess

Self-Assessment

Have students complete the **Take Another Look** questions on this page. Answers are provided below.

Reteaching

Ask students to explain the symbolism Frost used in his poem. Ask: What are the two roads describing?

Enrichment

Have students find and view Grant Wood's most famous painting, *American Gothic.* Have them research the painting and report to the class on what it shows about regional life in America and why the artist gave it the title he did. L2

4 Close

Ask students what they think the overall message is in this poem.

MAKE THE CONNECTION

Take Another Look Student answers will vary, but may include the following:

1. He takes the second road, leaving the first for another day. He chooses this road because it is less worn than the first road.
2. They stand for decisions.
3. Other similarities might include the observation that there are no other people present in either scene or that both are in the countryside.

Architectural Design

(pages 168–169)

1 Focus

Objectives

After completing this lesson, students will be able to:

- Understand what architects do.
- Define the *Rococo style* of art.
- Understand that home designs, like other forms of art, have a variety of styles.

2 Teach

Motivator

Tell students to assume that they are architects and have been asked to design a house or apartment building. What must they take into account when working on a design like this? Explain that architects must first make certain that their buildings are tailored to meet the practical purposes for which they are intended. A house, for example, must provide adequate space for the daily needs of the family. However, there is no reason why a design cannot be *both* functional and attractive.

Aesthetics

Ask each student to identify on a sheet of paper a building in their community that they feel is both functional and attractive. Collect and list these on the board. Did the list include buildings serving a variety of different functions? Was one building mentioned more than others? If so, discuss reasons why this building proved to be so well regarded. L1

LESSON 3

Architectural Design

Think about the word *home*. Where do you head when you "go home"? For some people, "home" is a cozy apartment. For others, it is a sprawling mansion. For still others, it is a shelter made of straw or fabric. These are just some of the forms that dwellings have taken since the earliest people set up housekeeping in caves.

In this lesson, you will expand your understanding of the place called *home*. You will also learn about some of the challenges of home design facing **architects**—*artists who plan and create buildings.*

A Home of the Past

Imagine that you are going to design a house for yourself, and money is no object. What sort of dwelling would you build? What kinds of features would you include inside? It was precisely these questions that faced a king who ruled France in the 1700s. This king, Louis XIV, had very lavish tastes. His answers to part of these questions appear in the photograph in **Figure 9–6.**

This is a single room in the house Louis XIV had built for himself. The building, the Palace

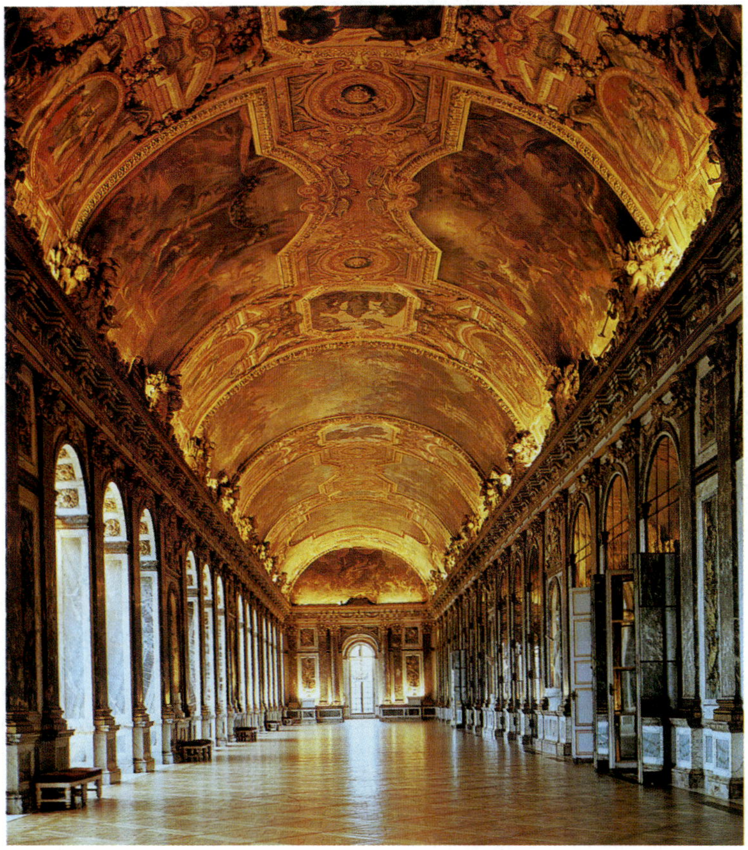

◆ **Figure 9–6** How do you think this room demonstrates Louis XIV's goal of building his power as king of France?

Louis Le Vau and Jules Hardouin-Mansart. The Hall of Mirrors at the Palace at Versailles, France. 1646–1708. Erich Lessing/Art Resource, NY.

COMMUNITY CONNECTION

Building Design Plan a trip to a local shopping mall with your class. Divide the class into four different working groups. The first group will travel outside the mall, photographing interesting architectural features of the overall building. The second group can visit several of their favorite stores and make sketches of the store's logos and designs. The third group can take photos of storefront window designs, paying attention to the furnishings and mannequins. The fourth group can do some research of the mall's history and the history of the architecture in your area. They will redesign the mall front using a different architectural style.

at Versailles (vuhr-**sye**), was named for the Paris suburb where it was built. Study the room. It is interesting not only for what it reveals about the king. It is also interesting for the new art style it launched. That style was called **Rococo** (roh-**koh**-koh). This is *an art style of the 1700s that emphasized graceful movement, curving lines, and delicate colors.* Rococo architecture relied on the heavy use—sometimes overuse—of pattern. Notice how every surface is covered in one kind of rich decoration or another. What words would you use to describe this room?

A Home of the Twentieth Century

Compare the two buildings in Figures 9–6 and **9–7.** What differences do you detect?

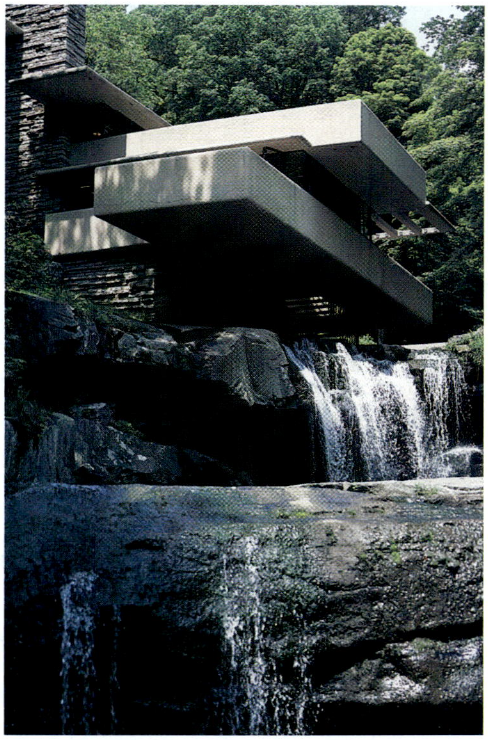

◆ **Figure 9–7** Notice the use of vertical and horizontal lines on the exterior of this building. What would you expect the inside of this house to look like?

Frank Lloyd Wright. *Fallingwater House*, Bear Run, Pennsylvania. 1936.

Time & Place

Prairie-Style Architecture

Historical connection. During the Industrial Revolution of the 1800s, mass production enabled the United States to become an industrial society. With mass production, however, the level of artistic quality declined. In architecture, Frank Lloyd Wright's prairie style was a reaction against this loss of artistry.

The prairie style, was intended to promote an old-fashioned lifestyle and a sense of art and individuality. Prairie houses were built low to the ground, emphasized horizontal lines, and were designed to blend in with the landscape. The interior featured an open floor plan where one room flowed into another. Wright's later architecture reflected many of these design principles (see **Figure 9–7**).

Obviously, the house on this page has much simpler and cleaner lines. The most striking thing about it, though, is its location. It was built on a rocky ledge directly above a small waterfall. The house, designed by twentieth-century architect Frank Lloyd Wright, even earned a nickname based on its unusual setting: "Fallingwater."

Notice the way in which the house blends into its natural surroundings. Its horizontal lines echo the natural rock formations, its vertical ones the cascading water. Wright once commented, "A house should not be *on* a hill, it should be *of* a hill." What do you think the architect meant by these words? How is this idea reflected in Figure 9–7?

✓ Check Your Understanding

1. How is Rococo style captured in the Palace at Versailles?
2. How did architect Frank Lloyd Wright make *Fallingwater House* feel like part of nature?

Time & Place

Have students compare the architectural styles shown in **Figures 9–6** and **9–7.** Ask them in which of the two buildings they would prefer to live. Have them give reasons for their answers. Finally, have students offer their judgments of both buildings.

3 Assess

Self-Assessment

Have students complete the **Check Your Understanding** questions on this page. Answers are provided below.

Reteaching

Work with individual students to identify the particular features of the Rococo art style found in Figure 9–6.

Enrichment

Bring in a variety of architectural books. Show students the astonishing variety and scope of building design in different cultures and in different times. Invite students to pick an architectural achievement to research in more depth. Ask students to share their research with the class and to compare the building designs from a variety of cultures. L2

4 Close

In pairs, have students discuss the challenges architects face in designing a home.

✓ Answers to Check Your Understanding

1. The Rococo style is evident in the heavy use of pattern and decoration. Every surface is covered in one kind of rich, curvilinear decoration or another.
2. The house was built on a rocky ledge directly above a small waterfall. It blends into its natural surroundings by means of horizontal lines echoing the natural rock formations, and vertical lines that seem to echo or repeat the lines of cascading water.

Creating a Fanciful Exterior

(pages 170–171)
Lesson Time: 2 hours 30 minutes

1 Focus

Objectives

After completing this lesson, students will be able to:

- Identify the building features found in Victorian style houses.
- Demonstrate technical skills effectively by using a variety of art materials to draw an elevation of a Victorian house, including such features as arches, towers, and columns.
- Describe, analyze, interpret, and judge their drawings.

Supplies
Refer to **What You Will Need** in the Student Edition.

2 Teach

Motivator

Ask students to explain what a "fad" is. *(An interest or activity that is very popular, but only for a short time.)* Direct their attention to **Figure 9–8**. What features of this house design are a fad?

Vocabulary

Explain that the term *façade* comes from an Italian word meaning "face." An *elevation* drawing can show any outside view of a building. Explain that in this lesson, students will draw the outside view of a home that *faces* the street.

LESSON 4

Creating a Fanciful Exterior

If you thought gingerbread houses were the stuff of fairy tales, think again. The buildings in **Figures 9–8** and **9–9** both look as though they might be made of gingerbread. Yet, both are real structures, made of hard materials. The house in Figure 9–8 represents a style of architecture popular in the 1800s. The building with the onion-shaped domes is even older. It was built in the city of Moscow in Russia during the 1500s. The structure was a cathedral and has now been turned into a museum.

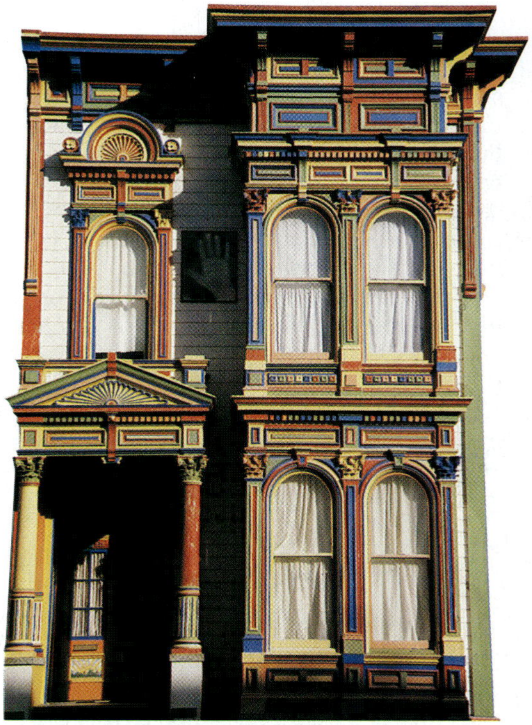

◆ **Figure 9–8** What kinds of shapes have been used to decorate this house?

Victorian "Painted Lady" (gingerbread house).

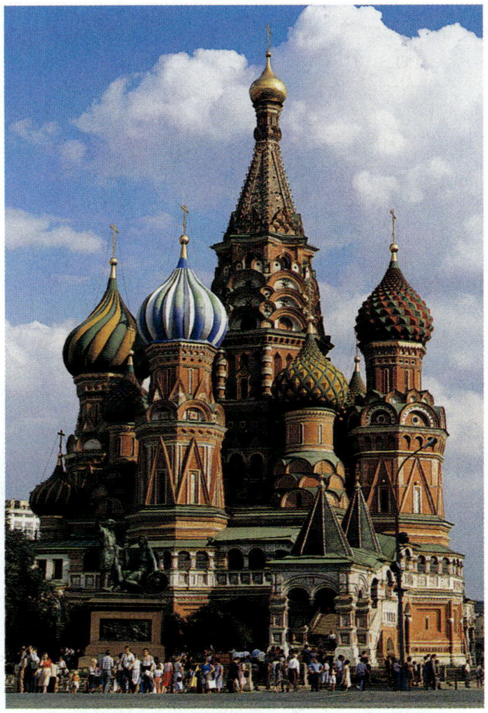

◆ **Figure 9–9** This is a cathedral in Russia. Identify and analyze how the art elements of texture, shape and color have been used to decorate this structure. How are the principles of pattern and rhythm used?

St. Basil's Cathedral, Moscow. 1551–60.

What You Will Learn

You will make an elevation of a house like the one in Figure 9–8. An **elevation** is *a drawing of an outside view of a building.* Your elevation will show the **façade** (fuh-**sahd**). This is *the front of a building.* In your design, you will include a porch and other features of the house. You will use a combination of lines and shapes to decorate the surfaces. Finally, you will make a decorative border for your drawing with cut geometric shapes. These will follow a regular rhythm, which is explained in Chapter 2, page 33.

MORE ABOUT...

St. Basil's Cathedral This cathedral is an example of the *Byzantine* style of architecture. The Byzantine style is distinguished by its distinctive use of domes and by an interior design that often features beautiful colored marble, magnificent murals and frescoes, and stunning glass mosaic designs. St. Basil's was built in 1554 in the center of Moscow—in Red Square near the Kremlin. Each of its eight bulblike domes is different, and all of the domes are painted in brilliant colors. Recently this old Russian church was converted into a museum.

What You Will Need

- Pencil and sketch paper
- Assorted colors of construction paper, 12 x 18 inches
- Oil pastels or crayons
- Small sheet of paper or paper towel
- Scraps of construction paper
- White glue

What You Will Do

1. Study the house in the picture. Complete several quick sketches of a similar house. Begin with simple shapes such as squares, triangles, rectangles, and half circles. Use these to build arches, towers, and **columns.** These are *vertical posts that rise to support another structure.* Add a porch and a variety of window and door shapes.
2. Choose your best sketch. Using oil pastels, transfer your design to a sheet of construction paper. Begin with a light color of pastel. Use this to draw the lines and shapes of the house, doors, and windows. While you work, place a small sheet of paper or a paper towel under your hand. This will prevent the colors from smearing.
3. Add railings and decorative touches like the ones in Figure 9–8. Use different combinations of repeated lines—straight, zigzag, curved—and shapes to invent patterns, natural rhythms, and textures. Decorate every surface of the house.
4. After your drawing is complete, make a border for the picture. Use small squares of construction paper for this. Choose colors that complement your house design. For variety, you may want to cut some of the squares into triangles, circles, diamonds, or other shapes. Layer the shapes and colors to make a regular or alternating rhythm around the picture. Glue them down.

Evaluating Your Work

- **Describe** Does your house have features and decorations like those in Figure 9–8?
- **Analyze** Did you use a variety of patterns, textures, and details to decorate all the spaces of the house?
- **Interpret** What part of the house looks the most important? What details contribute to this feeling?
- **Judge** Compare your house with the one in Figure 9–8. Explain how they are alike and how they are different. Is your design successful?

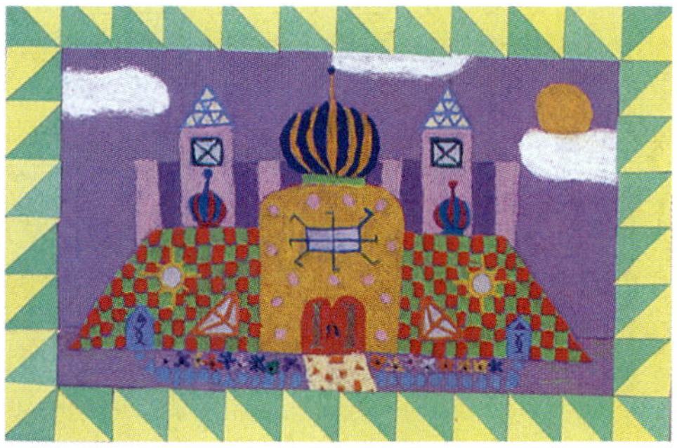

◆ **Figure 9–10** Student work. A fanciful exterior.

Studio Option

Demonstrate technical skills effectively to produce a ceramic version of your fanciful exterior. Use the slab method to make the base of your façade. Attach various architectural details to your base creating a relief. Finally, use glaze or paint to enhance it with color. Refer to Technique Tips on page 285.

Visual Art Journal

Conduct in-progress analyses of personal artworks. As you begin step 2, analyze your work and select your best sketch. Keep the other sketches in your portfolio to show your progression as an artist.

Understanding Art History

Explain that the kind of design in Figure 9–8 is called *Victorian.* The term is applied to a style of architecture that was popular during the reign of Queen Victoria in England, 1837–1901. Victoria was extremely influential and served as monarch longer than any other English ruler. The Victorian style emerged as a reaction to the dull, dark, and heavy classical Georgian style that preceded it.

Art Criticism

Have students describe and analyze the building designs in Figures 9–8 and 9–9. Ask: Which elements and principles of art play the most important role in each? What feeling or mood does each design communicate? Is each work successful? Why or why not? L1

3 Assess

Self-Assessment

Have students use **Evaluating Your Work** to conduct an in-progress critique of their artwork.

Enrichment

Many old buildings are destroyed to make room for newer structures. Others are preserved as landmarks. Ask students to identify and research any historic landmark buildings in their community. What qualifies a building for landmark status? Why is it important to save old buildings? L2

4 Close

Have students explain how their decorative façades are similar in style to the building in Figure 9–8.

Resources Beyond the Classroom

Home Tours Many communities sponsor tours of private homes in connection with real estate agents, architects, builders, and interior designers. Certain homes, designated "show homes," are specifically built and decorated to show off the talents of the people and companies involved. Other tours serve to celebrate and rediscover timeless design styles. Home tours are excellent opportunities for students to study architectural forms and building construction techniques more closely. These tours can also give students a clearer understanding of some art-related careers.

Cityscapes

(pages 172–173)

1 Focus

Objectives

After completing this lesson, students will be able to:

- Define *cityscape.*
- Understand the contributions to modern-day architecture made by architects like Louis H. Sullivan.
- Demonstrate technical skills effectively by drawing a sketch of a building detail.

SUPPLIES

- Viewfinders made by combining two L-shaped pieces cut from poster board
- Pencils and sketch paper
- Rulers or straightedges
- White drawing paper, 9 x 12 inches

2 Teach

Motivator

Instruct students to examine **Figure 9–11.** Ask if they think Sheeler included everything in the scene before him when he painted the picture. Would his painting have been more effective if he had made it wider or taller to include more of the scene? Is it important for an artist to decide just how much of a scene to include in a painting? Tell students that the artist must develop a "selective eye," that is, skill in deciding exactly what to put in or leave out of a picture.

LESSON 5

Cityscapes

Cities have been around in one form or another for more than 7,000 years. Like rooms, however, they have begun to appear as subjects of art only recently. In this lesson, you will learn about various ways in which artists have viewed and portrayed cities. You will also learn about the contributions of architects to the changing face of cities.

The City in Art

Factories, traffic jams, and high-rise apartment buildings are all part of modern city life. They are also a theme in some cityscapes. A **cityscape** is *a drawing or painting focusing on large buildings and other objects found in cities.* As an art form, the cityscape dates back to the early 1700s.

At the beginning of the twentieth century, the focus of the cityscape began to shift. Many artists began concentrating on the less glamorous aspects of the inner city. Such a painting appears in **Figure 9–11.** On its surface, the painting is a realistic picture of an industrial scene. Included are plant buildings, loading docks, girders, pipes, and assorted heavy machinery. The painting does not stop there, however. Notice its organization. Observe the use of geometric forms and shapes. Count the many horizontals, verticals, and diagonals. Note the careful combination of light and dark values of a single hue. In what way can this painting be said to be greater than the sum of its parts?

The Art of the Skyscraper

Ancient cities were located in spacious river valleys such as along the Nile in Egypt. They had plenty of room to spread out. This

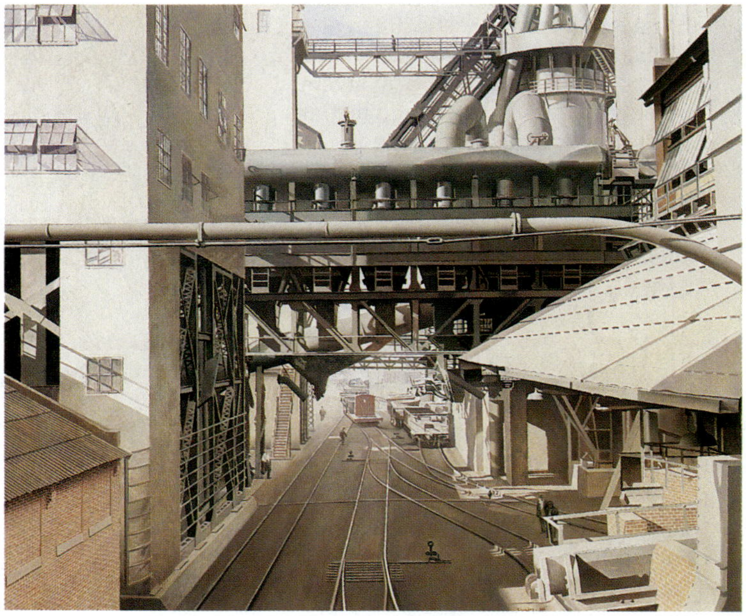

◆ **Figure 9–11** Find the pipe running across the center of this carefully composed work. What other object follows a straight path, then veers off at the last instant? What other "echoes" of lines and shapes can you find?

Charles Sheeler. *City Interior.* 1936. Aqueous adhesive and oil on composition board. 56.2 × 68.4 cm (22 × 27"). Worcester Art Museum, Worcester, Massachusetts. Elizabeth M. Sawyer Fund in memory of Jonathan and Elizabeth M. Sawyer.

MORE ABOUT...

SKYSCRAPERS In 1871, the Great Chicago Fire destroyed much of the city. Devastating as it was, the disaster gave architects a challenge and an opportunity to create stronger, more durable structures. Architect William Jenney designed the first metal-frame skyscraper, the Home Insurance Building in Chicago (1885). One young associate of his, Louis H. Sullivan, gained fame for his innovative crossbeam, steel-framed designs. Sullivan soon became the leader of the *Chicago School* style of architecture. He argued that "form follows function," and that good design embraces nature, society, and humanity.

is not true of modern urban centers such as New York, London, and Tokyo. In the last hundred years, these overcrowded cities have had only one direction in which to go. That direction is up.

The solution to the problem of limited space was solved toward the close of the 1800s. The person credited with the solution was a pioneering Chicago architect. His name was Louis H. Sullivan. Sullivan hit upon the idea of a steel frame made of crisscrossing beams. To this day, Sullivan's steel "skeleton" is at the heart of every skyscraper. An example of this modern architectural wonder appears in **Figure 9–12.** What steps has the architect taken to make this structure less boxlike than other skyscrapers you may have seen?

Studio Activity

Drawing a Building Detail

Use direct observation. Organize ideas from the environment. With sketchbook in hand, walk through your community. Be on the lookout for buildings with interesting or unusual designs. Once you find such a building, make a detailed sketch of a section of it. You might concentrate on a single floor, a corner, or even a window or door. Illustrate as many different types of lines and textures as you can.

PORTFOLIO

Take a photograph of the detail you selected to draw. Put it in your portfolio with your drawing. Use the photo to refresh your memory if you decide to redraw your artwork at a later time.

Check Your Understanding

1. What is a *cityscape?*
2. What was Louis H. Sullivan's contribution to modern-day architecture?

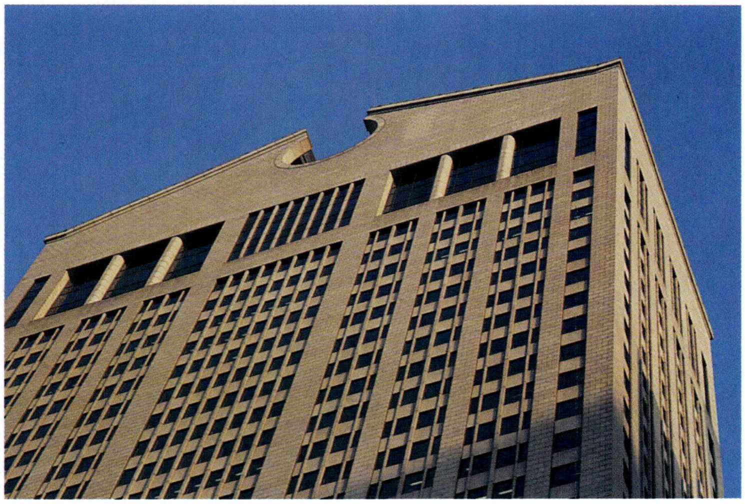

◆ **Figure 9–12** Compare and contrast this architectural design with that in Figure 9–7.

Philip Johnson and Associates. AT&T Building, New York, New York.

Answers to Check Your Understanding

1. A cityscape is a drawing or painting focusing on large buildings and other objects found in cities.
2. Louis H. Sullivan developed the idea of using a steel frame made of crisscrossed beams to create the building's structure. To this day, Sullivan's steel skeleton is at the heart of every skyscraper.

Studio Activity

Drawing a Building Detail

Show slides of local buildings and demonstrate how to use a viewfinder to identify an interesting portion of a building. (See Technique Tip 8 on page 283 in the Handbook.) Then show on the board how such a detail can be used as the basis for an interesting drawing, adding details, light and dark values, and textures. L1 ELL

Aesthetics

Ask students to identify a work in the book that they feel demonstrates the artist's use of a "selective eye." Discuss things the artist *might* have included in the work but chose to leave out. Are there any works in the book that students feel might have been more successful if the artist had been more selective? Have students explain. L1 ELL

3 Assess

Self-Assessment

Have students complete the **Check Your Understanding** questions on this page. Answers are provided below.

Reteaching

Ask students to explain how architects have solved the problem of limited space.

4 Close

Have students explain how architects like Louis H. Sullivan changed the "face" of modern cities.

Creating a Mixed-Media Cityscape

(pages 174–175)
Lesson Time: 90 minutes

1 Focus

Objectives

After completing this lesson, students will be able to:

- Demonstrate technical skills effectively by combining watercolor and texture-rubbing techniques to create a mixed-media cityscape.
- Conduct an in-progress critique of their mixed-media cityscape.
- Describe, analyze, interpret, and judge their artwork.

SUPPLIES
Refer to **What You Will Need** in the Student Edition.

2 Teach

Motivator

Have students examine **Figure 9–13.** Ask: What is the season and time of day represented? Why are so few people on the city streets? What hints does the artist provide to suggest that the "real" action of the city is taking place elsewhere? Have students speculate on where the artist must have been to view this scene. How is space suggested? Point out the artist's use of size, color, and placement of building shapes to create the illusion of space. Tell students that they will use these same techniques in their own mixed-media cityscapes.

Creating a Mixed-Media Cityscape

There is something magical about the sights and sounds of the big city. Some cities, even at night, seem to give off energy and electricity. One such place is the focus of **Figure 9–13.** Do you recognize this city? It is New York. One artist who fell under its spell was a painter named John Sloan. Sloan belonged to *a group of American Realists who worked at the beginning of the twentieth century.* Because there were eight in the group, they referred to themselves simply as **The Eight.**

In their paintings, The Eight realistically recorded the images of everyday life in the big city. Look closely at the cityscape in Figure 9–13. At its center, an elevated commuter train roars around a curve partially hidden by a low-rise building.

WHAT YOU WILL LEARN

You will create a city skyline. Your work will be made up of buildings cut from construction paper in a variety of hues. These will be set against a watercolor background suggesting day or night. To create a sense of space, you will place darker-colored buildings in the bottom foreground. These will overlap lighter-colored buildings placed higher in the picture plane.

WHAT YOU WILL NEED

- Pencil and sketch paper
- White drawing paper, 12 x 18 inches
- Water container
- Watercolor paints
- Large brush

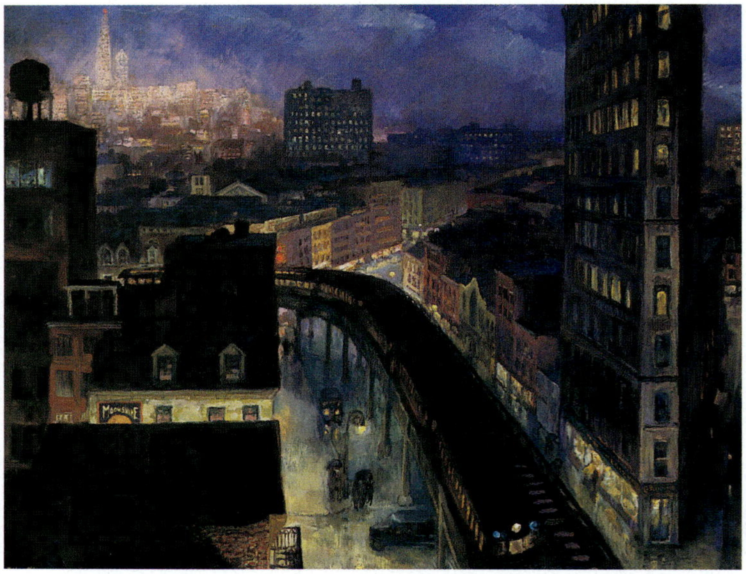

◆ **Figure 9–13** Critics, scornful of the subject matter of The Eight's work, dubbed the group the *Ashcan School*. What other art movements have you learned about with similar stories?

John Sloan. *The City from Greenwich Village.* 1922. Oil on canvas. 66 × 85.7 cm (26 × 33¾"). National Gallery of Art, Washington, D.C. Gift of Helen Farr Sloan.

TEACHER TO TEACHER

STUDENTS OF DIVERSE BACKGROUNDS You may find that many of your students have a firm understanding of and familiarity with a large metropolitan city. Others may be less experienced or familiar with the look and feel of the big city. For students with a rural or more suburban upbringing, provide a "tour" through a real city, showing travel movies or slides of a large metropolis. Help all students get a feeling of the noise, the pulse, and the congestion of a large city before they begin to work on their mixed-media cityscapes. The more prior knowledge each student has, the more interesting and detailed his or her artwork will be.

- Colored construction paper
- Crayons or oil pastels
- Ruler or other straightedge
- Scissors, white glue

What You Will Do

1. Complete several sketches of city skylines. Include overlapping buildings of different sizes and shapes. Add details such as windows and signs.
2. With the brush, cover the sheet of white drawing paper evenly with water. Decide whether your scene will take place at night or during the day. Depending on your choice, load a brush with a dark (for night) or light hue of watercolor paint. Add color to the wet paper. Do not worry that the color "bleeds," or runs. In fact, you may wish to use two or more colors, allowing them to mix together.
3. Set your watercolor painting aside to dry.
4. Referring to your sketches, cut out different building shapes from colored construction paper. Use a straightedge and scissors for this task. Cut larger buildings from the darker paper and smaller buildings from the lighter ones.
5. Arrange your cut-out buildings on the dry watercolored sheet. About a third of the way down from the top of the sheet, start arranging the smaller, lighter-colored buildings. Place the darker buildings closer to the bottom of the sheet—in the "foreground." Do these last, so that they overlap the lighter buildings. When you are satisfied with the placement of your buildings, glue them down.
6. Draw windows, signs, and other details with oil pastels or crayons.

Evaluating Your Work

- **Describe** Does your picture look like a city skyline?
- **Analyze** Do the sizes, colors, and placement of your buildings create the feeling of space?
- **Interpret** Does the sky suggest a particular time of day?
- **Judge** Are you pleased with your picture? What do you like best about it?

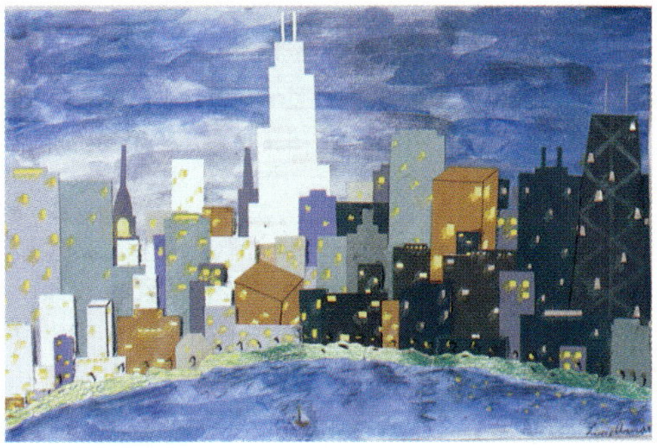

◆ **Figure 9–14** Student work. A mixed-media cityscape.

Reflective Thinking

Critical Evaluation. Analyze the original portfolios of your peers. Select a few of their artworks and form conclusions about formal properties and historical and cultural contexts. How have they applied the elements and principles of art to communicate their ideas? Do you notice any form of improvements in their skills?

Visual Art Journal

Express a variety of ideas based on direct observation. Walk around your neighborhood. Sketch details of interesting shapes and objects, such as street lamps, park benches, fences, etc. Think of different adjectives you could use to describe your neighborhood.

Art Criticism

Explain that when the artists of the Ashcan School first exhibited their paintings in New York in 1908, they were laughed at by critics and the viewing public. Tell students to pretend they are art critics for a newspaper and they must write a newspaper review in which they express their view of the Ashcan artists' work. Is it serious art, worthy of merit, or is it unworthy of serious consideration as art? Tell students to use Sloan's painting to support one of those views.

Studio Skills

Make sure that students arrange their building shapes using the techniques of placement, overlapping, and color to suggest space. Stress the importance of details to give the buildings a more interesting and realistic appearance. L1 ELL

3 Assess

Peer Assessment

Have students analyze their peers mixed-media cityscapes to form conclusions about formal properties—the elements and principles of art.

Reteaching

In pairs, have students compare techniques used to create the feeling of space in their pictures. L1 ELL

4 Close

Have students explain how details in their cityscapes provide a realistic view of a big city.

Career Opportunities in Art

Architecture Students who enjoy the creativity in planning and designing the buildings in their cityscape might be interested in learning more about architecture. Explain that the goal of an architect is to design buildings that are well-constructed, aesthetically pleasing, and functional. Encourage students to learn more about this career and to compare the different types of occupations in architecture, such as a building architect, landscape architect, and urban planner. Refer students to the Web site at **art.glencoe.com** and to the Career Spotlights section in the Handbook.

The Outdoors

(pages 176–177)

1 Focus

Objectives

After completing this lesson, students will be able to:

- Define *panorama.*
- Describe and compare landscapes and seascapes.
- Form generalizations about the interdependence of the art elements line and color and principles movement and variety in artworks depicting landscapes and seascapes.

2 Teach

Motivator

Ask students to use their imaginations and describe the things they might see out the window of an automobile during a leisurely drive through the countryside. Have a student list these on the board. Did students include the *road* on which they were driving? Direct students' attention to Hockney's painting in **Figure 9–15.** Can they easily identify the road referred to in the title of this painting?

Vocabulary

Tell students that the word *panorama* comes from the Greek *pan-* meaning "across" and *-horama,* meaning "sight."

The Outdoors

The invention of the airplane in 1903 by the Wright Brothers changed the way people viewed their world. From the air, nothing on earth seemed as powerful or important as it did at eye level. Cars, buildings, and even entire cities looked like toys. Roads and rivers looked like small ribbons. Plowed fields became so many squares on an endless patchwork quilt.

As you will see, this new view of our world was to have a lasting impact on another world. That was the world of art.

Landscapes

As noted in Chapter 6, successful *landscapes*—representations of scenes from nature—invite the viewer in. They tempt you with their shapes and colors.

A very different approach to landscape painting was taken by the artist responsible for **Figure 9–15.** This landscape, completed in 1980, does not invite you *into* it. Rather, it begs your eye to move *across* it. In this artwork, you follow the line of a road that winds through the countryside. On your journey, you pass clumps of trees, tennis courts, and houses. What sets this painting apart is the ever-shifting point of view and brilliant analogous colors—purples, reds, oranges. The subject is a well-known stretch of road in southern California. The artist has attempted to capture not only how the scenery looks to him but also how it feels. Notice that you may start your trip at either the left edge or right edge of the painting. What differences do you detect when you view the work beginning from one side or the other?

Seascapes

Even before the invention of the airplane, artists were recording broad vistas and panoramas. A **panorama** is *a complete view of an area in all directions.* One popular panoramic subject is exhibited in **Figure 9–16.** This work is a **seascape,** a *drawing or painting of the ocean and objects found on or around it.*

This particular seascape was completed just four years before the Wright Brothers

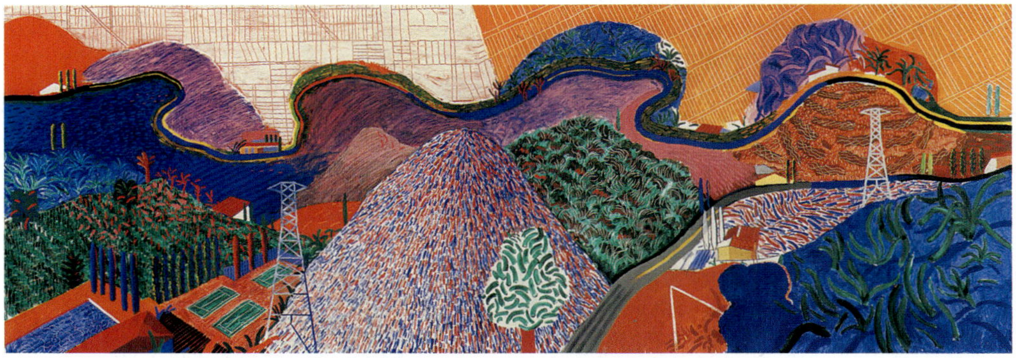

◆ **Figure 9–15** **Analyze the interdependence of the art element line and principle movement. What feeling does this painting evoke?**

David Hockney. *Mulholland Drive: The Road to the Studio.* 1980. Acrylic on canvas. 218.4 × 617.2 cm (86 × 243″). Los Angeles County Museum of Art, Los Angeles, California. Purchased with the funds provided by the F. Patrick Burnes Bequest.

TECHNOLOGY STRATEGIES IN THE ART CLASSROOM

Electronic Media-Generated Art Have students choose a scene for a panoramic view. The view can be a landscape or cityscape. Encourage them to consider a full 360-degree view. After deciding on a viewpoint, mark the spot with a plus sign on a sheet of paper to represent north, south, east, and west. Stand in the center. Take eight overlapping photographs using the mark as a guide. With photo imaging or art application, alter each view. Change colors, textures, or filters. Remind students to unify the panoramic view with a consistent color scheme, texture, or line that connects the sections.

took to the sky. Examine the painting. Much of the work is given over to an endless expanse of blue-green water, its surface flecked with whitecaps. The centerpiece, of course, is a small boat. Did you notice that the craft's mast is missing? It and its lone occupant are in trouble as the boat bobs helplessly on the water. The danger is made greater by a school of sharks circling the boat. Did you notice the creatures' black fins jutting above the water? Look even more carefully, and you will also notice a ship on the horizon. Its sails are barely visible as gray shapes against the white of the clouds. The artist, it seems, has provided a faint ray of hope—or has he? It is up to you, the viewer, to decide how this drama unfolds. Will the ship rescue the man before it is too late? Are those on board even aware of his presence?

Meet the Artist

Winslow Homer (1836–1910)

Cultural connection. Winslow Homer was a nineteenth-century American artist best known for his realistic and dramatic paintings of the sea. Homer was born in Boston, Massachusetts, in 1836. At age 19, he worked as an apprentice to a lithographer and then became a freelance illustrator a few years later. During the American Civil War, he illustrated scenes from the battlefields for *Harper's Weekly* magazine.

In 1866, Homer traveled to France and stayed for nearly a year. His work was not noticeably different upon his return. In 1881, however, a trip to Tynemouth, England, did evoke a change in his art. After visiting Tynemouth, a small fishing port, the sea became the focus of Homer's work (see **Figure 9–16**). On returning to the United States, Homer moved to Prouts Neck, a coastal fishing village in Maine. There, he created many of his most well-known seascapes.

To learn more about Homer and his work, click on Artist Profiles at art.glencoe.com.

Check Your Understanding

1. What is a panorama? Describe the panoramas in the two paintings on these pages.
2. Describe all the dangers facing the figure in the seascape on this page.

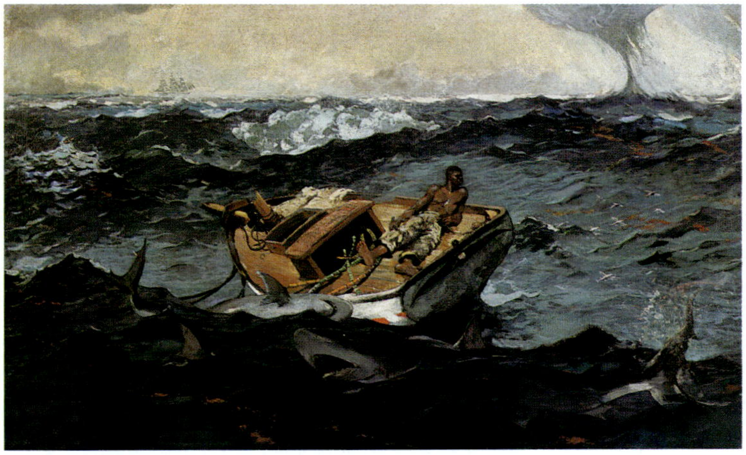

◆ **Figure 9–16** What do you feel poses the greatest threat to the man on the boat?

Winslow Homer. *The Gulf Stream.* 1899. Oil on canvas. 71.4 × 124.8 cm (28⅛ × 49⅛″). The Metropolitan Museum of Art, New York, New York. Catherine Lorillard Wolfe Collection, Wolfe Fund, 1906.

Meet the Artist

Invite students to look back at Winslow Homer's *Crossing the Pasture* in Chapter 4, Lesson 2, page 66. Have them compare it with the work shown in **Figure 9–16.** Ask students if they think Homer's experience as a war artist influenced his work. Have them explain their thinking.

Art Criticism

Use the following art-criticism questions to lead a discussion of Hockney's painting:

- What do you see below the road in this painting? What is above the road?
- How many different colors can you name? Can you find any straight lines? Where are most of these straight lines found? How is line used to unify this composition? How many different textures can you point out?
- Could Hockney's painting be said to show the passing of time? How so?
- Is Hockney's painting successful? Explain your reasoning. L1

3 Assess

Self-Assessment

Have students complete the **Check Your Understanding** questions on this page. Answers are provided below.

4 Close

Have students evaluate David Hockney's painting in terms of color and texture.

Answers to Check Your Understanding

1. A panorama is a complete view of an area in all directions. Hockney's panorama captures the scenery and feel of a stretch of road in southern California. Homer's panorama shows an endless expanse of blue-green water, with a small boat in distress in the center. Sharks have encircled the boat, but another ship is visible in the far distance.
2. The dangers include drowning, starving, or being devoured by sharks.

Creating a Seasonal Panorama

(pages 178–179)
Lesson Time: 90 minutes

1 Focus

Objectives

After completing this lesson, students will be able to:

- Demonstrate technical skills effectively by using a variety of art materials to produce a painting of a panoramic landscape that shows a particular season.
- Describe, analyze, interpret, and judge their paintings.

Supplies
Refer to **What You Will Need** in the Student Edition.

2 Teach

Motivator

List the four seasons on the board. Under each, have students identify various weather conditions associated with each—hot, cold, balmy, rainy, windy, icy, and so on. Direct students' attention to **Figure 9–17.** Ask them if the artist succeeded in showing a particular time of the year and have them explain how he did this.

Vocabulary

As a review, ask students to identify the warm and cool colors. Ask them why these colors are referred to as warm and cool. In Corot's painting, how are the shadowed areas indicated? How are the sunlit areas shown?

LESSON 8

Creating a Seasonal Panorama

You have examined panoramic views of land and of water. The painting in **Figure 9–17** gives you two vistas in one. In the near distance, just below the hill on which the viewer is standing, is a city—Genoa, Italy. Beyond is a stretch of sea rippling and shimmering in the sunlight. Notice how the strong Mediterranean sun glints off the stark white houses. What do you think it would be like to visit this combined city-seascape in person? Do you think cooling breezes from the sea might counter the noonday heat?

In making this painting, the artist faced a challenge. That challenge was capturing the dazzling effects of bright sunlight and its reflected light on a clear summer day. In this lesson, you will face a similar challenge.

What You Will Learn

You will paint a landscape that shows a particular season. You will begin by selecting hues, values, and intensities that suggest heat or cold, sunlight or shade. You will choose warm or cool hues and vary value and intensity depending on your purpose. For more on hue, value, and intensity, see pages 8–10 in Chapter 1.

What You Will Need

- Pencils and sketch paper
- White drawing paper, 9 x 12 inches or larger
- Tempera paints
- Brushes
- Mixing tray
- Paint cloth

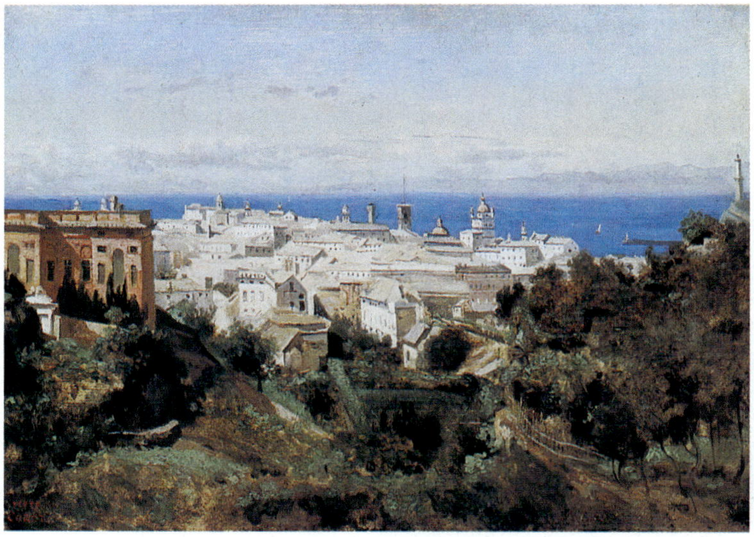

◆ **Figure 9–17** Which part of the painting is your eye drawn to first? Why do you think this is?

Jean-Baptiste-Camille Corot. *View of Genoa.* 1834. Oil on paper mounted on canvas. 29.5 × 41.7 cm (11⅝ × 16⅜″). Art Institute of Chicago, Chicago, Illinois. Mr. and Mrs. Martin A. Ryerson Collection, 1973.1017.

Teacher to Teacher

Value and Intensity Have students look at the colors, values, and intensities in Figure 9–17, Corot's *View of Genoa.* Point out how the most intense colors are in the foreground and how the atmosphere between the viewer and the background makes the colors in the distance less intense. Have students analyze their peers' artworks using the four steps of art criticism. Ask what students have done in their seasonal panorama to convey the particular season. Students should focus on the use of color and value.

What You Will Do

1. You will demonstrate technical skills effectively using a variety of art media and materials to produce a painting of a seasonal panorama. Brainstorm with classmates a list of objects associated with landscapes, cityscapes, and seascapes.
2. Choose one of the four seasons. Make several sketches of a panoramic outdoor scene that shows this season. It may be a landscape, seascape, or cityscape. Include at least four objects from the list you made. Tailor your choices to the season you have selected.
3. Transfer your best sketch to the white drawing paper. Paint your scene with colors that will help convey the season. Choose light values of high-intensity warm colors for warmer seasons. Choose dark values of low-intensity cool colors for colder seasons.

Evaluating Your Work

- **Describe** Did you use at least four objects selected from the list you brainstormed? Can these objects be easily identified?
- **Analyze** How did you use warm or cool colors to suggest heat or cold? How did you use light and dark values and bright and dull intensities to show sunlight and shadow?
- **Interpret** How did your color choices contribute to the mood in your painting?
- **Judge** Are you pleased with your picture? What is its best feature?

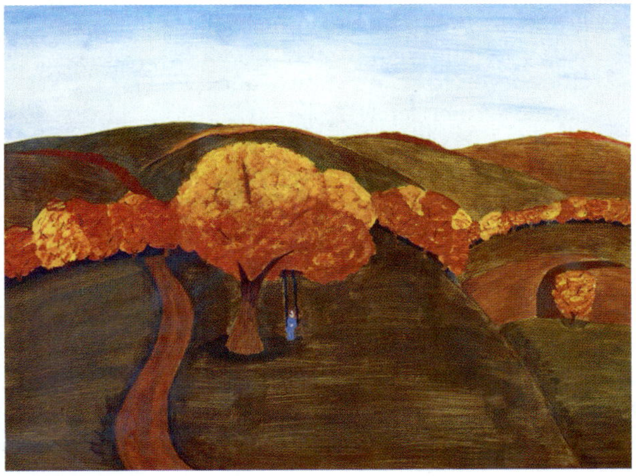

◆ **Figure 9–18** Student work. A seasonal panorama.

PORTFOLIO IDEAS

Find an artwork in this chapter that has a dramatic feeling. What elements of art did the artist use to create the artwork's expressive qualities? What principles of art were used? Create an artwork for your portfolio that expresses a dramatic feeling. Include your preliminary sketches and any notes you made to explain the technical skills you demonstrated.

Art Online

For additional activities, check out our Web site at **art.glencoe.com**. There you will also find:

- Artist Profiles
- Interactive Games
- Museum Web Links
- Studio Activities

ART IN EVERYDAY LIFE

Point out to students that weather conditions provide opportunities for "note taking." Encourage them to use their sketchbooks as weather journals, observing and sketching outdoor conditions as the seasons change.

Art Criticism

Have students describe Corot's painting. Ask: What has the artist done to guide the viewer's eye to the distant city? How has he suggested the brightness of a clear, sunny day? L1

Studio Skills

Encourage students to experiment with color mixing and point out how reds, oranges, and other warm colors can be changed to seem cool rather than warm. Black lines made with pen, marker, or india ink may be used to strengthen contour lines or to add details to their pictures. L1 ELL

3 Assess

Self-Assessment

Have students use **Evaluating Your Work** to conduct an in-progress critique of their seasonal panoramas.

Reteaching

Have small groups of students discuss their paintings and categorize each type of panorama as landscape, cityscape, and so on. L1

4 Close

Let students work in pairs to discuss what they learned in creating a seasonal panorama.

DEVELOPING A PORTFOLIO

Art-Criticism Entries Whether students critique their own artwork, the work of another student, or the work of a famous artist, art-criticism entries kept in their portfolios provide excellent opportunities to demonstrate their knowledge of the elements and principles of art. It also allows them to share their personal views in a written format. There are no right or wrong answers, but students do need to provide facts to support their opinions. Encourage students to periodically review their art-criticism entries to determine whether they have seen any growth in their art knowledge.

Ashcan Artists Paint the Town

1 Focus

Objectives

After completing this lesson, students will be able to:

- Paint a scene from their own city, town, or neighborhood.
- Create a Venn diagram comparing the works of two Ashcan artists.

2 Teach

Teaching the Feature

1. Have students recall what they have read about the Ashcan School. Then guide them in describing and discussing the two artworks, *The White Way* and *Election Night.*
2. Have students work with partners to read the article. Ask: What was Sloan's attitude toward city life? How do his paintings illustrate that attitude?

Activity

In a brief class discussion, let students share their own ideas about life in their city, town, or neighborhood. Ask: How could you best show life there in a painting? After the discussion, have students plan and create original paintings of their hometown.

Ashcan Artists Paint the Town

Some painters made gritty city life their subject.

When a critic labeled a group of artists the "Ashcan School," he was talking about the gritty, urban images these artists painted. Ashcan School paintings departed from those of the previous period. In the late nineteenth century, painters had portrayed peaceful and calm landscapes of the American countryside.

In the early twentieth century, urban centers like New York City became the new American "frontier." European immigration, industrialization, and migration from farms to cities began to change how—and where—Americans lived.

It was this "new" America that John Sloan (1871–1951) and other Ashcan artists depicted. Sloan painted "ordinary" people and their daily lives enjoying the dance halls and parks of New York City. Sloan's thick, quick brushstrokes reflect the fast-paced lives that city dwellers led. Although Sloan painted people, he was less fascinated by them than the busy, noisy city in which they lived.

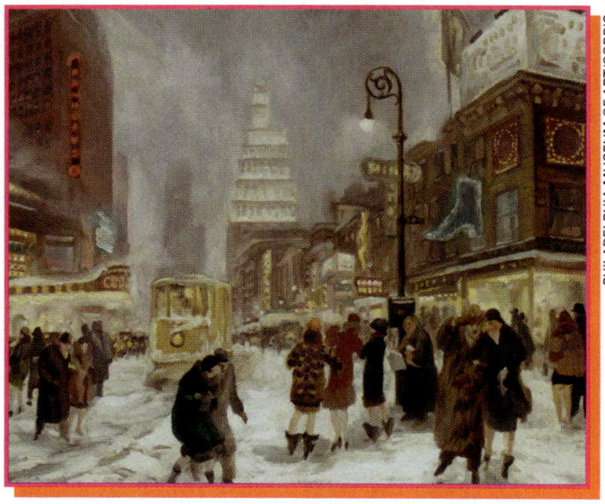

PHILADELPHIA MUSEUM OF ART/CORBIS

John Sloan. *The White Way.* 1922. The painting shows Times Square in Manhattan during a snow storm.

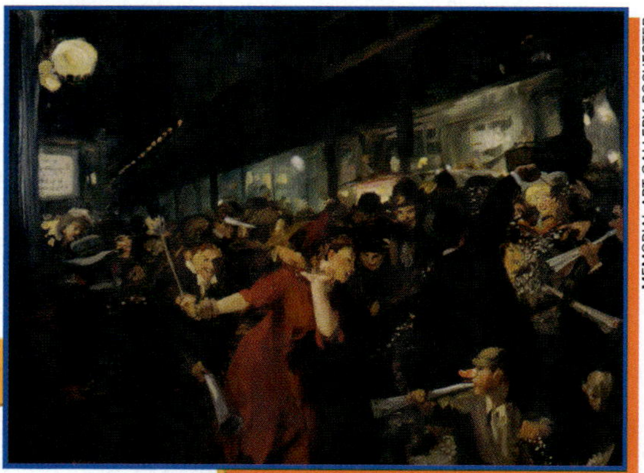

MEMORIAL ART GALLERY, ROCHESTER

John Sloan. *Election Night.* 1907. John Sloan described his experience of Election Day in his diary on November 5, 1907: "After dinner . . . out again and saw the noisy trumpet blowers. . . . A good humorous crowd, so dense in places that it was impossible to control one's movement."

TIME TO CONNECT

Some artists in the United States explored the everyday life of the cities, and some depicted pastoral scenes of the country.

- **Compare and contrast artworks of artists such as John Sloan, George Bellows, Isabel Bishop, and others with artists like Albert Bierstadt and Thomas Moran.**
- **Create a Venn diagram depicting their differences in style and subject matter and what the artists might have shared in common.**

TIME TO CONNECT

Have students work with partners to discuss the similarities and differences between artists in the two groups. Then ask partners to record their ideas in a Venn diagram. Suggest they ask themselves these questions:

- How are the styles of these artists alike?
- How are the subjects of these artists' paintings similar?
- What are the most important differences in the subjects painted by these artists?

Chapter 9 Review

BUILDING VOCABULARY

Number a sheet of paper from 1 to 10. After each number, write the term from the list that best matches each description below.

architects	façade
cityscape	panorama
columns	Rococo
The Eight	seascape
elevation	staged photograph

1. Vertical posts that rise to support another structure.
2. An art style of the 1700s that emphasized graceful movement, curving lines, and delicate colors.
3. The front of a building.
4. A complete view of an area in all directions.
5. A drawing or painting focusing on large buildings and other objects found in cities.
6. A drawing or painting of the ocean and objects found on or around it.
7. A group of American Realists who worked at the beginning of the twentieth century.
8. Artists who plan and create buildings.
9. A photographic composition that makes use of artificial images or processes.
10. A drawing of an outside view of a building.

REVIEWING ART FACTS

Number a sheet of paper from 11 to 14. Answer each question in a complete sentence.

11. Why did van Gogh choose to paint a picture of his room?
12. What is the name of the palace Louis XIV had built for him? What side of the king's personality does this palace reflect?
13. What change took place in the painting of cityscapes at the turn of the twentieth century?
14. What was the contribution of Louis H. Sullivan to the look of cities today?

CROSS-CURRICULUM CONNECTIONS

15. **Language Arts.** Imagine that you are a real estate agent. Your job is to describe homes that are for sale. Choose one of the dwellings in Figures 9–6, 9–7, or 9–8. Write a paragraph describing the structure. Identify the type of individual who might feel at home in the dwelling you have chosen. Explain how you came to this conclusion.
16. **Geography.** Genoa, Italy—the city shown in Figure 9–17—has a celebrated past. Using an encyclopedia or other resource, find out more about Genoa's past and present. What is the city most noted for today? Write your findings in a report.

Web Museum Activity

Los Angeles County Museum of Art, Los Angeles, California

In this chapter, you learned how places inspire artists and how artists represent these special places. Artists illustrate their personal view of the world in their artwork. You can visit different places across the world through an artist's eyes. Explore the various destinations by going to **art.glencoe.com** and clicking on the Los Angeles County Museum of Art link.

Through a variety of artworks, you will discover new places and revisit others in a new way. What did you learn when exploring these places? What did it reveal about the artist? After reading this chapter, why do you think artists represent places?

ANSWERS TO Chapter 9 Review

Building Vocabulary

1. columns
2. Rococo
3. façade
4. panorama
5. cityscape
6. seascape
7. The Eight
8. architects
9. staged photograph
10. elevation

Reviewing Art Facts

11. Van Gogh led a troubled life, and his room was a place where he felt safe.
12. It is the Palace at Versailles. The palace, with its ornate design and expensive furnishings, reveals the king's lavish tastes.
13. The subject matter shifted away from grandeur and toward more realistic subjects, such as factories.
14. He designed the steel cross-beam "skeleton" used for the framework of modern skyscrapers.

Cross-Curriculum Connections

15. Students' paragraphs will vary, but should include a detailed description of the structure and for what type of individual it would suit best.
16. Student reports may include that Genoa is one of Italy's largest cities and its main commercial seaport. Many regard Genoa as having the largest historic city center in Europe as a result of having been, for centuries, a powerful commercial center seaport and city-state.

Web Museum Activity

Before you have students go online, visit the Web site to preview the museum's online content, collection, and any online exhibit that might be of interest. Have students click on the images shown and answer the following questions for each artwork:

- What place is being represented?
- How does the artist illustrate that place?
- Describe the artwork. What stands out most?

Have students explain why they think artists represent places. Ask them which place they would represent in their artwork, and why.

Chapter Resources

Features	Standards for Chapter: National	Standards for Chapter: State/Local	Reproducible Masters
Quick Write *page 183* TIME ART SCENE "Extraordinary Glass" *page 200* ***Web Museum Activity*** *page 201*	**1.** (a, b) **2.** (a, b, c) **3.** (a) **4.** (a, b, c) **5.** (a, b) **6.** (b)		Guided Reading and Practice 10–1 Application Activity 10–2 Studio Activity 10–3 Artist Profile 10–4 Historical and Cultural Heritage 10–5 Enrichment Activity 10–6, 10–7 Lesson Plans

Lesson Resources

Lessons	Standards per Lesson: National	Standards per Lesson: State/Local	Reproducible Masters
1 ***Objects in Nature*** *(pages 184–185)*	4a, 5b		Application Activity 10–2
2 **ART & MATH** *(pages 186–187)*	2b, 5b, 6b		
3 ***Grouping Objects*** *(pages 188–189)*	1b, 2a, 4a		Studio Activity 10–3
4 ***Painting a Watercolor Still Life*** *(pages 190–191)*	1a, 1b, 2a, 3a		Artist Profile 10–4
5 ***Art Objects*** *(pages 192–193)*	1a, 1b, 2a, 4a, 4c		Historical and Cultural Heritage 10–5
6 ***Building a Clay Musical Instrument*** *(pages 194–195)*	1a, 1b, 2a, 2c, 5c		Enrichment Activity 10–6
7 ***Decorative Arts*** *(pages 196–197)*	4a, 4b, 5b		Enrichment Activity 10–7
8 ***Creating a Pendant*** *(pages 198–199)*	1a, 1b, 2a, 3a		

Assessment	Technology
Testing Program: Chapter Test 10–8 Portfolio and Assessment Techniques	Artsource Performing Arts Package, Kurt Jooss (DVD or VHS Segment 13) National Museum of Women in the Arts Interactive Lesson Planner Fine Art Transparency CC-10 *Lidded Jaguar Vessel* Fine Art Transparency 10 *Covered Bowls with Floral Scrolls*

Activities/Features
Meet the Artist: Georgia O'Keeffe
Make the Connection
Studio Activity: Experimenting with Form and Value
Evaluating Your Work Portfolio Ideas Visual Art Journal
Studio Activity: Creating an Object Design
Evaluating Your Work Reflective Thinking Visual Art Journal
Time & Place: Sixteenth-Century England
Evaluating Your Work Computer Option Art Online

KEY TO ABILITY LEVELS

Teaching strategies have been coded.

- **L1** Activities for all students; teacher direction required
- **L2** Activities for average to above-average students; some teacher direction needed
- **L3** Activities for students able and willing to work independently
- **ELL** English Language Learner activities

FEATURED ARTISTS

- Charles Demuth
- M. C. Escher
- Lik'an
- Georgia O'Keeffe
- Charles Sheeler
- Suzuki Kiitsu

FINE ART PRINTS

Fine Art Print 16, *Watch* by Gerald Murphy

Timesaving Technology

Interactive Lesson Planner

Make planning easy. Use this interactive software to organize your week, month, semester, or year and access all *Introducing Art* reproducible resources.

KEY TO LESSON RESOURCES

- Narrative Lesson
- Studio Lesson

Chapter 10

Examining Objects

(pages 182–201)

Chapter Overview

All around us are common objects that have intrinsic beauty, if we learn to perceive beauty as artists do. In this chapter, students will learn about artworks as objects—objects from different cultures and different times.

Discussing the Artwork

Focus On ◆ **Figure 10–1** This artwork is from New Ireland, an island that is part of Papua New Guinea, an island country in the southwest Pacific. Masks like this were used in ritual ceremonies that marked important events such as death. The people of northern New Ireland, Papua New Guinea, honor the dead through malagan ceremonies. According to malagan tradition, these ceremonies assist the souls of the dead to pass into the spirit world. *Malagan* refers to both the memorial ceremonies carried out after burial and mourning as well as the masks, figures, and posts made for use in these ceremonies. Malagan sculpture is notable for its openwork carving, projecting forms, and lively painting.

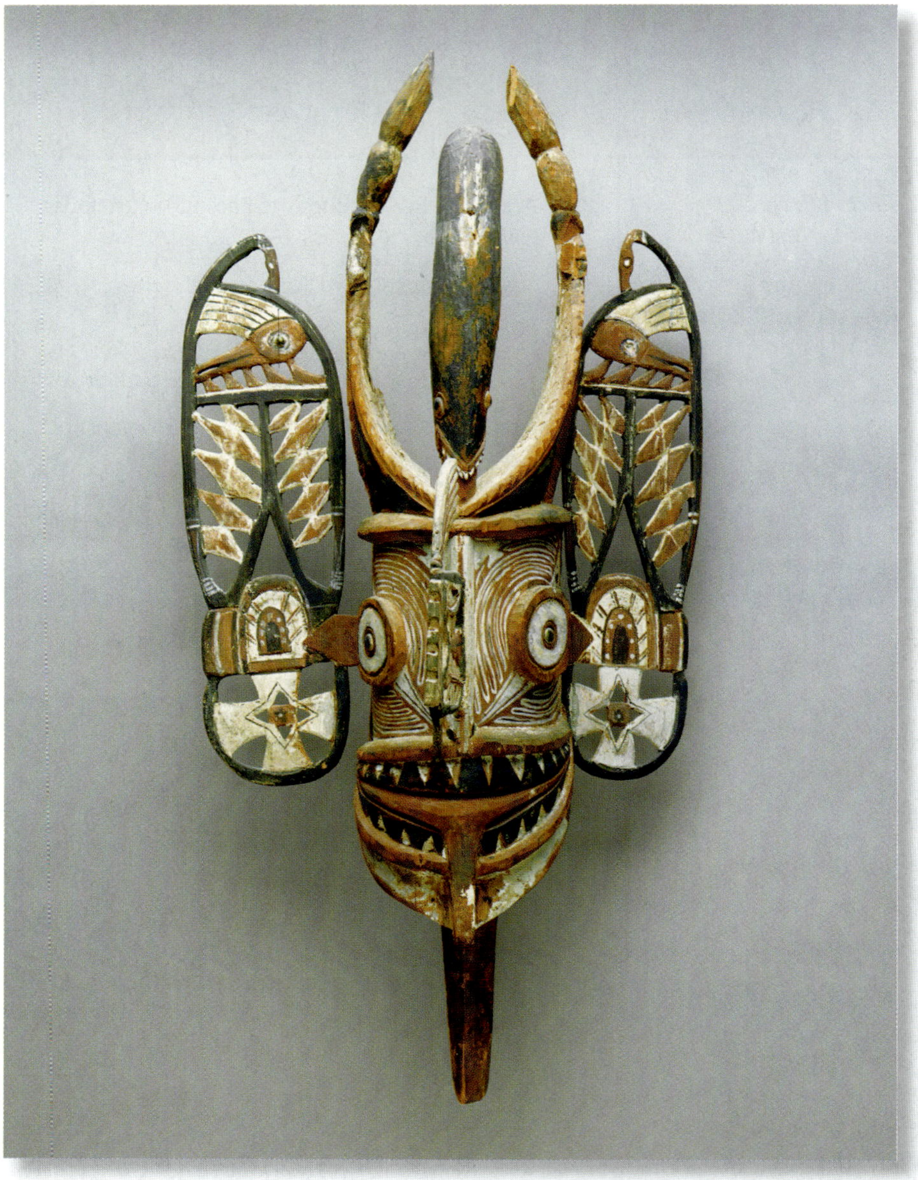

Focus On ◆ **Figure 10–1** **Tribal art has very personal and symbolic meaning to the people who make them. Look for the bird images and the rich patterns created with repeated lines and shapes.**

Melanesia, New Ireland, northwestern region. *Head of a malagan figure.* Early twentieth century. Wood, paint, and opercula. 97.8 × 46.4 × 31.1 cm (38½ × 18¼ × 12¼"). Dallas Museum of Art, Dallas, Texas. The Roberta Coke Camp Fund.

182

ART SOURCE ARTSOURCE

Linking to the Performing Arts

Dance/Theatre "Staging" a play or dance is similar to grouping objects for the visual artist. The principles of balance and composition are used when setting the stage. "The Green Table," choreographed by Kurt Jooss, is an example of a large set placed in the middle of a stage, with dancers grouped around the far end and the two sides. Have students read about the dance, "The Green Table," in the **Performing Arts Handbook** on page 319. To enrich student understanding, play the DVD or videotape (segment 13) in the **Performing Arts Package.**

Chapter 10

Examining Objects

"Culture is something that evolves out of the simple, enduring elements of everyday life; elements most truthfully expressed in the folk arts and crafts of a nation."

—Thor Hansen, paleontologist

Some objects are prized possessions. Certain prized possessions are also valuable items, like a rare coin or stamp. Others can hold value only to their owner. You might have a most prized possession, such as a torn ticket stub, an old toy, or a tarnished locket.

It is this second, hidden meaning of objects that makes them candidates for art subjects. In this chapter, you will learn about ways in which artists see the inner beauty in ordinary things. You will also discover how artists give these objects special significance by painting them or shaping them from clay or precious metals and gems.

After completing this chapter, you will be able to:

- Explain how artists perceive objects from their environment.
- Define the term *applied art.*
- Compare art objects from a variety of cultures.
- Use a variety of media to create original art objects.

Quick Write

Interpreting the Quote
Look at **Figure 10–1** and then read the quote. Write about the objects and symbols that define your culture today. What will you want to transmit to future generations?

Key Terms

perceive
watercolorist
applied art
vessel
pendant
pottery
slip
kiln
jewelry

Quick Write

Interpreting the Quote
Have students read the quote and start a class discussion on the different cultures students represent. What objects or symbols define those cultures? Next, have students complete the Quick Write activity. L1

Chapter Motivator

Instruct students to think about common objects they see every day—athletic shoes, their backpack, a baseball cap, a teacher's desktop, a geranium on the window sill, and so on. Ask them to describe the object, listing as many details as possible. Were they able to provide lots of details? Explain that in this chapter, students will improve their skills as observers of familiar objects in order to see that even common, everyday things have special meaning and beauty.

Art Online

Visit **art.glencoe.com**, the Web site for Glencoe's art programs. This site offers insightful resources for you and your students. Explore the many resources this site has to offer, such as:

- Art Advocacy
- Artist Profiles
- Career Corner
- Interactive Games
- Professional Development Articles

National Standards for Arts Education

This chapter addresses the following National Standards for the Visual Arts:

1. (a, b)
2. (a, b, c)
3. (a)
4. (a, b, c)
5. (a, b)
6. (b)

Objects in Nature

(pages 184–185)

1 Focus

Objectives

After completing this lesson, students will be able to:

- Define the word *perceive.*
- Explain why American artist Georgia O'Keeffe painted flowers on a large scale.
- Tell why the Chinese artist Lik'an chose to paint pictures of bamboo.

2 Teach

Motivator

Make available a collection of small, ordinary objects and instruct each student to select one. Call on several students to describe the object they selected. Then ask them to examine the objects with a magnifying glass. Did the closer examination reveal details that were overlooked at first? Direct attention to the two artworks in this lesson. Point out that both works were done by artists who took time to find beauty in the kinds of common objects we often take for granted.

Vocabulary

Tell students that Chinese painting is closely related to writing and *calligraphy.* Review the characteristics of calligraphy (see Chapter 7, Lesson 5). Point out how the lines of Lik'an's painting are made with the same kind of rapid, confident brushstrokes as those used in calligraphy.

LESSON 1

Objects in Nature

Artists have a special way of looking at things. They look at the ordinary and see the extraordinary. They look at a rain-slicked fence in the countryside and see a study in color and form and texture. They look at a battered old shoe and see a wholeness—a unity—that goes beyond the scuffed leather and tattered laces.

Some artists are born with this ability to "see." Others are trained to **perceive**—to *become aware through the senses of the special nature of objects.* In this chapter, you will share several artists' one-of-a-kind visions of objects in the world around them. You will also sharpen your ability to perceive.

Nature Studies

"Stop and smell the roses." Are you familiar with this saying? It underscores the idea that there is much that is beautiful and exciting in nature, if only we take the time to notice it.

Artists have been seeking out and perceiving the beauty in nature throughout the ages. The works on these pages are the result of two stops to "smell the roses." The paintings were made at different times and in different places. Yet, a common link exists between them. Both record objects found in nature.

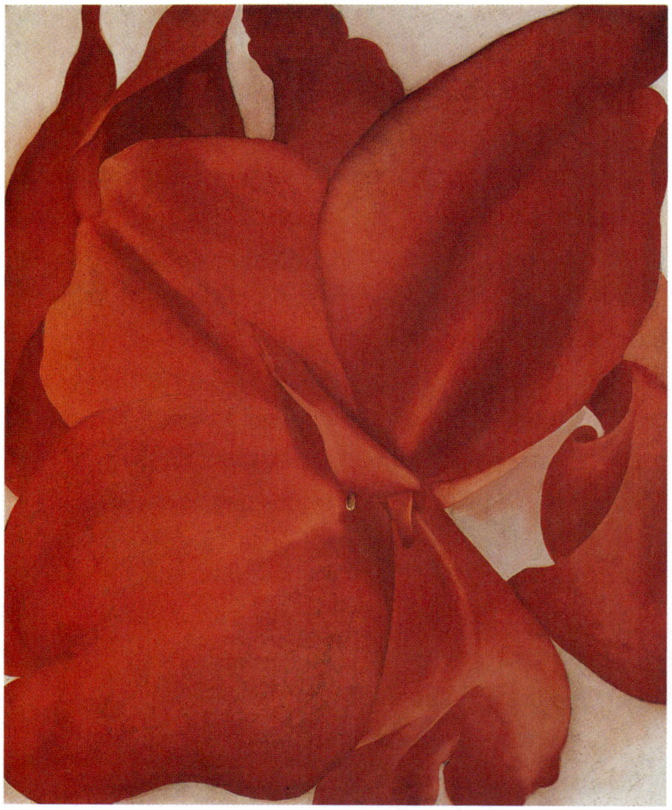

◆ **Figure 10–2** **Analyze the interdependence of color and value in this painting.**

Georgia O'Keeffe. *Red Cannas.* 1927. Oil on canvas. 91.8 × 76.5 cm (36⅛ × 30⅛"). Amon Carter Museum, Fort Worth, Texas. © 1997 The Georgia O'Keeffe Foundation/Artists Rights Society (ARS), New York, NY.

CURRICULUM CONNECTIONS

Botany Trees are a common part of our existence—graceful, useful, and important to our lives. Have students take a tree tour of their neighborhood. Have them collect samples of various species and compile a directory of trees in the area. Demonstrate how to press and mount the leaves between sheets of paper. Then, using a simple tree guidebook available at the library, have students identify each species with the common and scientific name. Ask students to study the characteristics of each leaf in detail and to compare the patterns and variations in shape, color, and line. What differences and similarities do they perceive?

An Object Up Close

The subject of the painting in **Figure 10–2** is an object of a type you have seen. Did you immediately recognize it as a brightly colored tropical flower? If you did not, the reason may have to do with the way in which the artist represented it. Notice the size of the painting. Why would any artist choose to magnify an image of a flower many hundreds of times?

The answer rests with events of the period in which the artist, Georgia O'Keeffe, lived. O'Keeffe was active in the early 1900s. The world was changing fast. Tall buildings were going up in big cities such as New York, where O'Keeffe lived. Convinced that people had begun to overlook nature's wonders, O'Keeffe painted her subjects larger than life, just like the buildings.

An Object from Long Ago

The painting in **Figure 10–3** focuses on a plant native to the artist's homeland. In this case, the plant is bamboo. The artist was from China. Look closely at this work. See the care given to each small leaf. The elegant lines call to mind calligraphy (kuh-**lig**-ruh-fee)—the art of beautiful writing. In fact, the artist was a noted calligrapher in his day. What quality of this work do you think prompted some viewers to call it a portrait of an actual plant?

Meet the Artist

Georgia O'Keeffe (1887–1986)

Cultural connection. Georgia O'Keeffe was deeply inspired by nature. Her most famous works are her flower paintings (see **Figure 10–2**). Born in Wisconsin in 1887, O'Keeffe knew from an early age that she wanted to be a painter.

Following her dream, she studied at the Art Institute of Chicago and the Art Students League of New York. O'Keeffe spent a great deal of time in New Mexico and moved there permanently after the death of her husband, artist Alfred Stieglitz.

In New Mexico, she created many paintings of natural forms in and around the desert, including animal bones, rocks, shells, and mountains. Compare the use of color and value in O'Keeffe's artwork, *Red Cannas*, with Figure 10–3.

To learn more about O'Keeffe and her work, click on Artist Profiles at **art.glencoe.com**.

Check Your Understanding

1. Define the term *perceive*.
2. Why did Georgia O'Keeffe paint flowers on such a large scale?

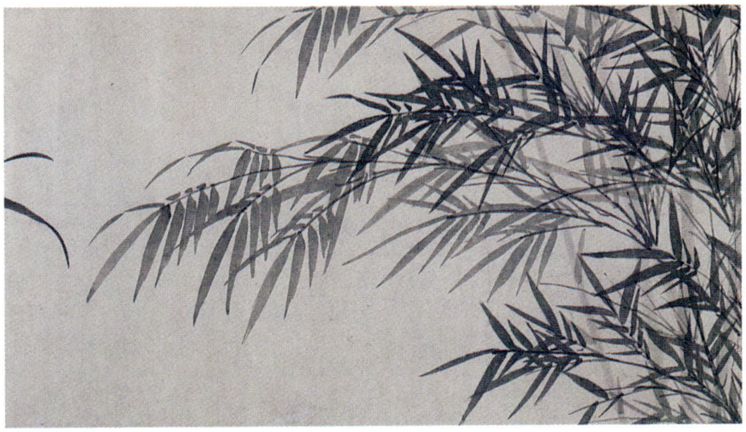

◆ **Figure 10–3** This ink painting of an actual bamboo plant shows many of its characteristics. How has the artist made some leaves look near and others look farther away?

Lik'an. *Ink-Bamboo*. (Detail.) 1308. Handscroll, ink on paper. 37.5 × 236.2 cm (14¾″ × 7′ 9″). The Nelson-Atkins Museum of Art, Kansas City, Missouri. Purchase: Nelson Trust.

Meet the Artist

Georgia O'Keeffe

O'Keeffe's use of color and value is very vibrant in her enlarged image of a flower. Lik'an's use of color is more muted and less defined.

Art Criticism

Divide the class into two groups, assigning each group one of the artworks in this lesson. Have students use the following questions to examine each work:

- How would you describe the artwork in a single, detailed sentence?
- Which work emphasizes line and value? Which emphasizes shape and color? How do both demonstrate variety and harmony?
- What ideas and feelings does the work communicate to you?
- Do you think this work is successful? Explain. L1 ELL

3 Assess

Self-Assessment

Have students complete the **Check Your Understanding** questions on this page. Answers are provided below.

Reteaching

Ask students to explain what senses they use when they try to *perceive*.

4 Close

Have students explain how a person can detect the extraordinary in ordinary objects.

Answers to Check Your Understanding

1. To *perceive* is to become aware through the senses of the special nature of objects.
2. Georgia O'Keeffe was convinced that people had begun to overlook nature's wonders. As a result, she painted objects larger than life so that no one could ignore them or fail to see their beauty.

Impossible Objects

(pages 186–187)

1 Focus

Objectives

After completing this lesson, students will be able to:

- Identify geometric forms in an artwork.
- Explain the mathematical basis behind an artwork depicting an impossible structure.
- Compare and contrast artworks in terms of style.
- Sketch a building using geometric concepts.

2 Teach

Motivator

Ask volunteers to recount movies they have seen or books they have read where impossible events occur. After several accounts, ask students what makes these types of events impossible. Note that in this lesson, they will encounter a work by one artist famous for his impossible structures.

Critical Thinking

Have students study the artwork in **Figure 10–4.** Have them trace the course of the water from its source at the bottom of the wheel to the top of the spillway. Ask: What makes this event impossible? *(The water appears to be running uphill.)*

Impossible Objects

When searching for new ideas, artists turn to a variety of sources. Sometimes they find inspiration in current events. Other times, they turn to literature or music.

The artwork in **Figure 10–4** was inspired by an unlikely source—geometry. This was true of almost all the works by this artist, M. C. Escher. Look at the artwork again. It shows a seemingly ordinary waterwheel. When you study this object closely, however, you begin to see a few odd things. Notice how the water seems to be running uphill. It is defying the laws of gravity. Another problem can be found in the path of the channel carrying the water. Try tracing this path with your finger. Begin at the bottom of the water wheel. Look at how the channel runs backward, then

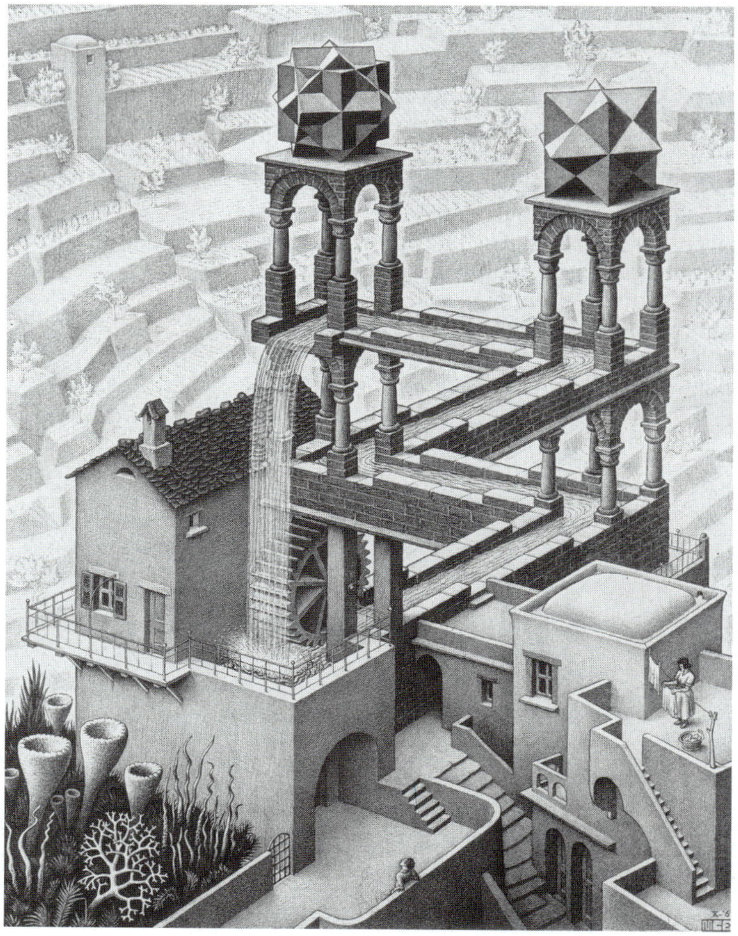

◆ **Figure 10–4** Escher used an impossible object as the basis of this artwork.

M. C. Escher. *Waterfall.* 1961. Lithograph.

MORE ABOUT...

M. C. Escher (1898–1972) Graphic artist Maurits Cornelius Escher is noted for his distinctive prints depicting intricate interlocking patterns and optical illusions. His earliest works were mainly landscapes and city scenes. By the mid-1930s, he began experimenting with repeating patterns and spatial illusions. From 1940 on, his work became more fantasy-oriented and included bizarre buildings that toyed with the viewer's perceptions such as the structure in Figure 10–4.

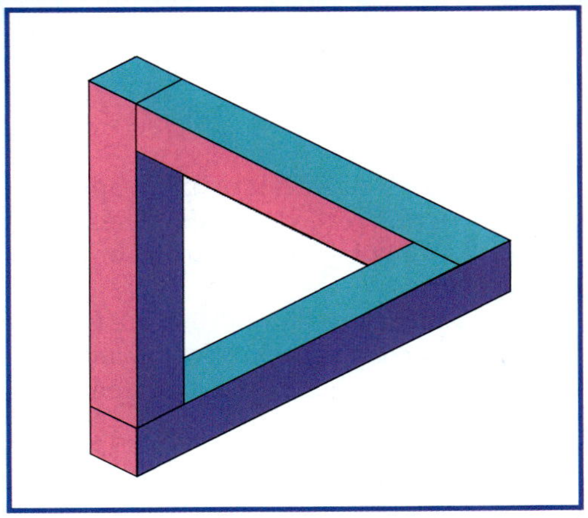

◆ **Figure 10–5** The Penrose triangle.

makes a 90-degree turn to the left. Somehow, strangely, the water is now above the point where it started!

Impossible Forms

Escher came up with the idea for this impossible structure after viewing the form shown in **Figure 10–5.** This object was created by a British mathematician named Roger Penrose. It looks at first like an ordinary triangle. Look carefully, however, and you will notice that this triangle has three right angles. You may recall learning the following two geometry facts:

- A right angle has 90 degrees.
- The sum of the angles in a triangle equals 180 degrees.

Here lies the mystery—and impossibility—of Escher's unusual water wheel. It is an impossible structure because it is based on an impossible object.

MAKE THE CONNECTION

Take Another Look

1. Look again at Figure 10–4. Escher used the Penrose triangle three times in this artwork. Can you locate them?
2. Add the sum of the three right angles in Figure 10–5. How is this number different from the sum of the angles in a real triangle?

ART & MATH

Sketch an impossible object. Practice sketching the Penrose triangle. You may find it difficult to draw at first. Once you have mastered this geometric form, try creating a building made from it. Share your completed building with classmates.

Using Math Skills

Ask students to define the math term "right angle." *(It is an angle with 90 degrees.)* Have students identify examples of right angles in their immediate environment. They might note that each of the four corners of their textbook forms a right angle, that the classroom walls probably form right angles, and so on. How many right angles can students count in the triangular form in **Figure 10–5?** How many of these triangles are repeated in the waterfall in Figure 10–4?

3 Assess

Self-Assessment

Have students complete the **Take Another Look** questions on this page. Answers are provided below.

Reteaching

Have small groups of students look through their books for other artworks that display triangular forms. Have group members compare these forms with the ones in Figure 10–4.

4 Close

Have students discuss whether an actual waterwheel could be designed in which the path of the water was triangular.

MAKE THE CONNECTION

Take Another Look Student answers will vary, but may include the following:

1. Urge students to find these triangles in the lower and upper pathways within the sluice.
2. The three right angles add up to 270 degrees. A conventional triangle has only 180 degrees.

LESSON 3

Grouping Objects

(pages 188–189)

1 Focus

Objectives

After completing this lesson, students will be able to:

- Define *still life* as an art form.
- Compare and contrast a Western and an Eastern still life painting.
- Understand and demonstrate how to use graduated changes in value to achieve a three-dimensional appearance.

Supplies

- Several common objects such as fruit, eggs, jars, bottles
- Large, square sticks of charcoal
- White drawing paper
- Tissues

2 Teach

Vocabulary

Explain that artists often choose to paint *still lifes,* pictures of ordinary objects, because they are mainly interested in composition. (See Chapters 1 and 2 for a review of composition.) Such works are meant to be quietly pleasing rather than loudly dramatic or shocking. Point out how Charles Sheeler's painting, for example, is a thoughtful arrangement of a few rounded objects.

LESSON 3

Grouping Objects

Have you ever been warned that "you can't mix apples and oranges"? Artists have been ignoring this piece of advice for well over 2,000 years. Their works have mixed apples, oranges, and countless other fruits and objects. In this lesson, you will look at two such mixtures. After careful examination, you may decide that the whole can be greater than the sum of its parts.

Objects in Still Lifes

An important scholar once noted that there are no new ideas, just new combinations of old ones. This statement certainly applies to the works of art called still lifes. These are paintings or drawings of inanimate, or nonmoving, objects.

The objects depicted in still lifes are familiar. What is unfamiliar is their combination—their arrangement. Each still life presents its subject matter in a new, startling way.

A Western Still Life

As a Western art form, the still life is one of the oldest. Descriptions of realistic paintings of grouped objects appear in Greek writings dating back to about 2400 B.C.

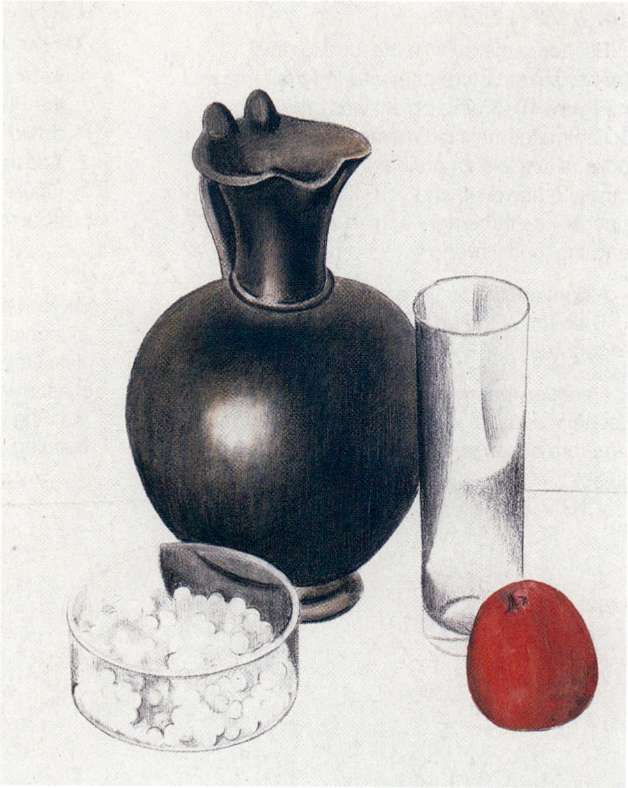

◆ **Figure 10–6** Compare this still life with the one in Figure 1–2 on page 4. What similarities do you detect? What differences?

Charles Sheeler. *Suspended Forms.* 1922. Charcoal, black and brown chalk, watercolor. 48.2 × 38.7 cm (19 × 15¼"). The Saint Louis Art Museum, St. Louis, Missouri. Bequest of Marie Setz Hertslet, 123:1972.

TECHNOLOGY STRATEGIES IN THE ART CLASSROOM

Digital Value Scale There are several ways to change the color value to make objects look three-dimensional when working with electronic media-generated artworks. Gradient options found under color or other menu tools are usually available with the bucket fill. Have students explore choices for the lighting sources. Have them make digital values scales exploring options, such as preprogrammed patterns, lines, and colors. Using art software, ask them to arrange and draw a simple still life with three objects. Have them apply changes in value techniques to make the objects appear three-dimensional.

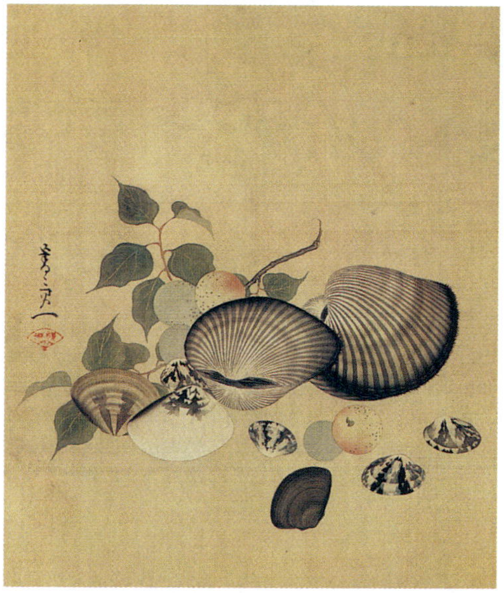

◆ **Figure 10–7** **Notice the arrangement of the objects in this still life.**

Suzuki Kiitsu. *Seashells and Plums.* Japanese. Edo Period. Nineteenth century. Color on silk. 34.6 × 29.2 cm (13⅝ × 11½"). Los Angeles County Museum of Art, Los Angeles, California. Etsuko and Joe Price Collection.

A painting fitting this description is shown in **Figure 10–6**. This still life, however, was completed in the twentieth century. Its artist, moreover, was American. Examine the work. It is a detailed, lifelike painting of several ordinary objects. Notice their placement. Would you say they have been arranged haphazardly or with care? Find the single horizontal line in the picture. What does this line represent?

An Eastern Still Life

Like the artworks you learned about in Lesson 1, the two on these pages are separated by time and place. The still life in **Figure 10–7** was completed more than a century before the one in Figure 10–6. The artist who made this second painting was from Japan. The work, in fact, gives us a sense of traditional Japanese design. It also provides an insight into Japanese culture.

Studio Activity

Experimenting with Form and Value

Demonstrate your technical skills. Look again at Figure 10–6. The artist has created a sense of three-dimensional form mainly through *value*. By changing little by little from dark to light values, he makes the objects appear solid and round.

Experiment with this method yourself. Arrange several objects, such as apples, eggs, and jars, on a tabletop. Step back and study this arrangement carefully. Then draw the composition with charcoal. Show gradual changes of value.

PORTFOLIO

In a short paragraph, evaluate the result of the shading technique you achieved with charcoal.

Examine the contents of the painting. These are summed up neatly in the title. What do the first of these items, the shells, reveal about Japan's geography? Look next at the still life's composition. How would you describe the arrangement of the objects? How similar is this arrangement to the one in Figure 10–6? As you study this work, it becomes clear that the artist's goal was to create an elegant, balanced design. Do you think he has succeeded?

Check Your Understanding

1. What is a still life?
2. In what ways are the still lifes on these pages similar? How are they different?

Studio Activity

Experimenting with Form and Value Supervise students as they arrange their objects. Tell them to fill the paper with their drawing. Demonstrate how the charcoal can be smudged with a piece of tissue to create gradual changes in value. Areas that appear to be too dark can be lightened using a soft or kneaded eraser.

Art Criticism

Have students describe each of the still lifes shown. Have them analyze both works by identifing the principles of art used to organize the elements. Students should use art vocabulary appropriately. L1

3 Assess

Self-Assessment

Have students complete the **Check Your Understanding** questions on this page. Answers are provided below.

Enrichment

While still in his teens, Suzuki Kiitsu was accepted as a student by the famous painter Sakai Hoitsu. Hoitsu made certain that Kiitsu's studies included poetry and the tea ceremony. Ask students to discuss how such a broad education might be helpful to an artist's success.

4 Close

Have students conduct an in-progress critique of their still lifes.

Answers to Check Your Understanding

1. A still life is a painting or drawing of inanimate, or nonmoving, objects.
2. Kiitsu and Sheeler both painted still-life objects to look three-dimensional. They both have little background detail. The subject matter of each is different.

Painting a Watercolor Still Life

(pages 190–191)
Lesson Time: 90 minutes

1 Focus

Objectives

After completing this lesson, students will be able to:

- Demonstrate technical skills effectively by using a variety of art materials to produce a watercolor still life.
- Describe, analyze, interpret, and judge their work.

SUPPLIES
Refer to **What You Will Need** in the Student Edition.

2 Teach

Motivator

Ask students to identify the kinds of subjects they think make the "best" paintings. List these on the board. Then ask if students can think of subjects that would not make an interesting painting. Direct attention to **Figure 10–8.** Do they think this is an interesting work? A successful work? What can be learned from this painting that features such humble subject matter?

Painting a Watercolor Still Life

To the average person, an eggplant and a green bell pepper are ingredients of a meal. To artist Charles Demuth, these simple vegetables were ingredients of a still life (**Figure 10–8**). Study this work. It helped secure Demuth's reputation as a great watercolorist. A **watercolorist** is *a painter who works in watercolor.*

In this lesson, you will create your own still life using watercolor and ink. Like the painting in Figure 10–8, yours will feature ordinary vegetables. See if you can paint them in a way that pleases even viewers who usually don't like vegetables!

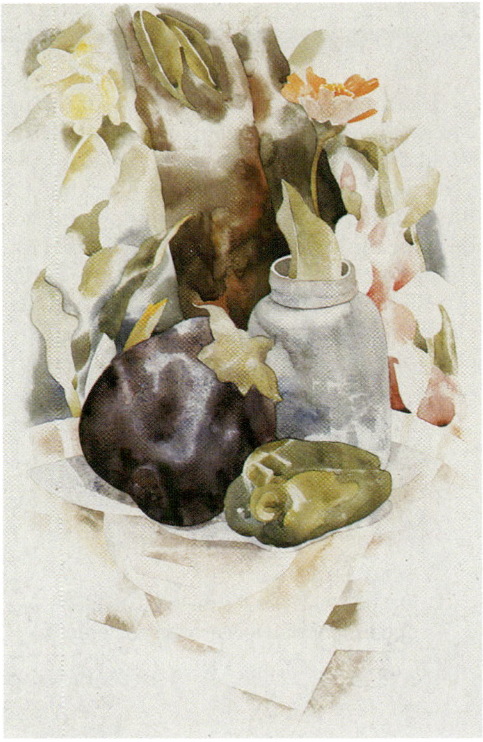

◆ **Figure 10–8** **Describe the techniques the artist applied to create this painting.**

Charles Demuth. *Eggplant and Green Pepper.* 1925. Watercolor with graphite. 45.7 × 27.9 cm (18 × 11″). The Saint Louis Art Museum, St. Louis, Missouri. Eliza McMillan Fund, 2:1948.

What You Will Learn

You will complete a watercolor-and-ink painting of two vegetables and a jar or bottle. Create highlights within your painting by leaving some areas of the paper unpainted. Use broken ink lines to strengthen contour lines and to create details and textures.

What You Will Need

- Two different vegetables and a jar or bottle as props
- A length of colorful cloth (optional)
- Pencil
- White drawing paper, 12 x 18 inches
- Watercolor paint
- Large flat brush
- Mixing tray
- Paint cloth
- A wooden skewer
- Black india ink

What You Will Do

1. You will demonstrate technical skills effectively using a variety of art materials to produce a still life painting. Begin by studying the watercolor in Figure 10–8. Notice that the artist has left some parts of the paper unpainted. Observe how this helps to suggest highlights, while adding a refreshing sparkle to the entire picture.

TEACHER TO TEACHER

DRY-BRUSH TECHNIQUE WITH WATERCOLOR AND INK Demonstrate to students what is meant by a dry-brush technique. Point out how this technique gives unpainted areas freshness in watercolor paintings. Demonstrate how painting a given area over and over again muddles the color. Also show how a broken ink line made with a pointed stick can be used to define contours and add detail and texture. Caution students not to use too many lines, which might add confusion to their pictures.

2. With several classmates, select and bring to class two ordinary vegetables and a jar or bottle. These are to be used as subjects for your still life. You may also wish to bring a colorful piece of cloth to serve as a backdrop. Place these objects on a tabletop. Strive for an interesting arrangement.
3. Using light pencil lines, complete a drawing of the still life. Make sure to fill the entire sheet of drawing paper.
4. With a large flat brush, paint your still life. Work with lighter hues first and add darker hues little by little. Use a dry brush technique to apply the paint with single brush strokes. Avoid scrubbing over painted areas. As you move your dry brush over the surface of the paper, some portions will remain unpainted. Leave them this way.
5. Dip the wooden skewer into black india ink. Use this to create broken lines to emphasize contours or edges and to add details and textures.

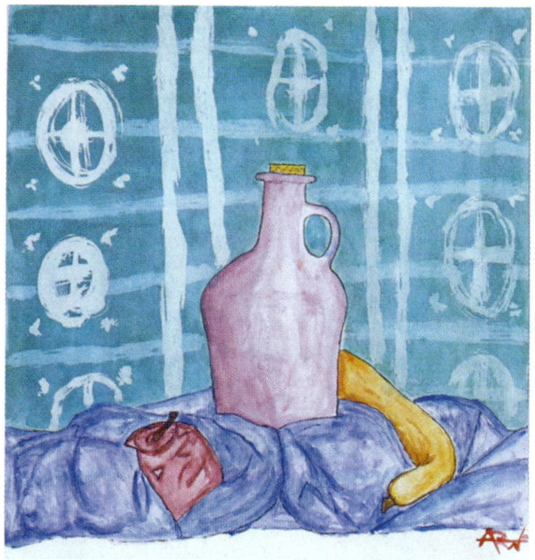

◆ **Figure 10–9** Student work. Watercolor still life.

Evaluating Your Work

- **Describe** Identify all the objects in your painting.
- **Analyze** Did you leave areas of your picture unpainted to suggest highlights and give your work a fresh look? Did you use broken ink lines to sharpen contours and add details and textures?
- **Interpret** Would you describe your work as light and fresh-looking, or dark and somber?
- **Judge** Do you think you succeeded in making a visually appealing painting using ordinary vegetables? Why or why not?

PORTFOLIO IDEAS

From time to time, review your portfolio contents. If you have been using it to hold all your notes, sketches, and finished artworks, you might want to review your selections and replace some of your entries. Remember, your goal is to present a portfolio of works that communicates your growth as an artist.

Visual Art Journal

Form generalizations about the interdependence of the art elements and principles in Figure 10–8. Next, describe in your journal your use of the art elements and principles in your still life.

Art On A Shoestring

Some watercolor rendering papers can be bought less expensively in rolls or by the foot than by the sheet or pad. A 100% rag, twenty-pound vellum is pretty tough, and you can iron the back of it to smooth it after using liquid media.

3 Assess

Self-Assessment

Have students use **Evaluating Your Work** to conduct an in-progress critique of their watercolor still lifes.

Reteaching

In pairs, have students identify the ways Demuth achieved texture and space in his painting. L1

Enrichment

Both Charles Sheeler and Charles Demuth practiced a style of art known as Precisionism. Have a student look up the definition for *precision* and read it to the class. Ask how the painting by Demuth in this lesson and the one by Sheeler in Lesson 3 conform to that definition. Ask students if they think Precisionism is a good name for the style of art both practiced. L2

4 Close

Have students brainstorm a list of techniques they found effective in painting their watercolor still lifes.

DEVELOPING A PORTFOLIO

Building A Storage System Actual physical construction of a portfolio case or folder can become a design assignment in itself. If you anticipate the type of assignments, including size, materials, and durability of the resulting artwork, you can establish some guidelines for the construction of a practical portfolio case. Then you can discuss the ways in which the work might be organized for storage within the classroom. This helps the students appreciate keeping a portfolio and is the beginning of establishing group expectations for their portfolios.

Art Objects

(pages 192–193)

1 Focus

Objectives

After completing this lesson, students will be able to:

- Explain the function of a *vessel* and identify examples of vessels.
- Understand that applied art objects serve a dual purpose.

SUPPLIES
- Pencils and sketch paper
- White drawing paper

2 Teach

Motivator

Ask students to express their opinions about **Figure 10–10.** How many discussed it in terms of its function? How many referred to it and discussed it as a work of art? Explain that the item pictured in Figure 10–10 is an example of *applied art,* an artwork that serves a practical function yet is visually pleasing. Have students analyze the interdependence of the art element form and principle proportion. Students should use art vocabulary appropriately.

Vocabulary

Explain that the ancient Persians typically crafted *rhytons* in the form of an animal's head or body. When the ancient Greeks invaded Persia, they were greatly influenced by Persian arts and crafts. Tell students that such *vessels* as the rhyton were eventually crafted in Greece as well.

LESSON 5

Art Objects

The artworks you have examined thus far in this chapter were created with a common purpose. That purpose is to appeal to the viewer in terms of its subject, content, or composition. Most fine art shares this purpose. However, some art serves an everyday use as well. Such *works of art that are made to be useful as well as visually pleasing* are known as **applied art**.

Vessel from Long Ago

Look at **Figure 10–10.** This art object is a **vessel**, a *hollow utensil made to hold something.* Vessels come in all shapes and sizes. They also serve a wide variety of purposes. The vessel pictured here was used for drinking. Pitchers and vases are other examples of vessels.

Look closely at Figure 10–10. This drinking vessel is called a *rhyton.* It was created about 2,500 years ago in the ancient kingdom of Persia. The object is made mostly from a single piece of gold. A gold liner at the base of the cup prevented liquid from flowing into the body of the animal. Notice the *flutings,* or bands of rings, etched into the surface of the cup. What other patterns have been used to decorate this object? What do you think was the social standing of the person for whom it was crafted?

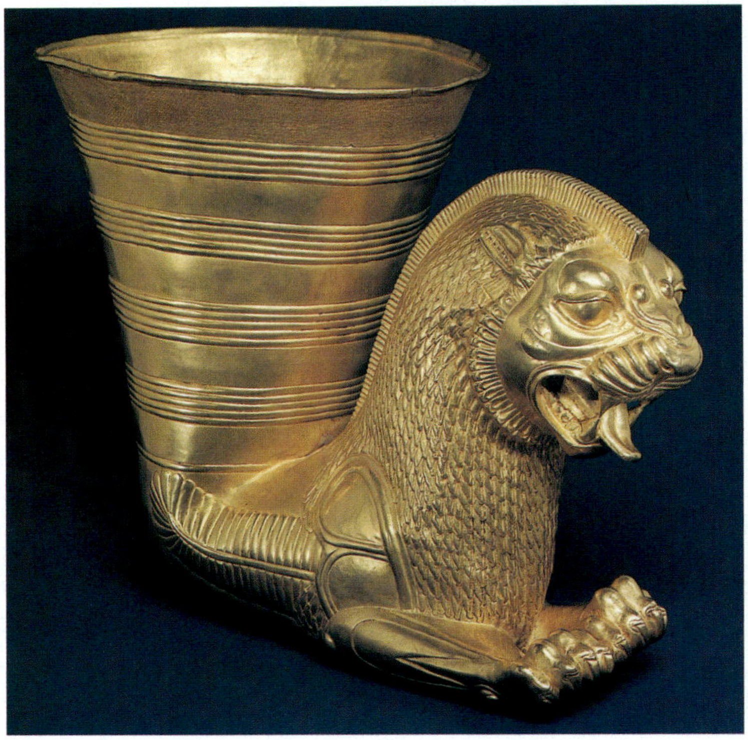

◆ **Figure 10–10** What animal is depicted on this object? What does that subject and the medium suggest about the person for whom the object was created?

Hamadan (Iran). *Rhyton Vessel in the Form of a Lion.* Fifth century B.C. Gold. 17 × 23 cm (6⅝ × 9″). The Metropolitan Museum of Art, New York, New York. Fletcher Fund, 1954.

CURRICULUM CONNECTIONS

GEOGRAPHY Ancient Persia was a kingdom located in an area that is now called Iran. The Persian Empire reached its peak around 500 B.C. This expansive empire extended from North Africa and southeastern Europe in the west to India in the east, and from the Gulf of Oman in the south to the southern boundaries of what is now Kazakhstan in the north. Much of the trade between central Asia and Europe passed through the Persian Empire, especially silk, spices, pottery, textiles, and precious stones. Have students research more about the ancient Persians and their culture and draw a map of the empire at its height.

Pendant from Long Ago

An altogether different function was served by the object in **Figure 10–11**. Like the rhyton, this pendant was fashioned entirely from gold. A **pendant** is *a jewelry item worn suspended from the neck on a string or chain.* Notice its size. For a piece of jewelry that is only 2⅝″, the artist has managed to include an amazing amount of detail. Study this object. It portrays a man who projects outward in high relief. Notice the expression on the man's face and the direction of his gaze. What feeling does this portrait communicate?

Check Your Understanding

1. What is a vessel? What are some examples of vessels?
2. Could the work in Figure 10–11 be regarded as both fine art and applied art? Why or why not?

Studio Activity

Creating an Object Design

Develop your technical skills. Imagine that you were a goldsmith in Persia, and you were asked to fashion a drinking vessel. Imagine, moreover, that the request was for an original design—something like no other drinking vessel seen before.

Complete a detailed pencil drawing of a cup with a handle. Make your drawing large enough to fill a 9 x 12-inch sheet of white drawing paper. Use shading to accent the details of your design and to emphasize its three-dimensional form.

PORTFOLIO

Write a paragraph telling how you fulfilled the challenge to create an original drinking vessel. Put it in your portfolio with your drawing.

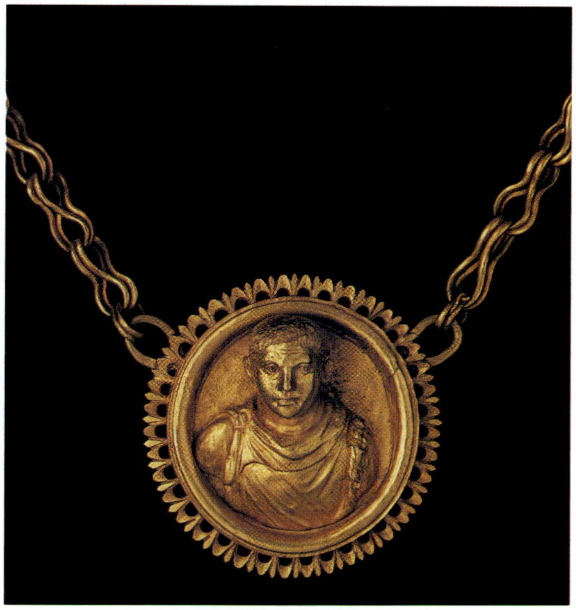

◆ **Figure 10–11** Compare the patterns on this object with those adorning the rhyton. How many objects can you identify in this tiny piece of art?

Roman. *Chain with a Portrait Medallion.* A.D. 238–243. Gold. 6.7 cm (2⅝″) in diameter. (Detail.) The Nelson-Atkins Museum of Art, Kansas City, Missouri. Purchase, Nelson Trust.

Studio Activity

Creating an Object Design

Tell students to give free reign to their imaginations in order to arrive at a truly original design. Emphasize the need for originality.

Team Building Activities

Divide the class into four or five groups. Pass out slips of paper that say either "for" or "against." Explain that each group is a museum committee formed to decide whether their museum should add the rhyton (illustrated in Figure 10–10) to their permanent collection. Each "committee" is to provide reasons why they are for or against the purchase of the rhyton. Tell groups to make specific references to features of the rhyton when giving their reasons. L1 ELL

3 Assess

Self-Assessment

Have students complete the **Check Your Understanding** questions on this page. Answers are provided below.

Reteaching

Ask students to brainstorm examples of vessels, explaining the function of each.

4 Close

Have students explain how the pendant in Figure 10–11 is an example of applied art.

Answers to Check Your Understanding

1. A vessel is a hollow utensil made to hold something. Some examples of vessels are a rhyton, a vase, and a pitcher.
2. Answers will vary. In one sense, it can be considered fine art because on its own it is pleasing to look at. However, it also serves a function as something to be worn, as part of one's costume or apparel. In that regard, it can be considered applied art.

Building a Clay Musical Instrument

(pages 194–195)
Lesson Time: 4 hours

1 Focus

Objectives

After completing this lesson, students will be able to:

- Demonstrate technical skills effectively by using clay to create a musical instrument in the form of a real or imaginary animal.
- Describe, analyze, interpret, and judge their clay object as both musical instrument and artwork.

SUPPLIES
Refer to **What You Will Need** in the Student Edition.

2 Teach

Motivator

Ask students to examine **Figure 10–12.** Discuss it as both art object and musical instrument. Point out the large fish-form of the work illustrated and discuss possible forms their own musical instruments might take.

Vocabulary

Inform students that there are several terms they will learn in this lesson. *Sound chamber* refers to the air pocket in the center of their musical instrument. *Windway* is the term used to describe the opening to the sound chamber through which one blows to produce sound. *Air vents* are holes that pierce the sound chamber.

LESSON 6

Building a Clay Musical Instrument

Applied art objects, as you have learned, are meant to serve an everyday function. The object in **Figure 10–12** goes a step further. It was designed to have two functions. The first, as the credit line reveals, was as a vessel. Can you guess its second function? Would it help you to know that its spout is adorned with finger holes, much like those found on a flute?

What You Will Learn

In this lesson, you will demonstrate technical skills effectively using a variety of art media and materials to produce a ceramic artwork. You will make your own musical wind instrument. Like the object in Figure 10–12, yours will be an example of **pottery**. This is *art, and the craft of making art, from clay.* Your instrument will not only create sound. It will also have the appearance of a real or imaginary bird, animal, fish, or person. You will use a variety of different textures to add interest to your instrument.

What You Will Need

- Sketch paper and pencil
- Water-based clay
- Clay modeling tools
- A fingernail file, coffee stirrer, or other flat instrument
- A round plastic drinking straw

What You Will Do

1. Make several sketches of animals that might serve as the shape of your pottery object. Choose your best sketch. Set it aside.
2. Make two clay pinch pots in the shape of bowls. The pots should be the same size. With a modeling tool, score—make shallow lines in—the lip of each pot. Add **slip**, *clay with enough added water to give it a runny, liquid consistency.* The slip will function as a kind of glue. Join the edges together firmly.
3. Lightly tap the resulting hollow clay sphere on your work surface. Shape the ball into the form that most resembles the body of the animal you have chosen. Use additional clay to fashion the details for your creature.

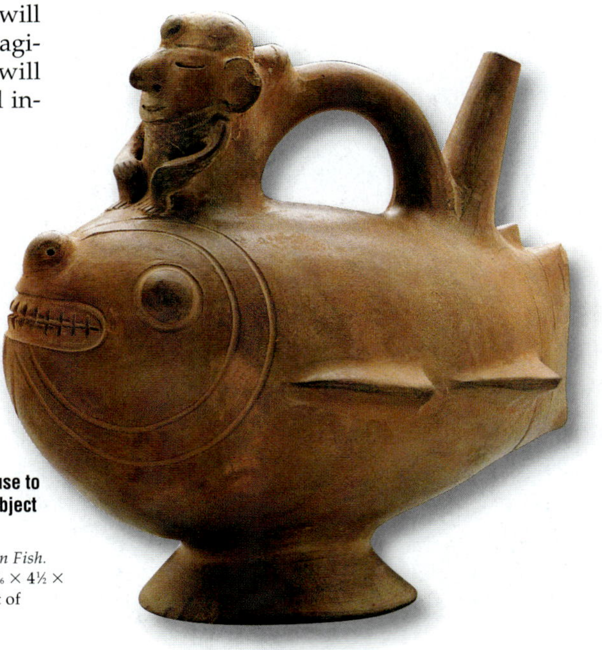

◆ **Figure 10–12** **What words would you use to describe this object? What feeling does this object summon up?**

Peru. *Spouted Vessel with Tubular Handle: Man on Fish.* 300–100 B.C. Ceramics. 18.7 × 11.4 × 22 cm (7⁵⁄₁₆ × 4½ × 8⅝″). Dallas Museum of Art, Dallas, Texas. Gift of Mrs. Nora Wise.

INCLUSION STRATEGIES

PHYSICALLY IMPAIRED For some students who are physically impaired, the task of making and joining the two pinch pots to create a sphere, as well as adjusting the windway and making the holes, may pose a challenge. In order for such students to more fully understand the separate steps involved in making the finished project, they might hold in their hands and examine a finished, fired clay musical instrument prior to making their own. They may need assistance in some of the more intricate steps of the project.

4. Choose a body feature to serve as the *windway.* This is the tube or channel of a musical instrument through which air is blown to produce sound. A tail, leg, or mouth will make a good windway.
5. With a fingernail file or coffee stirrer, push a flat hole through the windway. The hole should extend all the way into the body cavity, or *sound chamber.*
6. Push a plastic drinking straw into the opening to create a vertical shaft. This should run perpendicular, or at a right angle, to the windway. Returning to the flat instrument, angle the vertical clay wall opposite the windway.
7. Test the instrument at this stage by blowing into the opening. You should hear a whistle-like sound. If no sound comes out, adjust the clay tip opposite the windway until you can make a sound.
8. Pierce the sound chamber with the straw several times. This will create finger holes. You will want to place them where you can reach them easily with your fingers. Use the clay modeling tools to add small details and textures to the surface.
9. Allow your musical instrument to dry completely. Then, with your teacher's help, bake, or fire, the instrument in a **kiln**. This is *a special hot oven in which pottery objects are fired.* After firing, apply a glaze carefully. Make sure you do not cover the finger holes. Fire your object a second time.

Evaluating Your Work

- **Describe** Is the subject of your clay musical instrument recognizable?
- **Analyze** Did you use a variety of textures to add visual interest to your instrument?
- **Interpret** Is your creature pleasing to look at? Does the object produce sounds, and are these pleasing to the ear?
- **Judge** Is your work successful as an example of applied art?

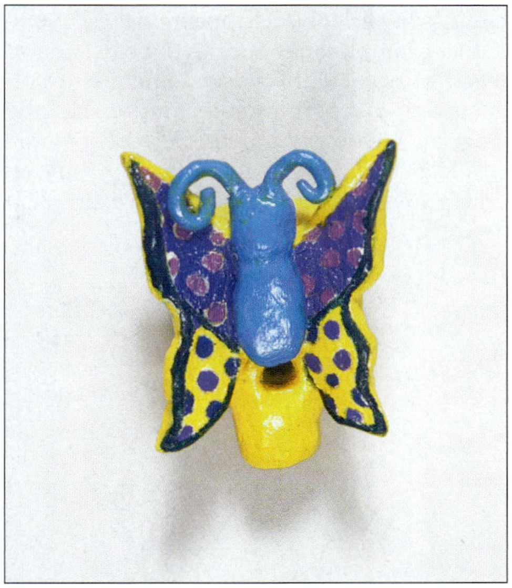

◆ **Figure 10–13** Student work. A musical instrument.

REFLECTIVE THINKING

Critical Evaluation. Analyze the original artworks of your peers. Examine the clay musical instrument they built and form conclusions about formal properties. For example, how did they use texture to create interest to their instrument? Does their pottery object function as a musical instrument?

Visual Art Journal

In your journal, describe in detail a variety of practical applications for design ideas. Apply these ideas as you plan your next art project.

Studio Skills

Demonstrate the clay hand-building process to form the two pinch pots. For each, use an amount of clay that fits neatly into the palm of the hand. Tell students to work *slowly* using thumbs and fingers. Show them how to score the edges and add slip to join the two pinch pots together. Demonstrate how the windway and air vents are made. Have students test the whistle, telling them that if it does not produce sound when wet, it will not work later when dry. L1 ELL

3 Assess

Peer Assessment

Have students analyze the clay musical instruments created by their peers to form conclusions about formal properties—the elements and principles of art.

Reteaching

In pairs, have students explain how their musical instruments work.

Enrichment

Appoint a team of students to conduct a search for information about sound instruments representing different cultures. Have them present their findings to the class and compare the different types of instruments. L2

4 Close

Have students demonstrate how their finished musical instruments make sounds.

MORE ABOUT...

CERAMICS Pottery is any object made from clay and is also the craft of making such objects. A word for both is *ceramics.* Before becoming a finished piece of pottery, clay takes six different forms:

- Plastic clay—clay that hold its shape.
- Slip—clay with enough water added to make it runny.
- Leather-hard clay—clay that is still damp but too hard to model.
- Greenware—dry clay.
- Bisqueware—fired pottery.
- Glazeware—pottery with a hard, glasslike finish.

LESSON 7

Decorative Arts

(pages 196–197)

1 Focus

Objectives

After completing this lesson, students will be able to:

- Define *jewelry.*
- Explain how a timepiece serves a dual purpose.
- Identify the influence of historical and political events in an artwork.

2 Teach

Motivator

Have students look at what they and their classmates are wearing. Ask if anything they are wearing could be classified as an adornment. Encourage them to point out earrings, belt buckles, watches, and necklaces. Explain that these items are simple objects of art made to be worn. These are objects labeled as jewelry.

Vocabulary

Explain that *châtelaine* is a French word that originally referred to the mistress of a castle or any large household. This woman wore an ornamental chain or clasp, usually at the waist. On the chain were the keys to the manse, a watch, and sometimes a small purse.

Decorative Arts

The success of applied art objects is not measured only in terms of beauty. A second yardstick is how well they do the job for which they were intended.

In this lesson, you will learn about objects whose job is to *adorn,* or decorate.

JEWELRY

Some art is made to be worn. Several examples of such objects appear on these pages. Other examples may adorn your ears, fingers, neck, or waist at this very moment. Such objects are grouped together under the label jewelry. **Jewelry** is *art, and the craft of making art, to be worn.* The pendant that you studied in Figure 10–11 on page 193 is an example of jewelry.

The earliest jewelry can be traced to the time of cave dwellers. These objects consisted mostly of shells or feathers strung together on woven leaves or vines. Since that time, the category of jewelry items has been expanded to include rings, earrings, necklaces and pins. Some, though not all, jewelry contains precious stones or metals.

Jewelry from the 1500s

Imagine that you are living in England during the late 1500s. You have been invited to a ball. At such gala events, you were likely to see numerous figures dressed up like the woman in **Figure 10–14.** Inspect this period portrait. How many jewels and baubles can you find glinting and sparkling on this grand lady's person? Notice that these adornments

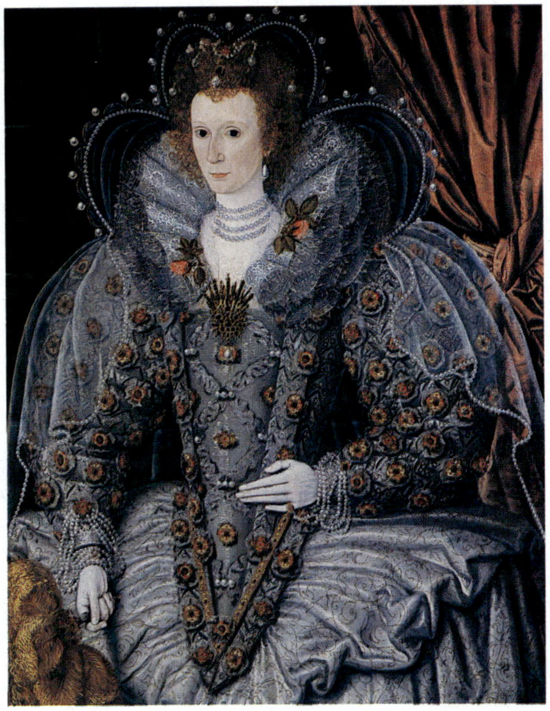

◆ **Figure 10–14** Describe how the artist used texture and pattern in the woman's dress.

Unknown British painter. *Portrait of a Noblewoman.* Late sixteenth century. Oil on wood. 113 × 88.3 cm (44½ × 34¾"). The Metropolitan Museum of Art, New York, New York. Gift of J. Pierpont Morgan, 1911.

MORE ABOUT...

JEWELRY IN TIME Prehistoric jewelry was probably worn for religious purposes or to show rank in the group. Crude necklaces and bracelets were made of bone, shells, feathers, and teeth. In the Bronze Age, people began using silver, copper, and bronze to shape ornamental objects. The ancient Egyptians believed that gemstones held magical powers, so gems were used in their headdresses, pendants, rings, brooches, and bracelets. The ancient Greeks preferred fine metalwork for their jewelry. In Europe in the 1500s, it was popular to weave precious gems into one's hair or sew them on to clothing.

are not limited to her splendid silk dress. Jeweled trinkets and pearls sparkle in her hair and on her ears, hands, and neck as well. How would you describe the look of this woman in all her splendor?

Jewelry from the 1700s

In Lesson 6, you learned that applied art objects serve a dual function. At least one item of jewelry shares this distinction. That item is a timepiece, or watch.

Such an object appears in **Figure 10–15**. The timepiece is the circular item at the very bottom of the photograph. The rest of the image is given over to a popular jewelry object of the day called a *châtelaine* (shaht-eh-**len**). This châtelaine contains a key, the watch, and a seal. Notice the repeating gemstone motif. Do you think this repetition adds harmony to the art object? How has the artist introduced variety?

Time & Place

Sixteenth-Century England

Historical connection. The sixteenth century was a period of great reform in England. During the first half of the century, King Henry VIII ruled the country. King Henry had Parliament pass a law declaring that the king, instead of the pope, headed the church in England. At the same time, a religious movement called the Reformation was spreading throughout Europe. The Reformation eventually led to Protestantism.

During the second half of the sixteenth century, Henry's daughter Elizabeth became the queen of England. Elizabeth I's reign is often referred to as England's Golden Age. It was a period of exploration, prosperity, military victory, and great literature. Look at **Figure 10–14**. How do the woman's clothing and jewelry reflect the prosperity of the time period? Compare and contrast Figures 10–14 and 8–2.

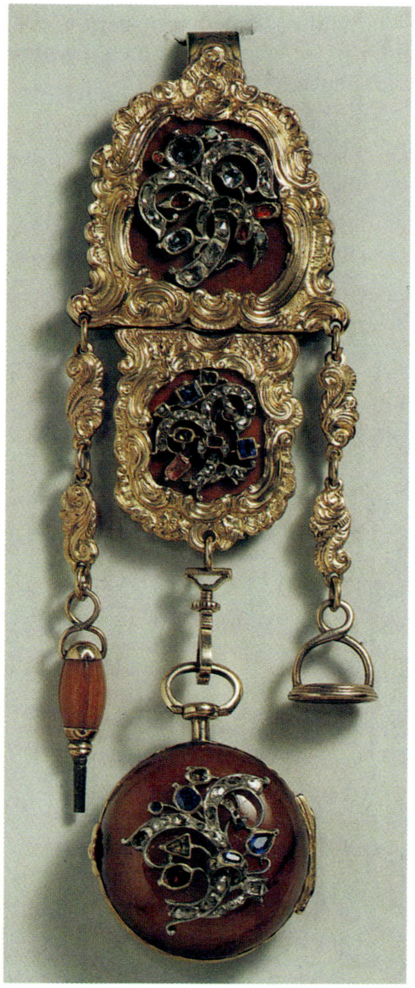

◆ **Figure 10–15** **This object was worn attached to a belt. What objects are suggested in these arrangements?**

German. *Watch and Châtelaine.* Eighteenth century, third quarter. Agate, gold, gemstone. 15.3 cm (6″). The Metropolitan Museum of Art, New York, New York. Collection of Giovanni P. Morosini, presented by his daughter, Giulia, 1932.

Check Your Understanding

1. What does the portrait in Figure 10–14 reveal about life in the 1500s?
2. What two functions are served by watches?

Time & Place

The woman's clothing and jewelry are very opulent and reveal the flourishing era of that time period. Both **Figures 10–14** and 8–2 are similar for their wealthy subjects, who also have the same type of demure expression.

Aesthetics

Ask students to compare the images in Figure 10–14 and **Figure 10–15.** In what way is the use of gems similar? In what way is it different? Does the fact that these objects are worn diminish their worth as art? Have students explain their responses.

3 Assess

Self-Assessment

Have students complete the **Check Your Understanding** questions on this page. Answers are provided below.

Enrichment

Divide students into two groups and assign one of the artworks in this lesson to each. Ask both groups to investigate why the work assigned to them has historical value. Have them use a variety of resource materials as they research the time and place of each artwork. Ask students to share their findings with the class.

4 Close

Have students name items of jewelry that serve a dual purpose.

Answers to Check Your Understanding

1. The portrait in Figure 10–14 reveals that there were social events that took place in the 1500s in which women wore highly ornamented dresses as well as splendid, sparkling jewelry in their hair and on their ears, hands, and necks.
2. Wristwatches function as timepieces. They also function as works of art.

Creating a Pendant

(pages 198–199)
Lesson Time: 90 minutes

1 Focus

Objectives

After completing this lesson, students will be able to:

- Demonstrate technical skills effectively by using a variety of art media to produce a design for a pendant.
- Describe, analyze, interpret, and judge their design.

Supplies
Refer to **What You Will Need** in the Student Edition.

2 Teach

Motivator

Discover what kinds of jewelry students like to wear. Have them study the jewelry items in **Figure 10–16.** Point out that the bolo-slide tie is a type of tie worn in the Southwest, but it was actually introduced from South America. A cord rather than cloth becomes the tie, and the decorative slide is made from precious metals and stones found in the Southwest and West—Arizona, New Mexico, Utah, California, and Nevada. Can students identify the figures in two of the slides? Besides a tie slide, what other ways could these jewelry forms be used?

Vocabulary

Review the term *relief,* a type of sculpture in which forms are slightly raised or project from a flat surface, and only viewed from the front.

LESSON 8

Creating a Pendant

Jewelry, like other art, varies from culture to culture. This is true not only of the specific kinds of items crafted but of their design. The three objects in **Figure 10–16** are bolo slides. You may have seen objects like these. They are decorative jewelry made to wear with string neckties.

Study these objects. Notice the geometric shapes. These are typical of rugs, baskets, pottery, and other art objects of native cultures of the Southwest. Can you identify the simplified figures in these pieces?

What You Will Learn

You will create a design for a pendant. You learned in Lesson 5 that a pendant is a jewelry item worn suspended from the neck on a string or chain. Like the bolo slides in Figure 10–16, your pendant will use geometric shapes. These will be cut from tagboard. Begin with a single simple shape. Then layer other smaller shapes on top to build a relief design. You will organize your work to create a center of interest by using contrasting geometric shapes.

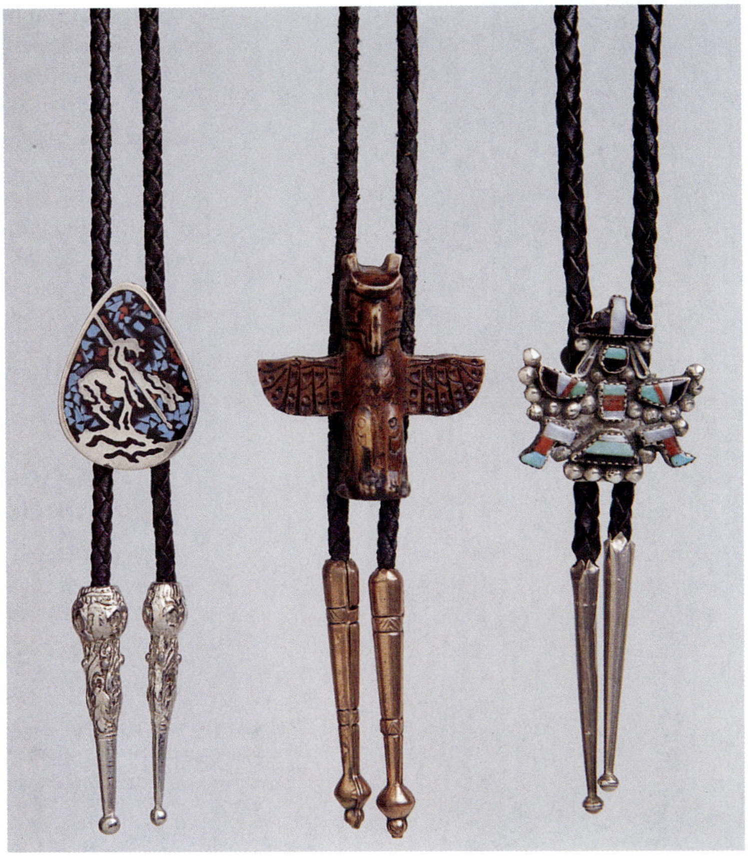

◆ **Figure 10–16** These bolo slides were crafted by Native American artisans. What figures or objects do you recognize?

Bolo Slides. Left: *Trail of Tears* (Colorado). Middle: *The Eagle* (Alaska). Right: *Yee, Sun Spirit* (Arizona). Contemporary. Silver, turquoise, coral, wood. Approx. 2.5–3.8 cm (1–1½″). Private Collection.

MORE ABOUT...

Jewelry Design of the Southwest Jewelry in the Southwest tradition used wrought, overlay, sand cast, or inlay techniques and followed traditional techniques until a few innovative artists began experimenting with gold and new methods in the 1950s. Tourist trade influenced the design of much Native American jewelry, rugs, and pottery. In about 1949, the Hickok Leather Company of Rochester introduced bolo-tie designs. They were based on the South American gaucho's string ties with ornaments. The handsome bolo-tie slides in Figure 10–16 are made from wood and silver inlaid with turquoise, coral, shell, and jet.

What You Will Need

- Sketch paper and pencil
- Tagboard scraps in a variety of sizes, ranging from approximately 2 inches to ⅜ inch on a side.
- Scissors
- White glue
- Paper towels
- Small stiff-bristle brush
- Foil paper or aluminum foil
- Cord or yarn

What You Will Do

1. Create several sketches of pendant designs. Your design should consist of layered geometric shapes.
2. Choose one of the largest tagboard scraps for the base. Following your design, cut the tagboard into a circle, oval, square, rectangle, or other geometric shape.
3. Layer smaller geometric shapes on top of the base. Attach the shapes with white glue. Carefully blot away any excess glue with a lightly dampened paper towel. Work little by little from larger shapes to smaller ones. Make small round shapes with a hole punch. Repeat similar shapes. Create a center of interest by using contrasting shapes or by introducing a pattern.
4. Use a stiff brush to cover the completed design with a layer of thin white glue. Carefully apply a sheet of silver or gold foil paper or aluminum foil. Using your finger, gently push the foil into the corners and creases of the design.
5. Fold back any foil paper edges that extend beyond the borders of the tagboard. Glue these to the back of your ornament. Attach cord or yarn to your pendant.

Evaluating Your Work

- **Describe** Describe the shapes and textures in your design. Identify the purpose of the jewelry.
- **Analyze** Explain how you organized the design to create a center of interest. What shape or patterns add contrast?
- **Interpret** Could your pendant be worn every day, or does it appear to be better suited for special events? Why?
- **Judge** Is your work a success? Explain why or why not.

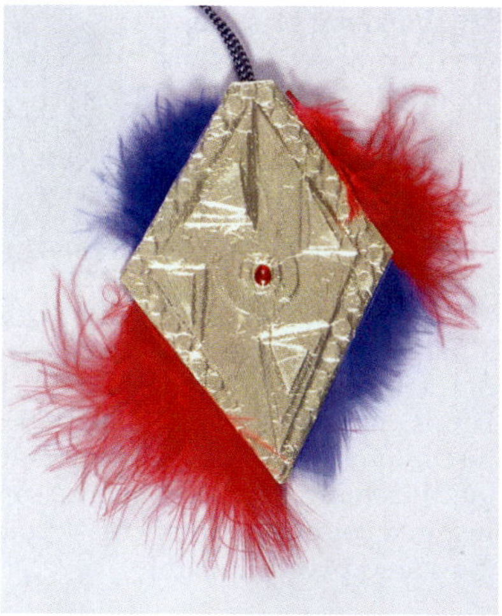

◆ **Figure 10–17** Student work. Pendant.

Computer Option

Produce an electronic media-generated version of your pendant. Choose from the Shape and Line tools and draw a large geometric shape with a thick line. Add smaller geometric shapes on top to layer the design. Create a center of interest by using a contrasting shape. Select the Color tool and a hue to match bronze, gold, or silver metal.

Art Online

For additional activities, visit our Web site at **art.glencoe.com**. There you will find:

- Artist Profiles
- Career Corner
- Interactive Games
- Student Art Gallery

Historical/Cultural Heritage

Native American and Inuit artists made these bolo slides in 1979. Have students investigate and discover what important art forms and styles are attributed to the Inuit and Native American tribe of their choice, what common natural materials are used by the group they choose, and what the purposes are of the artworks they focus on. Have them compare and contrast art forms from each culture. L2

3 Assess

Self-Assessment

Have students use **Evaluate Your Work** to conduct an in-progress critique of their pendants.

Reteaching

In pairs, have students identify the geometric shapes they used in their pendants. L1 ELL

Enrichment

Divide the class into small groups and assign each group a Native American tribe. Ask each group to research their tribe, finding out what kinds of jewelry are (and were) designed and worn by members of the tribe, and what purpose jewelry has in the tribe. Ask students to share their research, providing sketches of the jewelry or reproductions. L1 ELL

4 Close

Have students analyze each other's designs in terms of contrast, texture, and shape.

Resources Beyond the Classroom

Art Councils Area art councils make excellent partners in education. They can help raise awareness of the need for art education both in the classroom and outside of it. Artists and art patrons who are associated with art councils will usually donate time for instructing and educating students. Art councils sponsor such activities as art camps for students, arts and crafts workshops for children, and seminars and workshops for adults, including teachers. They may also be interested in cosponsoring student exhibits or hosting artist-student meetings.

Extraordinary Glass

1 Focus

Objectives

After completing this lesson, students will be able to:

- Draw and color a design for a stained-glass window.
- Compose a poem describing Tiffany's artwork.

2 Teach

Teaching the Feature

1. Let volunteers describe the works shown in the photographs. Ask: What makes this window and this lampshade special? What medium did the artist use to create these works?
2. Let students meet in cooperative groups to read and discuss the article. Have group members share and compare their impressions of Tiffany's work.

Activity

Ask students to imagine they are able to create their own stained-glass windows. Have them draw designs for these windows, using black crayon or marker to outline the shapes within the window and then color the spaces between the lines.

Extraordinary Glass

Captivating objects of color and shape

When is glass not just glass? When it was fashioned by Louis Comfort Tiffany. Tiffany was a decorator, craftsperson, and glassmaker who designed extraordinary items for the home. His glass lampshades and stained-glass windows were beautiful and functional.

Born in 1848, Louis Comfort Tiffany trained as a painter until he discovered the art of glass. His technical advances to the art of making glass objects were as important as his superb design work.

For centuries, glassmakers had placed pieces of glass within lead frames. Tiffany changed that by incorporating metal strips directly into his designs. Tiffany also invented his own glass in many colors. It is Tiffany's intense palette and finishes that make his lamps and vases so special. By 1900, Tiffany said that he could use 5,000 mixes of colors to reproduce "vast [and] teeming…nature." Nature's images and its colors inspired countless Tiffany masterpieces that shimmer, glow, and play with light.

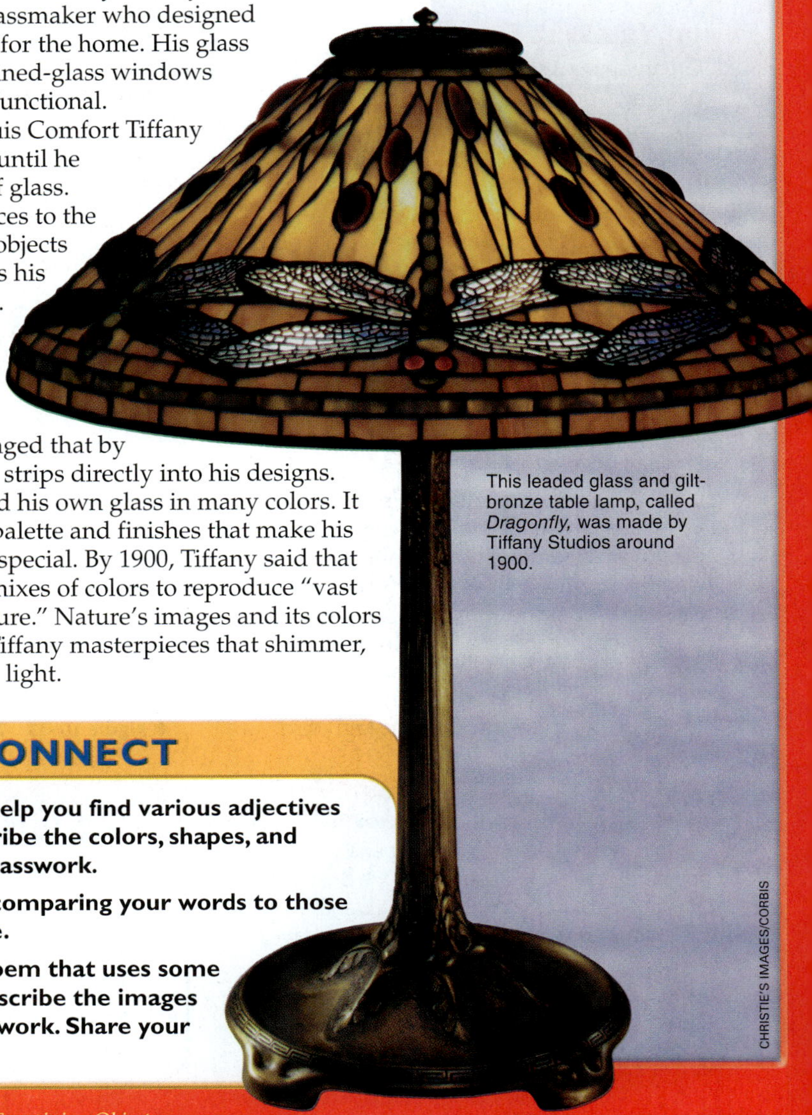

This leaded glass and gilt-bronze table lamp, called *Dragonfly*, was made by Tiffany Studios around 1900.

TIME TO CONNECT

- Use a thesaurus to help you find various adjectives and adverbs to describe the colors, shapes, and designs in Tiffany's glasswork.
- Expand your list by comparing your words to those found by a classmate.
- Draft and revise a poem that uses some of these words to describe the images found in Tiffany's artwork. Share your work with the class.

TIME TO CONNECT

Have students work in groups to generate lists of adjectives and adverbs. Students should use adjectives and adverbs appropriately to make their poems vivid and precise. As they write their poems, they should ask themselves these questions:

- What does this adjective or adverb contribute to the meaning or feeling of my poem?
- Should I replace this adjective or adverb with one that is more clear? If so, what word should I use?

Chapter 10 Review

BUILDING VOCABULARY

Number a sheet of paper from 1 to 9. After each number, write the term from the list that best matches each description below.

applied art	pottery
jewelry	slip
kiln	vessel
pendant	watercolorist
perceive	

1. Clay with enough added water to give it a runny, liquid consistency.
2. Art, and the craft of making art, to be worn.
3. A jewelry item worn suspended from the neck on a string or chain.
4. A painter who works in watercolor.
5. A hollow utensil made to hold something.
6. A special hot oven in which pottery objects are fired.
7. Works of art that are made to be useful as well as visually pleasing.
8. Art, and the craft of making art, from clay.
9. To become aware through the senses of the special nature of objects.

REVIEWING ART FACTS

Number a sheet of paper from 10 to 13. Answer each question in a complete sentence.

10. What events during her life prompted Georgia O'Keeffe to paint objects "larger than life"?
11. When were the first still lifes in the West produced? By whom were they produced?
12. Based on the objects shown in the still life in Figure 10–7 on page 189, what can we suppose to be true about the geography and culture of Japan?
13. Name two ways of judging applied art.

CROSS-CURRICULUM CONNECTIONS

14. **Language Arts.** Imagine that you are a poet in China during the 1300s. Your friend, Lik'an, has just completed a scroll painting of bamboo (see Figure 10–3 on page 185). Write a poem that sums up the feeling expressed by the painting.
15. **Language Arts.** Look back at Figures 10–7 and 10–8. Write a descriptive report comparing and contrasting the set of objects, colors, and media.

Web Museum Activity

Kimbell Art Museum, Fort Worth, Texas

In this chapter, you learned about the ways artists perceive objects and about art objects from various cultures and times.

Go to **art.glencoe.com** and take a closer look at some art objects by clicking on the Kimbell Art Museum link. You will discover the meaning and history behind the African and Oceanic objects from the museum's collection.

Select three different objects and describe their symbolism. What type of medium was used? Compare and contrast the objects you selected with what you learned in this chapter.

Web Museum Activity

Before you have students go online, visit the Web site to preview the museum's online content, collection, and any online exhibit that may be of interest. Student's responses will vary depending on the artworks they selected, but should include a description of the objects' symbolism and the art medium used. Responses should also reveal an understanding of this chapter's content.

ANSWERS TO Chapter 10 Review

Building Vocabulary

1. slip
2. jewelry
3. pendant
4. watercolorist
5. vessel
6. kiln
7. applied art
8. pottery
9. perceive

Reviewing Art Facts

10. During the early twentieth century, the pace of life quickened. O'Keeffe feared that people were moving too fast to notice the beauty in nature. She therefore made her paintings as large and attention-getting as the skyscrapers erected during this era.
11. They were produced as early as 2400 B.C. by the Greeks.
12. We can assume that the nation has a considerable seacoast and that shellfish play an important role in the Japanese diet.
13. Applied art is judged both on its aesthetic merits (beauty) and on its usefulness, or how well it functions.

Cross-Curriculum Connection

14. Students' poems will vary.
15. Reports will vary, but should mention that the differences include the media, the cultural clues evident in the two works, and the differences in style.

Chapter 11 *Recording Events*

Chapter Resources

Features	Standards for Chapter: National	Standards for Chapter: State/Local	Reproducible Masters
Quick Write *page 203* TIME ART SCENE "Photo Finish" *page 220* ***Web Museum Activity*** *page 221*	**1.** (a, b) **2.** (a, b, c) **3.** (a, b) **4.** (a, b, c) **5.** (a, b, c) **6.** (a, b)		Guided Reading and Practice 11–1 Studio Activity 11–2, 11–5 Enrichment Activity 11–3, 11–9 Application Activity 11–4, 11–6 Historical and Cultural Heritage 11–7 Cross-Curriculum Activity 11–8 Lesson Plans

Lesson Resources

Lessons	Standards per Lesson: National	Standards per Lesson: State/Local	Reproducible Masters
1 ***The Media of Visual Reporting*** *(pages 204–205)*	5b, 6b		Studio Activity 11–2 Enrichment Activity 11–3
2 ***Drawing a Sporting Event in Action*** *(pages 206–207)*	1a, 1b, 2a, 3a		Application Activity 11–4
3 ***The Artist as Historian*** *(pages 208–209)*	1a, 1b, 4b, 5a		Studio Activity 11–5 Application Activity 11–6
4 ***Drawing a Cartoon*** *(pages 210–211)*	1a, 1b, 2a, 3b		
5 ***Recording Exploration*** *(pages 212–213)*	4a, 4c, 6a		Historical and Cultural Heritage 11–7
6 **ART & SOCIAL STUDIES** *(pages 214–215)*	5c, 6a, 6b		
7 ***Advances in Visual Reporting*** *(pages 216–217)*	1a, 1b, 4c, 6b		Cross-Curriculum Activity 11–8
8 ***Making a Video Documentary*** *(pages 218–219)*	1a, 1b, 2a, 2c, 3a		Enrichment Activity 11–9

Assessment	Technology
Chapter Test 11–10 Portfolio and Assessment Techniques	Artsource Performing Arts Package, Vocalworks (Audio CD Track 9) National Museum of Women in the Arts Interactive Lesson Planner Fine Art Transparency CC–11 *Hmong Story Cloth* by Chaing Xiong Fine Art Transparency 11 *Building More Stately Mansions* by Aaron Douglas

Activities/Features
Meet the Artist: Jacob Lawrence
Evaluating Your Work Portfolio Ideas Art Online
Studio Activity: Recording a Historical Event
Evaluating Your Work Reflective Thinking Visual Art Journal
Time & Place: Mississippi River Exploration
Make the Connection
Studio Activity: Planning a Story Board
Evaluating Your Work Studio Option Visual Art Journal

KEY TO ABILITY LEVELS

Teaching strategies have been coded.

- L1 Activities for all students; teacher direction required
- L2 Activities for average to above-average students; some teacher direction needed
- L3 Activities for students able and willing to work independently
- ELL English Language Learner activities

FEATURED ARTISTS

- J. A. Holzer
- Kevin Kallaugher
- Jacob Lawrence
- Emanuel Leutze
- Marjorie Phillips

FINE ART PRINTS

Fine Art Print 17, *The Return of Ulysses* by Romare Bearden

Timesaving Technology

Interactive Lesson Planner

Make planning easy. Use this interactive software to organize your week, month, semester, or year and access all *Introducing Art* reproducible resources.

KEY TO LESSON RESOURCES

- Narrative Lesson
- Studio Lesson

Chapter 11

Recording Events

(pages 202–221)

Chapter Overview

In this chapter, students will explore the efforts and techniques artists have used over time and among different cultures to record events. Students will also have an opportunity to learn more about photography as an art form. In addition, they will create several works of their own that capture noteworthy events and activities.

Discussing the Artwork

Focus On ◆ **Figure 11–1** Considered one of the greatest American painters in the twentieth century, Jacob Lawrence used his work to depict the political and social struggles that African Americans endured throughout American history. Ask students to identify the influence of historical and political events in this artwork. The painting in Figure 11–1, *Strike,* was created to commemorate Jackie Robinson's integration into Major League Baseball. This was a major turning point in the history of American professional sports to include an African American in the baseball league. A closer look reveals that all the characters, players and fans alike, are African American.

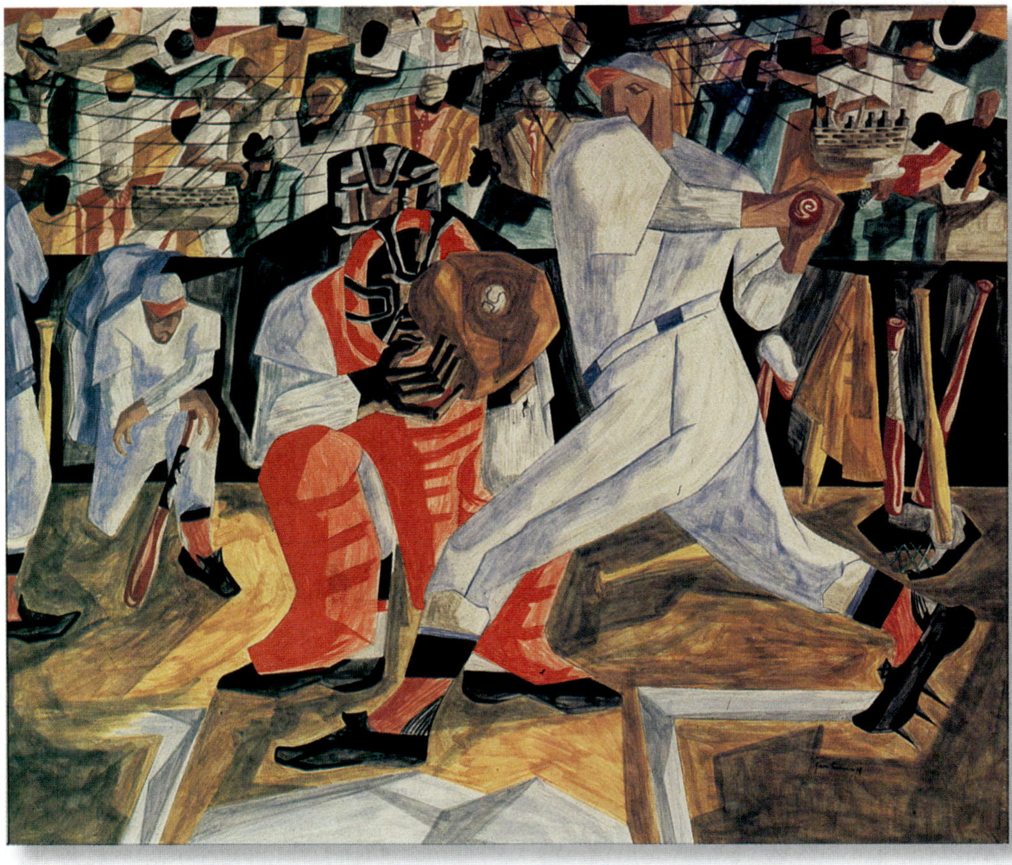

Focus On ◆ **Figure 11–1** **Explain how the artist has created movement in this painting. How do the elements of color and shape add to the excitement of this painting?**

Jacob Lawrence. *Strike.* 1949. Tempera on Masonite. 50.8 × 61 cm (20 × 24″). The Howard University Gallery of Art, Washington, D.C. Permanent collection.

ART SOURCE

Linking to the Performing Arts

Music Variety is a principle of art that applies to all art disciplines. Without variety, any work of art would be monotonous. It would be difficult to remain engaged because our minds would lose the stimulation that keeps us involved. In a reenactment of a radio program from the 1940s, *Vocalworks* brings to life the mood of the times by using a variety of segments and voices. Have students read how *Vocalworks* applies variety to their music in the **Performing Arts Handbook** on page 320. To enrich student understanding, play the audio CD (track 9) in the **Performing Arts Package.**

Chapter 11

Recording Events

"*When the subject is strong, simplicity is the only way to treat it.*"

—Jacob Lawrence (1917–2000)

Life is filled with events that impact us for better or worse. Some events affect people on a national or even global scale, such as wars or natural disasters. Others, like team championships or birthdays, affect individuals or smaller groups. We can capture these events in different forms of media.

In this chapter, you will explore and experiment with some of these media. You will learn about the various ways in which artists have recorded different personal and historical events.

After completing this chapter, you will be able to:

- Describe various art media and techniques that have been used to capture events.
- Compare how artists of different times and cultures have recorded events.
- Define *photography* and trace the development of this art form.
- Create several works of art that record personal and historic events.

Quick Write

Interpreting the Quote
Read the quote and look at **Figure 11–1.** In what ways do you think Lawrence used simplicity to depict his subject?

Key Terms

photography
gouache
caricature
frieze
mosaic
video documentary
story board
videographer
pan

Quick Write

Interpreting the Quote
Have students read the quote and complete the Quick Write activity. Student responses will vary, but may include that Lawrence used bright colors and geometric forms in this painting to depict his subject with simplicity. Lawrence tells stories and records events using flat, bold shapes, bright colors, and geometric patterns.

Chapter Motivator

Bring in several newspapers and newsmagazines and ask students to find examples of recorded events. Discuss the kinds of images that can be used to record events and tell students that, in this chapter, they will be learning about a variety of media and techniques used by artists to capture different events.

Art Online

Visit **art.glencoe.com**, the Web site for Glencoe's art programs. This site is designed to help you prepare for your classes and learn about the various opportunities in the art community. Explore the many teacher resources the site has to offer, such as:

- Arts Education Resources
- Galleries and Cultural Resources
- Professional Development Articles
- Teacher's Lounge

National Standards for Arts Education

This chapter addresses the following National Standards for the Visual Arts:

1. (a, b) **4.** (a, b, c)
2. (a, b, c) **5.** (a, b, c)
3. (a, b) **6.** (a, b)

The Media of Visual Reporting

(pages 204–205)

1 Focus

Objectives

After completing this lesson, students will be able to:

- Define *photography* as an art form.
- Understand that artists record events using photography and other media.
- Define the medium *gouache.*

2 Teach

Motivator

Ask students to list inventions that have changed our lives. If possible, bring in an old camera; open it and show students the lens and the aperture (the adjustable lens that lets in light). Explain that the lens focuses on the subject while the aperture opens to let in much light on a dark day or little light on a bright day. The shutter opens to expose the film in the camera. To develop film, you must have controlled conditions to darken a room. Use a yellow or red bulb to illuminate the darkroom. A photo supply store can provide the photosensitive paper and the toner for developing the film.

Vocabulary

This lesson presents many new terms. Ask volunteers to take one term, find its definition, and write it on prepared 4 x 6-inch index cards (writing the terms on one set of cards and the definitions on the other). Play a game of connecting terms and definitions.

LESSON 1

The Media of Visual Reporting

In a way, artists who record events are like newspaper reporters. Like reporters, their goal is to get the whole story and to report the facts accurately and thoroughly. Like reporters, artists always seek out an interesting angle.

Unlike reporters, however, artists are not limited to words when capturing events. Rather, they have at their disposal a wide range of tools. In this chapter, you will learn about some of those tools. You will explore the media of visual reporting.

Photography

Open any newspaper or magazine today, and you are apt to see photographs. This wasn't always so. As an art form, **photography**—*the art of making images by exposing a chemically treated surface to light*—is in its infancy. The first photographs were produced just over 150 years ago.

Photograph of an Event

Throughout its brief history, photography has been a key tool of the visual reporter.

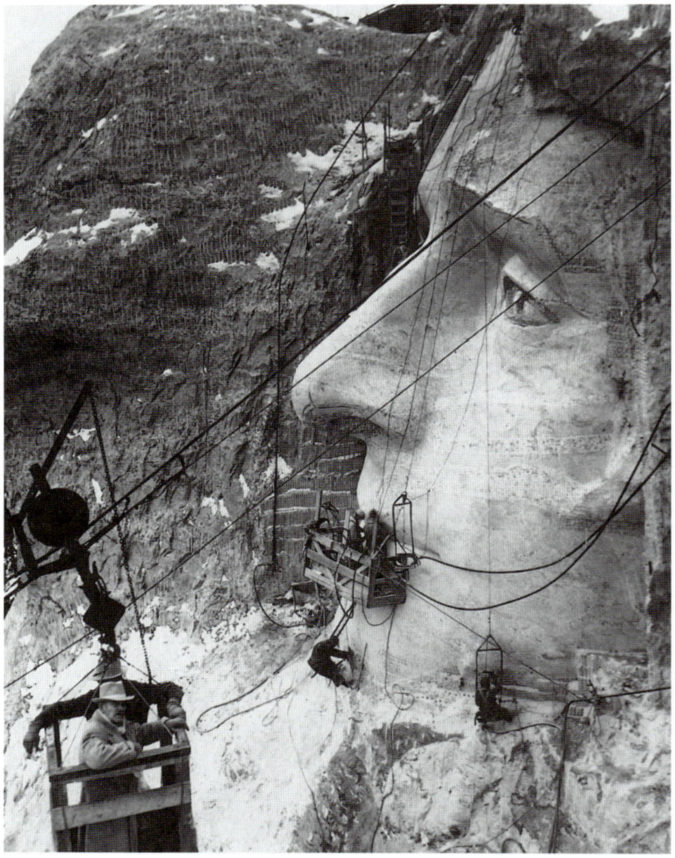

◆ **Figure 11–2** After Gutzon Borglum died, his son, Lincoln, took over this project. The last sculpture, of Theodore Roosevelt, remains unfinished to this day.

Workers on Mt. Rushmore. Photograph. Undated. Mt. Rushmore, South Dakota.

INCLUSION STRATEGIES

Physically Impaired For students who are physically impaired, drawing may be difficult. Photography can be a fulfilling activity and a source of pride and achievement. Investigate whether your school's Special Education service department has adapted devices that could enable students who are physically impaired to use a camera. Camera holders to attach a camera to a wheelchair and touch pads for shutter release are available or can be devised. Self-focusing cameras can help students with the focusing process. Always urge students, and especially those who tend to act impulsively, to carefully consider the composition of their photos.

Examine the compelling photograph in **Figure 11–2**. Like any good reporter, the photographer has answered the "four W's" of journalism—*who, what, when,* and *where.* Look carefully at the photo. The *who* is a crew of workers under the guidance of sculptor Gutzon Borglum. The *when* is 1937, the *where,* a mountaintop in the Black Hills of South Dakota. The *what* is a giant bust of a United States president carved out of the mountain's natural granite face.

Notice that the photographer has raised a fifth question—*how* to get the most interesting "angle." His answer was to take a personal risk and position himself on a rocky ledge a mile high in the sky.

Painting

An event no less dramatic is recorded in the painting in **Figure 11–3**. The *what, when,* and *where* are noted in the credit line below the artwork. The *who* is clear from the uniforms and batons. Study the expression on the faces of the front runners. Observe their body language. This is no ordinary relay race. It is a run for the Olympic gold medal. Each sprinter is searching for that burst of energy that will propel him forward across the finish line first.

Look again at the credit line below the picture, this time at the medium. That medium, **gouache (gwash)**, is *a form of watercolor that uses non-clear pigments.* Gouache creates flatter, more intense colors than normal watercolor paints. How do the flat areas of color in this painting help convey the intensity of the moment?

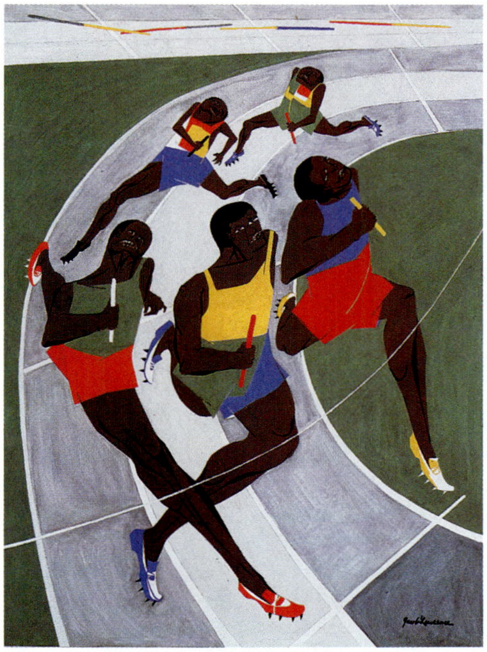

◆ **Figure 11–3** **The artist has used *abstraction* to record this event. Notice how he has simplified the shapes.**

Jacob Lawrence. *Study for the Munich Olympic Games Poster.* 1971. Gouache. 90.1 × 86.6 cm (35½ × 27″). Seattle Art Museum, Seattle, Washington. Purchased with funds from P.O.N.C.H.O.

Meet the Artist

Jacob Lawrence (1917–2000)

Cultural connection. Jacob Lawrence was a storyteller. Instead of using words, however, he used his paintings to tell stories about the lives of African Americans. Born in New Jersey in 1917, Lawrence grew up in Harlem—a section of New York City. In the mid-1930s, he began painting scenes of street life in Harlem. Lawrence focused on social concerns, including racism and discrimination, faced by African Americans during that time. He often used vivid colors in his work (see **Figure 11–3**). Although he later moved away from Harlem and became an art professor, Lawrence continued to paint until his death at age 82.

To learn more about Lawrence and his work, click on Artist Profiles at **art.glencoe.com**.

Check Your Understanding

1. In what way are artists, who record events, similar to newspaper reporters?
2. Each of the artworks on these pages captures a dramatic moment. Explain how each one succeeds.

Meet the Artist

Jacob Lawrence

Ask students to identify the influence of historical events in **Figure 11–3.** Lawrence is best known for his paintings of the history and struggles of African Americans. All the subjects in this painting and the one in Figure 11–1 are African American.

Aesthetics

Obtain books from the library for students on the subject of photographers from various cultures of the twentieth century. Note that they have many different approaches to photography and deal with many different subjects. Find photographs by Edward Weston (1886–1958), for example, whose elegant images of sand dunes, peppers, and many close-up forms of nature are considered among the classic works of photography.

3 Assess

Self-Assessment

Have students complete the **Check Your Understanding** questions on this page. Answers are provided below.

Reteaching

Have students explain the four W's of journalism shown in **Figure 11–2.** L1

4 Close

Ask students to discuss what they have learned about photography that will affect the way they look at photographs of events.

Answers to Check Your Understanding

1. Artists who record events are like newspaper reporters because, like reporters, the artists try to report the facts accurately and thoroughly. Like reporters, too, they seek out an interesting angle.
2. **Figure 11–2** captures a dramatic moment during the creation of Mt. Rushmore. The artwork succeeds in showing up close the danger and scope of the task. **Figure 11–3** captures a climactic moment of the Olympics in 1972. This artwork succeeds in communicating the intensity of the struggle of the runners to summon the strength and energy to win the race.

LESSON 2

Drawing a Sporting Event in Action

(pages 206–207)
Lesson Time: 2 hours 30 minutes

1 Focus

Objectives

After completing this lesson, students will be able to:

- Demonstrate technical skills effectively by using a variety of art materials to produce a drawing of a sporting event in action.
- Describe, analyze, interpret, and judge their artwork.

SUPPLIES
Refer to **What You Will Need** in the Student Edition.

2 Teach

Motivator

Review with students the techniques used in gesture drawing. See Chapter 3, Lesson 2, pages 44–45; or Technique Tip 1, page 281. Analyze the photographs that include a variety of men's and women's sports.

Many times the camera angle causes exaggeration of a gesture. Discuss how students can do this themselves as they draw.

Vocabulary

Ask volunteers to define concepts encountered in this lesson, such as *perspective, point of view, exaggeration, composition, overlapping,* and *proportion.* Refer them to the Glossary/Glosario, if necessary.

LESSON 2

Drawing a Sporting Event in Action

Look back at the painting in Figure 11–3 on page 205. Much of the drama can be traced to the subject matter—a foot race. **Figure 11–4** records another sporting event. It, too, is filled with intense action. Study this painting. Can you identify the event without looking at the title? Notice the feeling of movement suggested by the repeated shapes of the fans dotting the grandstand. Observe the abundant use of diagonals. Even if you've never attended a baseball game, you can sense the excitement as pitcher and batter prepare to compete.

WHAT YOU WILL LEARN

In this lesson, you will create your own artwork based on a sporting event. Begin by gathering magazine or newspaper photographs of baseball, basketball, or football games. Then select a sport. You will do a gesture drawing of a model in an action pose similar to one in a photo. Add background details based on the setting in the picture. Use bright colors in the foreground, dull colors in the background. Include diagonal lines and repetition to give a sense of movement to your drawing.

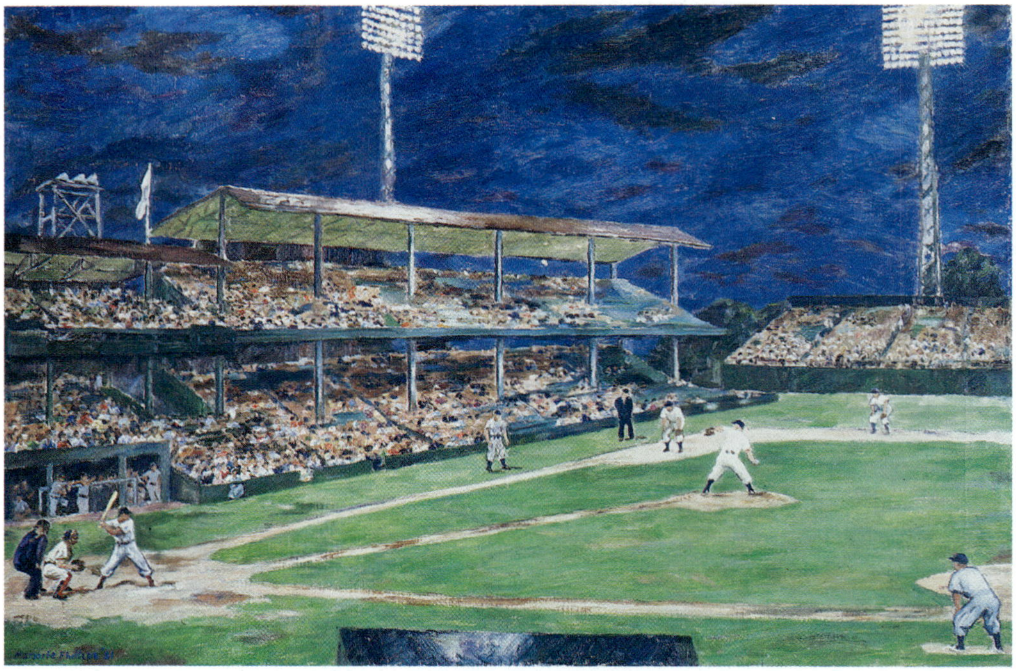

◆ **Figure 11–4** How many diagonal lines can you indentify in this painting? What objects have been repeated?

Marjorie Phillips. *Night Baseball.* 1951. Oil on canvas. 61.6 × 91.4 cm (24¼ × 36″). The Phillips Collection, Washington, D.C. Acquired c. 1951.

TEACHER TO TEACHER

FIGURE DRAWING Improving students' figure-drawing skills is a matter of encouragement and providing time for them to practice. Include exercises that help students master the use of proportion. Have students begin with quick gesture drawings or blind contour drawing as warm-ups. Encourage students to keep a sketchbook. Have them date drawings so they can see their progress. Occasionally, hold informal critiques so students receive constructive feedback and can correct recurring problems. It is important to get students into the habit of regularly drawing to improve their skills.

What You Will Need

- Photographs of sporting events
- Pencils and sketch paper
- White drawing paper, 12 x 18 inches
- Fine-tipped black felt marker
- Colored markers, charcoal, or colored drawing pencils

What You Will Do

1. Study the photographs you have gathered. Look for examples that show exciting action. Study the gestures and other body language of the athletes. Note the appearance and fixtures of the stadium or arena pictured.
2. Take turns posing with a fellow student. Ask your model to assume a pose similar to one in the picture. On sketch paper, do several rapid gesture drawings of your model.
3. Transfer your best sketch to white drawing paper. Still using pencil, add foreground and background details. Foreground details should include a uniform for your athlete and equipment. Background details should include crowds of fans and features of the setting. Include as many diagonals as you can.
4. With a fine-tipped black marker, retrace important contour lines. Use color to complete your drawing. Choose markers, charcoal, or colored drawing pencils. Consider bright colors that capture the mood of the game.

Evaluating Your Work

- **Describe** What sporting event does your work show? What moment in the event have you captured? What details of the setting have you included?
- **Analyze** Have you included diagonal lines? Have you used bright colors?
- **Interpret** Does you work communicate a sense of vivid action and movement?
- **Judge** Is your work successful? What would you do next time to increase the excitement of the sporting event?

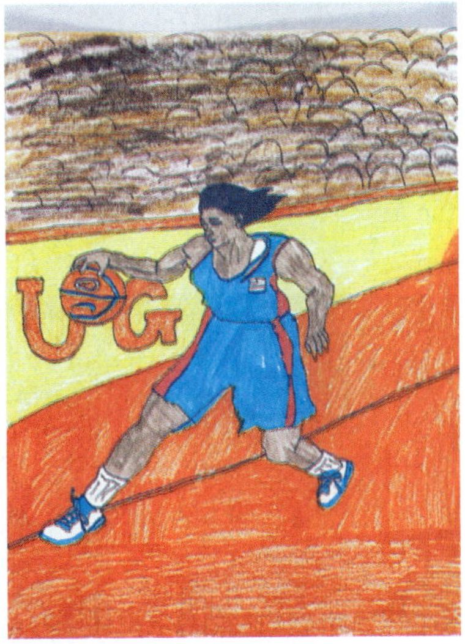

◆ **Figure 11–5** Student work. A sporting event.

PORTFOLIO IDEAS

To evaluate a project from your portfolio, begin by asking yourself questions such as:

- Does this artwork meet the assignment requirements?
- Does this artwork demonstrate how I have grown as an artist?
- What improvements could I make?

Art Online

For additional activities, check out our Web site at **art.glencoe.com**. There you will also find:

- Artist Profiles
- Career Corner
- Museum Web Links
- Student Art Gallery

Team Building Activity

Divide the class into groups of three or four. Distribute a variety of examples of illustration from magazines. Ask each group to compare and critique the various techniques used. Have each group decide why or why not the techniques are successful and take turns sharing their findings with the rest of the class. L1 ELL

Art Criticism

Bring in children's magazine illustrations and illustrated nonfiction children's books and have students compare the two kinds of illustration. Discuss the styles and techniques used in the books. How are they different from the magazine illustrations? Which techniques are most successful? Have students explain why they think one approach is more successful than another. L1

3 Assess

Self-Assessment

Have students use **Evaluating Your Work** to conduct an in-progress critique of their gesture drawing.

Reteaching

Encourage students to use their sketchbooks to improve their perceptual skills. Have them illustrate action-oriented themes using family members as their subjects.

4 Close

Let students work with peers to analyze their drawings. Have them evaluate the gesture drawings in terms of action and movement. L1 ELL

DEVELOPING A PORTFOLIO

Teacher Feedback Positive teacher feedback can be very encouraging for students. Keeping a portfolio of work over a period of time and monitoring one's growth is enlightening for students. Your written comments can inspire students to do so much more. Your challenge in the review process is to motivate students to pursue standards of good, thoughtful artwork. Established guidelines offer a framework for this, and the written reflections play a supporting role. Feedback can include recognition of demonstrated strengths in the portfolio, areas for future focus, and recognition of specific examples that stand out.

The Artist as Historian

(pages 208–209)

1 Focus

Objectives

After completing this lesson, students will be able to:

- Understand the role of the artist in recording historical events.
- "Read" the artist's message expressed by selection and emphasis.
- Identify the influence of historical and political events in artworks.
- Demonstrate technical skills effectively using a variety of art materials to produce a drawing of a traditional event.

SUPPLIES

- Pencils and sketch paper
- Newspapers
- White drawing paper
- Colored pencils, markers, or oil pastels

2 Teach

Motivator

Discuss the role of the artist in this age of photographic imagery and video and the immediacy of the media. Lead students to find examples of the special contribution artists can make, as in the roles of courtroom artists and law-enforcement artists.

LESSON 3

The Artist as Historian

"Today's news," someone once noted, "is tomorrow's history." Artists have long been mindful of this bit of wisdom. For centuries, they have used their talents and various tools to record events of the past and history in the making. In this lesson, you will examine some of the events they have captured in their art.

PAST EVENTS

Before the age of photography, portraits were used to provide "visual information" about leaders and celebrities. The painting in **Figure 11–6** provides another kind of historical record. Do you recognize the fourth figure from the left? He was a great military strategist who later became our nation's first president—George Washington.

In this page from history, General Washington is leading his troops across the Delaware River. The time of year is indicated by large chunks of ice around which the oar operators carefully maneuver. You might wonder why the party is venturing out under such frigid conditions. The answer is that they are planning a surprise attack on the British troops on the opposite shore. Notice that Washington stands taller than any other figure in the painting. The only object rising higher is the American flag. Observe that the diagonal lines of the oars and the flag lend movement to the scene. What do you think might have been the artist's reasons for

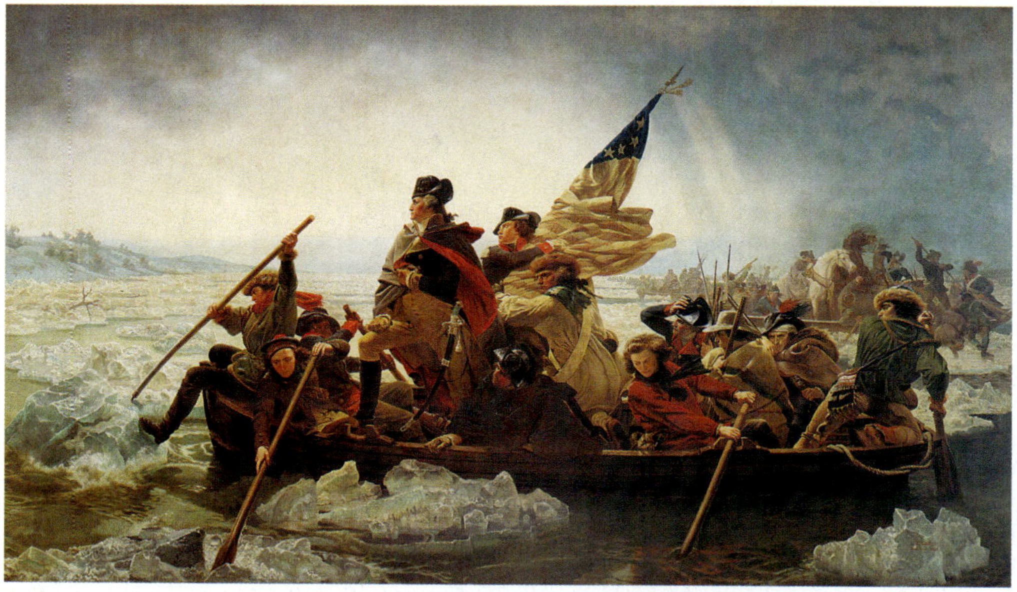

◆ **Figure 11–6** **Identify the influence of historical events in this painting. What details do you notice?**

Emanuel Leutze. *Washington Crossing the Delaware.* 1851. Oil on canvas. 378.5 × 647.7 cm (149 × 255"). The Metropolitan Museum of Art, New York, New York. Gift of John Stewart Kennedy, 1897.

CURRICULUM CONNECTIONS

SOCIAL STUDIES During the American Revolution, the fledgling Continental Army was poorly outfitted for the struggle for independence. On Christmas night, 1776, for example, when Washington led his forces across the Delaware to Trenton, many of his troops were suffering from frostbite and malnutrition. At Valley Forge, over 2,500 troops died of starvation or disease. Somehow Washington convinced his ragtag army to continue on. Have students locate other artworks depicting other events of the American Revolution.

recording the scene this way? How would you describe the future president's posture as he leads a nation-to-be to its destiny?

Recent Events

The tragedy of September 11, 2001, moved some art students in Houston, Texas to exercise their freedom of expression as Americans. They spoke loudly and vividly in the language of art as they created *The Eleventh Day* (**Figure 11–7**), a 12 x 30-foot mural on canvas.

Angry and confused over the events of 9/11, students were encouraged to express their feelings through art, by drawing and painting what they felt. They were inspired by Picasso's painting *Guernica,* as an example of how artists express their anger and frustrations over events they cannot control. The students chose to use the language of art to speak their thoughts, feelings, hopes, and dreams in response to the nation's tragedy. What feelings or mood does this mural convey?

Studio Activity

Recording a Historical Event

Identify the influence of historical events. With a group of students, brainstorm other events in national or local history. Illustrate themes from traditional events. Possibilities include the landing of the pilgrims at Plymouth and the founding of your own town or city. Look in an encyclopedia or similar resource to learn the *who, what, where,* and *when* of the event. Sketch the event you have selected. Complete your drawing using colored pencils, colored markers, or oil pastels.

PORTFOLIO

In several paragraphs, compose a description of your event and put it in your portfolio with your artwork.

Check Your Understanding

1. Which figure stands tallest in Figure 11–6?
2. What details and properties do you notice in Figure 11–7?

◆ **Figure 11–7** Encouraged to work in the style of Picasso, students were restricted to a palette of gray tones. How does this color scheme add to the painting's message?

Student work. *The Eleventh Day.*

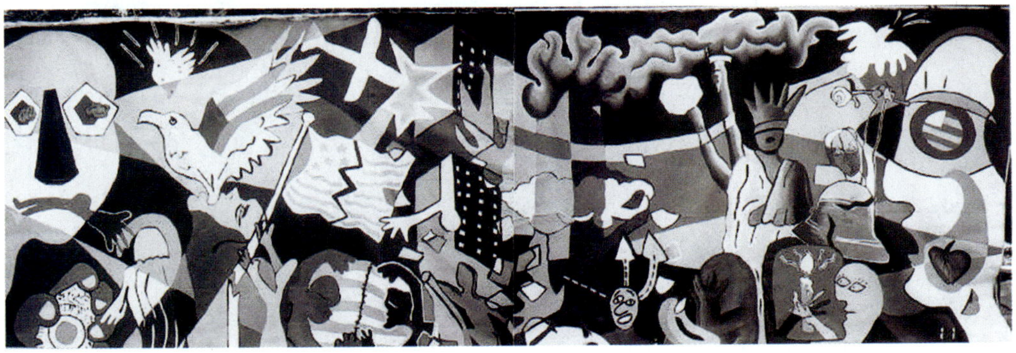

Answers to Check Your Understanding

1. George Washington stands tallest in the painting. The artist probably did this to emphasize the importance of George Washington as the leader of the troops and as the future president of a great nation.
2. Figure 11–7 depicts a very emotional portrayal of the events of September 11, 2001. The gray color scheme conveys this, as do all the images in the painting, such as the burning towers, the torn flag, and the blindfolded Statue of Liberty. Have students study the painting more closely and look for more details.

Aesthetics

There are many ways to represent current events for practical applications. Consider with your students the immediate rush of T-shirts, posters, framed photos, and so on that flood the market the moment a team wins a championship, the day a candidate announces he or she is running for an important political office, or at the release of a "hit" movie. Have students describe in detail design ideas used to promote a current event. L1

Art Criticism

Have students work with partners to evaluate the drawings they did of a historical event. Discuss their point of emphasis and the ways they kept that focus. Have them analyze each other's use of line, shape, and direction. L1 ELL

3 Assess

Self-Assessment

Have students complete the **Check Your Understanding** questions on this page. Answers are provided below.

Reteaching

In pairs, have students read to each other their descriptions of their events. Have them evaluate whether the four W's are clearly stated. L1

4 Close

Ask students to discuss ways in which artists help "capture" and interpret historical events.

Drawing a Cartoon

(pages 210–211)
Lesson Time: 60 minutes

1 Focus

Objectives

After completing this lesson, students will be able to:

- Understand the use of caricature or exaggeration to express an idea.
- Select significant features to symbolize an idea.
- Explain the Greek myth of Pandora's box.

SUPPLIES

Refer to **What You Will Need** in the Student Edition.

2 Teach

Motivator

Ask students what they know of the two symbols (elephant and donkey) seen in **Figure 11–8.** Review the concept of a mascot (see Chapter 7, page 125). Ask: How is this image used to symbolize the election? *(Perhaps it says that either party will have trouble governing, once elected.)* Ask about other mascots or symbols students are familiar with.

Vocabulary

The term *cartoon* originally referred to the preparatory sketch for a fresco, a tapestry, or a stained-glass window. The use of the word *caricature* is traced back to the nineteenth century in England, when a competition for fresco designs for Parliament was parodied in the magazine *Punch.*

LESSON 4

Drawing a Cartoon

During a political campaign, newspapers are filled with editorials—articles that try to persuade you to take a particular position. Television gives or sells time to candidates to speak about their positions. Cartoonists also use their art form to try to persuade their viewers. They use **caricature** (**kar**-ih-kuh-chur), *a humorous drawing that exaggerates features of a person to make fun of or criticize him or her.*

The cartoon in **Figure 11–8** uses the elephant and the donkey to symbolize the Republican and Democratic parties respectively. The cartoonist drew them as images on an ancient Greek vase because democracy began in ancient Greece. His title, *Pandora's Ballot Box,* adds another symbol. Do you know the ancient Greek myth of Pandora's Box? Pandora was a very curious girl who opened a forbidden box. By doing so she released troubles into our world. What does this say about the election?

What You Will Learn

In this lesson, you will create your own cartoon. Think of a neighborhood problem, such as littering, noise, or pollution. You might select a school problem, such as a playground bully. You will draw your characters using exaggeration of facial features, size, and expression to give meaning to your cartoon. You will add background details that help to set the scene and emphasize the problem.

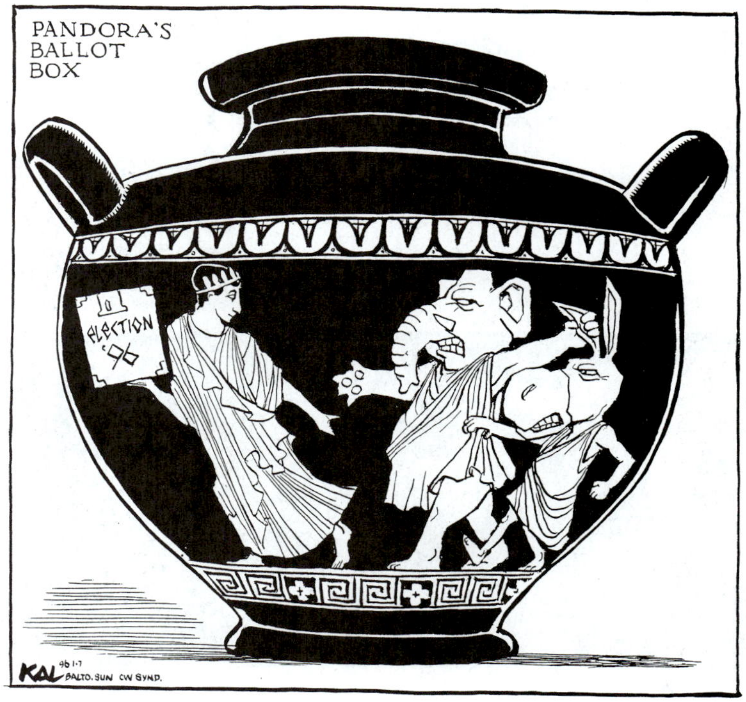

Cartoonists & Writers Syndicate

◆ **Figure 11–8** **Identify in this artwork the influence of political events.**

Kevin Kallaugher. *Pandora's Ballot Box.* 1996. Ink on paper. 15.2 × 16.5 cm (6 × 6½"). Cartoonists and Writers Syndicate.

CAREER OPPORTUNITIES IN ART

LOCAL BUSINESS TOURS Arrange for students to tour facilities where art-related work is produced. Examples might be a photography studio or an artist's studio, an advertising agency, or a publishing company. Discuss how the company uses art and artists as part of its business, and describe the range of careers available to individuals interested in art-related work. You might also arrange a career day that focuses on careers in art, and invite speakers from a variety of companies to talk about how they use art and artists to conduct business. Have students compare these different career opportunities in art.

What You Will Need

- Examples of cartoons from newspapers
- Pencils and sketch paper
- White drawing paper, 9 x 12 inches
- Fine-tipped black marker

What You Will Do

1. Study the cartoons to look for ways to use exaggeration.
2. Decide what you want your cartoon to say about the problem you want to solve.
3. Do several quick sketches, changing size and emphasizing the objects or persons to make your point. Decide whether you need any words in "balloons" or at the bottom of your cartoon.
4. Transfer your best sketch to white drawing paper. Still using pencil, draw your cartoon lightly, adding foreground and background details.
5. Use your fine-tipped black marker to go over all of your lines. Think about making some lines thicker for emphasis.

Evaluating Your Work

- **Describe** What are you saying in your cartoon? What persons or things have you used to make your point?
- **Analyze** How have you used caricature to exaggerate? How have you used symbols to express an idea?
- **Interpret** How well does your cartoon get its message across?
- **Judge** Ask your fellow students to decide if you have convinced them about your point.

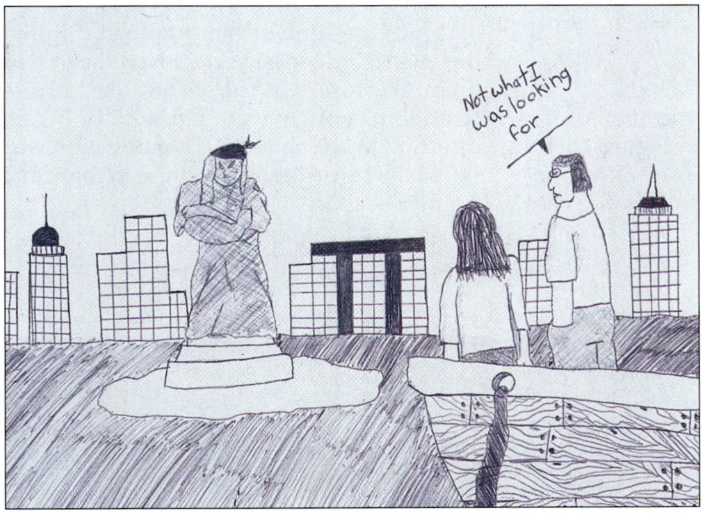

◆ **Figure 11–9** Student work. A cartoon.

REFLECTIVE THINKING

Critical Response. Analyze the original artworks of your peers. Study the cartoon they drew. Form conclusions about historical and cultural contexts, such as the problem they emphasized. How does their cartoon reveal this problem?

Visual Art Journal

Look in a mirror and do a caricature of your own face. Look for special features, like your nose, eyes, and mouth. Exaggerate one or two of your features. In your journal, write about the features you exaggerated.

Historical/Cultural Heritage

Discuss with students the kinds of subjects that lend themselves to caricature. Ask student volunteers to search through books and magazines to identify and select two different caricatures. Subjects may be related to history or politics. L2

3 Assess

Peer Assessment

Have students analyze the cartoons created by their peers to form conclusions about historical and cultural contexts. How successfully did they represent the particular problem?

Reteaching

Reinforce the meaning of caricature, myth, and symbol. Ask students to find examples of cartoons in books, newspapers, and magazines. L1 ELL

Enrichment

Encourage students to list the kinds of topics and issues that cartoons address: politics, personal relationships, ecology, discrimination, violence, social problems, and so on. Extend the meaning of *cartoon* to comic strips and animated films. Ask students to give examples of some of their favorites and explain why they appeal to them. L1

4 Close

Ask students to explain how their cartoons used exaggeration to express an idea.

INCLUSION STRATEGIES

English Language Learners The study of cartoons and caricatures provides an excellent opportunity for students who are less proficient in reading or speaking English. Many of the issues depicted in cartoons created for this age group are universal in their appeal. Have students bring in a favorite cartoon from a book or other source and read it and explain it to the class. Encourage all students to use body language and words in their presentations. Students who are struggling with English can practice their presentations with more proficient speakers. ELL

Recording Exploration

(pages 212–213)

1 Focus

Objectives

After completing this lesson, students will be able to:

- Explain what a *frieze* is.
- Understand what the term *mosaic* means.
- Understand that artists create visual records of explorations.
- Identify the influence of historical events in artworks.

2 Teach

Motivator

Engage students in a discussion of some of the explorations they have studied in social studies. Ask them how we know about those travels. Point out that artists have provided visual records to complement the written documents that tell about those events.

Vocabulary

Have students look up *frieze* in a dictionary. Ask students to explain the distinction between frieze and an architectural frieze. Have students try to identify an example of any kind of frieze they have seen and describe it to the class.

LESSON 5

Recording Exploration

For as long as there have been people, there have been explorers. There have also been countless stories of the brave men and women who ventured into the unknown and forged new paths. In this lesson, you will view visual records of two explorations. You will also learn about the media used to create such records.

Past Exploration

The first explorers were probably cave dwellers curious to know what lay beyond the next hill. It was not until around 1500 that exploration got under way in earnest. During this century, pioneers began embarking on journeys that would, in the end, make the world seem smaller.

Mosaic Frieze

One of these pioneering expeditions is the subject of the colorful work in **Figure 11–10**. This work is a **frieze** (**freez**), *a decorative band running across the upper part of a wall.* This frieze recounts the adventures of French-Canadian explorers Jacques Marquette and Louis Joliet. The two set out in the late 1600s on a quest to locate the source of the Mississippi River. Look closely at the work. All the figures and objects are made up of *pictures made with small cubes of colored marble, glass, or tile set into cement.* This art medium and the art form that results are known as **mosaic** (moh-**zay**-ik). Notice the care with which the artist mixed and matched pieces to create subtle shadings and depth. Can you find the lifelike images of the two explorers?

Recent Exploration

Since the time of Marquette and Joliet, our planet's deepest secrets have been laid open. Explorers of the second half of the twentieth century were left with only one direction in which to go. That direction was up. Many turned their attention to the "final frontier"—space.

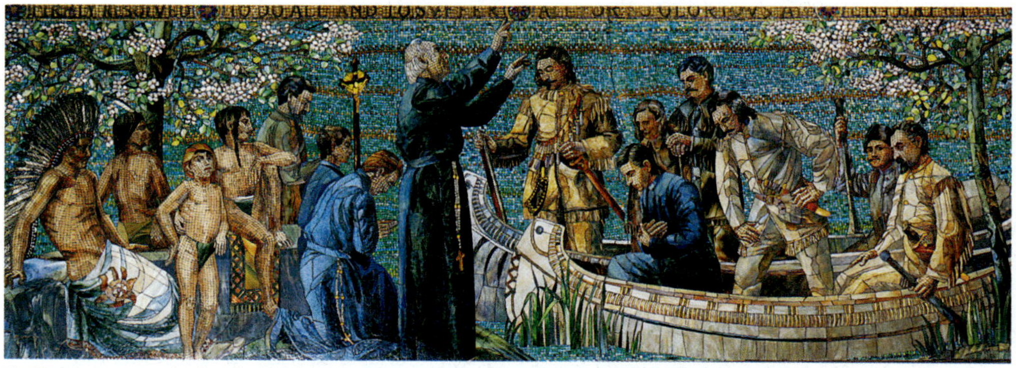

◆ **Figure 11–10** **Look at the detail in this mosaic. What do you think are some of the challenges facing artists working in this medium?**

J. A. Holzer. *Departure of Marquette and Joliet from St. Ignace on Their First Voyage to Illinois.* 1895. 1.2 × 2.7 m (4 × 9′). Harr, © Hedrich-Blessing.

MORE ABOUT...

Mosaics Mosaic art is found in cultures throughout the world. The Greeks, the Romans, and the Byzantines all used mosaics to decorate the walls, ceilings, floors, and interior walls of churches, public buildings, and exterior pavements. Muslims of India and Persia used mosaic art in their temples, as did the Aztec and Mayan peoples of Central and South America. Provide students opportunities to explore the history and use of mosaics. Have them visit the school or local library to find additional resources on mosaics.

Figure 11–11 shows an outpost in this realm of exploration. It is a photo of one of the nine planets in our solar system. It was taken during a spacecraft "fly-by." Do you recognize this planet? Notice the vivid colors in the photo. What do they reveal about the effects of recent technology on the art of photography?

Check Your Understanding

1. What medium was used for the frieze in Figure 11–10? Describe this medium.
2. What does the photo in Figure 11–11 reveal about the changing face of exploration?

Time & Place

Mississippi River Exploration

Historical connection. In the 1600s, the area that is now Canada was a French province called New France. Native Americans inhabited some parts of North America, but much of the land remained unexplored wilderness. The Native Americans mentioned a great river that they called *Mississippi*—a Native American word meaning "big river." In 1673, the governor general of New France sent Louis Joliet and Jacques Marquette to explore the Mississippi and trace its course. Joliet and Marquette set out with a party of five other explorers. On their journey, the explorers met many friendly Native Americans (see **Figure 11–10**). Identify the influence of historical events in Figure 11–10.

◆ **Figure 11–11** This photograph was taken by a camera on a spacecraft. How do you suppose this view differs from ones available to scientists of past centuries?

Jupiter. Photo by NASA.

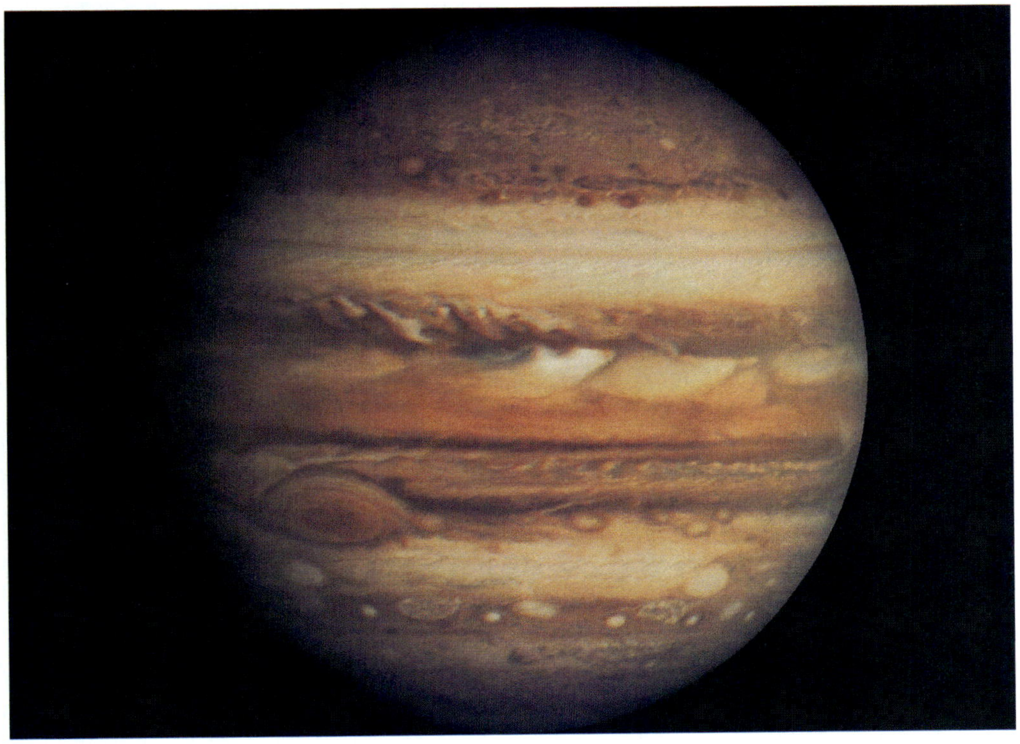

Time & Place

Mississippi River Exploration

The Mosaic portrays the Native Americans meeting the explorers Louis Joliet and Jacques Marquette as they departed from St. Ignace.

Understanding Art History

Bring in to the class several books about Greek architecture. Have students identify an example of a frieze from one of the books and compare that frieze with the one pictured in **Figure 11–10.** What do each of the friezes communicate? L2

3 Assess

Self-Assessment

Have students complete the **Check Your Understanding** questions on this page. Answers are provided below.

Reteaching

Have pairs of students design a frieze to decorate the classroom.

Enrichment

Ask volunteers to become explorers themselves and find out more about the story behind the mosaics in the Marquette Building in Chicago. Have them research the four W's of this artwork and report back to the class. L3

4 Close

Have students give examples of explorations that artists have recorded in their art.

Answers to Check Your Understanding

1. Mosaic is the art medium used in Figure 11–10. Mosaic is a medium and art form made up of pictures made with small cubes of colored marble, glass, or tile set into cement.
2. The photo in Figure 11–11 reveals that the "final frontier" is outer space.

Historical Events in Pictures and Words

(pages 214–215)

1 Focus

Objectives

After completing this lesson students will be able to:

- Explain the contributions to art and history of twentieth-century artist Jacob Lawrence.
- Identify the way in which shape and repetition can be used to suggest movement in an artwork.
- Identify the influence of a historical event in an artwork.

2 Teach

Motivator

Write the term "hero" on the board. Ask students to name acts that might be described as heroic. Write several of their responses on the board. Then add the following to the list: "Rescuing people being held against their will and guiding them to safety." Ask whether students agree that this is an act of heroism. Tell them that they are about to examine an artwork depicting a scene from the life of a famous historical figure noted for this very act.

LESSON 6
ART & SOCIAL STUDIES

Historical Events in Pictures and Words

Artists, as you have seen, can function as historians and storytellers. Few have enjoyed more success in both areas than twentieth-century African American artist Jacob Lawrence. Early in his career, Lawrence created several narrative art series based on historical figures.

The most inspirational of these was his 1939 series *The Life of Harriet Tubman.* Harriet Tubman herself, of course, is an inspiring figure in American history. Born into slavery, she escaped to freedom through the now-famous Underground Railroad. She then returned to the South, endangering her life to rescue countless other enslaved African Americans. Lawrence wrote the narrative in **Figure 11–12** for his work on the Harriet Tubman series.

Excerpt from "The Life of Harriet Tubman"

In leading many Black slaves out of bondage, Tubman encouraged crowds of slaves to follow her on faith, hastening across unfamiliar territories to freedom. The darkness of the night protected them and their numbers sustained these fleeing bands of men and women. The lesson of sustenance from group action is realized in subsequent images.

◆ **Figure 11–12** A narrative by Jacob Lawrence on his series "The Life of Harriet Tubman."

MORE ABOUT...

The Harlem Renaissance In the late 1920s and early 1930s an African American cultural movement emerged that was centered in the Harlem neighborhood of New York City. This period brought great developments in African American literature, music, theater, art, and politics. The Harlem Renaissance marked the first time that mainstream publishers and critics gave serious regard to African American literature and arts. The works that were produced through this movement attracted significant attention throughout the nation. It was the artists from this movement that inspired the work of Jacob Lawrence.

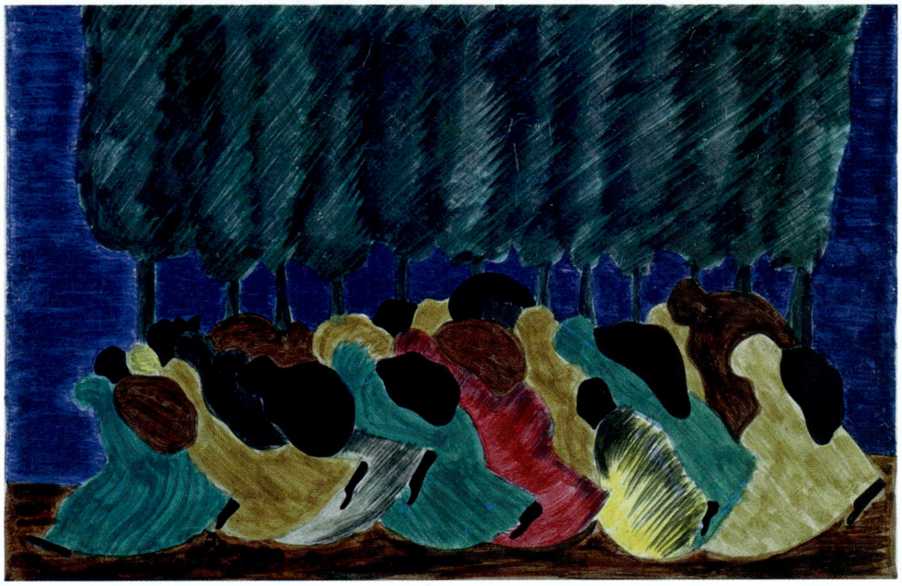

◆ **Figure 11–13** Notice Lawrence's use of alternating colors to achieve a sense of movement and action.

Jacob Lawrence. *Harriet Tubman Series No. 16.* 1939–40. Casein tempera on gessoed hardboard 30.5 × 45.4 cm (12 × 17⅞″). Hampton University Museum, Hampton, Virginia.

The Harriet Tubman Series

Lawrence's series on Tubman consists of 31 paintings. One of these paintings from approximately midway through the series appears in **Figure 11–13.**

Examine the work for visual clues about the specific event it depicts. Pay attention to important details such as the time of day. Notice, too, the hunched shoulders and long strides taken by the figures shown. What do these details suggest about their pace?

MAKE THE CONNECTION

Take Another Look

1. The story of Harriet Tubman's life teaches many lessons about important human values. Two are mentioned in Jacob Lawrence's narrative. One is the importance of faith. The second is the lesson of sustenance—a renewal of spirit—that comes from teamwork. Explain why these would be important.
2. How do you think Lawrence portrayed these values in his artwork?

ART & SOCIAL STUDIES

Re-creating a historical event. Imagine that you were going to create an inspirational historical artwork of your own. What event or figure from history would you show? What moral lesson would your work emphasize? Write a one- to two-page description of your historical artwork.

Art Criticism

Have students study the painting shown in **Figure 11–13.** Note that Jacob Lawrence uses repeated shapes in different colors in the painting. What feeling or sense does this accomplish? *(Answers might include that it conveys a sense of movement and urgency on the part of the escapees.)* L1

3 Assess

Self-Assessment

Have students complete the **Take Another Look** questions on this page. Answers are provided below.

Reteaching

Challenge students to identify a specific sentence in the text passage in **Figure 11–12** that corresponds to the scene depicted in the painting in **Figure 11–13.** Have students summarize the text in their own words to depict the scene Lawrence painted in Figure 11–13.

Enrichment

Note that Jacob Lawrence was a member of the early twentieth-century cultural movement known as the Harlem Renaissance. Explain that this was an awakening in all areas of the arts based in New York City's Harlem community. Invite students to learn more about this dynamic period, focusing on other artists as well as musicians and writers. L2

4 Close

Have students explain the role Harriet Tubman played in American history.

MAKE THE CONNECTION

Take Another Look Student answers will vary, but may include the following:

1. It was vital that Harriet Tubman's charges trusted her. Hence, the importance of faith. Cooperation was important in the face of danger during the years of the Underground Railroad.
2. The repeated posture of the members is an indicator that they were members of a "team."

LESSON 7

Advances in Visual Reporting

(pages 216–217)

1 Focus

Objectives

After completing this lesson, students will be able to:

- Understand the role of video in today's society.
- Evaluate the aesthetic quality of video programming.
- Appreciate the marvels of video technology.

SUPPLIES
- Pencils
- White drawing paper

2 Teach

Motivator

Discuss with students the place that film and television have in the lives of people today and how we rely on television to get news and other information. Ask students to talk about the kinds of motion pictures and television programs they watch and why.

Historical/Cultural Heritage

Many motion pictures and video documentaries provide an excellent means of learning about and understanding other cultures. Try to find a few video documentaries from various cultures and show them to the class. Ask the class to compare and critique the videos on their artistic merits. L2

LESSON 7

Advances in Visual Reporting

Technology and art have always been partners. The invention of paint in tubes in the mid-1800s freed artists for the first time to go outdoors and paint. Advances of the past hundred years have had equal importance and impact. In this lesson you will look at some of these advances and their effect on the field of visual reporting.

MOTION PICTURES

The visual records of generations past, as you have seen, were created using a variety of media. Yet, all shared a common limitation. All, even the camera, provided "frozen" views of an action event. If a still image is worth a thousand words, how many words could be expressed by a *moving* visual record?

An answer to this question came shortly before the beginning of the twentieth century. It was delivered in the form of the technological breakthrough pictured in **Figure 11–14.** This item, the *kinetoscope* (kuh-**net**-uh-skohp), was a forerunner of the modern movie projector. It was invented by the same person who gave us the electric lightbulb. His name was Thomas Edison. Examine this device. Do any of the parts look familiar? Can you guess what any of them do?

THE VIDEO REVOLUTION

The kinetoscope produced moving images by rapidly stringing together still ones. This same principle is at work in today's movie and video cameras. In the last few years, video cameras have advanced to digital video cameras. Digital video cameras increase creativity by expanding ways to quickly and easily edit and rearrange images, sound, and text.

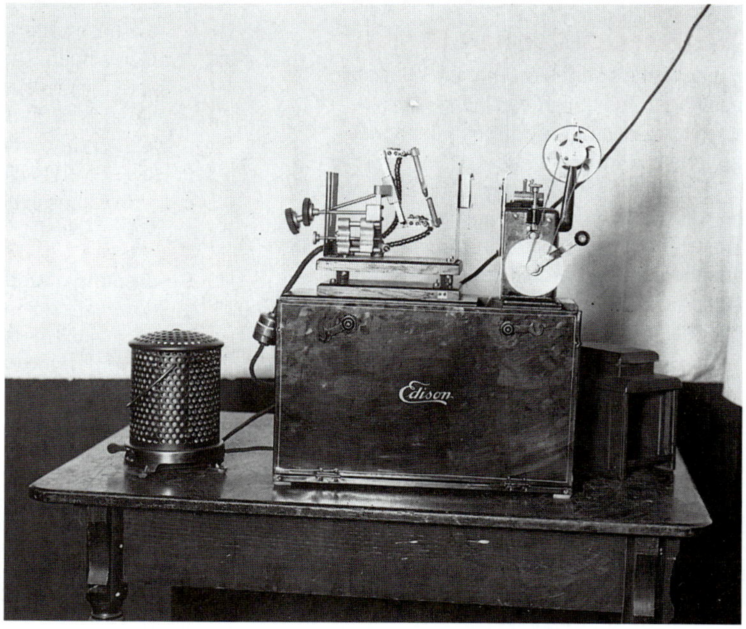

◆ **Figure 11–14** How has the making of motion pictures changed since the days of this device?

A moving picture machine invented by Thomas Edison. 1915. UPI/Corbis-Bettman.

TEACHER TO TEACHER

PLANNING A VIDEO Topics or themes for movies should motivate students and inspire their creativity. Throughout the school year there are opportunities to record school events, interview people, or demonstrate how something is made. Have students brainstorm possibilities. Generate lists of topics and concerns that relate to individual students, the school, city, country, or world. Challenge students to select a topic that interests them and has many opportunities for innovation. If choosing a topic that is global, uncover local concerns about the issue. Investigate the situation and solutions. Present different points of view.

The Video Documentary

The video camera has introduced an exciting new type of visual record. This is the video documentary. A **video documentary** is *an in-depth study of a person, place, thing, or event.* Today, there are many sources of excellent documentary programming. Nature videos are at the top of the list for artistry. These works have brought the viewer up close to the wonders and mysteries of nature. They have recorded the habits of the tiniest insect to the endless marvels of the vast oceans. See **Figure 11–15** for an example of a video documentary crew in action.

Check Your Understanding

1. What advances in the visual reporting of events have occurred in the last hundred years?
2. What is a video documentary?

Studio Activity

Planning a Story Board

Practical applications for design ideas. The first step to planning a video documentary is the creation of a **story board.** This is *a frame-by-frame plan of a video production.*

Think about a video documentary you might like to make. Consider your subject and the points of interest you might emphasize. Think about your audience as well. Then draw lines to divide a 12 x 18-inch sheet of drawing paper into six sections. In each section, sketch a scene in your documentary. Include the beginning, middle, and end of your documentary in your story board. Plan the characters, setting, situation, or problem, and solution. Write a script to accompany your images.

PORTFOLIO

Put your story board in your portfolio with your script.

◆ **Figure 11–15** This camera crew is about to film a video documentary. What do you suppose is around the bend in the path?

Photo by Kurtis Productions, Chicago, Illinois.

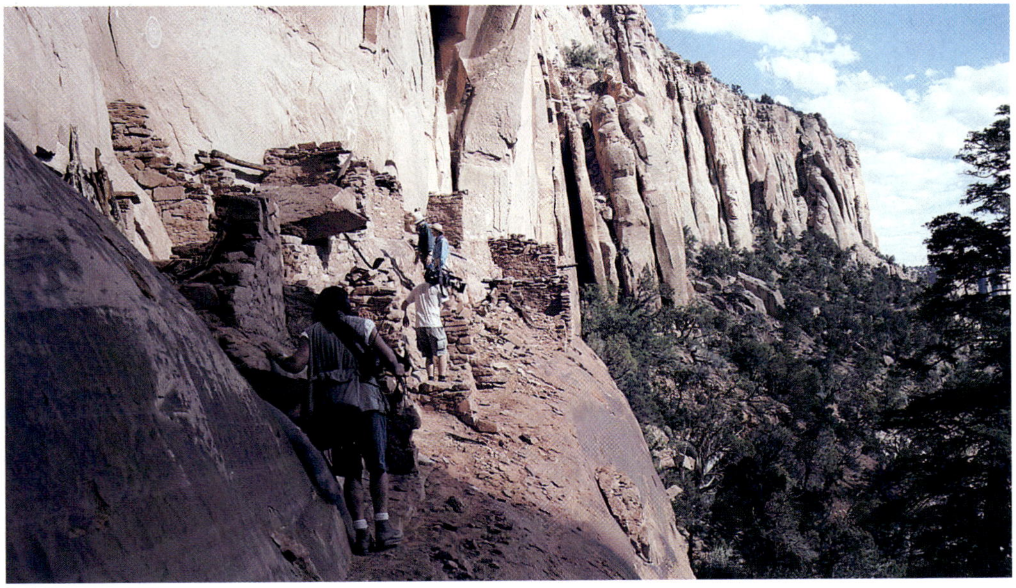

Studio Skills

Sketching ideas in a story board is good experience for students to gain confidence in expressing their ideas. Finished drawings are not necessary as long as the ideas are clear. Suggest drawing lightly. Have students use the story board as a thinking medium. L1 ELL

3 Assess

Self-Assessment

Have students complete the **Check Your Understanding** questions on this page. Answers are provided below.

Reteaching

Have students work in pairs to analyze their story board designs. Ask partners to provide constructive criticism to suggest ways of clarifying ideas. L1

Enrichment

Ask a group of students to study television program guides for one week and make a list of recommended programs. Their list should include mostly video documentaries if possible. Before they make their list, have them establish viewing goals or guidelines. L2

4 Close

Ask students to discuss the importance of being selective in their viewing of television and motion pictures.

Answers to Check Your Understanding

1. Some of the advances in visual reporting that have occurred in the last hundred years are the invention of the kinetoscope, a forerunner of the modern movie projector, the video camera and camcorder, and the video documentary.
2. A video documentary is an in-depth study of a person, place, thing, or event.

Making a Video Documentary

(pages 218–219)
Lesson Time: 90 minutes

1 Focus

Objectives

After completing this lesson, students will be able to:

- Organize ideas into a sequential plan to design and videotape a documentary video.
- Work with composing space in a lens and zooming in for close-up views of their subject.
- Demonstrate technical skills effectively by using a videocamera to produce a video documentary.

SUPPLIES

Refer to **What You Will Need** in the Student Edition.

2 Teach

Motivator

Ask which students in the class have had experience with digital and video cameras. Form teams with these students as instructors. Experiment with camera use and playback. Discuss theme and list on the board several possible themes for a documentary. When students have chosen a theme (a place or event that they can get to), have them list at least ten images that could be parts of the video.

Vocabulary

Introduce the terms *close-ups, long shots,* and *pans.* Demonstrate how to achieve each technique and discuss when and why a videographer uses these techniques.

Making a Video Documentary

When you watch a documentary on TV, do you imagine yourself as the **videographer**—the *person who operates a video camera?* Do you picture yourself trekking deep into the heart of Africa on a safari? Maybe you see yourself scaling a snow-capped mountain peak. In this lesson, you will have the chance to be a videographer. You will probably have to limit your travel to within your own town or city, however. **Figure 11–16** shows a student your age "on location" using a video camera. Can you identify her subject?

What You Will Learn

You will design and videotape your own documentary video. You will begin by choosing a subject. You will then plan and draw a story board. In it, you will identify images that will help give viewers a broad picture of the place or event. Based on your story board, you will shoot your video. You will use a variety of video techniques, including close-ups, long shots, and pans. A **pan** is *a slow, steady, sideways movement of the video camera to capture details in a panorama.*

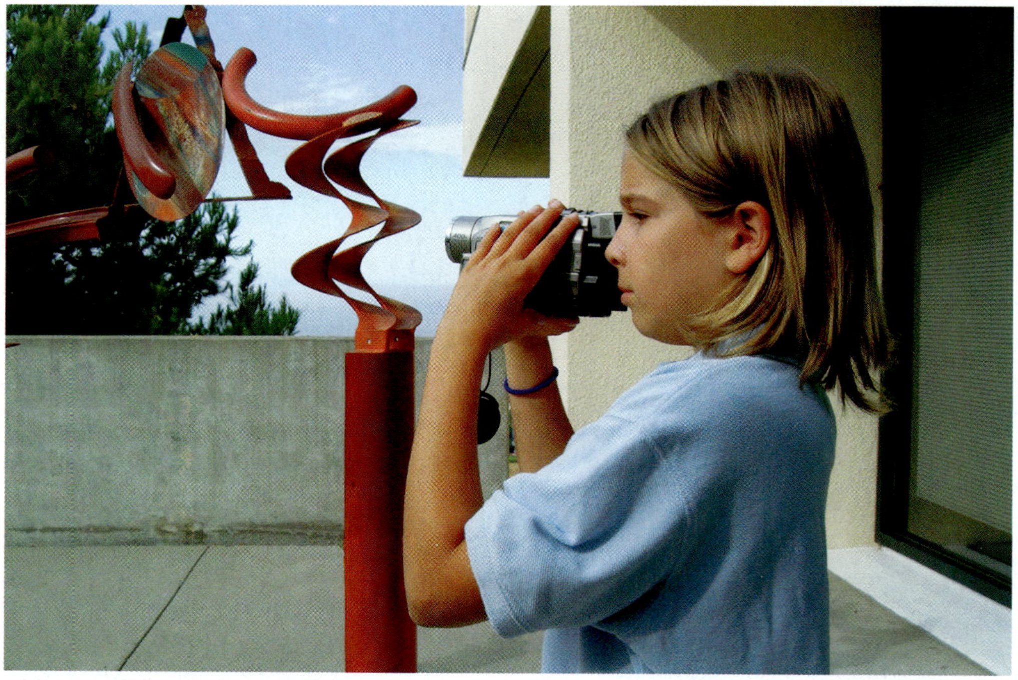

◆ **Figure 11–16** Student using video camera.

COMMUNITY CONNECTION

PRESENT THE NEWS Ask students to watch and keep a written record of the events that the local news reports. Have students create a story board for one of each kind of news segment, including world news, local news, sports, and weather. Working with partners, they should decide which stories are most important and brainstorm ways that they can best communicate these features to the class. Suggest that they visit their local news station and job shadow the news anchor or videographer for some tips. Students should make a poster describing the steps to create a news program.

What You Will Need

- Writing pad and pencil
- Yardstick or other long straight edge
- Sheet of white drawing paper, 18 x 24 inches
- Markers
- Camcorder
- VHS videotape cassette
- Tripod (optional)

What You Will Do

1. You will demonstrate technical skills effectively using a video camera to produce electronic media-generated art. With a group of students, brainstorm possible events that would make good topics for a video documentary. Choose subjects and locations that are realistic.
2. After choosing an event, make a list of ten or more images that are important to your subject. Note these on the writing pad. Organize your images into an outline.
3. Create a story board. With the pencil and yardstick or other straight edge, draw lines to divide a large sheet of drawing paper into 16 sections. In each section, sketch a scene from your outline. Use markers to add color to your story board.
4. Write an introduction to your documentary. Make sure the camcorder has been loaded with a videotape cassette and that the battery is charged. Set up the camcorder on a tripod if you wish, and tape yourself reading the introduction. Alternatively, you might ask a friend to serve as your narrator.
5. Following your story board, shoot your video scene by scene. Tell what you see as you tape to provide a running commentary. Include close-ups, long shots, and pans.
6. Plan your closing. Include a wrap-up commentary.

Evaluating Your Work

- **Describe** Did you plan your documentary? Did you create a story board to help organize the action?
- **Analyze** Did you add variety to your video by including close-ups, long shots, and pans?
- **Interpret** Did you cover the event you set out to cover? How did you capture the mood or emotion of the event?
- **Judge** Hold an "Academy Awards" ceremony for your class. Vote on awards for winners in the following categories: Most Interesting Topic; Most Original Coverage; Most Skillful Use of Equipment.

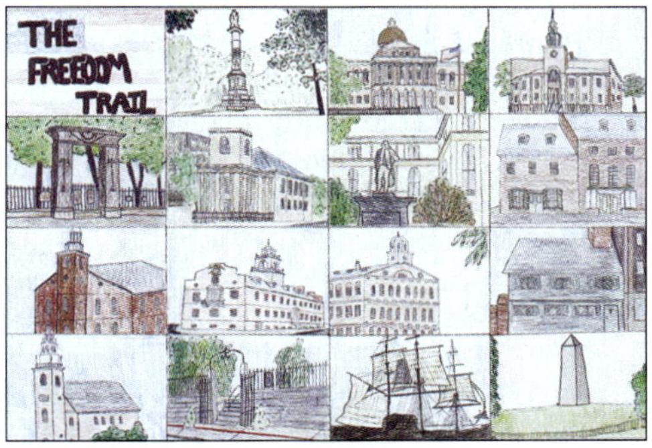

◆ **Figure 11–17** Student work. A story board.

Studio Option

Do a video interview with a member of your class. Prepare a list of questions to ask that will bring out the interests and talents of your subject. Videotape your interview.

Visual Art Journal

In your journal, describe in detail the process you used to create your video documentary. What did you learn? What would you do differently next time?

Aesthetics

Tape a documentary aired on television and show it in class. Analyze its organization, sequence, images, and commentary. Decide what makes a successful video documentary.

Studio Skills

Have students work in pairs so that one can introduce and narrate as the other films. If taping is to be done at a site other than the school, have students go with a designated adult. If cameras are used, follow the same plan of using the story board to plot images. Suggest that the finished pictures be mounted in a handmade book with written commentary. L1 ELL

3 Assess

Self-Assessment

Have students use **Evaluating Your Work** to conduct an in-progress critique of their video documentary.

Reteaching

Ask students to write a set of step-by-step directions for others to follow when doing a video documentary.

4 Close

Have a showing of student videos for various classes in the school. Have students make posters to advertise showings and titles.

Safety Tip

Care of Equipment As you demonstrate the use of video or camera equipment, spend some time discussing the care of such equipment. Make sure students understand that video equipment should be handled very carefully. You may want to touch base with the school administration to be sure to follow permission procedures for student use of school equipment off school grounds.

Privacy Issues Before students begin videotaping or taking pictures, discuss the importance of respecting other people's privacy. Students should not enter restricted or private areas without appropriate permission.

Photo Finish

1 Focus

Objectives

After completing this lesson, students will be able to:

- Create a flip book to show a moving image.
- Plan, write, revise, and share a radio broadcast.

2 Teach

Teaching the Feature

1. Before students open their books, ask: When a horse gallops, are all four hooves off the ground at the same time? Let students share their ideas. Then ask: How could you prove that your idea is correct?
2. Have students look at the photographs. Let them briefly discuss what the photographs show about the hooves of galloping horses.
3. Ask partners to read and discuss the article, "Photo Finish." Have partners be prepared to identify Muybridge's most important contributions.

Activity

Show students a small flip book; let them riffle the pages and watch the images "move." Then have each student draw the same figure on at least eight very small pieces of paper. The image should be in a slightly different position in each drawing. Have students staple their drawings together to create their own flip books.

Photo Finish

An early photographer comes up with the first motion picture.

A single event in 1872 helped pave the way for the invention of motion pictures. Leland Stanford, a tycoon and former governor of California, hired British-born Eadweard Muybridge to photograph Stanford's prized racehorse. The event ended up settling a bet, proving that there was a moment when a galloping horse had all four hooves off the ground at the same time.

That assignment spurred Muybridge's interest in photographing moving objects. For his next challenge, he lined up 12 cameras along the sides of a racetrack. He attached to each camera shutter a string that stretched across the track. As the horses galloped by, each camera caught the next split second of motion. Muybridge ran his still photos through a machine that flipped the photos one by one in order. This may have been the first "moving" picture!

Muybridge photographed other animals and humans in action. He published a series of books containing more than 100,000 of his photos. Both artists and scientists used his photos to study and analyze people and animals in action.

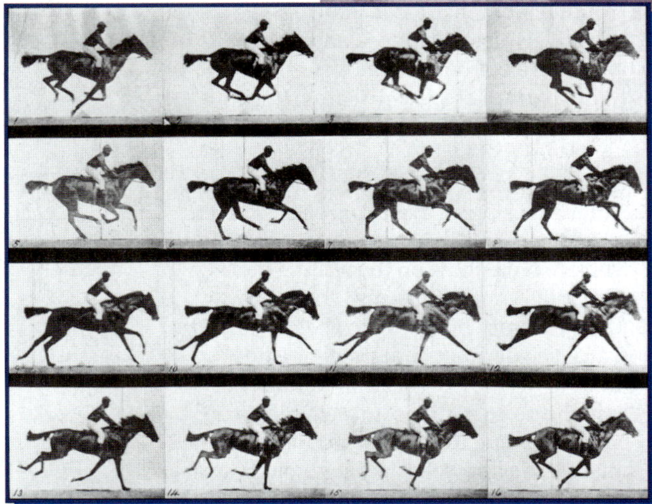

EADWEARD MUYBRIDGE

Eadweard Muybridge took a series of photos called *Galloping Horse* in 1878.

TIME TO CONNECT

- **Imagine that you are watching a race being run by the horse in Muybridge's *Galloping Horse*.**
- **Create a radio broadcast of this race. Write, edit, and peer-review a script. Check for correct grammar, spelling, punctuation, and descriptive language.**
- **Practice your script and take turns presenting your writing with other classmates. Can the class visualize what is going on based on your script?**

TIME TO CONNECT

Encourage student partners to discuss their ideas for a broadcast. Then have students write independently. As they compose and revise their scripts, ask them to keep these questions in mind:

- Is the action clear in each part of my broadcast?
- Am I using appropriate word choice and descriptive language?
- Am I using varied sentence structure in my script?

Chapter 11 Review

BUILDING VOCABULARY

Number a sheet of paper from 1 to 9. After each number, write the term from the list that matches each description below.

caricature	photography
frieze	story board
gouache	video documentary
mosaic	videographer
pan	

1. The art of making images by exposing a chemically treated surface to light.
2. A form of watercolor that uses non-clear pigments.
3. An in-depth study of a person, place, thing, or event.
4. A slow, steady, sideways movement of the video camera to capture details in a panorama.
5. Person who operates a video camera.
6. Pictures made with small cubes of colored marble, glass, or tile set into cement.
7. A decorative band running across the upper part of a wall.
8. A frame-by-frame plan of a video production.
9. A humorous drawing that exaggerates features of a person to make fun of or criticize him or her.

REVIEWING ART FACTS

Number a sheet of paper from 10 to 14. Answer each question in a complete sentence.

10. What are the four W's of visual reporting?
11. What personal risk was taken by the photographer of Figure 11–2 to record the event from the best angle?
12. What reasons might the painter of Figure 11–6 have had for making George Washington the tallest figure in the painting?
13. What event was recorded in the frieze in Figure 11–10?
14. When was the kinetoscope invented and by whom?

CROSS-CURRICULUM CONNECTIONS

15. **Language Arts.** Poets are also noted for adding color and immediacy to events from history. At your school or local library, find a copy of the ballad *Paul Revere's Ride* by Henry Wadsworth Longfellow. Read this colorful poem aloud to appreciate its rhythm. Study the "visual record" of this historical event.
16. **Science.** The image in Figure 11–11 was taken by a NASA space probe. Use online or library resources to learn more about NASA. Try to learn when NASA was founded, where it is headquartered, and what type of work it does. Write your findings in a report.

Web Museum Activity

The J. Paul Getty Museum, Los Angeles, California

In this chapter, you learned how artists of different times and cultures have recorded events. You discovered how photography developed as an art form. To explore further the use of photography in recording events, go to **art.glencoe.com**. Click on The Getty Museum link and view the different images of historical events.

What do these images reveal? What are the significant moments captured on film? Explain the "four W's" for each photograph.

ANSWERS TO Chapter 11 Review

Building Vocabulary

1. photography
2. gouache
3. video documentary
4. pan
5. videographer
6. mosaic
7. frieze
8. story board
9. caricature

Reviewing Art Facts

10. These are who, what, where, and when.
11. He placed himself on a rock ledge a mile up.
12. This may have been done to emphasize Washington's status as supreme commander of the Continental Army.
13. The event was the search by Marquette and Joliet for the source of the Mississippi River.
14. It was invented just before the turn of the century by Thomas Edison.

Cross-Curriculum Connection

15. Have student volunteers bring the poem to class and read it aloud.
16. Student reports will vary.

Web Museum Activity

Before you have students go online, visit the Web site to preview the museum's online content, collection, and any online exhibit that may be of interest. Student's responses should include the four W's for each photograph. Encourage students to use additional resources when explaining the four W's.

Chapter 12 *Telling a Story*

Chapter Resources

Features	Standards for Chapter		Reproducible Masters
	National	State/Local	
Quick Write *page 223* TIME ART SCENE "Kids Sew Stories of the Future" *page 240* *Web Museum Activity* *page 241*	**1.** (a, b) **2.** (a, b) **4.** (a, b) **5.** (a, b) **6.** (a, b)		Guided Reading and Practice 12–1 Studio Activity 12–2, 12–11 Enrichment Activity 12–3, 12–4, 12–9 Application Activity 12–5, 12–8 Historical and Cultural Heritage 12–6 Cross–Curriculum Activity 12–7 Artist Profile 12–10 Lesson Plans

Lesson Resources

Lessons	Standards per Lesson		Reproducible Masters
	National	State/Local	
1 *Picture Languages* (*pages 224–225*)	1a, 1b, 5a, 6a		Studio Activity 12–2 Enrichment Activity 12–3, 12–4
2 *Making a Visual Autobiography* (*pages 226–227*)	1a, 1b, 2a		
3 *Myths and Legends* (*pages 228–229*)	4a, 4b, 6a		Application Activity 12–5 Historical and Cultural Heritage 12–6
4 *Creating a Mythical Creature* (*pages 230–231*)	1a, 1b, 2a, 2b, 4a		Cross–Curriculum Activity 12–7
5 *Art Stories Larger than Life* (*pages 232–233*)	4a, 6a		Application Activity 12–8
6 ART & READING (*pages 234–235*)	5b, 6a, 6b		
7 *Book Illustration* (*pages 236–237*)	4a, 5b, 6a		Enrichment Activity 12–9
8 *Creating a Book Cover* (*pages 238–239*)	1a, 1b, 2a		Artist Profile 12–10 Studio Activity 12–11

Assessment	Technology
Testing Program: Chapter Test 12–12 *Portfolio and Assessment Techniques*	Artsource Performing Arts Package, The Joffrey Ballet of Chicago (DVD or VHS segment 3) National Museum of Women in the Arts Interactive Lesson Planner Fine Art Transparency CC–12, *I and the Village* by Marc Chagall Fine Art Transparency 12, *Dorothea and Francesca* by Cecilia Beaux

Activities/Features
Studio Activity: Designing a Cartouche
Evaluating Your Work Computer Option Visual Art Journal
Time & Place: Chinese New Year
Evaluating Your Work Portfolio Ideas Art Online
Meet the Artist: Diego Rivera
Make the Connection
Meet the Artist: Leo and Diane Dillon
Evaluating Your Work Reflective Thinking Visual Art Journal

KEY TO ABILITY LEVELS

Teaching strategies have been coded.

- **L1** Activities for all students; teacher direction required
- **L2** Activities for average to above-average students; some teacher direction needed
- **L3** Activities for students able and willing to work independently
- **ELL** English Language Learner activities

FEATURED ARTISTS

- Leo and Diane Dillon
- Marina Gutierrez
- L. Joe
- Faith Ringgold
- Diego Rivera
- David Alfaro Siqueiros
- William John Wilgus

FINE ART PRINTS

Fine Art Print 18, *Sun Dance Ceremony* by George Washakie

Timesaving Technology

Interactive Lesson Planner

Make planning easy. Use this interactive software to organize your week, month, semester, or year and access all *Introducing Art* reproducible resources.

KEY TO LESSON RESOURCES

- Narrative Lesson
- Studio Lesson

Chapter 12

Telling a Story

(pages 222–241)

Chapter Overview

The art of the tale can take many forms. In this chapter, students will learn that stories can be told in a number of ways, even without the use of words. They will "read" the story that is to be told in some works of art. They will see that different cultures tell stories in their own unique ways.

Discussing the Artwork

FOCUS ON ◆ **Figure 12–1** Leo and Diane Dillon's illustrations reflect clean and precise lines, attention to detail, concern with accuracy and content, and an innovative use of color. In this illustration from the book *Aïda,* they pay close attention to the characters in the story to bring their illustration to life. The use of rich and bold color sets the mood of the scene. This scene illustrates Princess Amneris praying to the gods to forgive her. As she is praying, Princess Aïda and the warrior Radames die in each other's arms. Their image is portrayed in the smoke from the torch.

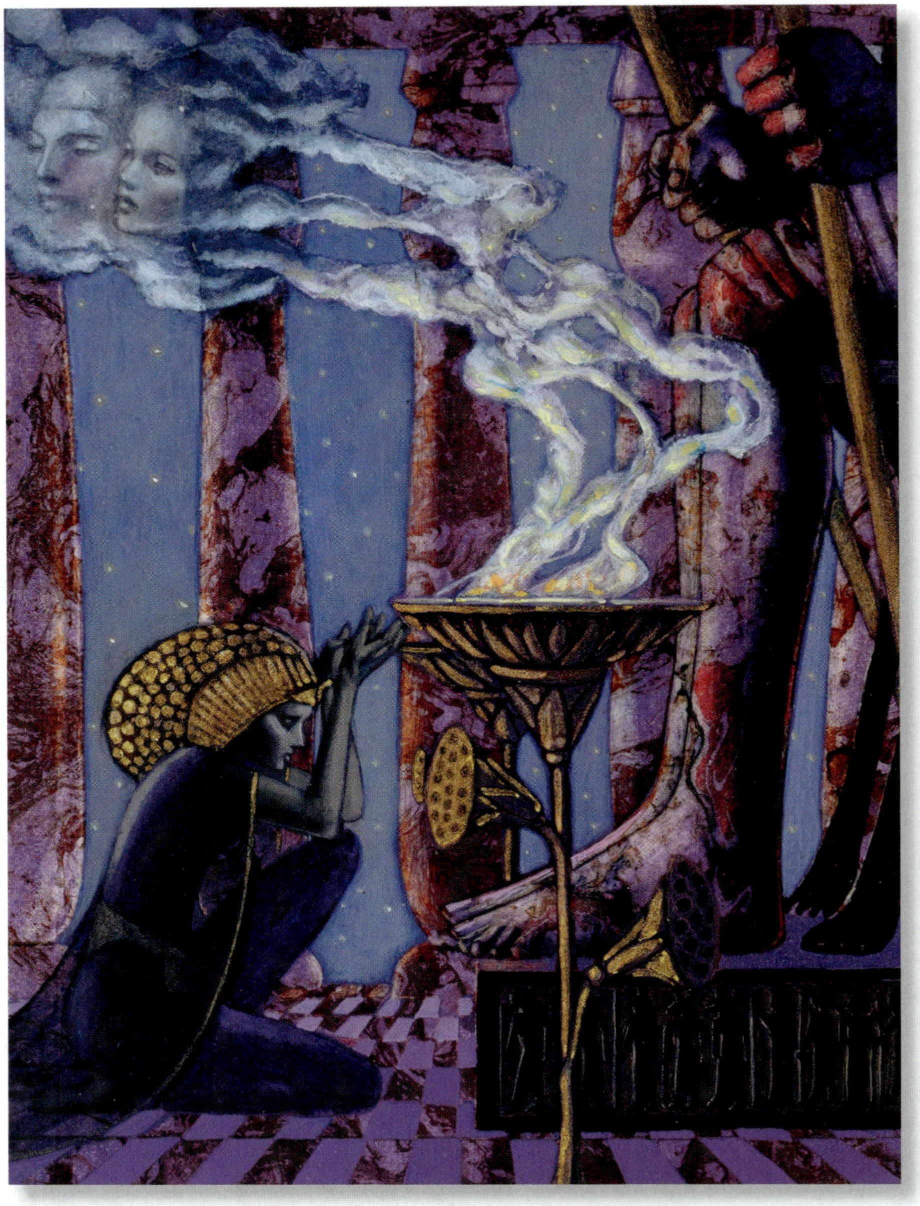

FOCUS ON ◆ **Figure 12–1** **What type of details can you learn from analyzing this book illustration of *Aïda?* Does the illustration invite you to read the story?**

Leo and Diane Dillon. Illustration from book *Aïda* by Leontyne Price. Harcourt Brace & Co., San Diego, California. 1990.

222

ART SOURCE ARTSOURCE

Linking to the Performing Arts

DANCE Stories can be told in many different forms. They can be expressed in words or pictures. Another way to tell a story is through dance. Dancers interpret stories by using their bodies to express a mood or feeling. *The Nutcracker and the Rat King* is the original story on which the ballet "The Nutcracker" is based. Have students see how The Joffrey Ballet of Chicago interprets this story in the **Performing Arts Handbook** on page 321. To enrich student understanding, play the DVD or videotape (segment 3) in the **Performing Arts Package.**

Chapter 12

Telling a Story

"An illustrator begins interpreting [the story] through his or her imagination. It's a magical process."

—Leo and Diane Dillon (b. 1933)

The art of storytelling is as old as humanity itself. Long before people could write, they were telling tales of intrigue and adventure. Some of these stories have been handed down through the ages and teach a lesson or moral. Others offer accounts of real people and events.

In this chapter, you will explore many approaches to storytelling. You will examine works by visual storytellers from a variety of times and places.

After completing this chapter, you will be able to:

- Recognize the story that runs through some artworks.
- Explain ways in which various cultures tell stories through art.
- Identify outside factors that impact the creation of visual stories.
- Tell stories using different art media and methods.

Quick Write

Interpreting the Quote
Read the quote and look at **Figure 12–1.** How do you interpret the illustration? Use your imagination and write a brief story describing the scene.

Key Terms

pictogram
cartouche
petroglyph
Kachina
fresco
cutaway
font

Quick Write

Interpreting the Quote
Have students read the quote and complete the Quick Write activity. Students' stories will vary, but encourage them to be creative as they imagine and describe the scene of the illustration in Figure 12–1.

Chapter Motivator

Choose a classic or contemporary wordless picture book to "read" to the class. Consult the school or public librarian for some suggestions. Show students each page as you present the book, allowing them time to study each picture carefully. After finishing the book, have students respond to the story. Tell them that in this chapter, they will learn about the ways artists tell stories without using words.

Art Online

Visit **art.glencoe.com**, the Web site for Glencoe's art programs. This site is designed to help you advance in your career as an art teacher and learn about the various opportunities in the art community. Explore the many teacher resources the site has to offer, such as:

- Art Conferences
- Student Art Contests
- Grants
- Educational Agencies

National Standards for Arts Education

This chapter addresses the following National Standards for the Visual Arts:

1. (a, b) **5.** (a, b)
2. (a, b) **6.** (a, b)
4. (a, b)

Picture Languages

(pages 224–225)

1 Focus

Objectives

After completing this lesson, students will be able to:

- Know the origin of hieroglyphic.
- Explain the history and purpose of petroglyphs.
- Define what a *cartouche* is.
- Demonstrate technical skills effectively by using a variety of art materials to produce a design of a cartouche.

SUPPLIES
- Brown butcher paper or several large brown paper bags
- Rulers, scissors
- Pencils, markers, crayons

2 Teach

Vocabulary

Connect picture stories to the history and meaning of names. For example, in English, *Smith* was originally the name for the village blacksmith, *Potter* was the maker of clay pots. Such meanings are found in most language groups. Explain to students that no matter what the ethnic origin of a name, there is a story to be told. Have them find names in any language and research the story of each.

Picture Languages

Ask people to define *story,* and most will mention "words." Few, if any, will include "pictures" in their definition. Yet, in a very real sense, all word stories *are* picture stories. If this statement is confusing, read on. On this page and the next, you will learn about and see examples of images that link the subject areas of writing and art.

EARLY PICTURE WRITING

Do you know someone who reads Korean, Chinese, or Japanese? Maybe you are able to yourself. If so, you are probably aware that these languages use not only letters but pictograms. A **pictogram** is *a small picture that stands for a word or an idea.* Early human languages were written entirely in pictograms. All alphabets today descend from collections of symbols such as these.

Egyptian Hieroglyphic

One of the earliest pictographic languages was used by the ancient Egyptians some 3,000 years ago. As noted in Chapter 5, this language was a type of *hieroglyphic* (hy-ruh-**glif**-ik), or form of picture writing.

Figure 12–2 shows an object that was common in Egyptian hieroglyphic. That object, a **cartouche** (kar-**toosh**), is *an oval or oblong containing an important person's name.* Study the two cartouches in the picture. Can you make out any familiar shapes? If you cannot, don't be discouraged. It took scholars many hundreds of years to crack the code of this complex language.

Native American Petroglyphs

Even older than the cartouche is the image shown in **Figure 12–3**. This object is a

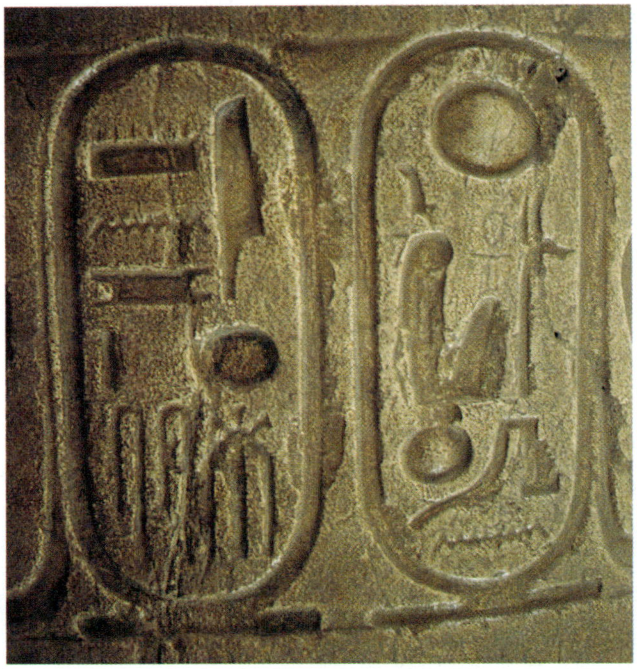

◆ **Figure 12–2** The picture writing in these ovals represents people's names. What images can you find?

Egypt. *Cartouche.*

INCLUSION STRATEGIES

SPECIAL LEARNING NEEDS Pictographs are a good way to maintain students' interest in writing. Especially for students with learning disabilities such as dysgraphia and dyslexia, combining hieroglyphic symbols with their own written words adds a lot of fun and creativity to a project integrating art and writing. Concerning measuring and cutting from butcher paper, it is possible that some students with special learning needs will have difficulty in figuring out measurements and in doing the cutting. Assistance may be required.

petroglyph (**peh**-truh-glif), *a symbolic rock carving or painting.* Objects of this kind were created long ago by Native American artists. Such images have been found in 41 of the 50 states and in Canada. Many petroglyphs are thought to date as far back as 8000 B.C., about 10,000 years ago.

Examine the petroglyph in this picture. Can you identify the creature shown? The four pairs of legs should provide a clue to its identity. It is a spider. Note that this is no ordinary spider. Rather, it is the Spider Woman. This is a goddess-like figure common to the teachings of the Hopi and Zuni peoples of the American Southwest. The petroglyph symbolizes the story of creation. According to this tale, the Spider Woman formed all living creatures out of clay using her many slender fingers. A second figure, the Sun God Tawa, sent glowing rays to warm the creatures, thus breathing life into them. How does this creation story compare with others you may have heard? What does it reveal about the role of nature in the Hopi and Zuni system of beliefs?

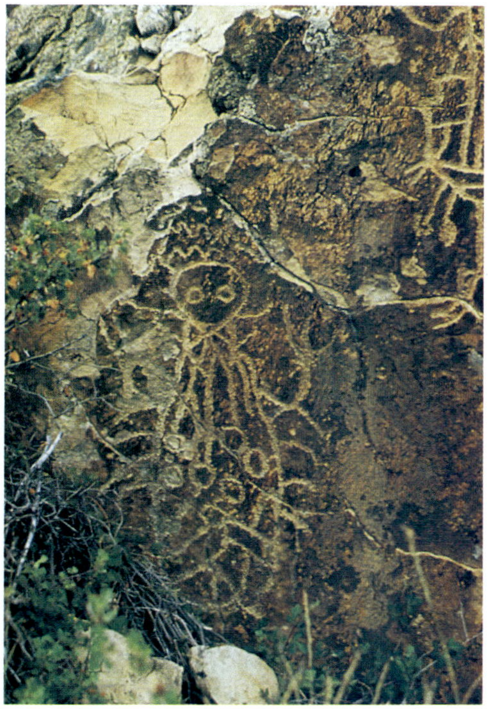

Studio Activity

Designing a Cartouche

Creative expression. Produce a design of your own personal cartouche. Begin by cutting a 4 x 9-inch rectangle from a large brown paper bag or from a sheet of brown butcher paper. Using pencil, draw an oval that fills most of the surface area. Within the oval, sketch images that correspond to letters in your name—a cat for *Catherine,* a car for *Carl.* Alternatively, sketch objects that symbolize your interests or hobbies. Go over all lines in fairly wide-tipped dark brown, red, and black markers. Allow a few minutes to make sure the markers have dried. Crumple the paper, then carefully smooth it out. The remaining creases will give your art an aged look.

PORTFOLIO

In self-reflection, write what you learned about symbolizing your name for a cartouche.

Check Your Understanding

1. What type of language was used by the ancient Egyptians?
2. What is a *cartouche?*
3. How were petroglyphs made?

◆ **Figure 12–3** What type of balance has been used in this image?

Native American. Petroglyph. *Spider Woman.* Nina River, Wyoming. Photo by Andrea Bush.

Understanding Art History

Have students learn about the Rosetta Stone, found in Rosetta, Egypt, in 1799 by an officer of Napoleon's army. Until this discovery, no one had been able to decipher Egyptian hieroglyphic. The Rosetta Stone has an inscription in hieroglyphic and the same one in Greek. From the Greek, two English scientists were able to find the key to understanding hieroglyphic. The Rosetta Stone is now in the British Museum.

3 Assess

Self-Assessment

Have students complete the **Check Your Understanding** questions on this page. Answers are provided below.

Reteaching

In pairs, have students study a display of their cartouches. Have them analyze their use of the art element color and principle emphasis. Were they able to identify the student's name? L1 ELL

Enrichment

Introduce students to sign language, which is a form of picture "writing." Signs for *love, happy, angry, see,* and *house,* for example, are easy to learn. Invite a teacher of signing to come to your class and teach some key words and phrases.

4 Close

Have students illustrate a story in pictures. Ask students to write in words what they "read" in each other's picture story. L1

Answers to Check Your Understanding

1. The written language used by the ancient Egyptians was hieroglyphic.
2. A cartouche is an oval or oblong containing a person's name in hieroglyphic form.
3. Petroglyphs were made by carving or painting symbolic images on rocks.

LESSON 2

Making a Visual Autobiography

(pages 226–227)
Lesson Time: 90 minutes

1 Focus

Objectives

After completing this lesson, students will be able to:

- Express a variety of ideas based on personal experience.
- Design and create a visual expression of who they are.
- Describe, analyze, interpret, and judge their visual autobiographies.

SUPPLIES
Refer to **What You Will Need** in the Student Edition.

2 Teach

Motivator

Discuss with students the Gutierrez self-portrait in **Figure 12–4**. Point out images and have students tell what they think each means. Then ask them to make a written list in three columns—persons, places, and things—they would like to include in their visual autobiography.

Vocabulary

Discuss the terms *biography* and *autobiography.* Note the difference in point of view. Also, have students talk about the difference between a self-portrait and a visual autobiography.

LESSON 2

Making a Visual Autobiography

Who am I? That question might at first seem easy for most of us to answer. Careful thought, however, reveals that each of us is a complex, one-of-a-kind individual. The person you see when you look into the mirror has a story to tell unlike anyone else's. Some writers have, in fact, written entire books about themselves and their lives. These are called *autobiographies.*

The painting in **Figure 12–4** is an autobiography of sorts. In this case, the artist has answered the question *Who am I?* without using words. Study the painting. The artist has painted herself three times. What differences can you find among the three self-portraits? Notice the images—an eye, a shoe, a factory, a chicken—which the artist has placed in front of her own image. What meaning do you suppose she wants us to "read" into these?

WHAT YOU WILL LEARN

You will create your own "visual autobiography" by illustrating themes from personal experience. Think of qualities and traits that make up the one-of-a-kind individual that is "you." Use a combination of found and original images to tell your story. You will emphasize the importance of events and objects in your picture through size and color contrast.

WHAT YOU WILL NEED

- Sheet of lined notebook paper and pencil
- Used magazines
- Scissors
- Sheet of white or colored drawing paper, 9 x 12 inches
- White glue
- Markers and oil pastels

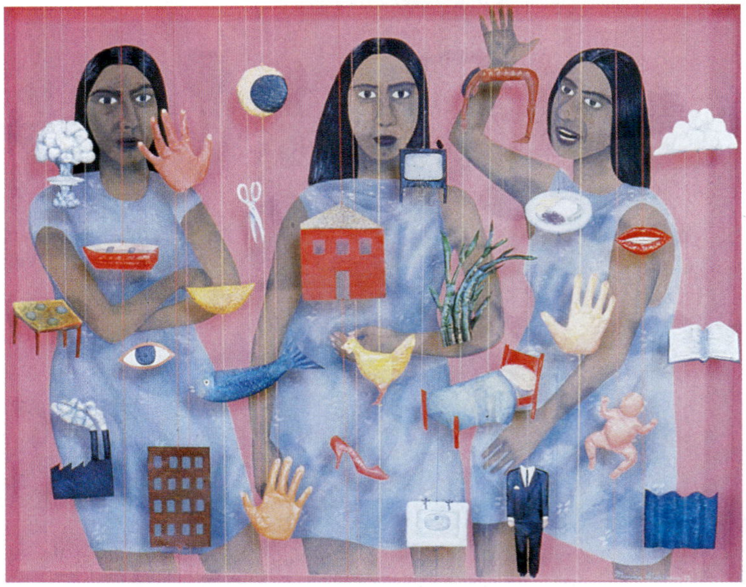

◆ **Figure 12–4** The images of hands and other objects are painted metal cutouts. They stand out in relief from the large triple self-portrait.

Marina Gutierrez. *Biography.* 1988. Acrylic on Masonite with painted metal. 122 × 183 × 15.2 cm (48 × 72 × 6″). Courtesy of the artist.

RESOURCES BEYOND THE CLASSROOM

GUEST SPEAKERS Don't overlook the importance of guest speakers in the art classroom. Guests can come from a variety of areas and can speak on a wide range of topics. For example, a career counselor can discuss art careers and how to prepare for them. An artist can demonstrate specific techniques. An art historian can talk about a certain historical period, while an art critic can help students understand various aesthetic approaches to understanding art. Speakers can be found at nearby community colleges, area art councils, and in community organizations.

What You Will Do

1. Divide a sheet of lined paper into two columns. In one column, list your hobbies, interests, likes, talents, and so on. Also include memories that have special meaning to you. Be sure to express a variety of ideas based on your personal experience. In the second column, note images that relate to the items in the first column. If you play an instrument, for example, you might draw several musical notes in the image column.
2. Look through old magazines for photographs of about half of the images you have recorded in your second column. Choose photos in a variety of sizes. Clip these out and arrange them in an interesting fashion on the sheet of drawing paper. When you are happy with the composition, glue the images in place.
3. Fill most of the remaining space on your paper with pencil sketches of other images from your list. Make some of the images larger than others. Leave some negative space between them. Write your name in a creative way between some of the images. Use block letters, squiggly lines, connected circles, and so forth.
4. Complete your illustrations with markers and oil pastels. Use bright hues for some images, contrasting duller hues for others.

Evaluating Your Work

- **Describe** What images appear in your artwork?
- **Analyze** How have you used size and color contrast to suggest the importance of some images?
- **Interpret** What does your artwork tell about you as a person? What title would you give your work?
- **Judge** Decide whether your autobiography is effective in terms of its design. Decide whether it is effective in telling about your life.

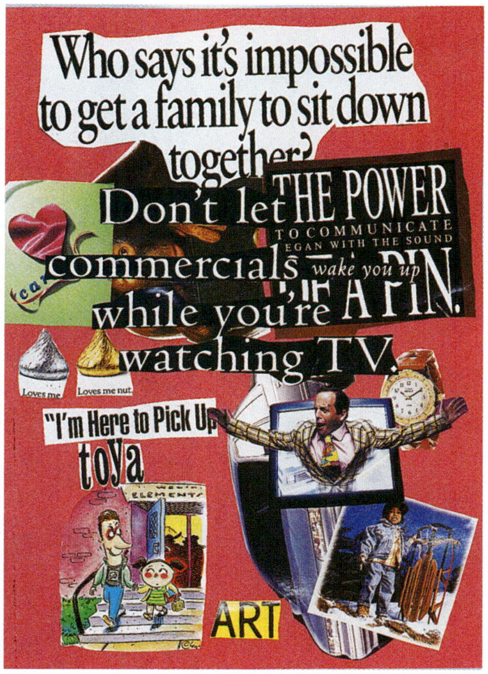

◆ **Figure 12–5** Student work. A visual autobiography.

Computer Option

Use a digital camera to produce photographic imagery. Have a friend capture a portrait of you. Title and save your image in an art application. On a new page, draw images that reveal your interests and traits. Copy and paste these images onto your portrait page. Resize and rearrange each image so they overlap your portrait.

Visual Art Journal

In your journal, describe your visual autobiography. What qualities and traits were most important for you to showcase? Why are these qualities valuable to you?

Studio Skills

Suggest starting the composition either by dividing the paper into sections with a ruler or by drawing a few large images. From there on, encourage students to recall pleasant memories to include anywhere on the paper. Encourage risking ideas. L1 ELL

Aesthetics

Have students analyze their peers' finished work just as a composition. They should analyze formal properties such as balance, emphasis, proportion, harmony, rhythm, and movement. Discuss the element of space in these works. L1

3 Assess

Self-Assessment

Have students use **Evaluating Your Work** to conduct an in-progress critique of their visual autobiography.

Reteaching

Have students discuss the difference between a self-portrait and a visual autobiography. L1

Enrichment

Ask students to choose a famous artist, writer, or other well-known, successful achiever whom they admire. Have students research important aspects of that person's life and create a visual biography of him or her. L2

4 Close

Discuss students' reactions to bringing together personal memories in a visual expression. How did they decide which were to be large and which small?

Technology Strategies in the Art Classroom

Electronic Media-Generated Art With a variety of digital tools, encourage students to create a personal autobiographical time line of important events in their life. Encourage students to take advantage of scanning and digital photography to record, copy, and print examples from family photo albums, early drawings, and writing. Students can include memorabilia and other important items. Remind students to create unity by using a consistent element, such as line, shape, color, texture, frame, or border. For more information on cameras, scanners, or software, refer students to the **Digital Media Guide.**

Myths and Legends

(pages 228–229)

1 Focus

Objectives

After completing this lesson, students will be able to:

- Understand the place of myth and legend in world cultures.
- Give examples of how myths and legends have appeared in visual art.
- Compare artworks depicting myths from different cultures.

2 Teach

Motivator

Discuss the many examples today of myth and legend in film and video. *Beauty and the Beast* and *The Lord of the Rings* are some examples. Find and compare myths and legends of various cultures in your library.

Vocabulary

Discuss the difference between *legendary* and *real.* Dinosaurs were real. The discovery of skeletal remains shows us the actual size and characteristics of these immense creatures. Legendary creatures, like dragons, come from stories and myths. Someone or something that might have once been real, such as Daniel Boone, can take on legendary qualities over time.

LESSON 3

Myths and Legends

Do you know the story of how the giraffe got its long neck? Maybe you are familiar with the legend of Hercules, the mighty Greek warrior. Myths and legends like these have been passed down through generations. They have also crossed many cultural boundaries.

In this lesson, you will learn about myths and legends from around the world. You will take a quick look at visual retellings of two such legends.

Legends Based on Human Traits

"They all lived happily ever after." You almost certainly know these words. You probably have heard them countless times at the end of bedtime stories when you were young. These words reflect our fondness for happy endings. They also reveal our desire to overcome evil, whether it is a wicked witch or the misdeeds of real people.

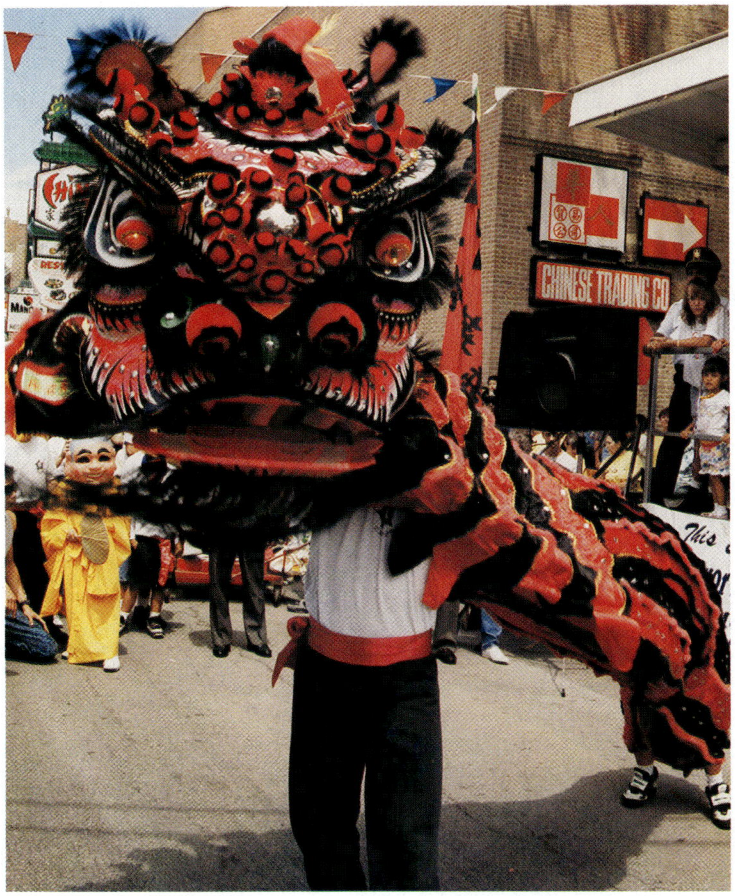

◆ **Figure 12–6** **Notice how balance is used to organize this object. Analyze the use of color.**

Chinese Dragon. Photo by Brian Lee.

MORE ABOUT...

Mythology Artists have depicted mythical creatures in their artwork since prehistoric times, but perhaps more than any other group of myths, the figures of Greek and Roman mythology have been particular favorites of Western artists. Ask students to research the system of gods and goddesses in Greek mythology. Then have them trace examples of these myths in artworks over the centuries. After students have a general understanding of *classical mythology,* as it is called, assign each student a mythological figure to identify in several different artists' works and bring copies of the works to class to show and discuss with others.

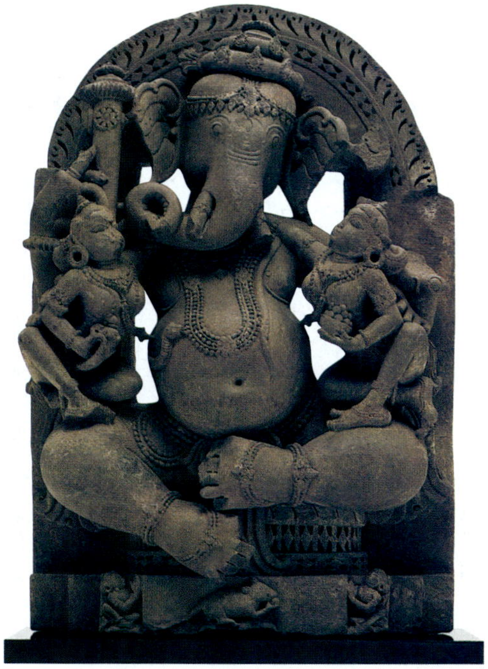

◆ **Figure 12–7** **Analyze the use of movement and form in this sculpture.**

The Hindu God Ganesha and His Consorts. Early eleventh century. Cream sandstone. 41.5 cm (16⅓″). John H. and Ernestine A. Payne Fund, Helen S. Coolidge Fund, Asiatic Curator's Fund, John Ware Willard Fund, and Marshall H. Gould Fund. Courtesy of Museum of Fine Arts, Boston, Massachusetts.

Object Based on Myth

The subject of **Figure 12–6** is a creature that is often used to represent evil in the legends of our own culture. Can you identify this mythical beast? It is a fire-breathing dragon. Study the menacing frown, flaring nostrils, and glowing red eyes. Don't bother looking for the brave knight you are accustomed to seeing wherever dragons lurk. In China, where this object was created, dragons are a symbol of good luck. A costume like this is typically worn by the lead figure in a parade to bring in the Chinese New Year. Can you think of other cultures you have learned about in which frightening masks are worn on happy occasions? How has the artist used the element of line to emphasize the dragon's fierceness?

Time & Place

Chinese New Year

Cultural connection. The traditional Chinese calendar is a lunar calendar, based on the cycles of the moon. Following this calendar, the new year begins somewhere between late January and early February. Although the Chinese have adopted the Western calendar, the lunar calendar is still used to celebrate festive occasions such as the Chinese New Year.

The traditional Chinese New Year celebration begins with the new moon on the first day of the new year. It lasts until the full moon 15 days later. On New Year's Eve, the Chinese shoot off firecrackers to symbolize driving away evil spirits. According to tradition, all doors and windows should be opened at midnight to allow the old year to go out. The Chinese New Year is celebrated with festivals and parades, highlighted by a dragon dance (see **Figure 12–6**). Compare the Chinese Dragon in Figure 12–6 with the Hindu sculpture in Figure 12–7.

Sculpture Based on Myth

The sculpture in **Figure 12–7** depicts another creature meant to bring luck. The work is a product of India.

This mythical figure is Ganesha, the ancient Hindu god of good fortune. Works like this once adorned the outsides of Hindu temples. What kind of creature is Ganesha? How did the sculptor go about breathing life and energy into this mythical being?

Check Your Understanding

1. Compare the two artworks on these pages and describe what they have in common.
2. What differences do you detect?

Time & Place

Chinese New Year

Both **Figures 12–6** and **12–7** are based on mythical creatures believed to bring luck. Although, they are different objects, they each represent a similar cultural belief.

Team Building Activity

Assign small groups of students to work collaboratively and go to the library or Internet to find examples of mythological creatures from many lands and cultures. Have each group choose one culture—Chinese, Japanese, Native American, Meso-American, for example—to read about and find artworks that tell about mythological figures from that culture. Prepare a myth hall of fame to display materials students bring in to share and compare these artworks. L1 ELL

3 Assess

Self-Assessment

Have students complete the **Check Your Understanding** questions on this page. Answers are provided below.

Enrichment

Invite students to research the legend of Ganesha and discuss their findings in class. L2

4 Close

Ask students to discuss what traits legendary creatures often have.

Answers to Check Your Understanding

1. These two artworks both depict symbolic, mythological creatures.
2. Ganesha is part imaginary animal, part real animal. The dragon is not at all real.

Creating a Mythical Creature

(pages 230–231)
Lesson Time: 90 minutes

1 Focus

Objectives

After completing this lesson, students will be able to:

- Create a mythical creature that exhibits formal balance and rhythm based on color and pattern.
- Understand the significance of Kachinas in the Hopi culture.
- Demonstrate technical skills effectively using a variety of art media and materials.
- Describe, analyze, interpret, and judge their artwork.

SUPPLIES
Refer to **What You Will Need** in the Student Edition.

2 Teach

Motivator

Every culture has its myths and legends. Ask students how every country, every race, every culture benefits from its particular myths and legends. *(They lend color and richness to the traditions of each group.)* Find many examples of Kachinas and have students read to learn about their meaning and the way that the Hopi culture is continued through these hand-crafted statuettes.

Creating a Mythical Creature

In the previous lesson, you learned about two mythical creatures. This lesson will teach you about another myth—a Hopi tradition and the legends connected with it.

Among the Hopi Indians of America's Southwest, it is believed that all things in the world have two forms, a visible object and a spirit essence. A **Kachina** (kuh-**chee**-nuh), a *hand-crafted statuette that represents spirits in Pueblo rituals,* represents the spirit essence. Kachinas are used to teach Native American children about the traditions of their people.

The *Eagle Kachina* in **Figure 12–8** is the spirit of the eagle. This is used in dances as a prayer for an increase of eagles. Examine the object closely. What features of the bird in the object's title are represented in this statuette? How would you describe the use of color?

What You Will Learn

You will design and construct your own Kachina. Everyday found objects will be used to construct your Kachina. Your finished object, like the one in Figure 12–8, will exhibit formal balance and rhythm based on color and pattern.

What You Will Need

- Sketch paper and pencil
- Three cardboard tubes from paper towels
- Colored construction paper
- Transparent tape
- Wrapping paper
- Scissors
- Work gloves (optional)
- Tempera paints, brushes
- Found objects, such as fabric scraps, raffia, and feathers
- Stapler or white glue
- Jewelry boxes or other small boxes

What You Will Do

1. You will demonstrate technical skills using a variety of art media and materials to produce a sculpture of a Kachina.

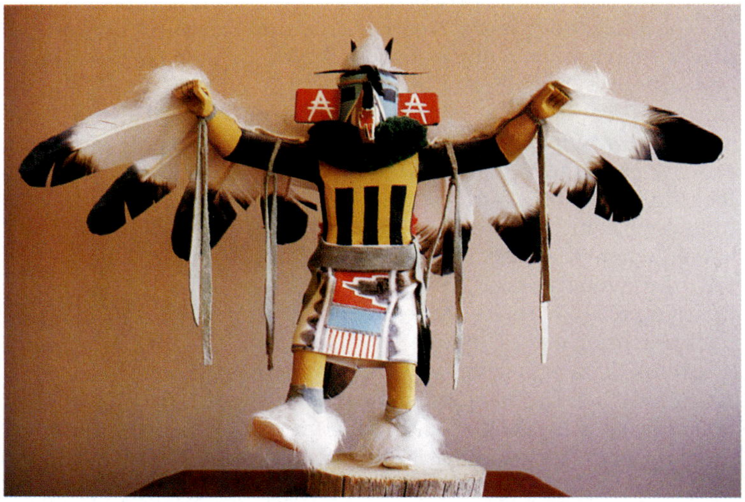

◆ **Figure 12–8** What details in this figure reflect the Native American culture?

L. Joe. *Eagle Kachina.* 1990. Wood, leather, feathers, yarn, and fur. 30 cm (12″). Private Collection.

MORE ABOUT...

THE HOPI The Hopi are one of the Pueblo tribes. Their towns in the arid mesa lands of northeast Arizona are some of the oldest continuously inhabited villages in the United States. The Hopi are a small, friendly group, tied together by their religious beliefs. The driving force of the Hopi religion is the need for water. The rain ritual, the planting ritual, and the corn-growing rituals are very important ceremonies. When clouds hang over the mountains, it is the rain-bringing Kachinas that are present. The Hopi do not worship these Kachinas but treat them as friends or partners who care about the Hopi people.

Begin construction by cutting one of the cardboard tubes in half lengthwise. The two narrow half-cylinders that result are to be the creature's legs. Wrap a scrap of brightly colored construction paper around the left leg. Secure it with transparent tape. Use a scrap of wrapping paper in a busy pattern to cover the right leg.

2. Follow a similar procedure with a second tube to form the arms. This time, begin by cutting away about 3 inches of the tube. Then cut the remaining part in half lengthwise. Again, attach colored paper and wrapping paper, this time to the opposite limbs. Attach the arms to the body with tape.
3. Cut two slits into the top of each leg. Slide the upper body down into the slits.
4. Create the Kachina's head by painting the top of the body tube. Use a medium brush to apply the base paint for the head. Add facial features—eyes, nose, mouth—with contrasting hues. Use a fine brush for this task. The features and other decorations should be highly geometric, as in Figure 12–8.
5. Use found objects such as fabric scraps, raffia, and feathers to create interesting features. Add the features to your Kachina with a stapler or white glue.
6. Use jewelry boxes or other small boxes for the Kachina's feet. Notch the bottoms of the legs and glue them to the boxes. Paint the feet.

Evaluating Your Work

- **Describe** Point out the arms, legs, and body of your figure. Identify wings, scales, or other such features.
- **Analyze** Does your Kachina exhibit formal balance and rhythm based on color and pattern?
- **Interpret** What feeling or mood is communicated by your Kachina?
- **Judge** What are the best features of your figure? What would you do differently if you were to repeat the lesson?

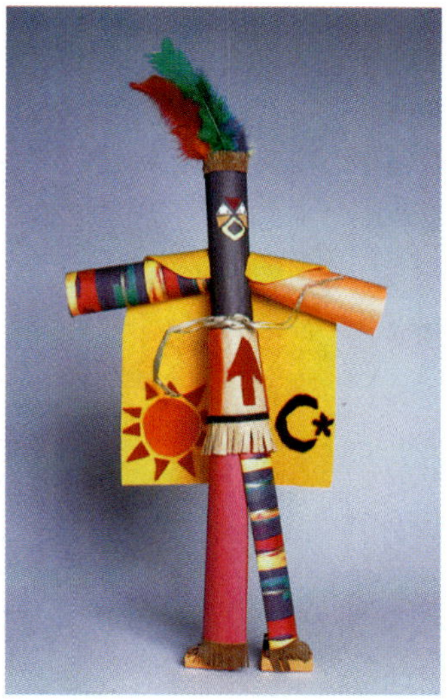

◆ **Figure 12–9** Student work. Kachina.

PORTFOLIO IDEAS

Artwork doesn't always fit into a folder or even a large portfolio. What if you worked with a group to make a three-dimensional sculpture or a mural? Photographs and drawings are one way to document the experience of working together. Another way is to write about it in detail. When describing work performed in groups, outline the goal and list each member's responsibility. Then focus on your own specific tasks for self-reflection and evaluation.

Art Online

For additional activities, check out our Web site at **art.glencoe.com**. There you will also find:

- Artist Profiles
- Career Corner
- Interactive Games
- Museum Web Links

DEVELOPING A PORTFOLIO

Group Projects When assigning group projects, discuss student responsibility and contribution to the group prior to the beginning of the project. Clear expectations of group members as well as the actual project will help students begin with a defined objective and clear focus. If there is to be an end project, consider how it can be documented in some way so that it can be included in all group members' portfolios. Group summaries of peers are often part of group projects. Rubrics provide a common point of reference for the students in completing the assignment and a clear understanding of what is expected.

Art Criticism

Find many examples and study their sculptu Some are carved fron ers are constructed of many mate rials. With students, analyze the principles of art in their design. Find the elements of line, shape, color, and texture in the Kachina examples and look for these also in the students' figures. L1

Historical/Cultural Heritage

Encourage students to learn more about the art and culture of Native American tribes. The use and significance of geometric shapes in pottery, rug design, sand painting, and other art forms is important. The Native American artist aims to restore harmony in natural forces. They live very close to nature, respecting it and caring for the earth.

3 Assess

Self-Assessment

Have students use **Evaluating Your Work** to conduct an in-progress critique of the Kachina they created.

Reteaching

Display students' artwork and have students assess its success. Ask students to compose a legend for their own Kachina.

4 Close

Ask students to describe their work and talk about its significance for them. Did they make a personal statement?

LESSON 5

Art Stories Larger Than Life

(pages 232–233)

1 Focus

Objectives

After completing this lesson, students will be able to:

- Understand the meaning and origin of the word *fresco.*
- Understand that frescoes and murals can both tell a story.

2 Teach

Motivator

Introduce the idea of large-scale stories. Ask students to talk about some of their favorite books and movies. Explain that art, too, can tell a grand story on a large scale. Direct students' attention to the Rivera fresco in **Figure 12–10.** Ask students to identify some of the "characters" in this story.

Historical/Cultural Heritage

Many of the city murals found in large cities of the United States are done by individuals who represent a large variety of ethnic groups. Find some examples (or ask students to find some) of these ethnic works in your own city or community. If possible, contact the muralists and arrange for them to visit the class. Remind students that a muralist must have permission from authorities before painting on any public structure.

LESSON 5

Art Stories Larger than Life

Some storytellers create short stories. These tell about an event or experience so specific that it may be recounted in just a few pages. Other stories are told on a much grander scale. These stories focus on events that are more complex or of great importance. They require hundreds and sometimes thousands of pages.

Visual stories, too, may be told on a large or small scale. In this lesson, you will look at stories that are larger than life.

FRESCOES

When you were little, you may have been scolded for drawing on the wall. Some professional artists make a living doing just that. They create frescoes (**fres**-kohz). A **fresco** is *a painting created when pigment is applied to a section of wall spread with fresh plaster.* The word fresco is Italian for "fresh." The technique of fresco painting got its start in Italy during the late Middle Ages.

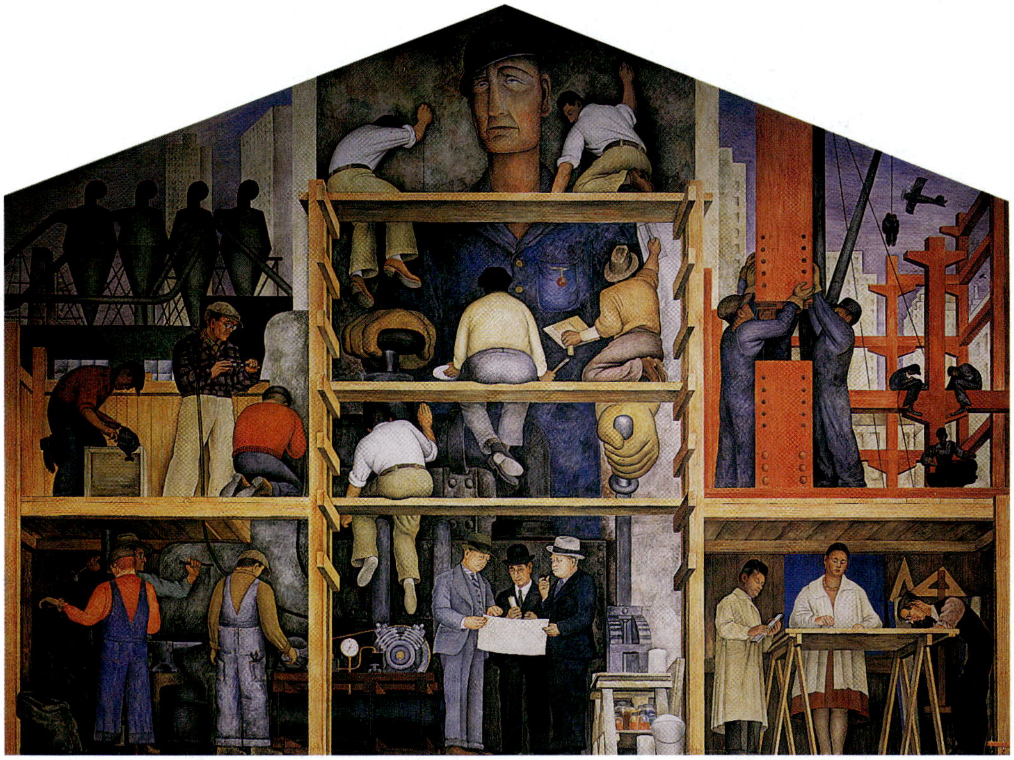

◆ **Figure 12–10** **Notice that the figures in the room at the viewer's lower right are wearing lab coats. What service do you think they provide to city dwellers?**

Diego Rivera. *The Making of a Fresco Showing the Building of a City.* 1931. Fresco. 6.9 × 9 m (22′ 7″ × 29′ 9″). Located at the San Francisco Art Institute, San Francisco, California.

INCLUSION STRATEGIES

SPECIAL LEARNING NEEDS Small group instruction and collaborative learning can be extremely beneficial to students who may learn at a slower pace. When assigning groups, make sure that there is a heterogeneous mix of abilities and personalities. Each group should have students who can offer direction, students who provide organization and order, students who risk ideas, and students who are willing contributors. Stress to the class that in group projects, each individual is important to the success of the group as a whole.

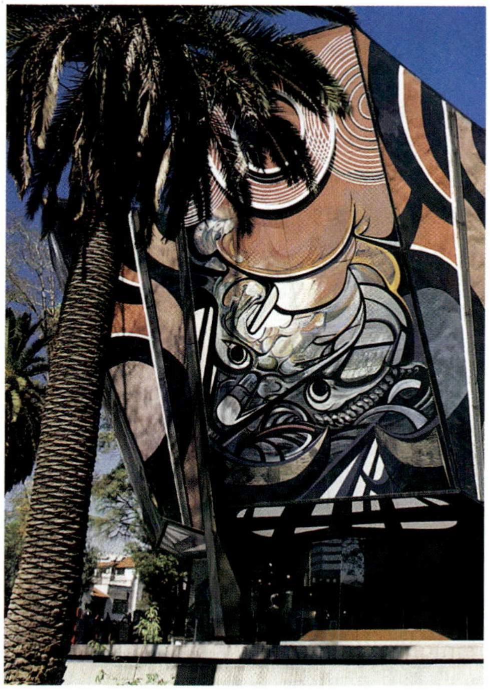

◆ **Figure 12–11** **This building, which was completed the year the artist died, bears his name. The mural shown covers 274 square meters.**

David Alfaro Siqueiros. *Poliforum.* 1974. Acrylic enamel on asbestos-cement and steel. 15 m (49′ 2½″). Mexico City, Mexico. Mexican Government Tourism Office, New York.

Frescoes that Tell a Story

The fresco in **Figure 12–10** was painted in the early 1930s. Observe the work's physical dimensions. The figures and objects in it have been painted life-size. Notice the painting's unusual shape. The artist has provided a **cutaway** of a house under construction. This is *a view in which an outside wall has been removed to reveal the scene within.* Most of the details in this painting are activities you would expect to find in such a scene. There are workers in coveralls laying foundations and men in business suits reviewing plans.

However, there is more to this painting than meets the eye. Notice the title. The fresco depicts not the building of a house but of a city. People from all walks of life work cooperatively toward a common goal. What is that goal? In what way is a house a fitting symbol of a city?

Meet the Artist

Diego Rivera (1886–1957)

Cultural connection. Diego Rivera is best known for painting large murals on the sides of public buildings. Many of his murals tell stories of his native Mexico, including its history and culture. Rivera often explored social and political themes in his work.

Born in Guanajuato, Mexico, in 1886, Rivera studied art at the Academy of San Carlos in Mexico City. He also took two trips to Europe to study art. When Rivera returned to his homeland in 1921, he began painting murals and frescoes (see **Figure 12–10**). His murals are found on many buildings in Mexico and also in the United States. Rivera died in 1957, leaving behind an unfinished mural for the National Palace in Mexico City.

To learn more about Rivera and his work, click on Artist Profiles at **art.glencoe.com**.

Murals

The artist who painted the fresco in Figure 12–10, Diego Rivera, was a notable Mexican artist. So was the individual responsible for the work in **Figure 12–11**. His name was David Alfaro Siqueiros (ahl-**far**-oh see-**cay**-rohs). This gigantic work is a *mural,* a type of public art done on a wall. The mural shown here graces the outside of an arts center in Mexico City. There are 12 such works, one for each of the sides of this oddly shaped building. Each mural addresses a different theme. Examine this giant artwork. What story does it tell? How would you describe its composition?

Check Your Understanding

1. What is a *fresco?* What is the origin of the word?
2. Compare ways in which the works on these pages are similar. How are the two different?

Answers to Check Your Understanding

1. A fresco is a painting created when pigment is applied to a section of wall spread with fresh plaster. The word *fresco* is Italian for "fresh."
2. They are similar in that they both are large and are public art. Their differences involve media and surface: Rivera's is a fresco painted on a wall; Siqueiros's is a mural painted on the outside of a building.

Meet the Artist

Diego Rivera

Most of Rivera's murals and frescoes deal with Mexican culture and history. Rivera was considered controversial because of his political views. Diego Rivera was commissioned by the Mexican government to paint many murals and frescoes; some of his best are in the National Palace in Mexico City. Ask students to locate examples of Diego's work and identify the influence of historical and political events in those artworks.

Aesthetics

Discuss with students the importance of murals in beautifying cities. Find examples of urban murals. They are often done in highly used or depressed areas of the city to give support to everyday people.

3 Assess

Self-Assessment

Have students complete the **Check Your Understanding** questions on this page. Answers are provided below.

Reteaching

In pairs, have students identify the differences between a fresco and a mural, finding examples of each in the book. L1

4 Close

Have students apply the four art-criticism questions to one of the artworks presented in this lesson. L1

Telling a Story Through Art

(pages 234–235)

1 Focus

Objectives

After completing this lesson students will be able to:

- Recognize sources of inspiration to which artists turn when searching for ideas for their work.
- Form generalizations about the interdependence of the art elements line and color and principles movement and rhythm in a work of art.
- Explain how writers and artists create a sense of action and movement.

2 Teach

Motivator

Write on the board, "A picture is worth a thousand words." Ask whether students are familiar with this saying. Explain that in this lesson, they will see an artist's visualization of a scene from a famous work of fiction.

Active Reading

Have students read the excerpt in **Figure 12–12.** Instruct students to attempt to capture the suspense of the passage by emphasizing colorful words in the passage. Students should recognize how style, tone, and mood contribute to the effect of the text.

Telling a Story Through Art

"Her words paint a vivid picture." "His painting tells a dramatic story." You have probably read descriptions like these. The first sentence describes a skillful writer, and the second describes a skillful artist. Sentences like these illustrate the tight bond that connects literature and art. These two forms of expression are so related that sometimes they overlap. In fact, many artworks are based on or inspired by literature.

Interpreting Literature

The passage in **Figure 12–12** is from Washington Irving's *The Legend of Sleepy Hollow.* In this scene, Ichabod Crane and his horse Gunpowder are being pursued by the dreaded Headless Horseman. Read Irving's excerpt. Pay close

Excerpt from "The Legend of Sleepy Hollow"

"If I can but reach that bridge," thought Ichabod, "I am safe." Just then he heard the black steed panting and blowing close behind him; he even fancied that he felt his hot breath. Another convulsive kick in the ribs, and old Gunpowder sprang upon the bridge; he thundered over the resounding planks . . . Ichabod cast a look behind . . . Just then he saw the goblin rising in his stirrups, and in the very act of hurling his head at him. Ichabod endeavored to dodge the horrible missile, but too late. It encountered his cranium with a tremendous crash—he was tumbled headlong into the dust, and Gunpowder, the black steed, and the goblin rider, passed by like a whirlwind."

◆ **Figure 12–12** Excerpt from "The Legend of Sleepy Hollow" by Washington Irving.

MORE ABOUT...

William John Wilgus (1819–53) As a teenager, William was sent to New York City to study art formally with Samuel F. B. Morse. *Ichabod Crane and the Headless Horsemen* was his first important painting. Wilgus painted a few landscapes, but his favorite subjects were portraiture and works depicting Native Americans of western New York. In the early 1840s, he opened a portrait studio in New York City, where he cultivated a reputation for his excellent likenesses. Ill health forced him to move to the South. His life and career were cut short by lung disease, to which he succumbed at the age of 34.

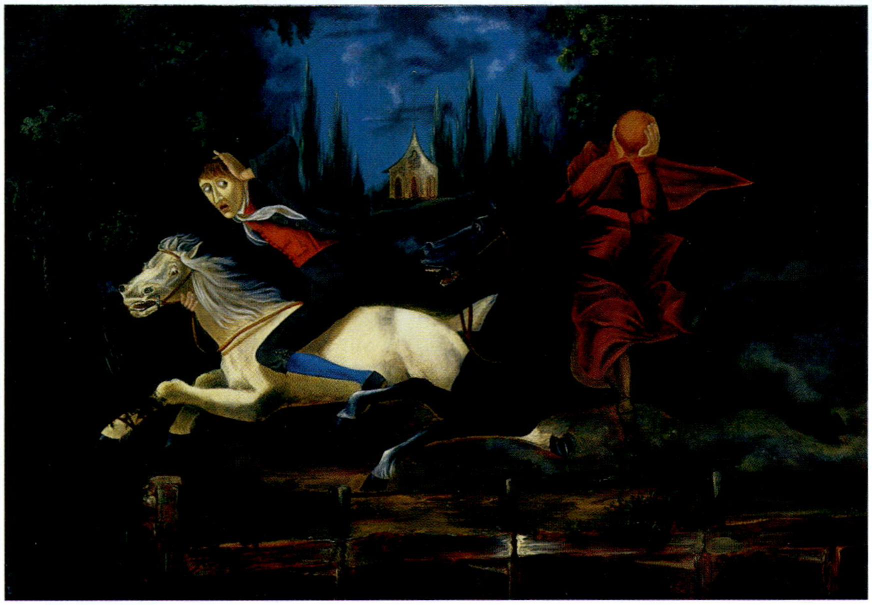

◆ **Figure 12–13**
Notice how the artist captures the action in Irving's story. What qualities add to the suspense and terror of the scene?

William John Wilgus. *Ichabod Crane and the Headless Horsemen*. c. 1855. Canvas. 53.3 × 76.7 cm (21 × 30.2″). National Gallery of Art, Washington, D.C. Gift of Edgar William and Bernice Chrysler Garbisch.

attention to how the author used descriptive words to paint an exciting, suspenseful scene.

Art Inspired by Literature

Now look at **Figure 12–13,** a painting by artist John William Wilgus. How does the artist capture the excitement and tension of Washington Irving's story? Both Irving's excerpt in Figure 12–12 and Wilgus's painting show the climax of the story. A climax is the point where a tale's dramatic tension reaches its high point. Why do you think Wilgus chose to paint this moment? Do you think he successfully portrayed Irving's story? Why or why not?

MAKE THE CONNECTION

Take Another Look

1. Reread the passage in Figure 12–12. Write down the adjectives that help create the mood. Next, write down the verbs that set the action.
2. Examine the painting in Figure 12–13. Next, write a paragraph describing the action and mood of the scene.
3. What elements and principles of art can you identify in Wilgus's painting? How do they contribute to the action and mood?

ART & READING

Sketch a scene from literature. Choose a scene from a favorite story of yours. Describe the setting, the characters, and explain what is happening. After describing the scene, draw a sketch using the appropriate elements and principles of art to express the mood of your scene.

MAKE THE CONNECTION

Take Another Look Student answers will vary, but may include the following:

1. Adjectives might include *hot, convulsive, resounding, horrible,* and *tremendous.* Verbs might include *panting, blowing, thundered, hurling, dodge,* and *tumble.*
2. Paragraphs should show originality and thought.
3. Students might mention the art principles movement or rhythm, which is evident in the repeated use of diagonal lines, as well as color contrast, which draws attention to the face on the schoolteacher.

Aesthetics

Point out that diagonal lines often create a feeling of unrest or tension in a work of art. Ask:

- Where does the artist, William John Wilgus, use diagonal lines in **Figure 12–13?** *(They are used in the figure of Ichabod Crane, the legs of both horses, and the arms of the Headless Horseman.)*
- How would the painting be different if the artist had not used these lines? *(It would lack the feeling of dynamic action suggested by these lines.)*

Art Criticism

Explain that Wilgus, in his visual retelling of the story, chose the most exciting moment. Have students imagine that he had chosen instead to depict events of the following morning. Ask: What might the subject of this painting be? Conclude by having students do sketches of their version of this scene. Allow time for comparison.

3 Assess

Self-Assessment

Have students complete the **Take Another Look** questions on this page. Answers are provided below.

Reteaching

Have students match up characters in the excerpt with figures in the painting.

4 Close

Create a gallery of the sketches students made for the "Art & Reading" assignment in this lesson.

Book Illustration

(pages 236–237)

1 Focus

Objectives

After completing this lesson, students will be able to:

- Understand the functions of book illuminations and the purpose of missals.
- Understand the functions of book illustrations.
- Recognize the differences in producing handmade and printed books.

2 Teach

Motivator

Ask students to imagine themselves in medieval times hand-lettering an entire book. Explain that the printing press made it possible to produce books faster and in greater quantities. More people learned to read. As a result, the role of books changed. Today, book illustrations still go beyond mere decoration. They serve to work with the text to communicate what the writer has to say.

Vocabulary

Have students recall terms introduced earlier: illuminations, woodcuts, miniatures.

LESSON 7

Book Illustration

As mentioned earlier, some stories are told in words, others in pictures. In this lesson, you will look at picture stories that co-exist successfully side by side with the printed word. Pictures of this kind appear scattered throughout the book you are holding at this moment. They are called *book illustrations.*

Manuscript Illustration

The practice of illustrating books goes back some 1,100 years. The earliest such illustrations were tiny paintings known as *illuminations.* They were so called because their job was to illuminate—or shed light on—the words on the page. Illuminations were common in Europe at a time when most people could not read. These illustrations thus served a function that went beyond mere decoration. Do you recall the name for art of this type?

The object in **Figure 12–14** is an illuminated page from a book produced around the turn of the fifteenth century. This book was called a *missal* (**mis**-uhl). Its purpose was to teach. The bulk of the instruction was provided by miniature framed images of the sort appearing at the top of the page shown. Notice the richly colored border of fanciful plants and creatures. Each of these objects was individually hand-painted. What kind of lessons do you think missals taught? Do you know the story narrated by the framed picture on this missal page?

Book Illustration of Today

The invention of the printing press in the 1400s changed for all time the way books were made and illustrated. At first, all illustrations were done as woodcuts.

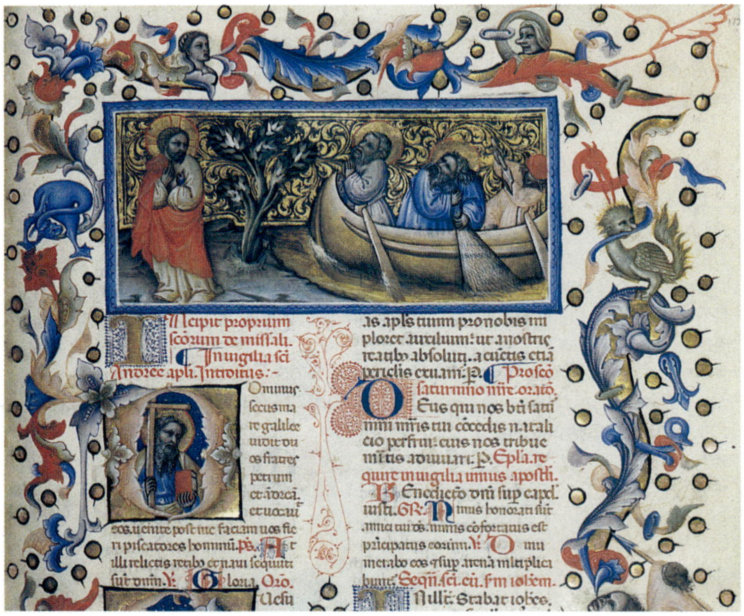

◆ **Figure 12–14** In what ways is this book page similar to others you have seen? How is it different?

Artist unknown. Missal. 1389–1404. Tempera colors, gold leaf and gold paint on vellum in a medieval, blind-stamped binding. 33 × 24 cm (13 × 9$\frac{7}{16}$″). The J. Paul Getty Museum, Los Angeles, California.

COMMUNITY CONNECTION

Create a Story Book Have students listen to a story told to them by a parent, grandparent, or family friend. Students should ask their storyteller how old they were when they first heard the story and why the story was important to them. What elements made it so memorable? While taking notes, students should ask their storyteller what visual images come to mind when they share it. Students should re-create the story in the form of a poem, or rewrite the story using the images as they see them in their own minds. Students should then take their illustrated poem or story and bind it into a small book and present it to the class.

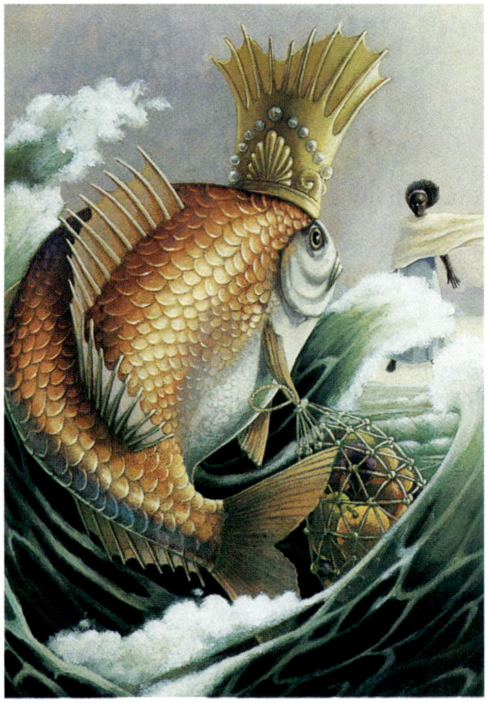

◆ **Figure 12–15** **The artists have used the art element of line to suggest action. What role does proportion play in this book illustration?**

Leo and Diane Dillon. *Marie and Redfish.* Illustration by Leo and Diane Dillon from *Her Stories: African American Folktales, Fairy Tales and True Tales* by Virginia Hamilton. Illustrations copyright © 1995 by Leo and Diane Dillon. Reprinted by permission of Scholastic, Inc.

The printing plates for such illustrations could be arranged conveniently alongside the type.

In time, changes brought about through advances in technology simplified this process. Artists today are free to create book illustrations in any medium they choose. One recent illustration appears in **Figure 12–15**. Examine this artwork. It was created to accompany a story titled "Marie and Redfish." The story tells of a teenager whose path crosses that of a prince. Find the "prince" in the picture. In what ways does this creature remind you of the mythical beasts you learned about in Lesson 3? In what ways does this illustration help the story come alive in the same way as the missal illustrations did?

Meet the Artist

Leo and Diane Dillon (b. 1933)

Cultural connection. Leo and Diane Dillon share a special distinction: They are the only artists to win the Caldecott Medal two years in a row. The Caldecott Medal is a prestigious award given to children's book illustrators. Since 1957, the Dillons have worked together to create many book illustrations, such as the one in **Figure 12–15**.

Leo Dillon was born in Brooklyn, New York, in 1933. Just 11 days later, his future wife Diane was born in Glendale, California. Leo and Diane met in 1953 while studying at the Parsons School of Design in New York City. Although their relationship began with an intense rivalry, they eventually fell in love and then married in 1957. Ever since, they have collaborated not only on book illustrations but also on posters, advertisements, and album covers. The Dillons work as a team, passing a piece back and forth, with each artist adding to and improving upon the work in progress. The end result is a unique combination that neither artist could have created individually. Compare and analyze the illustrations in Figures 12–14 and 12–15.

Check Your Understanding

1. What is an illumination? What is a missal?
2. How have book illustrations changed since the Middle Ages?

Answers to Check Your Understanding

1. An illumination is a tiny painting that was painted on the page of a hand-lettered book. Illuminations were meant to shed light on, or illuminate, the words on the page. A missal was a book that had many illuminations. The purpose of a missal was to teach.
2. Book illustrations are no longer hand-painted in each book. The printing press changed the way books were made and illustrated. Artists today are free to create book illustrations in any medium.

Meet the Artist

Leo and Diane Dillon

The artwork in **Figure 12–15** uses only a picture to describe a scene in the story, while the illustrations in **Figure 12–14** are meant to help instruct the reader.

ART IN EVERYDAY LIFE

Mention that illustrations can be found in most textbooks, newspapers, and magazines they read. Ask students to stop to evaluate illustrations whenever they see them to determine whether they simply embellish the text or help communicate ideas.

3 Assess

Self-Assessment

Have students complete the **Check Your Understanding** questions on this page. Answers are provided below.

Reteaching

Ask students to evaluate a map, poster, or drawing they created for a math, science, or other class. How was the visual effective? L1

Enrichment

Have students research different book illustrations from various cultures. Ask them to describe and compare each one. L1

4 Close

Have students choose a book that they think is beautifully illustrated. Ask them to explain why they chose that book. L1 ELL

Creating a Book Cover

(pages 238–239)
Lesson Time: 90 minutes

1 Focus

Objectives

After completing this lesson, students will be able to:

- Demonstrate technical skills effectively by using a variety of art media and materials to plan and design a book cover.
- Describe, analyze, interpret, and judge their book cover designs.

Supplies
Refer to **What You Will Need** in the Student Edition.

2 Teach

Motivator

Gather and display a variety of books from the library and discuss what makes a good design in book covers. Have students discuss which books are more appealing than others and explain why.

Vocabulary

To help students understand the word *avocational,* explain its three parts: the prefix *a–* means "not"; *vocation* means "a particular profession"; the suffix *–al* changes the noun *avocation* ("hobby") into an adjective.

LESSON 8

Creating a Book Cover

Despite what you may have heard, you *can* tell a book by its cover. For proof, examine the center portion of the quilt in **Figure 12–16.** It was used for a book cover. The group is having a "picnic" on the tar roof—the "tar beach"—of an apartment building in a big city. Notice how the illustration draws you right into the story. Do you think this art makes a good book cover?

What You Will Learn

In this lesson, you will design a book cover of your own. Begin by finding a story or making one up. Then plan a cover design that will invite readers to pick up your book and read it. You will create the title and author's name in a type style that suits the story theme or topic. The colors used for the title and the author's name should contrast with the colors of the illustration. Complete a picture to fit your chosen theme or topic.

What You Will Need

- Sketch paper and pencil
- Sheet of white drawing paper, 9 x 12 inches
- Sheet of colored construction paper
- Colored markers, crayons, or tempera paints and brushes

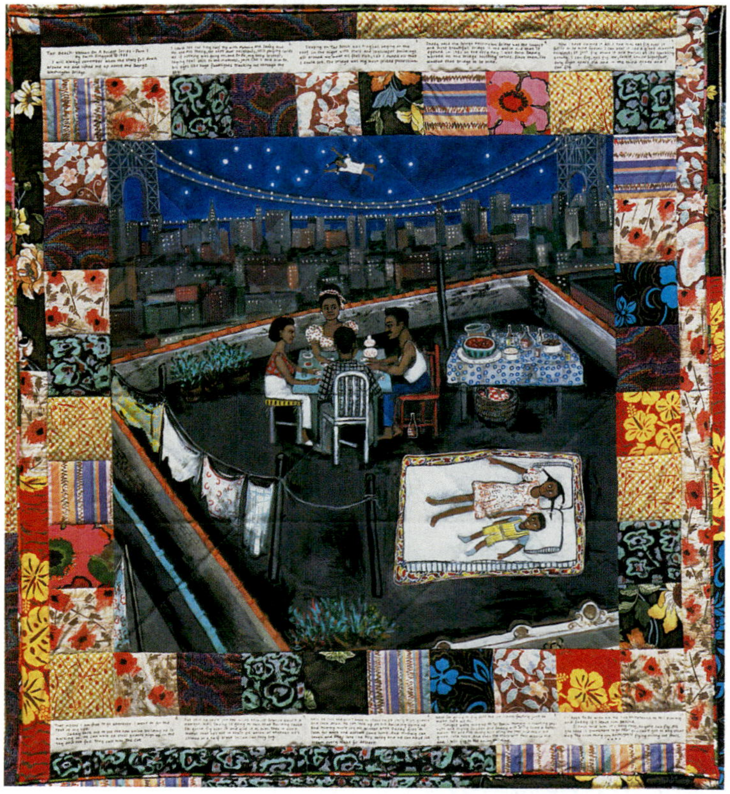

◆ **Figure 12–16** How would you describe the style of this artwork? How does the artist draw your attention to the figures?

Faith Ringgold. *Tar Beach.* 1988. Pieced and printed fabric. 188 × 175.3 cm (74 × 69″). Faith Ringgold, Inc. © Solomon Guggenheim Collection.

TECHNOLOGY STRATEGIES IN THE ART CLASSROOM

Electronic media-generated art Have students explore the Text Tool and different fonts, styles, colors, and special effects their program provides. Students can begin by making an original drawing on the computer, scan images, or take photographs. All of these images can be combined on the computer or combined in a collage to make the book cover. Encourage students to explore Word Art options so words can change direction: vertical, horizontal, diagonal, or curved, and can include perspective, shadows, and other possibilities.

- Ruler, compass
- Scissors, white glue

What You Will Do

1. In the school library, examine several books. Notice the covers or book jackets. Pay attention to the cover illustration and to the **font,** or *typeface.*
2. Choose a book that you like. If you prefer, you may make up a story and title.
3. Think of a picture that will attract readers to your book. Decide how large your picture will be. Make several sketches. Transfer your best sketch to a sheet of white drawing paper. Complete your illustration using markers, crayons, or tempera paints.
4. Think next about lettering styles for the title. Look through books for fonts that fit in with your story. If the story is humorous, you might choose rounded letters. A frightening story might call for tall, pointed letters.
5. Imitating the font you have chosen, carefully letter your title on colored construction paper. Choose a color that will stand out against your illustration. To control the height, measure and cut a strip from the construction paper about 1-inch wide. Draw the title on this strip. Use a ruler for the straight edges on letters such as *m* or *t*. Make the round parts of *p* and other letters by using a compass. Draw letters for the author's name in a similar fashion. These should be smaller than the title. Cut a half-inch-wide strip of construction paper to help guide you. With scissors, cut out the letters when you have finished.
6. Organize the design of your book cover. Experiment placing the words in relation to the illustration. When you are satisfied, glue the words in place.

Evaluating Your Work

- **Describe** What part of the story did you choose for the cover picture? What images appear in this illustration? What kind of font did you choose?
- **Analyze** Does color of the lettering in your title stand out vividly against colors of the illustration? Is the author's name smaller than the title?
- **Interpret** Does the font you chose fit the theme or message of your story? Is the message clear?
- **Judge** Tell whether your book cover would draw readers in and why.

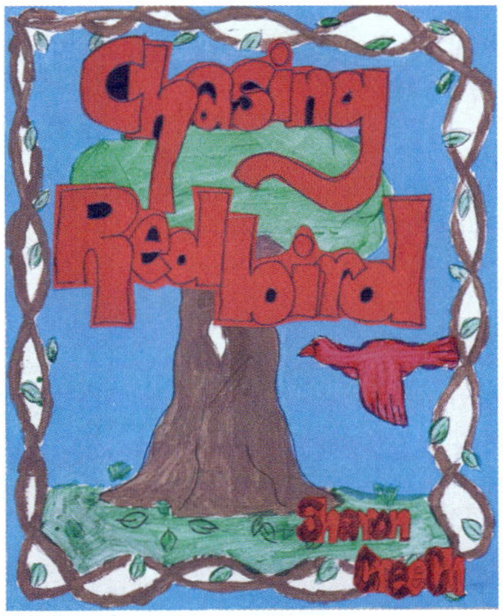

◆ **Figure 12–17** Student work. A book cover.

Reflective Thinking

Critical Evaluation. After your class displays their artworks, analyze the original exhibition of your peers' book designs. Form conclusions about formal properties and historical and cultural contexts. For example, how did they use color? What is the book's theme?

Visual Art Journal

Compare different avocational opportunities in art, such as visiting museums, taking art classes, creating art as a hobby. List those that interest you most.

Studio Skills

Work on letter design by helping students measure and cut a 1 to 2-inch strip of paper, so the height of the letters will be uniform. Students can use rulers and compasses to achieve the straight and curved lines and shapes of the letters. Suggest the choice of a colored background paper as an alternative to white. Students can draw their illustration on a separate piece of paper and glue it in place, or they may draw directly on the cover paper. As students develop and execute their designs, remind them to keep the total composition of the page in mind. L1 ELL

Art Criticism

Have students study magazines and books for the format used. Have them look for the use of space, margins, and placement of visuals.

3 Assess

Self-Assessment

Have students analyze the original artworks of their peers to form conclusions about formal properties—the elements and principles of art.

Enrichment

Bring library books to class that have received the Caldecott Medal for good design. Ask students to discuss what qualities in these books contributed to their award-winning design. L1

4 Close

Have students discuss how their study of book design may affect their reading choices in the future. Are they now more aware of different formats and styles? Will they look for well-designed books?

Inclusion Strategies

Special Learning Needs Students with disabilities in reading and writing will enjoy and may greatly benefit from using the computer to create special lettering effects. They can use different fonts in a variety of sizes and fill letters with colors and textures. The fusion of visual and verbal communication can have a powerful learning effect. Acquaint students who are visually impaired with the computer's zoom function so they can see their work enlarged.

Kids Sew Stories of the Future

1 Focus

Objectives

After completing this lesson, students will be able to:

- Draw a picture showing what life might be like in the year 2050.
- Plan, write, revise, and share an essay about local issues.

2 Teach

Teaching the Feature

1. Let several volunteers describe the quilt squares shown in the photographs: Ask: What do you think the purpose of this quilt might be?
2. Have students meet in cooperative groups to read and discuss the article. Encourage group members to share their opinions of the quilt project and of the quilt squares described and shown.
3. Have students describe in detail a variety of practical applications for creating quilts, such as for family celebrations, holidays, or local events. Have them make a sketch of their quilt and describe other design ideas.

Activity

Have group members discuss the futuristic ideas they would choose to depict in the quilt project. After students have shared their ideas, let them work independently to draw pictures showing what they think life might be like in the year 2050.

TIME ART SCENE — Language Arts

Kids Sew Stories of the Future

Kids' visions are sewn into a brilliant quilt.

Later this century, a shopping trip to the moon or a stay in an underwater hotel might be possible. Perhaps alien ships will land on Earth. If this sounds like a patchwork of wild ideas, you're right.

The Museum of Arts and Design in New York City challenged students to create quilt squares depicting their visions of life in the year 2050. Students from more than 250 schools sent in 19-inch squares in which they had stitched their dreams of the future. Judges picked one square from each state. Then, expert quilters sewed the squares together into a 12-foot-high, 22-foot-wide, three-panel quilt.

Holly Hotchner, director of the Museum of Arts and Design, says the quilt project introduced students to a traditional art form while giving them a chance to show off their positive, futuristic outlook. "The squares show a wonderful variety of views," says Hotchner, "and a great vision of life."

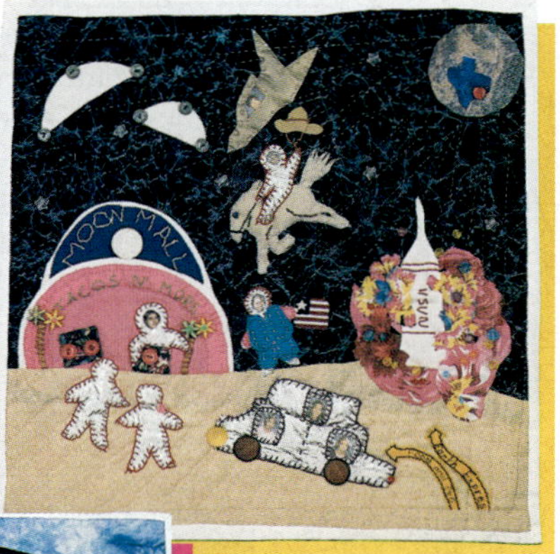

ABOVE: Texas kids are ready to live on the moon, with a nice view of folks back home.

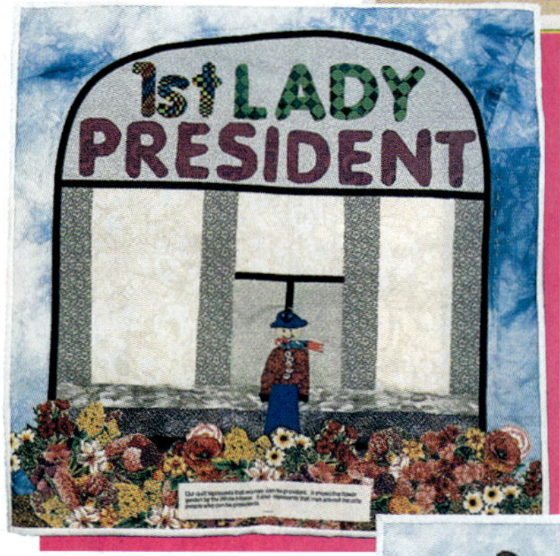

LEFT: Young quilters from Illinois say it's high time a woman ran the country.

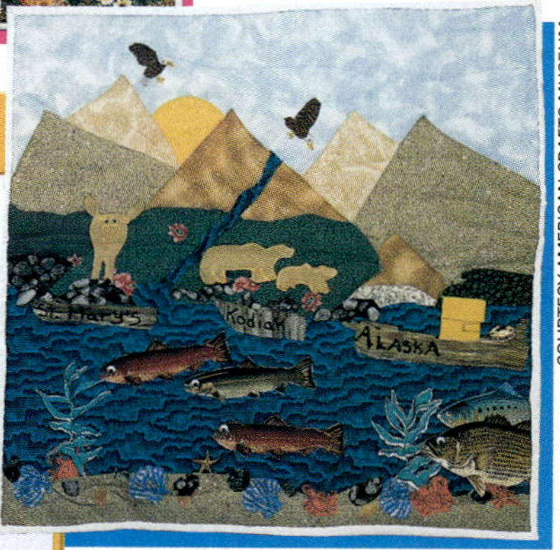

BELOW: The Alaska square shows wildlife, mountains, and clean water.

COURTESY AMERICAN CRAFTS MUSEUM

TIME TO CONNECT

- **Investigate a current issue in your town or city that interests you. Topics might relate to social issues, politics, or the environment.**
- **Outline and then draft an essay that presents the concern as well as your idea for a future solution.**
- **Translate your solution into visual form, drawing it on a piece of paper. These can be taped together to create a class paper quilt.**

240 Chapter 12 *Telling a Story*

TIME TO CONNECT

In groups, have students discuss the central problem and a possible solution to a local current issue. Then have students plan and write their essays independently. As they revise their compositions, have them keep these questions in mind:

- What can I add to make my writing more clear?
- Does every part of my essay help make my ideas clear? If not, how should I rearrange the text?

Chapter 12 Review

BUILDING VOCABULARY

Number a sheet of paper from 1 to 7. After each number, write the term from the list that matches each description below.

cartouche	Kachina
cutaway	petroglyph
font	pictogram
fresco	

1. A view in which an outside wall has been removed to reveal the scene within.
2. Typeface.
3. A symbolic rock carving or painting.
4. A painting created when pigment is applied to a section of wall spread with fresh plaster.
5. A hand-crafted statuette that represents spirits in Pueblo rituals.
6. An oval or oblong containing an important person's name.
7. A small picture that stands for a word or an idea.

REVIEWING ART FACTS

Number a sheet of paper from 8 to 13. Answer each question in one or two complete sentences.

8. What is a hieroglyphic? When did ancient Egyptian hieroglyphic come into being?
9. How old are Native American petroglyphs?
10. How is the dragon viewed in the Chinese culture?
11. What are Kachinas believed to represent?
12. From what language does the word *fresco* come? What does it mean in that language?
13. Why were illuminations common in the Middle Ages?

CROSS-CURRICULUM CONNECTIONS

14. **Language Arts.** Write a report describing how the art of visual storytelling has changed from earliest times through the present.
15. **Language Arts.** At your school or local library, find a poem about mythical creatures, such as "Dragon" by Karla Kuskin or "Ganesha, Ganesh" by Myra Cohn Livingston. Compare the poem's subject and meaning with what you learned in the lesson about such mythical creatures. Share your findings with the class.

Web Museum Activity

DeCordova Museum and Sculpture Park, Lincoln, Massachussetts

This chapter demonstrates the many ways artists tell stories through their art. Children's book illustrations are a good example of telling stories through pictures.

Go to **art.glencoe.com** and click on the DeCordova Museum link to take a look at the art of children's book illustrations. You will view different book illustrations ranging in subjects and themes from alphabet books, myths, folk and fairy tales, to fantasy, adventure, mystery, and drama.

Select three different illustrations and explain how they reveal the story's theme. Describe the style of the different illustrations. What techniques did the artists use to create the illustrations? Were you able to identify the book's subject or theme by only looking at the illustration?

ANSWERS TO Chapter 12 Review

Building Vocabulary

1. cutaway
2. font
3. petroglyph
4. fresco
5. Kachina
6. cartouche
7. pictogram

Reviewing Art Facts

8. Hieroglyphic is a form of picture writing. The ancient Egyptians perfected their hieroglyphic about 3,000 years ago.
9. Many are thought to be about 10,000 years old.
10. It is seen as an object of good luck.
11. They are thought to embody spirits who once dwelled among the Pueblo.
12. The word is Italian for "fresh."
13. This was a time when many people were unable to read. The illuminated books served as a source of information to these people.

Cross-Curriculum Connections

14. Student reports will vary, but may include the influences of technology and changes in styles of art. They might also identify different uses for story-telling pictures, such as the use of such works as book illustrations.
15. Responses will vary.

Web Museum Activity

Before you have students go online, visit the Web site to preview the museum's online content, collection, and any online exhibit that may be of interest. Students' responses will vary according to the illustrations they selected. Their responses should reflect an understanding of the techniques the artists used and the book's subjects or themes. Have students write a critique on the illustrations they selected.

Chapter Resources

Features	Standards for Chapter: National	Standards for Chapter: State/Local	Reproducible Masters
Quick Write *page 243* TIME ART SCENE "Everyone Loves a Parade" *page 260* ***Web Museum Activity*** *page 261*	**1.** (a, b) **2.** (a) **3.** (a, b) **4.** (a, b, c) **5.** (a) **6.** (a, b)		Guided Reading and Practice 13–1 Historical and Cultural Heritage 13–2, 13–5, 13–7 Application Activity 13–3, 13–4 Enrichment Activity 13–6, 13–8, 13–9 Studio Activity 13–10 Lesson Plans

Lesson Resources

Lessons	Standards per Lesson: National	Standards per Lesson: State/Local	Reproducible Masters
1 ***Holiday Celebrations*** *(pages 244–245)*	1a, 1b, 3b, 5a		Historical and Cultural Heritage 13–2 Application Activity 13–3
2 ***Creating an "Event" Quilt*** *(pages 246–247)*	1a, 1b, 2a, 5b		Application Activity 13–4
3 ***Celebration Dances in Art*** *(pages 248–249)*	4a, 5a, 6a		Historical and Cultural Heritage 13–5
4 ***Creating Kinetic "Festival" Art*** *(pages 250–251)*	1a, 1b, 2a, 3a, 3b		Enrichment Activity 13–6
5 ***Celebrating Rites of Passage*** *(pages 252–253)*	1a, 1b, 2a, 5a		Historical and Cultural Heritage 13–7 Enrichment Activity 13–8
6 **ART & SOCIAL STUDIES** *(pages 254–255)*	4c, 5b, 6a, 6b		
7 ***Art That Celebrates Life*** *(pages 256–257)*	4a, 4b		Enrichment Activity 13–9 Studio Activity 13–10
8 ***Celebrating a Role Model*** *(pages 258–259)*	1a, 1b, 2a, 5a		

Assessment	Technology
Testing Program: Chapter Test 13–11 *Portfolio and Assessment Techniques*	Artsource Performing Arts Package, Japanese Festival Sounds (DVD or Video Segment 8) National Museum of Women in the Arts Interactive Lesson Planner Fine Art Transparency CC-13 *Music in the Plaza* by John Sloan Fine Art Transparency 13, *Luncheon of the Boating Party* by Pierre Auguste Renoir

Activities/Features
Studio Activity: Making a Tricolor
Evaluating Your Work Studio Option Visual Art Journal
Time & Place: Hopi Ceremonies
Evaluating Your Work Portfolio Ideas Visual Art Journal
Studio Activity: Making a Hat
Make the Connection
Meet the Artist: Rie Muñoz
Evaluating Your Work Reflective Thinking Art Online

KEY TO ABILITY LEVELS

Teaching strategies have been coded.

- L1 Activities for all students; teacher direction required
- L2 Activities for average to above-average students; some teacher direction needed
- L3 Activities for students able and willing to work independently
- ELL English Language Learner activities

FEATURED ARTISTS

- Everald Brown
- Bing Davis
- Aurelio and Francisco Flores
- Childe Hassam
- Alfred C. Howland
- Fred Kabotie
- Rie Muñoz
- James Phillips
- Faith Ringgold
- Antonio M. Ruiz

FINE ART PRINTS

Fine Art Print 19, *In Celebration* by Sam Gilliam

Timesaving Technology

Interactive Lesson Planner

Make planning easy. Use this interactive software to organize your week, month, semester, or year and access all *Introducing Art* reproducible resources.

KEY TO LESSON RESOURCES

Narrative Lesson

Studio Lesson

Chapter 13

Celebrations

(pages 242–261)

Chapter Overview

The word *celebration* can refer to performing a ceremony, to commemorating an event, to honoring someone or something, or to marking a special occasion. In this chapter, students will learn how artists capture a variety of celebrations. They will also have opportunities to create their own artworks that celebrate what is meaningful to them.

Discussing the Artwork

Focus On ◆ **Figure 13–1** This candelabra is an example of Mexican folk sculpture that grew out of a traditional craft form. Introduced by the Europeans, candlesticks and candelabras were used throughout colonial Mexico to provide light and offer reverence to images of the saints. These sculpted candelabras were also used for religious ceremonies such as weddings and funerals, when they were placed on special altars or carried in processions. The candelabra shown here was used by families when they announced the engagement of a young couple. This ceremony was held in front of an altar adorned with the candelabra. The central figure on the front stem of the piece was the archangel San Raphael, and other images of angels, flowers, and birds are dispersed on the projecting arms.

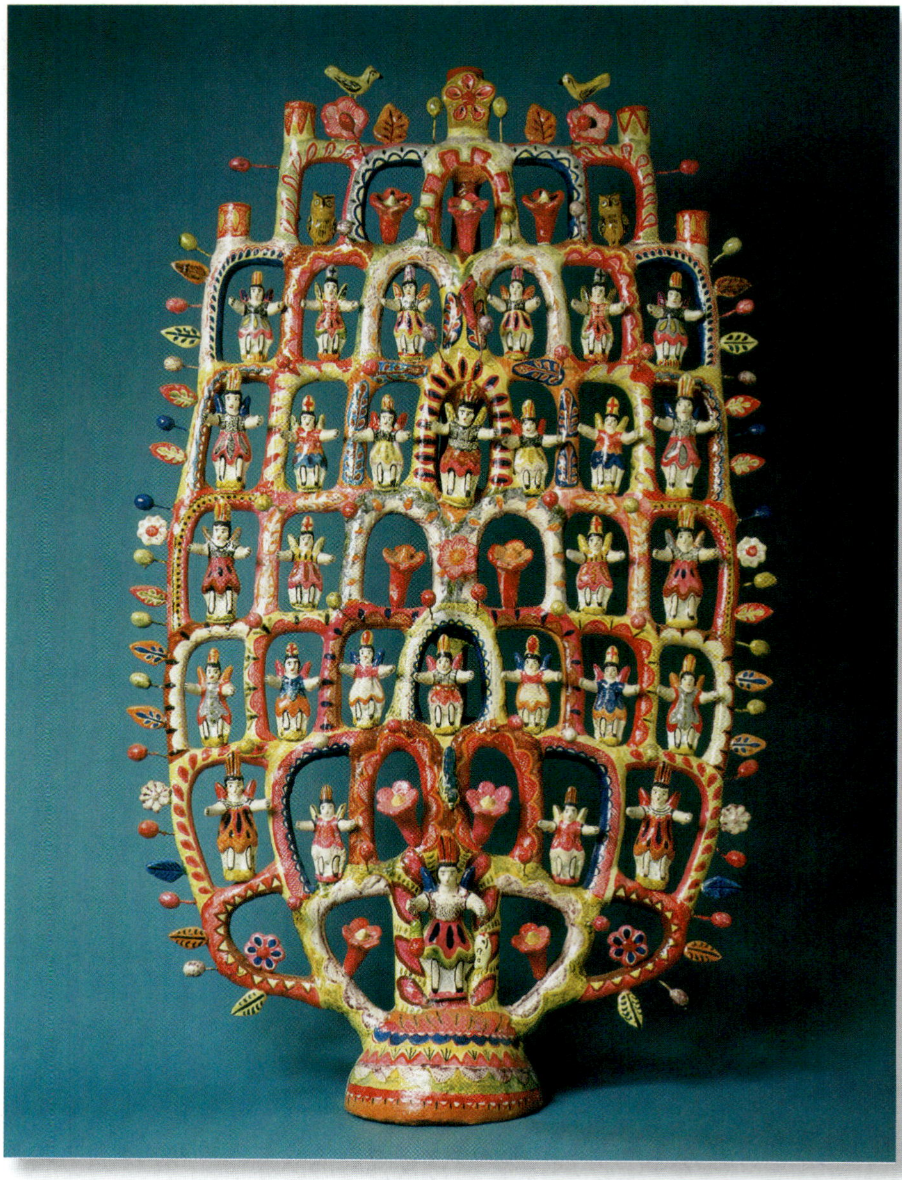

Focus On ◆ **Figure 13–1** **This ceramic candelabra was made in Izucar de Matamoros, Mexico, for a wedding engagement celebration.**

Aurelio and Francesco Flores. *Candelabra.* c. 1980. Hand-molded, fired, painted; clay, paint, wire. 106.7 × 66 × 21 cm (42 × 26 × $8\frac{1}{4}$″). © Museum of International Folk Art/Museum of New Mexico. Neutrogena Collection. Photo: Pat Pollard.

242

ARTSOURCE

Linking to the Performing Arts

Music Taiko drumming is a powerful expression of rhythmic sounds that resonate throughout the body. The players are completely focused on their playing and use powerful, purposeful movement to bring the strongest sounds out of their drums. Taiko drummer, Johnny Mori is a third-generation Japanese American who established a group called *Japanese Festival Sounds.* Have students read about Japanese Festival Sounds in the **Performing Arts Handbook** on page 322. To enrich student understanding, play the DVD or videotape (segment 8) in the **Performing Arts Package.**

Chapter 13

Celebrations

"Art must be an expression of love or it is nothing."
—Marc Chagall (1887–1985)

What do you think of first when you hear the word *celebration?* Do you think of food, music, or dancing? These are usually part of a celebration. However, celebrations also involve rituals, traditions, rites of passage, and victories.

In this chapter, you will learn about many ways in which art enriches our celebrations and records them to preserve memories. You will glimpse visual celebrations of many cultures.

After completing this chapter, you will be able to:

- Describe the different media and methods artists have used to illustrate celebrations.
- Identify the influence of various cultures and historical events in depicting celebrations.
- Create several works of art that focus on celebrations.

Quick Write

Interpreting the Quote
Read the quote and look at **Figure 13–1.** How is the candelabra an expression of love? Describe any symbolic meaning you notice in the artwork.

KEY TERMS

tricolor
seal
pueblo
shadow puppet
kinetic art
adenla

Quick Write

Interpreting the Quote
Have students read the quote and complete the Quick Write activity. Student responses will vary. Encourage students to study the candelabra and notice the use of color. Ask:

- What does the dominant color of pink suggest?
- For what other occasions can this artwork be used?

Ask students to describe any symbolic meaning they notice in the artwork.

Chapter Motivator

Students may tend to think that celebrations focus only on holidays. Point out that holidays are certainly a cause for celebration, but the word goes beyond just holidays. For example, tell students that when teammates give each other a "high five," a slap on the back, or some other congratulatory gesture after their team makes a goal in a sport, even that is a sign of celebration. Explain that in this chapter, they will discover how artists of different times and from many different places have captured the spirit of human celebration.

Art Online

Visit **art.glencoe.com**, the Web site for Glencoe's art programs. This site offers general student resources to help guide your students as they learn about art and artists. Encourage your students to visit this site and explore the various resources and activities. The general student resources include the following:

- Artist Profiles
- Interactive Games
- Student Art Gallery
- Web Links

National Standards for Arts Education

This chapter addresses the following National Standards for the Visual Arts:

1. (a, b)
2. (a)
3. (a, b)
4. (a, b, c)
5. (a)
6. (a, b)

Holiday Celebrations

(pages 244–245)

1 Focus

Objectives

After completing this lesson, students will be able to:

- Recognize that artists depict holiday celebrations to capture the emotions and setting of the event.
- Demonstrate technical skills effectively by using a variety of art materials to produce a flag for a group or community.

SUPPLIES
- Pencils
- White paper
- Assorted sizes and colors of construction paper
- Scissors, white glue
- Markers

2 Teach

Motivator

Ask students to identify their favorite holiday other than a religious holiday. Chart class responses to discover which holidays are more popular. Ask students to speculate if there are any months that do not have a patriotic, religious, or seasonal event celebrated by different groups of people. Direct student attention to the two artworks. Both are Independence Day pictures. Ask: What similarities and differences can you find in the paintings?

Holiday Celebrations

Every culture around the world celebrates holidays. Some holiday celebrations are joyous occasions. They are marked by parades, decorations, and possibly the exchange of gifts. Other holidays are times of solemn remembrance.

One common link among all holiday celebrations is the frequency with which they have turned up through the centuries as art subjects.

CELEBRATION ART

If you look up *celebrate* in a dictionary, you discover that the word has many meanings. One of these is "to rejoice." The artwork that opened this chapter is used for celebrating Mexican wedding engagements. The candelabra is used by families when they announce the engagement of a young couple. Celebrating a special event or a holiday is a time to rejoice.

Art Celebrating American Independence

A rejoicing of a different sort is pictured in **Figure 13–2**. The subject is obvious from the title. Even without glancing at the credit line, you can probably guess the year this work was done. The clothing styles and presence of horse-drawn vehicles offer clues.

Take a moment to study this painting. Notice how the artist has used lighter color values to focus the viewer's attention on the parade. A careful inspection reveals that this is no well-disciplined, uniformed marching band. Rather, it is a random gathering of townspeople. They are simply bound together

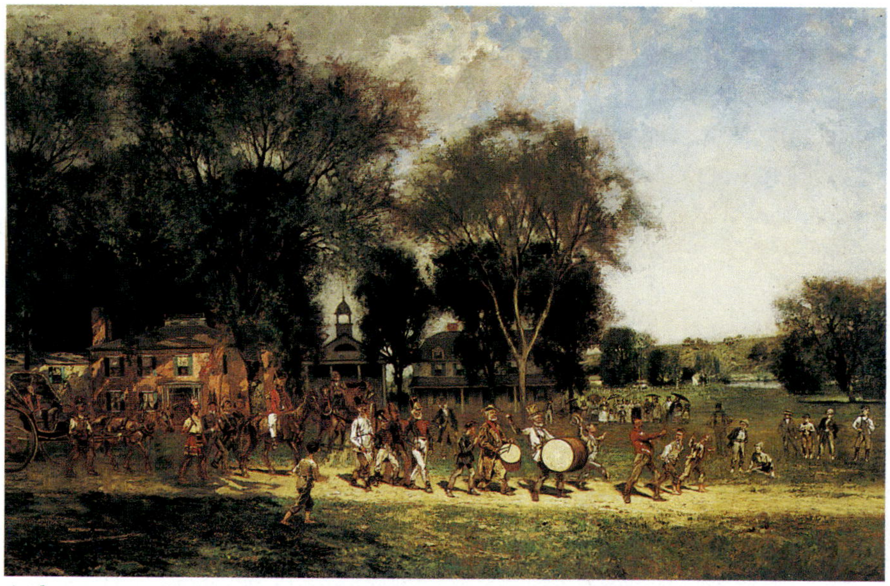

◆ **Figure 13–2** What colorful associations do you have with the holiday shown in this painting? Would you describe this work as realistic?

Alfred C. Howland. *The Fourth of July*. 1886. Oil on canvas. 61 × 91.6 cm (24 × 36$\frac{1}{16}$″). High Museum of Art, Atlanta, Georgia. Gift of Life Insurance Company of Georgia in celebration of the Nation's Bicentennial.

STORY BEHIND THE ARTWORK

RUIZ'S SCHOOL CHILDREN ON PARADE The setting of the painting shown in Figure 13–3 is the town of Tepetlaoxtoc, whose name appears on the flag with the portrait of Miguel Hidalgo Costilla, the priest who first declared Mexican independence from Spain in 1810. A gazebo repeats the same light colors of the paraders and of the buildings in the background. This emphasizes the main feature of the event—the parade. Ruiz loves to include contrasts. Notice the European dress of the boy on the bike on the right and the blue dress of the woman on the left.

by their patriotic spirit and the steady boom of the bass drums. What mood or feeling does this work bring to mind?

Art Celebrating Mexican Independence

Compare the style and subject matter of Figure 13–2 with those of **Figure 13–3**. This work celebrates Mexico's Independence Day. Both artworks focus on a parade. Unlike Figure 13–2, the marchers in Figure 13–3 are schoolchildren. All are dressed in white, and each child carries a miniature Mexican **tricolor** (**try-kuhl-uhr**). This is *a flag with three broad bands of color.* In stark contrast to the children's costumes is the black suit worn by the man leading the procession. Note the serious expressions on the people's faces. What do these suggest about the tone or mood of the celebration?

Studio Activity

Making a Tricolor

Practical applications. Design a tricolor to represent your class, school, or community. Choose colors with symbolic value. Use red, for example, for courage, blue for loyalty. Begin with a 9 x 12-inch sheet of paper. Divide it into three geometric shapes—squares, circles, rectangles, triangles, or a combination. Measure and cut from colored construction paper the three shapes in the colors of your choice. Using white glue, attach these so as to fill the sheet of drawing paper. Complete your flag by creating an official **seal**—*a symbolic image or emblem*—on a sheet of white paper. Color the seal with markers. Cut it out and glue it to the center of your tricolor.

PORTFOLIO

Write a short paragraph describing what your tricolor symbolizes and what each color stands for. Put the paragraph in your portfolio along with the tricolor.

Check Your Understanding

1. How does the artist of Figure 13–2 draw your attention to the parade?
2. What difference in mood do you detect between the paintings in Figures 13–2 and 13–3?

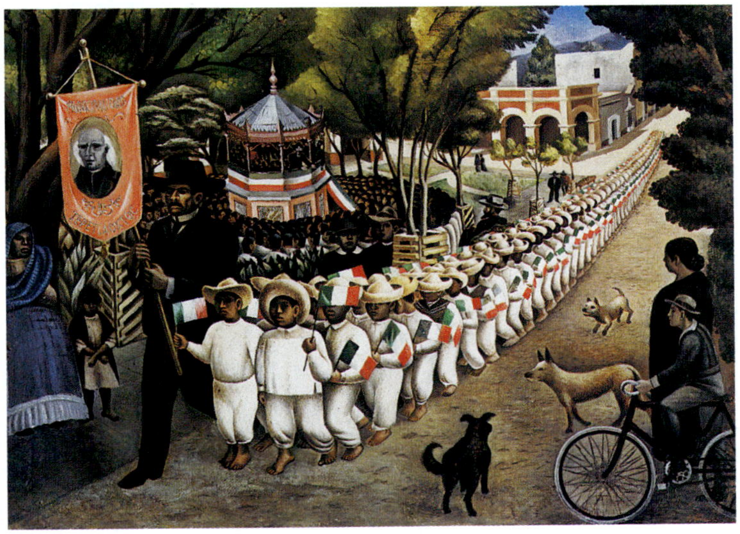

◆ **Figure 13–3** Compare this Mexican celebration with the American celebration in Figure 13–2. How are they different?

Antonio M. Ruiz. *School Children on Parade.* 1936. Oil on canvas. 24 × 33.7 cm (9½ × 13¼"). The Metropolitan Museum of Art. Secretaria de Hacienda y Credito Publico, Mexico City, Mexico.

Art Criticism

Have students use the four steps of art criticism for both paintings. Have them decide if both paintings are successful and explain which aesthetic theory their judgment supports. L1

3 Assess

Self-Assessment

Have students complete the **Check Your Understanding** questions on this page. Answers are provided below.

Reteaching

Ask students to describe what a *seal* on a flag is.

Enrichment

Both artworks in this lesson celebrate a nation's independence. Have students identify in **Figure 13–3** the influence of historical events. In Ruiz's work, the Mexican flag is prominent. Ask students to research the history of the Mexican flag. Have them discover what other flags preceded this one and why the colors are important. Students may also want to research the history of their state flag or that of a neighboring state. Have them share their findings with the class. L2

4 Close

Have students explain why it is useful to study artworks like the two pieces shown in this lesson.

Answers to Check Your Understanding

1. Howland uses contrasting lines and lighter hues to create a spotlight effect that draws the eye to the paraders as they march. The lines of the marchers contrast with the vertical and horizontal lines of the houses, people, and trees in the background.
2. The spontaneous activity and chaotic atmosphere characterizes Howland's *The Fourth of July.* In *School Children on Parade,* there is a more serious mood brought about by the repetition of clothing, position, and color of the many rows of marchers.

Creating an "Event" Quilt

(pages 246–247)
Lesson Time: 10 hours

1 Focus

Objectives

After completing this lesson, students will be able to:

- Demonstrate technical skills effectively by creating a quilt square and border from fabric, then work together with classmates to assemble the quilt.
- Describe, analyze, interpret, and judge their artwork.

SUPPLIES
Refer to **What You Will Need** in the Student Edition.

2 Teach

Motivator

Engage students in a discussion of quilts. Ask them to describe what they know about quilts: how they are made, what they are used for, what kind of art they represent. Ask them to tell what a quilting bee is. Explain that quilts were traditionally created as bedcoverings, but many have evolved into outstanding examples of folk art.

Understanding Art History

Have students research the history of quilts in this country and find out what styles and designs were common. Have them discover which are considered important artworks and why. L2

Creating an "Event" Quilt

The painting you looked at in Figure 13–2 celebrates a milestone in the growth of our nation. The work in **Figure 13–4** celebrates *eight* such milestones. On the surface, the painting shows a simple and distinctly American pastime—a quilting bee. Eight women appear seated around the quilt they have sewn. A deeper meaning begins to form when the viewer learns the identities of these individuals. The figure in the blue suit at the center is Harriet Tubman. The person in the polka-dot dress to her left is Rosa Parks. What personal sacrifices did these women make? What did they fight for?

What You Will Learn

A quilt is a fitting symbol for the contributions of people who are working together in a group effort. With classmates, you will make a quilt that celebrates an important group effort you or others in your community have made. Working alone, each of you will create a quilt square from fabric scraps and paint. This will help introduce variety. All the pieces will then be glued or sewn together. You will complete your quilt by creating a large frame or border that adds harmony and unifies the work, as in Figure 13–4.

What You Will Need

- Sketch paper and pencil
- Assorted scraps of fabric
- Fabric pieces (to be the basis for the quilt)
- Fabric glue or fusible webbing
- Needle and thread
- Fabric paint

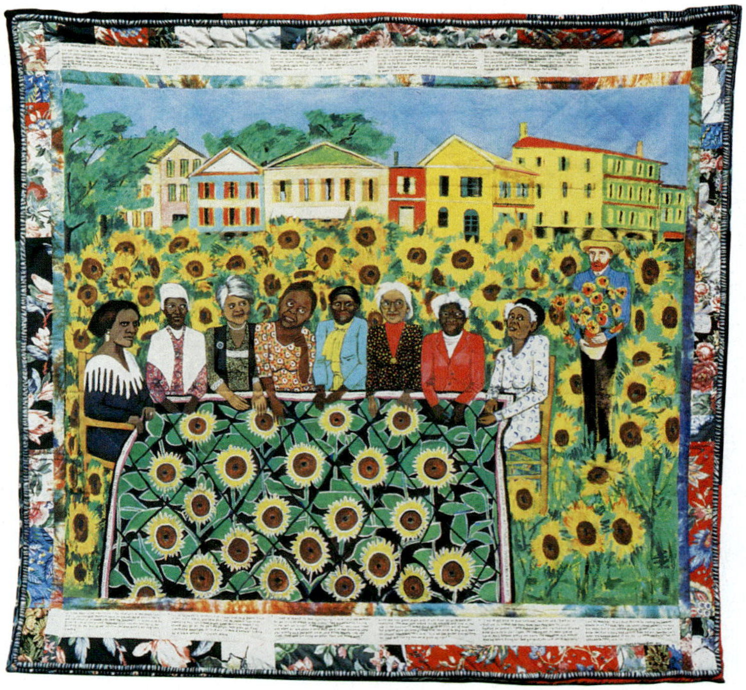

◆ **Figure 13–4** How has the artist added harmony to this busy painting? How has she introduced variety? Can you appreciate why this scene is an impossible one?

Faith Ringgold. *#4 The Sunflowers Quilting Bee at Arles.* 1991. Acrylic on canvas, pieced fabric border. 188 × 203.2 cm (74 × 80″). Faith Ringgold Inc., © Oprah Winfrey Collection.

MORE ABOUT...

Ringgold's Quilting Bee Ask students to study **Figure 13–4** in detail. Ringgold's composition is a comment on the way many male artists work alone, while women quilters work together as a team. Prominent women in African American history are portrayed: (left to right) Madame Walker, Sojourner Truth, Ida B. Wells, Fannie Lou Hamer, Harriet Tubman, Rosa Parks, Mary McLoed Bethune, Ella Baker, and standing alone in the field—Vincent van Gogh. Have volunteers choose one of the women pictured and report on her role in African American history.

What You Will Do

1. You will demonstrate technical skills effectively using a variety of art media and materials to produce a quilt, an example of fiberart. With group members, brainstorm an event to celebrate. Possibilities include a successful school fund-raising drive, a cleanup campaign, or an effort to save a local park.
2. After choosing an event, select colors and materials that reflect the theme and help create the mood. For example, you might choose green and blue for a Save the Earth campaign.
3. Working by yourself, make several pencil sketches for a quilt square. Look through the fabric pieces to see if any of the designs suggest ideas. Decide whether you will cut out figures and objects or use shapes and symbols to express the theme.
4. Using your best sketch as a guide, cut out shapes from a variety of fabrics. Arrange and overlap these on a piece of fabric. Attach the shapes using either fabric glue, fusible webbing, or needle and thread.
5. Decide if a title will be part of the entire quilt design. Letters may be cut from felt or fabric. The letters could be accented with hand sewn stitches or fabric paint.
6. Stitch all the quilt squares together. Make an overall border for the entire quilt out of fabric scraps.

Evaluating Your Work

- **Describe** Identify the objects and figures in your quilt square. Identify the event the quilt celebrates.
- **Analyze** Explain how you organized the art elements in your quilt to create harmony, variety, and unity.
- **Interpret** Explain how your square helps capture the event. Describe the mood and idea your square communicates.
- **Judge** Were you successful in creating a quilt that celebrates an event?

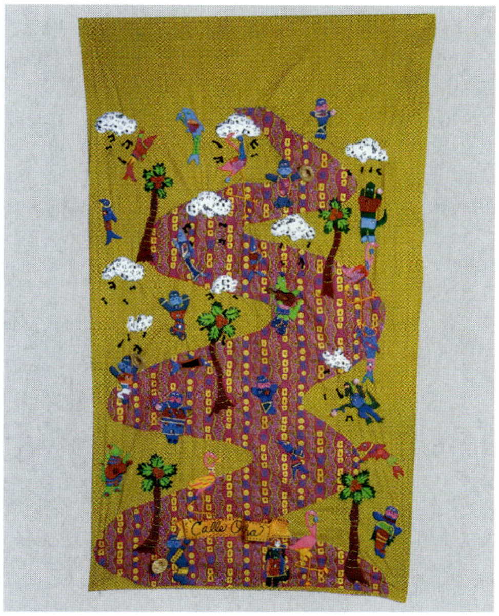

◆ **Figure 13–5** Student work. Quilt.

Studio Option

Make a paper quilt that tells a story. Express a variety of ideas based on personal experience. Choose colors and textures to emphasize the idea and mood. Use a variety of paper media. Cut out and layer shapes, symbols, or objects that relate to your story. Imitate cross-stitches by drawing parallel diagonal lines or X's with pen or paint.

Visual Art Journal

In your journal, write about working together with your classmates to create the "event" quilt. What did you like most about this project. Describe how you and your classmates proceeded to make the quilt.

Safety Tip

Using a Glue Gun If you choose to use a glue gun for this Studio Lesson, be certain to caution students about the safe use of this appliance. Supervise the location and use of the hot glue and make sure students understand that they must be extremely careful or risk burning themselves. Follow the manufacturer's directions carefully. If using fusible interfacing, show students how to place it between two layers of fabric and use the iron to fuse the fabrics.

Studio Skills

As a group, have students brainstorm ideas for a commemorative quilt. If the class is particularly large, you may want to divide into two quilting groups. Help students decide on the size of the overall quilt and compute the size of the individual sections and the width of border needed. L1 ELL

Art On A Shoestring

Contact local fabric stores or clothing manufacturers for possible donations of fabric remnants. If possible, invite a local quilter to give students some practical advice.

3 Assess

Self-Assessment

Have students use **Evaluating Your Work** to conduct an in-progress critique of the quilt they created with classmates.

Enrichment

Bring in books from the library that show some of the many quilting patterns that exist. Have students choose a geometric pattern and reproduce one quilting square using a medium of their choice. Display the squares as individual wall hangings. L1 ELL

4 Close

Have students write a brief summary of what they think the group's quilt communicates.

Celebration Dances in Art

(pages 248–249)

1 Focus

Objectives

After completing this lesson, students will be able to:

- Recognize the role of dance in important celebrations.
- Understand artistic interpretations of dances that are a part of celebrations.

2 Teach

Motivator

Engage students in a discussion of current dance styles. What kinds of dances do they like to do? Many students may not be into social dancing yet, but most will have an appreciation for the cultural role dance plays in our lives. Explain that dancing is not only a social event. In some cultures, dances are featured in important rituals and celebrations. Direct students' attention to **Figure 13–6**. Ask:

- What kind of music do you think the people hear?
- Compare this dance to that shown in **Figure 13–7**. How does Brown represent rhythm in his painting? *(Through use of lines, shapes, and color.)*

Vocabulary

Students may be familiar with the term *pueblo* from social studies classes. Remind them that the word not only refers to a dried-clay dwelling but also is the name of the Pueblo people who inhabit those dwellings. Ask students to find on a map the area of the U.S. where the Pueblo peoples make their home. *(New Mexico and Arizona.)*

Celebration Dances in Art

Does your school sponsor dances? Maybe a youth or social club in your community does. With few exceptions, such events in our society are leisure-time activities. Yet, in some cultures, dance plays a featured role in important celebrations.

In this lesson, you will explore two such celebrations. You will view artistic interpretations of dances that are part of these events.

A Nature Dance

Most of our dances are recreational. A few, however, have some special meaning. The opposite is true for the Hopi people of the American Southwest. In their culture, only a small number of dances are considered social events. The majority occupy an important place in rituals celebrating their people's oneness with nature.

One of these, the Green Corn Dance, is pictured in **Figure 13–6**. Examine this painting. Did you find your eye drawn to the sweeping curve formed by the ceremonial procession on the right side? The people in this line are the dancers. They are dressed in traditional clothing. Within the semicircle is a second, smaller group that includes a drummer. Notice the dancers' upright posture. What does their body language suggest or tell about the tempo, or speed, of the music? Find the figure in the feathered headdress standing atop the **pueblo** (pweh-**bloh**), or *dried-clay dwelling*. Who do you think this person is?

A Victory Dance

Some dances, like the one in Figure 13–6, are calm and dignified. Others are fast-paced and frenzied. How would you characterize

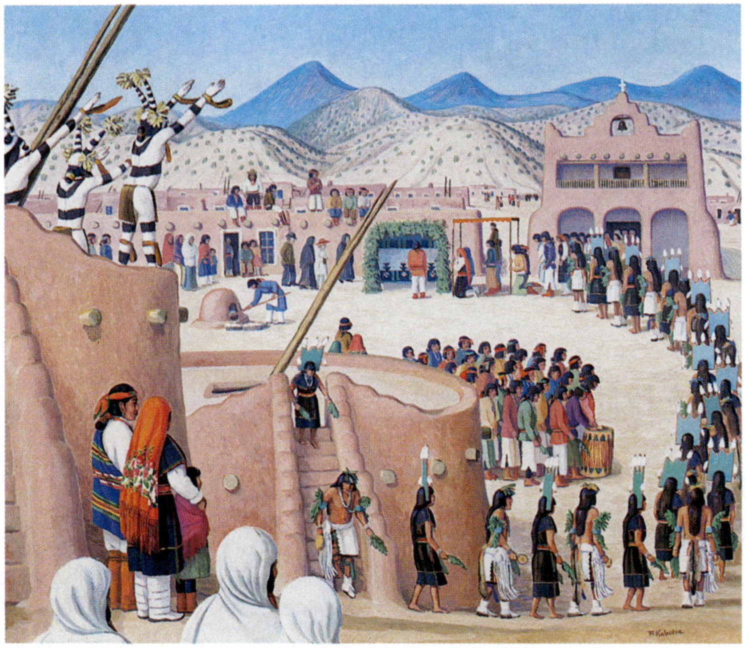

◆ **Figure 13–6** What do you think is the purpose of this dance? What role do the repetition of colors and forms and the use of vertical lines play in creating the painting's mood?

Fred Kaboti. *Pueblo Green Corn Dance, Hopi*. 1947. Oil on canvas. 74.7 × 64.8 cm (29½ × 25½"). The Thomas Gilcrease Institute of American History and Art, Tulsa, Oklahoma.

COMMUNITY CONNECTION

Plan a Celebration Have students plan a celebration or faire from their favorite culture or time period. Egyptian Day, Colonial Day, Western Day, or a Renaissance Faire are some examples. Students should research and find out about what foods, dances, games, and traditions occur at these celebrations. Students will create simple costumes and accessories to give their celebration a feeling of authenticity. They will then prepare and demonstrate crafts and arts that would be traditionally used at the celebration that they have chosen. Invite other classes, parents, and your principal to your class celebration.

the dance pictured in **Figure 13–7**? Without looking at the title, you can probably sense the joyous mood and high energy level of the dancers. The painting captures a part of a victory celebration in the artist's native island of Jamaica. Can you think of a dance or "ball" with a similar purpose in our own country?

Look closely at this painting. It is divided into three main sections. The top and bottom thirds of the picture plane are given over to musicians in brightly colored costumes. At the center are the dancers, framed against a field of vivid orange. Observe how the angled lines of their arms, legs, and bodies help convey a strong sense of urgent movement. Notice the array of bold colors that make up the buildings and plant life. What art principle has the artist used to control the many colors and shapes in this action-filled painting?

Check Your Understanding

1. What do most Hopi dances celebrate?
2. What event is the focus of the painting in Figure 13–7?

Time & Place

Hopi Ceremonies

Cultural connection. The Hopi, which means good, peaceful, or wise, are a group of Pueblo Indians who live on the mesas in northeastern Arizona. A *mesa* is an isolated hill with a flat top. The Hopi live in pueblo structures made of stone and mud. Their way of life revolves around farming, and corn is their main crop.

Hopi women and men have distinct responsibilities. Women take care of the home and children, weave baskets, and make pottery. Men farm, herd, build houses, weave clothing and blankets, and perform ceremonies.

Many of these ceremonies, such as the one illustrated in **Figure 13–6**, focus on corn and the need for rain to help the crops grow. In the Kachina ceremonies, Hopi men wear colorful masks and clothing to impersonate the Kachina spirits. How is the dance ceremony depicted in Figure 13–6 different from that in Figure13–7?

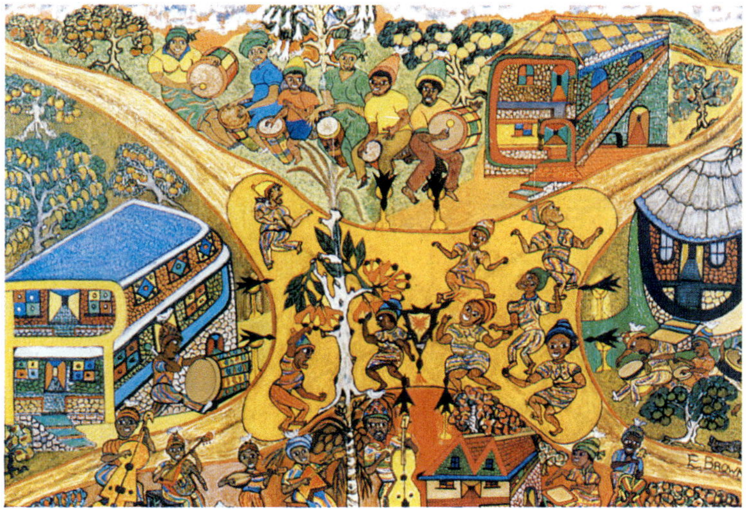

◆ **Figure 13–7** **Would you describe this treatment as realistic? Has the artist used linear perspective or any of the other space-giving techniques described in Chapter 1?**

Everald Brown. *Victory Dance.* 1976. Oil on canvas. 83.8 × 124.5 cm (33 × 49″). Organization of American States Museum, Washington, D.C. Collection of the Art Museum of the Americas.

Time & Place

Hopi Ceremonies

The *Pueblo Green Corn Dance, Hopi,* shows a traditional Hopi dance. The participants are walking in an orderly fashion, which makes the dance appear to be more calm and serious. The dance ceremony in *Victory Dance* is fast-paced and the dancers appear more lively.

Aesthetics

Have students analyze the interdependence of the art elements color and form and the principles of movement and repetition in both paintings. Students should use art vocabulary appropriately.

Team Building Activity

Have students work in groups of five or six so that they can share resources and ideas for portraying a celebration. Have students create a mood for the celebration they enact—using music, instruments, and found objects to create sound and rhythm—and share with the class. L1 ELL

3 Assess

Self-Assessment

Have students complete the **Check Your Understanding** questions on this page. Answers are provided below.

Reteaching

Have students find examples of movement in each painting.

4 Close

Have students explain the role of dance as an art form and as a means of celebration.

Answers to Check Your Understanding

1. Most Hopi dances celebrate their people's sense of "oneness" with nature.
2. The focus of the painting in Figure 13–7 is a victory celebration on the artist's native island of Jamaica.

Creating Kinetic "Festival" Art

(pages 250–251)
Lesson Time: 90 minutes

1 Focus

Objectives

After completing this lesson, students will be able to:

- Demonstrate technical skills effectively by using a variety of art materials to design and create a piece of kinetic art for a festival.
- Describe, analyze, interpret, and judge their artwork.

SUPPLIES
Refer to **What You Will Need** in the Student Edition.

2 Teach

Motivator

Have students make a list on the board of festivals they know about or have studied. Include on the list local festivals as well as the more universal ones. Ask students to share their experiences with festivals, telling what they like about them. Ask students to examine the fish in **Figure 13–8.** Have them imagine the festival associated with such a colorful creature.

Vocabulary

You may want to demonstrate the concept of a *shadow puppet* to students. Invite a few volunteers to set up a demonstration for the class. Point out that such moveable art is described as *kinetic.*

Creating Kinetic "Festival" Art

The Pueblo Green Corn Dance in Figure 13–6 is part of a Hopi *festival*. Festivals are colorful events that include food, music, dancing, and other forms of entertainment. They are celebrated in every culture. The purpose of some festivals is to usher in a new year. Others are meant to ensure a bountiful harvest.

No festival would be complete without live performances. The "performer" in **Figure 13–8** is a **shadow puppet**. This is *an art object in the shape of an animal or human attached to a wand or stick.* Shadow puppets are popular throughout much of Asia, where they are featured in special events known as *shadow dances.* In these events, the puppets are made to sway gracefully to and fro behind a screen on which a bright light has been trained. Each figure appears to be dancing with its shadowy partner. Can you guess the type of festival to which this art object relates?

What You Will Learn

Shadow puppets are an example of **kinetic** (kuh-**net**-ik) **art.** This is *an art style in which parts of a work are set into motion by a form of energy.* In this lesson, you will design and create your own piece of kinetic art for a festival. You will begin by deciding what form your art object will take. Then you will create the object out of tagboard. You will add visual texture to emphasize a specific part. You will repeat lines or shapes to create rhythm, as in Figure 13–8.

What You Will Need

- Sketch paper and pencil
- Sheet of tagboard, 14 x 22 inches

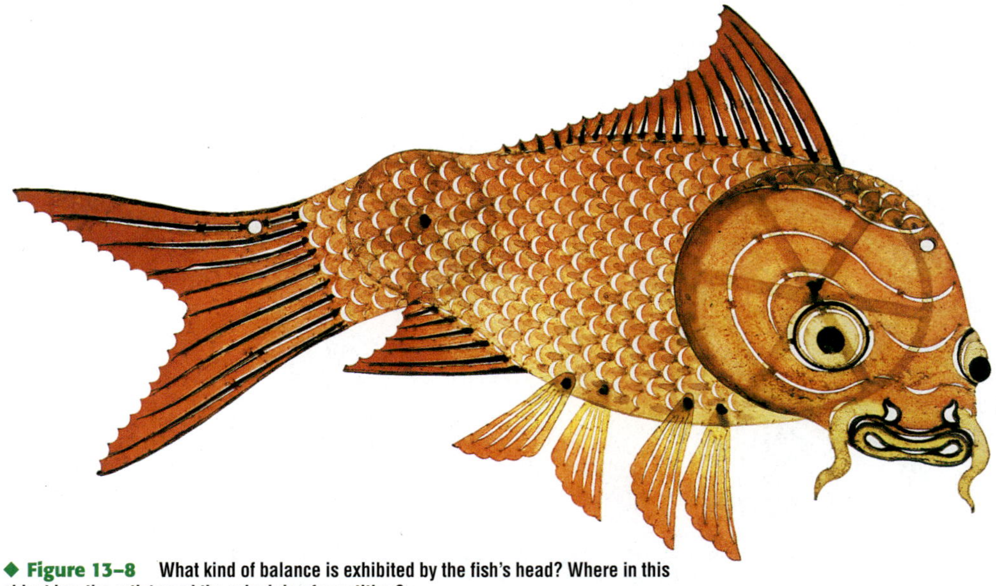

◆ **Figure 13–8** **What kind of balance is exhibited by the fish's head? Where in this object has the artist used the principle of repetition?**

China. *Fish Shadow Puppet.* c. 1900. Leather with color. 13.5 × 30.5 cm (5⁵⁄₁₆ × 12″). Museum of International Folk Art, a unit of The Museum of New Mexico, Santa Fe, New Mexico. The Girard Foundation Collection.

INCLUSION STRATEGIES

SPECIAL LEARNING NEEDS Puppetry is a good activity for students with disabilities because of its potential for creative expression. However, some disabled students may have difficulty tying strings for the shadow puppets or using a hole punch and brads. In general, it is best for students to make a project using their own initiative and abilities even if it means using other techniques or processes than those outlined in the directions. Well-meaning helpers sometimes inadvertently foster dependence rather than independence.

- Pens, watercolors, or markers
- Brushes
- Scissors
- Hole punch, book brads
- String or wooden dowel ¼ inch or less in diameter

What You Will Do

1. With classmates, brainstorm a list of joyous festivals. Exchange information on animal shapes and other images associated with these festivals.
2. Working alone, choose a festival. Make several sketches of an image connected with it. The image should be one that has potential for a kinetic art project. Your object should have at least two parts, such as a body and tail (see Figure 13–8). Arms, legs, and a head are other possibilities.
3. Transfer your best sketch to tagboard. Draw outline shapes for all of the parts of your object. Fill as much of the surface as possible. Add details and color with pens, watercolors, or markers. Cover the entire surface of each part with color. Repeat lines and shapes to create a rhythmic pattern. Emphasize one part by introducing visual texture.
4. With scissors, carefully cut all parts out of the tagboard. Use a hole punch to make holes at the points where the parts will be joined. Use book brads to attach the parts. Make an additional hole in either the top or bottom of your creation. Tie string through this hole if your object is to be hung. Insert a wooden dowel as support if your object is a shadow puppet.

Evaluating Your Work

- **Describe** Identify the type of kinetic art you have created. Indicate the energy source—the wind or muscle power, for example.
- **Analyze** Tell whether you repeated lines and shapes to create a rhythmic pattern. Point to a part you emphasized by adding visual texture.
- **Interpret** Explain how the art object will be used. State whether it expresses the joyous mood of the festival.
- **Judge** Explain whether your artwork is successful. Tell whether the parts move freely.

5. Share your work with classmates. Can they identify the festival you have chosen?

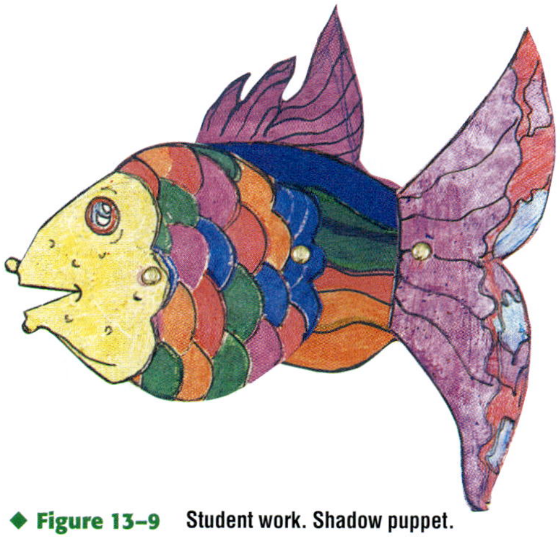

◆ **Figure 13–9** Student work. Shadow puppet.

PORTFOLIO IDEAS

The work you include in your portfolio will demonstrate what you have done and how you did it. Written self-reflections help you define goals and recognize achievements. A teacher may use your portfolio to evaluate your progress too. A portfolio is evidence of your participation, understanding, and growth as an artist.

Visual Art Journal

Conduct in-progress analyses of personal artworks. As you begin step 3, analyze your work and select your best sketch. Keep the other sketches in you portfolio to show your progression as an artist.

Historical/Cultural Heritage

Ask students to think of kinetic art they have seen from different cultures. One example is the Japanese kite. Another is the Chinese lantern. Have students find out about these and other examples of kinetic art and the festivals they are associated with, and bring in pictures to share with the class. L2

Studio Skills

Help students brainstorm their lists of festivals as well as animal shapes and other images. Bring in books about festivals to help inspire them. As students begin to sketch their objects, remind them to choose an area of emphasis and to add visual texture to that area. Demonstrate how to tighten the book brads so that the parts move freely but don't hang limp. L1 ELL

3 Assess

Self-Assessment

Have students use **Evaluating Your Work** to conduct an in-progress critique of their kinetic "festival" artwork.

Reteaching

In pairs, have students demonstrate to each other the energy source used by their kinetic art. L1 ELL

4 Close

Have pairs of students take turns using shadow puppets in a shadow dance.

DEVELOPING A PORTFOLIO

Rubrics for Assessment When using a rubric to assess a portfolio, it is meaningful to have more than one reviewer. If you have two or three people review the work independently, then come together to determine what student work looks like at each level of the rubric, you have set *benchmarks.* Benchmarks for specific assignments or portfolios offer concrete examples for students at each level of the rubric. You need a large pool of student work to make this effective. For more information on the use of rubrics for portfolios, refer to the booklet *Portfolio and Assessment Techniques* that accompanies this program.

Celebrating Rites of Passage

(pages 252–253)

1 Focus

Objectives

After completing this lesson, students will be able to:

- Recognize that rites of passage are celebrations of special achievements or honors.
- Understand that the Chinese Coming of Age Hat and the Yoruba *adenla* are examples of headdresses used in coming-of-age rituals.

SUPPLIES
- Assorted construction paper or tagboard
- Construction paper scraps
- Beads, trims, lace, yarn, and small found objects
- Scissors, white glue

2 Teach

Motivator

Ask students what age they would like to be if they could be older. What additional privileges would they have at that age? Discuss the rewards that come with hard work and achievement, and point out that the Chinese Coming of Age Hat, for example, is simply earned by growing older. The *adenla,* on the other hand, can only be worn by someone born into a royal family.

Vocabulary

Have students look up the word *rite* in a dictionary. Ask students to give examples of rites they are familiar with in their daily lives.

Celebrating Rites of Passage

Of all the events you celebrate, probably none is more special to you than the anniversary of the day you were born. On your birthday, *you* are the "celebrity." Friends and loved ones gather around you. Bearing presents and good wishes, they help you celebrate your passage into another year of life.

The special quality of birthdays and other "passages" is not lost on artists. In this lesson, you will look at two art objects celebrating rites, or ceremonies, of passage.

Rite of Passage Art

What do you plan to be when you grow up? This is a question you probably have been asked many times. You may have asked it of yourself as well. Growing into adulthood is a big step. With it come more privileges and more responsibilities. Many cultures observe this "coming of age" with a special celebration. Graduating, obtaining a driver's license, and being able to vote are examples of coming of age that bring a feeling of excitement and a desire to celebrate.

Chinese Rite of Passage Object

In some cultures, rites of passage include the wearing of special articles of clothing. One such article appears in **Figure 13–10.** Did you recognize this colorful creation as a hat? In China, it is a tradition—and an honor—to wear a hat like this on the birthday marking one's passage into adulthood. You may be reminded of the paper hats you wore at birthday parties when you were younger.

Examine this festive object. It has been richly embroidered with beads. Notice the

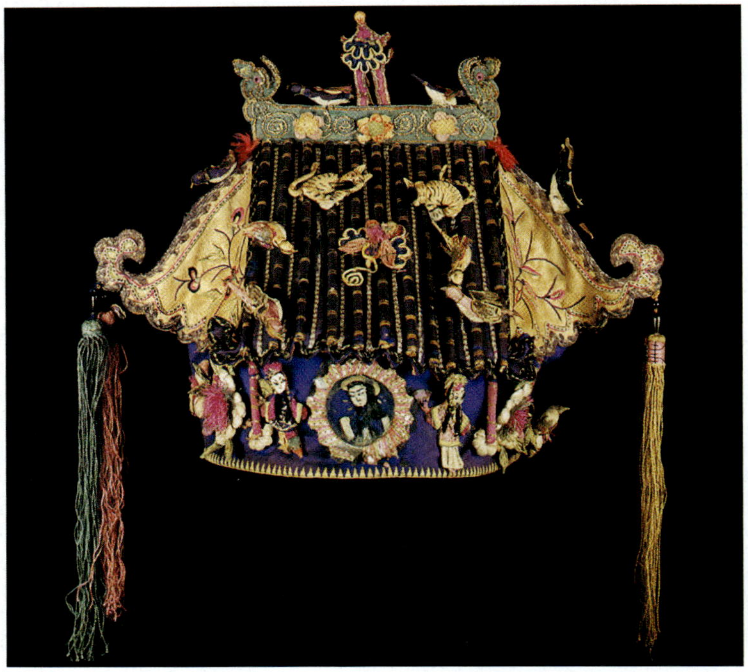

◆ **Figure 13–10** **Color helps create visual interest in this object. What other art elements contribute?**

China. *Coming of Age Hat.* Mixed media, embroidery. 31 × 38 cm (12 × 15″). Private Collection.

MORE ABOUT...

Ceremonial Hats Many cultures celebrate the age of puberty, about twelve or thirteen years old, as the "coming-of-age" period for young people. This is the time when they pass from childhood to adulthood, learning to accept the responsibilities that face adults.

In the Chinese hat shown in **Figure 13–10,** point out the elaborate stitchery and symbols used, including good luck charms and wishes. Ask students to compare this hat with birthday customs from their own ethnic or religious background.

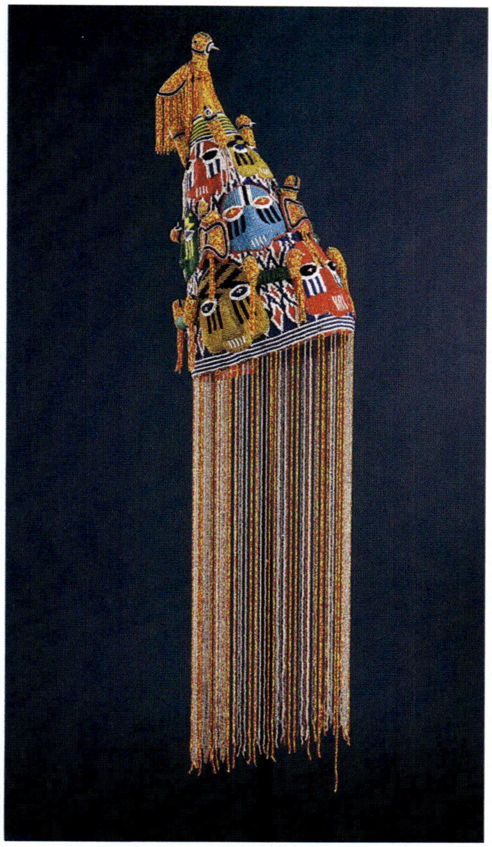

◆ **Figure 13–11** **What kinds of shapes appear throughout this object? How would you describe the colors that have been used? What steps has the artist taken to achieve harmony?**

Africa. Yoruba. *King's Crown (adenla).* c. 1930. Bamboo framework, beads, cloth, leather. H: 50.8 cm plus 58.4 cm beaded fringe (20″ plus 23″ fringe). Diameter: 31 cm (12¼″). The Saint Louis Museum of Art, St. Louis, Missouri. Purchase: Museum Shop Fund.

attention to detail. Who do you suppose the human figures toward the base of the hat might be?

African Rite of Passage Object

The custom of wearing a birthday hat in China is widespread. The "hat" in **Figure 13–11**, by contrast, is worn by a chosen few. This object is an adenla (uh-**den**-luh), or "King's Crown." It was created by an artist of the Yoruba people of West Africa. An **adenla** is *a sculpted ceremonial headdress used in rites of passage.* The privilege of wearing an adenla is reserved for royalty.

As you study this object, take note of the birdlike figure at the top. Many Yoruban adenla are decorated with woodpeckers. These are symbolic of the class structure—the "pecking order"—in this West African society. The long-beaded threads extending from the brim form a *veil* of sorts. The purpose is not to protect the new king from curious glances. Rather, it is to force his own gaze inward, to remind him of his obligation to serve his people well.

STUDIO ACTIVITY

Making a Hat

Demonstrate your technical skills. Use a variety of art media to produce a design of a hat or headdress for a special event in your life. Begin by cutting a circle from construction paper and then cutting a slit from the outer edge to the center. Pull together the "flaps" on either side of the cut to make a cone. Fasten with staples or transparent tape. Decorate your hat with beads, lace, and other found objects that convey the theme and mood of your chosen event.

PORTFOLIO

Write an evaluation of how well your hat or headdress reflects the theme and mood of the event. Add this to your portfolio with a photograph of the hat.

Check Your Understanding

1. Compare and contrast Figures 13–10 and 13–11.
2. Identify the influence of Yoruban political structure in an adenla.

Aesthetics

Both hats pictured in this lesson took time and skill to make and were made for important ceremonies. Ask students if they think these hats would be as valuable if they were made for everyday wear instead. Have them explain why or why not. L1

Understanding Art History

The King's Crown was made in the 1930s in Nigeria, by the Yoruba people. Divide the class into small groups and assign each group one of the following: geography, climate, crops, economic conditions, historical events, government, people. Have groups research the history of this artwork with particular focus on the assigned area. L2

3 Assess

Self-Assessment

Have students complete the **Check Your Understanding** questions on this page. Answers are provided below.

Reteaching

Have students brainstorm rituals that celebrate or honor other achievements.

Enrichment

Headdresses are part of many different rituals and ceremonies in many cultures. Have students research the role and significance of the headdress in a different ritual, such as weddings, or in another rite-of-passage ritual. L2

4 Close

Ask students to explain the significance of an *adenla* to a young person in Nigeria.

Answers to Check Your Understanding

1. The two headdresses are similar in that they both are worn on the head during a special ceremony. They are different in the media used, design, and in that one is worn by many, the other is worn by only a chosen few.
2. The adenla is decorated with woodpeckers, which is symbolic to the Yoruban class structure. They suggest the "pecking order" in that society. The long-beaded threads are to symbolize how the king should gaze inward to remind him of his obligation to serve his people well.

A Cause for Celebration

(pages 254–255)

1 Focus

Objectives

After completing this lesson, students will be able to:

- Demonstrate an understanding of historical and political influences on issues, events, and artworks.
- Compare and contrast artworks in terms of style.
- Describe and draw a celebration of their own.

2 Teach

Motivator

Ask students what type of event is depicted in the painting in **Figure 13–13** *(a parade).* Ask: What is the purpose of parades? *(They celebrate or commemorate something joyous or positive.)* Explain that in this lesson students will learn about the celebration portrayed in this artwork.

Art Criticism

Remind students that different lines give off different feelings or sensations. Ask: Which objects in Figure 13–13 make use of diagonals? *(The flags.)* Why do you think the artist chose to emphasize these objects? *(They are central to the meaning of the painting, which commemorates the United States becoming an ally of England and France during World War I.)*

A Cause for Celebration

There are many reasons to celebrate, and art embraces them all. Some celebrations, as you've read so far in this chapter, occur on a personal level. These include birthdays and rites of passage. Other causes for celebration occur on a national level. The passage in **Figure 13–12** describes such an event. This passage expresses the nation's mood in 1917 regarding World War I.

Celebrating Historical Events

In a special session of Congress held on April 2, 1917, President Woodrow Wilson delivered his "War Message." Four days later, Congress overwhelmingly passed the War Resolution, which brought the United States into World War I. Within a month of Congress' war declaration, joyous parades were held.

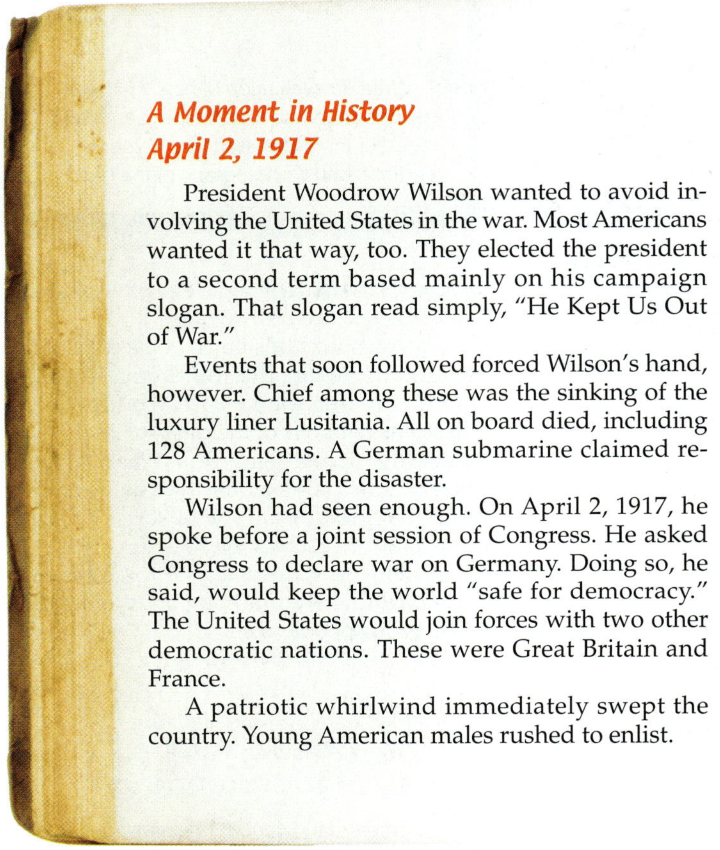

A Moment in History
April 2, 1917

President Woodrow Wilson wanted to avoid involving the United States in the war. Most Americans wanted it that way, too. They elected the president to a second term based mainly on his campaign slogan. That slogan read simply, "He Kept Us Out of War."

Events that soon followed forced Wilson's hand, however. Chief among these was the sinking of the luxury liner Lusitania. All on board died, including 128 Americans. A German submarine claimed responsibility for the disaster.

Wilson had seen enough. On April 2, 1917, he spoke before a joint session of Congress. He asked Congress to declare war on Germany. Doing so, he said, would keep the world "safe for democracy." The United States would join forces with two other democratic nations. These were Great Britain and France.

A patriotic whirlwind immediately swept the country. Young American males rushed to enlist.

◆ **Figure 13–12** Adapted from President Woodrow Wilson's "War Message."

MORE ABOUT...

Childe Hassam (1859–1935) Frederick Childe Hassam was born on the outskirts of Boston. He studied art at the Boston Art School and the École des Beaux-Arts in Paris. In France, he fell under the influence of the Impressionists and began to paint in their style. He subsequently became the leader of the American Impressionist movement. Most of Hassam's subjects were rural scenes from his native New England, though occasionally he chose urban subjects.

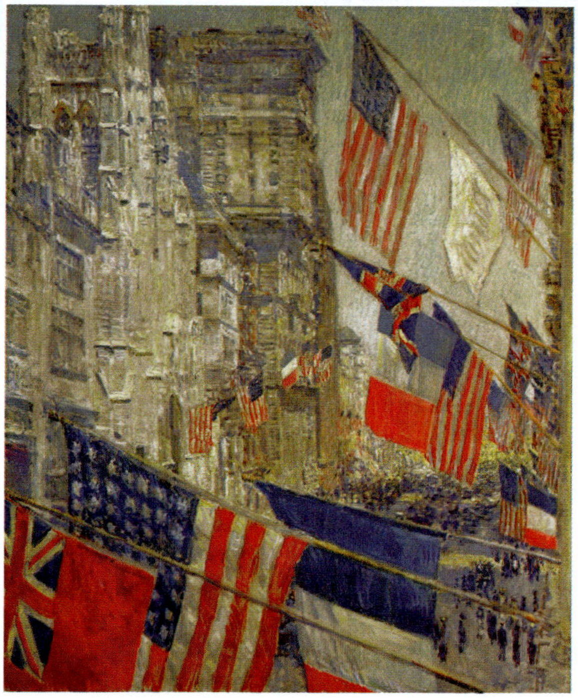

◆ **Figure 13–13** Notice Hassam's use of color in this painting. What colors stand out most?

Childe Hassam. *Allies Day, May 1917.* Oil on canvas. 92.7 × 76.8 cm (36½ × 30¼") National Gallery of Art, Washington, D.C. Gift of Ethelyn McKinney in memory of her brother, Glenn Ford McKinney.

The Colors of Patriotism

The scene shown in **Figure 13–13** illustrates a parade down Fifth Avenue in New York City. This painting is by American artist Childe Hassam (1859–1935). As noted in the credit line, the title of the work is *Allies Day, May 1917.* Childe Hassam happened to be present at the parade depicted in his painting. Hassam dedicated this artwork "to the coming together of [our] three peoples in the fight for democracy." Notice the colors that dominate. They are found in the many flags that hang from windows high above the street. The Stars and Stripes, which appears several times, is the largest. It is joined by the British Union Jack and the French Tricolor. By a lucky coincidence, all draw upon the same three colors.

MAKE THE CONNECTION

Take Another Look

1. After reading the passage in Figure 13–12, is the artwork effective in expressing that moment in history?
2. Look again at Figure 13–13. What feeling does the painting evoke? What is a dominant feature in this artwork?

ART & SOCIAL STUDIES

Depicting a celebration. Think about another cause for celebration. This may be a national event, or it may relate to family. Write a description of the event you selected. What is it celebrating? What is special about the particular scene you're describing? Next, draw several sketches of events related to this celebration.

MAKE THE CONNECTION

Take Another Look Student answers will vary, but may include the following:

1. The specific moment recorded in the painting is the one reflected in the final paragraph of the reading passage in Figure 13–12. Most students will agree that the work effectively records this celebratory moment.
2. The feeling might be described as joy, happiness, or patriotism. The dominant feature used to evoke that feeling is the flags.

Active Reading

Have students read the text in **Figure 13–12.** Ask them to summarize the text. What details stand out the most?

Critical Thinking

Observe that all three nations' flags make use of the same colors. Ask students what relationship among these powers might have led to the decision to use the same three hues.

3 Assess

Self-Assessment

Have students complete the **Take Another Look** questions on this page. Answers are provided below.

Reteaching

Ask students to find the part in the reading passage that most clearly reflects the scene in the painting.

Enrichment

Have students explore artworks that show other parades. Encourage them to use online or print resources. They should identify (1) the cause celebrated in the work they have chosen, (2) the artist, and (3) the manner in which the work is similar to and different from Childe Hassam's painting.

4 Close

Have students describe the dominant mood in this painting, noting the way in which the artist has used the elements of line and color to achieve that feeling.

Art That Celebrates Life

(pages 256–257)

1 Focus

Objectives

After completing this lesson, students will be able to:

- Recognize Rie Muñoz as an Alaskan painter who uses color, shape, and form to make expressive paintings.
- Explain how James Phillips's artwork celebrates his heritage in the rhythms created by lines, shapes, and colors.

2 Teach

Motivator

Have students recall the excitement of the first celebration they remember. Then have them look closely at Muñoz's painting in **Figure 13–14.** Ask: What are the figures celebrating? How does the artist create movement in this artwork? Then have students study Phillips's painting with circles. Point out that Phillips paints the strong colors, shapes, and rhythms from his African heritage. Ask students if they can almost hear the beat of music as they view his work.

Art Criticism

Have students use the four steps of art criticism to evaluate and compare the two paintings in this lesson. Have them use a Venn diagram to list commonalities as well as differences. Have students decide whether each artist's intent was the same. Finally, have them determine whether each painting is a successful work of art and explain why or why not. L1

Art that Celebrates Life

In this chapter, the focus has been on celebrations that relate to important dates on the calendar. Not all celebrations, however, revolve around "red-letter days." Some causes for celebration are simple, everyday events—skating with friends on a perfect fall afternoon, gazing out the window at a gentle spring rain, or waking up to the first snow. Can you think of similar occasions that made you feel glad just to be alive?

Every now and then life serves up such priceless moments. These celebrations of life know no cultural boundaries. In this lesson, you will look at two artists' views of such celebrations.

Inuit Subjects

The painting in **Figure 13–14** captures a rare moment for both the artist and her subjects. Study the work. In it, two Inuit women appear. The similarity of their positions indicates that they are celebrating. Imagine the artist's delight in creating this scene. She expresses her feelings by recording a celebration in a symbolic way. Notice the stylized use of shape and color.

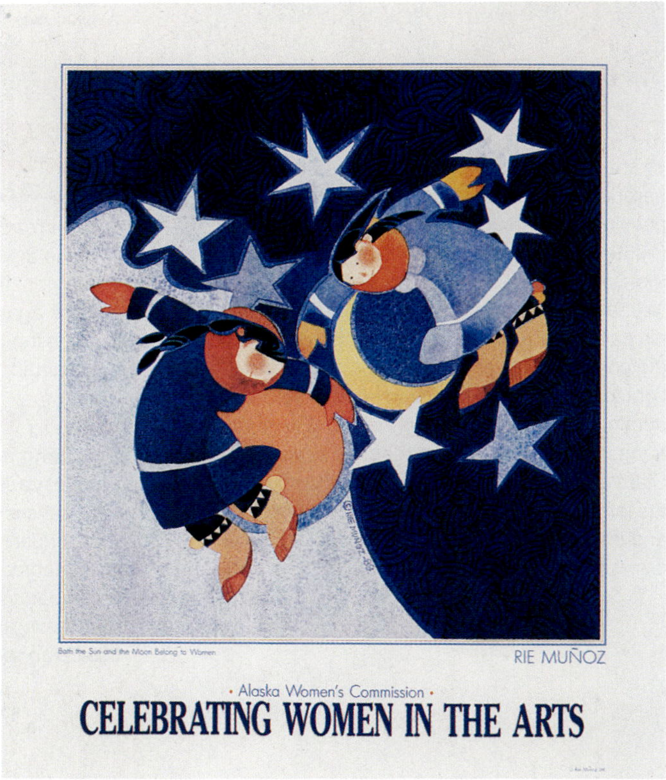

◆ **Figure 13–14** Notice how the artist uses the sun, moon, and stars to symbolize the universal nature of artistic expression. How has she used color to symbolize day and night?

Rie Muñoz. *Both the Sun and Moon Belong to Women.* 1990. Watercolor. 48.2 × 55.9 cm (19 × 22"). Rie Muñoz Ltd., Juneau, Alaska.

TEACHER TO TEACHER

Radial Designs Have students make a radial design with simple shapes and thick and thin lines. Begin the design at a center point on the paper, working evenly around axis lines that dissect the circle into even sections. Or, give students a pie shape that represents one-sixth or one-eighth of the circle. Have students draw their design on this slice. Then redraw this section repeatedly around the circle, using carbon paper or soft lead pencil. Add color with crayons, colored markers, colored pencils, oil pastels, or watercolors.

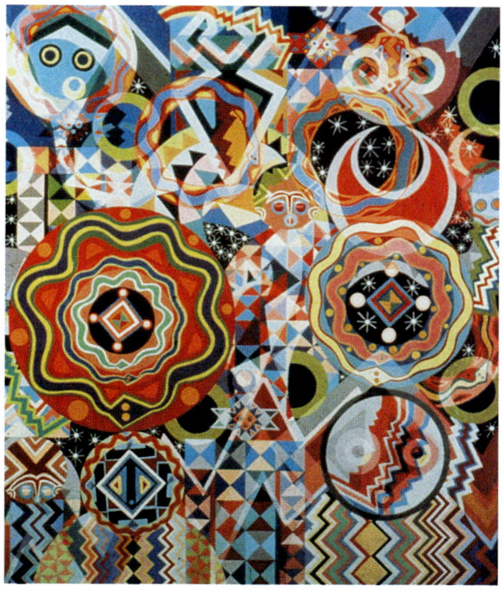

◆ **Figure 13–15** **Can you find objects in this painting that exhibit radial balance? What other art principles are evident in this work?**

James Phillips. *Ancestral Dream.* 1991. Acrylic on paper. 120.7 × 108 cm (47½ × 42½″). Private Collection.

African American Paintings

Some celebrations of life do not come from how we feel. They come instead from a sense of pride in who we are. The abstract artwork in **Figure 13–15** is such a "celebration." The work celebrates the artist's African roots.

As you explore this busy painting, your eye never stays in one place for long. It is forever moving, much like the pulsing colors and vibrating geometric shapes that make up the work. Pause for a moment to focus on the yellow-and-black bull's-eyes nested within the blue circle at the upper left. These objects may remind you of a face. If so, this is no accident. Similar arrangements throughout this painting are efforts to re-create, at least in spirit, the ritual masks of the artist's African ancestors.

Meet the Artist

Rie Muñoz

Cultural connection. Although Rie (short for Marie) Muñoz was born and raised in California, she is one of Alaska's most well-known artists. She paints scenes of everyday life in an Alaskan village, including such activities as fishing, hunting, and playing winter sports. Her watercolor paintings are filled with a sense of humor and whimsy (see **Figure 13–14**).

Muñoz is the daughter of Dutch parents who immigrated to California. She studied art at Washington and Lee University in Virginia and later at the University of Alaska-Juneau. In 1950, Muñoz took a steamship up Alaska's Inside Passage. She fell in love with the capital city of Juneau and decided to make it her home. Ever since, Muñoz has lived and painted there. She has had many jobs, including teacher, commercial artist, and museum curator, but eventually settled on full-time painter. Even now—in her seventies—Muñoz finishes between 50 and 60 paintings every year. Identify in Figure 13–14 any influences of Inuit culture.

Check Your Understanding

1. What event is celebrated in the painting in Figure 13–14?
2. What kinds of cultural images appear in Figure 13–15?

Understanding Art History

Divide the class into small groups of three or four. Assign half the groups Rie Muñoz and the other half James Phillips. Ask each group to research the world events that occurred at the time the artist's painting was made. Can they identify the influence of such events in the artworks? Have them include information about other local artists and art forms in drama, writing, music, and dance. Ask groups to share their findings. L1

3 Assess

Self-Assessment

Have students complete the **Check Your Understanding** questions on this page. Answers are provided below.

Reteaching

In pairs, have students explain the mood and feelings expressed in each painting in the lesson. L1 ELL

Enrichment

Have students investigate the lives and customs of the Inuit people. Have them concentrate on their art and culture, but also encourage students to discover the social history of these northern people. L2

4 Close

Ask students to explain how simple, everyday events can be a cause for celebration.

Answers to Check Your Understanding

1. The painting celebrates women in the arts.
2. The African masks of the artist's ancestors, including faces, repeated geometric shapes, and bright colors.

Celebrating a Role Model

(pages 258–259)
Lesson Time: 90 minutes

1 Focus

Objectives

After completing this lesson, students will be able to:

- Identify the significance of rituals and artworks to honor achievements.
- Demonstrate technical skills effectively by using a variety of art media and materials to produce a ritual wall hanging honoring a special role model or admired person.
- Conduct an in-progress critique of their artwork.

SUPPLIES
Refer to **What You Will Need** in the Student Edition.

2 Teach

Motivator

Ask students if they have a skill or talent they practice every day. Is there a person they admire who inspires them to work harder at their skill? Tell students that everyday rituals or routines usually lead to celebrations of larger achievements, such as the "first" concert or art exhibit, athletic award, passing grades, and a diploma. These events can in turn lead to new rituals or rehearsals for new goals.

LESSON 8

Celebrating a Role Model

Are there grownups whose footsteps you hope to follow in someday? Maybe your role model is a person like the one whose sculpted likeness appears at the center of the work in **Figure 13–16**. This man is C. J. McLin. He was the first African American to be elected to public office in the artist's home state of Ohio. The work is the artist's personal tribute to McLin. It is more than just that, however. It is also intended as a message to young people—a call to them to find heroes truly worthy of admiration. What qualities of this work reveal the artist's admiration for a leader and pioneer?

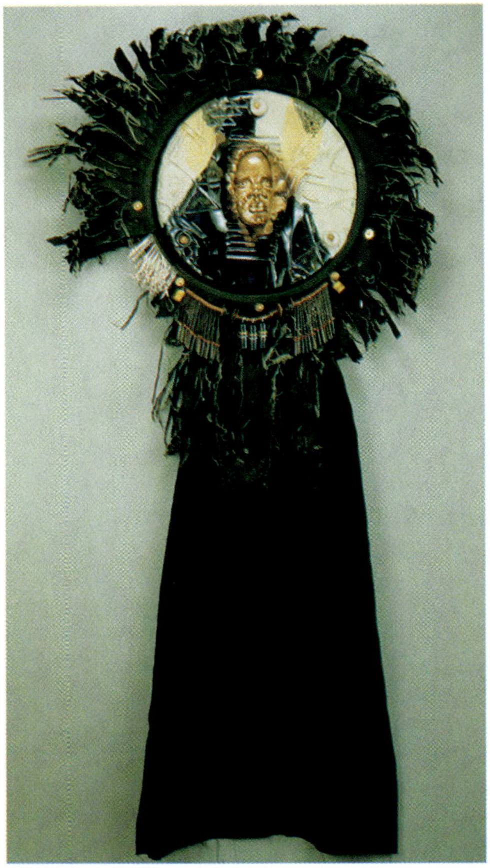

WHAT YOU WILL LEARN

You will create a three-dimensional mixed-media tribute that honors a person whose life or work inspires you. Your design will include a variety of media. The objects you choose will connect in some way with your theme. Your design will include colored yarn or paper strips that create harmony with the rest of the media. The yarn will be woven and arranged in an interesting pattern.

WHAT YOU WILL NEED

- Photographs and old magazines
- Compass
- Sheet of construction paper, 9 x 12 inches
- Scissors
- White glue
- Tissue paper, gold or aluminum foil
- Assorted yarns, colored paper, or colored markers
- Plastic lid from an ice-cream or coffee container

◆ **Figure 13–16** **How does the artist emphasize the image of the figure whose achievements this work celebrates?**

Bing Davis. *Puberty Ritual Image #10*. 1992. Clay and found objects. 91.3 × 45.7 cm (36 × 18″). Private Collection.

STORY BEHIND THE ARTWORK

PUBERTY RITUAL IMAGE # 10 To capture the spirit of his heritage, Bing Davis returned to his African roots. Some of the African art forms he discovered include fabric designs, carvings, music, dance, costumes, masks, and storytelling. Davis uses a wide variety of media to capture his feelings through symbols. Transforming everyday recycled objects into the meaning of his artwork is a special process for Davis. Discarded objects such as the shredded tire become the halo for the face in the center of the work. The tire represents the journey of life and the ancient rite of passage.

What You Will Do

1. Select a person whom you admire. This might be a relative, a leader in your community or state, a teacher, or anyone else who inspires you.
2. Think about images that communicate information about this person's appearance and accomplishments. These might include photographs and pictures clipped from magazines that symbolize the person's importance to you. Gather an assortment of such materials.
3. Trace a circle that will fit the outside measurement of the lid on colored construction paper. Choose a color that is in keeping with your tribute. Make a second circle the same size on a thin sheet of cardboard. Cut out both circles. Glue them together.
4. Arrange the photographs and images you have gathered on the colored construction paper circle. When you are satisfied with the arrangement, glue these in place. Fill the negative spaces between and around the images with strips of tissue paper, gold foil, or colored lines. Be creative! Set this object aside to dry.
5. Gather strands of thin yarn or cut paper strips in several colors. These should blend with those of the construction paper and images, so as to create harmony. Form an interesting pattern with the yarn or paper strips and glue them to the edge of the plastic lid to make a border and add repetition to the work.
6. Glue your circle to the flat surface of the lid.

Evaluating Your Work

- **Describe** Describe the materials used in your tribute. Identify the individual you are honoring.
- **Analyze** Does your work achieve harmony through the use of color? Have you used interesting patterns in the border as an organizing principle?
- **Interpret** Explain the idea, mood, and message your work expresses about its subject.
- **Judge** How does your work compare with that in Figure 13–16? In what ways is it similar? How is it different?

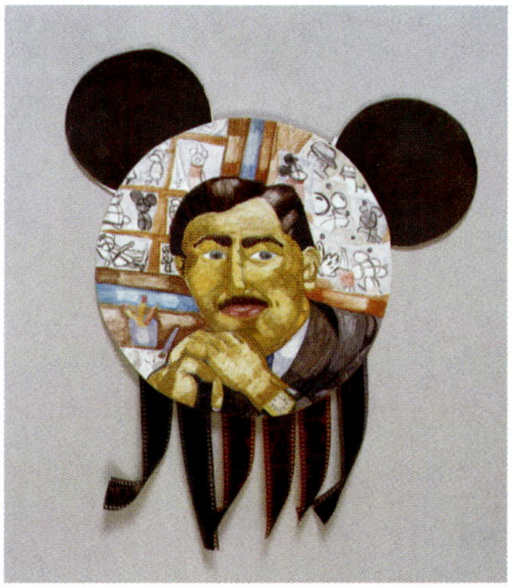

◆ **Figure 13–17** Student work. A role model.

Reflective Thinking

Critical Evaluation. Analyze the original artworks of your peers. Examine the mixed-media tribute to a role-model they created and form conclusions about formal properties. For example, how did they apply variety and harmony in their design?

Art Online

Careers in art. To learn more about art-related careers, visit our Web site at **art.glencoe.com** and click on Career Corner. Compare the different career opportunities and make note of those that interest you.

Aesthetics

Ask students to explain what Bing Davis does in this artwork that is different from other artists who reflect their heritage in their message. What features are unique? Does this uniqueness make it a better or poorer design? Have students explain their opinions. L1

Historical/Cultural Heritage

The *Puberty Ritual Image #10* was made in 1989 in Ohio to honor a prominent African American statesman. Have students research other African Americans as well as leaders from other cultural backgrounds, male and female, who made significant contributions in the 1980s. Include science, medicine, politics, the arts, and sports. L2

3 Assess

Peer Assessment

Have students analyze the mixed-media tribute their peers created to form conclusions about formal properties—the elements and principles of art.

Reteaching

Have pairs of students share with each other the message they were trying to convey in their artwork. L1 ELL

4 Close

Have students explain the theme of Bing Davis's wall hanging.

Resources Beyond the Classroom

Exhibitions and Competitions Community colleges, art schools, and universities often sponsor student exhibitions and competitions. Younger students who view such exhibits and competitions will be exposed to a wide variety of skill levels, techniques, and media. On occasion, schools and colleges invite younger students to submit artworks for exhibit; they may also invite students to participate in a competition in a special category. Students who see and participate in such exhibits and competitions are more encouraged to continue to create art throughout their lives.

Everyone Loves a Parade

Objectives

After completing this lesson, students will be able to:

- Draw a float or balloon that could be included in the Macy's Thanksgiving Day Parade.
- Write, share, and revise a journal entry.

Teaching the Feature

1. Have students read the article title, "Everyone Loves a Parade," and share their responses to it. Ask: What parades have you seen in person? What parades have you seen on TV? How did you feel about those parades?
2. Guide students in reading and discussing the article. Encourage volunteers to share their ideas about the work John Piper does.

Activity

Help students discuss their ideas for new—and unusual—floats and balloons for the Macy's Thanksgiving Day Parade. Then have students use markers or crayons to draw their favorite idea for a special addition to the parade.

TIME ART SCENE Language Arts

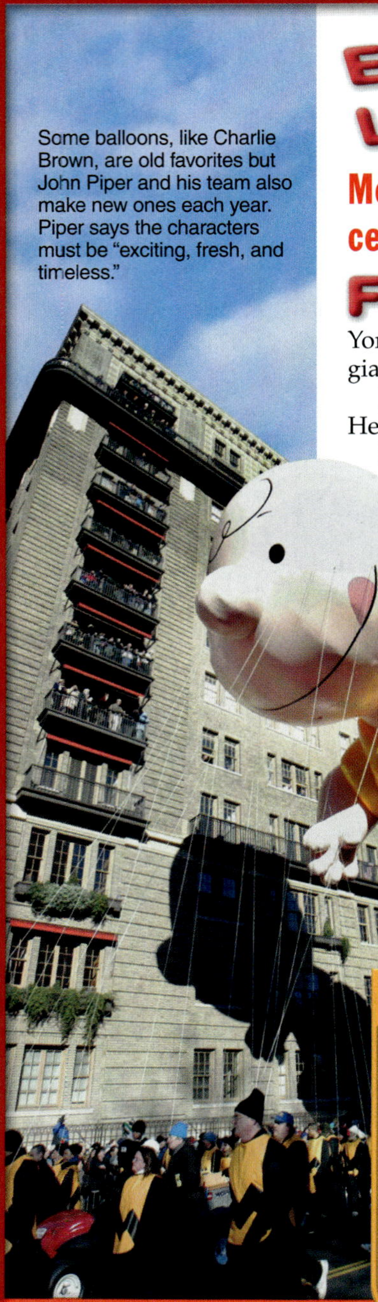

Some balloons, like Charlie Brown, are old favorites but John Piper and his team also make new ones each year. Piper says the characters must be "exciting, fresh, and timeless."

REUTERS NEWMEDIA INC./CORBIS

EVERYONE LOVES A PARADE

Meet the man behind a world-famous celebration.

For many people, Thanksgiving wouldn't be the same without the Macy's Thanksgiving Day Parade in New York City. Millions of people gaze at the colorful floats and giant balloons that soar among the city's skyscrapers.

John Piper is the man behind the floats and balloons. He designs them all and oversees the 20 people who help him dream up the holiday displays. In a warehouse in Hoboken, New Jersey, Piper and his team sketch ideas and make small models before building full-scale versions.

At parade time, Piper's staff grows to more than 300 people. It takes them about two hours to fill each balloon with helium. Workers keep the balloons grounded with nets and sandbags. "The curtain goes up at 9 A.M. Thanksgiving morning, no matter what," he says. But the crowd's response to the works of art rolling or floating by "lifts the spirits above and beyond everything else."

TIME TO CONNECT

- **Imagine attending or viewing the Macy's Thanksgiving Day Parade. Write a journal entry that describes what you found most interesting and impressive about the floats and balloons as they passed by.**
- **How do the size, form, color, and movement of the floats add to the sense of celebration? Share your work with the class for feedback. Revise your entry to make sure you've communicated a vivid sense of your reactions to the parade.**

TIME TO CONNECT

After students have written and shared their journal entries, have them work with partners to proofread their entries. As they proofread, have students answer these questions:

- Are all proper nouns correctly capitalized?
- Do any commas or quotation marks need to be added? Should any be taken out?
- Does the verb in each sentence go with the sentence subject?
- Are correct pronoun forms used?

Chapter 13 Review

BUILDING VOCABULARY

Number a sheet of paper from 1 to 6. After each number, write the term from the list that matches each description below.

adenla	seal
kinetic art	shadow puppet
pueblo	tricolor

1. An art style in which parts of a work are set into motion by a form of energy.
2. An art object in the shape of an animal or human attached to a wand or stick.
3. Dried-clay dwelling.
4. A sculpted ceremonial headdress used in rites of passage.
5. A flag with three broad bands of color.
6. A symbolic image or emblem.

REVIEWING ART FACTS

Number a sheet of paper from 7 to 11. Answer each question in a complete sentence.

7. What are the paintings in Figures 13–2 and 13–3 rejoicing?
8. In what ways might Figure 13–4 be said to be an example of *impossible art?*
9. What two types of dance are featured in Hopi culture? Which type is most common?
10. Name two purposes of festivals in various cultures of the world.
11. What is a rite of passage?

CROSS-CURRICULUM CONNECTIONS

12. **Social Studies.** One of the historical figures celebrated in Figure 13–4 is Rosa Parks. Using various resources, research Rosa Parks's life. Present your findings to the class. Include readings from stories people have written about her life.
13. **Social Studies.** Different states and locales have their own specific holidays. Residents of Massachusetts, for example, celebrate Patriot's Day. Find out about holidays specific to your town or community, such as Founder's Day. Learn about their meaning and what they represent. Design and create visual materials—posters and a logo, for example—for the next celebration of this event. Share your creations with your classmates.

Web Museum Activity

The Museum of Fine Arts, Houston, Texas

In this chapter, you learned about the different ways artists have recorded celebrations through the ages. Go to **art.glencoe.com** and click on the Museum of Fine Arts, Houston link to explore different types of celebrations from various cultures.

You will discover different forms of celebrations and understand the meaning of these special events. Examine the different images. What is being celebrated in each of these artworks? How do the artworks depict the particular celebration? Describe the meaning behind the festival or celebration.

ANSWERS TO Chapter 13 Review

Building Vocabulary

1. kinetic art
2. shadow puppet
3. pueblo
4. adenla
5. tricolor
6. seal

Reviewing Art Facts

7. Both works celebrate their nations' struggle for independence and the courage and dedication of those who participated in this struggle.
8. The work is impossible in that the figures shown represent different centuries and places.
9. The two types are social dances and dances that celebrate the oneness of people with nature. Dances of the second type are more common.
10. Some festivals celebrate the new year. Others are meant to ensure a good harvest.
11. It is a ritual that celebrates an important passage in life, such as the passage from childhood into adulthood.

Cross-Curriculum Connections

12. Student presentations will vary.
13. Student designs will vary depending on the holiday they have chosen.

Web Museum Activity

Before you have students go online, visit the Web site to preview the museum's online content, collection, and any online exhibit that may be of interest. Students' written responses will vary according to the images they selected. Students should include a clear description of the meaning behind the festival or celebration artworks they have chosen.

Chapter Resources

Features	Standards for Chapter		Reproducible Masters
	National	State/Local	
Quick Write *page 263* TIME ART SCENE "Making Movies" *page 276* Web Museum Activity *page 277*	**1.** (a, b) **2.** (a, b) **3.** (a, b) **4.** (a, c) **5.** (b) **6.** (a, b)		Guided Reading and Practice 14–1 Enrichment Activity 14–2 Studio Activity 14–3 Historical and Cultural Heritage 14–4, 14–6 Application Activity 14–5 Lesson Plans

Lesson Resources

Lessons	Standards per Lesson		Reproducible Masters
	National	State/Local	
1 ***Dreams and Nightmares*** *(pages 264–265)*	1a, 1b, 4c, 5b		Enrichment Activity 14–2
2 ***Creating a Fantasy Bird Collage*** *(pages 266–267)*	1a, 1b, 2a		Studio Activity 14–3 Historical and Cultural Heritage 14–4
3 ***Puzzling Paintings*** *(pages 268–269)*	1a, 1b, 5b		Application Activity 14–5
4 ***Creating Your Own Picture Puzzle*** *(pages 270–271)*	1a, 1b, 2a, 2b, 3a		Historical and Cultural Heritage 14–6
5 ***Impossible Images*** *(pages 272–273)*	4a, 5b, 6a		
6 **ART & READING** *(pages 274–275)*	5b, 6a, 6b		

Assessment	Technology
Testing Program: Chapter Test 14–7 *Portfolio and Assessment Techniques*	Artsource Performing Arts Package, Diavolo (DVD or Video Segment 6) National Museum of Women in the Arts Interactive Lesson Planner Fine Art Transparency CC-14 *Second Thoughts* by Yves Tanguy Fine Art Transparency 14 *Lily and the Sparrows* by Philip Evergood

Activities/Features
Studio Activity: A Drawing in the Surrealist Style
Evaluating Your Work Reflective Thinking Visual Art Journal
Studio Activity: Extending an Image
Evaluating Your Work Portfolio Ideas Art Online
Meet the Artist: M. C. Escher
Make the Connection

FEATURED ARTISTS

- Thomas Cole
- M. C. Escher
- René Magritte
- Joan Miró
- William Rimmer
- Lydia Rubio
- Kay Sage
- Rufino Tamayo
- George Tooker
- Lisbeth Zwerger

FINE ART PRINTS

Fine Art Print 20, *Paris Through the Window* by Marc Chagall

Timesaving Technology

Interactive Lesson Planner

Make planning easy. Use this interactive software to organize your week, month, semester, or year and access all *Introducing Art* reproducible resources.

KEY TO ABILITY LEVELS

Teaching strategies have been coded.

L1 Activities for all students; teacher direction required

L2 Activities for average to above-average students; some teacher direction needed

L3 Activities for students able and willing to work independently

ELL English Language Learner activities

KEY TO LESSON RESOURCES

Narrative Lesson

Studio Lesson

Chapter 14

Creating Fantasy

(pages 262–277)

Chapter Overview

This chapter deals with the power of imagination. Students will learn about fantasy art and the work of the Surrealists, and they will have an opportunity to explore fantasy art across time and place.

Discussing the Artwork

FOCUS ON ◆ **Figure 14–1** Joan Miró created a Surrealist painting, a style that expresses dreams, fantasy, and the subconscious in the subject matter. *Dutch Interior (I)* shows a man playing the guitar at a table. There are animals and a woman sitting around him listening to the music. Miró used a wide array of colors, especially green and white, to emphasize a happy day. The playful and humorous forms in this painting have a strange and whimsical quality. His paintings were Surrealistic images inspired by memory and fantasy. Have students study the painting. Ask them what it reminds them of. Explain that Surrealist artworks can mean a variety of things to different people because the subject is not defined. Miró is acknowledged as one of the most original artists of the twentieth century.

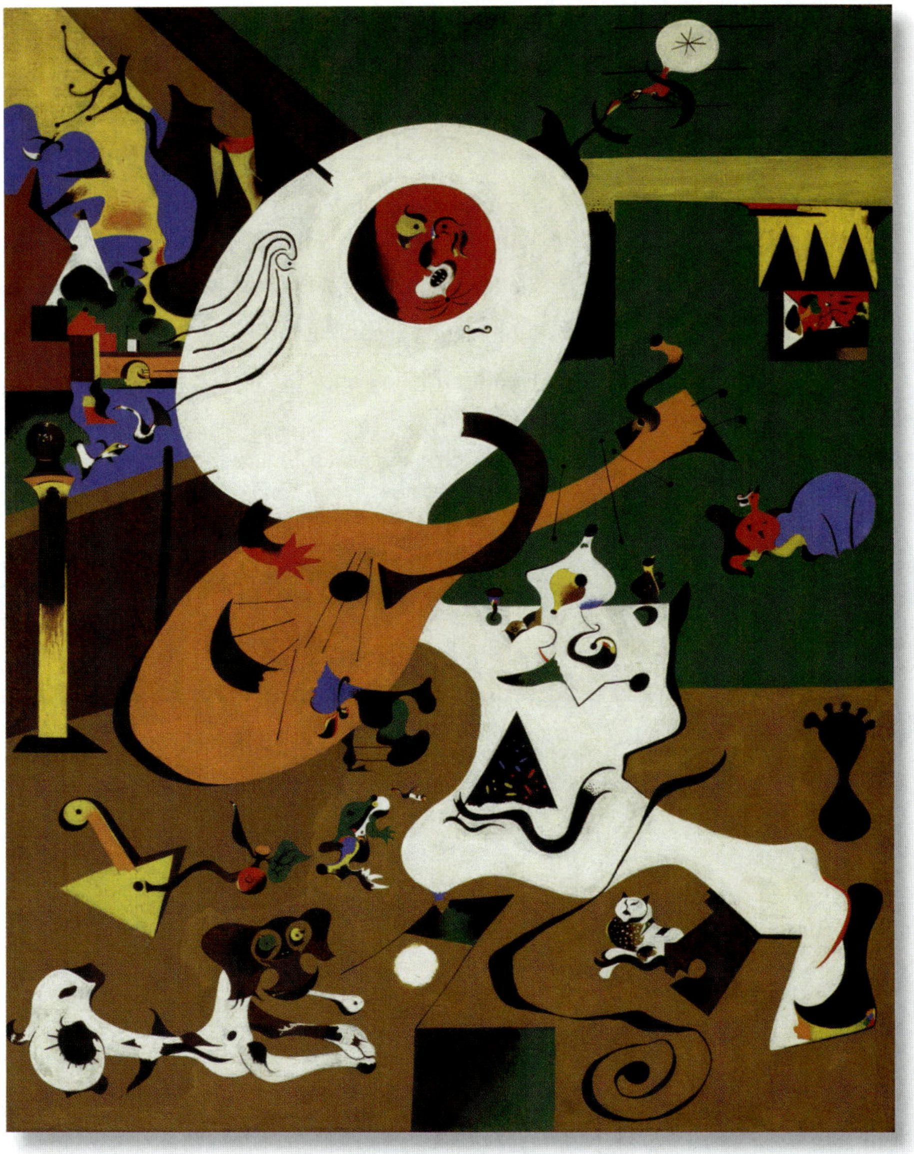

FOCUS ON ◆ **Figure 14–1** **Look at the fun image Miró creates with colors and shapes. Do you notice a dog and a window in the painting? What other objects has the artist included?**

Joan Miró. *Dutch Interior (I).* 1928. Oil on canvas. 91.8 × 73 cm (36⅛ × 28¾″). The Museum of Modern Art, New York, New York. Mrs. Simon Guggenheim Fund. © ARS, NY.

ART SOURCE

Linking to the Performing Arts

DANCE/THEATRE Diavolo is a dance company composed of dancers, gymnasts, and actors who work on and around outrageous, Surrealistic sets and structures. Their piece, "Tête en l'Air," is a signature work, inspired by the works of surrealist painter René Magritte and filmmaker Jacques Heim. Have students read about Jacques Heim, the creator and director of Diavolo, in the **Performing Arts Handbook** on page 323. To enrich student understanding, play the DVD or videotape (segment 6) in the **Performing Arts Package.**

Chapter 14

Creating Fantasy

"I try to apply colors like words that shape poems, like notes that shape music."

—Joan Miró (1893–1983)

The imagination is a wonderful and exciting thing. Artists use their imaginations to create and invent new forms of poetry, music, dance, painting, sculpture, and architecture. When you were a child, you could transform a box into a castle, or a stuffed animal into a living, talking friend. Now you can use that same imagination to unlock the door to creative ideas and to solve problems.

In this chapter, you will look at many artworks that play with your imagination. Open your mind to them and enjoy.

After completing this chapter, you will be able to:

- Define *fantasy art.*
- Determine what the Surrealists were trying to accomplish.
- Identify links between fantasy art and the influence of historical events.
- Complete several fantasy artworks using different media and techniques.

Quick Write

Interpreting the Quote
Look at **Figure 14–1** and read the quote. Describe how Miró's use of colors and shapes are like that of poetry and music.

Key Terms

fantasy art
Surrealists
juxtapose
social protest painting
architectural rendering
belvedere

Quick Write

Interpreting the Quote
Have students read the quote and complete the Quick Write activity. In his quote, Joan Miró is telling us to "read" his paintings like poetry, to "listen" to his paintings like music. Encourage students to let their imaginations run free. Have them study Miró's use of color and shape in this painting. Ask students to reflect on how they are an expression of poetry and music.

Chapter Motivator

Explain that, in this chapter, students will be expanding their understanding of what the word *imagination* means. Tell them that they will explore the outer limits of imagination of some recognized artists. They will study the artistic style of the Surrealists and compare such artworks. Students will also have an opportunity to create several fantastic artworks using a variety of art media and techniques.

Art Online

Visit art.glencoe.com, the Web site for Glencoe's art programs. This site offers general student resources to help guide your students as they learn about art and artists. Encourage your students to visit this site and explore the various resources and activities, such as:

- Art History
- Museum Links
- Technique Tips
- Studio Activities

National Standards for Arts Education

This chapter addresses the following National Standards for the Visual Arts:

1. (a, b)	4. (a, c)
2. (a, b)	5. (b)
3. (a, b)	6. (a, b)

Dreams and Nightmares
(pages 264–265)

1 Focus

Objectives

After completing this lesson, students will be able to:

- Define *fantasy art.*
- Understand the Surrealist art movement.
- Demonstrate technical skills effectively by using a variety of art materials to produce a Surrealist drawing.

SUPPLIES
- Pencils and lined paper
- White drawing paper, 9 x 12 inches
- Crayons, markers, or oil pastels

2 Teach

Motivator

Ask students to share some of the images they remember from scary dreams. What do some of the images have in common? Have students examine the paintings in **Figures 14–2** and **14–3.** Do either of these artworks have similarly strange images? Encourage students to discuss some of the themes that reappear in nightmares and dreams. Tell them that this lesson is a reflection of the strange images that can be experienced during sleep.

Dreams and Nightmares

Do you remember what you dreamed last night—or if you dreamed? Dreams are our lone connection with a world that is otherwise lost to us. This is the hidden world of sleep. It is a place where we spend 8 of every 24 hours each day—a full third of our lives. Is it any wonder that this uncharted territory has long held fascination for artists?

In this lesson, you will look at two "dreamscapes." You will explore visual interpretations of the strange kinds of images that visit us during our slumber.

Dream Art of the Past

Depicting dreams in art is nothing new. As a branch of **fantasy art**—*art that focuses on make-believe or imaginary subjects*—dream art dates at least to the time of the ancient Greeks. During the Middle Ages, demons and other "night visitors" were frequent subjects of paintings and illustrations.

The work in **Figure 14–2** was created in 1872. The artist, who was active during the mid-1800s, worked chiefly as a sculptor. The painting is based on a dream he actually

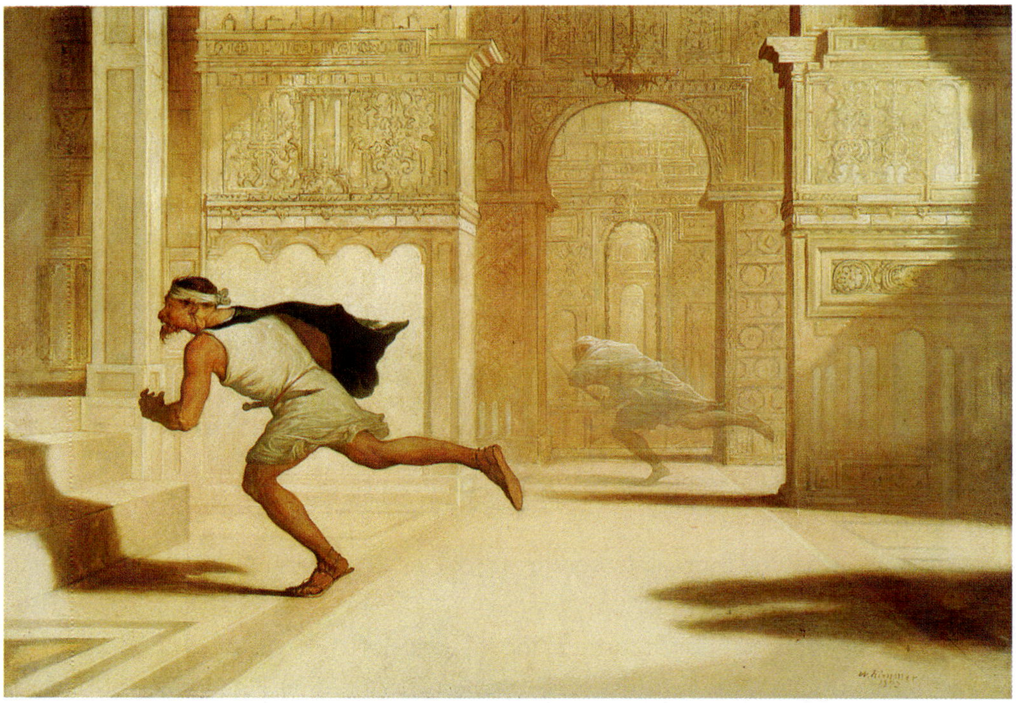

◆ **Figure 14–2** Look at the title and then at the painting. What principle of art has been used to heighten the suspense in this work?

William Rimmer. *Flight and Pursuit.* 1872. Oil on canvas. 46 × 66.7 cm (18 × 26½"). Museum of Fine Arts, Boston, Massachusetts. Bequest of Miss Edith Nichols.

STORY BEHIND THE ARTIST

KAY SAGE The life of Kay Sage was as surreal as her paintings. The daughter of a wealthy family, she married an Italian prince and moved to Rome when she was 27 years old. When her marriage ended ten years later, she began to write and paint. While living in Paris, she attracted the attention of Surrealist painter Yves Tanguy, whom she later married in 1940. The death of her husband in 1955 and her failing eyesight led to a period of depression and seclusion.

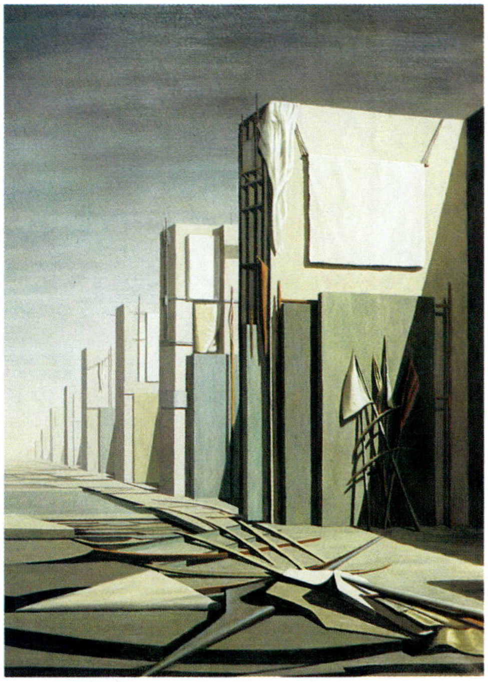

◆ **Figure 14–3** What properties are shared by this painting and the one opposite? How has the artist of this work suggested deep space?

Kay Sage. *No Passing.* 1954. Oil on canvas. 130.2 × 96.5 cm (51¼ × 38″). Collection of Whitney Museum of American Art, New York, New York. Purchase.

had. In the dream and the painting, the figure running in the foreground is the artist. That he is being chased by someone is clear not only from the title. It is equally evident from the scary shadows on the floor behind him. Who is chasing the artist? Why are they after him? Most baffling of all is the ghostlike image in parallel stride in the background. From whom is he running?

Recent Dream Art

During the first half of the twentieth century, artists struck out in many bold new directions. Some turned to their conscience for inspiration and subject matter. Others looked to their emotions. Yet others probed the inner workings of the mind. This *group of artists who explored the realm of dreams and the subconscious* called themselves **Surrealists** (suh-**ree**-uh-lists). The name comes from a word whose initial part, *sur-*, means "beyond or above."

The painting in **Figure 14–3** was created by a Surrealist. Examine this unusual work. Beneath a sullen sky, collections of flat building-high objects (some wrapped in what looks like canvas) stretch endlessly to the horizon. Scraps of these same materials litter the ground, providing a possible clue to the work's title. Typical of Surrealist art, this "landscape" is bathed in an unnatural light that casts shadows on some of the towering structures. What is the source of this light? The answer to that question, like the meaning of the odd shapes themselves, remains a mystery.

Studio Activity

A Drawing in the Surrealist Style

Creative expression. Express a variety of ideas based on personal experience and imagination to come up with an image you might expect to find in a nightmare. On a sheet of lined paper, note details of this image. Using pencil, sketch your image lightly on a sheet of drawing paper. Imitate as much as possible the style of the painting on this page and in Figure 14–2. Use colored pencils, markers, or oil pastels to complete your work. Choose hues that help communicate a sense of fear.

PORTFOLIO

Describe your nightmarish image and the Surrealist style you used to portray it.

Check Your Understanding

1. What is fantasy art? What are its roots?
2. To what did the Surrealists turn for inspiration?

Art Criticism

Use the following art-criticism questions to lead a discussion on Kay Sage's painting in Figure 14–3.

- What first captures your attention in this artwork? What images can you identify?
- What elements of art are most noticeable? What principles have been used to organize those elements?
- How would you describe the mood of this painting?
- Do you enjoy viewing fantasy pictures like this? Are you more attracted to pictures based on real people, objects, and events? Do you think it is possible to enjoy both fantasy and realism in art? Why or why not? L1

3 Assess

Self-Assessment

Have students complete the **Check Your Understanding** questions on this page. Answers are provided below.

Reteaching

Ask students to work in pairs to analyze each other's Surrealist drawing. What art elements and principles were used? L1 ELL

4 Close

Ask students to explain what makes the Surrealist art movement different from other movements they have studied.

Answers to Check Your Understanding

1. Fantasy art is art that focuses on make-believe or imaginary subjects. Fantasy art dates back at least to the time of the ancient Greeks.
2. The Surrealists turned to the realm of dreams and the subconscious for their inspiration.

LESSON 2

Creating a Fantasy Bird Collage

(pages 266–267)
Lesson Time: 90 minutes

1 Focus

Objectives

After completing this lesson, students will be able to:

- Use their imaginations to create fantasy birds that arouse emotion in viewers yet exhibit some real birdlike qualities.
- Demonstrate technical skills effectively by using a variety of art media and materials to produce a bird collage.
- Describe, analyze, interpret, and judge their artwork.

Supplies
Refer to **What You Will Need** in the Student Edition.

2 Teach

Motivator

Ask students whether they have ever had an experience or a feeling that they found hard to describe in words. Have them demonstrate how they might express such feelings as terror, anger, joy, or sadness without the aid of language. Explain that the twentieth-century Mexican artist Rufino Tamayo found it difficult to express his feelings with the usual images painters use. He needed a new visual language. He created this new visual language by combining abstract shapes and bold colors with a dash of mystery.

LESSON 2

Creating a Fantasy Bird Collage

The world of fantasy art is filled with curious creatures. Study the painting in **Figure 14–4.** Without glancing at the title, you can still sense the girl's sheer terror. Have you ever seen a bird like this? Perhaps the artist saw it in a dream.

What You Will Learn

In this lesson you will have a chance to use your imagination and create an image of a bird. You will use this image, along with an assortment of art media, to create a collage. Begin by discussing with classmates the various features of birds. A class member will list these features on the board. For each feature the class will brainstorm descriptive words. These will be written next to the feature. Using this list as a starting point, make several pencil sketches of birds. Transfer the best of these to drawing paper. You will use tissue paper and other materials to give your bird color and texture.

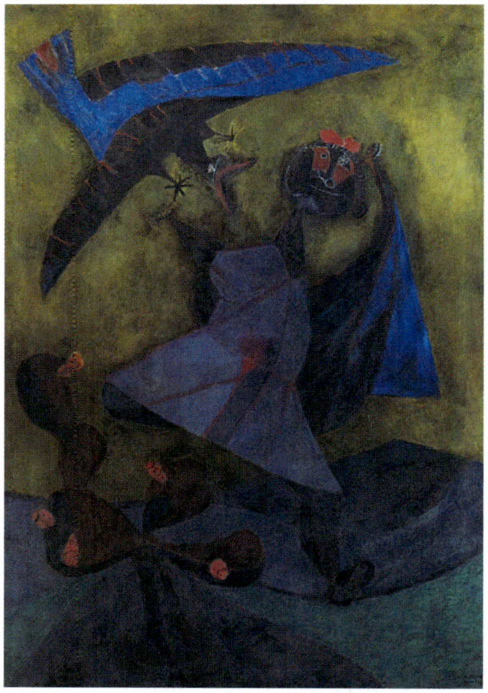

◆ **Figure 14–4** **Describe the artist's use of color and shape in this painting. What type of feeling does this artwork communicate?**

Rufino Tamayo. *Girl Attacked by a Strange Bird.* 1947. Oil on canvas. 178 × 127.3 cm (70 × 50⅛"). The Museum of Modern Art, New York, New York. Gift of Mr. and Mrs. Charles Zadok.

What You Will Need

- Pencil and sketch paper
- White drawing paper, 12 x 18 inches
- Scissors
- Sheets of colored tissue paper
- White glue, water, brush
- Yarn
- Black markers or pen and black ink

What You Will Do

1. Working with classmates, discuss features common to birds. These might include wings, legs, claws, beak, and feathers. One class member is to write these features on the board. Space for additional words is to be left alongside each feature.
2. Still working as a class, brainstorm words to describe each feature. Let your imagination run free. For *eyes,* for example, you might mention words such as *large, narrow,* and *yellow.* The volunteer at the board should list suggested words in the space after each feature.
3. Working alone, use the lists on the board to form a picture of a bird in your "mind's

MORE ABOUT...

Rufino Tamayo Because Tamayo was not concerned with expressing political views and preferred to create easel paintings rather than murals, for a long time he found it difficult to gain recognition in his native Mexico. However, the murals he created in 1952–53 for the Palace of Fine Arts in Mexico City changed that. Though placed alongside those of the famous muralists Rivera, Orozco, and Siqueiros, his murals more than held their own. They were widely praised, and Tamayo was added to the list of great Mexican painters.

eye." Your bird might terrify your viewers or it may make them smile and even laugh. Make several sketches of your bird.

4. Using your best sketch as a model, redraw your bird on a sheet of drawing paper. Make sure that the drawing fills the paper. Use a firm, continuous line.
5. Cut a variety of large and small shapes from sheets of colored tissue paper. When you have enough to cover your drawing, glue these carefully in place. Use white glue thinned with water for this purpose. Then lay the tissue paper on the damp surface. Smooth it out gently with your hand. Then carefully brush a second coat of glue across the surface of the tissue. If your brush picks up any color from the wet tissue, wipe it off on a paper towel.
6. Continue in this fashion, adding layer upon layer of tissue paper. Always glue the darkest colors of tissue in place first. Add subtle shadings of color by adding pieces of lighter tissue over pieces of darker ones.
7. When all the tissue is dry, add lines to suggest feathers or other designs. Do this with lengths of colored yarn or with a black marker or pen, or with both.

Evaluating Your Work

- **Describe** Is your drawing easily identified as a bird? Can you point to the different features of your bird?
- **Analyze** Is your bird large and colorful? Does it contain a variety of textures?
- **Interpret** What kinds of emotions or feelings do you think your bird collage will arouse in viewers?
- **Judge** Do you think your bird is a success? Do you feel it can be described as fantasy art?

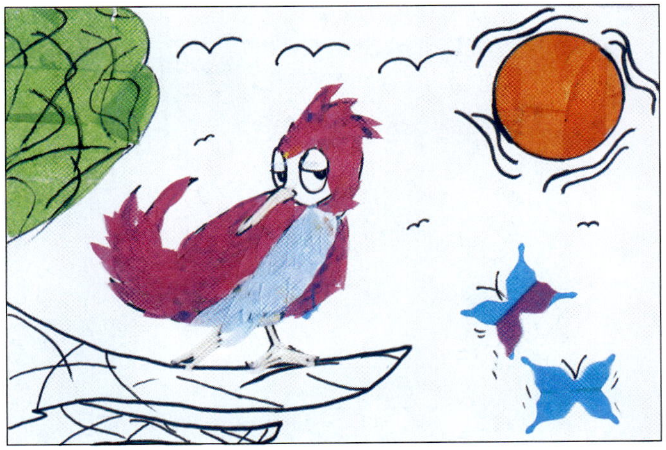

◆ **Figure 14–5** Student work. Fantasy bird collage.

REFLECTIVE THINKING

Critical Evaluation. Analyze the original portfolios of your peers to form conclusions about formal properties and historical and cultural contexts. Select a few of their artworks and evaluate how they communicated their ideas.

Visual Art Journal

In your journal, describe your fantasy bird. What would you do differently next time? Explain your reasons.

Aesthetics

Ask students to express their opinions about Tamayo's painting. What do they find most pleasing about it? What features do they object to? Why? L1

Sparking Creativity

Before involving students in the studio portion of this lesson, have each student write a four-line poem that reflects the same mood as Tamayo's painting. Ask students to read their poems in class. Have them discuss how Tamayo's painting inspired them to use language creatively to express that mood.

3 Assess

Peer Assessment

Have students analyze the fantasy bird collage of their peers to form conclusions about formal properties—the elements and principles of art.

Reteaching

Have students use gestures and body language to describe the feeling and mood of **Figure 14–4.** L1 ELL

4 Close

Ask students to explain how their fantasy bird collage qualifies as fantasy art.

INCLUSION STRATEGIES

English Language Learners For students who speak English as a second language, some of the vocabulary in this chapter may seem challenging at first. You may want to pair less proficient speakers of English with more proficient students who can help them understand the terms and concepts introduced in the text. In addition, encourage any student who may be struggling, to use the artworks themselves as nonverbal forms of communication. ELL

Puzzling Paintings

(pages 268–269)

1 Focus

Objectives

After completing this lesson, students will be able to:

- Recognize that because all the images in Magritte's picture are painted, none can be accurately referred to as "real."
- Point out that both paintings in this lesson make use of a picture-within-a-picture and impossible relationships.
- Demonstrate technical skills effectively by using a variety of art media to produce a picture that blends a photographic image and a pencil drawing.

SUPPLIES
- Pencils
- Old magazines with black-and-white photos and pictures of landscapes and seascapes
- Scissors, glue
- White drawing paper

2 Teach

Motivator

Begin this lesson by having students examine the painting by René Magritte in **Figure 14–6**. On the board, have them compile a list of everything in the work. Then ask them to circle everything that seems strange or unusual. Do the same with the painting by Lydia Rubio in **Figure 14–7**. Ask students why the artists may have introduced the unusual elements into their works.

LESSON 3

Puzzling Paintings

You wouldn't think much of it if you saw a car go by. You might sit up and take notice, however, if the driver were an elephant! Familiar images can seem unfamiliar—even strange—when they are placed in unexpected settings. Artists sometimes surprise viewers by doing just that. They **juxtapose** (**juks**-tuh-pohz), or *place side by side,* objects that look unusual or interesting when viewed together. In this lesson, you will look at two such works.

A Puzzling Painting from the 1930s

The images juxtaposed in an artwork often have little in common. In the painting in **Figure 14–6**, they have too much in common. This work was created by a Belgian Surrealist famous for his imaginative use of juxtaposition. His name was René Magritte (ren-**ay** mah-**greet**).

Examine this painting. If you were asked to describe it, what would you say? Maybe you would identify its subject simply as a window opening onto a nature scene. Look more closely, however. Find the small object in the shape of an upside-down *T* juxtaposed against a cloud. It takes some viewers a moment to realize that this seemingly out-of-place object is actually part of an easel. On the easel is an unframed landscape painting that blends perfectly with the scene beyond. With your finger, trace the outline of this "painting within a painting." What statement

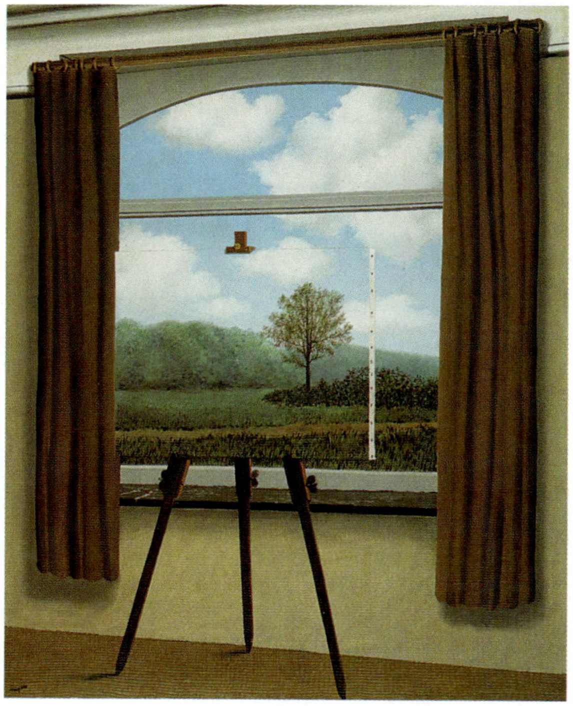

◆ **Figure 14–6** What two images are juxtaposed in this painting? Would such a juxtaposition be possible in real life?

René Magritte. *The Human Condition.* 1934. Oil on canvas. 100 × 81 × 1.6 cm (39⅜ × 31⅞ × ⅝″). National Gallery of Art, Washington, D.C. Gift of the Collectors Committee.

MORE ABOUT...

MAGRITTE AND RUBIO In the 1920s, Belgian artist René Magritte abandoned his abstract painting style after seeing a painting by Giorgio de Chirico. De Chirico was an Italian painter whose work greatly influenced the Surrealist painters who followed. If possible, show students examples of de Chirico's work.

Lydia Rubio was born in Havana, Cuba, and lived there until she was thirteen. Trained as an architect, she turned to painting in 1980. She explained her shift in careers by saying, "For me, painting is a far more personal and spiritual activity than architecture."

might the artist be making? Notice the title. Maybe this artwork is a comment on the inability of some people to tell where reality begins and ends. Can you think of advances in our own time that have helped blur the line between fantasy and reality?

A Puzzling Painting from the 1980s

Compare the painting in **Figure 14–7** with the one just analyzed. The work on this page was completed fifty-five years later. Yet, the two share a similar theme. Both, moreover, present "pictures within a picture."

As you study Figure 14–7, you find once again that first impressions can be deceiving. At first glance, this painting appears to be nothing more than a pleasant seascape. On closer inspection, you begin noticing details that are hard to explain. A trio of gently swaying palm trees at the left, for example, appears rooted to a wooden tabletop. On the right side is an open sketchbook propped against a mountain. As if these images weren't puzzling enough, what are we to make of the painting that floats in mid air? How about the one in the sketchbook that continues the scene behind it? Again, the title is a partial key to such mysteries. It hints at the possibility that the work is a picture album of events in the artist's life—past, present, and to come.

Studio Activity

Extending an Image

Demonstrate technical skills. Look through magazines for black-and-white photographs of landscapes or seascapes. With scissors, trim one such photograph to measure about 3 x 5 inches. Glue this photograph at or near the center of a 9 x 12-inch sheet of white drawing paper. Use pencil to "continue" the image in the photograph onto the white paper. Juxtapose unusual objects. Add details to the scene as you draw.

PORTFOLIO

What did you learn from extending the photograph? What would you do differently?

Check Your Understanding

1. What does *juxtapose* mean?
2. Name two things that the paintings on these pages have in common.

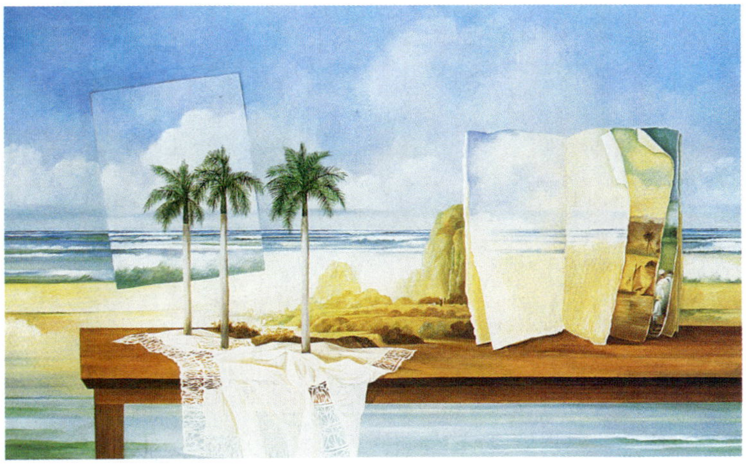

◆ **Figure 14–7** This artwork reflects the artist's fond memories of a grandmother who introduced her to painting when she was young.

Lydia Rubio. *Ella Pintaba Paisajes (She Painted Landscapes).* 1989. Oil on canvas. 91.3 × 234 cm (36 × 92″). Private Collection.

Vocabulary

Make sure students have a clear understanding of the term *juxtapose,* meaning "to place side by side." Have students use the word *juxtapose* or *juxtaposition* in a sentence.

Aesthetics

Ask students to express their initial reactions to the paintings by Magritte and Rubio. Did they find that the unusual features of these pictures caused them immediately to react in a negative manner, or did the strange features of the works arouse their curiosity and cause them to look at the works more closely? Have them compare these two artworks and note the similarities and differences. L1

3 Assess

Self-Assessment

Have students complete the **Check Your Understanding** questions on this page. Answers are provided below.

Reteaching

Ask students to work in small groups to examine each painting in the lesson and identify the pictures-within-the-pictures. L1 ELL

4 Close

Have students discuss the ways in which the works of Magritte and Rubio conform to the objectives of Surrealism. *(Both connect unrelated images in strange, dreamlike ways.)*

Answers to Check Your Understanding

1. Juxtapose means "to place side by side."
2. Both paintings include a picture within the picture. They also both make use of imaginative juxtaposition.

Creating Your Own Picture Puzzle

(pages 270–271)
Lesson Time: 90 minutes

1 Focus

Objectives

After completing this lesson, students will be able to:

- Create a "picture puzzle" that targets a problem in modern society.
- Demonstrate technical skills effectively by using a variety of art media and materials to produce a "picture puzzle."
- Describe, analyze, interpret, and judge their artwork.

Supplies
Refer to **What You Will Need** in the Student Edition.

2 Teach

Motivator

Ask students to brainstorm some of the problems that plague modern society. Write their ideas on the board. Ask students to discuss whether these problems are universal or limited to a general area or a specific group of people. Explain that social protest painting is an art style dedicated to criticizing the problems of big-city life and modern society.

Direct students' attention to **Figure 14–8.** Ask them to discuss some of the problems that Tooker is attacking in his painting. Ask: In what way is Tooker making a strong statement?

LESSON 4

Creating Your Own Picture Puzzle

Some picture puzzles, as you have seen, make statements of a general nature. Others operate on a more personal plane. What sort of comment or message does the picture puzzle on this page deliver?

Before you attempt an answer, it may help to know that the work is an example of **social protest painting**. Emerging in the 1930s, this was *an art style dedicated to attacking the ills of big-city life.* A frequent target of social protest paintings are current-day problems. Look again at the thought-provoking picture in **Figure 14–8**. What problem of big-city life do you think this work highlights? What "surreal" or fantasy images and objects can you find?

What You Will Learn

In this lesson, you will create a picture puzzle of your own. Like the painting in Figure 14–8, your work will target a problem of modern life. Begin by thinking about possible themes. Make sketches that juxtapose images that relate to your theme but not

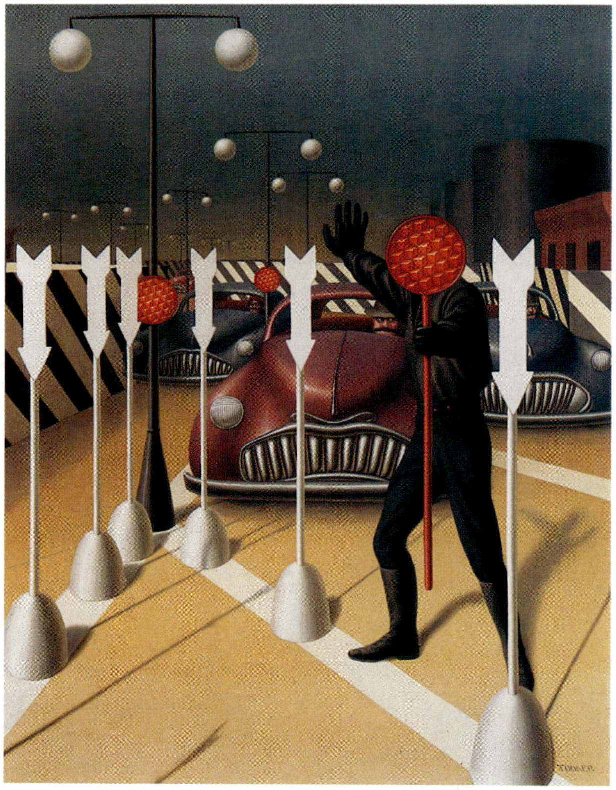

◆ **Figure 14–8** **Notice the moody sky and downward-pointing arrows. What feelings do they communicate?**

George Tooker. *Highway.* 1953. Tempera on panel. 58 × 45.4 cm (22⅞ × 17⅞″). Courtesy of Terra Museum of American Art, Chicago, Illinois. Terra Foundation for the Arts, Daniel J. Terra Collection.

Technology Strategies in the Art Classroom

Electronic Media-Generated Art Follow directions for creating a picture puzzle that is connected to a social or environmental issue. Scan images or take digital photos. Use the transformation tools in your art software to select and stretch, distort, or place images so they emphasize the idea or statement you want to make. Explore different kinds of brushes, colors, and filters. Work in layers to overlap images and apply different effects to each layer. Remind students to use brushes and filters so they can repeat results they like. Soften the edges of images so they look like one image rather than a collage.

ordinarily to each other. Use the best of your sketches as the basis of an oil pastel drawing. Add images clipped from magazines. Make one image larger than all the others to emphasize its importance.

What You Will Need

- Pencil and sketch paper
- Sheet of white drawing paper, 9 x 12 inches
- Oil pastels
- Old magazines
- Scissors
- White glue

What You Will Do

1. Think of a problem you feel strongly about or have learned about. Make a list of images that might be connected with the problem. Be creative.
2. On sketch paper, experiment with juxtaposing images from your list that usually are not related but which, together, make a strong statement. Decide on one image that is central to your theme. Draw this image the largest.
3. Transfer your best sketch to a sheet of white drawing paper. Complete your drawing using oil pastels. Choose colors that suit your theme.
4. Thumb through old magazines for additional images. Clip four or five pictures. Experiment placing these at various points on the surface of your drawing.
5. When you are happy with your arrangement, glue the images in place.

Evaluating Your Work

- **Describe** List the images that appear in your work.
- **Analyze** Did you emphasize one image by making it larger than the others? Does your picture contain an interesting juxtaposition?
- **Interpret** What is the mood of your work? What statement does the work make?
- **Judge** Are you pleased with your picture? Were your classmates able to identify the problem your work attacks?

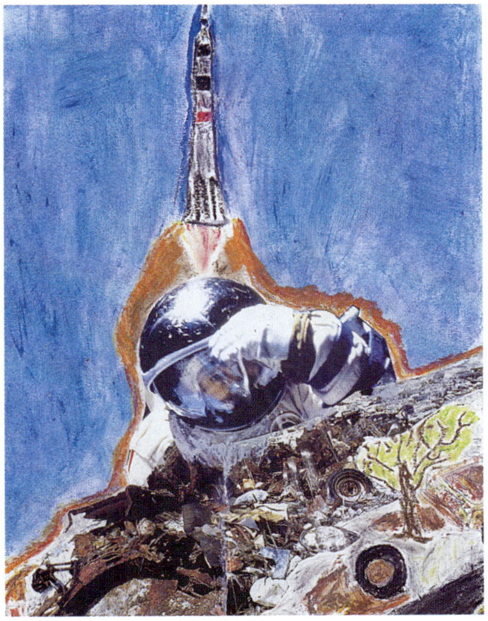

◆ **Figure 14–9** Student work. Current-day problem.

PORTFOLIO IDEAS

When you have completed this class, your portfolio will be evidence of all you have learned about art. Use it as a motivation to continue communicating your ideas and feelings through new artworks. As long as you continue to work, you will continue to grow as an artist.

Art Online

For additional activities, check out our Web site at art.glencoe.com. There you will also find:

- Artist Profiles
- Career Corner
- Interactive Games
- Student Art Gallery

Team Building Activity

Have students form groups of four or five and choose an area of social protest to research. Groups might choose nuclear waste, air pollution, overuse of insecticides, homelessness, or some other social issue that is often in the news. Ask each group to divide the research tasks equitably, then decide how to share their found information with the class. Hold a "social protest" session to allow groups to present their findings to the class. L1 ELL

3 Assess

Self-Assessment

Have students use **Evaluating Your Work** to conduct an in-progress critique of their picture puzzle.

Reteaching

Ask students to explain what it means when images are juxtaposed. L1

Enrichment

Bring in several different newspapers from various cities or regions of the country and have students identify news articles that reflect areas of social protest. Ask students to cut out the articles and mount them, then draw pictures to expand on the theme presented in the article. Hang the articles and pictures in a "hall" of social protest. Have students identify in the artworks the influence of political events. L1 ELL

4 Close

Ask students to discuss why they chose the problem they did and how they expressed their views.

DEVELOPING A PORTFOLIO

Using the Rubrics Both students and teachers need to fully understand the established rubric to be used for portfolio review. Post it or give a copy to each student for reference as the portfolio is developed. Will the portfolio show growth over time, or will it demonstrate acquired skills and accomplishments? The difference is important and directly impacts what the student chooses to include in the portfolio. Remind students throughout the grading period to review the rubric as they work on their portfolios to get them into the habit of considering expectations and standards.

Impossible Images

(pages 272–273)

1 Focus

Objectives

After completing this lesson, students will be able to:

- Define *architectural rendering.*
- Recognize a belvedere.
- Identify strange juxtapositions in artworks by M. C. Escher and Thomas Cole.

2 Teach

Motivator

Ask students to suggest examples of optical illusions they have come across in art or elsewhere. Invite them to bring in examples if they can. Then direct students' attention to Escher's print shown in **Figure 14–10.** Ask them to describe what they see. What is "wrong" or "impossible" about this picture? Lead students to an awareness of the juxtaposition of the first and second floors of the belvedere. Explain that artists like M. C. Escher specialized in creating such thoughtful, puzzling images.

Vocabulary

Locate and bring in examples of authentic *architectural renderings.* If possible, invite an architect in to show some renderings and show some examples of well-known *belvedere* structures.

LESSON 5

Impossible Images

"Seeing," it is said, "is believing." Generally, there is much truth to this statement. Sometimes, however, our eyes play tricks on us. They cause us to see imaginary pools of water shimmering in the distance when the weather is hot. They confuse us by making images appear to shift and change no matter how long we stare at them. You have probably seen optical illusions that will not "stay still."

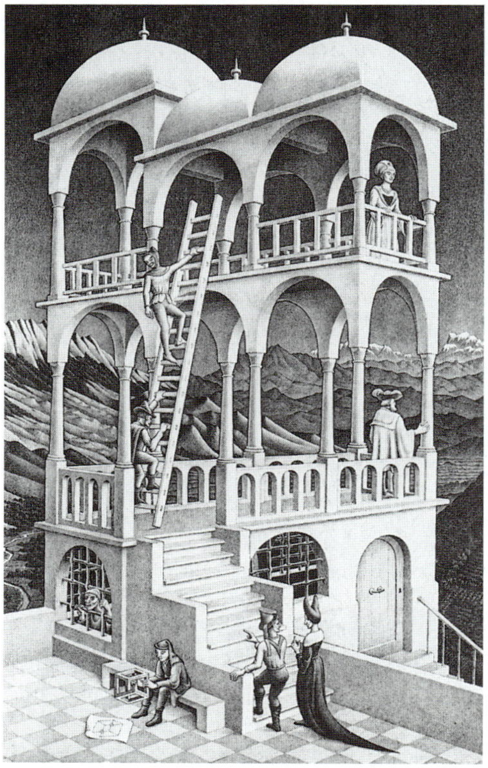

◆ **Figure 14–10** **The artist was fond of such visual puzzles. Another of his prints appears in Figure 2–10 on page 34. What similarities can you find between these two works?**

M. C. Escher. *Belvedere.* 1958. Lithograph. 46.2 × 29.5 cm (18 × 11⅔"). © 1996 Cordon Art, Baarn, Holland. All rights reserved.

In this lesson, you will look at an image that, like such illusions, fools the eye. You will examine a second work that looks impossible for entirely different reasons.

An Impossible Building

Some of the works you have looked at in this chapter contain ghostly beings. Others show eerie, surreal landscapes. The fine art print in **Figure 14–10** fits neither of these descriptions. It focuses, rather, on a perfectly straightforward subject. The work may be seen as a kind of **architectural rendering**. This is *a detailed, realistic two-dimensional representation of a proposed three-dimensional structure.* In this case, the proposal is for a **belvedere** (**bel**-vuh-deer), *a building designed to provide a view of its surroundings.* The word is a blend of the Italian roots *bel,* or "beautiful," and *vedere,* "view."

Look closely at this print. It doesn't take long before you notice that something is terribly wrong. To pinpoint the problem, locate the two figures—one on each level—gazing out at the scenery. Both stand at a railing along the narrow end on the structure's right. Yet, each faces in a different direction. The first and second floors of the belvedere have been juxtaposed at right angles! Note that a model for this impossible design is located conveniently within the print. It appears in the hands of the perplexed-looking figure seated on the bench near the bottom of the picture. Could such an object really exist in three dimensions? If you were the architect's client, would you approve this plan?

An Impossible Cityscape

In contrast to the confusing world shown in Figure 14–10, the painting in **Figure 14–11** appears to promise welcome relief. The feeling that you are on solid ground does not last for long, however.

RESOURCES BEYOND THE CLASSROOM

Local Libraries Use the library—either the school or the public library—as a convenient source of information about the elements and principles of art, art techniques, and art history. Not only are reference books available but also biographies, full-color art books, art magazines, and art journals, plus museum catalogs and other relevant information, all in a variety of media. Libraries can help students research how certain techniques are done or learn more about the artistic style of any artist not discussed in the textbook. Helping students learn to use library resources will be of benefit to them beyond the art class.

Focus your attention on the triangular shape looming on the horizon. You have probably seen photographs of this structure before. It is one of the great pyramids of ancient Egypt. In and of itself, there is nothing strange about this landmark. It is when we look elsewhere in the painting that a sense of having left reality behind begins to emerge. Notice the building at the left with the sharply pointed steeple. Buildings of this type are not found in or near Egypt. Do you know where such structures are found? Do you know what they are called? Can you understand what makes this cityscape impossible?

Check Your Understanding

1. What is an architectural rendering?
2. What makes the image in Figure 14–10 impossible? How about the painting in Figure 14–11?

Meet the Artist

M. C. Escher (1898–1972)

Cultural connection. M. C. Escher had no formal training in math or science, and he did not think of himself as an artist or a mathematician. Even so, his artwork is analyzed and appreciated by mathematicians and scientists, as well as artists and the general public.

Maurits Cornelis Escher was born in 1898 in Leeuwarden, the Netherlands. He planned to become an architect and studied at the School of Architecture and Decorative Arts in Haarlem. His interest soon switched to graphic arts, however. Escher is best known for prints that combine precise, realistic detail with optical illusions, repeating geometric patterns, and impossible spaces (see **Figure 14–10**).

Compare the strange juxtapositions in the work in Figure 14–10 with Figure 14–11.

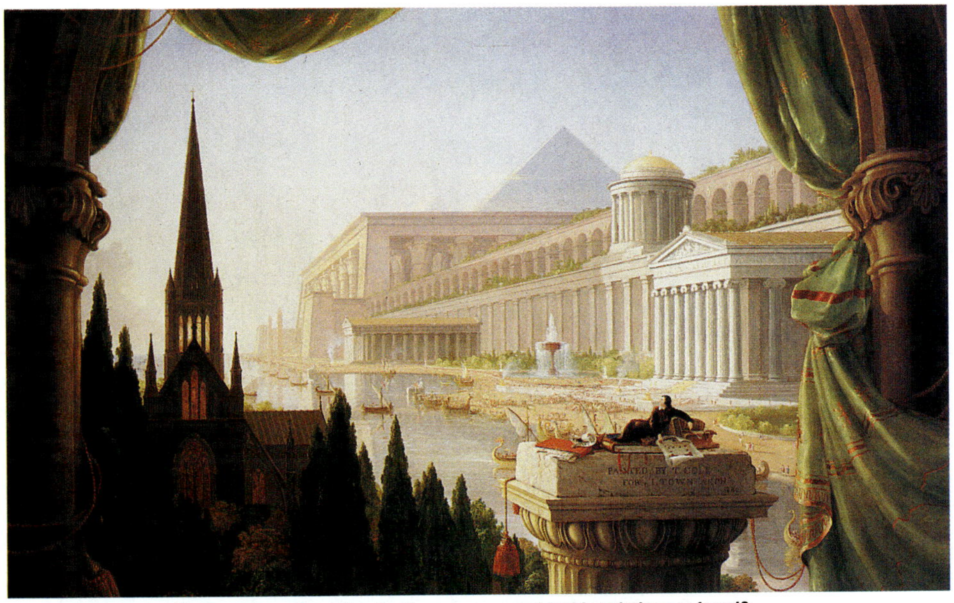

◆ **Figure 14–11** **Can you place where the structures represented in this painting are found?**

Thomas Cole. *The Architect's Dream.* 1840. Oil on canvas. 134.7 × 213.6 cm (53 × 84⅟₁₆″). Toledo Museum of Art, Toledo, Ohio. Gift of Florence Scott Libbey.

Meet the Artist

M. C. Escher

The strange juxtapositions and other techniques used by Escher and Cole are meant to create confusion and illusion. The image in Figure 14–10 is strange because it is based on an impossible design. In **Figure 14–11** the image is impossible because of the landmarks portrayed. The location of these landmarks is not accurate.

Aesthetics

Instruct students to identify the artwork in this lesson that they personally prefer. Then, in a single sentence, have them explain the reason for their choice. Ask them to form generalizations about the art elements and principles in that artwork. Collect the papers and tabulate the results on the board. How many favored the Escher work? How many preferred the Cole piece? What reason did students cite most often in support of their choice? L1

3 Assess

Self-Assessment

Have students complete the **Check Your Understanding** questions on this page. Answers are provided below.

Reteaching

In pairs, have students work together to produce an architectural rendering of a proposed addition to their school. L1 ELL

4 Close

Ask students to explain how an artwork can be "impossible."

Answers to Check Your Understanding

1. An architectural rendering is a detailed, realistic two-dimensional representation of a proposed three-dimensional structure.
2. The first and second floors of the belvedere have been juxtaposed at right angles. Buildings and structures from different times and locations have been juxtaposed in Cole's painting.

Fantasy in Pictures and Words

(pages 274–275)

1 Focus

Objectives

After completing this lesson, students will be able to:

- Explain how the choice of colors can affect an artwork's meaning and mood.
- Identify the artist's goal in completing a work.

2 Teach

Motivator

Explain that dreams often provide a starting point for creating artworks that deal in fantasy. Reveal that in this lesson, students will discover that dreams also fuel fantastic works of literature.

Art Criticism

Direct students' attention to the artwork shown in **Figure 14–12.** What event is taking place in this scene? What is the setting or location? Who are the figures shown in the painting?

Active Reading

In groups of three to four students, have each group read the passage in **Figure 14–13.** Ask students to recognize how the text's style, tone, and mood contribute to the effect of the text. How is this revealed in the illustration?

Fantasy in Pictures and Words

Artists and writers have vivid imaginations. Both are capable of creating wondrous images and weaving remarkable tales when they turn their minds loose. Although they use different media in their work, artists and writers sometimes cross paths professionally. To see this for yourself, examine the artwork in **Figure 14–12.** Do you recognize the characters in this illustration? They are straight out of a literary fantasy that became a movie classic. The characters are, of course, the Tin Man and Dorothy. The story is *The Wizard of Oz.*

You may have seen the movie version of *The Wizard of Oz.* Have you ever read the book that the film was based on? **Figure 14–13** contains a short passage from the book by L. Frank Baum. It's the very scene illustrated in Figure 14–12. After reading the excerpt, look again at the artwork in Figure 14–12. Notice how economically the artist has captured this description. She portrays in a single image what took the author almost 200 words to say. Such is the power of art!

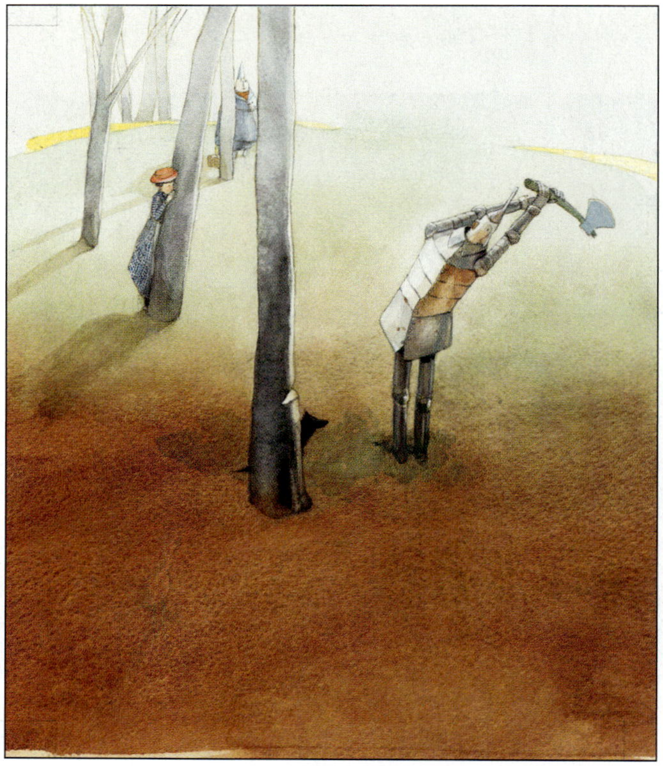

◆ **Figure 14–12** How would you describe the characters illustrated in this scene?

Lisbeth Zwerger. "The Tin Man." Illustration from *The Wizard of Oz* by L. Frank Baum. 1996 edition.

MORE ABOUT...

Lisbeth Zwerger Some artists learn their craft from artists of the past. One such individual is Austrian illustrator Lisbeth Zwerger. She was inspired by a book illustrated by the great nineteenth-century English artist Arthur Rackham. Since that inspirational moment, Zwerger has been awarded many prizes, including the highest international award for lifetime achievement, the Hans Christian Andersen Medal. Her artwork combines technical mastery with an insight and captivating wit. Her work in *The Wizard of Oz* has been praised for its haunting style and careful characterization.

Excerpt from The Wonderful Wizard of Oz

When [Dorothy] had finished her meal, and was about to go back to the road of yellow brick, she was startled to hear a deep groan near by.

"What was that?" she asked timidly.

"I cannot imagine," replied the Scarecrow; "but we can go and see."

Just then another groan reached their ears, and the sound seemed to come from behind them. They turned and walked through the forest a few steps, when Dorothy discovered something shining in a ray of sunshine that fell between the trees. She ran to the place and then stopped short, with a little cry of surprise.

One of the big trees had been partly chopped through, and standing beside it, with an uplifted axe in his hands, was a man made entirely of tin. His head and arms and legs were jointed upon his body, but he stood perfectly motionless, as if he could not stir at all.

Dorothy looked at him in amazement, and so did the Scarecrow, while Toto barked sharply and made a snap at the tin legs, which hurt his teeth.

◆ **Figure 14–13** Excerpt from *The Wonderful Wizard of Oz* by L. Frank Baum.

MAKE THE CONNECTION

Take Another Look

1. Figure 14–12 is from the 1996 edition of *The Wizard of Oz.* The artist, Lisbeth Zwerger, chose pale, misty, dreamlike colors for her illustrations. Do you think this was an appropriate choice? Why or why not?
2. In the 1900 edition of his book, author L. Frank Baum stated this as his goal: "solely to please children." Do you think the artist approached her work with the same goal in mind?
3. The passage in Figure 14–13 awakens several of the reader's senses. Notice that you can hear as well as see what is happening. Would you agree that the artist achieves the same effects in her work? If so, how?

ART & READING

Fantasy writing. People made of tin and talking scarecrows are possible only in a fantasy world. Reread the passage in Figure 14–13. Then write and illustrate your own fantasy passage. You may, if you like, choose another scene from *The Wizard of Oz.* Include at least one improbable creature.

MAKE THE CONNECTION

Take Another Look Student answers will vary, but may include the following:

1. The style is compatible not only with a fantasy tale, but one in which a character is in the midst of a dream.
2. Students might agree that the artist's goal was, indeed, the same.
3. The depiction of the Tin Man in the foreground allows the viewer to almost hear the creaky rusting noise of the wind playing against his frozen metal frame.

Art History

Refer students again to Figure 14–12. Ask: Do you think the artist was striving for stark realism? Why or why not? How does her style compare with that of the painting in Figure 14–11? *(Students will note that the work in Figure 14–12 has a more playful quality that the painting by Thomas Cole in Figure 14–11. Both, however, use the same misty quality to suggest a dreamlike fantasy environment.)*

3 Assess

Self-Assessment

Have students complete the **Take Another Look** questions on this page. Answers are provided below.

Enrichment

Observe that other works of literature dealing in fantasy have served as the basis for films. Have groups of students select such a work with which they are familiar, such as *The Lord of the Rings* trilogy, or the *Harry Potter* series. Invite them to select a passage from one of the works and design a movie poster based on that scene.

4 Close

Allow time for students to share the fantasy passages and scenes they created, as instructed under "Art & Reading." If time permits, allow volunteers to present their works and read their passages aloud.

Making Movies

1 Focus

Objectives

After completing this lesson, students will be able to:

- Draw an original comic book character.
- Write and illustrate a poem about the future.

2 Teach

Teaching the Feature

1. Encourage students to share what they know about the *Star Wars* films. Ask: Which *Star Wars* films have you seen? Which parts of these films do you like most? Why?
2. Have students work with partners to read and discuss the article. Ask the students in each pair to identify what they consider George Lucas's most important accomplishment.

Activity

Point out that George Lucas originally drew inspiration from comic book characters. Have each student use pencils or colored pencils to draw an original comic book character. Provide time for students to share their drawings and to discuss the stories each character might be part of.

MAKING MOVIES

George Lucas brings fantasy to the big screen.

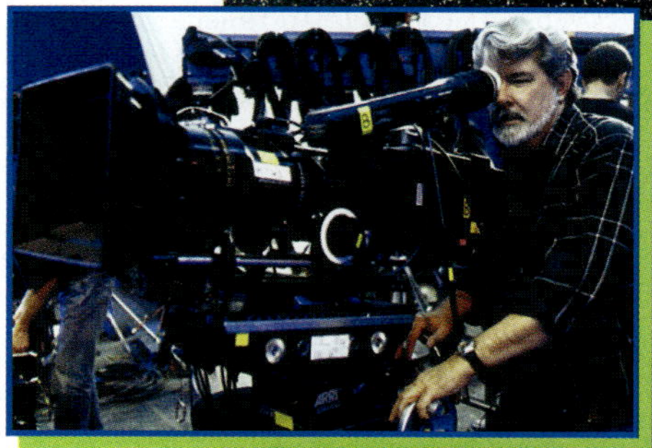

George Lucas's *Star Wars* movies reveal his lifelong love of fantasy. The film director was inspired by comic books and films that he enjoyed as a young boy. He also studied fairy tales and ancient mythology. He turned these and other bits of his space-age dreams into *Star Wars*.

Star Wars broke new technical ground. Lucas had to start his own special-effects laboratory, Industrial Light and Magic, to invent new ways of creating fantasy. His 2002 *Star Wars* film, *Attack of the Clones*, was the first major movie to use digital high-definition video cameras. To film his vision, Lucas had to convince two companies to build the new cameras from scratch. The success of Lucas's experiment allowed film technology to rapidly evolve. As the film animator Jason Barlow explains, "Now with digital technology real magic can happen."

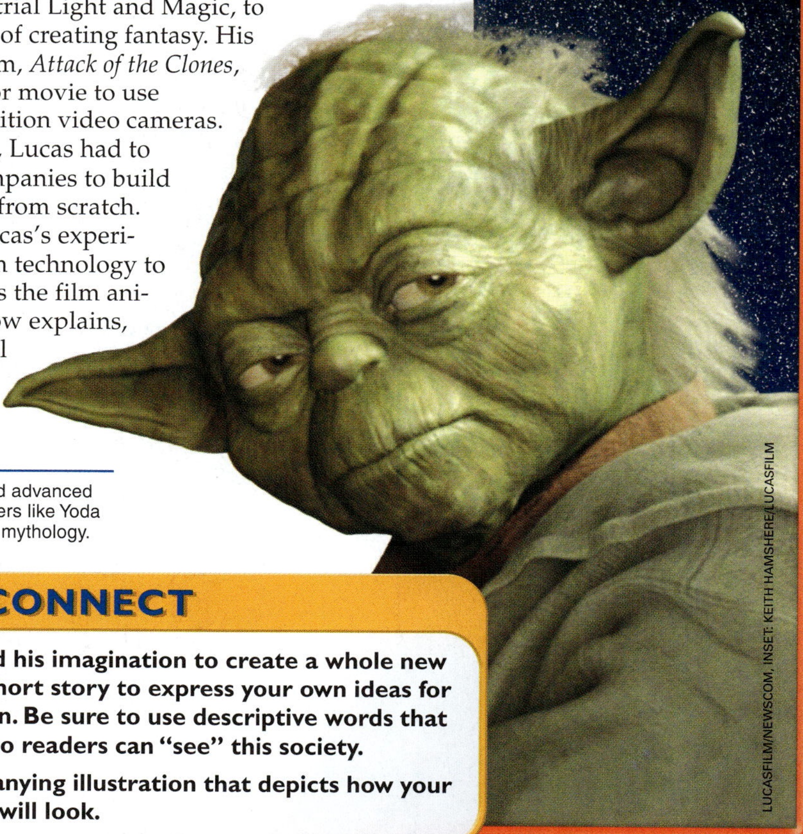

Lucas (TOP PHOTO) used advanced technology and characters like Yoda (RIGHT) to create a new mythology.

LUCASFILM/NEWSCOM, INSET: KEITH HAMSHERE/LUCASFILM

TIME TO CONNECT

- **Lucas used film and his imagination to create a whole new universe. Write a short story to express your own ideas for a fantasy civilization. Be sure to use descriptive words that evoke visual ideas so readers can "see" this society.**
- **Create an accompanying illustration that depicts how your fantasy civilization will look.**

TIME TO CONNECT

In a brief class discussion, help students share their ideas about a "fantasy" civilization. Let students brainstorm a list of vivid words and phrases that could be used in describing these civilizations. Record their ideas on the board. Then have students write their poems, keeping these suggestions in mind:

- Be sure each part of the poem contributes to a clear description.
- Consider the organization of details, to be sure the poem will entertain your readers.

Chapter 14 Review

BUILDING VOCABULARY

Number a sheet of paper from 1 to 6. After each number, write the term from the list that matches each description below.

architectural rendering
belvedere
fantasy art
juxtapose
social protest painting
Surrealists

1. A building designed to provide a view of its surroundings.
2. A detailed, realistic two-dimensional representation of a proposed three-dimensional structure.
3. Group of artists who explored the realm of dreams and the subconscious.
4. Place side by side.
5. An art style dedicated to attacking the ills of big-city life.
6. Art that focuses on make-believe or imaginary subjects.

REVIEWING ART FACTS

Number a sheet of paper from 7 to 12. Answer each question in a complete sentence.

7. What fantasy images turned up often in art of the Middle Ages?
8. When did the Surrealists work?
9. Who was René Magritte? For what is he best noted?
10. What is the significance of the title of Figure 14–7?
11. What did social protest artists frequently criticize in their works?
12. What makes the print in Figure 14–10 "impossible"?

CROSS-CURRICULUM CONNECTIONS

13. **Language Arts.** Look back at Figure 14–4 on page 266. Notice the manner in which the painting seems to suggest a story. Think about the story the artwork tells. Then write a short poem that captures the action and emotions.
14. **Social Studies.** Use library or online resources to learn more about the Great Depression and its aftermath. In the course of your research, answer the following questions: What caused this economic disaster? Which nations were affected by it? What measures were taken in this country to recover from its effects? Share your findings in the form of an oral report. Find images by Ben Shahn, Reginald Marsh, and other social protest painters to display during your presentation.

Web Museum Activity

The J. Paul Getty Museum, Los Angeles, California

In this chapter, you learned how artists use their imagination to create fantasy art. Many artists have imagined and expressed their idea of life in outer space. Go to **art.glencoe.com** and click on The Getty museum link to explore the different images of space through art.

You will discover how different cultures have expressed their vision of the universe. Through a variety of artworks, you will explore different images of the universe. What did you learn about the universe when looking at and reading about these images?

Describe your vision of outer space. Do any of the images reveal a similar vision?

ANSWERS TO Chapter 14 Review

Building Vocabulary

1. belvedere
2. architectural rendering
3. Surrealists
4. juxtapose
5. social protest painting
6. fantasy art

Reviewing Art Facts

7. The artworks depicted demons and other "night visitors."
8. Surrealists painted in the first half of the twentieth century.
9. He was a Belgian Surrealist. He is famous for his imaginative use of juxtaposition.
10. The work is an autobiographical glimpse of the painter's past and present, as well as her future.
11. They often target current-day problems.
12. The second floor of the building is arranged at a right angle to the first floor.

Cross-Curriculum Connections

13. Student poems will vary.
14. Reports will vary.

Web Museum Activity

Before you have students go online, visit the Web site to preview the museum's online content, collection, and any online exhibit that may be of interest. Students' descriptions will vary. Encourage students to be creative as they write about their vision of outer space. Their visions can be based on scientific facts or by their imagination. Have students share their descriptions with the class.

Using the Handbook

The Handbook is a convenient reference section which offers students step-by-step procedures for using traditional media, a separate section on guidelines for using digital media, and information on art-related careers. This material is designed to complement and enrich the narrative and studio lessons that appear in the book. The Handbook is divided into the following sections:

- Techniques Tips
- Digital Media Guide
- Career Spotlights

The Handbook can be used in conjunction with specific chapters and lessons, or as a reference guide. Regardless of the way you integrate the material, the Teacher Wraparound Edition offers additional information in the outside column to help you teach, apply, and reinforce these materials.

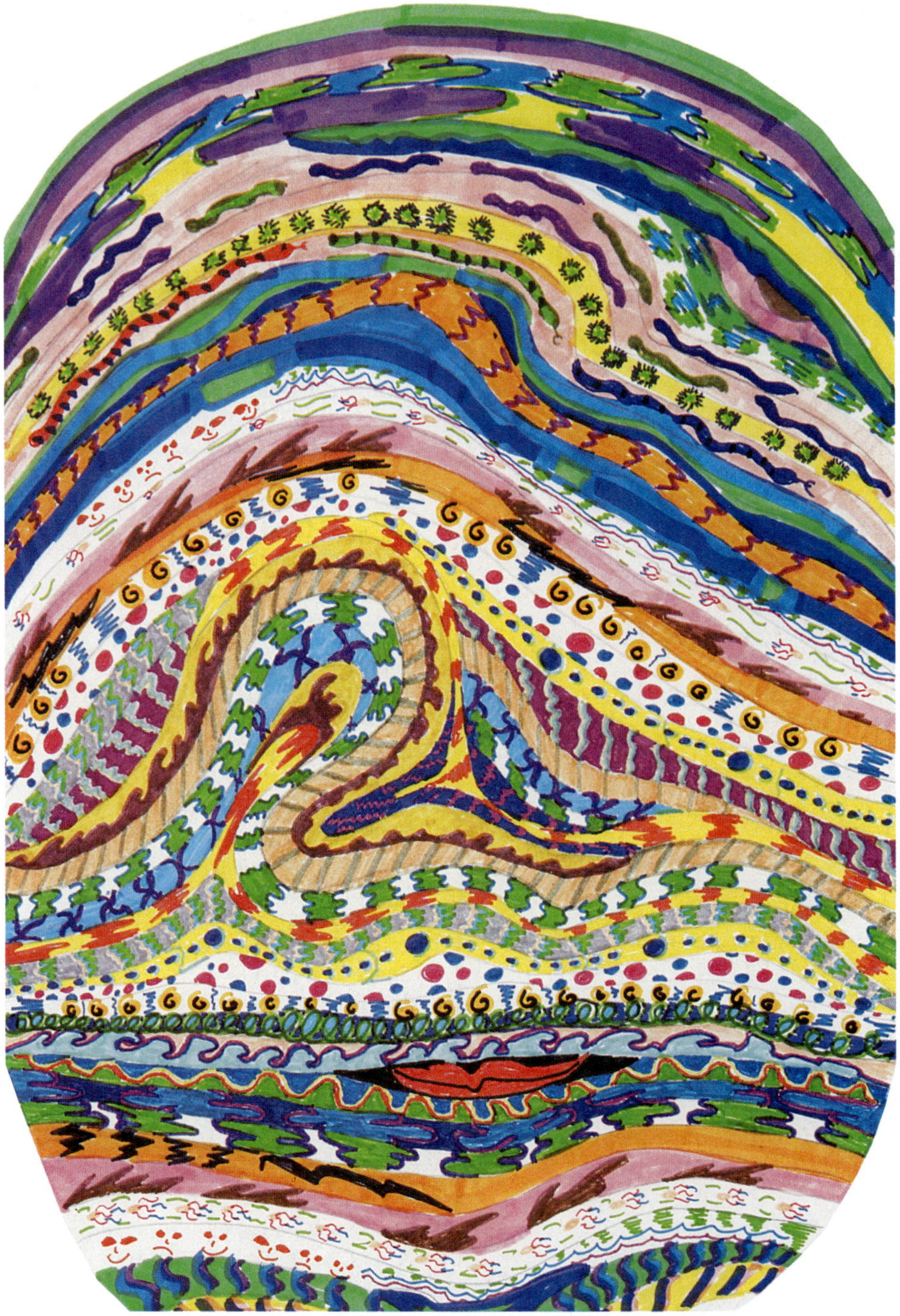

Looking at an object up close can reveal surprising details. This thumbprint was created by a student. Notice the use of line, color, and texture.

Handbook Contents

Technique Tips

DRAWING TIPS

PAINTING TIPS

PRINTMAKING TIPS

SCULPTING TIPS

OTHER TIPS

Digital Media Guide

Technique Tips

This section offers students step-by-step procedures on how to do specific skills related to the areas of drawing, printmaking, painting, and sculpting. General techniques in these areas are described and, when appropriate, illustrated with the drawings. Other general skills, such as making a mat or using glue, are included in this reference section.

Digital Media Guide

This section offers students guidelines and procedures on how to use digital tools to create artworks of their own. Although the computer cannot—and should not—replace traditional media, it can provide numerous additional visual solutions. In the art classroom, as in the artist's studio, technology can introduce more tools to the traditional artist's toolboxes. Using digital tools involves new strategies, higher-order thinking skills, and problem-solving skills.

Career Spotlights

The information provided in this section introduces students to 14 careers in art-related fields. Students are presented with an overview of the type of work and personal qualifications required of a person working in the featured occupation. In the Teacher Wraparound Edition, addresses are provided so that students can research and obtain further information about the careers that interest them.

Handbook Contents

Career Spotlights

TEACHER TO TEACHER

Stretch Your School Budget

Check with the local art club to see if it has a benevolence fund for aid to education. Check with the local art directors' club, designers' association, or society of illustrators (in cities larger than 300,000). Tracing vellum and some watercolor rendering papers can be bought less expensively in rolls or by the foot than by the sheet or pads. A 100% rag, twenty-pound vellum is pretty tough—and you can iron the back of it to smooth it after using liquid media.

DRAWING TIPS

1. Making Gesture Drawings

Gesture drawing is a way of showing movement in a sketch. Gesture drawings have no outlines or details. You are not expected to draw the figure. Instead, you are expected to draw the movement, or what the figure is doing. Follow these guidelines:

- Use the side of the drawing tool. Do not hold the medium as you would if you were writing.
- Find the lines of movement that show the direction in which the figure is bending. Draw the main line showing this movement.
- Use quickly drawn lines to build up the shape of the person.

2. Making Contour Drawings

Contour drawing is a way of capturing the feel of a subject. When doing a contour drawing, remember the following pointers:

- If you accidentally pick up your pen or pencil, don't stop working. Place your pen or pencil back where you stopped. Begin again from that point.
- If you have trouble keeping your eyes off the paper, ask a friend to hold a piece of paper between your eyes and your drawing paper. Another trick is to place your drawing paper inside a large paper bag as you work.
- Tape your paper to the table, so it will not slide around. With a finger of your free hand, trace an outline of the object. Record the movement with your drawing hand.
- Contour lines show ridges and wrinkles in addition to outlines. Adding these lines gives roundness to the object.

3. Drawing with Oil Pastels

Oil pastels are sticks of pigment held together with an oily binder. The colors are brighter than wax crayon colors. If you press heavily, you will make a brilliant-colored line. If you press lightly, you will create a fuzzy line. You can fill in shapes with the brilliant colors. You can blend a variety of color combinations. For example, you can fill a shape with a soft layer of a hue and then color over the hue with a heavy layer of white to create a unique tint of that hue.

If you use oil pastels on colored paper, you can put a layer of white under the layer of hue to block the color of the paper.

4. Drawing Thin Lines with a Brush

Drawing thin lines with a brush can be learned with a little practice. Just follow these steps:

1. Dip your brush in the ink or paint. Wipe the brush slowly against the side, twirling it between your fingers until the bristles form a point.
2. Hold the brush at the beginning of the metal band near the tip. Hold the brush straight up and down.
3. Imagine that the brush is a pencil with a very sharp point. Pretend that pressing too hard will break the point. Now touch the paper lightly with the tip of the brush and draw a line. The line should be quite thin.

   To make a thinner line still, lift up on the brush as you draw. After a while, you will be able to make lines in a variety of thicknesses.

5. Making a Grid for Enlarging

Sometimes the need arises to make a bigger version of a small drawing. An example is when you create a mural based on a small sketch. Follow these steps:

1. Using a ruler, draw evenly spaced lines across and up and down your original drawing (Figure T–1). Count the number of squares you

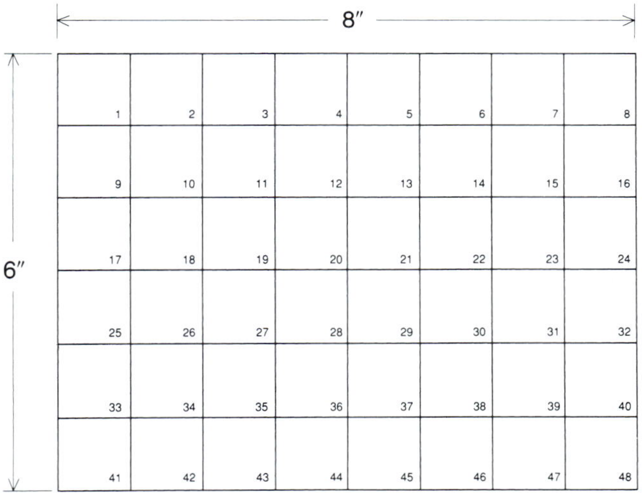

▲ **Figure T–1**

TECHNIQUE TIPS

TECHNIQUE TIPS

Using the Technique Tips

The technique tips listed on this and the following pages give students helpful hints for handling different media and tools. There are two types of technique tips. One type offers students step-by-step procedures which should be followed sequentially in order to achieve optimal results. The other type contains procedures and helpful suggestions that students may use as required by their individual studio projects.

Using The Drawing Tips

- Making Gesture Drawings
  Use with:
  Gesture Drawing, page 44
- Drawing with Oil Pastels
  Use with:
  Drawing a Still Life, page 18
  Creating a Portrait, page 48
- Drawing Thin Lines with a Brush
  Use with:
  Painting a Storm, page 118

TEACHER TO TEACHER

DRAWINGS Some drawings look better without a mat. A backing board with a lightweight acetate covering will do the trick. If the drawing is on tracing paper or vellum, however, a piece of inexpensive white poster or tagboard needs to go between the corrugated board and the drawing. The corrugated board will discolor any drawing in a few years. Thin paper shows the corrugation ridges from the backing.

- Using Shading Techniques
  Use with:
  Drawing a Still Life, page 18
- Using Sighting Techniques
  Use with:
  Drawing a Sporting Event in Action, page 206
  Creating a Diorama, page 94
  Creating a Nature Scene, page 106
- Using a Viewing Frame
  Use with:
  Drawing a Building Detail, Studio Activity, page 173
- Using a Ruler
  Use with:
  Abstraction in Art, page 98

made from side to side. Count the number of squares running up and down.

2. Measure the width of the surface to which the drawing is to be transferred. Divide that figure by the number of side-to-side squares. The resulting number will be the horizontal measure of each square. You may work in inches or centimeters. Using a ruler or yardstick, mark off the squares. Draw in light rules.
3. Measure the height of the surface to which the drawing is to be transferred. Divide that figure by the number of up-and-down squares. The resulting number will be the vertical measure of each square. Mark off the squares. Draw in pencil lines.
4. Starting at the upper left, number each square on the original drawing. Give the same number to each square on the large grid. Working a square at a time, transfer your image. (See Figure T–2.)

6. Using Shading Techniques

When using shading techniques, keep in mind the following:

- Lines or dots placed close together create dark values.
- Lines or dots placed far apart, on the other hand, create light values. To show a change from light to dark, start with lines or dots far apart and little by little bring them close together.
- Use care also to follow the shape of the object when adding lines. Straight lines are used to shade an object with a flat surface. Rounded lines are used to shade an object with a curved surface.

7. Using Sighting Techniques

Sighting is a technique that will help you draw objects in proportion.

1. Face the object you plan to draw. Hold a pencil straight up and down at arm's length. Your thumb should rest against the side of the pencil and be even with the tip.
2. Close one eye. With your other eye, focus on the object.
3. Slide your thumb down the pencil until the exposed part of the pencil matches the object's height. (See Figure T–3.)

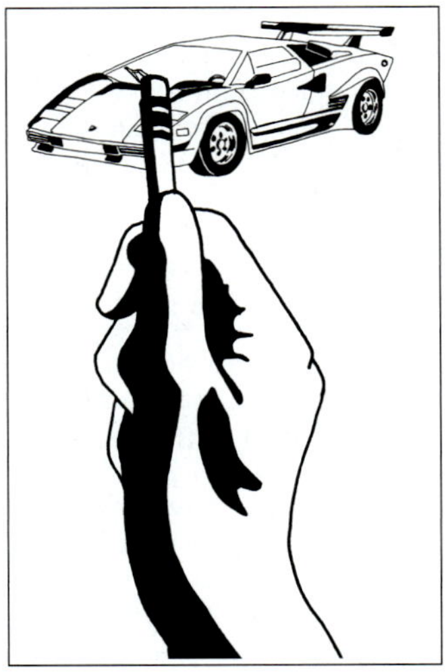

▲ **Figure T–3**

4. Now, without moving your thumb or bending you arm, turn the pencil sideways.
5. Focus on the width of the object. If the height is greater, figure out how many "widths" will fit in one "height." If the width is greater, figure out how many "heights" will fit in one "width."

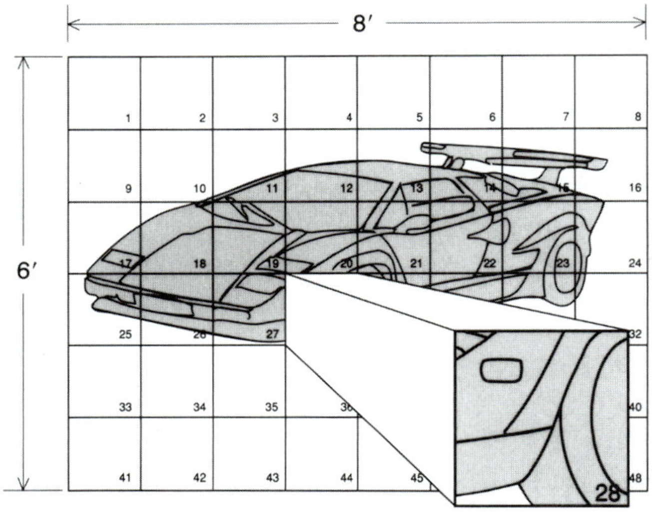

▲ **Figure T–2**

TEACHER TO TEACHER

Thumbnail Sketches Tell students that thumbnail sketches are small sketches drawn quickly to record ideas for a finished drawing. They are called thumbnail because they are almost small enough to have been drawn on a thumbnail. They are usually done with pen and ink. Have students think about situations in which the artist would prefer to use thumbnail sketches. For example, graphic artists and illustrators use them to record ideas and also to show ideas to other artists and art directors. Have students develop a series of thumbnail sketches that could be used to plan a series of paintings of animal totems or symbols of ancestry.

8. Using a Viewing Frame

Much in the way a camera is used to focus on one area of a scene, you can better zero in on an object you plan to draw by using a viewing frame (Figure T–4). To make a viewing frame, do the following:

1. Cut a rectangular hole in a piece of paper about 2 inches in from the paper's edges.
2. Hold the paper at arm's length and look through the hole at your subject. Imagine that the hole represents your drawing paper.
3. Decide how much of the subject you want to have in your drawing.
4. By moving the frame up, down, sideways, nearer or farther, you can change the focus of your drawing.

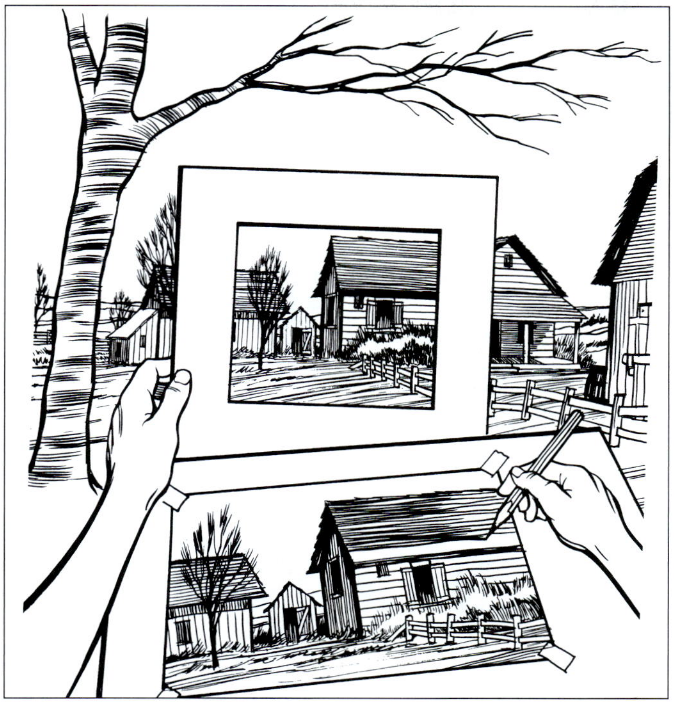

▲ Figure T–4

9. Using a Ruler

There are times when you need to draw a crisp, straight line. By using the following techniques, you will be able to do so.

1. Hold the ruler with one hand and the pencil with the other.
2. Place the ruler where you wish to draw a straight line.
3. Hold the ruler with your thumb and first two fingers. Be careful that your fingers do not stick out beyond the edge of the ruler.
4. Press heavily on the ruler so it will not slide while you're drawing.
5. Hold the pencil lightly against the ruler.
6. Pull the pencil quickly and lightly along the edge of the ruler. The object is to keep the ruler from moving while the pencil moves along its edge.

PAINTING TIPS

10. Cleaning a Paintbrush

Cleaning a paint brush properly helps it last a long time. Always:

1. Rinse the thick paint out of the brush under running water. Do not use hot water.
2. Gently paint the brush over a cake of mild soap, or dip it in a mild liquid detergent (Figure T–5).

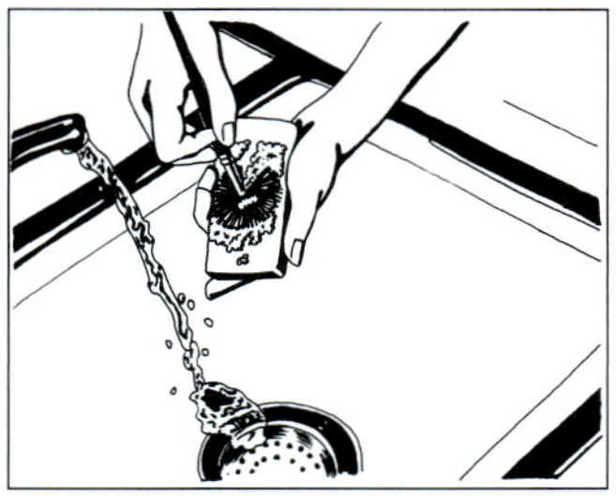

▲ Figure T–5

■ Cleaning a Paint Brush

Use with:

Mixing Colors, page 12
Creating an Expressive Word Design, page 74
Egyptian Tomb Painting, page 86
Painting a Storm, page 118

TEACHER TO TEACHER

Perceptual Skills Tell students that seeing the item they are drawing as a whole rather than just a collection of parts results in more successful drawings. The fact that we naturally see things as a whole was discovered in 1912 by German psychologist Max Wertheimer. He founded a branch of psychology called Gestalt. The German word *gestalt* means pattern or form. According to Gestalt psychology, we only recognize objects by seeing total patterns or forms, not by adding up the individual parts we see. Tell students that in making most drawings, they should do the large shapes first and add the details later.

- Making Natural Earth Pigments
  Use with:
  Creating a Nature Scene, page 106
- Mixing Paint to Change the Value of Color
  Use with:
  Creating a Realistic Painting, page 72
  Creating a Mixed-Media Cityscape, page 174
  Creating Your Own Picture Puzzle, page 270
- Working with Poster Paints
  Use with:
  Mixing Colors, page 12
  Creating an Expressive Word Design, page 74
  Egyptian Tomb Painting, page 86
  Using Abstraction in Art, page 98
  Drawing a Figure in Action, page 150
- Working with Watercolors
  Use with:
  Painting a Watercolor Still Life, page 190

3. Gently scrub the brush against the palm of your hand to work the soap into the brush. This removes paint you may not have realized was still in the brush.
4. Rinse the brush under running water while you continue to scrub your palm against it (Figure T–6).
5. Repeat steps 2, 3, and 4 as needed.

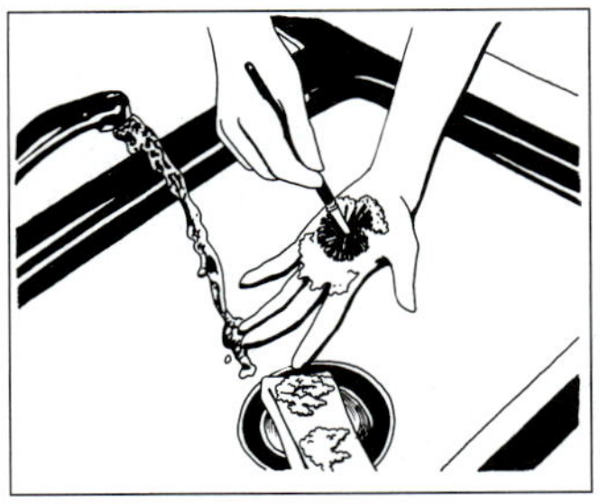

▲ **Figure T–6**

When it is thoroughly rinsed and excess water has been squeezed from the brush, shape your brush into a point with your fingers (Figure T–7). Place the brush in a container with the bristles up so that it will keep its shape as it dries.

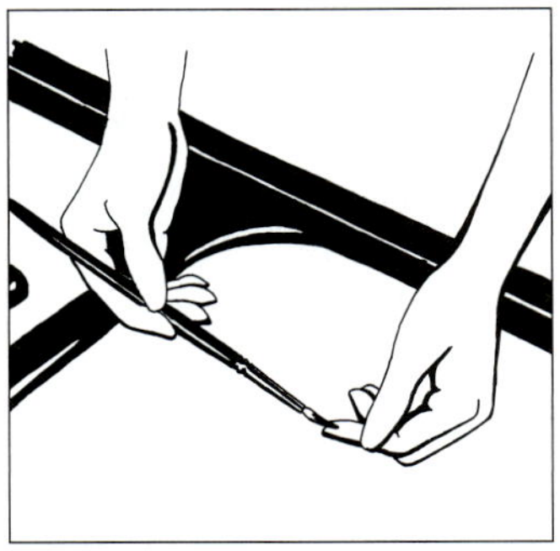

▲ **Figure T–7**

11. Making Natural Earth Pigments

Anywhere there is dirt, clay, or sand, there is natural pigment. To create your own pigments, gather as many different kinds of earth colors as you can. Grind these as finely as possible. (If you can, borrow a mortar and pestle.) (See Figure T–8.) Do not worry if the pigment is slightly gritty.

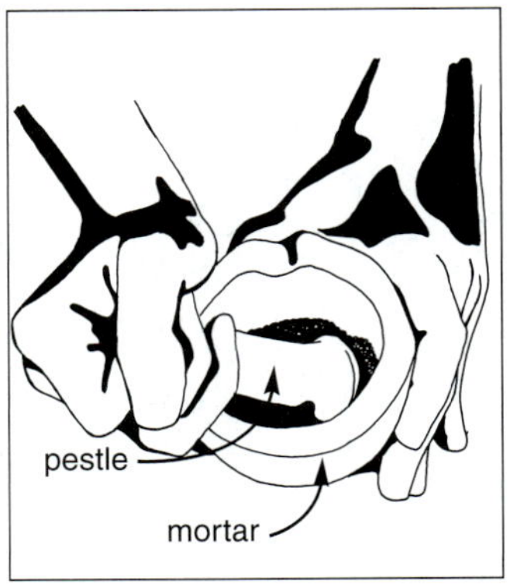

▲ **Figure T–8**

To make the binder, mix equal parts of white glue and water. Place a few spoonfuls of your powdered pigment into a small jar. Add a little of the binder. Experiment with different amounts of each.

When you work with natural pigments, remember to always wash the brushes before the paint in them has a chance to dry. The glue from the binder can ruin a brush. As you work, stir the paint every now and then. This will keep the grains of pigment from settling to the bottom of the jar.

Make a fresh batch each time you paint.

12. Mixing Paint to Change the Value of Color

You can better control the colors in your work when you mix your own paint. In mixing paints, treat opaque paints (for example, tempera) differently from transparent paints (for example, watercolors).

- *For light values of opaque paints.* Mix only a small amount of the hue to white. The color can always be made stronger by adding more of the hue.
- *For dark values of opaque paints.* Add a small amount of black to the hue. Never add the hue to black.
- *For light values of transparent paints.* Thin a shaded area with water (Figure T–9). This allows more of the white of the paper to show through.
- *For dark values of transparent paints.* Carefully add a small amount of black to the hue.

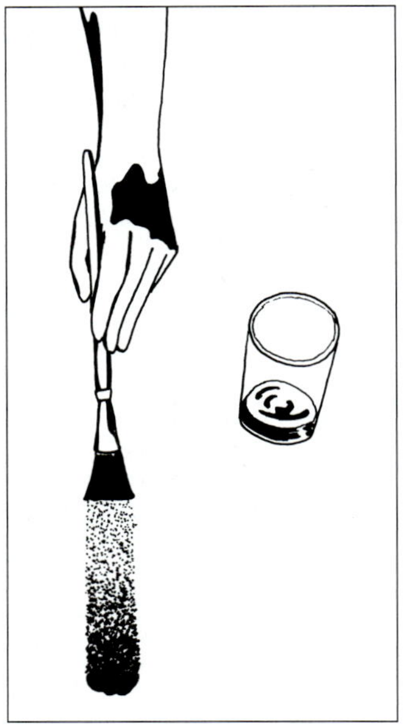

▲ **Figure T–9**

SAFETY TIP

ART SAFETY RESOURCES The need to direct time and effort to safeguarding the health of students in the art studio cannot be ignored. The Art and Creative Materials Institute (ACMI) is a national clearinghouse for research and information on health hazards in the arts. It publishes a newsletter which covers a range of topics including new hazards, precautions, government regulations, lawsuits, and a calendar of events. Those interested teachers can write to the following address: The Arts and Crafts Materials Institute (ACMI), P.O. Box 479, Hanson, MA 02341-0479

13. Working with Tempera

When using tempera, remember the following:

- Tempera paints run when wet. To keep this from happening, make sure one shape is dry before painting a wet color next to it.

14. Working with Watercolors

- If you apply wet paint to damp paper, you create lines and shapes with soft edges.
- If you apply wet paint to dry paper, you create lines and shapes with sharp, clear edges.
- If you dip a dry brush into damp paint and then brush across dry paper, you achieve a fuzzy effect.
- School watercolors come in semi-moist cakes. Before you use them, place a drop of water on each cake to let the paint soften. Watercolor paints are transparent. You can see the white paper through the paint. If you want a light value of a hue, dilute the paint with a large amount of water. If you want a bright hue, you must dissolve more pigment by swirling your brush around in the cake of paint until you have dissolved a great deal of paint. The paint you apply to the paper can be as bright as the paint in the cake.

PRINTMAKING TIPS

15. Making a Stamp Printing

A stamp print is an easy way to make repetitive designs. The following are a few suggestions for making a stamp and printing with it. You may develop some other ideas after reading these hints. Remember, printing reverses your design, so if you use letters, be certain to cut or carve them backwards.

- Cut a simple design into the flat surface of an eraser with a knife that has a fine, precision blade.
- Cut a potato, carrot, or turnip in half. Use a paring knife to carve a design into the flat surface of the vegetable.
- Glue yarn to a bottle cap or a jar lid.
- Glue found objects to a piece of corrugated cardboard. Make a design with paper clips, washers, nuts, leaves, feathers, or anything else you can find. Whatever object you use should have a fairly flat surface. Make a handle for the block with masking tape.
- Cut shapes out of a piece of inner tube material. Glue the shapes to a piece of heavy cardboard.

There are several ways to apply ink or paint to a stamp:

- Roll water-based printing ink on the stamp with a soft brayer.
- Roll water-based printing ink on a plate and press the stamp into the ink.
- Apply tempera paint or school acrylic to the stamp with a bristle brush.

SCULPTING TIPS

16. Working with Clay

To make your work with clay go smoothly, always do the following:

1. Dip one or two fingers in water.
2. Spread the moisture from your fingers over your palms.

Never dip your hands in water. Too much moisture turns clay into mud.

17. Joining Clay

If you are creating a piece of sculpture that requires joining pieces, do the following:

1. Gather the materials you will need. These include clay, slip, (a creamy mixture of clay and water), a paint brush, a scoring tool, (perhaps a kitchen fork) and clay tools.
2. Rough up or scratch the two surfaces to be joined (Figure T–10).

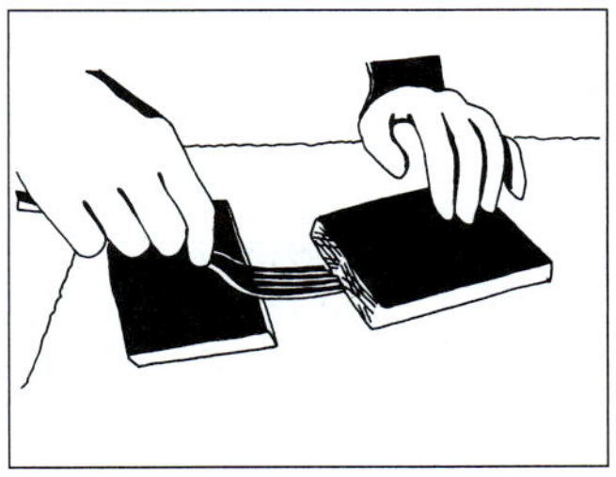

▲ **Figure T–10**

Using the Sculpting Tips

- Working with Clay
  Use with:
  Making a Mask with Formal Balance, page 28
  Making an Animal Sculpture, page 134
  Building a Clay Musical Instrument, page 194

SAFETY TIP

PRINTING Remind students to always wipe any remaining ink from a block and brayer after they have finished printing. If using a water-based printing ink, they can use water for cleaning. If using oil-based ink, however, they should use a solvent such as turpentine. Remember that if they use a solvent, they should be careful not to get it on their skin, or let it come in contact with their eyes.

USING KILNS Place kilns in a separate room. If that is not possible, locate the kiln in an out-of-the-way part of the room where students are not likely to come into contact with it when it is in operation. In addition, all kilns should have local exhaust ventilation.

■ Joining Clay
Use with:
Making a Mask with Formal Balance, page 28
Making an Animal Sculpture, page 134
Building a Clay Musical Instrument, page 194

3. Apply slip to one of the two surfaces using a paint brush or your fingers (Figure T–11).

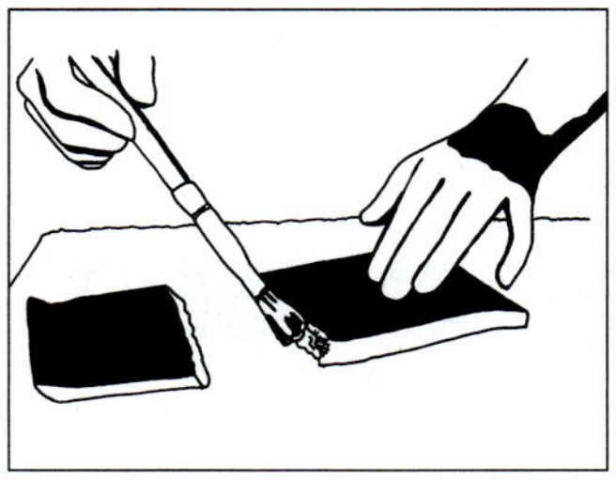

▲ **Figure T–11**

4. Gently press the two surfaces together so the slip oozes out of the joining seam (Figure T–12).

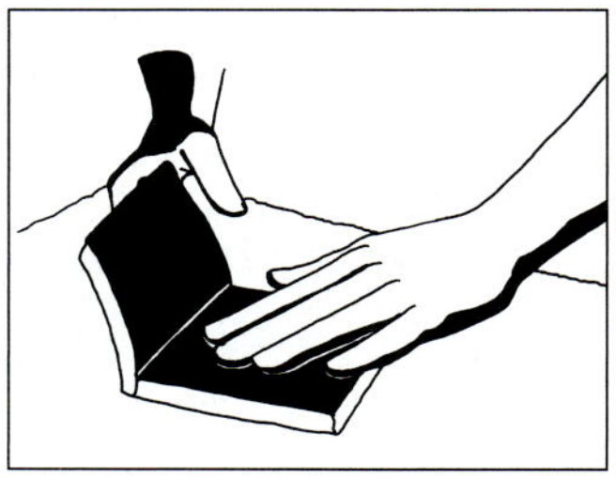

▲ **Figure T–12**

5. Using clay tools and/or your fingers, smooth away the slip that has oozed out of the seam (Figure T–13). You may smooth out the seam as well, or you may leave it for decorative purposes.

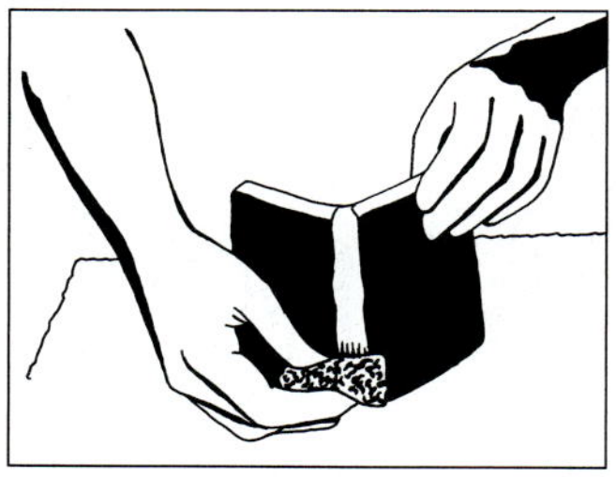

▲ **Figure T–13**

18. Making a Clay Mold for a Plaster Relief

One of the easiest ways to make a plaster relief is with a clay mold. When making a clay mold, remember the following:

- Plaster poured into the mold will come out with the opposite image. Design details cut into the mold will appear raised on the relief. Details built up within the mold will appear indented in the relief.
- Do not make impressions in your mold that have *undercuts* (Figure T–14). Undercuts trap plaster, which will break off when the relief is removed. When cutting impressions, keep the deepest parts the narrowest.
- In carving a raised area in the mold, take care not to create a reverse undercut (Figure T–15).

If you want to change the mold, simply smooth the area with your fingers.

19. Mixing Plaster

Mixing plaster requires some technique and a certain amount of caution. It can also be a very simple matter when you are prepared. Always do the following:

- Use caution when working with dry plaster. Wear a dust mask or work in a well-ventilated room.
- Cover your work space to keep the dust from spreading.
- Always use a plastic bowl and a stick for mixing. Never use silverware you will later eat from.
- Always use plaster that is fine, like sifted flour. Plaster should never be grainy when dry.
- Always add water to the bowl first. Sift in the plaster. Stir slowly.
- Never pour unused plaster down a drain. Allow it to dry in the bowl. To remove the dried plaster, twist the bowl. Crack the loose plaster into a lined trash can.

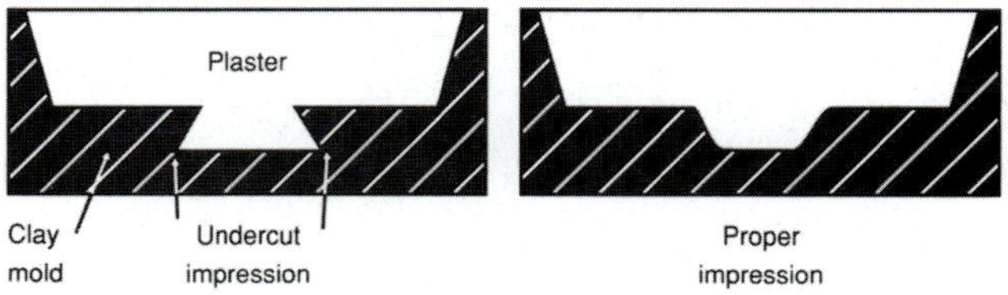

▲ **Figure T–14**

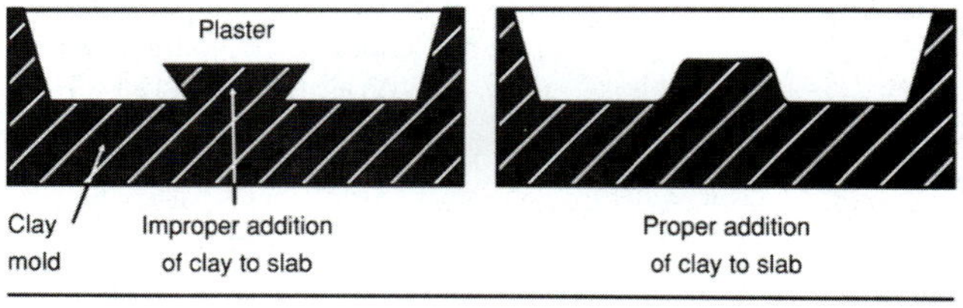

▲ **Figure T–15**

MORE ABOUT...

Pottery Before becoming finished pottery, clay takes six different forms. These are:

- Plastic clay
- Slip
- Leather hard clay
- Greenware
- Bisqueware
- Glazeware

Most ceramic objects are made hollow to avoid exploding or cracking during firing.

20. Working with Papier-Mâché

Papier-mâché (**pay**-puhr muh-**shay**) is a French term meaning "chewed paper." It is also the name of several sculpting methods using newspaper and liquid paste. These methods can be used to model tiny pieces of jewelry. They can also be used to create life-size creatures.

In creating papier-mâché sculptures, the paper-and-paste mixture is molded over a support. You will learn more about supports shortly. The molded newspaper dries to a hard finish. The following are three methods for working with papier-mâché:

- **Pulp Method**. Shred newspaper, paper towels, or tissue paper into tiny pieces. (Do not use glossy magazine paper: it will not soften.) Soak your paper in water overnight. Press the paper in a kitchen strainer to remove as much moisture as possible. Mix the mashed paper with commercially prepared papier-mâché paste or white glue. The mixture should have the consistency of soft clay. Add a few drops of oil of cloves to keep the mixture from spoiling. A spoonful of linseed oil makes the mixture smoother. (If needed, the mixture can be stored at this point in a plastic bag in the refrigerator.) Use the mixture to model small shapes. When your creations dry, they can be sanded. You will also be able to drill holes in them.
- **Strip Method.** Tear newspaper into strips. Either dip the strips in papier-mâché paste or rub paste on them. Apply the strips to your support (Figure T–16). If you do not want the strips to stick to your support, first cover it with plastic wrap. Use wide strips for large shapes. Use thin strips for smaller shapes. If you plan to remove your finished creation from the support, apply five or six layers. (Change directions with each layer so you can keep track of the number.) Otherwise, two or three layers should be enough. After applying the strips to your support, rub your fingers over the surface.

  As a last layer, use torn paper towels. The brown paper towels that are found in schools produce an uncomplicated surface on which to paint. Make sure no rough edges are sticking up. Store any unused paste mixture in the refrigerator to keep it from spoiling.

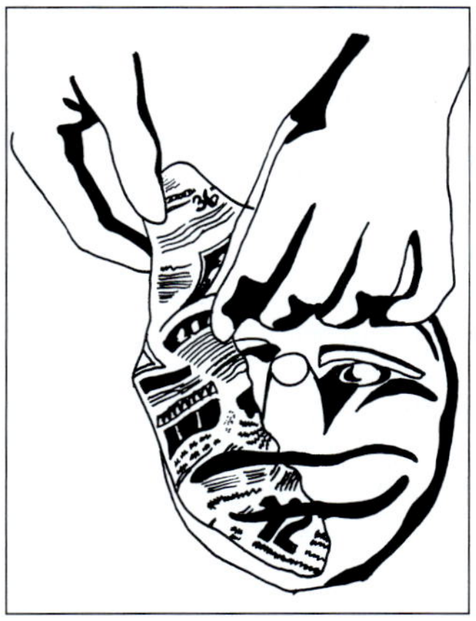

▲ **Figure T–16**

- **Draping Method.** Spread papier-mâché paste on newspaper. Lay a second sheet on top of the first. Smooth the layers. Add another layer of paste and another sheet of paper. Repeat until you have four or five layers of paper. Use this method for making drapery on a figure. (See Figure T–17.) If you allow the layers to dry for a day or two, they will become leathery. They can then be cut and molded as you like. Newspaper strips dipped in paste can be used to seal cracks.

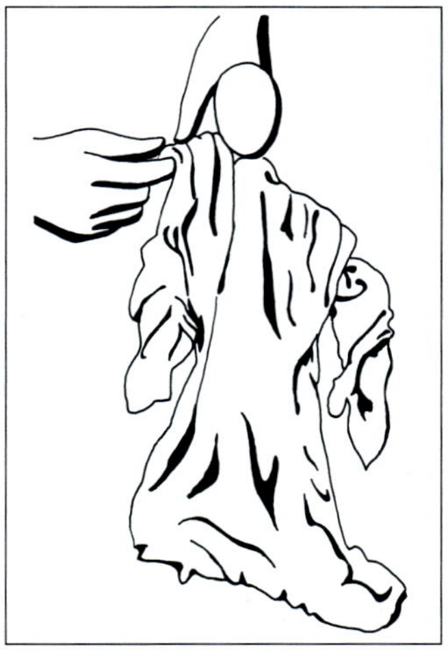

▲ **Figure T–17**

Like papier-mâché, support for papier-mâché creations can be made in several different ways. Dry newspaper may be wadded up and wrapped with string or tape (Figure T–18). Wire coat hangers may be padded with rags. For large figures, a wooden frame covered with chicken wire makes a good support.

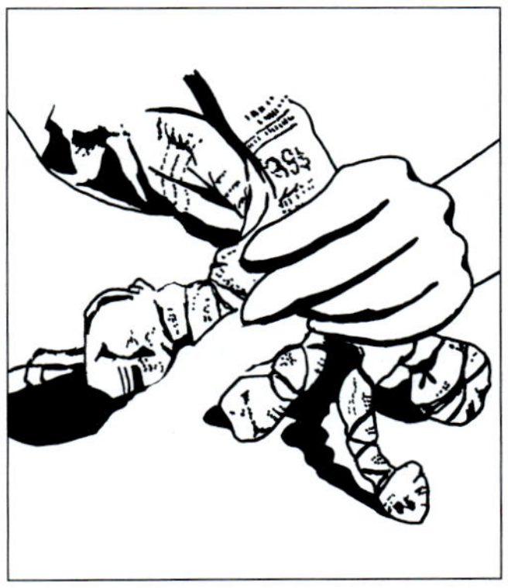

▲ **Figure T–18**

■ Working with Papier-Mâché
Use with:
Creating a Fantasy Creature, page 138

INCLUSION STRATEGIES

Physically Impaired Determine if any of your students are asthmatic, visually or hearing impaired, or on prescribed medication. Asthmatic students should not be exposed to dusts, fumes, or vapors because of breathing difficulties. Visually impaired students operate very close to their artwork, and as a consequence, are more likely to inhale dusts, vapors, and fumes. Students with hearing impairments should not be exposed to activities requiring noisy machinery. If students are on medication, seek a physician's advice regarding the potential harmful interaction between the prescribed medicine and art materials used in the class.

Other Tips

- **Measuring Rectangles**
  Use with:
  Making a Tessellation, page 34
  Creating a Fanciful Exterior, page 170

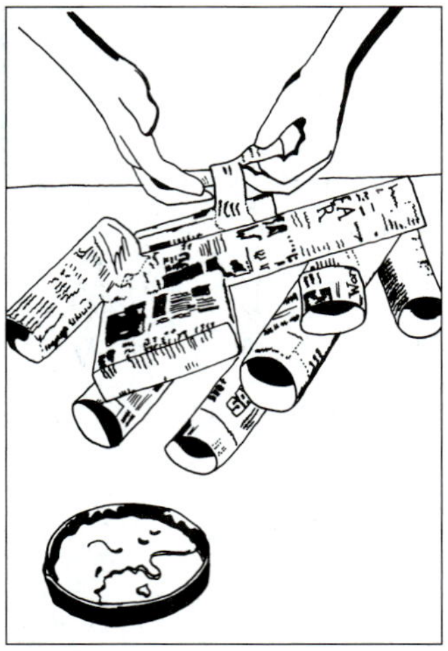

▲ **Figure T–19**

To create a base for your papier-mâché creations, tape together arrangements of found materials. Some materials you might combine are boxes, tubes, and bowls. (See Figure T–19.) Clay can also be modeled as a base. If clay is used, be sure there are no undercuts that would keep the papier-mâché from lifting off easily when dry. (For an explanation of undercuts, see Technique Tip 18, on page 286.)

Always allow time for your papier-mâché creations to dry. The material needs extra drying time when thick layers are used or when the weather is damp. An electric fan blowing air on the material can shorten the drying time.

21. Making a Paper Sculpture

Another name for paper sculpture is origami. The process originated in Japan and means "folding paper." Paper sculpture begins with a flat piece of paper. The paper is then curved or bent to produce more than a flat surface. Here are some ways to experiment with paper.

- **Scoring.** Place a square sheet of heavy construction paper, 12 by 12 inch, on a flat surface. Position a ruler on the paper so that it is close to the center and parallel to the sides. Holding the ruler in place, run the point of a knife or a pair of scissors along one of the ruler's edges. Press down firmly but take care not to cut through the paper. Gently crease the paper along the line you made. Hold your paper with the crease facing upward.
- **Pleating.** Take a piece of paper and fold it one inch from the edge. Then fold the paper in the other direction. Continue folding back and forth.
- **Curling.** Hold one end of a long strip of paper with the thumb and forefinger of one hand. At a point right below where you are holding the strip, grip it lightly between the side of a pencil and the thumb of your other hand. In a quick motion, run the pencil along the strip. This will cause the strip to curl back on itself. Don't apply too much pressure, or the strip will tear. (See Figure T–20.)

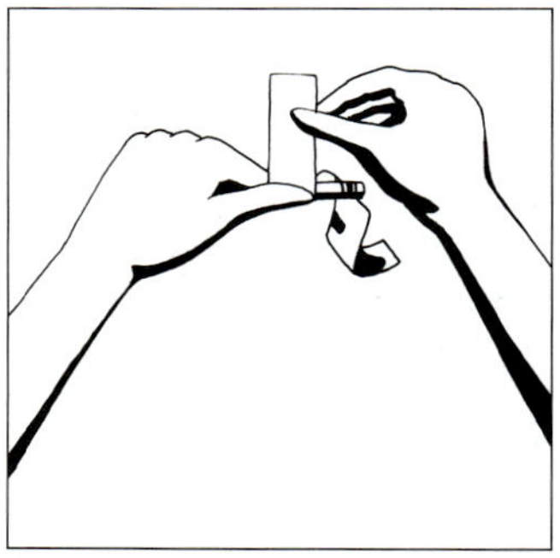

▲ **Figure T–20**

OTHER TIPS

22. Measuring Rectangles

Do you find it hard to create perfectly formed rectangles? Here is a way of getting the job done:

1. Make a light pencil dot near the long edge of a sheet of paper. With a ruler, measure the exact distance between the dot and the edge. Make three more dots the same distance in from the edge. (See Figure T–21.)

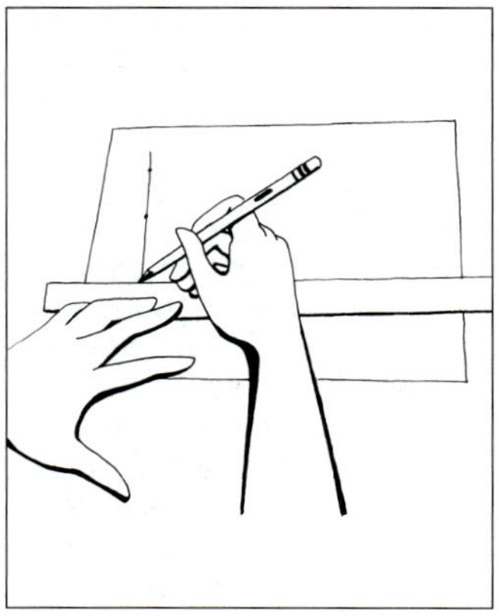

▲ **Figure T–21**

2. Line a ruler up along the dots. Make a light pencil line running the length of the paper.
3. Turn the paper so that a short side is facing you. Make four pencil dots equally distant from the short edge. Connect these with a light pencil rule. Stop when you reach the first line you drew. (See Figure T–22.)
4. Do the same for the remaining two sides. Erase any lines that may extend beyond the box you have made.
5. Trace over the lines with your ruler and pencil.

The box you have created will be a perfectly formed rectangle.

TEACHER TO TEACHER

Classroom Demonstrations Demonstration is an especially effective method of instruction when applied to studio activities. When preparing for a demonstration, always practice beforehand using the same materials students will be expected to use. Include continuous commentary by explaining in detail what you are doing and why you are doing it this way. To be of maximum value to students, the demonstration must be amplified by detailed explanation of every action. When this is done, students receive information by way of the eyes and ears, increasing the likelihood that this information will be understood and assimilated.

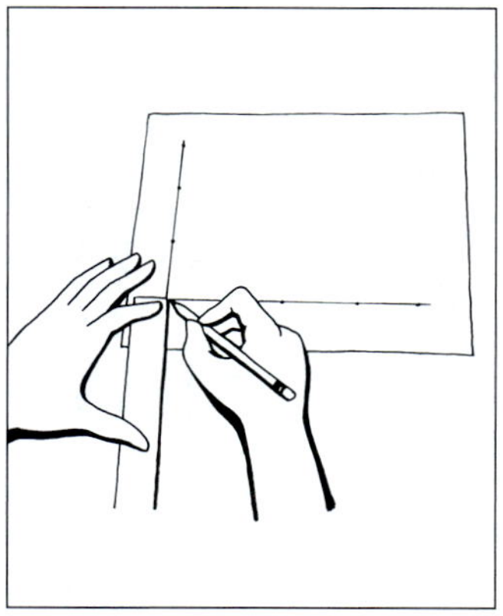

▲ Figure T–22

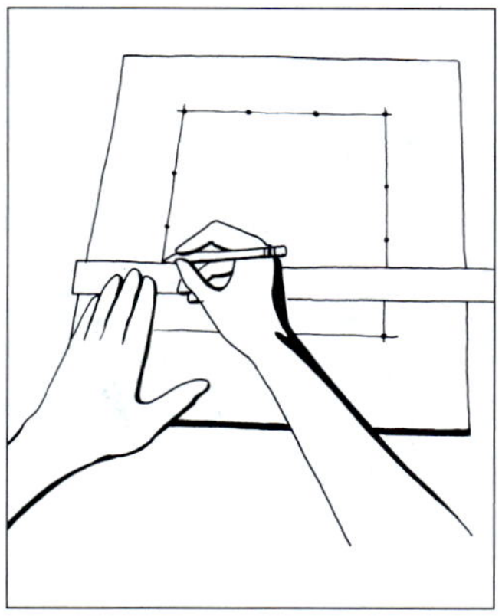

▲ Figure T–23

23. Making a Mat

You can add appeal to an art work by making a mat, using the following steps:

1. Gather the materials you will need. These include a metal rule, a pencil, mat board, cardboard backing, a sheet of heavy cardboard to protect your work surface, a mat knife with a sharp blade, and wide masking tape.
2. Wash you hands. Mat board should be kept very clean.
3. Measure the height and width of the work to be matted. Decide how large a border you want for your work. (A border of approximately 2½ inches on three sides with 3 inches on the bottom is aesthetically pleasing.) Your work will be behind the window you will cut.
4. Plan for the opening, or window, to be ¼ inch smaller on all sides than the size of your work. For example, if your work measures 9 by 12 inches, the mat window should measure 8½ inches (9 inches minus ¼ inch times two) by 11½ inches (12 inches minus ¼ inch times two). Using your metal rule and pencil, lightly draw your window rectangle on the back of the board 2½ inches from the top and left edge of the mat. (See Figure T–23.) Add a 2½ inch border to the right of the window and a 3 inch border to the bottom, lightly drawing cutting guidelines.

   Note: If you are working with metric measurements, the window should overlap your work by 0.5 cm (centimeters) on all sides. Therefore, if your work measures 24 by 30 cm, the mat window measures 23 cm (24 – [2 x 0.5]) by 29 cm (30 – [2 x 0.5]).

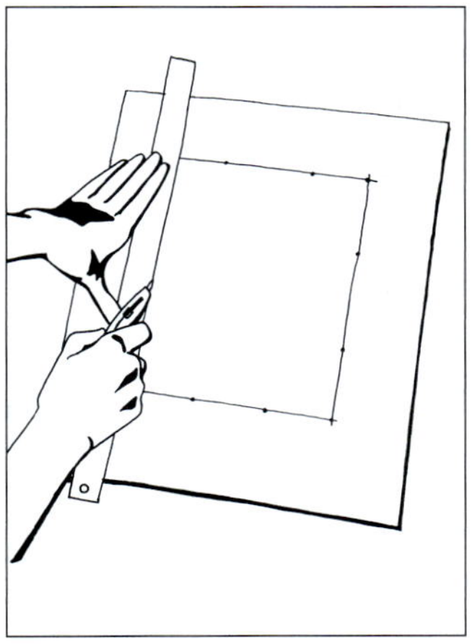

▲ Figure T–24

5. Place the sheet of heavy, protective cardboard on your work surface. Place the mat board, pencil marks up, over the cardboard. Holding the metal rule firmly in place, score the first line with your knife. Always place the metal rule so that your blade is away from the frame. (See Figure T–24.) In case you make an error, you will cut into the window hole or the extra mat that is not used for the frame. Do not try to cut through the board with one stroke. By the third or fourth stroke, you should be able to cut through the board easily.
6. Working in the same fashion, score and cut through the board along all the window lines. Be careful not to go beyond the lines. Remove the window.
7. Cut a cardboard backing for your art work that is slightly smaller than the overall size of your mat. Using a piece of broad masking tape, hinge the back of the mat to the backing. (See Figure T–25.)

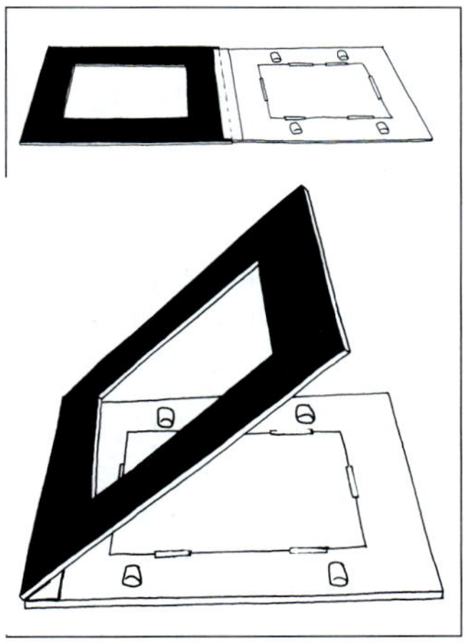

▲ Figure T–25

■ Making a Mat
Use with:
Creating a Nature Scene, page 106
Creating a Mixed-Media Cityscape, page 174
Creating a Seasonal Panorama, page 178
Making a Visual Autobiography, page 226

Safety Tip

Supervision in the Art Classroom Always supervise students carefully. Adequate supervision of students is required for both safety and liability reasons. Safety rules should be posted and explained at the start of each term—and these rules should be rigidly enforced. At no time should students be allowed to work in the classroom without direct supervision. Teachers should also make it a rule that students not bring to class and use their own art materials. It is possible that these art materials could contain unknown hazards.

- Mounting a Two-Dimensional Work
  Use with:
  Mixing Colors, page 12
  Egyptian Tomb Painting, page 86
  Painting a Storm, page 118
  Drawing a Figure in Action, page 150
  Painting a Watercolor Still Life, page 190

TECHNIQUE TIPS

Position your artwork between the backing and the mat and attach it with tape. Anchor the frame to the cardboard with a few pieces of rolled tape.

24. Mounting a Two-Dimensional Work

Mounting pictures that you make gives them a professional look. To mount a work, do the following:

1. Gather the materials you will need. These include a yardstick, a pencil, poster board, a sheet of heavy cardboard, a knife with a very sharp blade, a sheet of newspaper, and rubber cement.
2. Measure the height and width of the work to be mounted. Decide how large a border you want around the work. Plan your mount size using the work's measurements. To end up with a 3-inch border, for example, make your mount 6 inches wider and higher than your work. Record the measurements for your mount.
3. Using your yardstick and pencil, lightly draw your mount rectangle on the back of the poster board. Measure from the edges of the poster board. If you have a large paper cutter available, you may use it to cut your mount.
4. Place the sheet of heavy cardboard on your work surface. Place the poster board, pencil marks up, over the cardboard. Holding the yardstick firmly in place along one line, score the line with your knife. Do not try to cut through the board with one stroke. By the third try, you should be able to cut through the board.

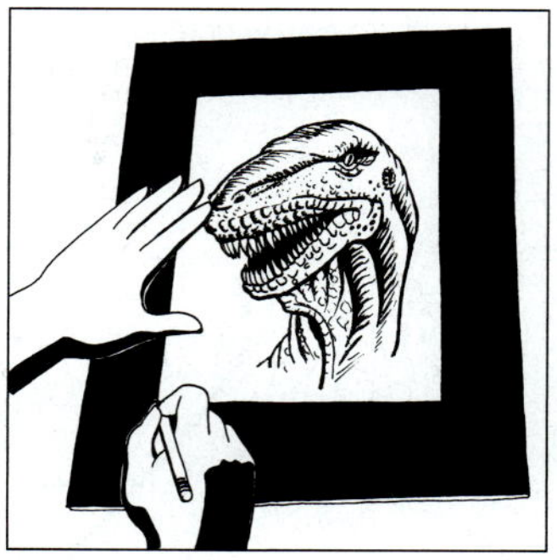

▲ Figure T–26

5. Place the artwork on the mount. Using the yardstick, center the work. Mark each corner with a dot. (See Figure T–26.)
6. Place the artwork, face down, on a sheet of newspaper. Coat the back of the work with rubber cement. (*Safety Note:* Always use rubber cement in a room with plenty of ventilation.) *If your mount is to be permanent, skip to Step 8.*
7. Line up the corners of your work with the dots on the mounting board. Smooth the work into place. *Skip to Step 9.*
8. After coating the back of your artwork, coat the poster board with rubber cement. Be careful not to add cement to the border area. Have a partner hold your artwork in the air by the two top corners. Once the two glued surfaces meet, you will not be able to change the position of the work. Grasp the lower two corners. Carefully lower the work to the mounting board. Line up the two corners with the bottom dots. Little by little, lower the work into place (Figure T–27). Press it smooth.

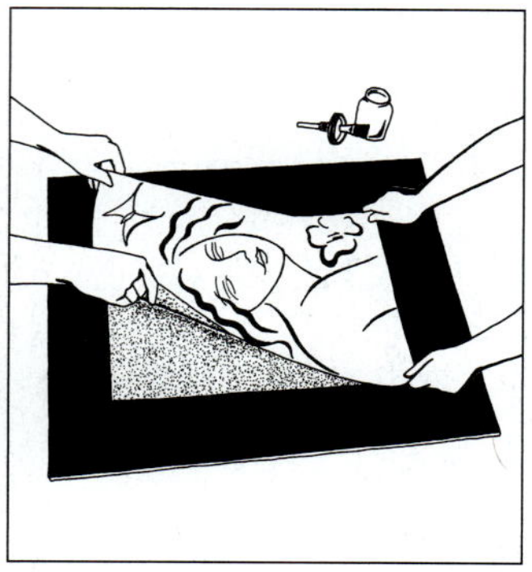

▲ Figure T–27

9. To remove any excess cement, create a small ball of nearly dry rubber cement. Use the ball of rubber cement to pick up excess cement.

25. Making Rubbings

Rubbings make interesting textures and designs. They may also be used with other media to create mixed-media art. To make a rubbing, place a sheet of thin paper on top of the surface to be rubbed. Hold the paper in place with one hand. With the other hand, rub the paper with the flat side of an unwrapped crayon. Always rub away from the hand holding the paper. Never rub back and forth, since this may cause the paper to slip.

26. Scoring Paper

The secret to creating neat, sharp folds in cardboard or paper is a technique called scoring. Here is how it is done:

1. Line up a ruler along the line you want to fold.
2. Lightly run a sharp knife or scissors along the fold line. Press down firmly enough to leave a light crease. Take care not to cut all the way through the paper. (Figure T–28).

Safety Tip

Clean-up Routines Remind students to clean up thoroughly and often. They should make certain to clean up spills immediately to prevent accidents. If dust results, have them use a wet mop or vacuum rather than a broom. Sweeping stirs up dust that could prove harmful to some students, particularly those who are asthmatic.

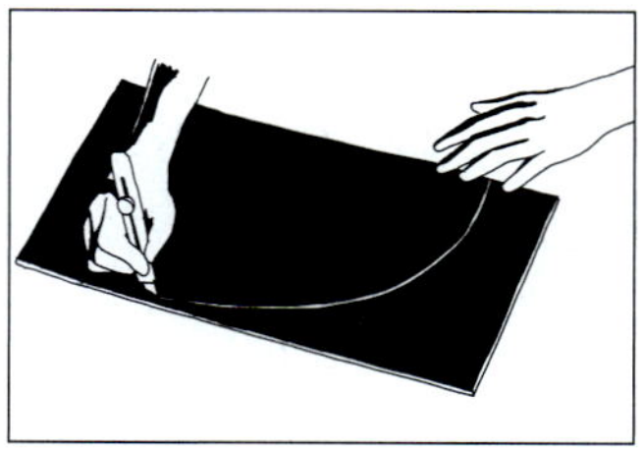

▲ **Figure T–28**

3. Gently crease the paper along the line you made.

To score curved lines, use the same technique. Make sure your curves are wide enough to ensure a clean fold. Too tight a curve will cause the paper to wrinkle (Figure T–29).

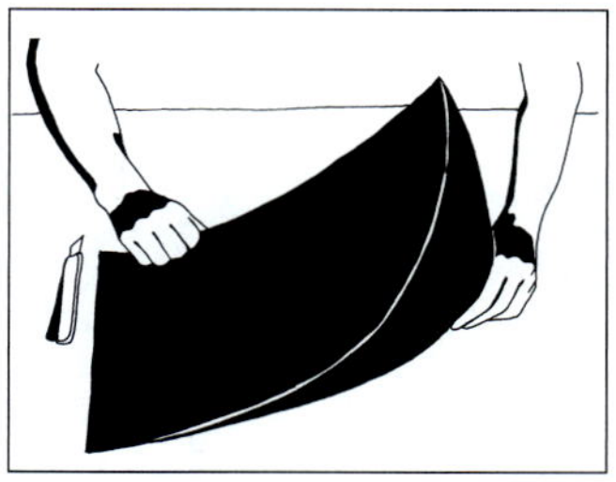

▲ **Figure T–29**

27. Making a Tissue Paper Collage

For your first experience with tissue, make a free design with the tissue colors. Start with the lightest colors of tissue first and save the darkest for last. It is difficult to change the color of dark tissue by overlapping it with other colors. If one area becomes too dark, you might cut out a piece of white paper, glue it over the dark area carefully, and apply new colors over the white area.

1. Apply a coat of adhesive to the area where you wish to place the tissue.
2. Place the tissue down carefully over the wet area (Figure T–30). Don't let your fingers get wet.
3. Then add another coat of adhesive over the tissue. If your brush picks up any color from the wet tissue, rinse your brush in water and let it dry before using it again.
4. Experiment by overlapping colors. Allow the tissue to wrinkle to create textures as you apply it. Be sure that all the loose edges of tissue are glued down.

28. Working with Glue

When applying glue, always start at the center of the surface you are coating and work outward.

- When gluing papers together, don't use a lot of glue, just a dot will do. Use dots in the corners and along the edges. Press the two surfaces together. Keep dots at least ½ inch in from the edge of your paper.
- Handle a glued surface carefully with only your fingertips. Make sure your hands are clean before pressing the glued surface into place.
- *Note:* The glue should be as thin as possible. Thick or beaded glue will create ridges on your work.

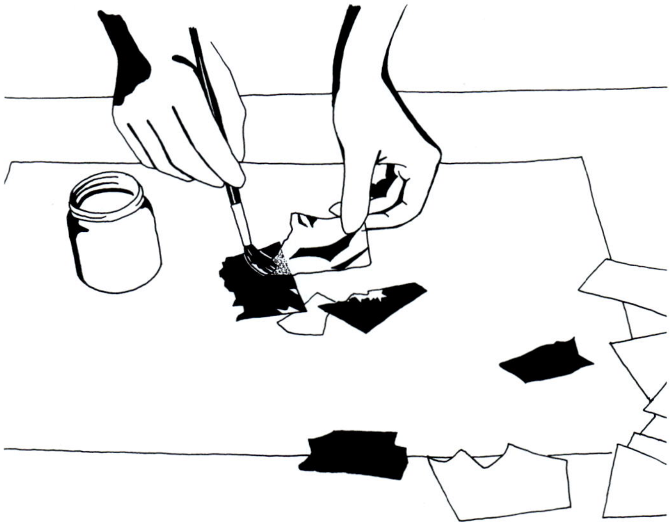

▲ **Figure T–30**

- Making Rubbings
  Use with:
  Making Rubbings for Texture, Studio Activity, page 21
- Making a Tissue Paper Collage
  Use with:
  Making a Collage, page 54
  Creating a Fantasy Bird Collage, page 266
- Working with Glue
  Use with:
  Making a Collage, page 54
  Creating an Expressive Face, page 146

TEACHER TO TEACHER

USING SPRAY FIXATIVES To protect drawings, you can spray them with fixative to prevent smearing. Test the spray first on a piece of scrap paper marked with the same drawing medium used in the drawing. Avoid getting the spray device too close to the drawing. Hold the spray device 12 to 18 inches from it. Keep the sprayer moving. Several light coats are better than one heavy one. Fixative dries rapidly. Spray fixative labeled *workable* is best. This term means that after you spray an area of a drawing lightly, you can still draw on it. Always use spray fixatives outside the studio in a well-ventilated area—outdoors, if possible.

Exploring Digital Media

When computers began to affect the way people communicated, artists began to explore how this new medium could be used to create and communicate art. At first, critics accused digital art media of doing all the "thinking," until they realized that these technologies were just new tools that artists could use to make some tasks easier. The artist makes the decisions, not the tool.

Table of Contents

MORE ABOUT...

IMITATING TRADITIONAL MEDIA While some art software programs imitate traditional media such as watercolor painting, or pen and ink, other programs create unique design styles that cannot be imitated by any other media. Digital technology saves time, paper, and paint by its ability to retain sketches of ideas that can be quickly recalled, edited, or deleted. The versatility of digital media increases their use among artists.

Scanners

Using Scanners

Whether you need to manipulate an artwork or insert a photo into a report, a scanner can be a useful tool. Scanners allow you to convert documents, illustrations, or photographs into digital image files on your computer. Once stored in a computer, these scanned files can be altered in an image-editing program.

Scanner Basics

Scanners come in a variety of shapes and sizes—from small, handheld devices to full-scaled, professional-quality drum scanners. Flatbed scanners are the most common household or schoolroom models. These machines include a flat, glass panel called the document table glass that is usually large enough to accommodate an 8½ × 110 image. Many scanners also come with film adapters to let you scan slides and negative or positive filmstrips.

Although individual makes and models will vary, there are some basic guidelines for using a flatbed scanner:

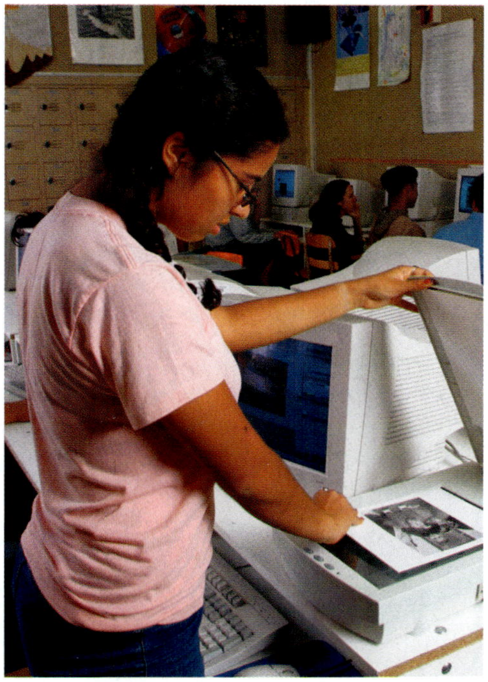

- Clean the glass to make sure there are no smudges or dirt.
- Open a host application on your computer—the program into which you plan to import the scanned image or document.
- Place the image facedown on the glass. Align with the appropriate corner markings.
- Adjust the settings in your host application program to specify the document source, image type, destination, resolution, and desired image size.

Always read the manual that came with your scanner for specific instructions and troubleshooting information.

Technology Notes

Resolution

Resolution is the fineness of detail that can be distinguished in an image. A basic rule of thumb is the finer the detail, the better the quality. In a high-quality image, even the smallest details can be distinguished. The resolution of a scanned image is measured in dpi (dots per inch). On a computer monitor, these dots are referred to as pixels. The more dots or pixels per inch, the better the quality. The recommended settings of dpi depend on the final output. For an image that will be seen on screen via e-mail or the Web, select a dpi between 72 and 96. For printing, the recommended settings vary depending on the type of image. Below are some typical settings which will vary depending upon the printer:

- **Color photo** — **300 dpi**
- **Text** — **400 dpi**
- **Text with images** — **400 dpi**
- **Line art** — **300 to 3200 dpi**

Discovering Scanners

From the beginning of Western or European art, one of its primary purposes was to record people, events, and ideas. Technology has changed and broadened avenues for expressing ideas. Scanners record an image by sending a beam of moving light across it and then translating the image into digital information. Have students think of creative ways to use the scanner beyond copying flat 2-D images. Try 3-D objects. Discover what happens if the objects move with the beam of light.

TEACHER TO TEACHER

ORGANIZING SAVED WORK Be sure students know how and where to save their work on the computer. Develop a consistent system for naming students' works. The name of each work, for example, might include the student's name, a number identifying the student's class period, and a short word or initials identifying the project name.

Scanning and Importing

Students can incorporate digital devices such as digital cameras, scanners, and computers into their growing knowledge of visual arts processes. Students can import their drawings and paintings into a computer paint or photo-editing program or create drawings and paintings with a computer paint program and print them for continued work by hand. Either way, the computer skills used can be assessed for techniques and final results. For more assessment strategies, refer to **Portfolio and Assessment Techniques** booklet.

Digital Cameras

Working with Digital Cameras

Digital cameras combine the features of the analog, or conventional, camera and the scanner. Like scanners, digital cameras allow you to download images to your computer's hard drive. Unlike scanners, digital cameras are cordless. They allow you to capture live images. Also, because the images are digital, you never need to buy film.

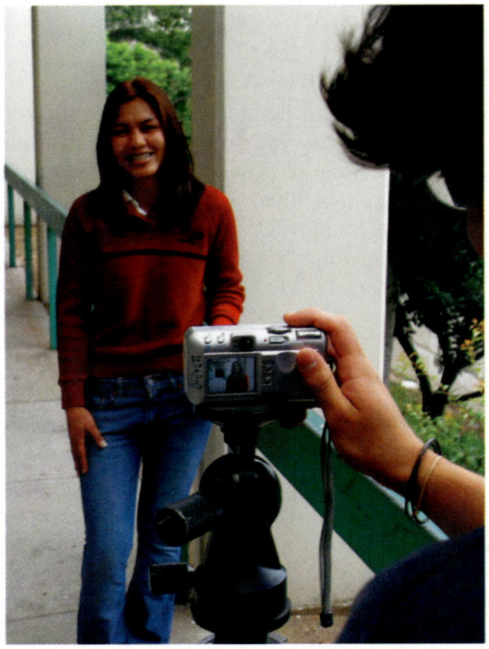

How Digital Cameras Work

Taking pictures with a digital camera is simple. If it is set on automatic focus, you just aim at your subject and click the shutter. Once you have taken a picture, you can download it to your computer. There, it can be edited, imported into a document, printed, or e-mailed.

Digital cameras vary widely in terms of features. One of the most important features is memory, or storage. The more memory the camera has, the more pictures you can take in a single session. (See "Technology Notes" for more on storage.) Other important features to look for include:

- **Software**. Most cameras come with software for downloading and manipulating images. Some lower-end cameras may not include software. Also, the quality of this software varies. Make sure the output file format is compatible with image-editing programs already installed on your computer.
- **Image quality.** Think about how you intend to use the camera. If you plan to take high-resolution pictures (pictures with very fine detail), you will need a better camera. For most art tasks and other student needs, medium resolution is usually fine.

Technology Notes

Storage

Storage is where your digital camera maintains digitized versions of the pictures you take. The least expensive models of digital cameras come with built-in *flash memory*. This type of storage cannot be upgraded. Flash memory can hold up to 25 images. These must be downloaded to your computer or erased before you can take more pictures.

The next step up in storage solutions is the *smart card*. A little like a floppy disk, a smart card is a removable flash memory module. The camera comes with one card, but you can buy additional cards as needed.

Top-of-the-line cameras have built-in hard disks that hold up to a gigabyte of data. Some newer cameras even come with writable CDs and DVDs.

MORE ABOUT...

Image Editing Professional photographers traditionally retouched, or altered, photographs in the darkroom until the invention of scanners and image editing software. Transformation is an important part of an image manipulation or editing. Transformations allow one to change the size or appearance of a photograph or just parts of a photograph to create different effects.

Graphics Tablets

Understanding Graphics Tablets

A graphics tablet is a high-tech version of drawing paper or a painter's canvas. Instead of brushes or other conventional media, you "draw" or "paint" on the tablet with an electronic pen. The image appears simultaneously on the computer screen. If you are unhappy with any pen stroke, you can simply select "Undo" from an on-screen menu. That portion of the drawing will disappear without a trace.

Tablet Fundamentals

Graphics tablets are as easy to install as they are to use. The tablet is plugged into the computer's USB (Universal Serial Bus) or serial port. There is no need to attach the pen, which is cordless. Once the accompanying software is installed, you are ready to draw. Graphics tablets may be used with all major paint and draw applications.

Tablets come in a range of sizes to suit different tasks. The smallest, which measure around 4 × 5″, are often used for sketches or to add objects to larger artworks. The largest tablets, at around 12 ×18″, are the size of a standard sheet of drawing paper. They can be used to create complete artworks.

The electronic pen is pressure sensitive. As with a conventional pen or brush, the harder you press, the darker and thicker the line. Some models boast as many as 1,024 levels of pressure sensitivity. Pressure sensitivity not only controls line thickness, but transparency and color as well. The higher the pressure sensitivity, the more natural your pen and tablet will feel.

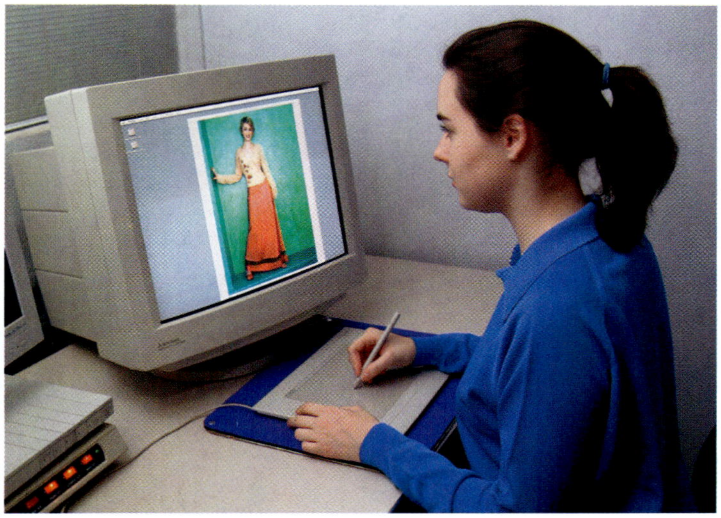

Technology Notes

Ergonomics

The term *ergonomics* refers to the application of science to the design of objects and environments for human use. In recent years, ergonomic engineers have been at work, developing computer tools that reduce the risk of repetitive stress injury. This is a type of injury affecting the nerves in the wrist and forearm.

Recent ergonomic developments include the cushioned electronic pen. The cushioned pen has a softer surface and weighs less than earlier pens. These features have been shown to reduce grip effort by up to 40 percent. The cushioned pen, thus, is more comfortable and safer to use.

DIGITAL MEDIA GUIDE

Investigating Line Tools

Have students investigate computer tools that create lines, such as the Pen, Pencil, or Brush. Try introducing a graphics tablet and stylus to students. Most models are pressure sensitive so that slow, heavy force produces a stronger line while faster, lighter strokes create thin, soft lines. Select a mood and have students use lines to convey the mood without obvious images, words, or symbols.

Applying Textures

Digital software offers a variety of textures that may be selected through Filter menus, Brush types, or Texture palettes. Or, you can create your own with just a Pencil tool and mouse or a stylus and graphic tablet. Have students practice by drawing natural objects that have distinct textures such as bark, leaves, and seedpods. Begin in black and white, so students focus on qualities and variations of lines and shapes in the texture.

MORE ABOUT...

Pressure-Sensitive Tablets These tablets, also known as graphics tablets, allow the artist to use a stylus just as a pen or pencil is used on paper. As the stylus is moved across the surface of the tablet, the line is recorded on the computer screen. There are many different sizes and types of graphics tablets. Some even offer the option of using your finger in place of a stylus.

Paint Tools

Paint tools provide a variety of choices for making lines and enhancing ones you want to emphasize in the image. Have students explore menu choices for Pencil, Brush, and Airbrush tools included in the software. Select settings that accentuate lines as you retrace them without making them appear too dominant. For example, if exploring the Airbrush tool, set the size of the dots of spray, the rate of flow, and the size of area it covers to match those in the image. Brush tools offer textures of special effects that can be applied. Or, select Brightness and Contrast under the Image menu, if available.

Using Color Palettes

In digital art programs, colors are presented in a palette rather than a color wheel. Most color palettes provide at least 256 color choices. Colors can be altered in value, intensity, hue, and saturation. Color seen on the screen, however, often does not match the printed image. While there are 256 screen colors, most printers only read 219 colors. As a result, certain colors are eliminated.

DIGITAL MEDIA GUIDE

Paint Software

Using Paint Software

Paint software programs offer new conveniences and capabilities to artists. Digital paints do not require any drying time. Not only is there no drying necessary, but paint mixing is a mathematical process. A digital artist has millions of colors in his or her palette. Previously used colors can be duplicated with ease and precision. Also, as with all art software, a painting can be easily erased and altered.

Paint Software Basics

In digital paint programs, images are created and stored as *bitmaps*. These are files made up of tiny dots called *pixels*. Since photographs downloaded to the computer have a similar format, paint programs do double duty as photo editors. A paint program can be used to brighten a dark photo, enhance its contrast, and so forth.

The main features of a paint program are:

- **A menu bar.** The menu bar contains file management commands (such as Open and Save), edit commands (such as Undo and Redo), and view commands (for example, Zoom).
- **The toolbox.** The toolbox contains art tools, such as brushes and pens, and image manipulation tools. These allow you to flip or rotate an image among many other options.
- **Palettes.** These are separate windows that allow you to control colors, brush tip sizes, line thickness, and the like.

Most paint programs also come with a variety of filters. These add special effects to an image or photo. One example is "feathering," which gives an image a wispy, cloudlike look.

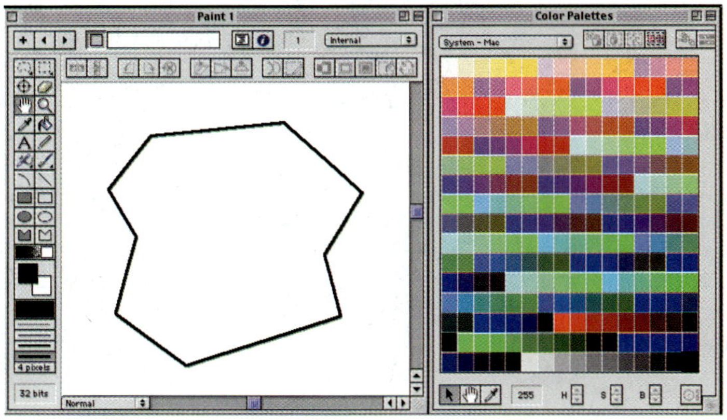

Technology Notes

Bitmap File Formats

One important aspect of working with paint programs is understanding file formats. There are many bitmap formats including JPEG, GIF, and PNG. It is worth noting that each of these formats has its own characteristics. JPEG images, for example, are compressed—stored in a smaller size. This means they take up less space on your computer's hard drive. GIF files are used for on-screen images. This format supports up to 256 colors and is often used for Web graphics. GIFs, however do not support print work. Finally, PNG images are increasingly turning up on Web sites and other environments shared by multiple computers and networks.

TEACHER TO TEACHER

PRACTICING PAINT TOOLS If students are not familiar with computer paint programs, allow them time to experiment. Encourage them to practice filling line drawings and closed shapes with color, exploring fill tools such as the Paint Brush, Bucket, Airbrush, and Gradients. Students learn quickly to make sure all lines connect before filling. A missing pixel can be located by using the Magnifying, Fatbits, or Zoom In tool.

Draw Software

Examining Draw Software

A cousin to paint software, draw software shares many of the same art tools and menus. Although draw programs lack some of the editing capabilities of paint programs, they are ideal for creating original artworks. They are especially well suited for creating logos, book or CD covers, and other art that combines images and text.

Draw Software Fundamentals

In draw programs, images are stored as mathematical formulas called *vectors.* These formulas carry information about the lines and curves that make up a particular drawing. Vector-based formats allow images to be *resized*—shrunk or enlarged—without distortion. This is one advantage of draw programs over paint programs. Paint programs produce images that cannot easily be resized without some loss of image quality.

Every object created by an artist using a draw program contains editable points and handles. By moving or dragging these elements, the artist can alter or smooth out shapes and curves with ease and precision. Digital illustrators often scan and import sketches into draw programs. This allows them to trace over the sketch with a mouse or stylus. They can then refine and color the sketch creating a digital illustration.

In addition to pens and brushes, the toolbox in a typical draw program contains assorted shape tools. For example, once shapes have been drawn, they can then be extended into three dimensions using an *extrude* command. Draw programs may include a selection of vector-based images that can be manipulated and used in other illustrations.

Recent draw software enhancements enable artists to work with bitmap images. Some sophisticated programs now come with filters, similar to the filters found in paint programs. These filters can be used for adding special effects to bitmap images.

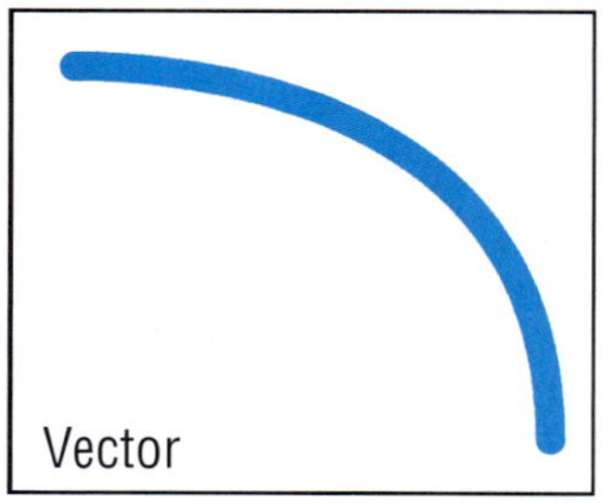

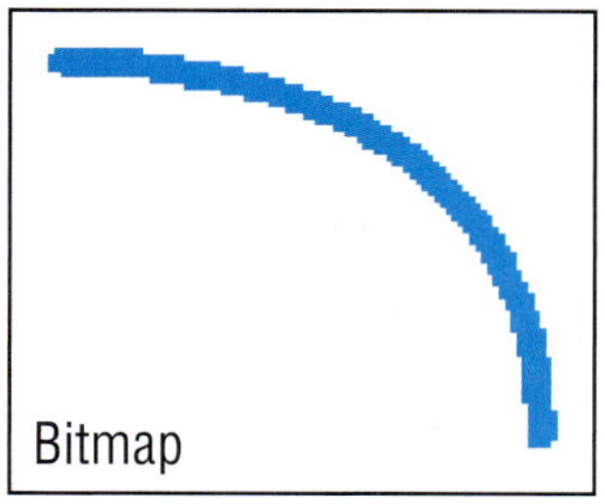

Technology Notes

Color Models

Color models are systems for arranging the colors of the visible spectrum so that they appear as the user intended when the image is viewed. The standard printing color model is CYMK. The letters are short for cyan (a greenish blue), yellow, magenta, and black. Most draw software comes preset for CYMK. Some artists instead work with the RGB (red, green, blue) model. For example, Web designers use the RGB model because their work is viewed on computer monitors. On monitors all the colors of the spectrum are created with only red, green, and blue.

Draw Programs

Draw software allows the artist to work in a vector graphics draw program, which means that paths are created in a connect-the-dots outline. One advantage is that draw images can be scaled to different sizes and still appear to have clear, smooth lines that retain crispness. In this environment, the artist can change, resize, or delete an object by clicking on it with an editing arrow.

MORE ABOUT...

Exploring Color Schemes Digital media are a great way for students to practice selecting and using color schemes to depict emotions without wasting materials. Remember to choose a CMYK color model for artworks that will be printed and RGB colors for artworks viewed only on a monitor or the Web. Have students select a mood that is not obvious. They should use simple shapes and brushes, and choose no more than five to ten colors from the color palette to express the emotion.

Using Perspective Techniques

Both paint and draw programs have tools and menus to create converging lines or to arrange, overlap, size, and manipulate details, color, and value without wasting paper or paint. With new 3-D graphics software, artists can render two-dimensional shapes as three-dimensional objects in a three-dimensional environment. 3-D graphics software is now easier to use and requires less memory than previous versions.

3-D Graphics Software

Examining 3-D Graphics Software

Creating art in three dimensions is nothing new. Creating *digital* art in three dimensions *is* relatively new. The ability to give form to computerized objects only became a reality some 15 years ago. That was when the first 3-D modeling programs arrived on the market. Since that time, the capabilities of these programs have been expanded dramatically. Today, digital artists can create entire animated movies using a single 3-D software package.

How 3-D Software Works

There are many types of 3-D graphics programs. Some are designed specifically for creating and editing 3-D images for use on Web sites and CD-ROMs, or print materials. Other 3-D modeling programs are designed for architects and engineers. These programs are used to create complex digital blueprints for buildings and other structures.

Like draw and paint programs, 3-D programs include tools for creating objects. Once created, objects are placed on a *stage.* The stage is similar to the *work area* in draw and paint programs. The stage has three surfaces, or *planes*—one for width (X), height (Y), and depth (Z). Each plane includes grid lines that allow the user to place objects at exact locations in space.

Similar to movies, 3-D programs include *lighting* and *camera* controls. Lighting allows the user to adjust the intensity and direction of the light source. The camera control determines the view and angle from which the object is seen.

Technology Notes

Rendering

When you see a movie on the big screen, you don't see the lighting, cameras, or film crew. The same is true of 3-D modeling and animation programs. The final product is the *rendered* scene or movie. *Rendering* is a process by which the program mathematically assigns shading, texture, and other art features to one or more bitmaps. Behind-the-scenes details do not appear in the rendered scene or movie.

Rendering can take anywhere from an hour to a day or more, depending on the resolution. If you are previewing a scene or movie, choose a low resolution. Make sure to allow ample rendering time for the final "cut."

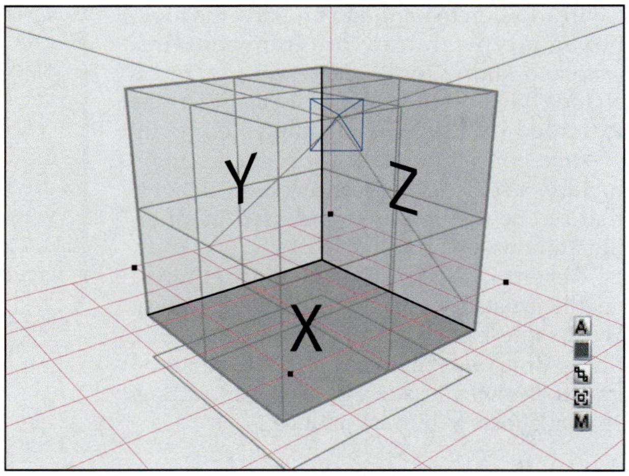

MORE ABOUT...

Enhancing Objects Computer paint or image-editing programs make it easy to enhance objects to make them appear three-dimensional. Shading and shadows are added with Brush, Airbrush, or Fill tools that provide control of flow, color, brush, size, density, and special effects. Light and dark hues can also be selected from color menus and palettes. Make gradients, or colors that gradually change value from light to dark, to add shading to objects to make them look three-dimensional. Explore tools and menus that affect color, value, intensity, and opacity.

Frame Animation Software

Understanding Frame Animation Software

In comic strips, the action occurs frame by frame. It is precisely this principle that is at work in frame animation software. Using this software, the digital artist is able to animate words and images quickly and easily. The programs even provide tools for "publishing" the finished movie on the Internet.

Frame Animation Basics

The first step in creating a frame animation is choosing your "actors." Objects, created in other graphics programs or by hand, may be imported. Frame animation software also includes tools for creating original simple objects and text.

Once the "cast" has been established, objects are placed on the *timeline.* This is a series of numbered frames beginning at zero. An object's position on the timeline determines the point at which it enters or exits the scene.

The third step in an animation is to create movement. An object can be made to move by means of one of the following:

- **A preset effect.** Animation software comes with a number of preset actions. These include *fade in, fade out, blur,* and *transform.* The last of these controls an object's size, angle, and so on.
- **A motion path.** The software also permits the user to create original motion paths. These tell an object where and how to move at any given moment.

Technology Notes

Sound

Animation software allows the addition of sounds and music to accompany the action. Sound files may be recorded using the computer's microphone. Another source of sounds is clip art Web sites, many of which offer free sound clips. Since sound files tend to be large, they can increase the size of the movie, possibly causing the action to pause. There are two ways of avoiding this:

- Looping sounds. This is having a single sound file, such as background music, repeated over and over.
- Using compressed sound files. AVI sound files tend to be larger because they are not compressed. Choose MPEG-3 files whenever possible. These require far less memory.

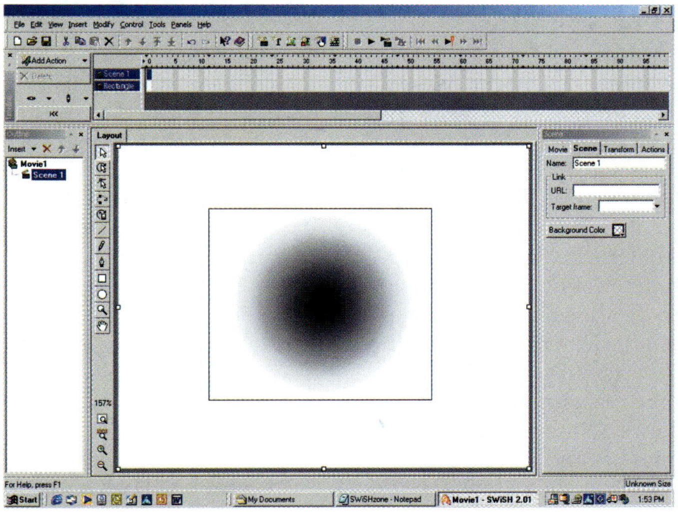

Sequencing Images

Developing a sequence of related images helps students become more proficient with the tools palette in a computer program. This task also allows for skill development assessment in both art and technology. The sequencing of three images may be chronological, seasonal, or developmental. Ask students to explain the tools and processes they used to achieve the sequence. The images can be imported into a computer slide show for class presentations. For more assessment techniques, refer to **Portfolio and Assessment Techniques** booklet.

TEACHER TO TEACHER

The One-Computer Classroom If your school provides only one computer in the art classroom, you may want to use computer time as a reward for students who complete quality work early. This "free time" can allow students to experiment with new approaches. You might suggest that students explore digital media to create the kinds of works they have made from traditional media; encourage them to compare and contrast the two outcomes.

Presentation Software

Have students create a slide show about balance in art using presentation software. Students can work in small groups to plan the show, take pictures, and scan images. Have students open the application and select New Slide Show. There are many templates to choose from. Have students insert the images, adding a new slide for each. Finally, students should include a title and closing page.

DIGITAL MEDIA GUIDE

Multimedia Presentation Software

Using Multimedia Presentation Software

Imagine viewing an exhibition of your own portfolio. With multimedia presentation software, there is no need to imagine. These remarkable programs allow you to create digital slideshows right on your computer. You can even add narration, background music, and special visual effects to your presentation.

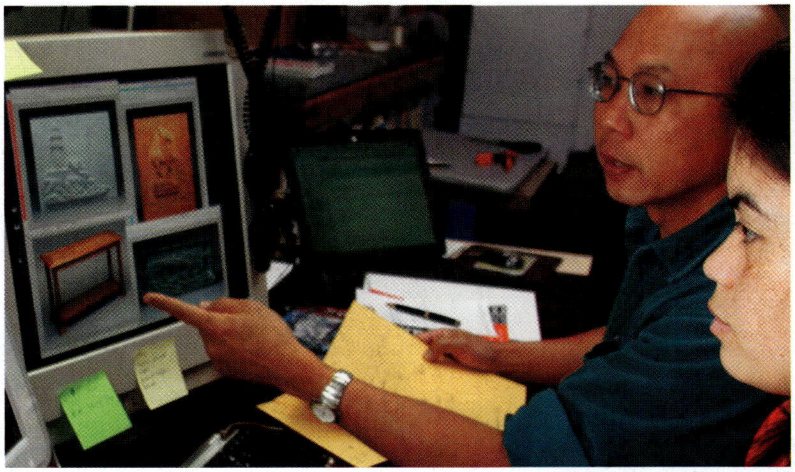

Multimedia Presentation Software Basics

The chief building block of the multimedia presentation is the *slide*. This is an individual screen containing a combination of multimedia *objects*. Objects are digital files that are *embedded*—contained within—a larger file. Sound, image, and animation files are all potential objects in a presentation.

In some multimedia presentation packages, objects can be added to a slide simply by dragging them from an *object bar*. In other programs, you use menus to embed objects.

Once you have created all the slides for your presentation, you are ready to *produce* your show. During the production phase, you attend to details such as the following:

- **Transitions**. *Transitions* are special effects between slides that add visual interest to your show. Known in some packages as "wipes," transitions include *dissolve* (one slide fading into another) and *explode* (a slide appearing to burst apart, revealing the next).
- **Timing.** This is the amount of time any given slide appears on the screen. Timing is one of the most important aspects of a multimedia presentation. If slides change too quickly, your viewers will not have a chance to appreciate each artwork fully. If a slide appears on the screen too long, the presentation may drag.

Technology Notes

Executable Files

Some multimedia presentation programs allow you to turn your shows into *executable files*. An executable file is a self-contained program that will open and run when double-clicked. All the icons on your system's desktop are executable files.

Executable files may be e-mailed or burned onto a CD or other portable medium. This permits viewers to run your slideshow even if they do not have presentation software installed on their computers.

MORE ABOUT...

Desktop Publishing Programs This kind of software allows the user to combine words and images, and to design pages for newspapers, yearbooks, and other graphic design products. As you and your students become more experienced in using the computer, you may want to explore programs for multimedia presentation, three-dimensional design development, animation, Web design, and video manipulation or editing.

Page Layout Software

Using Page Layout Software

The page you are reading right now was produced using page layout software. In the last two decades, this type of software has replaced earlier manual methods of page layout. It has revolutionized the process whereby printed materials are created.

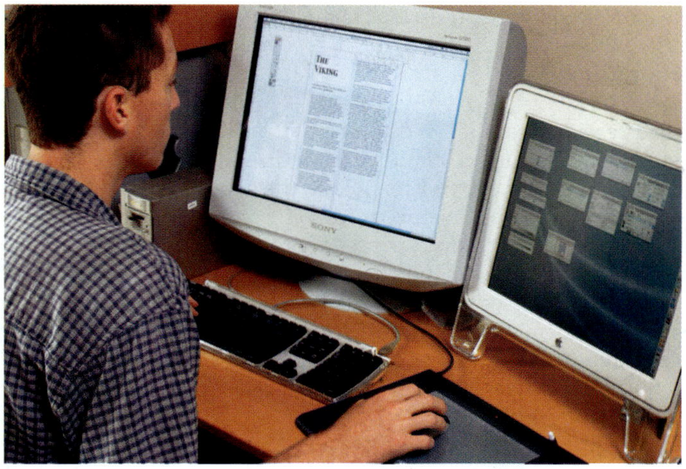

Page Layout Software Basics

Page layout software is one of the chief digital tools of the graphic artist. When the application is opened, a blank text page appears surrounded by *panes.* Panes are windows containing the tools used to manage and arrange text. The text is imported from a word processing program.

The first step in the layout process is to set specifications for the printed page. These include the number of columns, the size of margins, and whether the page will be vertical (portrait) or horizontal (landscape).

Next, the graphic artist adds *frames* to the page. Frames are blank rectangles with dotted outlines used to hold either text or pictures. In the simplest layout, the artist creates a single text frame and "pours in" the text file. This type of layout is used for novels and other books that consist entirely of running text. For more complex page layouts, several frames of different sizes may be added. The page you are looking at right now contains a picture box and several different text boxes.

The typeface, or *font,* used for a particular block of text is chosen from a list of typefaces in the text pane. The text pane also allows the artist to control such features as paragraph indents and line spacing.

Technology Notes

Style Sheets and Libraries

Page layout programs contain several powerful features that further streamline the graphic artist's work. Among these are *style sheets* and *libraries.* Style sheets are sets of user-defined instructions for how to treat a particular block of text or heading. They will include information including the font name, size and color, and the amount of vertical space above and below each line of text.

Libraries contain design elements like logos, and special features that are used repeatedly throughout the document. The artist simply drags a copy of the item from the library window into position on the page.

DIGITAL MEDIA GUIDE

Exploring Digital Options

Give students opportunities to explore the computer's many options by requiring them to use more than one medium in assignments. When combining images from a variety of sources, it is important to plan ahead. Remind students to consider page layout and orientation of the final image. If a horizontal or landscape view is required, this can usually be selected in the File menu under Page Setup.

MORE ABOUT...

Electronic Portfolios Similar to traditional portfolios, electronic or digital portfolios are great assessment tools. Establish the purpose of the portfolio—either to show work at a given point in time or to show growth over a period of time. Determine the interface of presentation program that will be used to create the portfolios. Have students import their selected images. Each image should be labeled with a title, the size, and media. Then have the artist add an introduction and closing reflection. For more assessment techniques, refer to ***Portfolio and Assessment Techniques*** booklet.

CAREER SPOTLIGHT

Using the Career Spotlights

On these pages, you will find teaching suggestions to help you introduce students to many art-related job opportunities and careers. At the bottom of the page, you will find a list of addresses of organizations that students can write for additional information.

Analyzing Advertisements

Divide students into small groups. Select a variety of magazines from different interest areas, such as fashion, mechanics, photography, architecture, teen life, current events, health, sports, science, science fiction, television, video games, computers, and so on. Have each group compare such things as the types of advertisements and the types of advertising techniques used to capture the attention of the specific audience. Have each group present their findings to the class.

Appreciating Architecture

Have students each sketch a building in their neighborhood. Then, have them examine the building materials used to create the structure they have drawn. Invite an architect in, if possible, to discuss such topics as the design process, the use of computer aided design programs, and how building materials are chosen for buildings in the area.

Advertising Artist

Advertising artists design the artwork that is used in advertisements. They usually work for an advertising agency. They may also work for a publication, such as a magazine or newspaper. Some advertising artists work in the advertising department of a large corporation, such as a store or restaurant chain.

Advertising artists work as part of a design team. This team includes an art director, designers, and copywriters. First, the art director develops a concept, or idea, for an advertisement. The copywriters write the words that will appear in the ad. Then the artist creates a design that works with both the art director's concept and the words. Many advertising artists use computers when creating their artwork.

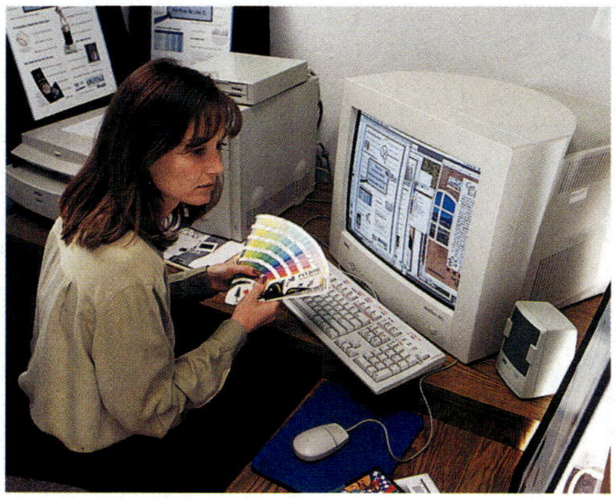

A career as an advertising artist usually requires a college education in art or design. Courses in computer design techniques are very valuable. Once they are hired, advertising artists may also receive on-the-job training.

Architect

An architect is an artist who designs buildings and other structures. Your home, school, and local shopping mall were all designed by architects. An architect prepares plans that show both the interior and exterior of a building. These sketches include floor plans that show the placement of rooms, hallways, doors, windows, closets, and other features. They also show the exterior walls on all sides of the building and a top-down drawing of the roof.

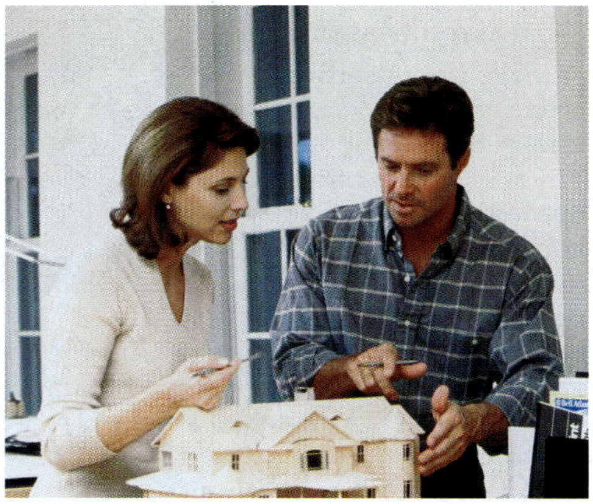

A building design must be not only visually pleasing but also functional and safe. When planning a building, architects must consider how the structure will be used. For example, the design for a home would be very different from the design for a restaurant or hospital. Architects must also keep in mind the needs of the people who will use the building. This includes such subjects as traffic patterns, living and work areas, and storage space. They must also know about heating and cooling, ventilation, and plumbing.

Architects need a college degree in architecture. They take courses in math, engineering, and drafting. Because many architects use computers to produce their designs, they also take courses in computer-aided design. In addition, they must pass an exam to become licensed.

RESOURCES BEYOND THE CLASSROOM

GUEST SPEAKERS Bring in resource people during the time that you are presenting careers. Students will be interested in learning from people who work directly in the art-related field. You may also invite the guidance counselor to discuss art-related careers and to talk about the various schools and colleges that specialize in art-related careers. If you live in an urban area, it will not be difficult to find people who work at some of these careers. Even the smallest newspaper in a rural area needs a layout person. The local television station will also employ someone who fits one of the career categories mentioned in this section.

Art Director

Art directors are responsible for the look of the advertisements that you see in newspapers, in magazines, and on television. They are also responsible for the style and design of magazines, and of books like this one. Art directors most often work in the fields of advertising and publishing.

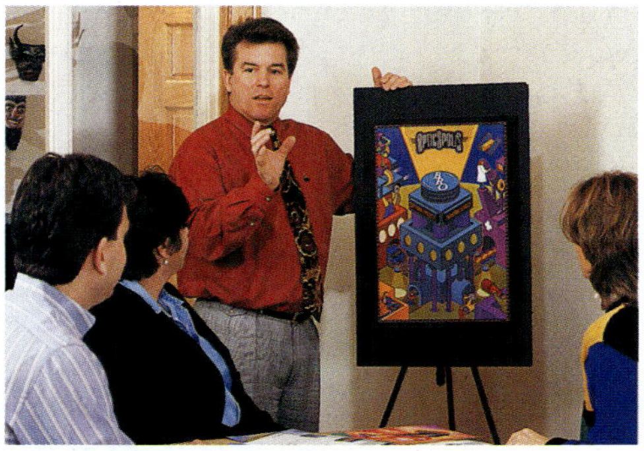

An art director studies the information that needs to be presented. He or she must decide how that information can be shown in a visually appealing way. The art director then works with a design team that includes artists, designers, and copywriters. The art director oversees the team's work and makes sure that the final printed material is satisfactory.

Most art directors have a college education. Courses should provide a well-rounded background in art and design. Art directors study graphic design, drafting, layout, photography, and computer design. Several years of on-the-job training are required before a person can become an art director.

Art Teacher

Art teachers instruct students in the use of various art materials and techniques. They also educate students in the theories and principles of art criticism, aesthetics, and art history. In middle schools, art teachers provide general art instruction. Art teachers in high schools may specialize in a specific area, such as painting, drawing, or crafts.

In a classroom, the art teacher helps students create their own artwork. Students are taught how to use a wide variety of media, such as pencils, charcoal, pastels, paints, and clay. The teacher encourages students to analyze their own work as well as the works of master artists.

Art teachers must have a college degree. Their educational background includes courses in both art and teaching. Many art teachers continue to study and exhibit their own artwork throughout their teaching careers. An essential part of being an art teacher is a love of art and a desire to encourage this appreciation in others.

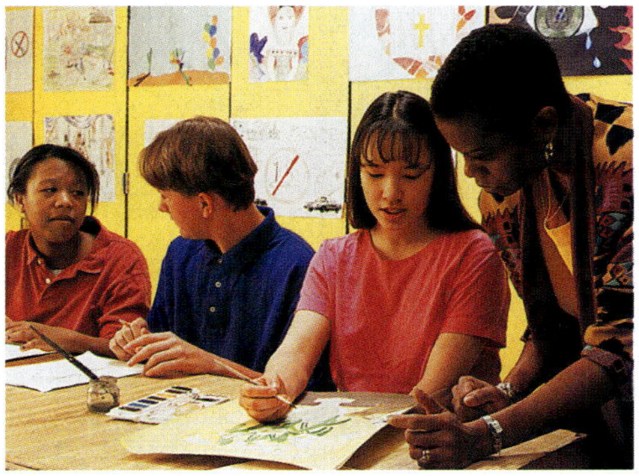

Art Directors

Explain that art directors often supervise teams of artists, designers, and production people. These teams may work in the same location or may work independently in their own studios in another location, even in another state. Ask students to explore ways that art directors might communicate with "outside" design teams and direct the work of several individuals and groups. Students might mention the use of scanners, modems, e-mail, phone conferencing, fax, and overnight express delivery services as means of ongoing, fast communication. Visit a local art director at a magazine or advertising agency, if possible, to have students observe a typical day in the life of an art director.

Art Teacher

Invite a school counselor to speak to the class and explain the requirements for attending art and design schools. Have the counselor explain the additional requirements for becoming an art teacher in your state.

Ask students to seek out art teachers who may work in park district programs, hospitals, retirement centers, or museums. Have students interview an art teacher to find out about that person's background, training, and areas of expertise.

MORE ABOUT...

ADVERTISING CAREERS You may wish to have students write to the following for information about careers in advertising management.

The American Advertising Federation
1101 Vermont Avenue NW
Washington, D.C. 20005-6306

TEACHER ASSOCIATIONS Have students contact the following organizations to learn more about teachers' unions and education-related issues:

American Federation of Teachers
555 New Jersey Avenue NW
Washington, D.C. 20001

Graphic Artist

Ask a graphic artist to come in and demonstrate some of the software and multimedia programs graphic artists often use or need to be familiar with, such as Photoshop, Quark, or Adobe PageMaker, for example.

Artist

Artists create works of art. Their work is usually classified as either fine art or applied art. Fine art, such as a painting, is created simply to be viewed and appreciated. Applied art, such as ceramics or other crafts objects, serves a more practical purpose.

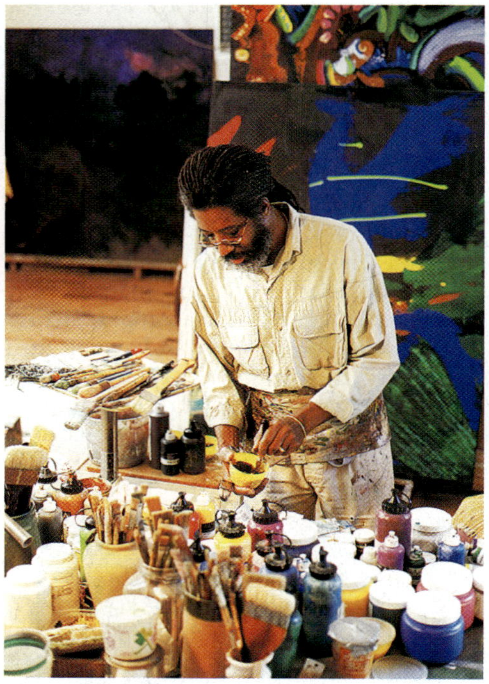

The work of an artist may involve a variety of media. The media are the materials used to create the art. A painter, for instance, might use oil, watercolor, or acrylic paint. A sculptor might create art out of stone, clay, or wood. Other artists might create jewelry, pottery, or furniture from such materials as metal, clay, or plastic.

Although not all artists have a college education, almost all have had formal art instruction. This training includes studio art classes, such as drawing, painting, and design. It also includes courses in art history. One of the most important requirements for a career as an artist is a natural talent in art.

Graphic Artist

Graphic artists design artwork for many types of products. These products might include packaging and promotional displays, brochures, advertisements, magazines, and books like the one you are reading. Graphic artists are often employed in the publishing or advertising fields. However, they may also work in other areas, such as designing the boxes that hold videos and computer games. They frequently work as part of a design team.

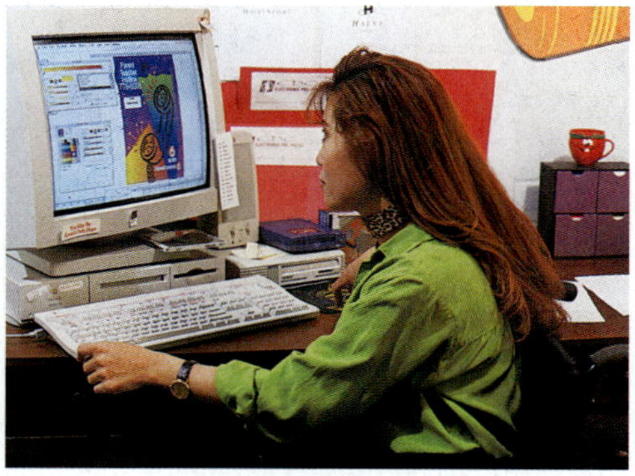

Most graphic artists use computers to help in the creation of their artwork. Computer technology saves time by performing some of the tasks that artists previously had to do by hand. For example, artists can use computer graphics to easily experiment with a variety of colors, shapes, and designs.

A career in graphic art generally requires a college education and formal art training. In addition, graphic artists must have an in-depth knowledge of computer graphics. Because the computer field changes so rapidly, graphic artists must continually learn about new technology.

MORE ABOUT...

Graphic Artists Careers Students may wish to write for more information on education and career resources in the field of graphics art and design. Have them contact the Special Interest Group on Computer Graphics (SIGGRAPH) at:

ACM SIGGRAPH
1515 Broadway, 17th Floor
New York, New York 10036

Illustrator

The work of an illustrator revolves around drawing. Illustrators may create many different types of artwork. Most specialize in one field, such as technical illustration. Illustrators often work in the publishing and advertising industries.

A technical illustrator specializes in drawing diagrams. These might be included in instructional manuals. They help explain how to use appliances or equipment, such as a computer or VCR. A fashion illustrator draws sketches of clothing and accessories. Fashion illustrations might appear in catalogs, advertisements, or magazines. A medical illustrator prepares detailed drawings of the human body. These drawings are often found in medical textbooks and journals.

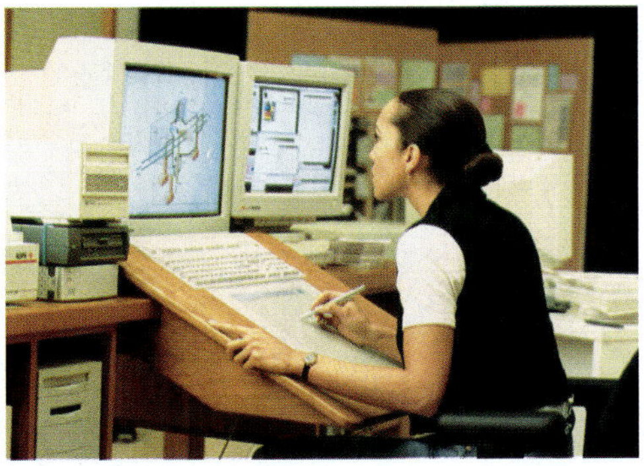

Most illustrators have a college degree in art. Besides drawing, they learn about design, composition, and perspective. Illustrators who want to concentrate on one area must also take courses related to that subject. For example, a medical illustrator must study biology and medicine.

Industrial Designer

Have you ever wondered who designed your favorite toys and electronic games? Those are the work of industrial designers. They design manufactured products, such as computers, kitchen appliances, and cars. Industrial designers usually work for large companies, such as toy or equipment manufacturers.

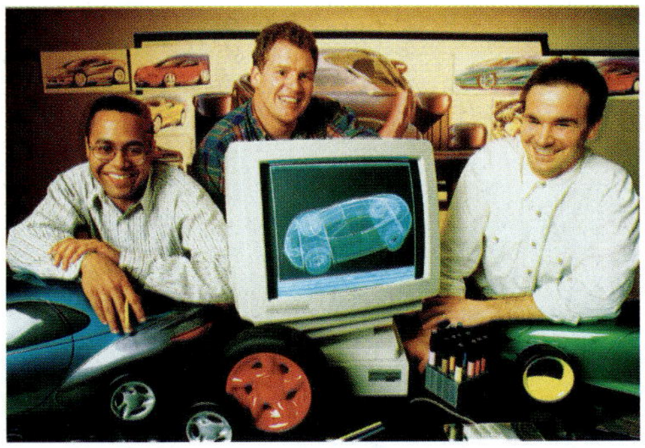

Industrial designers develop new products. They also make improvements to existing products, such as adding new features or changing the design of an automobile. When developing a product, industrial designers first do research. The designers need to know who will use the product and how they will use it. Industrial designers also must evaluate similar products that are already available. Then they combine this knowledge with their artistic ability. Their goal is to create products that will work well and be popular with consumers.

A career in industrial design requires a college education. In addition to art courses, industrial designers study computer-aided design. Many designers use computer technology when developing products.

Illustrator

Bring in examples of a variety of illustrators' work: medical illustration in journals, textbooks, and encyclopedias; technical illustration in manuals, brochures, and catalogs; and fashion illustrations appearing in catalogs and magazines. Also bring in a variety of trade books, textbooks, and children's books that are heavily illustrated. Ask students to choose one type of illustration to explore further, finding additional examples and researching the illustrators (if possible) responsible for the work.

Industrial Designer

Emphasize to students the broad spectrum of design included in the category of industrial design. Ask students to identify a few commonplace objects that they use every day, such as pens, backpacks, athletic shoes, bicycles, caps, doors, desks, refrigerators, and so on. Ask each student to choose an object to redesign or modify in some fashion, drawing their designs and writing a brief explanation of the purpose and appeal of their object. Have students share their designs and the process they used in their redesigns, and have them explain what improvements they think their particular design achieved.

MORE ABOUT...

ILLUSTRATIONS For information on careers in illustration have students contact:

The Society of Illustrators
128 East 63rd Street
New York, New York, 10021-7303

A brochure that describes careers in industrial design and lists academic programs in the field is available from the Industrial Designers Society of America. For price and ordering information write:

Industrial Designers Society of America
45195 Business Court, Suite 250
Dulles, VA 20166-6717

Interior Designer

Divide the class into small groups or pairs of students and have each group imagine that they are interior designers who have been asked to plan a student lounge for the school. Before they make their design, they should survey their classmates to see what they would like in a lounge and what they think the purpose and use of the lounge should be. Have them try to think of the lounge as a multipurpose area that could serve as space for a meeting, a party, art exhibits, and so on. What areas will they need to include? How should the spaces be furnished and decorated? Have students use their creativity. Have them make sketches for their lounge and include paint chips and wallpaper and floor covering samples to show the color scheme for the room.

Landscape Architect

Ask students to identify two buildings in the local area: one that has a pleasing landscape design and one that would benefit from an improved landscape plan. Ask students to analyze what they like about the first design and what is lacking in the second. Then ask students to make recommendations for an improved plan and create a small scale model of their plan using cardboard and found objects. As students work out their designs, remind them to think about color, shape, and form, and to consider what type of plants and construction materials they would use to help integrate the building with its surrounding environment.

Interior Designer

Interior designers plan the interior space of buildings. These buildings might include homes, offices, hotels, or restaurants. Sometimes interior designers plan renovations, or upgrades, to existing buildings. In addition to preparing drawings, interior designers choose furniture, carpeting, and window coverings. They also select lighting and color schemes. Interior designers must make sure that all of these individual parts work together as a whole and are aesthetically pleasing.

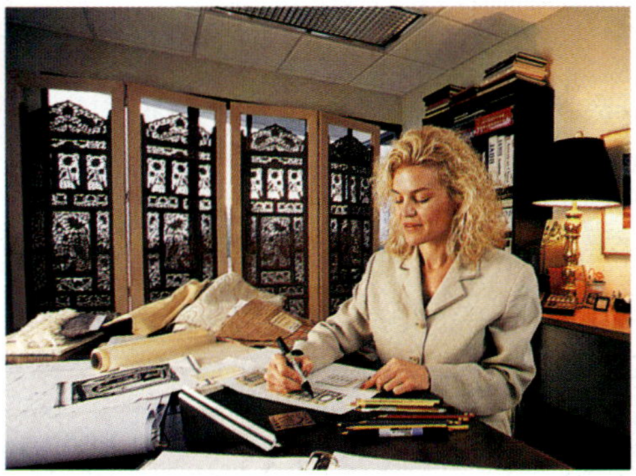

When planning an interior space, the interior designer must always consider the client's needs, tastes, and budget. Many designers use computer programs to create several versions of an interior plan. Using a computer also allows the designer to easily make design changes to suit the client's wishes.

To be an interior designer, you need a college education. Courses include drawing, design, and art history. Interior designers also must show creativity, a flair for color, and an eye for detail.

Landscape Architect

Landscape architects combine their love of nature and the environment with their artistic ability. They design outdoor areas such as those surrounding houses or apartment complexes, shopping centers, and office buildings.

Landscape architects choose which types of trees, bushes, and flowers are best suited for the location. Then they draw sketches of how these plants should be arranged. One goal of a landscape architect is to make sure that the design is not only functional but also attractive. Another goal is to make sure that the design works well with the natural environment. As in all design fields, more and more landscape architects are using computers to complete their work more efficiently.

A career in landscape architecture requires a college education. Courses include landscape design and construction, surveying, and city and regional planning. In addition, landscape architects study science and nature and take studio art courses.

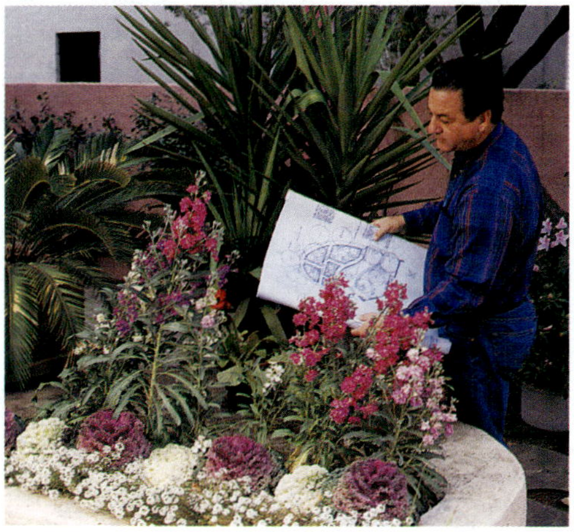

MORE ABOUT...

Interior Designers For information about careers in interior design, contact:

American Society of Interior Designers
608 Massachusetts Ave. N.E.
Washington D.C. 20002-6006

Museum Curator

Some people combine their love of art and museums to become museum employees. There are a wide variety of museums across the country. Some showcase artwork, such as paintings, sculpture, or photographs. Others house objects of historical value, such as antique clothing or furniture. Still others display items related to science or natural history, such as dinosaur skeletons.

People who work in museums may have several different types of jobs. A curator chooses and obtains the objects that will be displayed in the museum. An assistant curator helps the curator set up the museum exhibits. A conservator cares for and preserves the objects kept in the museum. A tour guide provides information about exhibits to the museum's visitors and answers their questions.

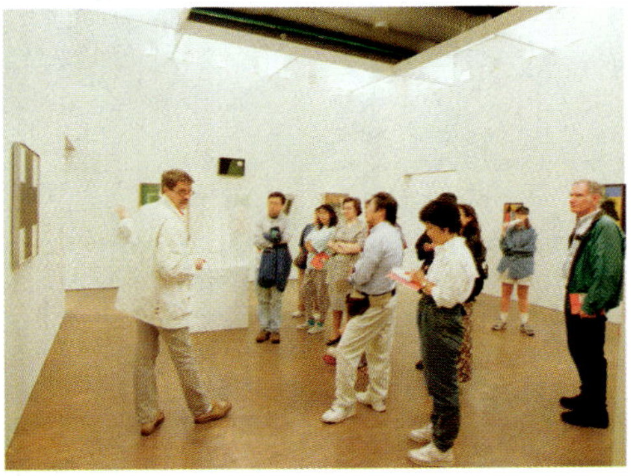

The degree of education required for a museum worker varies depending on the type of work. Most museum workers, however, are highly educated. Many have advanced college degrees and are considered experts in their field.

Photographer

Photographers are skilled artists who use their cameras to create artwork. Their work varies greatly depending on what type of photographs they take. For example, a catalog photographer works in a studio and takes pictures of objects such as food, clothing, or jewelry. A newspaper or magazine photographer works in the field, taking pictures of people and events in the news.

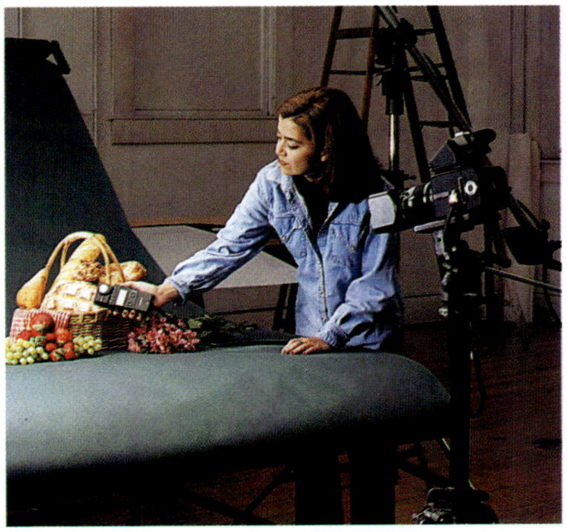

The work of photographers involves more than just taking the pictures. Photographers must first visualize the shot or set it up in an artistic way. After the pictures are taken, many photographers develop their own film in a darkroom. Then they print the slides or photographs.

A career as a photographer requires formal training in photography. Many photographers have a college degree in art. Photographers who specialize in certain areas, such as science, may need additional courses in that field. Beginning photographers sometimes receive training on the job by assisting a professional photographer.

Museum Curator

Invite a museum employee or volunteer who works at a local museum to come in and discuss what types of jobs exist locally. Encourage students to ask specific questions about day-to-day tasks.

If there is no museum close by, ask students to write a letter to any particular museum of their choice, anywhere in the country. Have students research different kinds of museums, with their locations and addresses. Before students write to a museum to ask about the work a museum employee does, have them draft a copy to share with the class. Encourage students to brainstorm pertinent questions to ask.

Photographer

Ask students to list kinds of publications in which they can observe photographs. They may mention newspapers, catalogs, magazines, fliers, books and textbooks, and encyclopedias. Have students look through such publications and notice the credit lines under the photographs. Ask them to discuss photographers whose names they see repeatedly and whether those individuals seem to specialize in one particular type of photography. Some examples of magazines students might examine for photos are *Time, Newsweek, National Geographic, Sports Illustrated, Discover, Architectural Digest, Smithsonian,* and various travel magazines.

MORE ABOUT...

Museum Curators For general information about careers as a curator and schools offering courses in curatorial science, contact:

American Association of Museums
1575 Eye St, N.W.
Suite 40
Washington D.C. 20005

Field Trips

Field trips contribute greatly to a course. If class field trips are not possible, individual trips that one or more students may take after school or on weekends might be arranged with the help and supervision of parents.

All trips will be more successful if you set up guidelines to help students understand the objectives. Research done prior to the trip and a follow-up evaluation will add to the value of the experience. Students should know what to look for and what to expect to gain from the experience. You might point out that the business people they visit may be possible employers some day. Appropriate conduct and dress on such trips is always in order. Students should also know what kind of follow-up will be expected, such as a written evaluation, a quiz, or class discussion.

Make the necessary arrangements for a field trip well in advance to ensure that students are welcome. Establish a time schedule and follow it carefully. While museums, organizations, and industries are usually happy to conduct tours of their facilities, the staff members usually have other responsibilities, and group tours must be prearranged in a thoughtful manner. In addition, keep the attention span and interests of your students in mind as you make such arrangements.

Textile Designer

The fabric of the clothes you are wearing was designed by a textile designer. The word *textile* refers to cloth or fabric. Textile designers create and draw patterns for fabric. The fabric may be used in clothing, furniture upholstery, draperies, or rugs. Textile designers sometimes create their own original designs. At other times, they may adapt a design or develop one based on a certain theme. Textile designers work for companies that manufacture fabric.

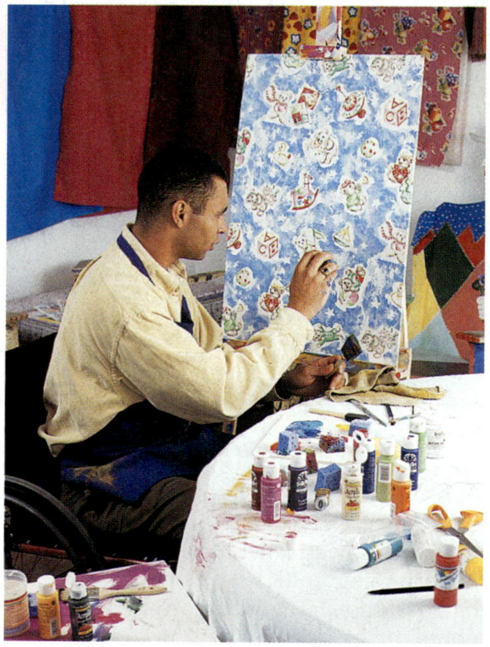

Like other artists, textile designers must have creativity and artistic skill. They must also understand how fabric is constructed and manufactured. In addition, they need to be aware of current fashion trends. With this knowledge, they are better able to create popular designs.

Textile designers generally need a college education. They study art, design, and textiles. Many textile designers also take courses in computer technology, including computer-aided design.

Web Designer

There are countless numbers of sites on the World Wide Web. These sites may be sponsored by companies, organizations, or individuals. They are most often used to provide information, promote products, and answer questions.

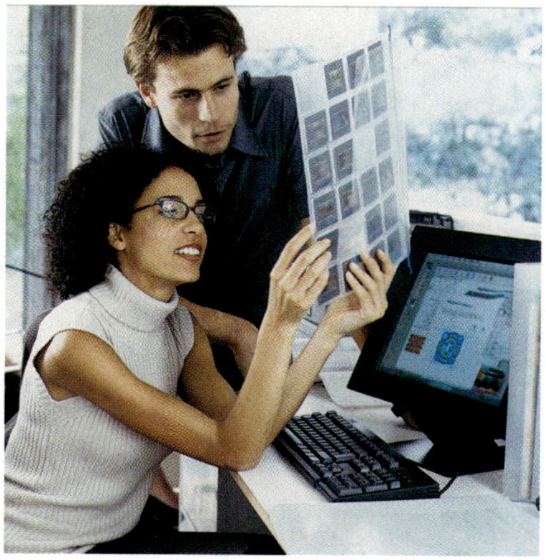

Web designers use computer software to create and maintain these sites. The work involves laying out web pages, designing graphic elements, and creating electronic links to other sites. Web designers may create sites for a large company or organization. They may also work for a design firm that creates sites for many companies.

To be a Web designer, a person must have a background in art, with an emphasis on design. A Web designer must also have technical training in computers and computer programming. Keeping current with the latest technology is an important part of the job.

MORE ABOUT...

Art and Design For a list of accredited schools of art and design, contact:

National Association of Schools of Art and Design
11250 Roger Bacon Drive, Suite 21
Reston, Virginia 20190

ARTSOURCE

Performing Arts Handbook

The following pages of content were excerpted from *Artsource®: The Center's Study Guide to the Performing Arts,* developed by the Music Center Education Division, an award-winning arts education program of the Music Center of Los Angeles County.

The following artists and groups are featured in the Performing Arts Handbook.

ARTSOURCE

MORE ABOUT...

ARTSOURCE The materials provided in the Performing Arts Handbook are excerpted from Artsource: The Center's Study Guide to the Performing Arts, developed by the Music Center Education Division. The Music Center of Los Angeles County, the largest performing arts center in the western United States, established the Music Center Education Division in 1979 to provide opportunities for life-long learning in the arts, and especially to bring the performing and visual arts into the classroom. The Education Division believes the arts enhances the quality of life for all people, but are crucial to the development of every child.

Artsource Performing Arts Handbook

(pages 310–324)

Purpose

The 15 features in the Performing Arts Handbook are designed to enrich students' learning by correlating what they learn about the visual arts to the performing arts—dance, music, and theatre. The featured performers and groups in this handbook were specifically chosen to supplement the chapters in the student text.

Using the Handbook

The following categories suggest ways to use the **Performing Arts Handbook.**

MINI-LESSONS Use the features as stand-alone lessons about dance, music, and theatre.

MOTIVATOR Use the features to introduce related chapters. Listed on each chapter opening page of your Teacher Wraparound Edition is a segment that correlates each chapter to this section. As you plan lessons, consider how you might use the Performing Arts Handbook as a way of introducing the chapter's content.

EXTENSION Refer to the recommended Artsource feature found on the chapter opening page of your Teacher Wraparound Edition, and use the appropriate feature to expand the study of that chapter. Students may volunteer for this Extension activity, or you might assign groups of students to read the feature, then complete the questions and activities on their own.

Alvin Ailey American Dance Theater

Setting the Stage

Direct students to read the paragraph about the Alvin Ailey American Dance Theater. Have students view the Artsource selection, if available.

OPTIONAL
Artsource: Performing Arts Package DVD or VHS segment 5 (Playing time 3:32)

Connecting the Arts

Using the Discussion Questions on this page, help students recognize that many artists have used difficult experiences to express a "revelation" in their work. Possible responses:

1. After experiencing a difficult struggle, life can often seem more precious.
2. Flock of birds—position of arms and their grouping; different level of dancers; people working together show a sense of unity and repetition.
3. Sense of humor, always late, caring, a good friend, likes basketball.

Extensions

- Have students complete the Creative Expression Activities.
- Use the Artsource: Performing Arts Package for more information about The Alvin Ailey American Dance Theatre and for additional related activities.

Dance Alvin Ailey American Dance Theater

The Alvin Ailey American Dance Theater performs classical ballet and modern works by well-known choreographers, but the group is best known for dances drawn from Alvin Ailey's African American background. These masterpieces capture the essence of his black experience in America and feature musical themes based on African American cultural heritage such as blues, spirituals, and jazz. "Revelations," the dance shown on this page, has become the "signature piece" for the company because it clearly captures the spirit and aesthetics of the company and its creator. The choreography includes different dances, all of which celebrate the human spirit and its ability to overcome adversity.

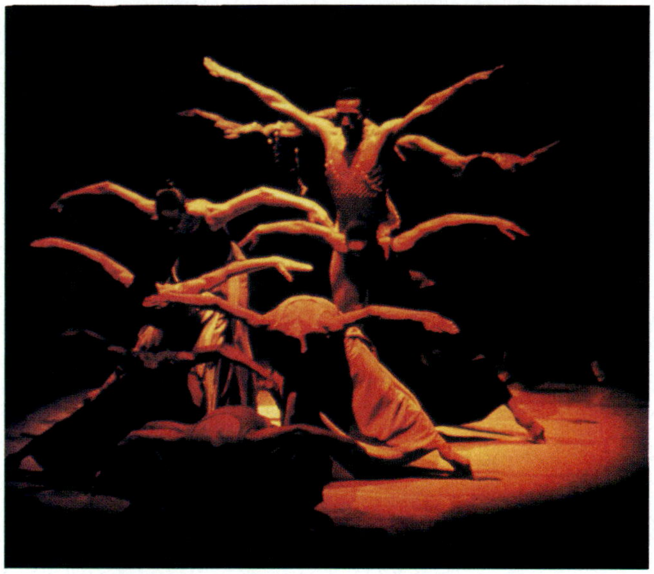

Alvin Ailey American Dance Theater. Alvin Ailey, founder and choreographer. "Revelations." Photo: Bill Hilton.

Discussion Questions

1. The word *revelation* means something that was unknown and is now revealed. Discuss a revelation a person might have while struggling through a difficult situation.
2. Look at the photo on this page. What images come to mind as you study the positions of the dancers? Discuss how unity and variety are demonstrated.
3. Imagine you are going to create a signature piece to represent yourself. Identify three to five traits that describe different aspects of your personality. Demonstrate these traits with a gesture or expressive movement. Which ones seem appropriate for your signature piece? Why?

Creative Expression Activities

Language Arts Think about Discussion Question 1. Write about a time when you or someone you know had a revelation.

Dance/Theatre After discussing Question 3, find gestural movements that can express each of the personal traits you listed. Choose one you like and abstract it in several different ways by exaggerating the size, doing it in slow motion, giving it a rhythmic pattern, adding a turn or change of level, or performing it as you walk. Share ideas with a partner and discuss what worked best.

APPRECIATING THE PERFORMING ARTS

DANCE "Revelations" was choreographed in 1960. In it there are several sections that evoke strong emotions. It expresses through movement the joy and strength of the music and captures a sense of personal freedom, wit, and humanity. The beginning formation of the dance is particularly memorable. A tight grouping of men and women reach out in unison, conveying powerful feelings of support, dignity, and hope. Alvin Ailey allowed the music he selected to influence his ideas and his choreography. Since his death in 1989, Judith Jamison, one of his most well-known dancers, has taken over as artistic director.

The Alley Cats is a "Doo Wop" quartet that blend four voices, bringing their own contemporary style to the tunes of the fifties and sixties. They formed their group in 1987 and began their musical journey with Disney's "Blast to the Past" salute. They have been featured performers on stages at Disneyland, Knott's Berry Farm, and the White House. "Doo Wop" is a vocal form that is done *a cappella,* singing without musical accompaniment. During the 1950s, young men and women began forming singing groups in their neighborhoods. Street corner singing soon gave birth to new ideas and the creation of "Doo Wop," a type of rhythm and blues technique using nonsense syllables in intricate, harmonic arrangements. "Sh-Boom," one of the most popular tunes of the fifties, uses meaningless sounds to fill the beats and create background chants. In between, there are fragments of poetic lyrics.

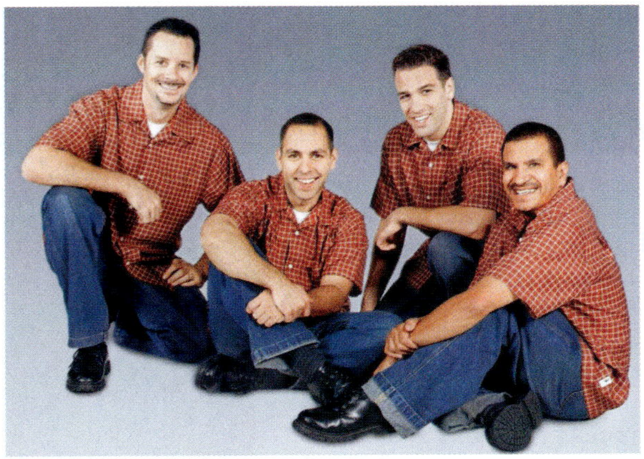

Photo: Skyline Displays.

ARTSOURCE

Discussion Questions

1. Like many modern pop songs, there are very few actual lyrics in "Sh-boom." Some of the words are "Life could be a dream, Sh-Boom, if I could take you to Paradise up above, Sh-Boom, and you would tell me that I'm the only one that you loved, my life could be a dream, sweetheart, hello, hello again, Sh-Boom, Sh-Boom." Think of a similar popular song you know and discuss comparisons between the lyrics.
2. What other facts do you know about the history and culture of the 1950s? What does this song express to you about the times and attitude of the people, as expressed through popular music?

Creative Expression Activities

Language Arts Write one line about love, friendship, sadness, or a wish. Say the line over several times until you can hear the scansion, or correct rhythm, for your line of verse. Once it feels right, begin to play with it by adding nonsense sounds that can precede, or fit in-between, the words. This can be alternated with doo-doo doo-ah, wop, sh, la-la, ding-a-ling-a-ding-dong, hello-hello again, chick-a-boom, wa-wa, or other combinations of syllables. As you continue to play with the rhythm and phrasing, the lyrical line will naturally begin to develop a melody. See how many variations you can find.

APPRECIATING THE PERFORMING ARTS

Music American culture often leads the world in terms of expression in popular music, songs, and fashion. It is most often created by the younger generation. New greetings, handshakes, gestures, and postures come into being and are exclusive to adolescents of a particular time. Researching and revisiting the popular arts of any modern generation gives us clues as to the influences and folk heroes that inspired much of popular expression and culture. The music of the 1950s was lighthearted, with a strong basic beat, and speaks of a time of relative calm and order.

The Alley Cats

Setting the Stage

Direct students to read the paragraph about The Alley Cats. Have students listen to the Artsource selection, if available.

OPTIONAL
Artsource: Performing Arts Package Audio CD track 7 (Playing time 2:12)

Connecting the Arts

Using the Discussion questions on this page, help students recognize that music can also be expressed without the use of any musical instruments. Student responses will vary.

Extensions

- Have students complete the Creative Expression Activities.
- Encourage students to share experiences that compare and contrast the aspects of their popular culture with the culture of another time period, such as the 1950s. They might also interview family members and ask them questions to identify the specific differences in music, dress, language, and dance that defined them as teenagers.
- Use the Artsource: Performing Arts Package for more information about The Alley Cats and for additional related activities.

The Chameleons

Setting the Stage

Direct students to read about The Chameleons and their mime play *Life Cycle.* Have students view the Artsource selection, if available.

OPTIONAL
Artsource: Performing Arts Package DVD or VHS segment 12 (Playing time 5:10)

Connecting the Arts

Using the Discussion Questions, help students recognize that there are cycles of action in many aspects of life. Possible responses are:

1. It's about the different stages of life from birth to death. Cycle means period of time when events repeat in the same order.
2. They want the audience to grasp the importance of life.
3. Sports: referees give hand signals to show the call, and athletes use hand movements to show the action or play. Gestures are a simple and direct way to communicate ideas clearly.

Extensions

- Have students complete the Creative Expression Activities.
- Encourage students to share experiences and knowledge about how gestures and mime are used in various aspects of their lives.
- Use the Artsource: Performing Arts Package for more information on The Chameleons and for additional related activities.

ARTSOURCE

Theatre The Chameleons

Life Cycle follows the relationship of two characters, one female and one male, from infancy through childhood, adolescence, courtship, marriage, parenthood, middle age, old age, death, and finally rebirth. On a bare stage and without costumes or props, Keith Berger and Sharon Diskin use pantomime and mime techniques to project a variety of human emotions and enact the rituals of friendship, love, and separation. Their work began with a desire to do a story about universal relationships. They began by improvising ways to create age changes by altering their posture, expressions, and attitudes.

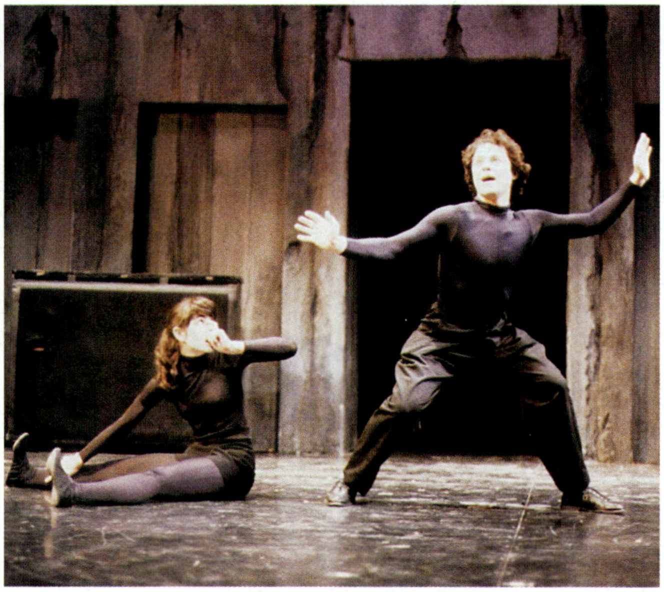

The Chameleons: Keith Berger and Sharon Diskin. *Life Cycle.* Photo © 1990, Craig Schwartz.

Discussion Questions

1. Why do you think Keith Berger and Sharon Diskin titled their mime piece *Life Cycle?* What does the term *cycle* mean, and how does this relate to the stages of life?
2. Study the photo on this page and describe the situation and what you think is being communicated by the two mimes.
3. Identify situations where people use gestures to communicate ideas rather than words. Discuss why this is done in each of the situations.

Creative Expression Activities

Pantomime Show the following ideas in mime movement: fishing, writing a letter, stirring cake batter, dealing cards, getting dressed, sewing a button on a shirt, and bowling.

Playwriting Create a mime scenario about a day in the life of a specific character. Then write an outline of the action to use as a mime script.

APPRECIATING THE PERFORMING ARTS

THEATRE Mime is the art of dramatic representation by movement and gestures only, without words. It can also refer to a performer specializing in this art. The Chameleons' performance style is characterized by strong emotions and natural characters involved in real-life dramas. They are masters of the traditional mime illusions and are acclaimed for their original mime repertoire. *Life Cycle,* a mime play, is performed to the music of Johann Pachelbel's "Canon in D Major." It was chosen as a score because it is repetitive and circular, underscoring the idea that life is a cycle with a beginning, middle, and end.

Dance Pilobolus Dance Theatre

Pilobolus Dance Theatre, an internationally acclaimed American dance company, was formed at Dartmouth College in 1971. Searching for a new dance style, they created a unique and highly original choreographic process that relied on trust, collaboration, and a weight-sharing approach to partnering. Each new dance project begins with several days of improvisation, where the dancers are called upon to find inventive movement through "creative play." This process, which has no rules, is guided by one or more of the four artistic directors. Dances that have emerged from this process feature a startling mixture of humor, artistry, and creativity. The name *Pilobolus* refers to a real-life phototrophic fungus found in pastures. This small mushroom has an eye that grows or moves in response to light. When ready to reproduce, it can project its spores nearly eight feet into the air. This little organism captures the essence of the way the company works and creates. Now over 30 years old, Pilobolus remains an original, influential, and versatile force in the dance world.

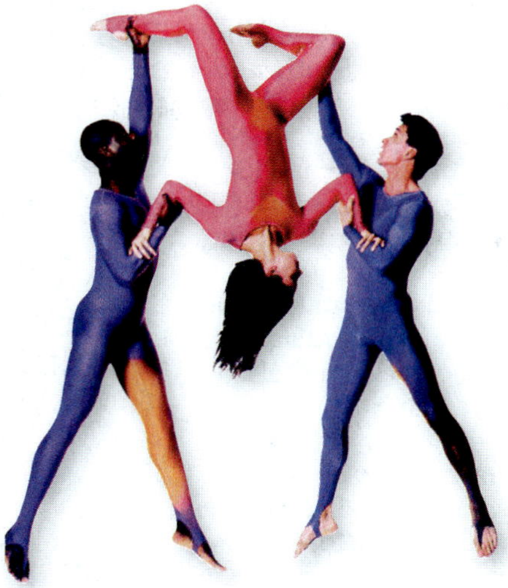

Pilobolus Dance Theatre performs "The Brass Ring." Photo: Howard Schatz.

ARTSOURCE

Discussion Questions

1. Discuss how dance can vary so much in purpose and style. Styles include: ceremonial, folk, ballet, jazz, modern, musical theatre, tap, and hip-hop. What do you think is the definition of *dance?* How many different reasons can you think of for why people dance?
2. Pilobolus's dancers collaborate to solve problems and find inventive solutions in order to create their work. Give examples of situations where you have improvised to solve a problem, either alone or in a group. How did collaboration help you and the group in this process? Were you inventive? What other organizations or systems use these ideas?

Creative Expression Activities

Language Arts/Dance Using verbs and adverbs as starting points for movement, write a selection of these words on cards. Pair each verb with an adverb. Arrange three to five sets in a sequence and design a small group dance study. Improvise the words using elements of dance, such as level, size, direction, energy, and tempo to make the movements interesting. Practice working as a team to find solutions to the problem. Verbs delineate the action sequence and adverbs tell how the action is to be done, i.e., turning slowly or running hesitantly. Prepositions can be added to define the relationships between the dancers.

APPRECIATING THE PERFORMING ARTS

Dance "The Brass Ring," choreographed by Pilobolus Dance Theatre, is a work about the relationship between dance, games, and athletics. It had its premiere at the 2000 Olympic Games in Salt Lake City, Utah. There are excerpts from nine different musical pieces that change the mood and energy of this evolving work. Each set of musical influences has a different affect of the dancers who work with each piece in a different way. It takes place under an imaginary night sky with bright stars. The dancers express grace and beauty as they perform an exquisite series of beautiful lifts and counterbalances.

Pilobolus Dance Theatre

Setting the Stage

Direct students to read the paragraph about Pilobolus Dance Theatre. Have students view the Artsource selection, if available.

Optional
Artsource: Performing Arts Package DVD or VHS Segment 11 (Playing time 3:15)

Connecting the Arts

Using the Discussion questions on this page, help students recognize how dance can vary in purpose and style. Possible responses are:

1. Dance is a way of expressing oneself through movement. People can dance for personal, social, cultural, and artistic reasons.
2. Responses will vary.

Extensions

- Have students complete the Creative Expression Activities.
- Ask students to name some of the physics principles they know about, such as balance, counterbalances, opposing forces that press and pull away from a center point, centrifical force, and chaos into order. Pose the question of how these ideas might be incorporated into either athletic or artistic body movement.
- Use the Artsource: Performing Arts Package for more information about Pilobolus Dance Theatre and for additional related activities.

Ballet Folklórico de Mexico

Setting the Stage

Direct students to read the paragraph about the Ballet Folklórico de Mexico and examine the photograph of the dancers. Have students view and listen to the Artsource selections, if available.

OPTIONAL
Artsource: Performing Arts Package
- **DVD or VHS segment 1 (Playing time 7:15)**
- **Audio CD track 1 (Playing time 3:10)**

Connecting the Arts

Using the Discussion Questions on this page, help students recognize the connections between visual and performing arts and that they are both expressions of a culture. Possible responses:

1. The sphere or sun.
2. Circle, rectangles, intersecting lines.

Extensions

- Have students complete the Creative Expression Activities.
- Have students work in groups to create three sun motifs. Then choose one and make a design that shows movement using eight repetitions of the motif.
- Use the Artsource: Performing Arts package for more information about the Ballet Folklórico de Mexico and for additional related activities.

For over 25 years, Ballet Folklórico de Mexico has presented authentic folk dances from different ethnic groups within Mexico. Amalia Hernández, the Artistic Director of the company, creates exciting dances based on ancient traditions. From the time of the Olmec Indians to the birth of modern Mexico, more than 30 distinct cultures have influenced Mexican culture. The dance shown in this photo is called "Los Mitos" and features the pageantry and ritual of these cultures before the arrival of the Spaniards.

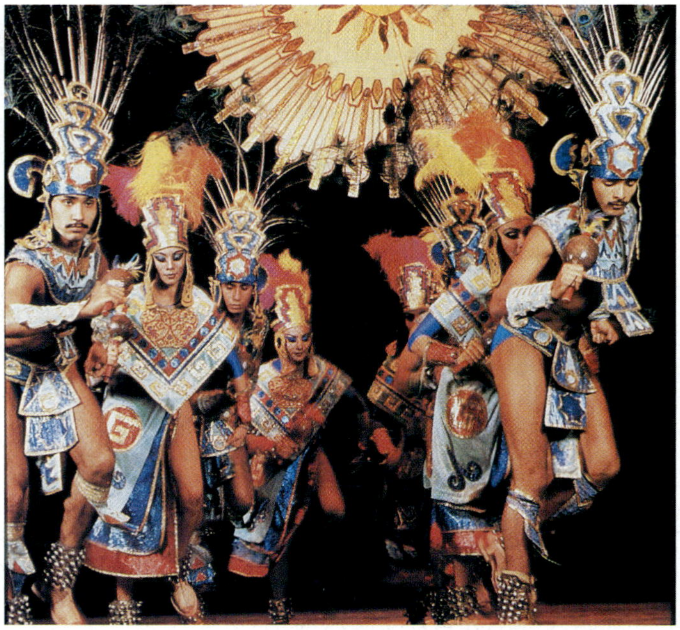

Ballet Folklórico de Mexico. "Los Mitos." Amalia Hernández, Artistic Director. Photo courtesy of Friedson Enterprises.

Discussion Questions

1. What symbolism do you see in the photo on this page that inspired ancient cultures of Mexico? What characteristics of the symbol can you name?
2. After viewing the video, describe how the dancers used geometric spatial designs.

Creative Expression Activities

Dance Stand in an open area with six to eight students and organize yourselves into three different geometric shapes, selecting from a circle, square, triangle, or the letter X. After your designs are organized, choose two that you like and walk or skip from one figure into another using eight counts to travel.

Language Arts Write a personal reflection of your impressions and feelings about either the images you see in the illustration on this page or of the dance in the video.

APPRECIATING THE PERFORMING ARTS

DANCE "Los Mitos" (the myths) is part of a suite of dances called *Los Concheros.* The suite is based on the ancient rituals of some of the indigenous cultures, such as the Toltecs and the Aztecs. These rituals connect each dancer to life and the universe. The title of the suite, *Los Concheros,* refers to the people who blow large conch shell trumpets during the ceremonial rites. Although the Concheros still enact their rituals today, the ceremonies now reflect the Spanish influence and have become a fusion of Christian and pre-Hispanic traditions.

Dance African American Dance Ensemble

ARTSOURCE

Based on extensive research, the African American Dance Ensemble performances are a blend of traditional African and African American styles. In African cultures, dance is not seen simply as an art form but as an integral part of the economic, political, social, and religious aspects of life. Artistic Director Dr. Chuck Davis and his company use dance and music to bring the message of "peace, love, and respect for everybody." His dance "Balante" is based on a post-initiation dance of the Jolas of the Casamance region of Senegal. It features the joyous, powerful dancing of young men who have completed their rites of passage, attaining the status of manhood.

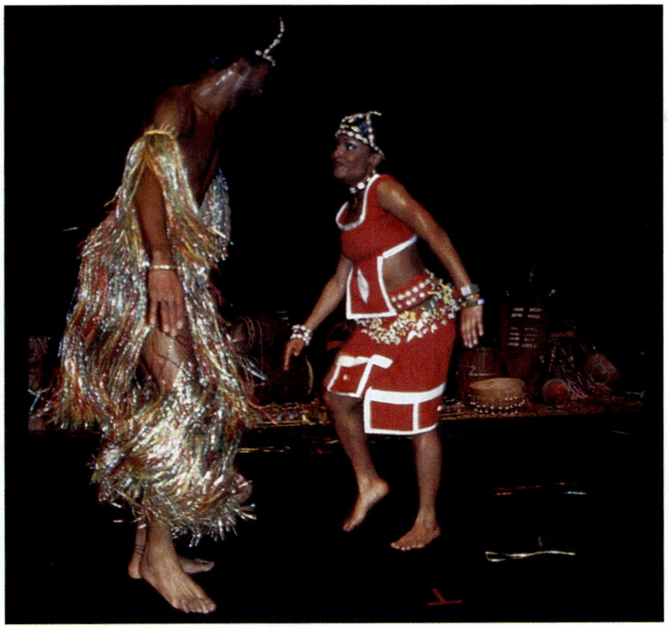

African American Dance Ensemble. "Balante." Dr. Chuck Davis, Artistic Director. Photo: Courtesy of African American Dance Ensemble.

ARTSOURCE

Discussion Questions

1. Initiates, in many traditional African societies, are expected to attain certain moral, intellectual, and spiritual qualities before they attain manhood. This "rite of passage" period is secret, and the boys and girls are separated from their tribe to undergo these instructions and challenges. Identify and discuss any rituals, activities, or accomplishments in our American society that serve as "rites of passage" for adolescent boys or girls.
2. What dance styles do you think have their roots in traditional African cultures? Give reasons for your answers.

Creative Expression Activities

Language Arts In many African ethnic groups, it is believed that wise people speak in proverbs and that everything has a place in life and a reason for being. Read the following proverbs, and then think of English equivalents: "Rain beats a leopard's skin, but it does not wash out the spots." (Ashanti); "When spider webs unite, they can tie up a lion." (Ethiopia); "Cross the river in a crowd and the crocodile won't eat you." (Kenya).

Social Studies Most African groups have ceremonies that celebrate life passages. Create a "Naming Ceremony" for you and your classmates. Select a name for yourself that tells something of your character, appearance, accomplishments, or history. Include a special song and movements.

African American Dance Ensemble

Setting the Stage

Direct students to read the paragraph about the African American Dance Ensemble. Have students view and listen to the Artsource selections, if available.

Optional
Artsource: Performing Arts Package
- **DVD or VHS segment 2 (Playing time 2:54)**
- **Audio CD Tracks 2, 3, 4 (Playing time 6:20)**

Connecting the Arts

Using the Discussion questions on this page, help students recognize the importance of dance and music in traditional African cultures. Possible responses are:

1. Student answers will vary.
2. Responses may include the dance styles from Brazil, Cuba, and Haiti.

Extensions

- Have students complete the Creative Expression Activities.
- Encourage students to share experiences and knowledge connected with traditional cultures in terms of ceremonies for birth, initiation, marriage, and death. How were music, dance, costume, and art incorporated?
- Use Artsource: Performing Arts Package for more information about the African American Dance Ensemble and for additional related activities.

APPRECIATING THE PERFORMING ARTS

Dance Dr. Chuck Davis researches the history of certain ethnic groups and learns how each dance is performed and connected to the society. Only when he knows this information can he incorporate the authentic movements into original African American work. Although he recognizes that movement takes on other meanings when it is removed from its roots, he is conscientious about paying homage to its origin. He sees himself as a "griot," or teacher and historian. He states, "I have gone to Africa and I have sat at the feet of elders and I have listened as their words poured like raindrops onto and into my being."

Eugene Friesen

Setting the Stage

Direct students to read the paragraph about Eugene Friesen. Have students view the Artsource selection, if available.

OPTIONAL
Artsource: Performing Arts Package DVD or VHS segment 4 (Playing time 8:56)

Connecting the Arts

Using the Discussion Questions on this page, help students recognize the unique creative quality of "Cello Man," a performance that combines mask theatre and music. Possible responses are:

1. The mask seems to depict a squirrel. The music might be high-pitched; it might have short, quick musical phrases.
2. A cello rests on the floor between the player's legs; its strings may be bowed or plucked. It has a deep sound that is mellow and pleasing to the ear.
3. The violin, the viola, the double bass, and the harp.

Extension

- Have students complete the Creative Expression Activities.
- Encourage students to recognize that stringed instruments are found in cultures all over the world, from ancient to modern times.
- Use the Artsource: Performing Arts Package for more information on Eugene Friesen and for additional related activities.

Music Eugene Friesen

ARTSOURCE

World-renowned cellist, Eugene Friesen, uses both his cello and his voice to create new music. He began playing the cello in his elementary school orchestra at age eight, pulling it to school in a little red wagon. By the time he got to high school he played in both school and community orchestras and began experimenting with an amplified cello to play rock and blues styles. A graduate of the Yale School of Music, Eugene moves out of the traditional classical world of the cello and into a creative, expressive one. The photo captures him playing in a solo performance called, "Cello Man," created in collaboration with Faustwork Mask Theater. In this show, Eugene weaves a spellbinding fabric composed of stories, songs, and inventive techniques on both the cello and electric cello. Using masks and costumes, he transforms himself into different characters that integrate with the music he is playing. This use of masks adds a dramatic element to the performance, which includes a duet with the recorded song of a humpback whale.

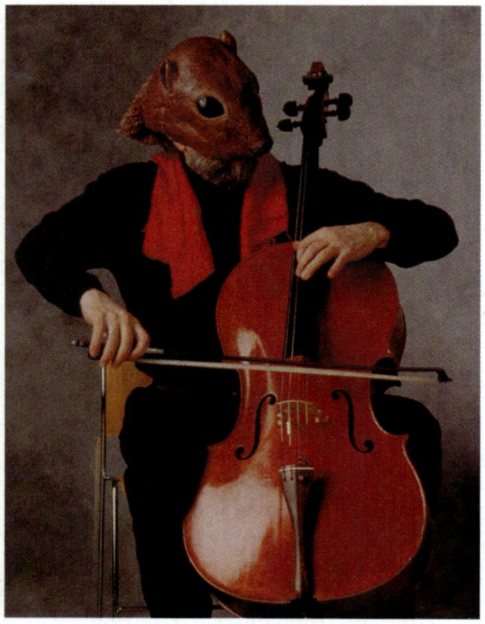

Eugene Friesen. "Cello Man." Photo: Craig Schwartz, © 1998.

Discussion Questions

1. Look at the photo and identify the animal depicted by the mask Eugene is wearing. Think of the characteristics of this animal and think about how they would translate into the tempo, quality, and melody of the music he is playing.
2. Do you know how a cello is played? Can you describe the sound a cello makes? How might this differ from the sound of an electric cello?
3. What other instruments can you name that are in the string family?

Creative Expression Activities

Language Arts Write a story that has a musical instrument as a main character. The instrument's character may be personified so that human traits and emotions are expressed. Also, think about the materials used in making the specific instrument and the way they might be included in describing the character.

Science Sound is produced by vibrations at different frequencies. Each stringed musical instrument produces different levels and speeds of vibrations that are created by bowing or plucking. The type of wood and the material of the strings and bow affect the type of sound that is produced. Research the differences in the sound qualities and textures of the violin, cello, and bass. What things impact the quality, texture, and pitch of the sound?

316 *Artsource: Performing Arts Handbook*

APPRECIATING THE PERFORMING ARTS

MUSIC Stringed instruments are important in many of the world's musical cultures. In ancient Egyptian, Greek, and Hebrew cultures, plucked string instruments such as the lyre and the harp came before the introduction of the bow. An instrument played with a bow necessitated an arched bridge and allowed for greater musical expression. Ancient Oriental and Near Eastern cultures, however, enjoyed both bowed and plucked instruments. Stringed keyboard instruments, such as the clavichord, harpsichord, and piano, which are technically members of the percussion family of musical instruments, evolved later in European history.

Choreographer Donald McKayle is a performing artist who has broken many barriers. He was the first African American male dancer selected to join the famous Martha Graham Dance Company. He also went with the company on its historic tour of Asia in the late 1950s. Among his many dances is a piece called "Rainbow 'Round My Shoulder," based on prisoners' dreams of freedom. McKayle focuses on prisoners in the South, who were chained together as they worked. In the dance he incorporates the strong, repetitive rhythm of work movements and prison songs. He believes that the more truthful artists are, the more their art will communicate to others. His dances, as well as his life, reflect this belief.

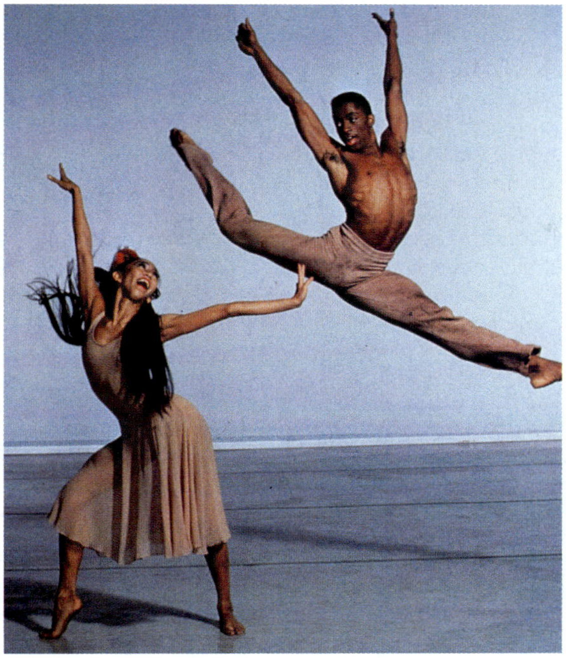

Alvin Ailey American Dance Theater. Donald McKayle, choreographer. "Rainbow 'Round My Shoulder." Featured dancers: Elizabeth Roxas and Desmond Richardson. Photo by Jack Mitchell.

ARTSOURCE

Discussion Questions

1. Share what you know about the life of prisoners working in a chain gang. What kind of movements would a choreographer use to portray a prisoner's hard and repetitive life? Explain your choices.
2. Look at the photo of the dancers on this page. What principles of art can you identify in the photo?
3. Why do you think a choreographer would choose the title "Rainbow 'Round My Shoulder" as a title for a dance about prisoners? What does a rainbow symbolize? What symbols would you choose if you were creating a work of art expressing a wish for freedom?

Creative Expression Activities

Dance Working with a partner or in small groups, think of movements that suggest actions associated with physical work. You might use such repetitive movements as hauling, dragging, pushing, pulling, lifting, carrying, and breaking rocks. Create several variations for each. Perform the movements for the class.

Language Arts List words that describe the feelings of someone who is imprisoned and longs for freedom. Use your list to write a poem or short story about this person and his or her feelings.

Donald McKayle

Setting the Stage

Direct students to read about Donald McKayle. Have students view the Artsource selection, if available.

OPTIONAL
Artsource: Performing Arts Package DVD or VHS segment 9 (Playing time 8:45)

Connecting the Arts

Using the Discussion Questions on this page, help students recognize that artists can make statements about political and social problems through their artworks. Possible responses are:

1. Road construction work—digging, shoveling, hauling, picking up heavy loads and passing them from one to the other, all walking in a coordinated way, pulling a heavy load with a rope.
2. Balance, unity, variety, and repetition.
3. A rainbow might mean hope, a pot of gold, or the end of a troubled time. Ideas for symbols will vary.

Extensions

- Have students complete the Creative Expression Activities.
- Encourage them to share their ideas about how to portray work movements or a social problem in a work of art. Have them take one specific idea and express it in a poem, dance, dramatic scene, or song.
- Use the Artsource: Performing Arts Package for additional related activities.

APPRECIATING THE PERFORMING ARTS

DANCE Choreographer Donald McKayle has a profound interest in African American heritage and has based this work "Rainbow 'Round My Shoulder" on related themes and styles. In this piece, the stage lighting creates the "crack of dawn" as five prisoners enter, performing strong, stark, and full-bodied movements. Although the movements of the men are forceful, they become weighted and weary as the day evolves. A woman appears, but she is really a vision representing freedom. The music, consisting of African American folk songs, is scripted to build emotional tension toward an explosive, sad ending.

Blue Palm

Setting the Stage

Direct students to read the paragraph about Blue Palm. Have students view the Artsource selection, if available.

OPTIONAL
Artsource: Performing Arts Package DVD or VHS segment 7 (Playing time 4:03)

Connecting the Arts

Using the Discussion questions on this page, help students recognize the role of storytelling in conveying emotions. Student responses will vary.

Extensions

- Have students complete the Creative Expression Activities.
- Ask students to name a movie or play they have seen and discuss one of the characters or situations with which they could identify. What did they discover or understand better after the experience and insight?
- Use the Artsource: Performing Arts Package for more information about Blue Palm and for additional related activities.

Theatre Blue Palm

ARTSOURCE

Prior to founding Blue Palm, Jackie Planeix and Tom Crocker, choreographers and performers, toured the world with the internationally renowned Béjart Ballet. Blue Palm creates original pieces focused on human dreams, fears, and flaws. Using a form called interdisciplinary theatre, they blend drama, dance, and humor. *Childhood* is composed of a series of scenes, each of which gives us a glimpse into the world of children, with its own whimsical logic. Blue Palm holds up a looking glass that lets us see how universal our feelings and struggles are. "The Lot" shows an adult reencountering a childhood friend who became lost in play and never grew up. The dialogue between them reveals each one's perspective and how these influenced the choices they made.

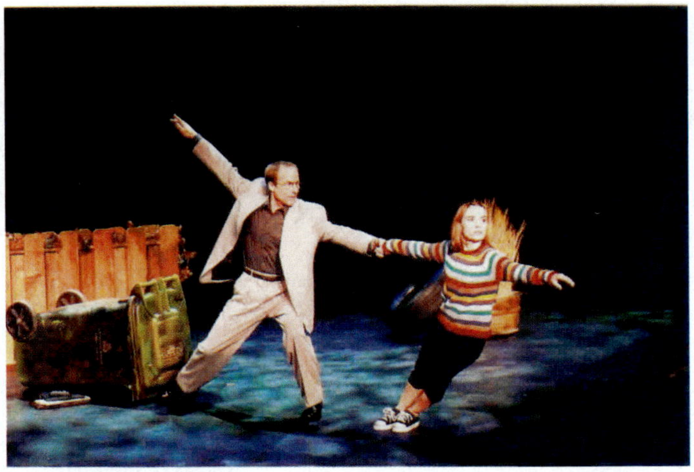

Blue Palm: Jackie Planeix and Tom Crocker. "The Lot" from *Childhood*. Photo: Brigitte Meuwissen.

The scene in the photo highlights the contrast between a child and an adult perspective, then the enduring bond that is friendship.

Discussion Questions

1. This performance examines the magical, yet sometimes complex, process of "growing up." What do you look forward to as you get older? What are the things that frighten you? What do you think will be your biggest strength? What might be your biggest challenge?
2. One of the characters in the play never grew up because she wanted to keep on playing. Imagine you could stop yourself from growing. Where would you choose to stop and stay? What would be the advantages and disadvantages?

Creative Expression Activities

Language Arts Recall a scenario from your own childhood that taught you something. Think of the setting you were in, your age, other people who were involved, and the emotions you were feeling. Imagine the beginning, middle, and ending of the scenario and see what happened and how you felt at the end. Was this feeling different than at the beginning or middle? Did you realize something or make a decision about something because of this event? Use your memory to write a short story that captures the scene, defines the characters, and describes the event. Share this with a partner. Did you learn something new in the writing or telling of your story?

APPRECIATING THE PERFORMING ARTS

THEATRE Through theatre we are able to look at events, situations and relationships and see them more clearly than we often can in real life. A playwright invites us to identify with different characters in a play and feel their emotions. As we watch a play we often are reminded of similar events or relationships in our own lives. Theatre has been a part of almost all cultures for thousands of years, providing people with a way to reenact events or journeys. The basic universal themes of love, hate, friendship, jealousy, longing, birth and old age remain common issues in plays as in life.

"The Green Table," created by choreographer Kurt Jooss in 1932, is a compassionate and powerful dance drama about the horrors of war. It features ten gentlemen in morning coats and spats standing and leaning around a rectangular green table. They posture and disagree until pistols emerge. A shot is fired, and war is declared. After the gun shot, the "Green Table" scene goes black and we see the figure of Death enter. In the scenes that follow, soldiers are called to fight, battles rage, refugees comfort one another, a profit-maker preys on the miseries of his fellow man, and a lone soldier holds watch. Through every scene, Death stalks the stage to find different companions, claiming victim after victim. These characters meet Death in their own ways, some swiftly and some slowly. Because of its universal themes of power, war and death, "The Green Table" continues to be performed around the world, making it the most performed of all dance works created in the twentieth century.

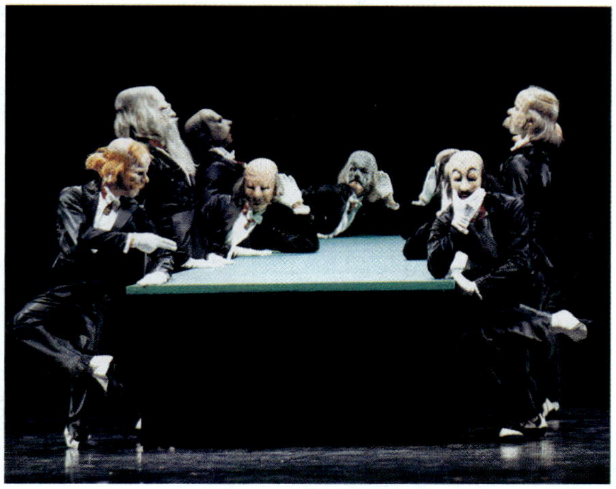

The Joffrey Ballet of Chicago performing "The Green Table." Kurt Jooss, choreographer. Photo: © Robert Migdoll, 1998.

ARTSOURCE

Discussion Questions

1. What do you think a dance drama is? How might this differ from a dance created to express music?
2. Why do you think the choreographer chose to have masks for the men at the green table? How might it have communicated something different without the masks?

Creative Expression Activities

Language Arts Some people feel that dance can't tell a dramatic work as well as a play that has the characters use words and dialogue. However, other people feel that emotions can be portrayed even more strongly when words are taken away and the characters communicate primarily through posture and movement. Write a short essay on the topic of war and how diplomats or statesmen make decisions that impact the ordinary citizen as well as soldiers. How would you portray the character of Death and how he claims his victims? What narration or dialogue would you use?

Kurt Jooss

Setting the Stage

Direct students to read the paragraph about Kurt Jooss. Have students view the Artsource selection, if available.

Optional
Artsource: Performing Arts Package DVD or VHS segment 13 (Playing time 4:22)

Connecting the Arts

Using the Discussion Questions on this page, help students think about and explore the idea of dance drama. Tell students that abstract ballet concentrates on dance for dance's sake. Narrative ballets play on simple emotions rather than intellect. A dance drama such as "The Green Table" portrays a complex idea that evolves emotion and intellect. Possible responses are:

1. Dance drama incorporates music and dance with words to express a story. Students may have seen dance productions that did not include the spoken word.
2. The masks represent figures that the performers want to portray. The masks also signify that the characters are not presenting their true faces.

Extension

- Have students complete the Creative Expression Activities.
- Use the Artsource: Performing Arts Package for more information about Kurt Jooss and "The Green Table" and for additional related activities.

APPRECIATING THE PERFORMING ARTS

Dance/Theatre Kurt Jooss first studied music, voice, and drama. A chance meeting with Rudolf van Laban, a renowned dance innovator, changed the direction of his life. Laban was searching for contemporary forms of movement. Jooss became his dancer, assistant, and choreographer. Interested in finding and developing a new language of movement, Jooss sought a form of dance that would serve as a way to handle contemporary themes. "The Green Table" is a conjunction of classical and modern dance. The choreographer approached dance from the intellectual angle, as well as the physical.

Vocalworks

Setting the Stage

Direct students to read the paragraph about Vocalworks. Have students listen to the Artsource selection, if available.

Optional
Artsource: Performing Arts Package Audio CD track 9 (Playing time 8:27)

Connecting the Arts

Using the Discussion Questions on this page, guide students in developing an understanding of swing music.

1. A washboard is being used as an instrument.
2. In a world of increasing complexity dominated by technology, many people look to the past for inspiration, and swing's message of buoyant optimism is particularly appealing.
3. Students answers will vary.

Extension

- Have students complete the Creative Expression Activities.
- One of the characteristics of swing jazz is scat singing, a series of vocal nonsense syllables created to express certain sounds. Encourage students to try using scat singing with a classmate.
- Use the Artsource: Performing Arts Package for more information about Vocalworks and for additional related activities.

ARTSOURCE

Music Vocalworks

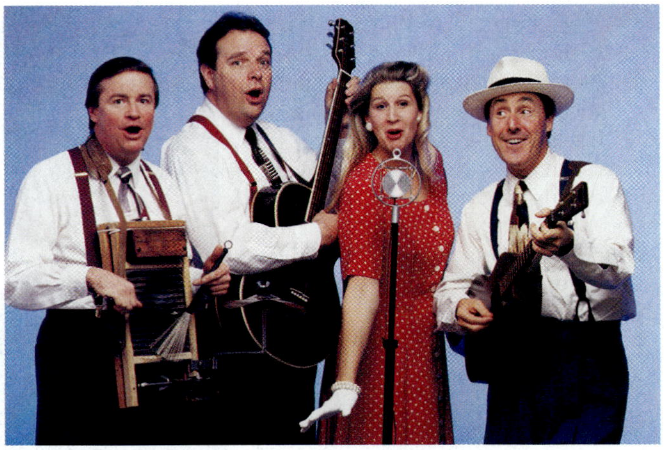

Vocalworks. Bruce Cooper, Michael Geiger, Debbie and Tim Reeder, and Dave Easthly perform "Vocalworks Radio Hour." Photo: Richard Hines, © 1998.

Vocalworks has brought the music of the 1930s and 1940s to modern audiences since 1983. Singing the music of the swing era, they note that their group has lasted longer than the swing era itself. In their show, "Vocalworks Radio Hour," they re-create a live radio broadcast from the period when home entertainment meant having the family gather around the radio in the living room to hear news, music, dramas, or comedy programs. Since no production would be authentic without a commercial, Vocalworks also includes singing commercials advertising toothpowder and dish soap. It is hard to believe, but there was no TV during that time—only phonographs, radios, and movies. The Great Depression and World War II were very difficult times for the American people. Concerned about their future and how they and their families would survive, they worried about retaining democracy and freedom as well as the economic and social stability of their country. Swing music was a wonderful escape that helped them forget their troubles for a while, just as music does for people today.

Discussion Questions

1. Improvisation is one of the characteristics of swing jazz. Look at the photo on this page and identify the instruments. Which ones do you think would be the ones most likely to be featured in the improvisation sections?
2. Swing music was characterized by its positive messages and upbeat rhythms during the Great Depression in the 1930s and World War II in the 1940s. Swing music and dance has gained a new popularity today. What do you think the reasons for this might be?
3. What type of popular music today raises your spirits and gives you renewed hope?

Creative Expression Activities

Social Studies Read about the Harlem Renaissance, 1919 to the early thirties. It was a time when African American life and experiences were dealt with from the perspective of African American artists, musicians, and writers. Much of it was inspired by life in Harlem, a small African American community in New York. Read about the Harlem Renaissance and its influence on jazz musicians, writers, poets and visual artists. Working in groups, present a choral verse reading of one of the following Langston Hughes poems to show how he was influenced by jazz: "The Weary Blues," or "Afro-American Fragment."

APPRECIATING THE PERFORMING ARTS

Music Swing is just one style in the continuum of jazz, which includes the blues, ragtime, Dixieland, boogie-woogie, and bebop. Many jazz specialists cite clarinetist and bandleader Benny Goodman's 1935 appearance at the Palomar Ballroom in Los Angeles as the opening of the swing era. Some who listen to swing today feel that all swing bands sound alike, but during the swing era there were so many bands that each one sought individuality by developing its own trademark sound. Although not confined exclusively to swing, the following are characteristic of the style: scat singing, repetition, syncopation, and call and response.

The Joffrey Ballet of Chicago

ARTSOURCE

The Joffrey Ballet of Chicago revives major historical ballets and features new choreography that draws from American life. "The Nutcracker," a traditional ballet, is based on the story *The Nutcracker and The King of the Mice* by E. T. A. Hoffmann. The original ballet premiered in St. Petersburg, Russia, in 1892. Begun by Marius Petipa and completed by Lev Ivanov, it was choreographed to a musical score by Peter Tchaikovsky. Set on Christmas Eve, "The Nutcracker" is a magical story about a young girl named Clara, who receives a nutcracker from her Uncle Drosselmeyer. Fritz, her jealous brother, breaks it. Although angry and sad, she repairs it with her uncle's help. However, when she checks on her nutcracker during the night, she sees him fighting off an attack by the Mouse King and his army. Clara helps the nutcracker, he thanks her, then magically turns into a prince. Snow begins to fall and soon they find themselves in "The Land of Sweets," where she meets the Sugar Plum Fairy and a host of toys, flowers, and dolls. After a delightful experience, she returns from her dream and awakens on Christmas morning.

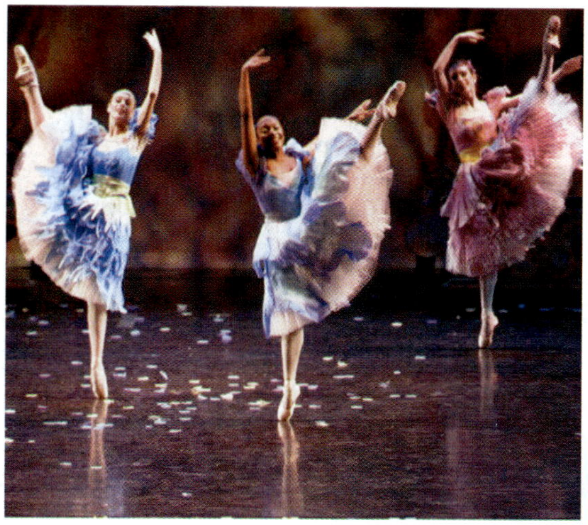

The Joffrey Ballet of Chicago performs 'Waltz of the Flowers,' from "The Nutcracker." Gerarld Arpino, artistic director. Photo: Herbert Migdoll.

Discussion Questions

1. Discuss other stories or fairy tales you know that focus on magical transformation. What do you think the role of magical power is in these tales? What purpose, if any, does it serve in our lives?
2. Have you ever seen a story enacted through dance? What would be the main differences between a story that is presented as a play and one that is presented as a dance? Which might be the more powerful? Give reasons why. Be very specific in your responses.

Creative Expression Activities

Language Arts Russian choreographer Michel Fokine said, "Man should and could be expressive from head to foot, yet even the greatest dancer must play his part as one member of a group—the ballet company." In small groups, discuss this idea and find connections to other group efforts such as sports, bands, and production crews.

Mime Create a mime or movement study based on toys and how they might move if animated. These might include: yo-yos, kites, balls, plastic clay; different types of dolls, jack-in-the-box, or action figures.

The Joffrey Ballet of Chicago

Setting the Stage

Direct students to read the paragraph about The Joffrey Ballet of Chicago. Have students view and listen to the Artsource selections, if available.

Optional
Artsource: Performing Arts Package
- **DVD or VHS segment 3 (Playing time 5:11)**
- **Audio CD track 5 (Playing time 6:32)**

Connecting the Arts

Using the Discussion questions on this page, help students recognize the role of storytelling through dance and music. Student responses will vary.

Extensions

- Have students complete the Creative Expression Activities.
- Encourage students to share other stories they have seen interpreted in dance.
- Use Artsource: Performing Arts Package for more information about The Joffrey Ballet of Chicago and for additional related activities.

APPRECIATING THE PERFORMING ARTS

Dance Classical ballet has its roots in the Italian and French Courts; it was in France that it became most important. The King of France, Louis XIII, danced in court ballets and sometimes even wrote the scenes and music. However, French court ballet reached its pinnacle under King Louis XIV, who reigned from 1643 to 1715. Greek myths were often the base of these ballets and courtiers would portray gods and heroes. A new form, *opéra-ballets* came into being in the 1700s in which singing, dancing, and acting were intermingled. As the 1800s approached, ballet became more popular and new themes were explored.

Japanese Festival Sounds

Setting the Stage

Direct students to read the paragraph about Johnny Mori and Japanese Festival Sounds. Have students view the Artsource selection, if available.

OPTIONAL
Artsource: Performing Arts Package DVD or VHS segment 8 (Playing time 7:36)

Connecting the Arts

Using the Discussion Questions on this page, help students recognize that while artistic forms and styles may begin in one culture, they are carried to other places in the world as people migrate. Possible responses:

1. India to Korea, China, Japan, and United States.
2. Athletes and dancers must show great discipline over mind, body, and spirit.
3. Many traditional cultures of Africa and Native Americans. Drumming is used for ritual, dance, ceremonies, battle, healing, and recreation.

Extensions

- Have students complete the Creative Expression Activities.
- Encourage students to understand how traditions change and evolve the further they are from their source.
- Use the Artsource: Performing Arts package for more information about Johnny Mori and his musical group and for additional related activities.

ARTSOURCE

Music Japanese Festival Sounds

Johnny Mori was fascinated by the Taiko drummer who accompanied the folk dancers at the annual Obon Buddhist Festival in Los Angeles, California. This inspired him to learn to play the drums. Today he blends traditional Taiko drumming with a modern Japanese American style. Taiko drumming originated in ancient India as part of religious ceremonies and celebrations. This form eventually found its way to Korea, China, and Japan. Traditionally, Taiko drums were included in ensembles with other instruments. In some cultures the drums were also used to perform functional roles, such as announcing the time of day or calling people to special gatherings. Today, Taiko is featured in performances with some ensembles composed solely of various sized drums.

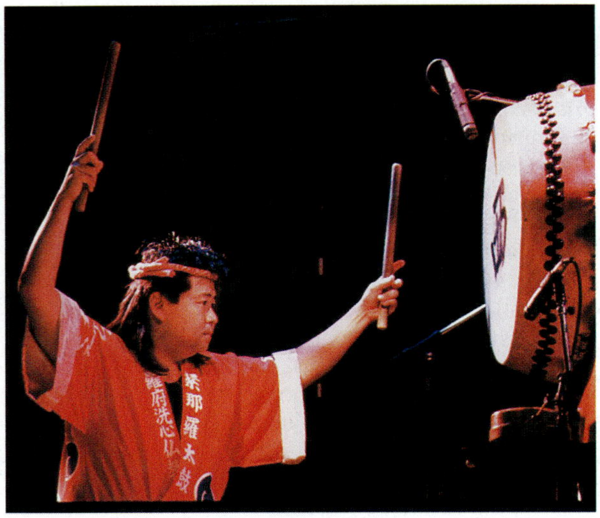

Japanese Festival Sounds. Johnny Mori, Artistic Director. Photo: Craig Schwartz © 1989.

Discussion Questions

1. Where did Taiko drumming originate? To what other countries did it spread?
2. Taiko performers demonstrate great skill and control in movement and drum technique. Their performance skills are a result of many hours of concentrated, vigorous work involving the mind, body, and spirit. Discuss how Taiko drummers are like athletes and dancers.
3. What other cultures place an emphasis on drumming? For what purposes are the drums used?

Creative Expression Activities

Language Arts The technique of learning drum patterns by vocalizing the sounds began in India and was transferred to many Asian cultures. Five basic syllables used in Taiko are: KA; KARA; DON; DOGO; and SU (which means *rest*). Combine the syllables in different patterns, saying them as you clap or beat out the rhythms. Repeat each pattern several times.

Geography Using a map or globe, trace the geographical and historical route of the Taiko drums from India through Asia to the United States.

APPRECIATING THE PERFORMING ARTS

MUSIC Humans have created musical instruments from a variety of materials found in their environment to produce many different sounds. Taiko drums are part of the percussion family of instruments that produce sounds when they are either hit, shaken, or scraped. Like other musical instruments, drums are designed in many sizes and shapes. The five basic drum stokes are: KA (a quarter note struck on the drum rim); KARA (two eighth notes struck on the rim); DON (a quarter note struck on the drum head); DOGO (two eighth notes on the head); SU (a rest).

Parisian born Jacques Heim is the dynamic creator and director of Diavolo, a dance and physical theatre group that takes a daring, compelling and uncompromising look at contemporary human life. Heim has studied dance, film, and choreography in France, the United States, and England and has an MFA in Theatre, Dance, and Film from the California Institute of the Arts. He created Diavolo in 1992 after graduating from Cal Arts in California. He states, "I try to convey an appreciation for movement by breaking down barriers to dance via a vocabulary based on everyday activities." Diavolo is composed of dancers, gymnasts, and actors, who work as teammates. In their collaborations, they work on and around outrageous, surrealistic sets and structures. Everyday items such as benches, doors, and ladders provide the backdrop for dramatic movement. In the dance, "Tête en l'Air," dancers leap from a staircase and roll down its steps, creating metaphors for the challenges of relationships while maintaining balance.

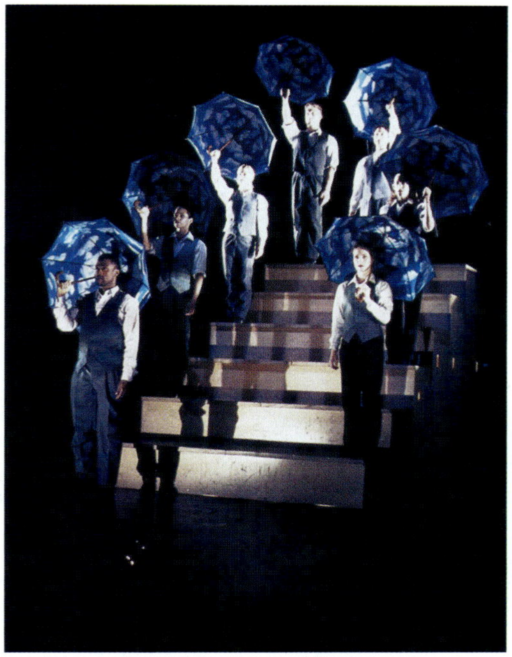

Diavolo performs "Tête en l'Air." Photo: Ed Krieger.

Discussion Questions

1. Can you think of an everyday object that would lend itself to a dance piece? Give reasons why you think this piece or structure would be interesting to dance with or on. How would you have the dancers interact with the object? What thematic ideas come to mind?
2. This dance takes place on and off a staircase structure. If you were the choreographer, how many different actions can you think of that you could incorporate into the dance movements? See if you can list at least ten.

Creative Expression Activities

Language Arts The word *Diavolo* has several possible meanings. A favorite, however, is *dia*—Spanish for "day" and *volo*—Latin for "I will fly." Write a paragraph titled, "The Day I Will Fly."

Science A theme in Diavolo's work is the relationship between gravity and weight. Choose three different objects of varying size and weight; for example, a ball, a book, a feather, or silk scarf. Drop each object from above your head and observe how each falls to the ground. Is the rate of speed at which they fall constant or does it fluctuate? What words would you use to describe the way each object fell in terms of energy qualities such as floating, bouncing, slamming, heavy and forceful, graceful.

ARTSOURCE

Diavolo

Setting the Stage

Direct students to read the paragraph about Diavolo. Have students view the Artsource selection, if available.

Optional
Artsource: Performing Arts Package DVD or VHS segment 6 (Playing time 5:41)

Connecting the Arts

Using the Discussion questions on this page, help students recognize how everyday objects can be incorporated into a dance. Possible responses are:

1. Large boxes could serve as a set in which dancers could dance on them at different levels, get inside them, hide behind them; a thematic idea would be "hide and seek."
2. Climbing, scooting down, falling, rolling, jumping or leaping off, sitting or standing in different poses, balancing and suspending, dragging self or others up, pushing or pulling others down or up.

Extensions

- Have students complete the Creative Expression Activities.
- Have students take an everyday structure and design it as a set for a dance. It can be realistic or abstract, and have designs and extensions.
- Use the Artsource: Performing Arts Package for more information about Diavolo and for additional related activities.

APPRECIATING THE PERFORMING ARTS

Dance/Theatre The work of Diavolo is the ultimate in artistic risk-taking. Company members are always teammates, collaborating on and around surrealistic sets and structures that allow them to create metaphors for the challenge of relationships, the absurdities of life and the struggle we all face in order to maintain our humanity in a technological world. Their piece, "Tête en l'Air" is a signature work, inspired by the works of surrealist painter René Magritte and filmmaker Jacques Tati. Whimsical interactions between performers, like passengers in a bizarre landscape of props and pratfalls, are the driving imagery in the work.

Xochimoki

Setting the Stage

Direct students to read about Xochimoki and to examine the photograph of the musicians. Have students listen to the Artsource selection, if available.

OPTIONAL
Artsource: Performing Arts Package Audio CD track 8 (Playing time 4:04)

Connecting the Arts

Using the Discussion Questions on this page, help students recognize that artworks give us historical and cultural information, and serve as inspiration for other artistic forms of expression. Possible responses are:

1. Brass trumpets, trombones, sousaphones, tubas; recorders; conga drums; slit drums; talking drums; xylophones; ankle bells from Middle East and maracas from Mexico.
2. Student responses will vary.

Extensions

- Have students complete the Creative Expression Activities.
- Encourage them to share experiences they have had with cultural or ancient music. Have them identify and describe the instruments used and give examples of the rhythm using body percussion or voice.
- Use the Artsource: Performing Arts Package for more information about Xochimoki and for additional related activities.

ARTSOURCE

Music Xochimoki

Xochiomoki (soh-shee-**moh**-kee) is a musical group that features unique musicians. Jim Berenholtz and Mazatl Galindo combine original music of pre-Colombian civilizations with contemporary acoustics and electronic instruments. The result is an interesting mix of the old with the new. One source of inspiration was found when they visited some of Mesoamerica's most exciting murals in the Lacandon rain forest near Yaxchilan. Here they studied artworks that depicted dancers and musicians of that ancient world. Using the murals to guide their creativity, Xochimoki composed "Bonampak," an original work using the same instruments illustrated in the murals.

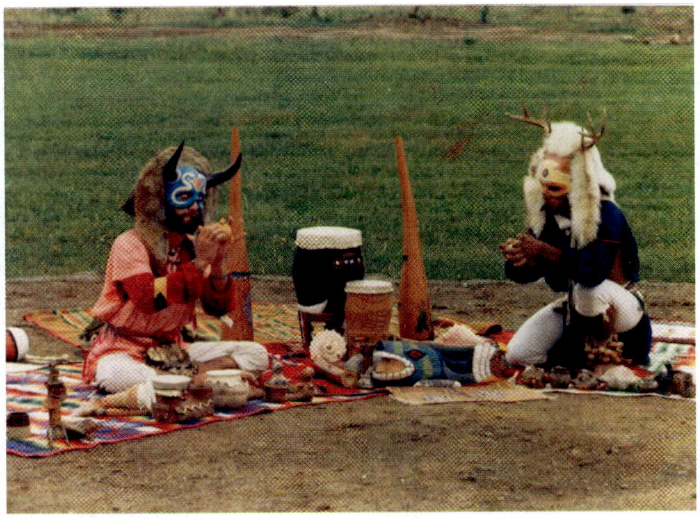

Xochimoki. Jim Berenholtz and Mazatl Galindo. Photo: Courtesy of Xochimoki.

Discussion Questions

1. In the mural described above, musicians are shown playing gourd trumpets, ocarinas, tall wooden drums with skin heads, log drums, turtle-shell drums struck with deer antlers, and seed-pod rattles worn on the ankles. What modern instruments do you think would be similar to these?
2. List types of music that are popular today and the instruments used to play this music. Explain how examples of these instruments or music would help future civilizations understand today's society.

Creative Expression Activities

Visual Arts Using the list created in Discussion Question 2, work with a partner or in a small group to design a mural that preserves contemporary music trends. Share your design with the class.

Language Arts Sketch your vision of musical instruments of the future. Let your artwork illustrate how the instruments are played as well as how they look. Write detailed descriptions of each, describing the sounds they produce, the materials from which they are made, and how they produce sounds.

APPRECIATING THE PERFORMING ARTS

Music The two artist-scholars who formed Xochimoki researched and collected valuable information, music, and instruments from the Hopi, Raramuri, Nahuatl, Maya, and Quechua communities. Murals provided images for reconstructing lost or unavailable instruments from these cultures in addition to dance postures, costumes, spatial groupings, and gestures. Xochimoki emphasizes the ancient traditions of the Americas as part of our Western hemispheric heritage. The name *Xochimoki* derives from the Nahuatl (Aztec) and Hopi languages.

Artists and Their Works

S

T

V

W

Glossary

A

Abstract Having a recognizable subject that is shown in an unrealistic manner. (p. 76)

Adenla (uh-**den**-luh) A sculpted ceremonial headdress used in rites of passage. (p. 253)

Aesthetics (es-**thet**-iks) The study of the nature of beauty and art. (p. 64)

Aesthetic view An idea or school of thought on what is most important in a work of art. (p. 64)

Ancestor figure An image carved in wood that was used as the resting place of a spirit. (p. 153)

Applied art Works of art made to be useful as well as visually pleasing. (pp. 83, 192)

Appliqué (ap-lih-**kay**) An art form in which cutout shapes are attached to a larger surface. (p. 129)

Architects Artists who plan and create buildings. (p. 168)

Architectural rendering A detailed, realistic two-dimensional representation of a proposed three-dimensional structure. (p. 272)

Architecture The art of planning and creating buildings. (p. 92)

Art critic A person whose job is studying, understanding, and judging works of art. (p. 66)

Art historians People who study art of different ages and cultures. (p. 82)

Artist A person who uses imagination and skill to communicate ideas in visual form. (p. 4)

Art medium A material used to create a work of art. (p. 42)

Art movement A trend formed when a group of artists band together. (p. 96)

Assemblage (ah-sem-**blahzh**) A three-dimensional artwork consisting of many pieces assembled together. (p. 106)

B

Balance A principle of art concerned with arranging the elements so that no one part of the work overpowers, or seems heavier than, any other part. (p. 26)

Belvedere (**bel**-vuh-deer) A building designed to provide a view of its surroundings. (p. 272)

Binder A liquid that holds together the grains of pigment. (p. 47)

Bust A sculpture that shows a person's head, shoulders, and upper chest. (p. 85)

C

Calligraphy (kuh-**lig**-ruh-fee) The art of beautiful writing. (p. 132)

Caricature (**kar**-ih-kuh-chur) A humorous drawing that exaggerates features of a person to make fun of or criticize him or her. (p. 210)

Cartouche (kar-**toosh**) An oval or oblong containing an important person's name. (p. 224)

Cityscape A drawing or painting focusing on large buildings and other objects found in cities. (p. 172)

Color What the eye sees when light is reflected off an object. (p. 8)

Columns Vertical posts that rise to support another structure. (p. 171)

Composition The way the principles are used to organize the elements of art. (p. 64)

Content The message, idea, or feeling expressed by a work of art. (p. 65)

Contours Outlines and surface ridges. (p. 87)

Credit line A listing of important facts about an artwork. (p. 69)

Cutaway A view in which an outside wall has been removed to reveal the scene within. (p. 233)

D

Diorama (dy-uh-**ram**-uh) A scenic representation in which miniature sculptures and other objects are displayed against a painted backdrop. (p. 94)

E

Eight, The A group of American realists who worked at the beginning of the twentieth century. (p. 174)

Elements of art The basic visual symbols an artists uses to create works of art. (p. 4)

Elevation A drawing of an outside view of a building. (p. 170)

Emphasis Making an element or an object in a work stand out. (p. 31)

Environment Surroundings. (p. 124)

F

Façade (fuh-**sahd**) The front of a building. (p. 170)

Fantasy art Art that focuses on make-believe or imaginary subjects. (p. 264)

Figure study A drawing that focuses on the human form. (p. 148)

Fine art Art made to be enjoyed visually, not used. (p. 83)

Folk art Art made by artists who have had no formal training. (p. 138)

Font Typeface. (p. 239)

Form An element of art that refers to an object with three dimensions. (p. 15)

Fresco (fres-**koh**) A painting created when pigment is applied to a section of wall spread with fresh plaster. (p. 232)

Frieze (**freez**) A decorative band running across the upper part of a wall. (p. 212)

G

Gesture drawing Drawing lines quickly and loosely to capture the form and actions of a subject. (p. 44)

Gouachev(**gwash**) A form of watercolor that uses non-clear pigments. (p. 205)

H

Harmony Combining the elements of art to accent their similarities. (p. 30)

Hieroglyphic (hy-ruh-**glif**-ik) An early form of picture writing. (p. 86)

Hue A color's name. (p. 8)

I

Illumination Hand-painted book illustration. (p. 132)

Intaglio (in-**tahl**-yoh) A printmaking technique in which the image to be printed is cut or scratched into a surface. (p. 51)

Intensity The brightness or dullness of a hue. (p. 10)

J

Jewelry Art, and the craft of making art, to be worn. (p. 196)

Juxtapose (**juks**-tuh-pohz) Place side by side. (p. 268)

K

Kachina (kuh-**chee**-nuh) Hand-crafted statuette that represents spirits in Pueblo rituals. (p. 230)

Kiln A special hot oven in which pottery objects are fired. (p. 195)

Kinetic (kuh-**net**-ik) **art** An art style in which parts of a work are set into motion by a form of energy. (p. 250)

L

Landscape A drawing or painting of mountains, trees, or other natural scenery. (p. 104)

Line The path of a dot through space. (p. 6)

Line quality The unique character of any line. (p. 7)

M

Mascot An animal or person used by a group as a sign of luck. (p. 125)

Monoprint A print made by applying ink or paint to a plate and then transferring the image by hand-rubbing. (p. 117)

Mosaic (moh-**zay**-ik) Pictures made with small cubes of colored marble, glass, or tile set into cement. (p. 212)

Motif Unit of repetition in a visual pattern. (p. 33)

Movement The principle of art that leads the viewer to sense action in a work, or it can be the path the viewer's eye follows through the work. (p. 33)

Murals Large two-dimensional works painted on walls. (p. 156)

N

Nature study A drawing used to help artists sharpen their perception of natural objects. (p. 108)

Negative space Empty spaces between the shapes or forms in two- and three-dimensional art. (p. 16)

Nonobjective Having no readily identifiable subjects or objects. (p. 71)

O

Old Stone Age The historical period that occurred between 30,000 and 10,000 B.C. (p. 124)

P

Painted screen An art object used as a wall or room divider. (p. 89)

Pan A slow, steady, sideways movement of the video camera to capture details in a panorama. (p. 218)

Panorama A complete view of an area in all directions. (p. 176)

Pattern A two-dimensional decorative visual representation. (p. 33)

Pendant A jewelry item worn suspended from the neck on a string or chain. (p. 193)

Perception An awareness of the elements of an environment by means of the senses. (p. 42)

Perceive Become aware through the senses of the special nature of objects. (p. 184)

Petroglyph (**peh**-truh-glif) Symbolic rock carving or painting. (p. 225)

Photography The art of making images by exposing a chemically treated surface to light. (p. 204)

Pictogram A small picture that stands for a word or an idea. (p. 224)

Picture plane The flat surface of a painting or drawing. (p. 30)

Pigment A finely ground powder that gives paint its color. (p. 46)

Point of view The angle from which the viewer sees the scene in an artwork. (p. 72)

Porcelain (**por**-suh-lihn) A fine-grained, high-quality form of pottery. (p. 128)

Portfolio A carefully selected collection of artwork kept by students and professionals. (p. 13)

Portrait A visual representation of a person at rest. (p. 48)

Portraiture (**pohr**-tray-chur) The art of making portraits. (p. 152)

Pottery Art, and the craft of making art, from clay. (p. 194)

Principles of art Guidelines that govern the way artists organize the elements of art. (p. 26)

Printmaking Transferring an image from an inked surface to create another surface. (p. 50)

Proportion How parts of a work relate to each other and to the whole. (p. 31)

Public art Art to be displayed in and enjoyed by a community. (p. 156)

Pueblo (**pweh**-bloh) Dried-clay dwelling. (p. 248)

R

Renaissance (ren-uh-**sahns**) Period of rebirth. (p. 93)

Rhythm The principle of art that indicates movement through the repetition of elements and objects. (p. 33)

Rococo (roh-**koh**-koh) An art style of the 1700s that emphasized graceful movement, curving lines, and delicate colors. (p. 169)

S

Sculpture A three-dimensional work of art. (p. 52)

Seal Symbolic image or emblem. (p. 245)

Seascape A drawing or painting of the ocean and objects found on or around it. (p. 176)

Self-portrait A painting or drawing of an artist's own image. (p. 147)

Shadow puppet An art object in the shape of an animal or human attached to a wand or a stick. (p. 250)

Shape An area clearly set off by one or more of the other five visual elements of art. (p. 14)

Slip Clay with enough added water to give it a runny, liquid consistency. (p. 194)

Social protest painting An art style dedicated to attacking the ills of big-city life. (p. 270)

Solvent A liquid used to control the thickness of thinness of the paint. (p. 47)

Space The distance or area between, around, above, below, and within things. (p. 15)

Staged photograph A photographic composition that makes use of artificial images or processes. (p. 165)

Still life A painting or drawing of nonmoving objects. (p. 17)

Story board A frame-by-frame plan of a video production. (p. 217)

Study A drawing used to plan a painting or other large project. (p. 108)

Style An artist's personal way of using the elements and principles of art to express feelings and ideas. (p. 144)

Stylized Simplified or exaggerated. (p. 105)

Subject An image viewers can easily identify. (p. 64)

Surrealists The group of artists who explored the realm of dreams and the subconscious. (p. 265)

Symbol An image used to stand for a quality or an idea. (p. 87)

T

Tapestry A woven wall hanging with decorative designs or colorful scenes. (p. 136)

Texture How things feel, or look as though they might feel if touched. (p. 20)

Totem An object that serves as an emblem or respected symbol. (p. 126)

Trait A personal characteristic. (p. 125)

Tricolor A flag with three broad bands of color. (p 245)

U

Unity The arrangement of elements and principles of art to create a feeling of completeness or wholeness. (p. 36)

V

Value The lightness or darkness of a hue. (p. 9)

Variety Combining one or more elements of art to create interest. (p. 30)

Vessel A hollow utensil made to hold something. (p. 192)

Video documentary An in-depth study of a person, place, thing, or event. (p. 217)

Videographer Person who operates a video camera. (p. 218)

W

Watercolorist A painter who works in watercolor. (p. 190)

Glosario

A

Abstract/Abstracto Mostrar un sujeto reconocible de forma no realista. (p. 76)

Adenla/Adenla Tocado ceremonial usado en rituales de transición. (p. 253)

Aesthetics/Estética Estudio de la naturaleza de la belleza y el arte. (p. 64)

Aesthetic view/Punto de vista estético Idea o escuela de pensamiento sobre qué es lo más importante en una obra de arte. (p. 64)

Ancestor figure/Figurín de un ancestro Imagen tallada en madera que se usaba como el lugar de descanso de un espíritu. (p. 153)

Applied art/Arte aplicado Obras de arte hechas con un fin utilitario además de ser agradables a la vista. (pp. 83, 192)

Appliqué/Appliqué Forma de arte en la que se adhieren recortes de material a una superficie más grande. (p. 129)

Architects/Arquitectos Artistas que planean y crean edificios. (p. 168)

Architectural rendering/Perspectiva arquitectónica realista Representación bidimensional realista y detallada de una estructura tridimensional propuesta. (p. 272)

Architecture/Arquitectura Arte de planear y crear edificios. (p. 92)

Art critic/Crítico de arte Aquella persona que se ocupa de estudiar, comprender y juzgar obras de arte. (p. 66)

Art historians/Historiadores de arte Aquellas personas que se ocupan de estudiar el arte de las distintas épocas y culturas. (p. 82)

Artist/Artista plástico Aquella persona que usa su imaginación y su habilidad para comunicar ideas de una forma visual. (p. 4)

Art medium/Medio artístico Material utilizado en la creación de una obra de arte. (p. 42)

Art movement/Movimiento artístico Tendencia que se manifiesta cuando se une un grupo de artistas. (p. 96)

Assemblage/Assemblage Obra de arte tridimensional que consiste en muchas piezas ensambladas entre sí. (p. 106)

B

Balance/Equilibrio Principio del arte que se refiere al arreglo de los elementos de manera tal que ninguna parte de la obra predomine o parezca tener más peso que cualquier otra parte. (p. 26)

Belvedere/Mirador Edificio diseñado para proveer una vista de sus alrededores. (p. 272)

Binder/Sustancia aglutinante Líquido que une los granos de pigmento. (p. 47)

Bust/Busto Escultura que muestra la cabeza, hombros y parte superior del pecho de una persona. (p. 85)

C

Calligraphy/Caligrafía Arte de escribir con letra bella. (p. 132)

Caricature/Caricatura Dibujo humorístico que exagera los rasgos de una persona para ridiculizarla o criticarla. (p. 210)

Cartouche/Tarjeta Forma oval u oblonga donde está inscripto el nombre de una persona importante. (p. 224)

Cityscape/Paisaje urbano Dibujo o pintura que muestra grandes edificios y otros objetos que se hallan en las ciudades. (p. 172)

Color/Color Lo que el ojo ve cuando un objeto refleja la luz. (p. 8)

Columns/Columnas Postes verticales que se elevan para proveer apoyo a otra estructura. (p. 171)

Composition/Composición Forma en que se utilizan los principios para organizar los elementos del arte. (p. 64)

Content/Contenido Mensaje, idea o sentimiento expresado por una obra de arte. (p. 65)

Contours/Contornos Bordes y aristas de una superficie. (p. 87)

Credit line/Resumen de datos Listado de información importante acerca de una obra de arte. (p. 69)

Cutaway/Sección Vista en la que se ha quitado una pared exterior para mostrar la escena del interior. (p. 233)

D

Diorama/Maqueta Representación escénica en la que esculturas en miniatura y otros objetos se muestran contra un fondo pintado. (p. 94)

E

Eight, The/Los Ocho Grupo de realistas estadounidenses que trabajaron a principios del siglo veinte. (p. 174)

Elements of art/Elementos del arte Los símbolos visuales básicos que usa un artista para crear obras de arte. (p. 4)

Elevation/Alzado Dibujo de la fachada de un edificio. (p. 170)

Emphasis/Énfasis Hacer que resalte un elemento o un objeto en una obra. (p. 31)

Environment/Ambiente Lo que rodea algo. (p. 124)

F

Façade/Fachada El frente de un edificio. (p. 170)

Fantasy art/Arte de fantasía Arte que se enfoca en sujetos ficticios o imaginarios. (p. 264)

Figure study/Estudio de figuras Dibujo que se enfoca en la figura humana. (p. 148)

Fine art/Bellas artes Obras hechas para el disfrute visual, no para ser utilizadas. (p. 83)

Folk art/Arte folklórico Obras realizadas por artistas que no han tenido capacitación formal. (p. 138)

Font/Fundición Conjunto de todos los moldes o letras de un tipo para imprimir. (p. 239)

Form/Forma Elemento del arte que se refiere a un objeto con tres dimensiones. (p. 15)

Fresco/Fresco Pintura creada al aplicar pigmento a una sección de una pared revocada con yeso fresco. (p. 232)

Frieze/Frisco Banda decorativa ubicada a lo largo de la parte superior de una pared. (p. 212)

G

Gesture drawing/Dibujo de gestos Dibujando líneas con rapidez y sin límites para capturar la forma y acciónes de un sujeto. (p. 44)

Gouache/Aguada Un tipo de acuarela que usa pigmentos no transparentes. (p. 205)

H

Harmony/Armonía Combinar los elementos del arte para acentuar sus similitudes. (p. 30)

Hieroglyphic/Jeroglífico Forma antigua de escritura basada en dibujos. (p. 86)

Hue/Tono El nombre de un color. (p. 8)

I

Illumination/Iluminación Ilustración pintada a mano en un libro. (p. 132)

Intaglio/Entallar Técnica de impresión en la cual se raspa o se corta sobre una superficie la imagen que ha de imprimirse. (p. 51)

Intensity/Intensidad Luminosidad u opacidad de un matiz. (p. 10)

J

Jewelry/Joyería Arte y oficio de realizar obras de arte que se llevan puestas. (p. 196)

Juxtapose/Yuxtaponer Poner lado a lado. (p. 268)

K

Kachina/Kachina Estatuilla hecha a mano que representa a los espíritus en los ritos de la cultura Pueblo. (p. 230)

Kiln/Horno Horno especial para cocer objetos de alfarería. (p. 195)

Kinetic art/Arte cinético Estilo artístico en el que se ponen en movimiento partes de una obra por medio de energía. (p. 250)

L

Landscape/Paisaje Dibujo o pintura de montañas, árboles u otra escena natural. (p. 104)

Line/Línea La trayectoria de un punto a través del espacio. (p. 6)

Line quality/Cualidad de la línea El carácter único de cualquier línea. (p. 7)

M

Mascot/Mascota Animal o persona utilizados por un grupo como signo de buena suerte. (p. 125)

Monoprint/Monocopia Estampa hecha al aplicar tinta o pintura sobre una plancha y luego transferir la imagen frotando con la mano. (p. 117)

Mosaic/Mosaico Ilustraciones hechas con pequeños trozos de mármol, vidrio o losa de colores asentados en cemento. (p. 212)

Motif/Motivo Unidad que se repite en un diseño. (p. 33)

Movement/Movimiento Principio del arte que hace que el espectador vea acción en una obra, o la trayectoria que sigue el ojo al mirar una obra. (p. 33)

Murals/Murales Obras bidimensionales grandes pintadas sobre paredes. (p. 156)

N

Nature study/Estudio del natural Dibujo realizado para ayudar al artista a realzar su percepción de los objetos naturales. (p. 108)

Negative space/Espacio negativo Espacios vacíos entre las formas o figuras de una obra bidimensional o tridimensional. (p. 16)

Nonobjective/No objetivo Que no tiene sujetos u objetos inmediatamente identificables. (p. 71)

O

Old Stone age/Edad de Piedra El período histórico que abarca del año 30,000 al 10,000 A.C. (p. 124)

P

Painted screen/Biombo Objeto de arte utilizado como pared o para dividir una habitación. (p. 89)

Pan/Toma panorámica Movimiento lateral lento y regular de la cámara de vídeo para captar los detalles de un panorama. (p. 218)

Panorama/Panorama Vista completa de un área en todas las direcciones. (p. 176)

Pattern/Diseño Representación visual bidimensional decorativa. (p. 33)

Pendant/Pendiente Artículo de joyería que se lleva alrededor del cuello colgado de un hilo o cadena. (p. 193)

Perception/Percepción Estar conciente de los elementos de un ambiente por medio de los sentidos. (p. 42)

Perceive/Percibir Tomar conciencia por medio de los sentidos de la naturaleza particular de los objetos. (p. 184)

Petroglyph/Petroglifo Grabado o pintura simbólicos sobre roca. (p. 225)

Photography/Fotografía Arte de crear imágenes al exponer a la luz una superficie tratada con sustancias químicas. (p. 204)

Pictogram/Pictograma Figura pequeña que representa una palabra o una idea. (p. 224)

Picture plane/Plano La superficie plana de una pintura o dibujo. (p. 30)

Pigment/Pigmento Polvo molido fino que da color a la pintura. (p. 46)

Point of view/Punto de vista Ángulo desde el cual el espectador ve la escena de una obra de arte. (p. 72)

Porcelain/Porcelana Forma de alfarería de grano fino y alta calidad. (p. 128)

Portfolio/Carpeta de trabajos Colección de obras cuidadosamente seleccionada de estudiantes y artistas profesionales. (p. 13)

Portrait/Retrato Representación visual de una persona en reposo. (p. 48)

Portraiture/Pintura de retratos El arte de hacer retratos. (p. 152)

Pottery/Alfarería Arte y oficio de hacer objetos de arte con arcilla. (p. 194)

Principles of art/Principios de arte Lineamientos que gobiernan el modo en que los artistas organizan los elementos del arte. (p. 26)

Printmaking/Grabado Acción de transferir una imagen de una superficie cubierta de tinta a otra superficie. (p. 50)

Proportion/Proporción Manera en que las partes de una obra se relacionan entre sí y con el todo. (p. 31)

Public art/Arte público Obra de arte expuesta para el disfrute de una comunidad. (p. 156)

Pueblo/Pueblo Vivienda de arcilla seca. (p. 248)

R

Renaissance/Renacimiento Período de renacimiento. (p. 93)

Rhythm/Ritmo El principio del arte que indica movimiento mediante la repetición de elementos y objetos. (p. 33)

Rococo/Rococó Estilo artístico del siglo dieciocho que enfatizaba la gracia del movimiento, las líneas curvas y los colores delicados. (p. 169)

S

Sculpture/Escultura Obra de arte tridimensional. (p. 52)

Seal/Sello Emblema o imagen simbólica. (p. 245)

Seascape/Paisaje marino Dibujo o pintura del océano y los objetos que se encuentran en él o a su alrededor. (p. 176)

Self-portrait/Autorretrato Dibujo o pintura de la imagen del propio artista. (p. 147)

Shadow puppet/Marioneta Objeto de arte de forma animal o humana unido al extremo de una varilla. (p. 250)

Shape/Contorno Área claramente delimitada por uno o más de los cinco elementos visuales del arte. (p. 14)

Slip/Arcilla blanda Arcilla con suficiente agua agregada como para darle una consistencia resbaladiza y blanda. (p. 194)

Social protest painting/Pintura de protesta social Estilo artístico dedicado a atacar los males de la vida en los grandes centros urbanos. (p. 270)

Solvent/Solvente Líquido usado para regular el espesor de la pintura. (p. 47)

Space/Espacio Distancia o área entre, alrededor, sobre, debajo y dentro de las cosas. (p. 15)

Staged photograph/Foto de estudio Composición fotográfica que usa imágenes o procesos artificiales. (p. 165)

Still life/Bodegón Dibujo o pintura de objetos inanimados. (p. 17)

Story board/Tablero de historieta Plan toma por toma de una producción de vídeo. (p. 217)

Study/Estudio Dibujo usado para planear una pintura u otro proyecto grande. (p. 108)

Style/Estilo Modo personal del artista de usar los elementos y principios del arte para expresar ideas y sentimientos. (p. 144)

Stylized/Estilizado Simplificado o exagerado. (p. 105)

Subject/Sujeto Imagen que el espectador puede identificar fácilmente. (p. 64)

Surrealists/Surrealistas Grupo de artistas que exploraron el mundo de los sueños y el subconsciente. (p. 265)

Symbol/Símbolo Imagen utilizada para representar una cualidad o una idea. (p. 87)

T

Tapestry/Tapiz Paño tejido con diseños decorativos o escenas coloridas que se cuelga de la pared. (p. 136)

Texture/Textura La forma en que algo se siente al tocarlo, o cómo parece que se sentiría al tocarlo. (p. 20)

Totem/Tótem Un objeto que sirve como emblema o símbolo respetado. (p. 126)

Trait/Rasgo Característica personal. (p. 125)

Tricolor/Tricolor Una bandera con tres franjas anchas de color. (p. 245)

U

Unity/Unidad El arreglo de elementos y principios del arte para lograr una sensación de consumación y totalidad. (p. 36)

V

Value/Opacidad La claridad u oscuridad de un color. (p. 9)

Variety/Variedad Combinar uno o más elementos del arte para generar interés. (p. 30)

Vessel/Recipiente Utensilio cóncavo destinado a guardar algo. (p. 192)

Video documentary/Documental de vídeo Estudio en profundidad de una persona, lugar, cosa o suceso. (p. 217)

Videographer/Camarógrafo Persona que opera una cámara de vídeo. (p. 218)

W

Watercolorist/Acuarelista Pintor que trabaja con acuarelas. (p. 190)

Index

A

B

C

G

H

I

M

INDEX

Q

R

S

Credits

Cover Illustration: Leo and Diane Dillon

Photo Credits: Courtesy of the African American Dance Ensemble 325; Art Resource, NY 97, 124, 138, 162; Digital Vision 308tr; Tim Fuller Photography, Tucson, AZ 302bl, 303(2), 304(2), 306(2), 307tr, 308bl; Giraudon/Art Resource, NY 86, 92t; Robert Homes/Corbis xi, 162, 307bl; Ed Krieger 333; Superstock 165, 170(2), 173; Alan Levenson/Getty Images 305bl; Robert Llewellyn/Image State 305tr; Brigitte Meuiwissen 328; Herbert Migdoll 323, 331; Michael Newman/Photo Edit 293, 294, 300; Alan Schein Photography/Corbis 6; Skyline Displays 321; Tom Stewart/Corbis 302tr; Keren Su/Corbis 154; Michael Tamborrino/The Stock Market 156; UPI/Corbis-Bettmann 216; Lee White Photography, Los Angeles, CA 218, 295, and all Student Art; David Young-Wolff/Photo Edit 301; Xochimoki. Jim Berenholtz and Mazatl Galindo 334.